The Film Genre Book

The Film Genre Book

John Sanders

auteur

John Sanders

is the Head of Film Studies at Bedford Modern School, Bedford, UK.

Dedication

For Saši, my lovely director, and Matej, Andrej and Natalia, my beautiful crew.

First published in 2009 by
Auteur, The Old Surgery, 9 Pulford Road, Leighton Buzzard LU7 1AB
www.auteur.co.uk
Copyright © Auteur 2009

Designed and set by Nikki Hamlett at AMP Ltd, Dunstable, Bedfordshire
Cover images: *The Searchers* © BFI Stills, Posters and Designs; *Goodfellas*, *Metropolis*, *The General* © Joel Finler Archive; *A Matter of Life and Death* © BFI / image.net; *Spider-Man 2* © Sony Pictures/image.net
Printed and bound in Poland
www.polskabook.co.uk

British Library Cataloguing-in-Publication Data
A catalogue record for this book is available from the British Library

ISBN 978-1-903663-90-5 (paperback)
ISBN 978-1-903663-91-2 (hardback)

Contents

Introduction

The inspiration for this book was twofold: my absolute love of film and the memory of trying to plan a scheme of work that would teach a range of films to students. My reaction to this task was one of fear. I had seen lots of films, but the dilemma of conjuring up sufficient examples to satisfy the various demands of different study modules seemed enormous. As I trawled through books and the Internet I was able to piece things together, but what energy and time I expended! There are *lots* of film guides and lots of in-depth texts on film; and, of course, the Internet can be a marvel (or a curse). Indeed, all these sources have helped me construct this book, but I could never quite find texts that hit me between the eyes, both user-friendly and with enough depth to satisfy students and the overworked and panicky teacher.

And so, an idea took root and you are holding the result. *The Film Genre Book* may not be a definitive text, but I wanted something that teachers, students and the film enthusiast (I count myself as all three) would be able to use constructively and enjoyably.

The assembly of the films herein is not based on my favourites, or often, the recognised classic of a particular genre (although many classics *are* covered); but of films that are ripe for analysis, which tell us something about the decade in which they were made and add something interesting to our definition of any particular genre. I have also tried to write about films that are widely available, that can be viewed, enjoyed and used to educate. It was a jigsaw, and some films slipped through whilst some surprises emerged (before I started writing I certainly never thought I would ever analyse *Young Guns* [1988]).

The term 'genre' is a slippery beast; it has a long literary heritage, stretching back to Aristotle's literary categories in *Poetics*. These divisions, and further permutations over the years, of comedy and tragedy have been used by writers, critics, publishers and readers/audiences for centuries, but what has happened with literary genres, as with film genres, is that many factors have conspired to blur genre definitions. Historical context, critical thinking, public preference and business interests have all played a part in reinventing genres and introducing new genre contenders. In the literary world today the range of genres would seem to be manifold. Any group of writers which seems to form a coherent voice can create a new genre; there is the 'Troubled Teenager' genre, for example, familiar to any teacher of English, and comparable to the 1950s upsurge in films revolving around alienated youths, notably Nicholas Ray's *Rebel Without A Cause* (1955). One could conceivably argue that the winners of the Booker Prize themselves constitute a type of novel ('literary prize-winners'?). And just as literary genres have mutated, so film genre structures have been challenged; time, production, criticism and taste have dictated this.

Genre, or type, or kind, is an ideal way for film companies to pigeonhole their products, to sell a set of codes and conventions to audiences who, in turn, crave the familiarity and predictable entertainment that genre films can deliver. Film critics have considered the notion of genre, tapping into literary tradition as I have mentioned, which embraces both the uses and the challenges of genre criticism. Initial divisions of film types resulted in the standard and widely agreed genres of the Western, the musical, the horror film, the comedy, the war film, the thriller, the crime film and the science fiction film; others have added the detective film, action/adventure, the epic and the biopic, amongst many others. In this book I have added drama, the blockbuster and fantasy film. And that, I think, underlines the appeal of genre study when it is not held only as a rigid structure; it is a flexible and ever-growing field that is forever open to interpretation.

This book stands as a window on the world of genre, and on the relationship between genre and audience, a relationship that is continually being refined and reconfigured through time. Many of these films contain multiple generic strands, what Hollywood likes to call 'hybrids', so beautifully parodied in the 'RomComZom' that is *Shaun of the Dead* (2004). But even those films that seem entirely comfortable in their generic pigeon-hole exhibit elements of other genres: *The Searchers* (1956) is, of course, a Western, but there are elements of comedy and romance lurking in its narrative. No genre is absolute. The other historically limiting notion of genre study is the idea that genres are purely the product of the Hollywood film factory; yes, the major studios and audiences have often been seduced by genre's charms, but casting an eye over the 63 films that comprise this book, it is clear that genre boundaries do not end at the United States' borders. World cinema, like Hollywood, is willing and able to both embrace genre and play with its possibilities.

I have delineated films into seven genre categories, but it has been done in part to illustrate just how genre changes through time, and how, in some ways, it stays the same. When one compares films in each genre here, the only outcome is debate: *Red River* (1948) or *Brokeback Mountain* (2005)? *Metropolis* (1927) or *ET* (1982)? *Cat People* (1942) or *A Nightmare on Elm Street* (1984)? *A Matter of Life and Death* (1946) or *Pan's Labyrinth* (2006)? Genre unites and divides, and that is what is so stimulating about its use as a tool in film criticism.

This would seem an appropriate point to make clear that this is not *The Film Genre* Theory *Book*. Although the book touches on theoretical concepts (such as genre hybrids, for example), it is not intended as a theoretical work *per se*. There are a number of classic scholarly works in this area, such as Steve Neale's *Genre* (1980) and Rick Altman's *Film/Genre* (1999), which you are directed towards if this volume has whetted your appetite for a greater engagement with the concept of genre. Rather, this book should be regarded as either an introduction to this area for the reader new to the formal study of film; or a more thought-provoking and challenging work of reference for the general reader.

Ultimately, genres have become so flexible and some of my decisions can certainly be debated, but this is only right as it helps to further our awareness of genre's limiting and liberating power. Like sonnets, genre is the form, to be embraced emphatically or to act as a structure to rebel against, to reform and reshape to make new meanings for new generations. The steady rhythm of the genre form imposes a discipline upon the film-maker, which is the springboard for creativity;

it is up to audiences to respond in kind, taking comfort from the familiarity of genre, but also to appreciate genre's manifold possibilities and follow its twists and turns.

Overall, I have tried to include a diverse range of films; some are 'classics' but some, I hope, you will discover for the first time. The list is dominated by Hollywood, which in some ways is inevitable with a genre-based book, but there *is* work from beyond those confines as well. It's not just about the films, but also the connections, the producers and the stars leading a merry dance through film history; the silent films, in particular, open up so many avenues of reflection, a world before the 'talkies', where film language was pure and uncompromised by dialogue.

How to use this book

The Film Genre Book has been designed to provide historical overviews of the development of 7 genres, from the early years of narrative cinema to the present day. This is achieved primarily by the close study of 9 films (one per decade from the 1920s onwards, with the exception of the DRAMA section, where the first film, *Intolerance*, was released in 1916), which are listed on the grid opposite.

Each case study begins with some production notes and a brief plot synopsis, followed by: a consideration of its historical context (both industrial context and wider societal issues); a select filmography of the key players (actors and/or technicians); a selection of other films that one might connect with the primary case study (linked either thematically or perhaps by the key personnel); a short analysis of the representation of one or more of the key themes or elements in the film; some short critical remarks about the film; and finally, but perhaps most significantly, an extended textual analysis of one or more key scenes.

In this way, it is hoped that the reader will gain a greater understanding of each of these films' importance within the development of the genre to which it most clearly belongs.

	WESTERN	DRAMA	SCIENCE FICTION	HORROR	COMEDY	FANTASY	BLOCKBUSTER
1916							Intolerance
1920s	The Iron Horse	Sunrise	Metropolis	Nosferatu	The General	Thief of Bagdad	
1930s	Stagecoach	Angels with Dirty Faces	Things To Come	Frankenstein	Duck Soup	King Kong	Gone with the Wind
1940s	Red River	The Killers	A Connecticut Yankee in King Arthur's Court	Cat People	Kind Hearts and Coronets	A Matter of Life and Death	Bambi
1950s	The Searchers	The 400 Blows	Invasion of the Body Snatchers	Night of the Hunter	Mon Oncle	Hidden Fortress	Ben-Hur
1960s	Once Upon a Time in the West	Saturday Night and Sunday Morning	2001	The Birds	The Graduate	Jason and the Argonauts	The Sound of Music
1970s	Pat Garrett and Billy the Kid	Apocalypse Now	Alien	Halloween	Young Frankenstein	Soylent Green	Jaws
1980s	Young Guns	Wings of Desire	ET	A Nightmare on Elm Street	Raising Arizona	Brazil	The Last Emperor
1990s	Unforgiven	Goodfellas	The Matrix	Silence of the Lambs	Delicatessen	Edward Scissorhands	Titanic
2000s	Brokeback Mountain	Crash	Children of Men	Dark Water	Shaun of the Dead	Pan's Labyrinth	Spider-Man 2

Approached another way, the book is so organised that at the same time it also offers the reader a snap-shot of the (primarily American) film industry in any given decade. By reading, say, each of the seven entries on films from the 1950s across all the genres, the reader will gain a wider understanding of the historical and industrial issues that were current at that time – from society's anxieties about the perceived Communist threat (see *Invasion of the Body Snatchers* [1956] in the SCIENCE FICTION section) to the industry's own concerns about, and responses to, the emergence of the TV threat to its bottom line (see *Ben-Hur* [1959] in the BLOCKBUSTER section).

So, *The Film Genre Book* also serves as a brief introduction to film history from the 1920s to as recently as 2006.

This book is a journey; I hope it opens up some films to the reader, the teacher and the student alike. I delight in the fact that it has allowed me to discuss films as diverse as *Bambi* (1942) and *Dark Water* (2002); although, when you think about it, perhaps they are not so different after all...

A note on style

The date of a film's release appears the first time a film is mentioned within the body of that section of the book. The chapters and timings that appear in parenthesis in the TEXTUAL ANALYSIS sections are of those from the Region 2 DVD of the film and are correct as of the date of first publication of this book (2009 – obviously we can't take account of possible future re-issues in which the numbering of chapters might change).

THE WESTERN

The Western genre is a favourite of mine, but the inclusion of three John Ford films was troubling. However, the facts, as I see them, are these: *The Searchers* (1956) had to be included for its vision and its poetry, a template for the modern Western and even films beyond this genre; *Stagecoach* (1939) is the only decent Western to emerge from the 1930s, and *The Iron Horse* (1924) is *the* silent Western, eclipsing all others. A Howard Hawks contribution was a must; his skill in many genres is unsurpassed, and if it was not to be his effortless work in *Rio Bravo* (1959), then it had to be *Red River* (1948). John Wayne looms large in this early part of the section, but for many a film-goer, 'Duke', as he was known, was the epitome of the Western star and an all-American hero. His three leading roles in this section defined the Western hero – and anti-hero – for all who followed. I am sad not to include an Anthony Mann film; his output of the 1950s is a delight, both in its visual beauty and complex characterisation, but *The Searchers* won out in the end.

If *Once Upon A Time In The West* (1968) had not existed then perhaps the flourishing of Westerns in the late 1960s and early 1970s may not have taken place. Sam Peckinpah would lead the Hollywood charge when it came to revisionist Westerns with his highly influential *The Wild Bunch* (1969), to be followed by, amongst others, Arthur Penn's *Little Big Man* (1970) and Clint Eastwood's *High Plains Drifter* (1973). But for the 1970s it was to Peckinpah that I was drawn; his list of Western credits charts a path from the traditional (*Ride The High Country*, 1962) to revisionism (*The Wild Bunch*) to the contemporary (*Junior Bonner*, 1972). The chosen film, *Pat Garrett and Billy the Kid* (1973), combines all three of these strands into a masterful deconstruction of the Old West. *Young Guns* (1988) revised and revived the genre for the MTV generation, although it was the next decade's choice, *Unforgiven* (1992), that was to forge a path for a new breed of Westerns, reworked for the end of the millennium and the next century.

As I wrote this section it became clear how flexible this genre can actually be; the films here say so much about so many different facets of life; it was Hollywood's backbone for so many years, but it is telling that even though the genre is at its lowest ebb in terms of quantity, it is still a force to be reckoned with. Even in its heyday the Western film only garnered one Best Picture Oscar, *Cimarron* in 1931, whereas in the last twenty years or so there have been two films, *Dances with Wolves* (1990) and *Unforgiven*, that have been multi-Oscar winners. And, just when you think that the genre is dead and buried along comes another intelligent Western vision: take your pick from *Open Range* (2003); *Three Burials of Melquiades Estrada* (2003); *The Missing* (2003); *Brokeback Mountain* (2005) and *The Assassination of Jesse James by the Coward Robert Ford* (2007). The Western is dead, long live the Western.

The Iron Horse

KEY FACTS

Release Date: 1924

Country of Origin: USA

Running Time: 133 minutes

PRODUCTION NOTES

Production Company

Fox Film Corporation

Distributor

Fox Film Corporation

Budget

$280,000 (estimated)

SYNOPSIS

The story begins with a surveyor named Brandon dreaming about building a railway from the east coast of the United States to the west. His friend, a contractor called Marsh, is less hopeful about the success of this endeavour, but Brandon sets out to find a way to achieve his dream. With his son, Davy, he discovers a pass that takes 200 miles off the journey. However, the father is killed by Cheyenne Native Americans, including a two-fingered white man who has joined the Cheyenne tribe, but a hidden Davy survives.

Many years later Brandon's dream starts to become reality as work starts on two railways, one from the east, the other from the west. Gangs of immigrant workers help lay the track but there is the constant threat of attack from Native Americans. Marsh is the main contractor. Running out of time to finish the railway, he must find a shorter route through the Black Hills. Jesson, his chief engineer, is engaged to Marsh's daughter, Miriam, but is seduced by a girl called Ruby who is working for local landowner Bauman, who does not want the railway to follow the shortcut.

Jesson agrees to help Bauman, and when Davy, now a pony express rider, appears with the key to the shortcut, Jesson tries to kill him as he dangles over a cliff, looking for the pass that he and his father discovered years before. Davy survives, and after a fight with Jesson, the shortcut is used and the two railways finally meet. Before this can happen, the workers endure another attack by the Native Americans, but they are rescued by people from the town that is growing up beside the track. Davy meets the Native American who murdered his father, finally kills him and avenges his father's death. As the golden spike is driven into the connecting pieces of track Davy embraces Miriam, the girl with whom he played as a young boy.

HISTORICAL CONTEXT

The Iron Horse was made just 55 years after the golden spike was driven into the track that united the Union Pacific and Central Pacific railways, the first transcontinental track in the United States. As such, it became a potent symbol of American achievement and 'white progress'. The 1920s was an era of optimism and hope; the First World War had been over for six years when *The Iron Horse* was made and the Great Depression was not yet on the horizon.

The United States had emerged from the war as an extremely powerful nation, full of energy and a desire to promote its democratic dreams. The focal event of the film, and the struggle to achieve the goal were relevant, then, to this age of contentment. The enterprises detailed in the film were also reflected in progress made during the 1920s: Henry Ford began to manufacture motor cars on a massive scale and plans for more skyscrapers came to fruition by the end of the decade and beginning of the next with the construction of New York's Chrysler Building and The Empire State Building.

However, the film can also be read in a different way; it can be seen as a message to those who were becoming too complacent about the mechanics of modern society: it was a time of unfettered enjoyment when caution was eschewed in favour of bourgeois superficiality and hedonism. The hard work and suffering of those who had built the country were being forgotten and the film stands as testament to that frontier spirit.

SELECT FILMOGRAPHY OF MAIN PRODUCERS AND CAST

John Ford, 1895–1973, Director

The Iron Horse, 1924

The Prisoner of Shark Island, 1936

Stagecoach, 1939

The Grapes of Wrath, 1940

How Green Was My Valley, 1941

My Darling Clementine, 1946

Fort Apache, 1948

She Wore a Yellow Ribbon, 1949

Rio Grande, 1950

The Quiet Man, 1952

The Searchers, 1956

The Man Who Shot Liberty Valance, 1962

Cheyenne Autumn, 1964

(and over 120 more films)

George O' Brien, 1899–1985, Actor

The Iron Horse, 1924

The Blue Eagle, 1926

Sunrise, 1927

East Side, West Side, 1927

Noah's Ark, 1928

Fort Apache, 1948

She Wore a Yellow Ribbon, 1949

Cheyenne Autumn, 1964

LINKS TO OTHER FILMS

La Bête Humaine (1938)

Jean Renoir's study of human weakness and violence uses trains and railways as symbols of the fate of those that are ruled by passions that lead them to commit acts of violence and murder.

The Lady Vanishes (1938), *Night Train to Munich* (1940), *Murder on the Orient Express* (1974), *Silver Streak* (1976)

These are just some of the many films that use trains as a backdrop for intrigue and murder; the nature of train transport adds to the claustrophobic atmosphere of these films, the narrow corridors and small spaces helping to intensify the excitement.

Union Pacific (1939)

Cecil B. DeMille's epic retelling of the building of the first transcontinental railway across the United States follows *The Iron Horse*'s narrative quite closely, although its flat direction does not match John Ford's poetic vision.

A Ticket to Tomahawk (1950)

Another Western that deals with the survival of railways against opposition. Here, like *The Iron Horse*, the film charts a railway's fight for survival against a ruthless stagecoach owner.

The Titfield Thunderbolt (1953)

In Charles Crichton's Ealing Studios' comedy the preservation of the past is characterised as a struggle over a rail branch line due for closure. The titular train is brought out of retirement from a museum and saves the day for a group of villagers fighting bureaucracy and big business.

The Train (1964)

In John Frankenheimer's war film a train is used as a symbol of defiance as railway workers and Resistance fighters try to prevent a train-load of French artworks being taken to Germany during World War II.

Closely Observed Trains (1966)

Another film set in World War II, but here the movement of trains through a small Czechoslovakian station under Nazi control is used as a backdrop for a young man's rite of passage into adulthood and as a symbol of events happening in the world at large.

Once Upon a Time in the West (1968)

See entry for this film (pg. 38) for link.

REPRESENTATION

Trains

Power, progress, communication; trains are represented in a particular way in Westerns. They connect the wilderness with civilisation and realise people's dreams of progress. This is all from a white perspective, of course; in the United States the indigenous peoples saw them as harbingers of misery and alien intrusions into their world; they were the lifeblood that fuelled an invasion of unwanted and hostile people. Tyranny or freedom depended on your skin colour.

Throughout *The Iron Horse* there are numerous shots of trains, understandable given the film's subject matter, but the amount of coverage makes the trains become characters in their own right. We see shots from the trains' point-of-view and the Native Americans seem to attack not only the people but the trains themselves: they try to catch them with ropes, arrows thud into their sides and they are encircled, but afford their white inhabitants protection from attack, or they come to the rescue of those that become stranded. The ending is, of course, the culmination of years of hard human toil, but the image of Davy and Miriam embracing is echoed in the two trains coming together, meeting like lovers about to kiss.

The film is a love letter to the train, with its solidity, power and romance (train travel has always had connotations of romance and excitement, beginning with the whistle of a steam train as it sets off). By referring to it as an 'iron horse', these very virtues are made explicit – it emphasises its strength and poetic associations over its mechanical functionality, linking it to nature and creating an image of harmony in a rapidly changing world. 'Iron Horse' is the Native American name for train. Flagging it up in the film's title inextricably links the machine and the indigenous population, a connection that would have negative ramifications for the Native Americans as white civilisation all but destroyed their lands and way of life.

'His climactic action scenes in particular, with hordes of Indians attacking one locomotive while another races to the rescue and at the same time hero and villain stage their own personal battle on the side, show Ford's editing skills and fluid camerawork at their best, even at this early stage in a long career.' Michael Parkinson & Clyde Jeavons, *A Pictorial History of Westerns*, Hamlyn, London, 1984

'The railroad is a means of restoring the unity of the nation ruptured by the Civil War, and the means whereby Manifest Destiny, the settlement of the entire continent, is to be achieved.' Edward Buscombe, '*The Iron Horse*' 100 Westerns, BFI, 2006

KEY SCENE TEXTUAL ANALYSIS

Attack on father and son (3/4 10:06)

The surveyor shows his son a pass where he thinks the train track will be laid. The image is a matte painting, but this only enhances the glamour and poetry of the image; like a Remington picture it conjures up a mythic West, one to which John Ford fully subscribed. The cutback to the father and son is also an image of an idyll, the father's hand rests lovingly on the boy's shoulder, their bodies joined in an image of paternal care and protection; the union is further emphasised by the clothes that they share: the hat and the waistcoat. The symmetry of the framing, figures at the centre and the two tree limbs pointing in the same direction, help to underpin the atmosphere of contentment and love.

The medium shot of the two sitting by the fire is also balanced, the smoke rising between them, a sense of equilibrium pervading the frame. The medium close-up of the father is also balanced and a portrait of fatherly sensibilities, but the jarring note of the axe, horribly foreshadowing events to come, disrupts the harmony. The pipe, which earlier seemed a symbol of the father's solidity and civility, is thrust away as the father hears something; the close-up on the branch being trodden on by a moccasin-clad foot signals danger, and the anonymity of that threat increases the audience's expectations of the horror that will unfold. The medium shot of father and boy is a visual reminder of the earlier harmonious hug, but here the father's hands are clasped around the boy's face as if his fingertips have been dipped in fear. More and more feet clamber over the same point and the embrace becomes heavy. A gentle kiss seals the father's decision as he hides the boy from sight.

The action is played out in a medium long shot, but the father is soon overwhelmed, a three-shot of the Native Americans stressing their dominance. The long shot of the Native Americans in the background and the captured surveyor in the foreground brings these two worlds together; the alternate shots previously give way to this shot which proclaims that the father will not escape. Just as the rifle in *Once Upon A Time In The West* (1968) signals the fate awaiting the McBain family, so the axe, foregrounding the son, suggests the violence to come. The juxtaposition of axe, mutilated hand and the horrified boy add to the suspense and menace of the moment. The long shot of the Native Americans closing in on the prone body of the father emphasises the threat to him, the axe remaining a potent symbol of violence and unspeakable horror for both man and boy. The shots of the mutilated Native American and father suggest their different positions at that moment: a slightly low angle on the Native American underpinning his superiority and a higher angle on the father highlighting his vulnerability. The hidden, but watching boy, is framed by the tree limbs around him, a natural protection, but the effect of the violent thrusting action of the Native American, as the axe descends on the father, is played out by the boy as he physically recoils and collapses, stressing the bond between father and son.

John Ford paints a chilling and stereotypical portrait of the 'savage Indian' with one observing Native American wearing a sinister smile, his body shining with sweat. The scene ends with a static long shot of the scalping and the Native American's triumphant retreat. It is all played out within the frame: the horror speaks for itself without the need for close-ups or camera movement.

Attack on the supply train (7)

The attack on the vulnerable father and son is replaced with one on the powerful train, a symbol of modernity and change, which is charging through Native American territory. The train comes steaming out of the distance, the track dissecting the frame and cutting through the wilderness with its strength and solidity. In comparison, the horse-riding Native Americans, carrying a frail rope

The nature of the relationship between the train and the Native Americans is again explored as a medium shot of the train, resplendent in the sunshine, is tainted by the shadows of the attackers, threateningly moving up the side of the train carriages. The long shot of the train in a hollow and Native Americans above it on a ridge demonstrate that, if there is a threat to progress, it is the Native Americans, albeit fleetingly. The shot of the shadows on the side is repeated to emphasise the malevolent nature of the Native American, a view perpetuated by the film industry through out to the 20th century. The final shot of the attack shows the Native Americans filling the frame, consuming the train in the background, dancing like the savages of stereotype. This is one small victory for the Native Americans; but the track remains and more trains will come.

between them across the track, appear insignificant and puny; the close-up of the train driver framed by his engine shows a man who is secure in his connection with this great machine in the face of the threat ahead.

The moving POV shot could be that of the driver, but it is also that of the train, with a personality of its own, strong and resolute, steadfastly moving forward, the track stretching to the horizon without interruption. The shot of the train hitting the Native Americans' rope and pulling them off their horses would have been designed to make a 1920s audience laugh, but it perfectly encapsulates the nature of the battle between this iron beast of white progress and the frail indigenous culture. But the train is stopped by an obstruction on the line, and the pace of the editing increases as the Native Americans attack.

A new and greater Cheyenne (15)

The building of a 'new and greater Cheyenne' is initiated by the establishing shot of the town, with track and trains dominating the frame, serving as an artery carrying the blood of life and progress. Every frame of this sequence is filled with vitality and movement as the people create a new community in the wilderness. Men carry parts of buildings up ladders, people flood into the town on trains, carriages, horseback and on foot. A sense of hysterical endeavour takes hold of the masses as a carriage careers wildly in circles and cowboys ride up to the train and gather women from it. The trappings of life back East are disgorged, furniture included, and then there is a cut to show the priorities of the people: men eagerly paint the saloon sign and items continue to be grabbed from the train with alacrity. It is frenzied activity, a violent birth, people desirous to clad themselves in the comfort of familiarity. The scene ends with broad humour. The mayor tells Wild Bill Hickok that order must be maintained yet the sight of a full-sized bar being carried behind them emphasises that their job will be difficult. Meanwhile, a divorce after a 10-hour marriage is granted and a tooth is pulled by the dentist/barber. This is a vignette of frontier town life, the mischievous, hot-headed and greedy sibling of long-established towns, where life and death vie with equal vigour.

A bar room brawl (18 1:29:32)

Another staple of the Western is played out in this scene, but the *mise-en-scène* helps add considerably to the sense of verisimilitude. The long shot comes from behind the bar, positioning the audience as detached observer. The saloon is a vast

on the wall and add to the disorientating and chaotic nature of the fight, the sort of technique that would be used many years later in Richard Burton and Elizabeth Taylor's fight scenes in Mike Nichols' *Who's Afraid of Virginia Woolf* (1966) or the boxing ring scenes in Martin Scorsese's *Raging Bull* (1980).

The frames of each shot are filled with people, shadows rolling over them and the two fighters, the camera almost fighting at times to get a glimpse, the audience brought right into the action as if part of the cheering crowd. The serious fight is juxtaposed with the onlookers who play out the fight on the sidelines until everything is brought to a halt by Miriam, who first sees the shadow play from the other side of the canvas. Here we see that it is just a tent, adding to the sense of this fight as spectacle for others' pleasure; she literally tears through

space, filled with an assortment of paraphernalia, a chaotic scene enriched by the swarming men. The roof is not solid, but a canopy resembling a big top, emphasised by the vertical pole in the centre of frame, appropriate for an arena where men will perform for each other in acts of drinking and fighting.

Dust fills the air to add to the general rugged image of the place, and then medium shots of the protagonists prepare the audience for the imminent encounter. The long shot shows the two men charging like wild beasts at each other and the room erupts; this is the stuff of true entertainment for the hardened audience in the saloon. A few men are holding lamps, and it is from these that it is suggested the light sources emanate. Davy falls back into the empty frame after a punch from Jeeson. The swinging lights cast moving shadows

the artifice as she slits the side of the tent and intervenes, stopping this particular performance.

Stagecoach

KEY FACTS

Release Date: 1939

Country of Origin: USA

Running Time: 96 minutes

PRODUCTION NOTES

Production Company

Walter Wanger Productions Inc.

Distributor

United Artists

Budget

$531,300 (estimated)

Awards

Best Supporting Actor Thomas Mitchell Academy Awards, USA

Best Music, Scoring Hageman, Harling, Leipold, Shuken Academy Awards, USA

Best Director John Ford New York Film Critics Circle

SYNOPSIS

The Ringo Kid is on the trail of the men who have killed his father and brother; he becomes caught up with an array of characters on a stagecoach journey to Lordsburg, including a prostitute, a drunkard doctor, a gambler and a crooked banker. After fending off a Native American attack the Ringo Kid gets the group to its journey's end and safety. Although he should be arrested for the eventual killings of those that he sought, The Ringo Kid is allowed to go free, a noble hero, taking with him the prostitute who is shown to be a more humane person than all the other so-called respectable travellers on the stagecoach.

HISTORICAL CONTEXT

The 1930s were a time of great hardship for those in the United States and throughout the world. Massive unemployment, poverty and great unrest created fertile breeding grounds for the rise of dictators like Hitler in Germany. *Stagecoach* appeared just months before the beginning of the Second World War (but two years before America's entry). Although its tale of a band of misfits brought together has more to do with what had already passed in the 1930s, a social critique of how the downtrodden and reviled in society can often be more noble than the well-to-do and the respectable, it does look forward to the trials that would bring together many disparate nations of the world. It also condemns capitalist corruption; many a big business exploited the workers of the 1930s. Finally, it pays tribute to the New Deal, an American government initiative which set out to right some of the economic wrongs, and thereby spread some of the wealth; indeed this notion of equality equates perfectly with the film's characters and its narrative.

SELECT FILMOGRAPHY OF MAIN PRODUCERS AND CAST

John Ford, 1895–1973, Director

See entry for *The Iron Horse* (pg. 14)

Walter Wanger, 1894–1968, Producer

You Only Live Once, 1937

Stagecoach, 1939

Foreign Correspondent, 1940

The Long Voyage Home, 1940

Scarlet Street, 1945

Joan of Arc, 1948

Invasion of the Body Snatchers, 1955

Cleopatra, 1962

Bert Glennon, 1893–1967, Director of Photography

Ten Commandments, 1923

Stagecoach, 1939

Drums Along the Mohawk, 1939

They Died With Their Boots On, 1941

House of Wax, 1953

Sergeant Routledge, 1960

Dudley Nichols, 1895–1960, Screenwriter

The Lost Patrol, 1934

The Informer, 1935

Bringing Up Baby, 1938

Stagecoach, 1939

The Long Voyage Home, 1940

For Whom the Bell Tolls, 1943

And Then There Were None, 1945

Scarlet Street, 1945

John Wayne, 1907–1979, Actor

Stagecoach, 1939

Red River, 1948

She Wore a Yellow River, 1949

The Quiet Man, 1952

Rio Bravo, 1959

The Alamo, 1960

True Grit, 1969

The Shootist, 1976

Claire Trevor, 1909–2000, Actress

Stagecoach, 1939

Murder My Sweet, 1944

Key Largo, 1948

LINKS TO OTHER FILMS

Grand Hotel (1932)

A film which also charts the shifting fortunes of a disparate group of people from a range of social backgrounds. Of course, they are not under attack from a band of Native Americans, but they are all playing their parts in the various social strata that we see in *Stagecoach*.

Lifeboat (1944)

The scenario in this Alfred Hitchcock film runs along similar lines as *Stagecoach* with its depiction of a group of survivors from a torpedoed ship adrift in the Atlantic Ocean during World War Two. The tensions and interplay between the protagonists, again from a mix of social backgrounds, is given a comparative atmosphere as they are preyed upon by the elements.

The Searchers (1956)

John Wayne plays the leads in both this film and *Stagecoach*, an outsider who eventually saves the day. Both characters are on the edge of society because of past deeds, but they use their sense of honour and humanity in order to force a positive outcome at the conclusion of both films. Where they differ is in their emotional complexity, perfectly suggested by their different fates; yes, they both head off into the wilderness, but Ethan Edwards in *The Searchers* is alone, forever destined to be an outcast; The Ringo Kid has company and a sense of a shared future.

REPRESENTATION

The Stagecoach

The train in the Western represents the onslaught of civilisation and the march of 'white progress'; in *Once Upon a Time in the West* the train dehumanises the Native Americans, transporting them like cattle. From a Native American point of view its track pulses with the lifeblood of the cities back east and pollutes the wilderness with its relentless movement westwards. The stagecoach, conversely, has more of the spirit of the wilderness. It takes a less rigid route than the train, and sits more comfortably in the wilderness. Pulled by horses and more open to the elements it places the white travellers on the same level as the Native Americans. A journey on a stagecoach connects the traveller with the land; they feel every contour and endure the hardships of a world beyond civilisation. Thus, in the film the characters are pitted against the Native Americans without the comfort and protection that a train would afford. They are ordinary people in an environment that is hostile to

them and one which acts as both a social leveller and as a vehicle for the best and worst of human traits.

Monument Valley

One of the key features of many of John Ford's Westerns was the use of Monument Valley in Utah, a landscape seen in not only *Stagecoach*, but also in *My Darling Clementine*, *Fort Apache*, *She Wore a Yellow Ribbon*, *The Searchers*, *Sergeant Rutledge* and *Cheyenne Autumn*. But it is more than a landscape, it has become a symbol of the American West, a mythic landscape which suggests majesty, freedom and wilderness. The fact that audiences now identify Westerns with the desert landscape underlines the power of this iconography, branded into our minds by so many Hollywood films. These landscapes speak of harshness, pushing humanity to the extreme and to its fringes; the Mittens of Monument Valley stand as vast monoliths, as potent a symbol of 'otherness' as the monolith in Stanley Kubrick's *2001* (1968).

When a director chooses a different locale for a Western it is often shocking and unsettling for the audience, but the choice often helps convey a message, in keeping with the more traditional arid backdrop. A popular alternative is a snow-filled frame, again the harsh elements mirroring the characters' interior landscapes, full of violence and pain. Notable examples of this kind are Raoul Walsh's *The Tall Men* (1955), André de Toth's *Day of the Outlaw*, and Sergio Corbucci's *The Great Silence* (1968); the latter film's snowscape matching its icy heart. Lush, green vistas were very much the experience of many cowboys, but are little seen on the big screen; to see a variation on the desert iconography there is none better than Anthony Mann's visions of the Old West, particularly *The Far Country* (1955).

'The film that gave such an impetus to the genre that it must be called the first modern Western.' Phil Hardy, *The Encyclopedia of Western Movies*, Octopus Books, London, 1984

'The contrast between the innocence of the wilderness and the ambiguous 'blessings of civilisation' are brilliantly stitched into a smoothly developed narrative.' Nigel Floyd *Time Out 14th Ed.*, Time Out Guides Ltd., London, 2006

KEY SCENE TEXTUAL ANALYSIS

A Proposal (9)

Whilst resting at Apache Wells, Ringo decides that he will make a proposal to Dallas. Ford begins this sequence by accentuating both the distance *and* the link between them by keeping a static shot and moving the characters within the filmic space. Dallas walks down a long corridor towards an exterior light source. It is the light of opportunity for Ringo, but she disappears at the end, although the depth of field created, keeping them held in the same space, even when not communicating, will be repeated later in this sequence.

Ringo's progress after her is halted by the proprietor as a new light source invades from a side passage. The medium close-up of the two fleshes out the story, informing Ringo that the people who killed his kin are at the stagecoach's destination.

The exterior again shows Ringo and Dallas in the same space but still apart. The shot has a fence post in the foreground, signifying a barrier; this device is used in the next shot as Dallas walks towards the camera. The shadows of trees also cross her face and the cut to Ringo shows him set against a barren and gnarled tree; love will not be easy for this outlaw and the prostitute.

The long shot of the couple again stresses the connection between the two as he walks some distance behind her. There is no cutting between the two figures now, just this expressionistic shot to highlight that these two breathe the same air. Both this and the corridor shot have also suggested that at this point they are trapped by their social stereotypes - the narrow corridor and then the walled/fenced path outside.

As she reaches the foreground her face is bathed in light, as is his when he nears her – they are illuminated now that they are together. As Ringo approaches, he moves to the other side of the fence that they have been walking along and so this barrier is now between them. But Ford uses this in two ways, just as he has with the deep focus photography. They are separated, but the fence allows Ringo to lean in towards Dallas in a most intimate way, without too much actual intimacy; they have only just met and his loving declaration needs both intimacy and decency. The cut to the two-shot intensifies the growing closeness but there is still the visual reminder of their problems with the vertical part of the fence prominent between them.

But as Ringo's romantic plea begins, the barrier is removed with a close-up of Ringo, cutting to one of Dallas, the pupils of her eyes illuminated by a light source, as if suggesting her sudden realisation that real love is on offer here.

Dallas' 'But you don't know me' signals her feelings of inadequacy and self-loathing, and Ford cuts again to the dissected two-shot to illustrate the returning sense of chasm between them. Unable to bear this honest love, Dallas walks out of their space, and the sense of a spectre hanging over this relationship is suggested by a cut to a mysterious figure approaching, in complete silhouette.

The next shot further emphasises the disruption to this relationship as Dallas runs into the background, leaving Ringo to face this interloper who invades their filmic space in the foreground. It is the sheriff who is taking Ringo back to jail, and he takes Dallas' place at the fence opposite Ringo, warning him not to stray too far. The receding figure is still part of Ringo's filmic space, just!

A gunfight? (15 1:24:04)

Although much of the film has detailed the stagecoach's perilous journey there is still the matter of Ringo's revenge and his relationship with Dallas. Ford takes an interesting approach by not actually showing the gunfight. This, of course, withholds information from the audience and increases the sense of tension. The old device of having the bad man walking after the shootout, and then dropping down dead, serves to increase our anticipation. However, it signals that Ford is not really interested in this as much as he is with Ringo and Dallas.

Ringo prepares for the shootout by accompanying Dallas to the place where she will stay, obviously in the red light district of town. The camera tracks with the couple, keeping them in the same space as they walk past a succession of bars and brothels. In a replay of the earlier scene discussed, the nature of their relationship is played out in filmic space. For the walk he remains close to her, providing support in this seedy part of town, although his inner struggle is perhaps suggested by his figure being consumed by shadow every few steps.

When they arrive at the destination she runs away in shame, but again Ford keeps the camera static and uses depth of field to underline their

dive towards a low angle camera cuts to Dallas, who runs from the back of the frame upwards to end in a close-up. She screams 'Ringo!' and Ford shows her desperately running through the space that Ringo has vacated, forever, as far as she knows at this point. We see the two reunited; she is clinging to a fence, reminiscent of a wooden cross. The camera tracks in as Ringo approaches and the space between them is finally brought to nothing as they embrace.

The cut to a long shot of the couple in each other's arms looks like the final shot of the film, and again Ford playfully, and frustratingly, interrupts their happiness again. The final 'happy ever after' shot is destroyed by horses and a wagon coming between us and them. Although they are finally united in their space, this wagon invades this serenity for it is the sheriff to take him off to jail. However, it is just a momentary frustration as the sheriff and Doctor Boone set them off on their journey to Ringo's ranch 'down South'.

problematic relationship; he is in the foreground and she is deep into the frame, suggesting estrangement and connection all at once.

Again, as in the first proposal, he catches up with her and this time remains on the same side of the fence; the intimate two-shots and single close-ups indicate that we are building up to another proposal, which does happen (in a cowboy kind of manner): 'I asked you to marry me, didn't I?' But his 'Wait here' frustrates the development of this scene as he goes off to do what a man's gotta do!

The meticulous build-up to the shootout, with some false starts, is cheekily curtailed as Ringo dives forward, firing off the first round of the gunfight, and we see no more of the battle. In fact, Ringo's

'Well, that saves them the blessings of civilisation,' says the doctor as the couple rides off; the framing of them in the stopover on the stagecoach journey and then at the destination has suggested their connection, but also their confinement whilst part of civilisation. The final shot, as they ride off into Monument Valley, shows the expanse that they are moving into; they are finally free, as the doctor suggests, free of injustice, prejudice and, indeed, free of Ford's framing devices; the camera remains static as they escape into the distance.

Red River

KEY FACTS

Release Date: 1948

Country of Origin: USA

Running Time: 133 minutes

PRODUCTION NOTES

Production Companies

Charles K. Feldman Group

Monterey Productions

Distributor

United Artists

Budget

$3,000,000 (estimated)

Awards

Nominated: Best Film Editing (Christian Nyby) American Academy Awards

Nominated: Best Writing (Borden Chase) American Academy Awards

Nominated: Outstanding Directorial Achievement in Motion Pictures (Howard Hawks) Directors Guild of America

SYNOPSIS

An account of the opening up of the Chisolm Trail following an authoritarian rancher, Thomas Dunson, with an assortment of cowboys and his adopted son. The epic drive begins in Texas and ends at the town of Abilene, charting the many hardships and setbacks involved. Along the way Dunson and his son come into conflict; Dunson thinks nothing of killing whilst his son has more liberal views. Eventually the son takes control of the herd and drives it to Abilene. Dunson catches up with him and tries to provoke a gunfight. The son refuses to be drawn into a fight to the death and Dunson resorts to punching him. The pair are finally reconciled after a bruising fight and the film acknowledges that both Dunson's good old-fashioned determination and his son's humanitarian views are the way forward.

HISTORICAL CONTEXT

The immediate post-war period brought a flourishing of the arts; in the theatre Tennessee Williams wrote *A Streetcar Named Desire*, the story of discontent in steamy New Orleans and Hollywood was dominated by the *film noir* cycle, dark journeys into the underbelly of American life. A year before *Red River* even the Western genre had succumbed to the film noir influence (see *The Killers*, pg. 90, for an example of *film noir*), in the shape of Raoul Walsh's *Pursued* (1947). Cruelty, deception and a bleak outlook were the hallmarks of much artistic production at the time, reflecting the post-war experience; the horrors that had been seen in war stayed in the memory of many men's minds. *Red River* is full of anger and violence, but it does suggest a new way forward, one embodied in Dunson's adopted son. If John Wayne's Dunson is symbolic of the damaged veteran then his adopted son does suggest that there is hope.

SELECT FILMOGRAPHY OF MAIN PRODUCERS AND CAST

Howard Hawks, 1896–1977, Director

The Dawn Patrol, 1930

Scarface, 1932

Bringing Up Baby, 1938

Only Angels Have Wings, 1939

His Girl Friday, 1940

To Have and Have Not, 1944

The Big Sleep, 1946

Red River, 1948

Gentlemen Prefer Blondes, 1953

Rio Bravo, 1958

Borden Chase, 1899–1971, Screenwriter

Red River, 1948

Bend of the River, 1952

Man without a Star, 1955

Russell Harlan, 1903–1974, Director of Photography

A Walk in the Sun, 1945

Red River, 1948

Riot in Cell Block 11, 1954

The Blackboard Jungle, 1955

Run Silent Run Deep, 1958

To Kill a Mockingbird, 1962

John Wayne, 1907–1979, Actor

See entry for *Stagecoach* (pg. 20)

Montgomery Clift, 1920–1966, Actor

The Search, 1948

Red River, 1948

A Place in the Sun, 1951

From Here to Eternity, 1953

The Misfits, 1960

Joanne Dru, 1922-1996, Actress

Abie's Irish Rose, 1946

Red River, 1948

All the King's Men, 1949

She Wore a Yellow Ribbon, 1949

Wagonmaster, 1950

LINKS TO OTHER FILMS

Rebel Without a Cause (1955)

The story of teenage angst and conflict between parents and children is played out in Nicholas Ray's seminal film; parallels can be drawn between this and *Red River* as the adopted son fights for his own identity and battles with his authoritarian father.

Cowboy (1958)

A naïve easterner buys into a cattle drive and encounters all sorts of problems along the way. The former hotel clerk learns many hard lessons as he travels the 2000-mile route from Chicago to the Rio Grande.

The Cowboys (1971)

John Wayne appears again as the head of a cattle drive, forced to take on a group of teenagers to help when his men run off to a gold rush, and he becomes their surrogate father. Here, the boys learn about the hardships of this life and eventually resort to violence, unlike the adopted son in *Red River*.

The Culpepper Cattle Company (1972)

Another teenager finds that life on the cattle drive is far from the idyllic one that he envisaged; the physical suffering and random violence present a bleak picture of life in the wilderness. The beginning of the cattle drive is an echo of *Red River*'s, as is the teenager's renunciation of violence.

REPRESENTATION

Cattle drives

The epic struggle to drive cattle for hundreds, if not thousands, of miles across harsh terrain and encountering many types of hardship, including Native American attacks, the elements, snakes, rustlers, stampedes and inhospitable land owners, make the symbol of the drive a very potent one indeed in Western film-making. It is representative of the human struggle within the wilderness, of our attempt to order the world around us. It also places man directly into the natural world as part of the natural order as he struggles alongside all living creatures to survive in the wilderness. There is a certain harmony about this struggle, as he is forced to work with nature rather than destroying it.

The journey structure of the cattle drive also helps it draw parallels with rights-of-passage narratives, emphasising the connection between the physical journey and the inner journey that naïve characters experience as they travel towards their goals; this

is not always positive: dreams are often dashed and the grim realities of life are often exposed. The man who conquers the cattle drive is seen as the most determined and professional, and in some cases, the most ruthless.

Fathers and sons

The Western is fertile ground for playing out family relationships, none more powerful than between father and son. In *Red River*, Dunson and his adopted son become increasingly hostile towards each other as the cattle drive progresses. It is a much-used conflict of values and beliefs where the notion of an alienated youth comes into conflict with his father. The battleground in Westerns focuses on the idea of masculinity; males are, in the extreme conditions of Western life, often required to be macho, strong and violent. Fathers usually perceive their sons as weak and incapable of surviving in the Western environment, a pressure that either makes the son become brutalised or find his own, more peaceful, way through life. *Red River* is one of many Westerns where the father/son dynamic follows this pattern or other permutations of this oft-represented scenario; others include *Shane* (1953), *Broken Lance* (1954) and John Wayne's last film, *The Shootist* (1976), which sees him again trying to educate a young man, here the son of his landlady, but this time with the idea of self-control rather than aggression.

'Hawks told me that he consciously imitated (John) Ford's visual style for some scenes in **Red River**.' Joseph McBride, *Searching For John Ford A Life*, Faber and Faber, London, 2003

'It's yet another variation on Hawk's perennial concern with the theme of self-respect and professionalism, and being part of the group.' Geoff Andrew *Time Out 14th Ed.*, Time Out Guides Ltd., London, 2006

KEY SCENE TEXTUAL ANALYSIS

The cattle drive begins (12)

A fade from black heralds the start of the cattle drive. It is dawn and a series of static shots emphasise the stillness in the half-light and the anticipation of the momentous task ahead. The rising sun creates a luminous aura around the cattle and the men, as if they are at the dawn of time, of something so awe-inspiring that even nature takes notice. The dream-like non-diegetic music adds to the unearthly nature of the scene.

Each new shot is reframed to close in on the cowboys and the fact that they are all staring in the same direction. There is something elemental, almost biblical, in this sequence; as if there is a messiah about to descend. And a messiah does come, not from above, but on horseback and he will attempt to lead them to the Promised Land, otherwise known as Missouri. Hollywood's

see. It certainly begins as a POV, but then comes almost full circle to reveal Dunson himself. Does this suggest an out-of-body experience as Dunson embarks on this superhuman task, worthy of an Old Testament story, seeing not only his men and his cattle, but also himself? Or does it perhaps suggest that he has both the power and authority to merit this grand POV, but indicating that he too is part of the journey, very much flesh and blood? Whatever the reason, the panorama created increases the tension of the moment and signifies to both us and Dunson the enormity of the task ahead.

Again, Dunson is afforded two one-shots, his face in shadow, helping to stress the mystery surrounding the man; the enigmatic and the cruel. His words again – 'Take 'em to Missouri, Mat' – are gently spoken and directed at Matthew. He signifies his trust in the young man to set the cattle drive in motion.

mythologising of the Old West is in full swing.

Thomas Dunson rides up to the gates of his ranch and the diegetic sound of the horse's hooves is accentuated to emphasise his importance in this moment. He is the only source of movement amidst the stillness; he will be the dynamo behind the cattle drive. It is he who will utter the first words of the sequence – 'Ready, Matthew?'– signifying his importance, but also his trust in the young cowboy, Matthew. Hawks reiterates Dunson's importance by giving him the only one-shot of the sequence thus far.

The next shot, as he surveys his kingdom of men and cattle, both of whom either remain transfixed or still whilst waiting for his command, appears to be a POV shot. This would be appropriate as it again signals that this man has authority over all he can

Matthew's primeval scream is appropriate in this setting. The dawn is awoken and so are the rest of the cowboys and the cattle; they literally jump into life. There then follows a quick 17-shot explosion of life. The pace of the editing has been leisurely until this point but then the rapid cutting between cowboy faces, as they yelp with elemental joy, releases the tension of the previous section.

Not only is the editing pace increased, but the camera becomes progressively closer to its protagonists, revelling in this moment of epiphany. Not only are they in close-up but they move dynamically within the frame, almost exploding out of it. The message is direct: these men are men of action, men of nature (they sound like coyotes) and they are ready to face colossal odds.

It is reminiscent of Eisenstein's famous lions' montage in *The Battleship Potemkin* (1925), as the still stone beasts seem to raise themselves in anger at the cruelty of the Bolsheviks. Not only is this the beginning of a cattle drive, which would account for their cries, but it helps Hawks remind the audience that these men of many different backgrounds (as we have seen in previous scenes) are inextricably bound together.

The non-diegetic music erupts at this sync point with a chorus of voices proclaiming the glory and hardships to come. As is usual for Hawks an element of comedy is introduced with old Groot's strangulated attempt to give a lusty cowboy yelp.

The sequence ends by cutting between long shots of the dynamic grandiose spectacle and the still static Dunson and Matthew, who are delineated from the rest as having the power, and time, to ruminate over their chances of success. Both in one of the long shots and in the two-shot of Dunson and Matthew, the camera is placed at a low angle, subtly forcing the audience to look up to these events and to these men. We should never forget, as Hawks intended, that these men are heroes.

The showdown (32)

By this point in the film Matthew has taken control of the cattle drive as Dunson has become increasingly unpredictable and ruthless. Dunson finally catches up with Matthew at the cattle drive's end in Abilene to carry out his promise of killing him.

The long shot of Dunson and his hired men riding towards the final showdown is foregrounded by a mass of cattle; they are the focus of the battle between Dunson and Matthew, and the latter is seen riding, and then striding through them, as if rebranding them as his own. But his surge through the cattle, his renewed dynamism accentuated by the tracking shots of him, suggest that his battle lies beyond the cattle and rests with his deep-seated hatred of Matthew.

It is noticeable that the cuts back to the waiting cowboys have them framed within a *mise-en-scène* that suggest domesticity and a new way of life;

Cherry and Melville stand next to an ornate front porch and Matthew stands in front of a wagon, full of domestic trappings (pots, pans, tablecloths), perhaps a suggestion of their futures.

The relentless movement of Dunson towards Matthew is underpinned by the non-diegetic music with its striding, marching, orchestral score, punctuated by blasts of brass instruments suggesting his madness; one such blast occurs as Cherry challenges him and Dunson fells him with a single shot, receiving a bullet himself as Cherry falls to the ground.

Visually, this shot tells us something about Dunson; the camera tracks with him and continues to do so even as the gunfight between him and Cherry takes place; Dunson barely pauses, just long enough to turn and shoot and take a bullet in his side, and then continue towards his quarry.

There is no cut here, indicating Dunson's insatiable desire to confront Matthew, and it is also interesting how the camera stays firmly focused on him, and how Cherry enters his space and is quickly dispatched, entirely fitting for a character who has dominated the narrative and tends to dominate the filmic space.

The medium long shot from behind Matthew states the nature of the conflict that will ensue: the railroad (progress) bisects both men, whilst next to Matthew is the 'domestic' wagon and next to Dunson is a horse (freedom, individuality). But this is not just a symbolic struggle - it is a very real struggle between stubborn men who have a father and son bond.

After the movement of the previous shot there is now this static frieze followed by a series of ever-increasing close-ups of the two protagonists. Hawks suggests the conflict by filling up the screen with Dunson's face, then Matthew's. Finally, the latter is as important as the former in filmic terms. Matthew also gains the upper hand by refusing to draw and remaining still whilst Dunson fires at him. The shots generally hit the wagon behind, noticeably hitting the objects of domesticity that the free-spirited cattle baron rejects. These close-ups end on Matthew's defiantly grinning face, as if he is the moral victor.

There is still the matter of the fist fight and after Matthew has taken a beating he finally fights back. For the final moment of Matthew's 'earning' of Dunson's respect he hits him with an upper cut. The camera is now behind and below Matthew, emphasising his resurgence and the cataclysmic nature of this physical outburst against his 'father'. After the second punch Dunon is dazed, but there is a nuance of admiration in his face. Another dramatic upper cut and some return punches from Dunson lead to Matthew charging him and both ending up crashing into the aforementioned wagon.

Pointedly, Dunson is covered with the artefacts of domesticity, and the other great Hollywood symbol of the home and security, the woman, intervenes at this point. Empowered with a gun, Matthew's love, Tess Millay, rails at them for their stupidity and because they love each other. She fires at them,

after all. The final shot of the new cattle brand drawn in the sand by Dunson denotes how they have an equal partnership at last, but also connotes the branding of the land by men. This is the beginning of a new America, based on economic wealth (the cattle), progress (the railroad), settling down (the woman and the wagon) and male professionalism/respect/friendship.

makes them see sense and then throws the gun back at one of the watching cowboys.

Initially, the men are seen from a high angle, disempowering them as they listen to Tess' passionate, but sensible, tirade. Dunson's comment, 'You'd better marry that girl, Matt' indicates her embodiment of all that it is suggested is needed in a frontier wife. Her constant wiping of her nose is probably a reference to Dunson's habit before embarking on important decisions. The final shots are now on a level with the two men, occupying equal space of the two-shot; they are now equals with mutual respect and the framing underlines this.

The film ends with individual close-ups of the two leads, with equal frame space for each. But Dunson has two shots and Matthew only one; Wayne was the big star and this was Mongomery Clift's debut

The Searchers

KEY FACTS

Release Date: 1956

Country of Origin: USA

Running Time: 119 minutes

PRODUCTION NOTES

Production Companies

C.V. Whitney Pictures

Warner Bros. Pictures

Distributor

Warner Bros. Pictures

Budget

$3,750,000 (estimated)

Awards

Nominated: Outstanding Directorial Achievement in Motion Pictures John Ford Directors Guild of America

SYNOPSIS

Texas, 1868. Confederate soldier Ethan Edwards returns to his brother and sister-in-law's isolated farmstead after many years' absence. Tragedy soon overtakes the reunion and Ethan joins a posse of Texas Rangers in pursuit of raiding Commanches, and all but his two nieces are killed by the Native Americans back at the farm. The nieces are kidnapped, and so begins Ethan's quest to find the girls with the help of Martin Pawlee, his brother's adopted one-eighth Native American son. The search lasts for many years and Ethan's obsession, racism and bitterness grow steadily as they encounter the brutality of the wilderness in its many forms - madness, treachery, and savagery. The finale comes after finding the elder niece's dead body and the younger Deborah as part of the Commanche chief's tribe. Her 'Indianisation' disgusts Ethan and his first instinct is to kill her. He ultimately transcends his racist feelings and returns her to friends, although he seems isolated from the happy ending.

HISTORICAL CONTEXT

The 1950s was a time of post-war prosperity and Cold War paranoia in the United States. In film terms it seemed that Hollywood was at last beginning to address the issue of the demonised Native American after many years portraying them as savages. A new liberal attitude prevailed, and it seemed it was time to address racial stereotyping. Indeed, after the horrors of Nazi Germany's ethnic cleansing, it was perhaps time for the United States to face up to its own tainted past.

Certainly, Hollywood had helped perpetuate the one-dimensional view of Native Americans through its many Westerns that portrayed them as uncivilised, preying on the heroic white settlers. Until the 1950s they were filmic gun fodder, but films such as *Broken Arrow* (1950) and *Apache* (1954) began to present a more sympathetic portrayal of the indigenous population. John Ford had directed many Westerns before *The Searchers*, including *The Iron Horse* (1924), *Stagecoach* (1939), *My Darling Clementine* (1946), *Fort Apache* (1948), *She Wore a Yellow Ribbon* (1949) and *Rio Grande* (1950), many of which contained the standard depiction of Native Americans.

The Searchers is something of a departure for Ford. There are still savages, but now we see more of their lifestyle and rituals, even a condemnation of a brutal cavalry attack on a Native American reservation. Most importantly, Ethan faces his own racist philosophy and finally accepts his part-Native American companion and his niece who has been raised by her captors. There are still many uncomfortable issues for a modern audience: the shameless degradation of Luck, Pawlee's inadvertently purchased wife (providing supposed comedy), and the explicit assertion that 'exposure' to a Native American way of life would taint a white person's moral character and sanity. Nevertheless, John Wayne's central performance does embody the 1950s and its troubled attempt to come to terms with its past, a struggle that would gather momentum in the following decade.

SELECT FILMOGRAPHY OF MAIN PRODUCERS AND CAST

John Ford, 1895-1973, Director

See entry for *The Iron Horse* (pg. 14)

Merian C Cooper, 1893–1973, Executive Producer

King Kong, 1933

Fort Apache, 1948

Rio Grande, 1950

The Quiet Man, 1952

The Searchers, 1956

Winton C Hoch, 1905–1979, Director of Photography

Joan of Arc, 1948

She Wore a Yellow Ribbon, 1949

The Quiet Man, 1952

The Searchers, 1956

John Wayne, 1907–1979, Actor

See entry for *Stagecoach* (pg. 20)

Jeffrey Hunter, 1925–1969, Actor

The Searchers, 1956

The True Story of Jesse James, 1957

King of Kings, 1961

The Longest Day, 1962

Natalie Wood, 1938–1981, Actress

Rebel without a Cause, 1955

The Searchers, 1956

West Side Story, 1961

Love with the Proper Stranger, 1964

LINKS TO OTHER FILMS

Broken Arrow (1950)

The treatment of the Native Americans is more sympathetic and positive here than in most previous Westerns, which had predominantly portrayed them as savage hordes, serving as targets for white settlers' guns. The representation is worthy, if rather patronising, and there are still white actors in Native American roles, Jeff Chandler being the most prominent example as Cochise, a role he would reprise in The Battle at Apache Pass (1952).

Apache (1954)

Another liberal Western which details Burt Lancaster's Native American character's attempt to fight against, escape from and ultimately settle away from white society. It is a positive representation of a way of life under threat, but is again undermined by the casting of white Lancaster in the central role. Conversely, it is certain that the film would not have been made without a star in the title role, and his desire to make such a film; Lancaster's own production company was behind the project. As such, it was a step to redress the stereotyped and biased representation that Hollywood had perpetuated for many years.

REPRESENTATION

Home and wilderness

There is a clear delineation between the worlds of home and the wilderness in the film. The white people here exist at the edge of society, walking a fine line between survival and extinction. When the Native Americans attack the homestead of Ethan's sister and brother-in-law the scene is shot almost entirely from the inside of the home. Its interior is imbued with the soft purplish light of a sunset, and domesticity and order seem to be thriving. The setting of the table, the ordered routines and the womb-like home are comforting, but then they become the rituals of the imprisoned, as it becomes clear that they are being surrounded by the Native Americans. The blowing out of the light and the mother's slap of the girl's face fracture the inner sanctum of the home and foreshadow its

destruction.

Of course, the wilderness is a white man's wilderness; it is the Native American's home. Only Ethan realises this: he shoots buffalo to cut off their food supply; he shoots at the eyes of an already-dead Native American who is buried out on the plains so he cannot enter their sacred land and a village is wiped out and Native American women killed. There is as much violation of the Native Americans as there is of the whites; one man's wilderness is another man's home.

The Native Americans

They are mostly portrayed as brutal killers, as embodied by the leader of the rampaging band, Scar. There is also the hapless daughter, Luck, who becomes Martin Pawlee's wife. She is mocked by Martin and Ethan, although her death at the hands of the cavalry is treated with tenderness. Most interesting is the treatment of Martin and Deborah. Martin is ridiculed from the start by Ethan for his dark complexion and unconventional manners, but it is he who is shown to have a loving spirit throughout the film and who prevents Ethan from killing Deborah at its dramatic climax. The niece herself is shown to be integrated into the Native American tribe by the end of the film and initially refuses to be 'rescued'. Ultimately, she embodies the inner demons within Ethan, someone whom he has loved, but has been soiled in his eyes by her long association with something that he detests, the savage Indian.

In accepting this new type of identity when he picks her up in his arms at the end, he reconciles his sense of otherness with that of the Native Americans. Like the Native Americans he has searched for an identity in an ever-changing world and becomes reconciled to his fate as an isolated member of society, as we shall see when examining two scenes in detail. The final point to make is that, like its predecessors, Apache and Broken Arrow, the film is somewhat compromised by its use of white actors in key Native American roles, a practice which took many years to be addressed.

'What makes The Searchers so successful...is Ford's confident handling of such complex material, his ability to mix frontier slapstick...mythic landscapes...and character exploration with telling economy.' Phil Hardy, *The Encyclopedia of Western Movies*, Octopus Books, London, 1984

'At the dawn of the second century of cinema The Searchers stands, by general assent, as a monument no less conspicuous than the towers of stone which dominate its landscapes. The strength yet delicacy of its mise en scène, the splendour of its vistas, the true timbre of its emotions, make it a touchstone of American cinema. The Searchers is one of those films by which Hollywood may be measured.' Edward Buscombe, The Searchers, BFI, 2000

KEY SCENE TEXTUAL ANALYSIS

The opening (2)

After the melancholy and elegiac tone of the title sequence's traditional cowboy music we are presented with the simple title card, Texas 1868. Like an inter-title card from the silent era of film, it has echoes of a lost era as is appropriate for a film which depicts the last moments of an America torn between its wild and dangerous mistress past and its safe and conformist family future. The title fades and we are left momentarily in darkness, until a door is opened and we emerge from the womb-like interior of the house. A woman's silhouette bars our way for a moment and then the camera tracks after her as she moves forward and through the door.

What faces her, and the audience, is an expanse of wilderness, the harsh world beyond the safety of the home. It is alien-like with monolithic rock formations, sparse vegetation and orange-hewed sand stretching into the distance. The emphasis is on the isolation and the immensity of the place. The wooden roof rafters look like parts of a skeleton, as if the house is associated with death. The house itself is rudimentary, elemental almost, as if nature might claim it back for its own at any moment. In the midst of this space a tiny figure on horseback nears the house.

Like the killers in *Once Upon A Time in the West*, this figure is visually linked to the wilderness. The shot which reveals the woman's face for the first time shows us an apron-wearing mother figure (the blue of her dress matched by the blue of the crockery in the next scene, firmly linking her with domesticity). She is buffeted by the wind and the glare coming from the wilderness causes her to shield her eyes, the tilt of her hand indicating not just protection from the bright sun, but also being reminiscent of the gesture made as one is about to faint. She is a home-maker, but it is a fragile home in a hostile environment, and fittingly the woman (Martha) is never seen straying beyond the house porch.

There follows a long shot to reinforce the stranger's connection to the wilderness. He is framed by two of the giant monolithic rock structures and it is noteworthy that the hitching post in the foreground has a large blanket draped over it, decorated with Native American designs, foreshadowing the profound effect that the Native Americans will have on these settlers' lives.

The woman's husband appears from the shadows and, disbelieving, utters the first word of the film: 'Ethan?' Who is Ethan? Where has he come from? What has he been doing? These are questions that are posed but never answered throughout the film. Indeed, the man himself is called into question throughout the film. The name and the man are riddles to all around him, to the audience and ultimately to himself. A question is a fitting beginning to a film charting a search for others and for self.

The next shot emphasises the connection between the home and the women. As the members of the household assemble on the porch to view the approaching figure, it is only the man who ventures beyond the confines of the house, leaving the women in a protected band within its boundaries. Indeed, throughout the film it is the men who search, who are active, but who are also aimless and troubled. The women are anchored, are carers and sustain the family unit, whatever travails they have to endure. The children move into position within the space of the medium shot as if choreographed, the young girl with her dolly and the boy carrying firewood, part of the rituals and routines of domesticity. The young girl, Deborah, is the only one of the children afforded a single shot, and the *mise-en-scène* is prophetic. She is

different; he is a soldier and there is no embrace from the family. They stand as if uncertain of him, maintaining their earlier positions.

The non-diegetic sound has continued throughout the sequence as a gentle orchestral piece, clearly from the Western genre with strings, strumming guitar and south-of-the-border brass. The next shot, a medium of Ethan and Martha, is tender and loving as he kisses her forehead, but this is immediately followed by a pause in the harmonious, if slightly melancholic score, and then quickly followed by a discordant note that quickly gives way to the harmony again. However, the sour note is there and musically prepares us for the difficult relationship that Ethan has with the notion of family.

the one who will be captured and reared by the Native Americans. Tellingly, there is another Native American rug hanging beside her. The doll that she clutches is the one that Ethan finds on his search, and the barking dog foreshadows his inadvertent betrayal of her as she hides by her grandmother's gravestone in the later attack. The cut from her back to Ethan helps to establish the connection between the two characters that will further develop throughout the film.

Ford has not shown the audience the approaching Ethan for some time and he gives us another tantalising glimpse as he dismounts, his face still obscured by his long-brimmed hat, before cutting back to Lucy's exclamation, 'That's your Uncle Ethan!' His name is confirmed but he still remains a mystery. He shakes the man's hand without a word and then the reverse long shot, from the perspective of the wilderness now sees Ethan as a central part of the family group. However, he is

Once kissed, Martha retreats back to the house, still facing Ethan. The strings swell as it cuts back to a long shot to continue this movement into the safe environs of the home. Ethan follows the smiling Martha, but her backward entry into the house could carry a number of interpretations: she cannot take her eyes off this enigmatic man whom she has not seen for many years; or are we being told that there is something dangerous about Ethan? Her retreat is certainly reminiscent of someone retreating from a monster or murderer. As the narrative unfolds Ethan is painted in many shades, and these are two that figure heavily throughout the film.

The ending (44)

The opening left us with the traditional structure of white family life entering the home. By the time we reach the climax that family has been all but decimated and we are left with a new family unit, but one from which Ethan is again estranged. The initial shot repeats the visual motif of the film's opening, a group of people gathered on a front porch, gazing out in anticipation at something unseen coming out of the wilderness. Except this time there is an older man and a woman, with a man seated (the eccentric Mose who has appeared child-like throughout the film and is possibly part-Native American). This time the house seems to be more solid: the wood is possibly painted, it has a fixed lantern and there are even decorative flourishes in the rafter supports. This appears much more stable than the homestead we see at the beginning of the film. A suitable place to house the new family unit that is approaching.

specially composed for the film) is heard once more. Mose is seen again, happily rocking in his chair, wearing his favourite hat, and then Ford closes proceedings by returning to the camera set-up that began the film, placing it on the porch of the house.

Ethan lovingly hands over Debbie to the Jorgensen's and it seems as if he might follow and become part of this new family group. The camera tracks back into the house as the Jorgensens guide a nervous Debbie inside. Notably, she is still in Native American dress: the 'enemy' is now embraced and crosses the white settlers' threshold in peace. Ethan moves aside, allowing Martin and Laurie to enter the house, hand in hand. Like the three who have just entered, they become silhouettes and

The next shot shows five horsemen nearing the house. The number is not the only difference from the beginning. In the background there is still the wilderness, but in the foreground, and much more the focus this time, is an expanse of water and happily grazing horses and cattle. This land is alive, unlike the beautiful but unforgiving landscape at the beginning.

Back at the house a young woman runs excitedly out onto the porch, and then, much more significantly, she races out into the wilderness and towards the riders. The apprehension of the opening scene is gone and the upbeat non-diegetic music underpins the harmonious atmosphere. The searchers are returning, Ethan at the front with Debbie cradled on his lap. Martin follows and it is to him that the young woman runs.

There is no dialogue, but as Ethan and Debbie dismount the traditional-sounding cowboy song which was played over the title sequence (although

anonymous, returning to safety, but this time as a group which has more in common with the land and the people of that land than those before them: a young girl brought up by Native Americans, the partly Cherokee Martin and his bride-to-be, with Mose left happily on the porch. They are the new everymen, and again Ethan is denied access.

His one step up onto the porch suggests his desire to be part of all this but instead he pauses and reaches across with his left hand and grabs his right arm. Although it has been well-documented that Wayne made this gesture as a tribute to a typical stance of old Western actor, Harry Carey Sr., it also neatly articulates a desire for human comfort or comforting himself from the chill of alienation within him, and a realisation that he can never be part of this new world.

So, Ethan does find Debbie and discovers an ability to overcome his hatred, but he will be forever excluded from the future because he is a man too much of the past.

The walk back into the wilderness perfectly illustrates this: there is no sign of the water or animals in the background, just a bleak expanse; the wind throws dust around him as he almost evaporates into the wilderness; and Wayne's own loping gait with trailing right foot encapsulates the melancholic feeling of otherness. The lyrics of the song evaporate too – 'Ride away, ride away' – and the closing door brings the film full circle. Ethan and the past remain outside while the others, with their futures, stay within.

C'era una volta il West (Once Upon a Time in the West)

KEY FACTS

Release Date: 1968

Country of Origin: Italy

Running Time: 165 minutes

PRODUCTION NOTES

Production Companies

Paramount Pictures

Rafran Cinematografica

San Marco Production

Distributor

Paramount Pictures

Budget

$5,000,000 (estimated)

Awards

Best Production Bino Cicogna David di Donatello Awards, Italy

SYNOPSIS

After an initial gunfight where only one man, Harmonica, survives and the McBain family is massacred, this epic tale charts the fortunes of the widowed Jill McBain as she struggles to fend off railroad boss Morton's attempts to wrestle her late husband's land from her control. Morton's henchman, Frank, we discover, had ordered Harmonica's death and is responsible for the deaths of the McBain family. Cheyenne, leader of a criminal gang, also becomes involved in the plot as his men are mistakenly suspected of the McBain killings. The complex narrative eventually reveals that Morton is trying to gain control of the McBain settlement, Sweetwater, as it has the only water supply for many miles around and his railroad must be built through this land.

Harmonica maintains a relentless pursuit of Frank, who we gradually learn in a series of flashbacks, has cruelly murdered his brother many years before. The denouement sees Frank murder Morton, in order to gain control of the railroad, and Harmonica eventually kills Frank. Cheyenne, fatally wounded in a gunfight with Frank near the end of the film, dies and Harmonica rides off, his job done. Jill is left to provide hope and support for the workers as the railroad, and civilisation, head west through her invaluable land.

HISTORICAL CONTEXT

Once Upon a Time in the West was made in the 1960s, a time of upheaval in the world: stirrings against Russian Communist rule in Eastern Europe and ongoing conflicts in the likes of Korea and Vietnam. It was also an age of personal and sexual discovery as the young challenged old taboos and restrictions. Certainly, Sergio Leone's 'Dollar' trilogy, and most particularly, *Once Upon a Time in the West*, presented a radically different view of the mythic Old West, as put forward by the likes of John Ford and Howard Hawks. Yes, they had depicted the conflict between the Old West and modern society, but never with such brutality.

The Western genre has its origins at the very beginning of film-making in Hollywood, but was in decline by the 1960s. The Western had always struggled for credibility in Hollywood, often regarded as fodder for Saturday morning serials and gangs of cowboy-playing children who flocked to the cinemas to act out their gunfighting dreams. The advent of the mass adoption of television in the United States during the 1950s put further pressure on their credibility: for every John Ford Western in the cinema there were countless TV Westerns (Steve McQueen's *Wanted Dead or Alive*, for example), using the old tired (sic) and tested formulas. There seemed very little left for the Western to do or say, particularly whilst 1950s America was gripped by a fascination with science fiction films. The Western seemed to be stuck in a rut, and even intelligent film Westerns like John Ford's *The Searchers* (1956) did only reasonable business at the box office.

Although popular American Westerns would emerge in the 1960s (*The Magnificent Seven*, 1960, stands as an obvious example) they were not plentiful and it was Leone who single-handedly reinvented and rejuvenated the genre, creating the sub-genre of the Spaghetti Western as he did so.

Leone adored Hollywood Westerns and used many of their conventions, but the moral uncertainty and the blurring of archetypal characters seem entirely in keeping with the 1960s. He imported American actors (Eastwood, Bronson, Fonda and Coburn) and exported back to America the sacred cow of genres, repackaged in a new and exhilarating form.

This form was often graphically violent, amoral, playful with its use and subversion of traditional Western genres (look at Leone's 'Dollar' trilogy for evidence of this), and were injected with a contemporary sensibility through their characterisation and use of electronic music, as scored by Ennio Morricone. The moral boundaries of earlier Westerns had become unclear, and Hollywood would learn from Leone, producing Westerns such as *The Wild Bunch* by the end of the decade.

Leone also helped to revitalise a flagging Italian film industry, which had been riding high on the success of the 'sword and sandal' epics of the 1950s and early 1960s, both home-grown (Leone's *The Colossus of Rhodes*, 1961) and Hollywood-financed (Mervyn LeRoy's *Quo Vadis*, 1951). However, massive financial flops like Joseph L Mankewicz's *Cleopatra* in 1963 helped put the Italian film industry into the doldrums, and the long-running cycle of Spaghetti Westerns which Leone initiated eventually revitalised Italian fortunes.

SELECT FILMOGRAPHY OF MAIN PRODUCERS AND CAST

Sergio Leone, 1921-1989, Director, Screenwriter

See LINKS TO OTHER FILMS below for details

Ennio Morricone, 1928, Composer

Leone's two trilogies

Days of Heaven, 1978

The Mission, 1986

The Untouchables, 1987

Cinema Paradiso, 1989

Claudia Cardinale, 1938, Actress

The Pink Panther, 1963

The Professionals, 1966

Once Upon a Time in the West, 1968

Fitzcarraldo, 1982

Henry Fonda, 1905-1982, Actor

Young Mr. Lincoln, 1939

The Grapes of Wrath, 1940

The Return of Frank James, 1940

My Darling Clementine, 1946

The Wrong Man, 1957

Twelve Angry Men, 1957

Once Upon a Time in the West, 1968

Charles Bronson, 1921-2003, Actor

The Magnificent Seven, 1960

The Great Escape, 1963

Once Upon a Time in the West, 1968

The Dirty Dozen, 1967

Death Wish, 1974

Jason Robards, 1922-2000, Actor

Hour of the Gun, 1967

Once Upon a Time in the West, 1968

Tora! Tora! Tora!, 1970

Pat Garrett and Billy the Kid, 1973

All the President's Men, 1976

Philadelphia, 1993

Enemy of the State, 1998

Magnolia, 1999

LINKS TO OTHER FILMS

A Fistful of Dollars (1964)/*For a Few Dollars* (1965)/*The Good, the Bad and the Ugly* (1966)

These Leone films form the 'Dollar' trilogy, which looks at the early part of the American West's creation, up to The American Civil War. It is a time of chaos, individualism and lack of coherence in society.

A Fistful of Dynamite (1971)/*Once Upon a Time in America* (1984)

Leone's second trilogy, which begins with *Once Upon a Time in the West*, charts the creation of modern America as the Old West dies, making way for the cities, industry and twentieth-century sensibilities which defined this new era. The succeeding instalments examine progress through revolution and criminal activity, seeing these as the origins of present day American society.

The Iron Horse (1924)

Leone loved American Westerns and his films contain many references to the Hollywood version of the American West. John Ford, in particular, he found to be an essential thematic and visual source. *The Iron Horse*'s recounting of a transcontinental railway is mirrored in *Once Upon a Time in the West*, examining the iconic status of the train in the creation of America.

The Searchers (1956)

Again, Leone acknowledges his debt to John Ford by shooting some scenes of *Once Upon a Time in the West* in Ford's favourite location, Monument Valley, the archetypal Western location. The McBain massacre, which we will look at in detail, also owes much to the massacre of Ethan's sister and her family in *The Searchers*. Both films clearly demonstrate the powerful connotations of the home and of the wilderness.

REPRESENTATION

Men

In Leone's earlier 'Dollar' films there is a blurring of the stereotypical representation of the all-American Western hero. These films depict the

Clint Eastwood character capable of the same level of brutality, cynicism and calculation as the bad guys. In *Once Upon a Time in the West*, the Jason Robards character is both a villain and a good guy, whilst the male hero, Charles Bronson, is not your typical cowboy: he is dark-skinned, taciturn and single-minded in his pursuit of Henry Fonda. The film has been called a revisionist Western, using some of the clichés of American Westerns and subverting them at the same time. It challenges the traditional representation of the American frontier as being formed by honest men (see also *Unforgiven*, pg. 58), and instead presents the full mix of people who were involved in this process: the good, the bad and the ugly.

Women

Women had been neglected in the first of Leone's Westerns, existing in the narrow confines of the mother/virgin/Madonna or whore archetypes. Here, Claudia Cardinale's character is more complex and she is, in fact, seen as combining the archetypal female character types, a strong person who provides hope for the future of this burgeoning and chaotic civilisation. Of course, here and later in Leone's work (notably, *Once Upon a Time in America*) Leone's treatment of women is problematic, supporting the idea of women in film being represented from the perspective of, in Laura Mulvey's words, 'the male gaze'. Jill McBain is alive and forms an integral part of the emerging world at the end of the film, unlike the other dead cowboys; but Jason Robards' words to her as she goes out to bring water to the railroad workers – 'And if one of them should pat your behind, just make believe it's nothing. They earned it' – are rather chauvinistic, to say the least, and invite a critical feminist reading.

The American West

Westerns are ripe for analysis when it comes to semiotics. Gunfights, good and bad cowboys, railroads, dusty towns and isolated homesteads are all representative of the Western and its depiction of the American West. Key symbols, like the McBain's Sweetwater homestead, represent a tiny

oasis of security amidst an unpredictable world of violence and death, as represented by Frank and the wilderness. Another staple of this genre is the Native American or 'Indians' as they were often termed. This is one aspect of Leone's Westerns which is almost totally under-represented, except for a fleeting, but telling, reference in the third sequence of the film; Jill McBain's arrival at the station. Here, a group of Native Americans are herded off the train down the same route as the cattle. That image, coupled with the words of a white cowboy – 'Get the lead outta your asses, you Redskin warriors' – signifies that this once free-roaming and spirited people have lost their independence and are subjugated by 'white progress'.

'Leone's masterpiece is the culmination of his distinctive contribution to the Western genre. In Leone's west, characters are driven by revenge, greed or lust, but never by a sense of community or a desire to civilise the wilderness. For the director, it's an opportunity to pursue aesthetic, not social ends. Indeed Once Upon a Time in the West is more about other Western movies than it is about the west itself.' Edward Buscombe, 'Once Upon a Time in the West', *100 Westerns*, BFI, 2006

'Close-ups have remained among the most powerful devices available to directors. Few have used them more dramatically than Sergio Leone in Once Upon a Time in the West.*'* Mark Cousins, *The Story of Film*, Pavillion Books, London, 2004

KEY SCENE TEXTUAL ANALYSIS

The McBain massacre (3/4)

The Hunt

The scene begins and ends with a gunshot, book-ending what is a very brutal scene. The iconic use of the gun, a staple of the Western genre, dominates the *mise-en-scène* of this sequence.

The extreme close-up of the rifle, making full use of the widescreen frame, identifies violence/death/killing as a major theme in the film: killing to eat, as here; killing for greed or killing for fun later on. The camera shakily depicts the killing of the unlucky bird, foreshadowing the murders to come. A man's face comes into the frame: it is an open face, kindly; there is warmth (contrast this with the iciness of the heartless killer's face).

Leone repeats and juxtaposes shots, creating a pattern of shots to further the visual message. For example, McBain's face makes the same movement from left to right as the rifle barrel, matching him to the killing device, followed by a cut to the young boy, linking him to the threat of violence as well.

The boy is half-hidden by the sagebrush, obscuring our view of him; is something or someone lurking there? The father watches as the son carefully walks through the sagebrush; our obscured view and the accentuated sound of insects and birds all add to the suspense.

The boy initiates the second of the scene's violent markers (the first being the initial gunshot) by suddenly jumping to make the birds fly off and mimicking his father's actions of violence. Two points to make: the fabric of this wilderness society is based on the gun for survival and here we see the son learning from the father; it also foreshadows the violence to come and chillingly juxtaposes with the boy's death at the end by a real gun (his game of death is closer to the real thing in the wilderness).

The boy is disappointed to be called by his father and the camera again traces the boys' arduous run through the scrub, carrying the spoils of his father's shooting (two lifeless birds; these are both necessary to eat and survive, but are also the boy's

playthings and link him to death). The environment is tough and hostile, and the sedate and revelatory crane shot presents us with a view of the antidote to the wilderness – the McBain's home.

The home and preparations for a celebration

Father and son, the hunter-gatherers, return to the house with their prizes. The house is solid, wooden and grand; we never see inside the house during this sequence (except, later in the scene, when we emerge from its darkness from the boy's POV). A tracking shot of the daughter is next, and the motion from wilderness to home of the men is contrasted with the female movement from within the home, thus identifying her with its connotations of safety, family and nourishment, as she carries out a huge bowl of corn husks.

The stereotyping of the genders is typical of the Western genre and may seem old-fashioned to viewers today, but does reflect the gender roles of this time. The scene is domestic with the prominent red gingham tablecloth covered with food. This movement of the domestic world to the outside is a brave step; this family is out in the wilderness and planning a celebration beneath the hot sun and biting wind (the meal never looks like it's going to be eaten with the wind blowing sand incessantly over the food).

Timmy, the little boy, and his sister are both redheads (as is the father) emphasising their Irish roots – Maureen also sings 'Danny Boy' later in the scene; these are identifiably immigrants with their roots in Europe. Like the father and son, Maureen has a kind and open face, adding to the audience's sympathy for these characters.

As well as the tablecloth and the red hair, the *mise-en-scène* is dominated by the colour red: the young boy's trousers, a stripe down his shirt, the red wine on the table, the terracotta earthenware, the older brother's hair and even his handkerchief. It is the colour of danger and of blood.

The red palette is also juxtaposed with the innocent, virginal white of Maureen's dress. She helps her father put on his shirt collar, identifying her not just as daughter, but also as substitute wife. The sounds of the wilderness, the birds and, particularly, the crickets, have been incessant throughout this scene; they are both a constant reminder of the wilderness' otherness but are also reassuring.

First signs of trouble

When the noise of the wilderness abruptly stops the natural order is disturbed and foreshadows the impending doom.

The only sound is that of the domesticated birds as the family look about them with great concern; these people who have settled in the wilderness have become in tune with nature, sensing danger. As the silence continues, Maureen continues to cut the bread; significantly, she cuts with a large knife moving its blade towards her body in a threatening manner.

hand on flesh; the son is angered by his father's comment that his 'mother' is arriving and that he will be late to pick her up. 'Our mother died six years ago' is the reply, which earns him the slap. The message is of a harsh world where mothers die and instant punishment is meted out (Brett and his two older children die because he has land valuable to the railroad and Timmy will die for hearing one of the killers carelessly utter their leader's name).

The father's casual violence towards his son is juxtaposed with his tenderness towards his daughter as he touches her face, and with his gentle tone as he describes his new bride's clothing to Patrick so that he will recognise her at the train station. This underpins the type of frontier society that existed then, brutality and love co-existing side by side.

There is one last moment of serenity for the McBains as Maureen goes back to laying the table,

The first close-up of Brett's face, as he listens, reveals the dead tree stump behind him; this is a remnant of their house building, but also points to death; the second has the house (the fruit of his labour and his sanctuary) behind him. The only 'guest' who sits down to the meal is Brett's rifle, and it is this rifle that dominates the *mise-en-scène* for the next part of the scene. As Timmy goes into the house to get washed the camera prowls to a position whereby the barrel of the rifle foregrounds and dominates the action, a reminder of the ever-present threat of violence.

The reason for the party has remained a mystery until this point, and the rather oblique conversation between father and daughter about their imminent change of fortune adds to the unease of the scene thus far.

When Brett hits Patrick in the face, the brutality is emphasised with the amplified sound of the

Patrick leads the horse and buggy out from the barn and Brett walks to the well to get some water. Leone allows the restless camera to become static for a moment, the serenity of the domestic scene underpinned by Maureen's gentle singing of 'Danny Boy'. But the undertone of violence is ever-present, with the rifle and holstered gun clearly seen in the foreground.

The build-up to the massacre

The next shot begins the build-up to the shooting as we have a long shot, with the scrub of the wilderness now beginning to reassert itself in the foreground and the heightened noise of the relentless wind. Their fleeting moment of domestic bliss, of Brett's dreams of a new life with his new wife and future wealth, are about to be shattered. The lurking threat in the wilderness is about to show itself; the three characters are all framed with the ropes of the well resembling a gallows.

The bucket creaks and squeaks as Brett pulls the rope (reminiscent of the squealing windmill which prefigures the violent gunfight in the preceding scene). If we are still unsure that something wicked this way comes, Leone draws the audience's attention to the rifle, placed squarely in the foreground as the camera tracks past Maureen.

Again, the noise of the crickets stops abruptly and all three characters look around uncertainly. The tension mounts rapidly; the bucket obscures Brett's face just as the truth of what's about to happen dawns on him. Leone affords us three close-up shots of the family in succession, to emphasise their fear but also for us to identify one last time with these sympathetic individuals.

The camera tracks around the back of Brett's head

hunt. The dark irony and true horror is revealed as Brett looks back towards his home.

Like a dying swan, almost as if she is being buffeted by the strong wind, Maureen drops to the ground. Brett's explosive shout of 'Maureen!' is propelled by a zoom to an extreme close-up of his mouth.

The camera then tracks Brett's race to Maureen; the pace, energy and desperation of his movement is underpinned by the camera movement. However, the tracking shot also indicates that his actions are being monitored as sagebrush obscures our view of him.

Two gunshots ring out and the father comes to rest next to his dead daughter, with Patrick unseated by a bullet. Brett crawls desperately towards his holstered gun but his death is sealed with one more blast, underpinned by the unsettling sound of squawking turkeys.

- who is watching him? It looks as if we will track around to his face, but Leone has Brett look around to match the camera movement, and we do not see his expression; our frustration mirrors his own anxiety.

The silence is broken by a return to the scene's opening with the flight of birds from the sagebrush: do even the animals fear what is coming? The next shot connects Maureen even more closely to death as she moves towards the barrel of the father's rifle and, in close-up, looks up lovingly towards the flying birds, her innocence contrasting with the horror to come.

The massacre

The next jolt comes again from the soundtrack as a gunshot is heard; Brett continues to watch the birds, expecting one to fall, echoing the earlier

As the youngest McBain runs from the dark, womb-like safety of the home, he is born into the brutal blinding light of violence, his family lying dead round him; the POV shot helps the audience to empathise with the boy, as does the desperate sounds of boot on wood and his frantic breathing.

The first use of non-diegetic sound corresponds with this moment of extreme terror and incomprehension, and is matched by a close-up of the boy's face; a mighty bell chimes and amplified electric guitars are played with violent intensity and a harmonica wistfully starting after a few chords. It is brutal, identifiably of the Western genre, but also a lament, and underscores the emergence of the killers from the sagebrush (it's called 'Like a Judgement').

The boy clutches a bottle of wine, a portentous red colour, as if it were his lifeblood; he is surrounded by empty glasses, without colour or life. The killers do not just show themselves, they seem to be the monstrous birth of the wilderness, their long jackets or 'dusters' the colour of the vegetation and sand that surrounds them. The music, a slow march of death, charts their gradual emergence, and strings propel what becomes a symphonic accompaniment to their walk towards the boy; the symbolic dead tree stump that we have seen so many times in the sequence foregrounds their entrance.

Choral voices add to their deathly majesty and the camera remains at ground level as they stride towards him, emphasising their power. The cut to the backs of the five men, with the small boy facing them in the background, accentuates their power and his frailty; they are converging not only on him, but also on the symbol of the boy's security, the home. Leone's full use of the widescreen process demonstrates the killers' total dominance of the frame.

The killers have thus far remained anonymous, and so all the more enigmatic. The cut to the shoulder of the middle gunman as he walks forward reinforces his position as leader, coupled with his handing of his rifle to one of the others as they began their walk, and his central position in the line.

The camera then tracks slowly around the face of this killer in a revelatory way to show us the face of evil. It is Henry Fonda! A 1968 audience would have had many more preconceptions about Fonda than today's audience. He was synonymous with good guy roles, such as Abraham Lincoln in *Young Mr. Lincoln* (1939) or Tom Joad in *The Grapes of Wrath* (1940); going against type was a casting coup and makes his character all the more chilling.

Frank's blue eyes are seen clearly in close-up as he and the boy face each other. The eyes are icy, and his malevolence is heightened by the chilling smile that slowly forms as he watches the boy. The boy's face, like those of his siblings, is open, kind and innocent. His freckles reinforce this, while the killers have weathered, hair-covered and brutal faces.

The remark 'What shall we do with this one, Frank?' from one of his men elicits a sinister expression and a close-up expulsion of tobacco and spittle, a nauseating gesture amidst a sickening sense of the men's amoral actions. Frank's chilling response – 'Now that you've called me by name...' – sets up a final unthinkable act; the cold-blooded killing of the young boy.

A close-up of Frank's hand, drawing a pistol and pointing it directly at the camera (and, thus, the audience) draws us ever more closely into this unfolding nightmare. The cold hard metal of the weapon is juxtaposed with the ruddy life of the boy in close-up. The sinister straining strings and the death bell chime underpin the horror as Fonda menacingly smiles at the boy.

Again, the close-up of the gun pointing at us, and then the roaring sound of gunshot and smoke, cut through the non-diegetic sound. Mercifully (and because there is no need; it is horrible enough to imagine the scene) we do not see the effect of the shot, but instead a rapid dissolve brings us to the blurred image of a train's engine stack, along with the piercing sound of its whistle. The audience is disorientated and shocked. The screeching whistle echoes the boy's cry and its power reinforces the outrage of the act.

The sequence ends as it began, with a gunshot. Both shots kill, but the final one takes away a young boy's life and helps further the enigma of the narrative (set up in the confusing initial gunfight), and is only resolved after a complex story of killing, revenge and greed has been played out.

Pat Garrett and Billy the Kid

KEY FACTS

Release Date: 1973

Country of Origin: USA

Running Time: 122 minutes (1988 restored version)

PRODUCTION NOTES

Production Company

Metro-Goldwyn-Mayer

Distributor

Metro-Goldwyn-Mayer

Budget

$4,638,783 (estimated)

Awards

Nominated: Best Newcomer Kris Kristofferson
BAFTA Awards, UK

Nominated: Anthony Asquith Award for Film Music
Bob Dylan BAFTA Awards, UK

SYNOPSIS

This is another telling of the Pat Garrett and Billy the Kid story, following on from many other versions of Billy the Kid's life in particular. The framing device at the beginning and end of the film (cut from the original release version) shows Pat Garrett's violent demise, bringing the story full circle and detailing how Garrett has become embroiled in the corruption of big business. The main story details Garrett's rejection of his outlaw past and his embracing of law and order, but a justice that seems more concerned with the rights of businessmen, in this case, Chisum, rather than the individual.

It begins with Garrett having one final parley with The Kid as his friend before announcing his intentions to bring him to justice as a newly made sheriff. Garrett eventually does capture his old friend and brings him to trial in the town of Lincoln where he is sentenced to death. The Kid cheats death by shooting two deputies and escaping, only to be later shot by Garrett at Fort Sumner; but not before The Kid has had a little more 'fun' with his gang of outlaws.

HISTORICAL CONTEXT

The early 1970s was a time that was still reeling from the impact of the social and political revolutions of the late 1960s. In the United States political thought had focused on the continuing US involvement in Vietnam, polarising views and leading to a massive peace movement; the final peace settlement was signed in the year *Pat Garrett and Billy the Kid* was released. Another major US political issue at the time was the 1972 Watergate political scandal. In the presidential campaign of that year a group of men, employed by the re-election organisation of Republican President Richard Nixon, were arrested whilst breaking into the Democratic party's headquarters in the Watergate building in Washington DC. The resulting scandal eventually resulted in the President's resignation.

Thus, it is within this context that the film can be viewed as an exploration of corruption within the Establishment and its attempts to suppress the individual. It is a Western also very much of its time, with an almost hippy ambience to the commune that is The Kid's hideout, with its emphasis on free love. The casting of Bob Dylan, an iconic music figure and political singer, adds to its 1970s sensibiliiy and his songs supply the soundtrack with its unmistakeable air of protest, freewheeling love and self-expression. The melancholy tone of these songs also connects with the idea that the Establishment is winning over the individual, again echoing the continued distrust of those in power.

SELECT FILMOGRAPHY OF MAIN PRODUCERS AND CAST

Sam Peckinpah, 1926–85, Director, Screenwriter

Ride the High Country, 1962

Major Dundee, 1965

The Wild Bunch, 1969

Straw Dogs, 1971

Junior Bonner, 1972

The Getaway, 1972

Pat Garrett and Billy the Kid, 1973

Bring Me the Head of Alfredo Garcia, 1974

Cross of Iron, 1977

Convoy, 1978

The Osterman Weekend, 1983

John Coquillon, 1933–1987, Director of Photography

Witchfinder General, 1968

Pat Garrett and Billy the Kid, 1973

Cross of Iron, 1977

The Osterman Weekend, 1983

Clockwise, 1985

James Coburn, 1928-2002, Actor

The Magnificent Seven, 1960

The Great Escape, 1963

Major Dundee, 1965

Our Man Flint, 1966

A Fistful of Dynamite, 1971

Pat Garrett and Billy the Kid, 1973

Cross of Iron, 1977

Kris Kristofferson, 1936, Actor

Pat Garrett and Billy the Kid, 1973

Bring Me the Head of Alfredo Garcia, 1974

Alice Doesn't Live Here Anymore, 1975

A Star is Born, 1976

Convoy, 1978

Heaven's Gate, 1980

LINKS TO OTHER FILMS

The Left Handed Gun (1958)

Just as the Billy the Kid in *Pat Garrett and Billy the Kid* is of his time, so Paul Newman's interpretation of the famous outlaw is a product of the 1950s. He is very much in the mould of James Dean's *Rebel Without a Cause*, a young man lashing out at society and coming into conflict with both the Establishment and fathers or father figures.

Easy Rider (1969)

Some of the characters in *Pat Garrett and Billy the Kid* seem to have walked off the set of Dennis Hopper's *Easy Rider*. The Kid's gang are a collection of misfits, akin to the generation who were encouraged to 'turn on, tune in and drop out'. They would not look out of place in the drug-ridden world inhabited by the motorcycling free spirits in *Easy Rider*.

The Wild Bunch (1969)

Made four years before *Pat Garrett and Billy the Kid*, this film also deals with characters who, like Billy the Kid, are becoming anachronous in a society which is becoming dominated by the 'civilising' forces of big business. Both the Wild Bunch and Billy the Kid present Sam Peckinpah's abiding themes of individualism, non-conformity and the decline of the old order.

Heaven's Gate (1980)

Michael Cimino's epic film details another slice of Western history where big business tries to eradicate the 'little man'. In this case it charts the Johnson County Wars of 1892, which deals with the Wyoming Cattleman's Association attempts to drive homesteaders off their land and out of the state.

REPRESENTATION

Law and order

As with many Hollywood Westerns the practice of mythologising the West and its heroes and outlaws is in evidence here. Billy the Kid is ascribed iconic anti-hero status. He is visually represented, as we shall see below, as a Christ-like figure when captured, and as a Western pop star as he escapes from the Lincoln County jail. Bob Dylan's ballads further add to the mythical status of this outlaw, but it is more about an overall thematic framework than a portrait of any one person.

The outlaw is certainly not above brutality and killing but he is true to himself, something which Pat Garrett most certainly is not. Garrett has tried to safeguard his future by joining with the forces of the Establishment, the framing device showing where that will eventually lead: death at the hands of those he had joined. He is shown as a confused man, compromised by the decisions that he has made. As such, he shares many traits with the Robert Ryan character in *The Wild Bunch*, a former friend to the gang and later part of the posse sent to kill them.

The second deputy, whom Billy kills as he escapes from the Lincoln County jail, is shown to be the perfect embodiment of law and order: a humourless and brutal man, lacking in humanity, a pillar of the Establishment.

Law and order exists under a thin veil of civility, but it is just as brutal as unlawful doings. Billy, his gang and even Garrett are all doomed to die, symbolised by the buried chickens at the opening of the film which are blown apart, just as, at the beginning of *The Wild Bunch*, the children drop the scorpions into the mass of ants: both are dangerous but the ants, a symbol of society's masses, will ultimately prevail.

In the Westerns examined in this section the notion of law and order often plays a key role in the film's narrative. Again and again, the forces of law and order are seen to be corrupt and repugnant: Little Bill in *Unforgiven* exercises a law which bends to his perverse and amoral will; in both *Young Guns* and *Once Upon a Time in the West* the Establishment exists in a law and order vacuum, filled by the greed of those in power; and *The Searchers* is dismissive of the capabilities of any dispensers of justice. It is Ethan who takes the law into his own hands in the latter film, just as characters in *Red River* and *Stagecoach* exist and survive in a world that is dominated more by the law of the wilderness than any man-made construct.

'Loosely based on the historical facts, the film emphasises the brutality of the west and the greed and power that lay beneath it, yet its ultimate effect is melancholic. Rather than being an exposé of the myth of the west, this is a film in which the characters enjoy posing, endlessly re-telling stories from the past.' Edward Buscombe, 'Pat Garrett and Billy the Kid', *100 Westerns*, BFI, 2006

'It both records and condemns the passage of time and the advent of progress.' Steve Grant *Time Out 14th Ed.*, Time Out Guides Ltd., London, 2006

KEY SCENE TEXTUAL ANALYSIS

Escape (6/7)

Prior to this scene we see Billy being captured by Garrett and the final image of the sequence presents Billy with both arms outstretched in a crucifixion-style pose. It is one of a number of religious references in the film associated with him. However, he immediately comes into conflict with the God-fearing sheriff during his short incarceration in the subsequent scenes. Peckinpah presents Billy as a single-minded, ruthless killer as well as a kind of celebrity gunslinger.

Billy has asked to go to the outhouse. A long scene shot within the confines of the jail precedes this, accentuating the claustrophobia of freewheeling Billy's predicament. In contrast, the first shot of this sequence shows two horses wildly rearing whilst corralled, mirroring Billy's frustration to escape.

The *mise-en-scène* is typically Western. The emphasis seems to be on authenticity: an old water-pump, broken wheel, firewood, foraging pigs, an old wagon, run-down buildings with exposed brick walls. It is chaotic and messy.

The two cowboys are distinct. Billy is long-haired with a flowing white shirt and unbuttoned waistcoat, suggesting his free-spirited and bohemian nature, whilst the lawman is dressed in a more strait-laced manner with black hat, black three-quarter length jacket, black boots, buttoned-up waistcoat and high-collared shirt. He is much more uptight and formal.

The ensuing conversation takes place in the outhouse, a skeletal, run-down building, full of gaping holes. The boundaries between public and private are blurred, just as they were in this chaotic moment in American history.

Billy is shown in intimate close-up as he sits down and discovers the hidden gun which will facilitate his escape, whilst Bill is shown in medium shot as he maintains his reverie; the contrasting intimacy, as borne out through their contrasting size in the frame, dictates the audience's connection with the characters.

Billy eventually moves into Bill's filmic space as he exits the outhouse, and his POV of the unsettled horses clearly defines his connection with these trapped animals and his desire to escape.

As the two men are consumed by the shadow at the side of the jail, there is a cut to the children playing on the gallows, one girl swinging from the noose; the juxtaposition of children and violence/death/cruelty is a common visual motif in Peckinpah's work (used at the start of *The Wild Bunch* and during Steve McQueen's decimation of a police car in *The Getaway*). The imagery presents a tension between innocence and corruption, but points to their interconnectedness. It is a chilling image and comes after Billy's denunciation of Chisolm and his ilk for their obsessive pursuit of land and power, the 'fencing off' of the country.

The shot of the puritanical sheriff smiling at the children links his religious bigotry within the ruling Establishment. His POV shot of the children is now reframed to incorporate the American flag; the juxtaposition of flag, gallows and children is one perspective and suggests the possible abuses committed in the name of a nation. The reading here could be of a nation perverting its most innocent by robbing them of their freedom from the start of their lives – a freedom that Billy personifies, and in this scene, manages to assert by breaking free of the Establishment's order. Meanwhile, Chisolm and his landowning friends murder and steal but these actions are legitimised by a corruption of the flag and its values (other representations of the flag can be interpreted later in the scene).

Throughout this scene the two men have been on the same level as they have walked around, but now Billy ascends the stairs to physically and mentally gain the upper hand. The diegetic sound of his chains is prominent, emphasising the reining in of his freedom, just as the sound of the horses neighing emphasised their captivity.

As Billy turns and points the gun at Bill he is shown from a low angle, suggesting the re-emergence of his dominance, and underlined by the high angle shot of Bill as the balance of power shifts.

offers the fullest expression of this approach to violence). Its detractors see this as a glorification of violence, whilst others see it as a *meditation* on violence, its graphic effect on the fragile human frame, the slowness of the moment emphasising the importance of the movement of death. For The Wild Bunch, their minutely observed deaths mark their moment of release from a world that has moved on, and left their free spirited ways behind.

A convention of the Western, that the hero or anti-hero would not shoot someone in the back is exploded here. Billy does what he has to. There is no room for niceties; it confronts the audience's expectations and beliefs by deconstructing the Western's conventions. With the killing, non-diegetic music is heard, a jumble of country music expressing the chaos and urgency of the action. Diegetic voices of the townspeople add to the mayhem.

The long shot of the two men confirms their relative positions within the frame and Billy's power; the reverse shot reiterates this and focuses the audience on the gun and the power that it bestows in this society.

The next three images are medium shots, showing both men in isolation, their respective fates now moving in different directions. There is one more two-shot as Billy gives Bill a final chance to come towards him and avoid death, but this is rejected and the gunshot and impact are separate shots, as is Bill's fall through the window. The two cannot be reconciled and so occupy different filmic spaces.

The gun shot, when it comes, is shown from almost face-on to Billy, the gun erupting as if part of his body, and part of Bill's fall is presented in slow motion, a regular motif of Peckinpah's depiction of violence (the climatic shootout in *The Wild Bunch*

The editing gathers pace as Billy arms himself and Bob advances towards the jail. The long shot of Billy frames him next to the American flag, presenting an alternate vision of society where freedom and action prevail. The moment that Billy takes aim and Bob stops synchronises with a slowing down of the music to a single guitar, strummed with an air of finality. The zoom, first towards Billy and then matched by one towards Bob, links the two men at the moment of confrontation and death, underpinning the intensity of the exchange (Bob has goaded Billy throughout the previous jail scenes about his Godlessness and Billy has responded in kind).

The cut to a medium shot of Billy and then a close-up of Bob draws the audience into this deadly moment; the low angle for Billy and the high angle looking down on Bob mirrors the previous killing and the power shift in Billy's favour.

The cut from Bob's face to the medium of Billy and the blast from the shotgun allows us to see Bob and Billy's essential humanness for a moment, both clearly associated with violence and death; the weapon is again seen as an extension of Billy's body as the camera gives us a face-on view of the blast, the slow motion helping us to recognise the coins that Bob himself had added to the cartridge in the hope that he could blast and shred Billy.

Instead, Bob is graphically killed, his body erupting in a mass of blood, again presented in slow motion; a moment of revenge for Billy and a portrayal of man's frailty. Billy's pay-off – 'Keep the change, Bob' – is pure Hollywood, but the shot of a static Billy contrasts with the twisting death of Bob; stillness in life and, ironically, movement in death.

The shot from behind Billy creates juxtaposition between Billy, alive and standing, Bob's prostrate body and the unused and redundant gallows behind. The victor surveys his territory below. Significantly, a half-finished church stands to Billy's left, lying somewhere between Bob's strict, unbending personification of religion and Billy's saviour/killer persona. Billy even breaks up Bob's gun, a symbol of his disgust for Bob's doctrines.

Only when the shooting has finished do the people emerge from the recesses of the town, all shot from a high angle, emphasising their weakness in contrast to Billy's vitality. They resemble an audience appearing before a deity, a celebrity or, as is soon seen, a singer. The shot from behind Billy's head, with flapping stars and stripes, again connects him with a possible vision of a different kind of America, where individual freedom prevails.

Noticeably, Billy calls upon the lone Mexican to bring him an axe; another outsider in this civilised town, the inhabitants of which gather around the dead body as if it were an exhibit rather than a human being.

Billy then performs again to the crowd, this time with a ballad which details his disdain for a town which was prepared to let the power of the Establishment exterminate any signs of rebellion or individuality. The Bob Dylan folksy non-diegetic music then begins as Billy exits the jail. The shootings, the escape and the ballad all position him as a maverick and free spirit.

Peckinpah does not allow his main protagonists the luxury of infallibility – they are human, warts and all. Thus, Billy's triumphant exit is undermined by being thrown from the horse that the Mexican has chosen for him (very similar to Steve McQueen's unceremonious dumping on the ground as he tries to get into a car in *The Getaway*). Even when he does leave, he forgets his blanket and rides back into town to collect it.

The camera finally pans with him as he leaves, but the camera loses track of him as he rides behind a building and alights on a roaring fire, a portentous symbol of his future demise perhaps. He is, however, afforded a grand exit in the final shot; a classic mythical crane shot as he rides out of the town and towards the wilderness beyond, the true home for such a free-wheeling individual. Peckinpah, then, both reinforces and deconstructs the near-mythical character of Billy the Kid throughout this sequence, and the film in general, with touches of authenticity, absurdity and Hollywood Western cliché.

Other scenes help develop these ideas; the poetry and surreal nature of death (Sheriff Baker's death in DVD Ch. 13); the ruthlessness and necessities of gunfights (Billy fails to observe the conventions of the 10 paces gunfight in Ch.18), and the randomness of events (Garratt's near gunfight with the occupants of a passing boat on a river by which he is camping in Ch. 22).

Young Guns

KEY FACTS

Release Date: 1988

Country of Origin: USA

Running Time: 107 minutes

PRODUCTION NOTES

Production Companies

20th Century Fox

Morgan Creek Productions

Distributor

20th Century Fox

Budget

$13,000,000 (estimated)

Awards

Nominated: Critics Award Christopher Cain
Deauville Film Festival, France

SYNOPSIS

Ranch owner John Tunstall hires a group of young men as regulators to guard his ranch and cattle, under threat from the local bad man and rancher, Murphy. These youths, all outsiders, count Billy the Kid and Doc Scurlock amongst their number, and after Tunstall is murdered they set out to avenge his death. Initially, they try to do this through lawful means as they are deputised and given warrants to serve on Murphy's men. But as they begin to catch up with the murderers they kill them and, as a result, start to operate outside of the law and are hunted by the authorities. Eventually, one of the group, Dick, is killed and they are all cornered by some soilders, who have been ordered to track down the now-famous gang. After a final shootout, all but Billy, Doc and Chavez are killed, but Billy does return momentarily to shoot Murphy between the eyes, finally avenging Tunstall's death and then riding off to continue his outlaw life until his death at the hands of Pat Garrett, an episode that does not appear in this film.

HISTORICAL CONTEXT

In Britain and the United States during the 1980s the aggressive monetarist policies of Margaret Thatcher and Ronald Reagan dominated society - capitalism and the pursuit of money were key values. There was very much a culture of individualism and related greed which was reflected most vividly in Oliver Stone's *Wall Street* (1987). *Young Guns* reflects a world where big business and the Establishment try to crush any maverick tendencies or free spirit in society.

The power of wealthy Murphy, supported by the law, all but destroys the community that Tunstall has tried to create. Billy does strike a final blow for the community when he shoots Murphy, but most of the freewheeling group are dead by this time and the rest are on the run, fully alienated from conventional society. The film, however, is not really interested in critiquing 1980s society, and its historical relevance seems more concerned with its 'Brat Pack' identity and homage/pastiche of the Western genre.

The 'Brat Pack' was a term coined to describe an emerging group of young actors and actresses who were in their late teens/early twenties and appeared in a glut of teen-orientated films. Their number included Emilio Estevez, Charlie Sheen, Rob Lowe, Andrew McCarthy, Michael J. Fox, Matthew Broderick, Ally Sheedy, Molly Ringwald and Demi Moore. These films, including *The Outsiders* (1983), *Red Dawn* (1984), *The Breakfast Club* (1985) and *Pretty in Pink* (1986) were vehicles for displays of teenage angst in a variety of genres.

By the late 1980s, the Western genre was no longer a Hollywood staple. The 1970s witnessed a late but brief flourishing of the genre, with a series of often downbeat films, at pains to convey a sense of verisimilitude. There was perhaps even hope amongst devotees that the genre might be revived. Two factors seemed to militate against this.

First was the advent of the blockbuster - where once boys had played with Smith and Westons, in 1977 they swapped them for light sabres. Horse opera had been replaced by the space opera. Second, the myth and reality surrounding Michael Cimino's *Heaven's Gate* helped undermine the

Western in the eyes of those who financed film production. The sweep of the film suggested that the Western could at least match the spectacle of the blockbuster, but the film's mounting costs and its comparative failure at the box office was enough to bring down United Artists (until it was resurrected by MGM), and create the impression that the Western genre was itself to blame for the film's failure. The fact that United Artists was already in financial freefall after the failures of earlier films was swept aside and the popular misconception that Westerns were now box office poison led to their near extinction.

Young Guns is, then, that rare breed: a successful 1980s Western. It borrows its narrative and look from not only classic Western conventions, but it has clear intertextual links to music videos (the 1980s seeing the flourishing of this particular phenomenon) and the action/adventure genre. It is a knowing take on the Western, merging it with 1980's sensibilities, as typified by its 'Brat Pack' cast and modern rock soundtrack.

SELECT FILMOGRAPHY OF MAIN PRODUCERS AND CAST

Christopher Cain, 1943, Director, Producer, Screenwriter

The Stone Boy, 1984

That Was Then...This Is Now, 1986

Young Guns, 1988

Gone Fishin', 1997

September Dawn, 2006

Emilio Estevez, 1962, Actor, Director

Repo Man, 1984

The Breakfast Club, 1984

St. Elmo's Fire, 1984

Stakeout, 1987

Young Guns, 1988

National Lampoon's Loaded Weapon 1, 1993

Bobby, 2006 (as Director)

Charlie Sheen, 1965, Actor

Red Dawn, 1984

Platoon, 1986

Wall Street, 1987

Young Guns, 1988

Major League, 1989

Hot Shots, 1991

The Three Musketeers, 1993

Terminal Velocity, 1994

Kiefer Sutherland, 1966, Actor

Stand by Me, 1986

The Lost Boys, 1987

Young Guns, 1988

Flatliners, 1990

Young Guns II, 1990

A Few Good Men, 1992

The Three Musketeers, 1993

Dark City, 1997

Phone Booth, 2002

Mirrors, 2008

Terence Stamp, 1939, Actor

Billy Budd, 1962

Far From the Madding Crowd, 1967

Superman II, 1981

The Hit, 1984

Wall Street, 1987

Young Guns, 1988

The Adventures of Priscilla Queen of the Desert, 1994

Jack Palance, 1919-2006, Actor

Panic in the Streets, 1950

Sudden Fear, 1952

Shane, 1953

The Big Knife, 1955

Attack, 1956

Le Mepris, 1963

The Professionals, 1966

Monte Walsh, 1970

Chato's Land, 1972

Hawk the Slayer, 1980

Young Guns, 1988

Batman, 1989

City Slickers, 1991

LINKS TO OTHER FILMS

The Magnificent Seven (1960)

Young Guns uses the archetypal narrative of the anti-heroes fighting against oppression. It mirrors *The Magnificent Seven* with its use of a band of mavericks – six in this case (seven, if one includes Tunstall) – following the classic earlier Western's depiction of them as alienated loners who come together to fight a common evil. In *Young Guns* it is Murphy and the Establishment that supports him; in *The Magnificent Seven* it is the Mexican bandits who are oppressing the villagers. Here, all but three of the gunfighters die fighting on the side of right, and the audience sympathises with them. The Magnificent Seven are portrayed as loners, drifters, eccentric and even psychotic, all displaced in a changing world that is becoming less tolerant of their nomadic and free-spirited ways. The characters in *Young Guns* are depicted in a very similar way, again with a Hollywood gloss that allows the audience to connect with them. It is, of course, debatable whether actual gunfighters would have acted in this way, and they certainly would have been more ruthless and less sympathetic.

The Outsiders (1983)

This is another story of misfits who rage against the Establishment, and is another example of a 'Brat Pack' film dealing in teenage angst and alienation. Familiar 'Bratpackers' are in the cast (Emilio Estevez and Rob Lowe, for example), and there are other actors, including Tom Cruise, who would go on to super-stardom. The group of mavericks are here called 'Greasers' and the setting is 1967 Tulsa, where the disenchanted and underprivileged young men clash against the wealthy and privileged 'Socs'. The film charts their camaraderie and trials, and also contains the kind of self-reflection that bubbles under the surface of *Young Guns*.

REPRESENTATION

Outlaws

The Hollywood Western has long mythologised and glamorised Western bad men, both real and fictional. Many of the Westerns discussed in this book have anti-heroes who are ultimately portrayed as honourable and noble: The Ringo Kid in *Stagecoach*; Ethan in *The Searchers*; Cheyenne in *Once Upon A Time in the West* and Billy the Kid in *Pat Garrett and Billy the Kid*.

Indeed, real outlaws have often been portrayed as not only the celebrities of their time, but also as wronged victims and/or romantic heroes. Key films of this type include *Jesse James* (1939), *Billy the Kid* (1941), the life of John Wesley Hardin in *The Lawless Breed* (1953), *The True Story of Jesse James* (1957) and *Butch Cassidy and the Sundance Kid* (1969). In *Young Guns* the outlaws are certainly wild, but seem more like disaffected youths than hardened gunfighters; there is something quite contemporary about their speech and actions, 'Bratpackers' playing at being cowboys rather than gritty realistic portrayals. The film's poster showing the six gunmen does not look authentic; they could just as easily be wearing the high school clothes of *The Breakfast Club* or the combat outfits of the Wolverines in *Red Dawn*.

This idea of disaffected youths appearing in genre films is not uniquely a 1980's phenomenon. Paul Newman is a similarly moody teenager in *The Left-Handed Gun*; Robert Wagner is a young romantic lead as the eponymous hero of *The True Story of Jesse James*. Even the biblical epic gets a teenage revamp in *King of Kings* (1961) with heartthrob Jeffrey Hunter as Jesus. The film was dubbed 'I Was a Teenage Jesus' by some critics at the time, alluding to its casting of Hunter, an actor aiming for the James Dean style in many of his early films, such *The Searchers* and *The True Story of Jesse James* (as Frank James), a film directed by Nicholas Ray, who directed the great staple of teenage angst, *Rebel Without a Cause*.

'In addition to the well-staged set-pieces, the dusty, wintry, subfusc look... and the fine ensemble acting, Young Guns is probably the most accurate account there has been of the Lincoln County War. It has a narrative coherence lacking in Peckinpah's movie [Pat Garret and Billy the Kid], and situates the characters within the currents of the times.' Philip French, *Westerns*, Carcanet, 2005

KEY SCENE TEXTUAL ANALYSIS

Title sequence (1)

The title sequence begins with a shot that has been altered in post-production. It is unclear at first, an unidentified landscape that seems to have smoke or sand blowing over it. The generated colour is of a brown hue with a grainy texture, while the non-diegetic music is a modern synthesiser sound resembling a heartbeat, with a faint wind sound.

Vegetation and mountains in the background can be faintly distinguished; knowing already that this is a Western indicates that this is a wilderness landscape.

Six figures then emerge from over the horizon. Most certainly they are cowboys. However, their identities are obscured by the fact that the colour saturation process renders them as ghostly white silhouettes. These phantoms from the past are then emblazoned with the film's title '*Young Guns*'.

The grainy texture does lend it an 'Old West' look, but the effect is actually closer to that found in music videos, a dominant media text of the 1980s, with all its trappings of fast and stylised visuals. The music gathers pace, and this is no old-style Western track, but 1980s rock music, with a modern Country and Western edge to it.

There is then a cut from the atmospheric long shot, which borrows from classic Western framing of other cowboy gangs (see *The Magnificent Seven* and *The Wild Bunch*); the attempt is to make this gang as mythical as previous fictionalised groups.

The cut to the medium close-up and then a zoom to a close-up of Billy the Kid are inherited from the modern Western, where the zoom and tight close-ups became the norm (see Sergio Leone's Spaghetti Westerns and *Ulzana's Raid* [1972]).

The close-up with the actor's name superimposed is pure soap opera; Dallas was one of the biggest soaps at the time and it employed this device in its title sequence (other references are the numerous TV Westerns, such as *Bonanza*). The sequence is of its day, it is tongue-in-cheek and self-effacing. The actors look directly at the camera, an act of defiance and rebellion as they break the 'fourth wall', visually linking the film to the shot of the outlaw looking and firing at the audience in Edwin S. Porter's *The Great Train Robbery* (1903).

This convention is repeated for all six main protagonists; some seem to be in character (Lou Diamond Phillips, for example) whilst others (Kiefer Sutherland) seem to be out of character as they look directly at the audience. This mixture of acting styles again points to the playful nature of this opening sequence.

The cut to the long shot again as they all draw guns and blast away at nothing in particular is underpinned by the pace of the electric guitar-led rock/country music increasing; the camera rapidly tracks up and down their line, with close-ups of the weapons as they fire. There have been references to other Western films and other genres in different media in the first two minutes, and the rest of the film is no exception; the scattergun approach to references is appropriate for a film that does not take itself too seriously, both respecting and

deconstructing the myths created by Westerns of the past.

The cut to black and then fade to a long shot of a Western town demarcates the stylised title sequence from its depiction of reality that follows. The initial long shot presents a typical Western town, with horses, wagons and cowboys. The initial exchange between Doc and Tunstall (Terence Stamp) is sweet and innocent, but it is soon replaced by what this film is keen to deliver – action. The sound of the electric guitar is also replaced by a lilting violin as we are momentarily shown a calm picture of frontier life.

But a gun shot and the pumping guitar signal a return to action, and if the audience was in any doubt that this is not a traditional Western then the fast track along the store fronts, as the camera follows a man running, and then the whip pan back to the pursuers, should again illustrate that this is an action movie in disguise. The *mise-en-scène* is familiar but a different heart beats beneath this familiar skin.

The escape for Billy the Kid is easily effected by Tunstall and the Doc after a number of rapid tracking shots, akin to something one would expect to see in a more modern chase from an action or thriller film.

Dusty action (19; 1:34:19)

The final sequence is reminiscent of such 'heroes totally outnumbered' Westerns as *The Wild Bunch*, *Butch Cassidy and the Sundance Kid* and *The Magnificent Seven*.

Taking the scene from the moment when a large trunk is pushed out of an upstairs window of the besieged house, it is clear that the sequence owes much to previous Westerns; it is, in fact, a clear expression of a postmodern text, playfully deconstructing itself through pastiche.

The low-angle shot of the burning building, as the trunk is pushed out, helps to highlight the serious predicament that the *Young Guns* find themselves in. It also bestows extra importance onto this trunk, and we see why in a moment.

The first of the group emerges in slow motion, representing the first of many echoes of Sam Peckinpah's *The Wild Bunch*, which was the first Western to employ this technique. The effect is of a balletic 'dance of death', described as both a glorification of, and a meditation on, violence in Peckinpah's work. Yet here the intention seems to be merely adding slickness to the blood-letting.

Not only are the visuals slowed down, but so is the diegetic sound, rendering the shouts and screams something of a primeval quality. Billy the Kid emerges from the trunk, screaming; this unorthodox means of leaving a building and his dramatic eruption from the trunk (with low-angle empowering shot) is reminiscent of action films of the time, particularly those of Arnold Schwarzenegger. There is little similarity here with traditional Westerns but everything to do with the increasing desire for film-makers to make cross-over productions, appealing to the young

The music is again modern rock, with mystical elements introduced when Chavez, the Native American/Mexican Young Gun arrives with the horses. The surrounding cowboys are all despatched fairly dispassionately but the *Young Guns* have a more melodramatic fanfare when they are shot; not only do they take the bullets in slow motion, but there is also a whizzing sound of the bullet introduced onto the soundtrack, emphasising the impact and pain for the recipient (this technique was used to similar effect in Walter Hill's *The Long Riders* [1980]). The effect can be justified in filmic terms; like the use of slow motion, it is a representation of a highly-charged moment: of killing and being killed. Of course, in action terms it also sounds pretty 'cool' and unsettling, and teenage audiences do love a slow-motion death.

For good measure, Alex is killed rather excessively by a gattling gun, again a prominent feature of *The Wild Bunch*. Bonney, Doc and Chavez make good

demographic that make or break films. *Young Guns* is, stylistically, a kissing cousin of the blockbuster cycle of films that had begun in the 1970s (*Jaws*, *Star Wars*, et al.).

The succeeding shots are all very short, in order to maintain a quick pace to their escape, with a mixture of slow motion and real time shots. One image of a cowboy being shot has faint spots of blood hitting the lens as the squib explodes; this sort of shot, which momentarily breaks the spell that we are watching a fiction, is intended to draw the audience into the heart of the action (see Steven Spielberg's opening sequence on Omaha Beach in *Saving Private Ryan* [1998]), but it also breaks down the barrier between the viewer and the viewed, disturbing that fine balance in a postmodern manner.

their escape (this was the decade when sequels really came into their own; *Young Guns 2* came out two years later), and the finale comes with Bonney's return and wonder shot which kills the baddie, Jack Palance's big businessman, Murphy.

The final shot of the three remaining Guns going their separate ways, with a voiceover lending the tale an air of authenticity (Billy the Kid did, of course, exist), and leaving the Kid to ride off into the distance is, in the context of the film, both an acknowledgement and pastiche of the standard Western finale.

Unforgiven

KEY FACTS

Release Date: 1992

Country of Origin: USA

Running Time: 131 minutes

PRODUCTION NOTES

Production Companies

Malpaso Productions

Warner Bros. Pictures

Distributor

Warner Bros. Pictures

Awards

Best Actor in a Supporting Role Gene Hackman Academy Awards, USA

Best Director Clint Eastwood Academy Awards, USA

Best Picture Clint Eastwood Academy Awards, USA

Best Film Editing Joel Cox Academy Awards, USA

Best Actor in a Supporting Role Gene Hackman BAFTA Awards, UK

Outstanding Directorial Achievement in Motion Pictures Clint Eastwood Directors Guild of America

Best Director Clint Eastwood Golden Globes, USA

Best Performance by an Actor in a Supporting Role in a Motion Picture Gene Hackman Golden Globes, USA

Film of the Year Clint Eastwood London Critics Circle Film Awards

Best Director Clint Eastwood National Society of Film Critics Awards, USA

Best Film Clint Eastwood National Society of Film Critics Awards, USA

Best Screenplay David Webb Peoples National Society of Film Critics Awards, USA

Best Supporting Actor Gene Hackman National Society of Film Critics Awards, USA

SYNOPSIS

Unforgiven charts the story of William Munny, a former killer who has renounced his murderous ways to marry and have children. At the beginning of the film we see that he has been widowed and is living in fairly impoverished conditions, his few pigs dying of swine fever. Munny, within this context, decides to go after some reward money offered by a prostitute in Big Whiskey for the killing of two cowboys, one of whom disfigured her after she joked about the size of his genitals. The cowboys are only fined by the brutal sheriff, Little Bill, hence her desire to see justice properly served. Together with a young would-be gunfighter, the Schofield Kid, and an old friend, Ned Logan, Munny sets off to claim the reward money.

Another gunfighter, English Bob, accompanied by a writer who is recording his memories and actions for a biography, arrives in the town to kill the two cowboys for the reward. Little Bill makes an example of him by beating him half to death, a warning to anyone else who might come looking for the cowboys. Upon Munny and his companions' arrival they are attacked by Little Bill and his men, but it is only Munny who they manage to capture and nearly kill.

After Munny has recuperated with the help of the prostitutes and his friends the Schofield Kid and Ned depart, wanting no more trouble. But en route home Ned is captured, beaten and finally dies of his wounds, his body placed in a coffin outside a bar, the focal point of all the violence. Munny discovers this and returns to town, killing Little Bill, some of his men and the owner of the bar, a man who also owns the prostitutes; a Western pimp. Munny's final words as he leaves the bar, and the town, for good, are a chilling warning of brutal violence to any that might stop him. The final words of the film inform the audience that he returns home and takes his children away to start a new life.

HISTORICAL CONTEXT

The 1990s were characterised by, as ever, conflicts throughout the world, such as the first Iraq War in 1991, Afghanistan throughout the 1990s, the war in Serbia/Bosnia from 1992-95 and in Rwanda in the mid-1990s. In this decade, war came closer to home. This was not archive footage but live images pumped into living rooms every day. There were not just wars in remote parts involving people we knew little about; these were wars in Europe and beyond, and they involved British and American troops.

Unforgiven was one of very few Westerns made in the 1990s, but it addressed itself to such elemental issues, particularly regarding the nature of violence, and it tuned into the prevailing zeitgeist. Its meditation on what makes someone violent and pushes them over into the kind of brutality we see here is charged with the atmosphere of extreme violence, of man's ability to commit multiple murder, a depravity that many had associated in modern history with the Nazis, but now seemed alive and well in the contemporary world. It is a 'revisionist' Western which attempts to deconstruct all the myths that have grown up around the Western and its depiction of a place, a time and its people.

Unforgiven not only received critical praise, but in a decade which really saw the near extinction of the genre, it managed to transcend any generic constraints to speak to a wide audience, garnering a plethora of awards, including four American Academy Awards. Ironically, in the light of the scarcity of Westerns, it was actually the second Western in three years to win the Academy Award for Best Picture (the first being *Dances with Wolves* in 1990).

SELECT FILMOGRAPHY OF MAIN PRODUCERS AND CAST

Clint Eastwood, 1930, Director, Producer, Actor

A Fistful of Dollars, 1964

For a Few Dollars More, 1965

The Good, the Bad and the Ugly, 1966

Play Misty for Me, 1971

High Plains Drifter, 1972

The Outlaw Josey Wales, 1976

Bronco Billy, 1980

Pale Rider, 1985

Bird, 1988

White Hunter, Black Heart, 1990

Unforgiven, 1992

A Perfect World, 1993

The Bridges of Madison County, 1995

Mystic River, 2003

Million Dollar Baby, 2004

Flags of Our Fathers, 2006

Letters from Iwo Jima, 2006

Changeling, 2008

Gran Torino, 2008

David Webb Peoples, 1940, Screenwriter

Blade Runner, 1982

Unforgiven, 1992

Twelve Monkeys, 1995

Gene Hackman, 1930, Actor

Bonnie and Clyde, 1967

The French Connection, 1971

The Poseiden Adventure, 1972

The Conversation, 1974

The French Connection II, 1975

Superman, 1978

Under Fire, 1983

No Way Out, 1986

Mississippi Burning, 1988

Unforgiven, 1992

The Firm, 1993

Wyatt Earp, 1994

Get Shorty, 1995

The Quick and the Dead, 1995

Enemy of the State, 1998

The Royal Tenenbaums, 2001

Morgan Freeman, 1937, Actor

Driving Miss Daisy, 1989

Glory, 1989

Robin Hood: Prince of Thieves, 1991

Unforgiven, 1992

The Shawshank Redemption, 1994

Amistad, 1997

Kiss the Girls, 1997

Deep Impact, 1998

Along Came a Spider, 2001

Bruce Almighty, 2003

Million Dollar Baby, 2004

Richard Harris, 1930-2002, Actor

This Sporting Life, 1963

Major Dundee, 1964

Camelot, 1967

The Molly Maguires, 1969

A Man Called Horse, 1970

Cromwell, 1970

The Return of a Man Called Horse, 1976

The Field, 1990

Unforgiven, 1992

Gladiator, 2000

Harry Potter and the Philosopher's Stone, 2001

Harry Potter and the Chamber of Secrets, 2002

LINKS TO OTHER FILMS

The Outlaw Josey Wales (1976)

The opening of this film, another of Eastwood's Westerns, resembles that of *Unforgiven*, in that we see a man resorting to his previous violent ways. The catalyst in *The Outlaw Josey Wales* is the killing of his wife and child and the destruction of his farm by mercenary soldiers at the beginning of the American Civil War. Both Munny and Wales reignite their brutal past, but the characters also return to the family unit, Munny to his children and Wales to his newly-created family of a rescued elderly woman and her granddaughter, an old Native American man and a young Native American woman.

Open Range (2003)

Just as Clint Eastwood has returned to the Western genre a number of times, so Kevin Costner made *Open Range* after directing *Dances with Wolves* in 1990 and producing *Wyatt Earp* in 1994. There is a sense of weariness about the cattlemen (played by Costner and Robert Duvall) as they have to resort to violence to settle the dispute between themselves and the land baron who does not want their cattle roaming freely. The brutal and realistic gunfight at the end echoes that in *Unforgiven*, and leaves the film with an atmosphere of senselessness and despair.

A History of Violence (2005)

A very similar narrative links this David Cronenberg film with *Unforgiven*. A family man's violent past resurfaces when he is rediscovered by people from his days as a criminal. This is another meditation on violence and its place in our psyche. Both films show the effects of brutality, but it is even more extreme in this film, with Cronenberg framing unflinching shots of the aftermath of violence.

REPRESENTATION

Violence

Violence in the Western is a staple convention, whether it is a gunfight, a massacre by, or of, Native Americans or a stagecoach/bank/train robbery. The mode of dying that prevailed in the silent Westerns, the serial Westerns of the 1920s and 1930s and the B Westerns of the 1930s was clean and without fuss, particularly if you were a Native American. As a cowboy good guy or a repentant bad guy you were perhaps afforded a few moments of pain or dramatic monologue. But there was very little blood and cowboys/soldiers/Native Americans tended to drop like flies. Death, it seems, was painless; at best, spectacular; at worst, boring.

The Second World War seemed to galvanise the Western into treating the notion and consequences of violence with a little more thought. The 1950s were replete with psychological Westerns, which began to show violence in more realistic and often sadistic terms. Violence became a philosophical concept: how men used violence and its effect on perpetrators and others. Anthony Mann's cycle of Westerns in this decade saw the actor James Stewart undergo a number of brutal trials.

In five films together, *Winchester '73* (1950), *Bend of the River* (1952), *The Naked Spur* (1953), *The Man from Laramie* (1955) and *The Far Country* (1955), the hero endures numerous violent incidents, from prolonged and vicious fights to being dragged by a horse through a camp fire. But it was not until the 1960s that audiences were really shown what a bullet or knife can do to a human body. Leone's Spaghetti Westerns led the way; violence was graphic but stylised and often comic. Then came *The Wild Bunch*, where the depiction of violence reached epic dimensions.

The Bunch's final deaths are redemptive, the bloodletting a symbol of the death of the individual in the face of the Establishment's overwhelming power. Violence here is shown to be within everyone, from the children who torment scorpions to the 'good guys' who accidentally kill innocent bystanders. Violence has been depicted as a way of condemning past wrongs (Arthur Penn's *Little Big Man* [1970]) or reflects other conflicts (both Ralph Nelson's *Soldier Blue* [1970] and Robert Aldrich's *Ulzana's Raid* [1972] echo the Vietnam War).

Unforgiven, like *Ulzana's Raid* before it, is also at pains to demythologise the Western as a 'realistic' representation of history. The latter shows both whites and Native Americans as brutal and ruthless, each prepared to commit atrocities to get the upper hand; it debunks the idea that the Native Americans were simply noble, the concept that the Hollywood Western had been trying to promote since its more liberal approach in the 1950s. *Unforgiven* shows violence erupting without warning; it is elemental, without nobility or heroics. No warnings are given before someone is shot and the aftermath affords no dignity to any of the characters, including Munny.

'Unforgiven stands out in that it takes the theme of melancholy not as a nostalgia for a lost age, nor for the genre itself. Rather it casts aside any sense that the story of the West or the way it has been told was noble. In its place is a stark portrait of an unmerciful world created by the violence that guns bring and that a misplaced sense of justice validates.' Michael Hammond, *'Unforgiven'*, in Williams, L. R. and Hammond, M. (eds) *Contemporary American Cinema*, McGraw Hill/Open University Press, 2006

'If the Western was to continue to be viable, it would need to be adapted to contemporary sensibilities, show that it was aware of its own past and in touch with the present. And that is precisely what Unforgiven tries to do, by turns drawing strength from the roots of the genre, the accreted meanings of character and convention, but then always inflecting them, adapting them, subverting them to refashion the genre into something viable for the modern age.' Edward Buscombe, *Unforgiven*, BFI, 2004

KEY SCENE TEXTUAL ANALYSIS

Shooting practice (7; 16:13)

The scene begins with an intimate interior shot of the inside of a keepsakes box. We snatch a glimpse of a woman's photograph – Munny's wife – and some jewellery, most notably a delicate cameo brooch. Munny's hand reaches in and removes the framed photograph before freeing another unseen object which seems to be hidden beneath his display of gentility and family love; it is a gun and he examines it in the half-light.

Beneath the façade of family and civility there lies Munny's brutal and uncivilised past. The gun's proximity to these keepsakes provides us with this analogy. He puts the photograph to one side and it is the gun that he takes away; a decision has been made.

The next long shot is an iconic Western moment: man attempts to fire gun at tin can. The composition of the shot reveals that Munny has his back to his children and the house, whilst the lifeless tree and the gravestone of his wife beneath are on the side that he is facing, symbolising a rejection of his present and a desire to embrace a future which may be bleak.

He fires and misses, and so begins a scene, like many others in this film, which implicitly tackles the myths that have been perpetuated by the Hollywood Western; it also deconstructs Clint Eastwood's iconic status as a Hollywood tough guy.

The next shot has the can in foreground close-up, with Munny on one side of the can in the background and the children/house on the other; again the choice that Munny is making, between family and violence, is underlined by the composition.

He again misses, and the medium shot, as he takes aim for his third attempt, has the children appear right next to the gun's barrel, with them in the background and it in the foreground; his actions are endangering his children and his future. The third miss is followed by close-ups of the can, Munny's frustrated face and then the children; there is incredulity that he cannot hit the can.

All this suggests Eastwood's desire to demythologise the Western; this ex-gunfighter cannot even hit a can and Eastwood, the actor, for so long seen to be the ultimate professional with a gun (*A Fistful of Dollars*, *Dirty Harry*), is shown as incompetent. A rapid succession of shots show him missing again and again, until he looks down at the gun in bewilderment. The daughter's question to her brother – 'Did Pa used to kill folks?' – again juxtaposes his children and their innocence with his growing desire to relearn his killing ways.

As Munny walks into and then out of the house, now brandishing a shotgun, he is flanked with more reminders of the genteel existence which he is rejecting – the lace cloth and girl's blouse hanging on the washing line. The emphatic shot of him blasting the can with a shotgun is a grim parody of both Munny's former gun-slinging and Eastwood's own film persona; both are now well past their sell-by date.

The next sequence shows him shaving and, smartly dressed, laying flowers on his wife's grave. He is preparing for a new life. The shot of the daughter in the doorway from within the house is reminiscent of the opening to *The Searchers* (see 1950s Western section) as Munny walks out and leaves domesticity and family life for a violent future.

The demythologising through parody continues as Munny attempts to mount his horse; it spins around as he comically flails and is unceremoniously dumped onto the ground. The long shot of this moment is humorous but also melancholy, for he is a solitary figure with just an old farm horse, a dilapidated cart and outside toilet making up the *mise-en-scène*; pathetic fragments of a life. Also key here is the barren landscape; there is no life visible, just a flat, monotonous horizon which promises little.

It is an anti-triumphant departure. As he wrestles with the horse and eventually climbs up, Munny eulogises the dead wife and mother; the children are shown in medium shot and close-up and the shots and the children are static; in fact, the only movement with them occurs in their final shot as the daughter moves within the frame towards her brother, indicating their new family unit as father

rides off. The departure is low-key, as is much of the film's action, a technique which adds to the verisimilitude of the scenes.

The final long shot, as Munny rides away, is the antithesis of most Western farewells and departures: it is ordinary; there is no non-diegetic musical accompaniment, as with this entire scene, and the only sounds are the diegetic noise of clucking chickens flanking Munny as he rides off. Again the reality of the scene is retained; a man is leaving his two young children to fend for themselves in order to kill two men for money. It is sad and brutal and needs no fanfare or visual excess.

A shooting (22)

Munny's first killing in the film is a sombre and anti-heroic affair. He and his partners catch up with the cowboy who attacked the prostitute at the beginning of the film. However, it is the innocent cowboy, Davy, who is shot in this scene.

It begins with a typical cowboy scene, the branding of a calf. It escapes and the first gunshot fells Davy's horse, trapping Davy beneath it. The first indication that this will be a messy and protracted killing is demonstrated by the mistaken killing of the horse. Eastwood portrays the whole scene as a demonstration that the reality of a gunfight is far from slick and noble.

The cowboys, at first, do not know what to do, eventually scrambling for cover. Munny and his partners are shown to be skulking behind rocks, hardly models of Western heroism. The first front-on medium shot of the three has all their faces in shadow; the strongly-lit hero is not apparent here. A fairly rapid pace of editing helps to show each of the main groups, their predicaments and the chaos of the situation. The short-sightedness of The Schofield Kid, and his constant questioning about what is happening, underlines the sense of absurdity of the situation.

After a series of medium shots, the close-up of Ned, focusing on his face and the gun, helps to accentuate his own growing unease about what is unfolding. The tension increases as Davy crawls towards the rocks, The Schofield Kid keeps questioning and Ned seems paralysed with fear. A shot of Munny with the barrel in the foreground foreshadows his eventual decision to take decisive and deadly action. That shot is repeated twice more until Ned pleads that he cannot shoot the prone boy and Munny stretches towards the front of the frame and grabs the gun. We then see the gun from his perspective; he has crossed the line back into the world of violence.

He fires and misses, and as his frustration rises he asks Ned how many more shots he has. He is now framed in medium shot by the Kid's arm and holster; it is the Kid who has spoken most about killing and wanting to kill, so it is appropriate that Munny is now seen framed by this representation from his violent past.

There is then a cut from the crawling Davy, desperate and frightened, to the medium shot of

But it does not end there; there is nothing clean about this death. Davy cries 'I'm dying, boys', as he clutches his stomach, and then pleads for water. Only the Kid shouts out in defiance of what they have done; the three-shot now shows Munny with head bowed.

The camera now focuses on the victim, as he screams in fear of his impending death and his need for water. Munny, in his despair, demands that Davy's friends give him water: the killer is also humane. The complex universe of the Western is again illustrated, in contrast to the countless bloodless shootings depicted in Westerns over the years.

As the camera tracks around the rock to reveal a cowboy giving water to Davy, it is as if this is a sight almost too painful to behold. When Davy is revealed, it is the stomach bullet wound that is centre frame, emphasising his pain and the fact that his life is ebbing away.

a determined Munny, the barrel of the rifle now a cold, metallic extension of Munny's mindset. He shoots and misses again, and the rapid cutting between Davy and his friends constantly reminds us of their plight, as humans in a terrible situation.

The final rifle shot hits Davy and Munny immediately gives the weapon to the Kid. The three-shot shows Munny and the Kid in active positions, filling much of the frame; Ned is tiny and crumpled behind them, a passive presence.

Munny is again framed within the Kid's body, and after exchanging a look of shame with Ned, he responds to the Kid's constant questioning as to whether Davy is dead – 'Yeah, we killed him, I guess'. The close-up on Munny and the sombre non-diegetic music highlight his fall back into brutality.

The return to the three-shot now shows all three with heads bowed, any bravado or commitment to the job now gone. They contemplate the enormity of what has happened. The scene's final shot of Ned looking at Munny stands as a perspective from a man who has finally rejected violence (Ned) on one who has returned to its savage pointlessness (Munny). In a later scene, Munny sums this up with characteristic insight: 'It's a helluva thing, killing a man. You take away all he's got and all he's ever gonna have.'

Brokeback Mountain

KEY FACTS

Release Date: 2005

Country of Origin: USA

Running Time: 134 minutes

PRODUCTION NOTES

Production Companies

Alberta Film Entertainment

Focus Features

Good Machine

Paramount Pictures

River Road Entertainment

Distributor

Focus Features

Budget

$14,000,000 (estimated)

Awards

Best Achievement in Directing Ang Lee

Academy Awards, USA

Best Adapted Screenplay Larry McMurty, Diana Ossana Academy Awards, USA

Best Achievement in Music Written for Motion Pictures, Original Score Gustavo Santaolalla Academy Awards, USA

Best Film Diana Ossana, James Schamus BAFTA Awards, UK

Best Performance by an Actor in a Supporting Role Jake Gyllenhall BAFTA Awards, UK

Best Adapted Screenplay Larry McMurty, Diana Ossana BAFTA Awards, UK

Outstanding Directorial Achievement in Motion Pictures Ang Lee Directors Guild of America

Best Director Ang Lee Golden Globes, USA

Best Motion Picture – Drama Golden Globes, USA

Best Original Song – Motion Picture Gustavo Santaolalla, Bernie Taupin Golden Globes, USA

Best Screenplay – Larry McMurty, Diana Ossana Golden Globes, USA

Golden Lion Ang Lee Venice Film Festival

SYNOPSIS

Two young cowboys sign up to tend sheep in a remote area of Wyoming, the taciturn strangers slowly getting to know each other as they lead their isolated existence in the wilderness. Eventually, after a drunken evening, Ennis and Jack begin a 20-year love affair, which barely survives the passage of time. Their lives away from Brokeback Mountain follow traditional lines: marriage, children, other jobs. They occasionally escape to the wilderness and live as their other selves, but each time they must return to their domestic lives and lies.

Ennis struggles through life, his marriage fails (his wife discovers the secret affair) and he ends up living in a caravan; Jack marries into a wealthy family but is as equally alienated as Ennis. Although Jack pleads with Ennis to move away together they never make the break, and when Jack is beaten to death (for being homosexual it is implied), Ennis is left with no more than his memories of Brokeback Mountain and a love which society was not able to accept.

HISTORICAL CONTEXT

The noughties have been characterised by more panics than any previous decade: global terrorism, global warming and bird flu to name just a few. Countries have been in a state of flux, whether caused by war or by mass migration, and an air of uncertainty pervades society, fuelled by the accessibility and saturation of information. In the cinema, CGI-filled blockbusters dominate box office takings. However, the big conglomerate film companies were starting to see a renewed interest in less escapist fare, dealing with quirky but ordinary people, which were very much character- and narrative-driven, compared with the staple spectacle and high concept films.

Certainly, after films such as *Alexander* (2004) and *Catwoman* (2004) failed to make money, they began to mimic the independent sector, creating their own arthouse divisions – Focus Features (Universal), W2 (Warners) and Fox Searchlight (20th Century Fox).

Films such as Alexander Payne's *Sideways* (2004) and Jonathan Dayton's and Valerie Faris' *Little Miss Sunshine* (2006) were not only critical successes but they made money; low budgets and high returns are just what the major Hollywood studios dream about.

Into this arena came *Brokeback Mountain* (from Focus Features), an intimate story that pushes back the barriers about the depiction of homosexuality in mainstream cinema. At a time of such uncertainty and where many previous taboos are being more fully addressed, it seems appropriate that the Western, a genre that epitomises maleness of a very rigid nature should, in this era, be the forum for a meditation on a love affair that has rarely entered bigger budget film-making in Hollywood. Coupled with the move towards making more films that were ordinarily the preserve of the independent sector, the time seemed opportune for such a film as this.

SELECT FILMOGRAPHY OF MAIN PRODUCERS AND CAST
Ang Lee, 1954, Director

The Wedding Banquet, 1993

Eat Drink Man Woman, 1995

Sense and Sensibility, 1995

The Ice Storm, 1997

Ride with the Devil, 1999

Crouching Tiger, Hidden Dragon, 2000

Hulk, 2003

Brokeback Mountain, 2005

Lust, Caution, 2007

James Schamus, 1959, Screenwriter, Producer

The Wedding Banquet, 1993

The Ice Storm, 1997

Ride with the Devil, 1999

Hulk, 2003

Brokeback Mountain, 2005

Heath Ledger, 1979–2008, Actor

10 Things I Hate About You, 1997

A Knight's Tale, 2001

The Four Feathers, 2002

Ned Kelly, 2003

Brokeback Mountain, 2005

The Brothers Grimm, 2005

The Dark Knight, 2008

Jake Gyllenhall, 1980, Actor

Donnie Darko, 2001

The Day After Tomorrow, 2004

Brokeback Mountain, 2005

Jarhead, 2005

Zodiac, 2007

LINKS TO OTHER FILMS

Bend of the River/The Naked Spur (1952)

Two Westerns directed by Anthony Mann which both use landscape as a central metaphor for the interior machinations of the characters in his films. Both these films, starring James Stewart, and his other Westerns of the 1950s, deal with psychologically scarred characters who undergo emotional trauma amidst breathtaking scenery, which contrasts with, and parallels, their behaviour. Brokeback Mountain plays a similar role in the Ang Lee film.

Lonely are the Brave (1962)/*Hud* (1963)/*Junior Bonner* (1972)

These films, directed by David Miller, Martin Ritt and Sam Peckinpah respectively, all use a modern setting for their Westerns, a context which further emphasises the cowboys' anachronistic existence, struggling to cope with a world which views them as dinosaurs.

The Last Picture Show (1971)

Peter Bogdanovich's film about 1950's small town America has the same melancholy atmosphere as *Brokeback Mountain*, as it depicts a dying community and a group of people who are desperately searching for meaning and comfort in their drab lives.

My Beautiful Launderette (1985)

Like *Brokeback Mountain*, this film is perhaps commonly regarded as a one-issue story: homosexuality. However, again like Lee's film, it actually deals with a number of issues. There is the powerful depiction of racism and its inherent complexity, exposing its ability to exist within all types of people. Thatcherite Britain in the 1980s is also strongly represented with its focus on the perceived importance of financial success and concomitant ruthlessness.

REPRESENTATION

Masculinity

Notions of masculinity have been depicted in fairly narrow terms by mainstream film-makers for many years. Men are seen time and again as the sexual predator, the provider and protector. Those that slip through the macho net are often viewed as weak or deviant. The Hollywood Alpha-male was white, charming and successful, either through guile or brawn – actors like Errol Flynn personified the classic broad brushstroke definition of masculinity.

Whether masculinity was a social construct or a result of biology, the representation was the same. This dominant model for masculinity could, of course, be embraced or rejected by the individual but the flow of received wisdom continued for many years from film to audience in cinemas around the world, particularly the western world. Whatever the genre, from Westerns to war films to science fiction, the archetypes were preserved; it was only with the navel-gazing of films like Nicholas Ray's *Bigger Than Life* (1956) that traditional male roles would come under scrutiny, to be redefined or rejected. Nearly 50 years later Todd Haynes would revisit the 1950s, when Hollywood's confrontation with its own notions of masculinity began. His study of American suburban artifice, *Far From Heaven* (2002), suggests an alternate, although by no means insincere, take on masculinity.

Of all the genres, Westerns are most closely associated with the archetypal models of masculinity. Cowboys were rugged, powerful, taciturn and heterosexual... or so the Hollywood myth would have you believe.

Brokeback Mountain suggests a more complex scenario. Although set in the 1960s, its use of traditional Western conventions gives it a timeless atmosphere, suggesting that this is a story about men that could easily have existed in the 1860s. Ennis and Jack are everything one would expect of cowboys in a Western, but they are so much more; they are humans, not stereotypes.

By presenting this story within a Western framework, the pressures on the men to conform to stereotype is all the more pronounced. They try to break free from society's structures in sexual terms just as the film itself tries to transcend decades of Western convention. Masculinity is here defined as something much more wide-ranging than has been seen within many of this genre's output. Like *Unforgiven* before it, there is an expression of masculinity which speaks more about the human condition than any narrow definition.

Solitude

It is not uncommon that Westerns have dealt with the solitude associated with being part of a vast, untamed wilderness, particularly from the point of view of the white settlers. The wilderness can often be seen as a place of death and wildness (see *The Searchers* for more detail), but it is also a place of refuge and freedom. For Ennis and Jack it is seen as initially a place of solitude, yet one that then fosters their friendship. It becomes clear that it is, in fact, in the towns and houses of civilisation that these two characters are most lonely. But it is not only the two cowboys who are victims of solitude; Ennis' wife, Alma, is abandoned emotionally and physically by her husband. Her solitude is emphasised by the shots of their forlorn house situated on vast plains, the washing on the line flapping in the incessant wind, a melancholy of domestic solitude.

'It is the story of a time and place where two men are forced to deny the only great passion either one will ever feel. Their tragedy is universal. It could be about two women, or lovers from different religious or ethnic groups—any "forbidden" love'. Roger Ebert http://rogerebert. suntimes.com

'The film is extremely moving, tragic even, and sensitive towards the feelings of the simple wives who attempt to understand their troubled husbands.' Philip French, *The Observer*, 8th January, 2006

KEY SCENE TEXTUAL ANALYSIS

Ennis arrives in Signal, Wyoming (1)

A huge panorama of the landscape begins this film, setting up its credentials in a true Western manner. The non-diegetic music is acoustic guitar-based and is identifiably of the Western/Country and Western variety - haunting and melancholy.

Director Lee wants to set up genre conventions because they will, of course, be deconstructed as the film progresses.

Just as a horse and rider are often placed in the midst of a vast vista to enhance their isolation, so a truck appears at the bottom right of the frame, dwarfed by the immensity of the landscape which stretches hypnotically to the horizon. In three shots the truck emerges from the dawn and stops and a cowboy (Ennis) emerges; a cowboy hitching a lift and travelling on a beast far removed from the traditional mode of transport for a cowboy. This, of course, is a modern Western, but Lee is emphasising his disconnection from his natural environment, the 'Great Outdoors'.

It is a long shot of Ennis as he walks away in a cowboy costume (for here, in this disempowered environment it is just that; not until he is in the mountains is he in his element), and a long lens is used as if to highlight his isolation. The audience is looking down a telescope at a dying breed, a rare specimen. There is no gun. Instead he carries just a brown paper bag containing his belongings, which adds to the pathos of the moment.

The next shot is a modern twist on the old one-horse Western town, with a few ramshackle buildings, no life and the framing giving emphasis to the immense sky. It is empty and without warmth. The long angle lens accentuates this emptiness and it is static/dead (compared with the later panoramas which are full of mystery and life, and over which the camera lovingly moves, caressing the landscape). Into this space comes the tiny figure of Ennis.

time is emblematic of a man with very little to his name.

The long shot looking down the street does not add any extra dimension to the town, but instead reinforces the lifelessness of the place, particularly with another rusting truck in the foreground.

It is not until the next shot that we see Ennis in close-up and actually see his face; up to this point we have seen only fragments of a person, fitting for a man who is incomplete at this point in the film. The entrance of a black truck animates the static scene, but the diegetic sounds of a spluttering motor, its comical wheel spin as its engine is turned off and the driver's obvious frustration with it, again speaks of decay.

The Western convention of the one-horse (truck) town has been established and now we see some more of the trappings of the Western: the newcomer (Jack) arrives in a black car (horse) and

The next medium shot is again static and the *mise-en-scène* is dominated by dullness such as the grey structure against which Ennis leans and the rusting truck to the right of frame. It is a picture of monotony and decay, in marked contrast to the life shown in later scenes on Brokeback Mountain. In this world Ennis cannot express himself, but he embraces life and self-knowledge in the wilderness; here he is seen, head down, almost part of the structure behind him.

We then see him from a distance, in long shot, but now with a rushing train in the foreground, affording the audience only a partial glimpse, just as the train's passengers might briefly glimpse this dejected figure who seems to be part of this dying town, and forgetting him instantly; such is Ennis' empty life. The medium shot of him smoking and then flicking off the ash to save the butt for another

wears a black hat, whereas Ennis sports a light-coloured Stetson.

Jack walks towards Ennis with hands on hips as if he is about to draw, but his expression is one of friendship. Ennis, however, responds by dropping his head again and inviting no chit-chat. It has echoes of a Western stand-off, but this world is stripped of any vitality and there is no progress made, either antagonistic or otherwise.

Lee cuts from medium shot to medium shot as each cowboy coyly glances at the other. Jack's head goes down, in mirror image of Ennis', and the non-showdown is complete; the film throughout deconstructs our expectations of cowboys and it begins that job here.

In fact, the only good glimpse that Jack gets of Ennis is in his truck's side mirror as he shaves;

he is interested by him but sullenness wins through at this point. Certainly, a taciturn nature is stereotypical for a cowboy and Ennis particularly conforms to this.

A third cowboy now enters the scene on his slightly more groomed steed, a polished car. The cowboy ignores the others, continuing this air of non-communication. The new arrival also wears a hat and sunglasses to add to his masculine iconography. The touch of having him carry a thermos flask instead of a gun is ironic, undermining his macho posturing and detailing perhaps how far this cowboy is removed from our perception of the rugged cowboys of old.

The sign on the door – 'Trespassers will be shot. Survivors will be shot again' – speaks of the idea of casual death, so typical of Westerns, but also shows how far removed from that old West these characters are at this point, similar to a thousand

tent together. The events of the previous evening have changed their lives forever.

Ennis emerges from the tent without a word. Ennis is next seen in the foreground, close to familiar things such as his horse and rifle. After a homosexual encounter, going against all that he has seen and been taught in a particularly macho tight-lipped world, it is too much to cope with at the moment. He has his back turned as Jack emerges from the tent and ritually checks his rifle, a recourse to the familiar cowboy world.

Ennis mounts the horse, with barely a look back at Jack, whose body language is much more friendly. He utters the only line – 'See you for supper'. Ennis rides off into nature, an escape, leaving a dejected Jack in lonely mid-shot. The cut to the medium shot of Ennis leaves him to the edge of the frame rather than the centre; the emptiness leaves room for his thoughts and confusion.

clichéd funny signs that appear in workplaces or homes.

Both Ennis and Jack are ignored by the owner of the office and he shuts the door as Ennis mounts the steps - superiority and humiliation still have currency. The new cowboy's return to the door and his derogatory words – 'Get your scrawny asses in here' – underlines this boss' superiority (these are the first words of the film, and they are harsh). His high angle POV does, for the first time, place Ennis and Jack together in close proximity (albeit with the latter in the foreground and the former behind); they are allied in their lowly station in life.

The morning after (4; 27:36)

The opening shot after their first sexual encounter is an intimate close-up of the two men lying in the

The next long shot is even more expressive of this mindset; he rides with a large empty space beside him. The grey, cold land rises ahead of him, brooding black clouds behind, melancholy, while shapeless non-diegetic music and the diegetic brutal wind underline his mood. As he climbs the hill the clouds darken. He seems listless until his eyes are drawn to something up ahead.

The rapid riding contrasts with the previous shots until he arrives at the ugly sight of a sheep, its stomach ripped out by coyotes (he should have been on guard on the mountain the previous night but his drunkenness and encounter with Jack have prevented him from carrying out his duty). The close-up of the sheep's insides and the cut back to Ennis' face connect the two; he too has bared his inner self. His thoughts of confusion must also include the question 'am I being punished for what I have done?'

This shot is then juxtaposed next to the virtually naked Jack as he washes his clothes in the stream. Jack is elemental in this naked state, as if this sexual encounter has freed him of society's constraints in the form of his clothes. Another reading could be explored as he is shown to be wringing out and thrashing his shirt; perhaps he is coming to terms with what has happened, not sure how to react. The bridge seems suspended above him, a great weight or threat.

The subsequent two shots of the dog and the sheep fur attached to a wooden stake are both contemplative, and then, in half-light (indeed their minds are full of light and shadow), Ennis re-enters Jack's life. The carrying of the gun still indicates Ennis' macho posture as he confronts what has happened with Jack.

Jack lays on his side and Ennis sits down to be on his level. The dialogue begins but Lee frames the two men to emphasise their discomfort and their edginess whilst connecting with their feelings; Jack is in profile (he is the more connected of the two) whilst the reticent Ennis is shot almost from behind. The conversation underlines their struggle to deny the truth of what has happened, to maintain their tough male cowboy persona:

> Ennis: This is a one-shot thing we got goin' on here.
>
> Jack: It's nobody's business but ours.
>
> Ennis: You know I ain't queer.
>
> Jack: Me neither.

The conversation ends with a two-shot, but from behind both men. They have not voiced their innermost feelings and so there is no face-on openness. They remain closed to themselves and their sexuality and the audience is denied access to them as well. Again, the landscape beyond contains their true thoughts and feelings. Of course, they are still cowboys whatever their sexuality, but in a society conditioned against this, they have no vocabulary to deal with their situation.

DRAMA

The drama genre; does it exist? There are a number of things to say here; I wanted to have a section which allowed the inclusion of a range of films that would otherwise have been neglected by my traditional genre approach, for without them the book's breadth of vision would have been somewhat narrowed. And, indeed, its inclusion helps promote a discussion about genre, an increasingly fluid concept in an era which prides itself on redefinition and the blurring of supposedly fixed ideas.

Most importantly, as I decided on the films and wrote about them I felt that they created their own sense of cohesion, their stories forming a timeline of human drama. Certainly, 'melodrama' has often been cited as a distinct genre, an early favourite of genre study, and the films that follow all certainly deal with heightened emotion and personal crises. The section begins with the sublime *Sunrise* (1927), a tale very much of human drama, told with a sumptuous visual language that puts many modern films to shame. Both *Angels With Dirty Faces* (1938) and *The Killers* (1946) focus on the choices made by individuals and the unavoidable fate that awaits them; the former comes from that wonderful stable of Warner Bros. films that emerged in the 1930s dealing with social issues and the cult of gangster celebrity and notoriety, whilst the latter is one of the purest expressions of what has become known as film noir. It belongs to a group of films that, by the sheer depth of their dark visual motifs and themes, is a strong contender to stand as its own genre. They can both be compared with the 1990s selection, Martin Scorsese's *Goodfellas* (1990), a film that both celebrates and revises audience reaction to gangsters, again emphasising characterisation amidst a bravura display of camerawork and editing. *The 400 Blows* (1959) and *Saturday Night and Sunday Morning* (1960) deal with alienation on either side of the English Channel, character studies of individuals trapped by their respective environments and powerless to escape by the time each film reaches its denouement. They are, of course, great examples of film-making techniques that were breathing new life into visual story-telling, capturing key moments in the New Waves that engulfed Europe in the late 1950s and 1960s.

Francis Coppola's *Apocalypse Now* (1979) stands as a symbol of the virtues in film-making and some of its follies in the 1970s; it was a last gasp for the maverick film-makers of that decade and both its production history and visual chaos perfectly mirror the horrors of war. By contrast, *Wings of Desire* (1987) is a far more low-key and sedate film, a work of great visual poetry which again explores the human condition in a virtuoso manner. Its director, Wim Wenders, like Coppola, tells stories on their own terms, allowing the audience to wallow in visual pleasure and eek out their own personal readings. *Crash* (2005) is very much a film of its decade, preoccupied with the results of a century of massive human migrations across the planet; it is a film that deals with the age-old issues of disharmony amongst different creeds and races; conflicts that grow in importance as the stakes get higher in global terms with humanity's increasing ability to destroy and self-destruct.

Sunrise: A Song of Two Humans

KEY FACTS

Release Date: 1927

Country of Origin: USA

Running Time: 91 minutes

PRODUCTION NOTES

Production Company

Fox Film Corporation

Distributor

Fox Film Corporation

Awards

Best Actress in a Leading Role Janet Gaynor
Academy Awards, USA

Best Cinematography Charles Rosher Karl Struss
Academy Awards, USA

Best Picture, Unique and Artistic Production
Academy Awards, USA

National Film Registry National Film Preservation
Board, USA

SYNOPSIS

In a small village a farmer (the man) is having an affair with a woman from the city and neglecting his spouse. The man meets his lover in the marshland outside the village and she tempts him with images of the city, telling him that he should kill his wife and run away with her. They concoct a plan that would make the wife's death look like an accident, and he agrees to carry it out. He takes his wife for a boat ride on the nearby lake, but as he is about to push her overboard he stops and is filled with remorse. They reach the far side of the lake and his wife, having realised his murderous intentions, rushes to a trolley car and jumps on, hotly pursued by her repentant husband.

They make the journey to the city and become reconciled after witnessing a wedding in a church. They spend the rest of the day in extreme happiness, reliving the early days of their marriage in a dreamlike euphoria. They have their photograph taken, eat, go to a funfair (where he catches a drunken pig that has escaped) and they dance, leaving the previous atmosphere of fear and distrust well behind them. On the journey back to the village their small rowing boat is capsized in a storm; she is feared drowned but he makes it back to shore. He is totally distraught and goes off to seek revenge on his former lover. As he is attempting to strangle her the shouts of the villagers from the lake stop him and he realises that his wife has been found. She is alive and they are reunited, whilst the woman returns to the city alone.

HISTORICAL CONTEXT

The First World War had ended in 1918 and, for the Americans at least, it was a time of frivolity and good times; it was the so-called Jazz Age. However, beneath the shimmer of fun, particularly in the cities, lay a decadent and superficial underbelly. F. Scott Fitzgerald perfectly recorded the duality of this age in his stories of excess and emptiness. In his novel, *The Great Gatsby* (1925), Fitzgerald describes the preparations for one of Gatsby's parties: 'Every Friday five crates of oranges and lemons arrived from a fruiterer in New York - every Monday these same oranges and lemons left his back door in a pyramid of pulpless halves.' In much the same way, his guests arrived each Friday and emptied themselves with hedonistic frivolity.

Sunrise shows the lure of the city; it is even enjoyed by the married couple but they ultimately return to the security of their village life. It is unsurprising that F.W. Murnau, who had witnessed the deprivations of post-war Germany, could see the parallels between this way of life and the feeling of invincibility felt by the Germans before the war. Prophetically, he shows this life to be a façade; indeed, with the Wall Street Crash of 1929 it all but evaporated.

Murnau was just one of a stream of European film-makers who made their way to the United States between the two world wars. Although his American adventure was cut short by his premature death in 1931, many others had long and/or influential careers in Hollywood, including the directing talents of Fritz Lang, Robert Siodmak and Michael Curtiz, and cameramen Karl Struss and John Alton. These are just a few of the many who arrived from Europe in the early part of the twentieth century; others would found film studios, like Louis B. Mayer (MGM) and the Warner brothers. Although they all brought their individual talents to the roles that they pursued, there was a collective work ethic that characterised these men, who had often escaped the turmoil that embroiled Europe at the beginning of the century.

Some also brought a strong legacy of film-making from their countries, particularly those from Germany and the Austro-Hungarian Empire where film-making techniques had developed rapidly. The influence of expressionist techniques, used in art, theatre, architecture, music and literature found their way into film-making, and this distortion of reality for emotional effect began to inform many a film's *mise-en-scène*. It was this stylistic influence that crept into Hollywood films as these Europeans began working in the studio system, from the silent period well into the century.

SELECT FILMOGRAPHY OF MAIN PRODUCERS AND CAST

F.W. Murnau, 1881–1931, Director

Nosferatu, eine Symphonie des Grauens, 1922

Der Letze Mann, 1924

Herr Tartüff, 1926

Faust, 1926

Sunrise, 1927

4 Devils, 1928

City Girl, 1928

Tabu, 1931

George O' Brien, 1899–1985, Actor

See *The Iron Horse* in WESTERN section (pg. 14)

Janet Gaynor, 1906–1984, Actress

The Blue Eagle, 1926

Seventh Heaven, 1927

Sunrise, 1927

Street Angel, 1928

4 Devils, 1928

Lucky Star, 1929

The Man Who Came Back, 1931

Merely Mary Ann, 1931

Adorable, 1933

Carolina, 1934

One More Spring, 1935

The Farmer Takes a Wife, 1935

Small Town Girl, 1936

Ladies in Love, 1936

A Star is Born, 1937

Three Loves Has Nancy, 1938

The Young in Heart, 1939

LINKS TO OTHER FILMS

The Crowd (1928)

A depiction of the way in which the big city consumes individuals, a city that is full of dreams but inevitably leads to anonymity. In *Sunrise*, the city and its people are often seen as anonymous hordes flocking around the towering structures which seem intent on engulfing them; the rural couple is only passing through.

Pandora's Box (1929)

Two years after *Sunrise*, another German director, G.W. Pabst, brought a story to the screen which contains a depiction of the archetypal vamp in the form of American Louise Brooks as Lulu. There is both a physical and emotional similarity between vamps of both films, although Lulu is a much more detailed characterisation.

Citizen Kane (1941)

Both Orson Welles' film and Murnau's are critically acclaimed, and the connection between the two lies firmly in their use of film language. They are innovative films in terms of the fluidity of camerawork, often expressing meanings beyond the literal. The influence of the cinematographers in each film is also crucial, all three of whom had pivotal parts to play in the productions - Charles Rosher and Karl Struss in *Sunrise* and Gregg Toland in *Citizen Kane*.

Double Indemnity (1944)

The vamp in *Sunrise* can be seen as a template for the femme fatales of the later film noir cycle in Hollywood (see pg.90 and *The Killers*). In Billy Wilder's film the woman is able to convince the man to actually carry out the murder of her husband. Her sexual guile is shown to enshroud the man, just as the vamp in Murnau's film tries to ensnare her man.

Beauty and the Beast (1946)

Jean Cocteau's beautiful reworking of the fairytale is replete with dreamlike imagery and mesmerising visuals which help translate the transcendental nature of the love between the two characters. *Sunrise* shares some of these traits as it strives to visually transmit the love, or as the subtitle of the film states, the *Song of Two Humans*, in a poetic form.

The Great Gatsby (1974)

This is the third attempt to transpose the poetic quality of F. Scott Fitzgerald's language onto screen. It goes some way to showing the kind of world that momentarily hypnotises the husband in *Sunrise*, and equally shows its empty promises.

Badlands (1973)/*Days of Heaven* (1978)/*The Thin Red Line* (1998)/*The New World* (2005)

All of Terrence Malick's films echo the beauty of the images and poetic vision that Murnau was able to present in *Sunrise*. Like Murnau, Malick has artistic control over his projects and the resultant films are more akin to visual tone poems than conventional Hollywood products. The directors share visions of life that can be layered upon genre narratives, but elevate them to new heights of artistic endeavour.

REPRESENTATION

Rural and urban life

The long trolley car ride between the rural and the urban, taken by the couple after the husband's aborted murder attempt, is a visual metaphor for the way that the two worlds, although separate, are inextricably linked. The rural idyll has been disrupted by the arrival of the woman from the city, and it is to the city that the couple must come in order to fully exorcise their demons. The city is presented as a chaotic place of unbridled fun and abandonment by the woman in tempting the man (see TEXTUAL ANALYSIS section), but when the married couple arrive they are initially accosted by the maelstrom of traffic.

When they are reconciled the traffic melts away and they are momentarily returned to their rural home as they walk into the road, oblivious to the noise around them. When they are eventually shaken from this love-filled reverie they find themselves surrounded by cars, blaring their horns in anger. But nothing can disturb the equilibrium, so firmly rooted in the rural, and although they partake in the trappings of urban living their otherness is actually celebrated. It is the man from the country who captures the escaped pig later on in the film and they perform a folk dance for the crowd, immune to any incongruity in the urban environment.

The superficiality of the urban world is underlined as a storm wind blows through the funfair and its environs, a world of levity which may be blown away at any time. In the village there is a European design to the *mise-en-scène*, resembling more a nineteenth century German village than anything to be found in twentieth century America. This antiquated and alien look emphasises its otherness, its total contrast to the urban world, and therefore a place where other values are promoted. This anachronistic *mise-en-scène* also suggests its almost fairy tale setting, a morality tale that emphasises its universality by the use of nominal titles for the three main characters.

However, it is not a simple case of urban bad, rural good. The village is seen at night and the interiors of the couple's house are in classic German expressionist mode, all shadows and unusual angles, just as in Robert Wiene's *Die Cabinet den Dr. Caligari* (1919) or Murnau's own *Nosferatu, eine Symphonie des Grauens* (1922). The only glimpse we have of a rural idyll is a flashback to show husband, wife and child in a daytime scene beneath

a tree with the wife's hair flowing and happiness on the faces of all three. They are a holy family of pastoral joy. It is the woman from the city who has cast a shadow over the rural scene and darkened and tainted the couple, and it is only with her departure that the sun rises again on their world.

'The last great movie of German silent cinema, voted the best film of all time by French film critics, was made in America. Sunrise...[was] about the contrasting values of country and the city.' Mark Cousins, *The Story of Film*, Pavillion Books, London, 2004

'If Sunrise causes us to regress, it is to our more innocent selves. Thus, it makes us lose our scepticism regarding the 'banalities' of human existence, and the potential for art to move us.' Eds. Lucy Fischer, *Sunrise A Song of Two Humans* BFI Film Classics, Bfi Publishing, London, 2002

"Sunrise *is a great film; a landmark in the use of a moving camera; and of crucial importance in showing how genre cinema may be complemented by the gravity of a true artist's feelings.'* David Thomson, *The New Biographical Dictionary of Film*, Little, Brown, London, 2002

KEY SCENE TEXTUAL ANALYSIS

Meeting the woman from the city (2/3)

The man leaves his wife behind for a rendezvous with the woman from the city; previously we have seen the difference between this worldly and vain woman and the homespun and devoted wife.

The camera tracks behind the man as if he is too ashamed to face the camera. The *mise-en-scène* shows him hunched over as he moves further into the darkness and mist. Guilt, danger and moral ruin seem to be his companions on this walk, but still he goes on. The moon shines brightly in the darkness, its hypnotic glow drawing him like the sexual allure of his lover.

The long tracking shot also suggests his journey into a dark place, both literally and metaphorically, his twists and turns through the trees and vegetation underlining the moral maze that he has entered with his decision to have an affair. He walks behind the fauna, obscuring our view of him, just as his mind's clarity has become confused by the sexual draw of this woman. His brief pause in the open as he climbs over a fence seems to be both

Their embrace is violent and elemental. The cut to the wife's embrace of their young child is juxtaposed with the illicit union. One is sexual and aggressive, the other is loving and gentle. These are two worlds at polar extremes with the man serving a self-imposed exile from his family. His world is transferred to the very edge of society, as underlined by the location of his affair. He exists in a limbo world, a swamp land which is neither land nor water. By contrast, the mother and child are evenly lit in the warm, nurturing atmosphere of the home. Their comforting, plain clothes act as symbols of a domestic, ordinary and honest life. The close-up of the wife's tearful face accentuates all her attributes: caring, simple and honest love, and virtue.

one final physical and mental demarcation between the two men that he has become; the husband and the lover.

He walks past the camera, which turns and then appears to be his POV as it moves through low-hanging branches of a tree. Through this final veil is the woman, framed with the moon, linking her closely with it and its associated mythology: sexuality, madness, enchantment. She waits like a predator deep within the trees. It is not, as we expected, the man's POV, which is rather disorientating (perhaps a suggestion of her effect on him). For a few moments the audience becomes voyeur, watching her as she prepares herself for his arrival. Her sheer, clinging, black dress is also suggestive of sexuality, of a predatory creature; there is something of the snake about her; in 1920s parlance she is a vamp. Her expression, as the man approaches, resembles a creature about to devour another living thing.

Pain is etched on her face, but she concentrates on her duties, lying the child down in bed. The cut back to the other couple again draws the audience's attention to the differences between the two relationships. However, the positioning of the figures in the frame also points to a similarity, for the man takes the position of the young child, whilst the two women are interchanged; the suggestion seems to be that he is the vulnerable one. As the mother repositions the child, so he is positioned by the woman. He is beneath her as this act of devouring continues. Both in medium shot and then close-up, he lies back like a helpless child whilst she caresses him, his eyes rolling as if in a drugged state. Sexual passion, ironically, seems to emasculate him, but also induces a state where he forgets his responsibilities as a carer for his wife and child.

The intertitles relate their conversation. As the man agrees that he belongs totally to the woman during her invitation to the city and his question about his wife, she grasps his head, pushing his face from the camera as if trying to hide it from those thoughts, enveloping him in her world, her hand covering his head like a claw.

The next intertitle – 'Couldn't she get drowned?' – with the 'drowned' fading on last, mimics the emerging thought from the darkest recesses of her mind. The intertitle itself then melts downwards, like a life slipping away or a representation of the drowning. Indeed, the title then dissolves to a 'flash forward' of the man drowning his wife.

In the next shot the man recoils from the woman, but her body thrusts itself into his filmic space. At first, he begins to choke her, but as he again fights to leave, she enters the frame once more, subduing

disorientating sequence which deliberately looks artificial. This vision is tempting but it is also just a façade, just as the woman's sexual allure is paper-thin.

The next sequence of multi-layered shots again disorientates the viewer, just as the man is being disorientated and drawn into this world of superficial excitement and narcissism. The camera moves on each separate element are, in themselves, chaotic and this is further enhanced by the blurring effect to suggest the impact these images are having on the naïve country man.

The single image of the band helps to underline the madness of the sequence; the frame is bursting with manic life, instruments obliterating the human figures, and the movements of the musicians

him with her clutching hands and devouring him with her lips; they fall to the ground and she is on top once more. The 'Come to the city' phrase in the next intertitle is repeated, the second appearing as larger text as she implores him and consumes him with her words.

As we return to the two-shot, her words conjure up a vision of the city before them. This process shot is a complex web of images, suggesting his further entrapment as she presents a world of urban delight, far removed from his country existence.

The process shot tracks through a neon city, a miniature, with cars racing around; the effect emphasises their journey into this world, and the temptations that it presents. The camera then whip pans, giving a glimpse of a variety of exciting and dynamic urban vistas until it cranes up a neon-lit building to show a cityscape with searchlights, a combination of models and matte paintings. It is a

choreographed to make them look like demented toys.

As we return to the couple in the foreground, and the vision fades, the woman begins to mimic this urban chaos with her manic and serpentine dance. He watches with fixated passion; her movements suggest sexual and moral abandon, a nihilistic dance of entrapment.

Overcome by desire, he grabs her and plunges his face into her stomach. He is possessed by the vision and the wild abandon that she presents. He eventually draws her down to the ground as he kisses her once more, only this time he is on top, signalling his full immersion into this world. She no longer has to draw him in; he is now a dominant force within this amoral universe.

The cut to a long shot of the village shows that the moon shines above it, linking their illicit passion with the village and reminding the audience of what he is leaving behind. The village is also mostly covered by darkness. The domination of the moon underlines the supremacy of the mad passion of the moon over the domestic love that can be found in the village. The camera then tracks after the couple, showing not their progress, but the deep imprint of their shoes in the thick mud; the implication seems to be that they are now both mired in the mud of lies, duplicity and infidelity; it is a moral quagmire.

As she picks bulrushes to aid his escape from the capsized boat (once the wife is drowned), we do not see the man's face; his back is turned from the camera as if he is too ashamed to face the audience. Murder may soon be added to his list of misdeeds. The shot dissolves to black, emphasising the darkness of their actions and their plans, which the camera can no longer bear to record.

As the man returns home Murnau presents his predicament in visual terms. We see him framed in front of a web of fishing nets; he is trapped in this new mindset, a mindset based on sexual passion, hedonism and plans of murder. His gait is now hunched, slow and heavy; his figure symbolises the burden of wrong-doing and he drags his feet as if he has been chained to iron balls of self-loathing, moral emptiness and guilt.

The cut to his wife shows her lying still in bed, simple, honest and guiltless. The shadow of the window frame casts the shape of a cross over her prostrate figure, identifying her with religious virtue. The juxtaposition of her open room and the clutter of the husband's filmic space underpins their two separate universes. We then see him covered by the shadows cast by the branches of the tree; they reflect the moral darkness and suggest the demons that are pursuing him.

Angels with Dirty Faces

KEY FACTS

Release Date: 1938

Country of Origin: USA

Running Time: 93 minutes

PRODUCTION NOTES

Production Companies

Warner Bros. Pictures

First National Pictures

Distributor

Warner Bros. Pictures

Awards

Nominated: Best Actor in a Leading Role James Cagney Academy Awards, USA

Nominated: Best Director Michael Curtiz Academy Awards, USA

Nominated: Best Writing, Original Story Rowland Brown Academy Awards, USA

Best Actor James Cagney New York Film Critics Circle Awards

SYNOPSIS

Two young lives go in very different directions as one youth is caught trying to steal from a train, whilst the other manages to escape. The former, Rocky Sullivan, grows up to be a gangster and the other, Jerry Connolly, becomes a priest. When Rocky returns to his old neighbourhood it is clear that the local boys, all would-be gangsters, idolise him, much to the consternation of his old friend who is trying to steer them away from a life of crime.

Rocky becomes involved with two corrupt associates, a lawyer called Frazier and a businessman named Keefer, who eventually turn on each another. When Fr. Jerry starts a crusade against corruption Frazier and Keefer target him to be killed. Rocky learns of this and kills them, and ultimately he is sentenced to death. Fr. Jerry asks Rocky to grant him a final favour, to act as a coward as he is led to the electric chair, thereby destroying his hero status in the eyes of the boys who worship him. Initially he does not agree but as he is led to his death Rocky begins to scream and squirm. This allows Fr. Jerry to return to the boys, tell them what has happened and put their hero-worship of the gangster to an end. The story finishes with Fr. Jerry and the boys in the church, with the inference that they may have been saved from a life of crime because of Rocky's final selfless act.

HISTORICAL CONTEXT

Prohibition – the banning of alcohol – lasted in the United States from 1920 until its repeal in 1933. A coalition of political parties and pressure groups had helped bring this amendment to the constitution, and the resulting rise in black market alcohol sales and illegal bars enabled organised crime to prosper. The country had just come out of the First World War and the new law divided American society. There was a sense that people wanted to enjoy themselves after the horrors of the war, but the law drove the enjoyment of alcohol underground, perhaps intensifying the level of enjoyment that people gleaned from drinking.

The excesses of lifestyle were forced to come to an end by the time of the Wall Street Crash in 1929, but it emerged as a romantic period, full of glamour and danger in the Hollywood vision. The gangster film became one of the most popular sub-genres, and certainly the staple genre for the Warner Brothers studio, which found its niche in the 1930s for producing a series of highly profitable gangster films, often starring James Cagney and Humphrey Bogart.

SELECT FILMOGRAPHY OF MAIN PRODUCERS AND CAST

Michael Curtiz, 1886–1962, Director

The Mad Genius, 1931

Doctor X, 1932

20,000 Years in Sing Sing, 1932

Mystery of the Wax Museum, 1933

Captain Blood, 1935

The Charge of the Light Brigade, 1935

Kid Galahad, 1937

The Adventures of Robin Hood, 1938

Angels with Dirty Faces, 1938

Dodge City, 1939

The Private Lives of Elizabeth and Essex, 1939

Santa Fe Trail, 1940

Virginia City, 1940

The Sea Hawk, 1940

The Sea Wolf, 1941

Yankee Doodle Dandy, 1942

Casablanca, 1942

Passage to Marseille, 1944

Mildred Pierce, 1945

Night and Day, 1946

Young Man with a Horn, 1950

White Christmas, 1954

We're No Angels, 1955

King Creole, 1958

The Adventures of Huckleberry Finn, 1960

James Cagney, 1899–1986, Actor

The Public Enemy, 1931

A Midsummer Night's Dream, 1936

Angels with Dirty Faces, 1938

The Oklahoma Kid, 1939

Each Dawn I Die, 1939

The Roaring Twenties, 1939

The Fighting 69th, 1940

The Strawberry Blonde, 1941

Yankee Doodle Dandy, 1942

Blood on the Sun, 1945

13 Rue Madeleine, 1947

White Heat, 1949

Kiss Tomorrow Goodbye, 1950

The Seven Little Foys, 1955

Mister Roberts, 1955

One, Two, Three, 1961

Ragtime, 1981

Pat O'Brien, 1899–1983, Actor

The Front Page, 1931

Angels with Dirty Faces, 1938

The Fighting 69th, 1940

Crack-up, 1946

Riffraff, 1947

The Boy with Green Hair, 1948

The People Against O'Hara, 1951

The Last Hurrah, 1958

Some Like it Hot, 1959

Ragtime, 1981

Humphrey Bogart, 1899–1957, Actor

The Petrified Forest, 1936

Kid Galahad, 1937

Angels with Dirty Faces, 1938

The Oklahoma Kid, 1939

The Roaring Twenties, 1939

Virginia City, 1940

They Drive by Night, 1940

High Sierra, 1941

The Maltese Falcon, 1941

Casablanca, 1942

Passage to Marseille, 1944

To Have and Have Not, 1944

The Big Sleep, 1946

Dark Passage, 1947

The Treasure of the Sierra Madre, 1948

Key Largo, 1948

In a Lonely Place, 1950

The Enforcer, 1951

The African Queen, 1951

The Caine Mutiny, 1954

Sabrina, 1954

We're No Angels, 1955

The Desperate Hours, 1955

LINKS TO OTHER FILMS

Little Caesar (1931)

Mervyn LeRoy's gangster film was made whilst prohibition was still in place, and it takes care to distance itself from glorifying the actions of a gangster as he rises to notoriety with a condemnation of criminals in an opening title.

The Public Enemy (1931)

This was James Cagney's breakthrough role, which follows a similar path to *Angels with Dirty Faces*. It traces a boy from his involvement in petty crime to a full criminal life when he is older. Both stories end badly for the main protagonist, reinforcing the message that crime does not pay.

The Roaring Twenties (1939)

Another of Warner Brothers' gangster films, again with James Cagney and Humphrey Bogart, but the fairly unglamorous deaths afforded the Cagney characters in earlier films are here replaced with a death scene of tragic proportions.

The Godfather (1972)

Francis Ford Coppola's seminal gangster saga redefined the sub-genre, breathing new life into the stories of criminal society, with its operatic violence and façade of respectability.

The Untouchables (1987)

Brian de Palma's film details the story of Elliot Ness, a federal agent, who sets about bringing crime boss, Al Capone, to trial. The film charts the effects of prohibition and the difficulty that the authorities encountered in trying to apprehend and prosecute the higher echelons of organised crime.

Sleepers (1996)

This resembles *Angels with Dirty Faces* in that it charts the story of young friends whose lives go awry early on, and catches up with them later in their careers, where crime is shown to have ruined them.

REPRESENTATION

1930s gangsters

There were early attempts to portray gangsters on screen as the unpleasant characters that they undoubtedly were; Edward G. Robinson's Rico (*Little Caesar*) was brutal, as was James Cagney's Tom Powers (*The Public Enemy*), with the latter's infamous thrusting of a grapefruit half into his girlfriend's face and his violent and ignominious death. As the 1930s progressed, though, the gangster was represented in an increasingly glamorous manner. In 1939 the character of Eddie Bartlett in *The Roaring Twenties* is a sympathetic portrayal of a criminal; his death scene (as stated in the LINKS TO OTHER FILMS section) breathes the same air as a tragedy. The final scene, as Panama Smith cradles Eddie on the steps of a church, has the look of a Pietà, the image of a dying Jesus in Mary's arms as He is taken down from the cross. Similarly, *Angels with Dirty Faces* shows Rocky's essential goodness with his final act as he is led to execution.

It was not until James Cagney returned in *White Heat* (1949) and *Kiss Tomorrow Goodbye* (1950) that the romantic edges were rubbed off to reveal psychopathically violent characters, perhaps far closer to the truth than his earlier gangster incarnations. The film noir cycle began in the early 1940s, and its relentlessly bleak narratives and characterisations undoubtedly had an influence on these later gangster films. At the same time it all but killed off this sub-genre for the next 20 years until *The Godfather* appeared and finally represented gangsters in the most complex

way that had been seen in films; the men were killers, businessmen, family men, and quite often, psychopathic.

But for all their complexity and the brutality of their acts, it is clear that gangsters were among the most popular character types brought to the screen. Their glamorous lives and daring escapades were enticing, the cult of celebrity growing quickly around them as early as Cagney's first forays into this territory. Indeed, *The Public Enemy* is prefaced with a message from Warner Bros.: 'It is the ambition of "The Public Enemy" to honestly depict an environment that exists in a certain strata of American life, rather than glorify the hoodlum or the criminal.'

Crime and poverty

Criminal activity is seen to be borne out of social deprivation in *Angels with Dirty Faces*; the environment in which the two boys live is poor and they are disadvantaged as a result. They have no positive role models, nobody to support and direct them, which leads them into petty crime. Indeed, they are both intelligent boys and are shown to do well in their respective fields, but these roles are very different. Rocky is caught, and it is depicted how he becomes institutionalised, a habitual re-offender; again there is no network of support in place to try and rehabilitate him. History seems to be repeating itself with the local boys, but this time Fr. Jerry is there to provide guidance and Rocky seems to realise this in the film's finale. This social commentary may seem simplistic at times, and indeed, its moralising tone can be difficult to accept, but it was key to Warners' film-making raison d'être in the 1930s, and Michael Curtiz was one of its chief advocates.

'A tough drama masquerading as social comment, and typical of the studio's belief that people are all victims of society.' Clive Hirschhorn, *The Warner Bros. Story*, Octopus Books, London, 1981

'*Michael Curtiz's films preach social responsibility, and* Angels with Dirty Faces *is his most powerful sermon.*' Martin Rubin, *1001 Movies You Must See Before You Die*, Cassell Illustrated, 2007

KEY SCENE TEXTUAL ANALYSIS

A vibrant city (1)

A close-up of a man reading a newspaper begins the film. Much of what occurs in the film will be reported by the newspapers as it depicts the cult of celebrity, the celebrity gangster in particular.

Even if the headline means nothing to a non-American audience, the diegetic music, a hurdy-gurdy, signals that this is an early period in American twentieth-century history; a news-vendor can also be heard shouting. The camera moves off the newspaper and a long crane shot ensues, capturing a multitude of actions, with a cacophony of sound helping to add to the general vibrancy of the scene. Women thrash quilts against the walls as they hang out of their balconies. It is a picture of domesticity and of a life lived in the public gaze. It is a working class area and there is a sense of community and shared endeavour.

The buildings are dressed with drying clothes and shop awnings, whilst below horses pull carts and market stalls display their wares. As the camera moves it captures even more of this world. The next building is almost obliterated by the sheets and mattresses, as are the streets and pavements with even more stalls. It is chaotic, but it transcends this to depict a community that is bound by its shared disregard for what looks nice, instead opting for the practical, borne out of necessity, a necessity that is further illustrated by the Bargain Store and the laundry van.

As the camera continues its observational and explorative journey, we see increasing numbers of people going about the hustle and bustle of everyday life and making an honest living. The camera cranes downwards to show their faces and clothes, essentially a melting pot of humanity.

The camera comes to rest at street level and we are momentarily part of this hectic world, full of movement. The sound of the hurdy-gurdy has grown louder and it now forms part of the frame, together with an audience, both young and old enjoying its simple pleasures.

The grand sweep of this crane shot, which lasts for nearly one and a half minutes, suggests that the people of this world are all linked by their common predicament and fate, whatever that might be in the future; filmically, they all occupy the same space, hence the one all-encompassing shot.

The cut comes at street level and reframes the shot of the hurdy-gurdy and its player; entertainment as a source of escape was extremely important to people at this level in society. The camera then begins to crane upwards to rest on two young men who are hanging over a balcony. Their postures suggest mischievousness and a relaxed attitude in this environment. They are the human equivalents of the brash, flapping sheets that adorn the buildings; their worn, dirty clothes highlight their social background, but their hats, worn at angles suggest defiance.

Their talk is of boredom and of films (the second reference to the media) and Rocky will become a matinee idol of sorts, sensationalised by the press and living a glamorous lifestyle, worthy of a film star.

Rocky's rise to notoriety: a montage (3; 06:03:00)

As Rocky tells his friend Gerry that he alone will take the 'rap' for their petty thieving there is a fade to black followed by a montage charting Rocky's journey from 15-year-old reform school boy to hardened criminal. It was a common Hollywood convention to include montages (see Byron Haskin's wonderful work in another Cagney gangster film, *The Roaring Twenties*), allowing the narrative to flow more quickly and often conveying large chunks of story in bite size pieces.

Here, the first shot is of Rocky's fingerprints being taken. The close-up of the document showing only his finger begins the dehumanising process that the institutions will have on him. He is reduced to two photographs, some fingerprints and basic statistics; he is becoming a number, just one in a vast number of statistics.

The dissolve to the next shot helps suggest a passage of time, showing a gang of young men involved in hard labour. It is impossible to pick out Rocky, which highlights his submersion into this world. Another dissolve reveals a layered shot: another fingerprint document, this time with no photographs (underlining his further descent into anonymity), is mixed with a shot of prisoners, highlighting their regimental way of life.

A further shot of prisoners moving in a uniform manner dissolves to more fingerprints; Rocky's

the image is frozen and then becomes part of a newspaper front page.

The journey from obscurity to notoriety is complete; he is now a celebrity and the remaining images extend the audience's knowledge of his celebrity lifestyle and nefarious activities. A roulette wheel is mixed with a shot of Rocky enjoying the high life, but it also suggests the fleeting nature of this existence, a life built on chance. The process shot of champagne glasses multiplied and rotated, overlaid on the shot of Rocky, highlight not only the excesses of his new life but the fact that its trappings may indeed become a complicated trap.

This theme of excess continues with the angles of drinks being poured, nightclub neon signs, dancing girls and musicians reiterating the frenzied nature

identity seems utterly obliterated in a sea of documentation and the structures of prison life.

Then his photograph reappears: Rocky has grown up and Cagney now plays the part; there are more layered shots of prison life before a close-up of two prisoners, one who shakes his head, as if to indicate that there is something wrong with him, followed by a rapid dolly move to a close-up of Rocky. He bites a chain, like an animal, and the fact that he is a loner is underlined. Rapid dissolves of older prisoners, still regimented and institutionalised, follow this until one of the archetypal images of Hollywood montage, the swirling newspaper front page, indicates Rocky's rise from obscurity, for he is becoming a celebrity.

His emergence from the world of the institution continues as we see him outside the walls for the first time, orchestrating illegal activities. He emerges out of the darkness in the next shot, this time like a hunted animal lashing out, firing a gun;

of this life. It is almost impossible to pick out where one image ends and another begins, such is the density of the layering. It disorientates the audience and gives us an idea of the social whirl into which Rocky has been sucked.

The montage returns to the flipside of this existence, the violence of crime. A building is blown up and another newspaper swirls through the ether, like a magic carpet, announcing Rocky's incarceration. He is back where he started, in prison, but now he is a celebrity, and we know that life has changed completely for him.

The dramatic and downbeat non-diegetic music matches the visuals with its opening and ending underlining the bleakness of the prison existence. The orchestral score only lightens for a moment when showing Rocky enjoying the rewards of his ill-gotten gains, but even there it is fairly chaotic; its musically layered texture matches the layering of images and the complex web in which the young

Rocky is being ensnared.

The vibrant city returns (4)

This shot reprises the long crane shot of the film's opening; Curtiz is inviting the audience to see the changes that have been wrought in the time that Rocky has been in jail and also to make some observations about the changes.

For the fourth time in about eight minutes a newspaper front page is seen; 'Flier Circles World 3 Days, 19 Hrs., 7 Min.' It shows a world that is changing and advancing and one where the sensational is far more newsworthy than more mundane matters such as politics.

The shot, however, reveals both similarities and

unexpected direction. After all the images of secular escape, the excess of gangster celebrity, both recreational and 'work' images, the camera moves the audience towards a church. It is another possible route for contentment, but one which Rocky will take the remainder of the film to embrace.

The static image of the church's interior, the softness of the lighting and the diegetic sound of angelic singing all juxtapose with what has gone on before, and stands as another way for Rocky, a way already taken by Jerry.

differences; women still put out their washing and the streets are packed with market stalls and people, yet the music is different. Upbeat contemporary jazz music plays, and as the camera moves the diegetic music is seen to be emanating from a van promoting radios. Just as the headline indicated, technology has moved on, the media's desire to be sensational and entertain has also become apparent. Also gone is the old-fashioned world of the hurdy-gurdy with its associations of communities based around oral tradition and traditional values. Here we see the world of mass communication, of a society moving away from community and towards isolation through music arriving into the front room.

For a film that has shown how a society was becoming preoccupied with entertainment and escape from the drudgeries of life, be it film, newspapers or radio, the crane shot cuts as it nears the radio car and then moves in an

The Killers

KEY FACTS

Release Date: 1946

Country of Origin: USA

Running Time: 105 minutes

PRODUCTION NOTES

Production Companies

Mark Hellinger Productions

Universal Pictures

Distributor

Universal Pictures

Awards

Nominated: Best Director Robert Siodmak Academy Awards, USA

Nominated: Best Film Editing Arthur Hilton Academy Awards, USA

Nominated: Best Music, Scoring of a Dramatic or Comedy Picture Academy Awards, USA

Nominated: Best Writing, Screenplay Anthony Veiller Academy Awards, USA

SYNOPSIS

The story begins with two hitmen on the trail of Andersen, otherwise known as the Swede, who works at a petrol station in a small town. It seems as if his past has caught up with him, and when the men find him in his room, the Swede makes no attempt to escape, despite being warned by a work colleague. He accepts his fate and is shot and killed by the men. The rest of the narrative charts the investigation by Jim Reardon into the Swede's life on behalf of the company with whom his life was insured. He reveals that the Swede was involved in criminal activities and inextricably linked to femme fatale, Kitty Collins. His murder seems to be connected with a payroll robbery, and with the help of Lt. Sam Lupinsky, he entraps the crime boss, Big Jim Colfax, and the men he hired to kill the Swede.

HISTORICAL CONTEXT

The 1940s were dominated by the Second World War and its aftermath, and Hollywood output was dominated by flag-waving films designed to boost public morale. However, another type of film emerged, to be termed 'film noir' by the French critic Nino Frank (for some it doesn't constitute a 'genre', rather a 'movement'). Films of this nature resolutely refused to bring any cheer; they were relentlessly bleak and dark-hued, both in terms of narrative and *mise-en-scène*.

John Huston's *The Maltese Falcon* (1941) is sometimes credited as the first film noir, but that distinction may well be held by Boris Ingster's *Stranger on the Third Floor* (1940). Other films made in 1940, like William Wyler's *The Letter* and Alfred Hitchcock's *Rebecca*, also contained noirish elements, particularly with regard to their chiaroscuro lighting, but the film noir template contains many elements. It includes an urban setting, criminals, a femme fatale, killings and double crossings, but it is a film movement that defies an ultimate definition, shifting like the shadows within its frames. For some, it is a film genre with enough common conventions to bind films together, but for others there are too many disparate elements for the films to be grouped. Whether genre or not, it provides a useful discussion point about the nature of genre.

Film noir also tapped into the horror and anxiety that people experienced in the time of war, the subsequent threat of nuclear annihilation and the displacement of returning veterans, with films such as Edward Dmytryk's *Crossfire* (1947) and Robert Aldrich's *Kiss Me Deadly* (1955) perfectly illuminating these terrors. Just as the horrors of the First World War had influenced German cinema, so Second World War atrocities were transposed to the dark underbelly of American life in a repackaged form. But film noir did not only come out of dark days; the films were also the successor to the gangster films of the 1930s with their tales of organised crime. More prosaically, they were a product of necessity: with reduced budgets affecting the quality and extent of sets it was inevitable that shadows would begin to hide a multitude of sins. The films connected

with American audiences. It was a way in which dark deeds and thoughts could be served up with a structure that was exciting and appealed to people's sense of schadenfreude; stories of lives out of control and men destined to die. How similar to the world at the time, and how reassuring to see it packaged up where right would come out on top - most of the time.

The films did not die out at the war's end, but continued well into the 1950s with films like Joseph H. Lewis' *The Big Combo* (1954) and Orson Welles' *Touch of Evil* (1958). Indeed, film noir lived on beyond its black and white days, revived in 'neo-noir' films such as Stephen Frears' *The Grifters* (1990), John Dahl's *The Last Seduction* (1994) and Joel Coen's *The Man Who Wasn't There* (2001).

SELECT FILMOGRAPHY OF MAIN PRODUCERS AND CAST

Robert Siodmak, 1900–1973, Director, Screenwriter, Producer

People on Sunday, 1930

The Spiral Staircase, 1945

The Killers, 1946

The Dark Mirror, 1946

Criss Cross, 1949

The File on Thelma Jordan, 1950

The Crimson Pirate, 1952

Custer of the West, 1967

Anthony Veiller, 1899–1986, Screenwriter

The Stranger, 1946

The Killers, 1946

State of the Union, 1948

Moulin Rouge, 1952

Solomon and Sheba, 1959

The Night of the Iguana, 1964

Mark Hellinger, 1903–1947, Producer, Actor

They Drive by Night, 1940

High Sierra, 1941

The Killers, 1946

Brute Force, 1947

The Naked City, 1948

Miklos Rozsa, 1907–1995, Composer

The Four Feathers, 1939

The Thief of Bagdad, 1940

Jungle Book, 1942

Double Indemnity, 1944

Spellbound, 1945

The Lost Weekend, 1945

The Killers, 1946

Brute Force, 1947

Secret Beyond the Door, 1948

The Naked City, 1948

Criss Cross, 1949

Adam's Rib, 1949

The Asphalt Jungle, 1950

Julius Caesar, 1953

Lust for Life, 1956

Ben-Hur, 1959

King of Kings, 1961

El Cid, 1961

Burt Lancaster, 1913–1994, Actor, Producer, Director

The Killers, 1946

Brute Force, 1947

Criss Cross, 1949

The Crimson Pirate, 1952

From Here to Eternity, 1953

Apache, 1954

Vera Cruz, 1954

Gunfight at the O.K. Corral, 1957

Sweet Smell of Success, 1957

Elmer Gantry, 1960

Birdman of Alcatraz, 1962

The Leopard, 1963

Seven Days in May, 1964

The Professionals, 1966

The Swimmer, 1968

Ulzana's Raid, 1972

1900, 1976

Atlantic City, 1980

Local Hero, 1983

The Osterman Weekend, 1983

Tough Guys, 1986

Ava Gardner, 1922–1990, Actress

The Killers, 1946

Pandora and the Flying Dutchman, 1951

The Snows of Kilimanjaro, 1952

Mogambo, 1953

The Barefoot Contessa, 1954

The Sun Also Rises, 1957

On the Beach, 1959

55 Days at Peking, 1963

Seven Days in May, 1964

The Night of the Iguana, 1964

The Bible: In the Beginning, 1966

The Life and Times of Judge Roy Bean, 1972

Earthquake, 1974

The Cassandra Crossing, 1976

LINKS TO OTHER FILMS

Double Indemnity (1944)

Billy Wilder's film tells the story of an insurance man who is ensnared by femme fatale, Phyllis Dietrichson, to kill her husband. The narrative unfolds in flashback and details another fated protagonist who must face death for making the wrong decisions.

Out of the Past (1947)

As with The Killers, Jacques Tourneur's film is also a story of a past life catching up with the main character. Like the Swede, Jeff Bailey is unable to start a new life, away from crime and a femme fatale, eventually resulting in his death.

The Asphalt Jungle (1950)

Dix, a gambler, who thinks that he can return to his life before crime after he joins in with a jewellery robbery, finds that fate will lead him in a different direction. He hopes to use the money from the robbery to buy back the farm that he lost during the Great Depression, but it all unravels and he dies, a broken man, at the end of the film. The atmosphere of frustration, desperation and discontent that pervades The Killers is strongly echoed in this film.

The Killers (1964)

The plot of this remake is very similar to the 1946 film, but its 1960's context, the fact that it is in colour and its more graphic violence help to distance the impact of Don Siegel's film from Robert Siodmak's original.

REPRESENTATION

Femmes fatales

The women in films noirs are stereotypically represented: they are duplicitous sexual predators and death is written all over them. Although the representation is negative, these women are certainly powerful. They manipulate men and are often a step ahead of them; there were very few films in the 1940s and 1950s that afforded women so much control. They are not just sexual objects, but are fully self-aware and use their sexuality to assert their authority. They kill, and are often a match for the men around them, with their capacity for mental sparring easily the equal of any hard-boiled man.

Characters such as Brigid O'Shaughnessy in John Huston's The Maltese Falcon (1941), Vera in Edgar G. Ulmer's Detour (1945) and the eponymous Gilda (1946) are all ruthless women, using their charms to exercise control (of course, men in films are able to seduce, cheat and kill, but they are usually regarded as anti-heroes, if not heroes). Kitty Collins in The Killers is seen as a deadly influence in the Swede's life, but she is a memorable character, vivid, with a force of nature that is elemental and exciting.

Often, it is the memory of the femme fatale that lingers longer for the audience. One of the most hideous manifestations of the femme fatale is the character of Ellen Berent Harland in John M. Stahl's Leave Her to Heaven (1945) who, amongst other things, kills her husband's disabled brother and deliberately induces her own miscarriage, all to keep her man. It is her that audiences remember, not the husband, and in many of the films noirs mentioned, the femmes fatales stand shoulder to shoulder with their male counterparts.

'The quality...[is] in the overall sensibility - the casting, the use of shadows, the composition alternating between paranoid long shots and hysterical close-ups... Worth attention as a '40s thriller, but more than that as a prime example of post-war pessimism and fatalism.' Tony Rayns, Time Out Film Guide 14th Ed., Time Out Guides Ltd., London, 2006

'If the film, shot by Woody Bredel, is a virtual inventory of film noir's low-key, expressionist cinematography, it is also a compendium of film noir plots.' Mark Bould, Film Noir, Wallflower, 2005

KEY SCENE TEXTUAL ANALYSIS

Opening scene (1)

The opening shot sets the tone and the enigma for the entire film: the audience takes the back seat in a car travelling into the night. The headlights illuminate just a slither of outside detail and the men in the shot are undefined, consumed by deep shadow.

The story will unfold in a series of fragmented flashbacks, making the audience (along with the private detective) piece together the Swede's life. This shot, with its back projection of the road, further emphasises the sense of dislocation with its extreme jerkiness, and sets the scene for the mysterious journey to follow.

As the director's credit appears the camera moves slowly and deliberately with, and towards them, as they walk towards and peer into a building. They then walk towards the camera, their hard faces illuminated starkly by the key light; one is plump, the other angular. As the men walk towards the diner, their dark figures move towards the light and the *mise-en-scène* is dominated by two giant shafts of darkness in the foreground. The building, with its row of low-lit windows, and the lone street light right in the middle of frame do not seem like beacons of hope, but just light that is about to be extinguished by the shadows. Throughout this scene the killers speak in hard-boiled dialogue, bullying and threatening the other characters, and the visuals help to underpin the growing sense of hostility.

The next shot takes us outside the car, and the headlights pick out the town limits sign for Brentwood, New Jersey. Its provincial message to 'Drive Carefully' seems totally at odds with the shadowy figures and the relentlessly pounding non-diegetic music, speaking of the danger and violence to come.

The third shot, which then carries the opening titles, is a street scene where the only strong source of light comes from behind one of the buildings. The resultant pools of darkness engulf much of the frame and again signals the film's sinister atmosphere; the non-diegetic music also erupts at this point, a frenzy of stabbing violin chords. As the titles near their end two shadows, followed by their more solid owners, appear from the back of the frame, deep from within the bowels of the noir world. They are nothing but silhouettes, just as they were in the car, their shadows like diabolical umbilical cords, feeding off the darkness.

The interior of the diner is lighter, but still is disfigured by shadows; its low ceiling emphasises the claustrophobic nature of the scene as these 'heavies' bully the owner, the cook and the one other customer. The camera tracks hurriedly along the counter as the two men sit down, as if eager to capture their first words, and to suggest the danger inherit in their presence. The cut to the other character, Nick Adams, rooted in the foreground of the frame, helps to establish not just their proximity to each other but also their developing relationship: the frame is cramped and it again points to the growing tensions in the room.

This is followed by a number of medium shots, encompassing the owner and the hitmen, his white jacket contrasting with their dark and dour suits. They also keep their hats on whilst inside, an uncharacteristic act, marking them out as outsiders not interested in integrating. The medium shots are also very busy with the frame full of bodies, allowing for little sense of freedom for the characters and indicating their inability to escape from these thugs.

The single shots of Nick Adams as he reacts to the two men's taunts help to illustrate both his vulnerability and isolation. It may, conversely, also foreshadow his separation from these men and his later action where he is proactive and warns the Swede.

The shot where one of the killers moves towards Nick, when the latter is instructed to go to the other side of the counter, strongly emphasises the threat through spatial juxtaposition. Again, Nick is firmly in the foreground of the frame, underpinning the frame's clutter and the inherent menace. Close-ups or rapid camera movement are not used here

music starts up again, heavy with threat and dread.

The killers go back into their natural hunting ground, the darkness, and Nick Adams, the Swede's petrol station attendant friend, plunges himself into its dangerous environs as he runs to warn his friend.

The urgency of the orchestral strings underpins his desperate flight through the night. The movement is captured with a tracking shot to help emphasise his speed and desperation as he leaps over white picket fences and through gardens. As he nears the house the aerial shot forms a dark tunnel, full of shadows, into which he must run. The shot tracks back and reframes in a room to show a prone figure on a bed in the shadows with his head obliterated by the darkness. It is someone who has already

to increase the threat or the tension, but the filling of the frame and the movement within it subtly suggests the undercurrents of aggression and fear.

The juxtaposition of the killers and the owner is shifted over the course of the next few shots, with their realignment working to emphasise their dominance over him: the three-shot becomes much more of a threat as one hovers behind him and the other sits like a sentinel in front.

When another customer comes in, his exit is followed by a quick pan back to the owner and the seated heavy. The owner is at the very edge of the frame as if desperate to break out. His existence is at the very edge of an abyss and any thought that he might escape is undermined, again, by his proximity to the killer; the frame speaks of his inextricable bond with these men and the fact that his fate lies in their hands. The owner, or 'bright boy' as they call him, is left unharmed, but only on the whim of the two heavies, and as they leave non-diegetic

been all but consumed by shadow; his identity is obscured, appropriate for a film where one man becomes obsessed by the search for another man's identity.

As Nick bursts into the room the frantic music stops and the camera follows him quickly as he breathlessly moves to the Swede's bedside; that camera movement and Nick's animated gesticulations signal his fear and sense of urgency, but the frame settles on both men and the body remains inert, suggestive of the Swede's inability to escape. Even Nick's shadow entreats him to move, but the man of shadows is trapped and his monotone responses further illustrate an acceptance of his fate.

Nick turns away from the Swede, unable to comprehend his inaction. The camera follows him, his face in darkness to symbolise his incomprehension. His movement out and into the light of the landing indicates his movement away from the darkness inhabited by the Swede and a melancholy score returns to underpin the inevitability of the tragic fate awaiting him.

We return to the Swede in medium close-up, the outline of his face more visible. But it is not until the camera tracks in further that we finally see his anguished face. The camera, then, becomes the audience's guide as it takes us further into the darkness to see the face of despair, which he covers and rubs with his large hands as if washing himself in the shadows that have long since engulfed him.

The camera remains still as it observes this face, a portrait of resignation and oblivion; the moment of reflection soon passes as the non-diegetic music reverts to its more sinister tones and he raises his head one last time towards the light as the diegetic sounds of a creaking door and ominous footsteps approach.

The cut to the staircase reveals the killers coming up from the gloom below and through the shadows towards their prey; the music gradually becomes a wall of sound that can only end in an eruption. The cut back to the Swede reveals a medium shot of him, his body swathed in shadows like the robes of Christ at the Pietà.

The killers' faces are again in shadow, suggesting their dark intentions, while the faster cutting between him and them accelerates the feeling of inevitable blood-letting. Its rhythm also underlines the connection between his world and theirs, and indicates that even the practice of contract killing has its own ritualistic rhythm.

They finally enter, like two dark demons devoid of human attributes, illuminated and brought to life briefly by the flashes of their guns as they bring death to the Swede. The camera shoots them from a low angle, empowering them in their act of killing, and the diegetic gun shots replace the non-diegetic music with a macabre rhythm all their own.

We see neither the Swede nor the aftermath of the murder, just his hand clasping the bedpost and sliding down, the last vestiges of life leaving his body. It is appropriate that a character who has a dark, mysterious past should die in this way:

unseen in the darkness, only a fragment of him illuminated, suggesting the hidden depths of his life. The final tight grip signifies his final struggle, the last hand gesture suggestive of a final peace, almost Christ-like in its gentleness.

The extraordinariness of the action is given a matter-of-fact veneer by the dropping of an object to the floor, the sound of footsteps on the stairs and the bedpost itself: murder is finally ordinary; it is anywhere and lies just beneath the surface of society.

Les Quatre cents coups (The 400 Blows)

KEY FACTS

Release Date: 1959

Country of Origin: French

Running Time: 95 minutes

PRODUCTION NOTES

Production Companies

Les Films du Carrosse

Sédif Productions

Distributor

Cocinor

Awards

Best Director François Truffaut Cannes Film Festival, France

OCIC Award François Truffaut Cannes Film Festival, France

Nominated: Palme d'Or Cannes Film Festival, France

Nominated: Best Writing, Story and Screenplay - Written Directly for the Screen François Truffaut Marcel Moussy Academy Awards, USA

Nominated: Best Film from any Source François Truffaut BAFTA Awards, UK

Nominated: Most Promising Newcomer to Leading Film Roles Jean-Pierre Léaud BAFTA Awards, UK

SYNOPSIS

Young Antoine is neglected at home by his mother and stepfather; he seems to be a constant source of irritation to them. At school he fares little better and is the focus of ridicule and anger from his teacher. He cannot keep out of trouble and is eventually caught by a night watchman after he steals, and then tries to return, a typewriter from his stepfather's office. This act prompts his mother to hand him over to the police. His parents are happy to let the authorities take control of his life and he is sent to a youth detention centre. After some time in captivity, he escapes and runs towards the sea, but once on the beach there is nowhere left for him to go.

HISTORICAL CONTEXT

Although France had emerged victorious from the Second World War with the help of its allies and Charles de Gaulle had returned from England to reclaim Paris, the following decade was not the happiest in political terms. In its weakened position, France struggled to maintain its worldwide stature as a major power, beginning to lose its colonies as countries struggled to gain their independence. In French Indochina there were heavy defeats and the troubles in Algeria were to be long, bloody and costly for France, not ceasing until its independence in 1962. The nation was insecure in these years, unsure of its place in the world and of its political leaders. *Les Quatre cents coups* is a very domestic drama, but perhaps it connects with this sense of disillusion and lack of direction, a general malaise afflicting the country. It is a damning indictment of a society that does not face up to its responsibilities; the Nazis may have been repelled but here we see the French imprisoning its youth.

The film came at the beginning of the movement dubbed the 'Nouvelle Vague' (New Wave), preceded only a year earlier by Claude Chabrol's *Le Beau Serge* (1959), widely regarded as the first example of the Nouvelle Vague philosophy. In some ways the movement is linked to the neo-realist film-makers of Italy, who produced films that stripped away any artifice from narratives; they filmed on the streets in real locations with non-actors, the accent being on verisimilitude.

The French New Wave went on to debunk classical narrative form, playing with film language and conventions and including jump cuts, asides to the camera and narratives bursting with rebellion. As with film noir, the term Nouvelle Vague was coined by French critics; the difference here was that there was more coherence to the movement in that some of these critics (Claude Chabrol, Eric Rohmer and Jacques Rivette) became film-makers themselves and applied the same basic principals to their work. As part of this new theoretical framework for film these critics, who wrote for the influential film magazine *Cahiers du cinéma*, proposed the auteur theory. This suggested that some film-makers were the sole authors of their films, each bound to the other by recurring motifs, themes and use of film language.

The other great exponent of this 'wave' was Jean Luc Godard, and although all these directors were individual film-makers, it is hard not to see these films as a reaction against the French Establishment, presiding over a number of reactionary and aggressive policies during this time. The Nouvelle Vague broke free of classical French cinema narrative and exclaimed its radical credentials on the screen. It chimed with the growing sense of discontent throughout Europe and beyond, as the yoke of Nazi oppression had been replaced by other dictatorships, particularly the Soviet regime. The French New Wave also paved the way for film-making revolutions throughout the world, including Czechoslovakia, Britain and the United States.

SELECT FILMOGRAPHY OF MAIN PRODUCERS AND CAST

François Truffaut, 1932–1984, Director, Screenwriter, Producer, Actor

Les Quatre cents coups, 1959

Tirez sur le pianiste, 1960

Jules et Jim, 1962

Antoine et Colette, 1962

Fahrenheit 451, 1965

Baisers volés, 1968

La sirène du Mississippi, 1969

Domicile conjugal, 1970

L'Enfant sauvage, 1970

La Nuit Américaine, 1973

L'Histoire d'Adèle H., 1975

L'Argent de poche, 1976

L'Homme qui aimait les femmes, 1977

L'Amour en fuite, 1979

Le Dernier métro, 1980

La Femme d'à côté, 1981

Vivement dimanche!, 1983

Jean-Pierre Léaud, 1899–1986, Actor

Les Quatre cents coups, 1959

Antoine et Colette, 1962

Made in U.S.A., 1966

Le départ, 1967

La Chinoise, 1967

Weekend, 1967

Dialog 20-40-60, 1968

Baisers volés, 1968

Le Gai Savoir, 1969

Porcile, 1969

Domicile conjugal, 1970

Os Herdeiros, 1970

Les Deux anglaises et le continent, 1971

Last Tango in Paris, 1973

La Nuit Américaine, 1973

L'Amour en fuite, 1979

Détective, 1985

Le Pornographe, 2001

J'ai vu tuer Ben Barka, 2005

LINKS TO OTHER FILMS

Zéro de conduite (1933)

Jean Vigo's film about boarding school life, as seen through the boys' eyes, and ending in rebellion against the adult structures that have been imposed on their young lives.

Whistle Down the Wind (1961)

A story of childhood innocence and essential goodness as three children discover a criminal in a barn and come to believe that he is Jesus. Their devotion and purity is contrasted with the jaded knowingness of the adults.

Kes (1969)

A boy, like Antoine, who seems to be something of an outcast at school, finds solace in a bird, whose abilities and freedom echoes the boy's aspirations. At home he also suffers from neglect and abuse, and the ending is a bleak study in despair when his brother kills the kestrel.

Les Choristes (2004)

A film that shows the difference that an enlightened adult can make in a child's life. A teacher at a school for problem children decides that singing may be a way to get through to them. No such adult exists in Antoine's world, who remains alienated from society.

REPRESENTATION

Childhood

Childhood is often depicted as a time of innocence by film-makers; in early Hollywood cinema the angelic faces of Shirley Temple, Judy Garland and Elizabeth Taylor dominated the representation of children. The 1950s really started the trend towards presenting children who felt neglected and alienated; any children in films who had been previously represented like this were usually derived from Victorian literature, such as Robert Stevenson's *Jane Eyre* (1944) or David Lean's *Oliver Twist* (1948). James Dean in Nicholas Ray's *Rebel without a Cause* (1955) set the template for youths who struggle to find a voice in society; Antoine, too, seems to desire this voice but there is no-one to support him. The difference between the two films, only four years between them, is the gritty reality of Truffaut's film with its New Wave intensity compared with the Hollywood gloss of Ray's film.

In earlier films where we see children going astray, like James Cagney's characters in *The Public Enemy* and *Angels with Dirty Faces*, their lives are brought to sorry conclusions. The poignancy of *Les Quatre cents coups* lies in the sense of emptiness, of nothingness. There is no chance of the glamour that Cagney's characters at least taste during their lives; childhood is a springboard to an abyss rather than future hopes and dreams.

Adults

The adults in this film do not face their responsibilities to the young; the mother is having an affair, neglecting her son and is only too eager to discard him. The stepfather takes scant notice of him, whilst the other adult male in his life, the teacher, does not have the generosity of spirit to understand and help the errant boy. The other adult figures, the police and those who run the detention centre, are faceless bureaucrats who lack any sensitivity to form a bridge between themselves and Antoine's needs. By the end Antoine is half-boy, half-adult, trapped in a limbo where he cannot go back to childhood and fears the spectre of adulthood.

> 'Truffaut had his film shot with only natural light on real Parisian streets. His story was loosely constructed, in a similar way to the work of the neo-realists...Truffaut was interested in the fleeting aspects of experience, life seen from the point of view of a passionate boy who was searching, like many of the New Wave characters, for something indefinable, a certain meaning or exhilaration or transcendence.' Mark Cousins, *The Story of Film*, Pavillion Books, London, 2004

> "The New Wave, spearheaded by the outspoken Francois Truffaut... was a reaction against the mainstream 'quality tradition' of the 1950s, condemned for being formulaic and studio-bound... These early films by the Cahiers directors had in common a casual approach to the 'rules' of mainstream cinema, a freer editing style, and loosely constructed scenarios.' Peter Graham, in Nowell-Smith (ed.), *The Oxford History of World Cinema*, OUP, 1997

KEY SCENE TEXTUAL ANALYSIS

Inside the house and then escape (4)

The film is full of images of entrapment; from early on the apartment where Antoine lives with his parents is shown to be cramped and claustrophobic. The boy is awoken by his mother in a room that seems nothing more than a glorified closet. The camera is at his level when the mother enters the room so the audience gets a sense of his world, one where adults invade his space and squeeze him to the side of the frame. There is nothing loving about the way the mother wakes him; it seems brutal even. The room and his pyjamas add to the general sense of neglect that is shown throughout the film: the room is chaotic, half-formed and has a transitory nature (it may even be a corridor-cum-bedroom). An adult's coat hangs down, again emphasising the boy's lack of ownership and anchorage in the house, while the large rip in his pyjama jacket is further testament to the atmosphere of neglect and degradation.

The dingy bathroom, the ominous teacher's voice that he hears in his head and the father's forbidding footsteps all combine to reiterate that the apartment is a place of unhappiness and perhaps even fear. The boy stares anxiously into the mirror. In fact, it is one of many images of looking in the film; looks of fear, realisation, innocence, happiness and desperation abound.

The rest of this short apartment scene is shot in close-up or medium shot with the figures tightly packed within the frame. But never is there a moment of actual human intimacy or affection. The boy is shown no love from his parents and leaves, alone in his own filmic space, hemmed in by the walls of the apartment. It is only the audience who is connected to him, for the camera is on his level again, allying us to him and not to the adults.

Once the film language turns to medium and long shots as the boy moves outside, light-hearted diegetic music begins, suggestive of freedom and carefree days, and the contrast with the cramped environs of the apartment is obvious.

However, even as he has fun with a friend spending the day missing school, there is a further image of this boy's desire to be free. They go to a fairground where he gets on a ride and is spun round in a circular room. As it gathers speed, the floor drops and he is left stuck to the wall. The camera records both him and his POV and the blurred faces of those watching as he speeds round and round. His feelings of disorientation, alienation and of being constantly observed by those who govern his life are suggested by these shots, as he tries to move but is prevented by an unstoppable force from making any headway. His grimaces and restricted movements are all reminiscent of the boy's feelings towards, and his place in, society. Even his joys are symbolically tainted by the *mise-en-scène*.

as a solitary figure behind bars. Here again, after his arrest for theft, we see him placed not just in a cell but one that is in a room where all the police officers are visible, free to move around and do as they wish. The camera draws away from Antoine and his companion as they sit together, outcasts in a world that does not even register their existence. Later, the camera tracks back to the bars to reveal Antoine asleep on the cell's floor; he is vulnerable and the last person that should be on the wrong side of the bars.

His isolation is further illustrated when he is removed from the larger cell, to make way for some prostitutes, to a one-person cell in the same

Claustrophobic (5)

This theme of claustrophobia is repeated visually in the next scene when the boy goes to bed; he lies in his sleeping bag as if it were a protective cocoon against the outside world. As before, the camera is low and the audience only sees events from his level. First, his step-father passes through the room with only his legs visible as if to emphasise that his parents are just passing strangers. Their lack of identity helps us to connect with the boy's sense of alienation, and he feigns sleep when his step-father comes back and forth. When his mother returns from her adulterous affair she steps over him like he is a mere piece of furniture; it again reinforces the idea that he hardly exists for his parents, and only in their argument is he mentioned, a scapegoat for the parents' guilt. Truffaut never takes the camera off Antoine, the close-up of his face accentuating his pain and our identification with his plight.

Behind bars and a photograph (16/17)

Antoine has been glimpsed many times in the film

room; the medium shot shows us the humiliating position that he has now reached. This cell and its young occupant paint a sad and pathetic picture - where love and nurture are needed, only isolation and cruelty are proffered. We are given a lengthy POV shot as Antoine surveys this hostile world; the board game that the officers play only serves as a salutary reminder of the innocent fun that Antoine should be enjoying. The camera again draws back from this spectacle, so as to underline his sense of otherness.

As he is transported from this holding cell to another place of isolation, we see a long sequence of Antoine in a prison van. The shots cut between Antoine looking out from behind yet more bars at the back of the van or his POV of the outside world. The boy framed by bars tells its own story and the POV offers up tantalising glimpses of freedom: the movement of people on the streets or the neon-lit building with the free-wheeling dodgem cars (a reminder of his fairground escape earlier in the film). But what Antoine sees is not simply a world that is free - some of the visions are of the tawdry adult futures that await him such as sex revues and sleazy clubs. The tears on his face speak not only of his incarceration but of a world that is morally bankrupt.

The non-diegetic music swells as this sequence progresses. The innocent refrain that underscored his earlier escapes now providing an ironic and dramatic counterpoint to his imprisonment.

At the prison fingerprints are taken, personal belongings confiscated and his processing is completed; the Establishment now has full control of his body, if not his mind. The cell is bare and impersonal, almost medieval with its rough-hewn rock walls. The final indignation comes at the end of this sequence when his photograph is taken. He looks directly at the stills camera, but then large

he runs down to the beach, however, the camera moves in again and we track with him. Once more he is imprisoned within the filmic space.

Throughout the sequence the music has maintained the familiar innocent, but melancholy, refrain heard earlier in the film, swelling at times with joyful innocence but then being pegged back by reality. As the sea is observed the music swells, but as we close in on him again and the physical space to run in quickly diminishes, the music's lightness now seems plaintive, almost desperate, in its stumbling search for harmony. The diegetic sound of his shoes on the ground has also permeated the sequence, their tread indicating his smallness amidst the vast unwelcome of life.

adult hands roughly force his head into profile; it is violatory and indicative of the controlling and disfiguring effect of society on this boy. The freeze-frame of this moment provides an everlasting image of society's brutality and his vulnerability and also foreshadows the freeze-frame at the film's end.

An escape? (20)

After some time at the correctional facility, Antoine makes his escape; his bid for freedom is visualised in a long tracking shot which captures him in the middle of the frame, running but not really moving away from the filmic space. He runs past gates, fences, signs, ordered rows of trees; even in the country there seems to be a degree of rigidity.

With the dissolve to the estuary, and then the sea beyond, Antoine finally seems to be making progress; he runs away from the camera and is seen in long shot after so many shots of him in medium and close-up during his imprisonment. As

He reaches the edge of the water as the final musical refrain sounds out like the last heartbeats of hope. He looks around but there is nowhere else to go. He has been running and running, but the journey has been pointless; there is an anticlimactic feeling of 'what now?' 'What is left for me?'

The camera tracks closer, imprisoning him even more with an optical zoom towards his face before the final freeze-frame. Again, it captures the moment, the intensity of the boy's humanity. The audience has been connected with Antoine throughout the film; we see what he sees and share his indignations at the hands of the adult system, but with this frame, as he stares directly at us, we become implicated within the system that has condemned him. It is a plea for help, crossing the invisible fourth wall into the audience's world, and it does allow us to really sense his pain. Ultimately, it forever freezes him in this moment of confusion, vulnerability and inescapable destiny, and it says: 'you are all part of this'.

Saturday Night and Sunday Morning

KEY FACTS

Release Date: 1960

Country of Origin: UK

Running Time: 89 minutes

PRODUCTION NOTES

Production Company

Woodfall Film Productions

Distributor

Bryanston Films Ltd.

Budget

£100,000 (estimated)

Awards

Best Film Karel Reisz BAFTA Awards, UK

Best British Actress Rachel Roberts BAFTA Awards, UK

Most Promising Newcomer to Leading Film Roles

Albert Finney BAFTA Awards, UK

SYNOPSIS

Arthur Seaton is a young, disenchanted and frustrated factory worker in Nottingham who, angry about the rut in which he finds himself, tries to blot out these thoughts with alcohol and anti-social behaviour. He is having an affair with a co-worker's wife, Brenda, and he also starts dating a single woman called Doreen. He asks his aunt to help procure an abortion for Brenda when she becomes pregnant with his child and also maintains a long-running feud with a neighbour by shooting her with an air rifle. When his co-worker, Jack, discovers the adulterous affair he gets his brother and a friend to give Arthur a severe beating. The film concludes with Arthur and Doreen sitting on the side of a hill, looking out over a new housing estate and contemplating their future together; Arthur seems destined to get married and settle down, but he remains angry at what he considers is a society trying to grind him down and make him conform.

HISTORICAL CONTEXT

Post-war euphoria soon turned to boredom and disappointment in Britain; with the war won there was a generation of men who seemed rudderless and frustrated. The feeling was exacerbated by the sense that the war was over, but hardship remained in the form of food rationing, which lasted until 1954 in Britain. British industry had been on a wartime footing, mass producing for the war effort. In the factories and on the fields there had been a sense of camaraderie against an evil foe. By the late 1950s the spark of rebellion against the Soviets was igniting in parts of Europe, but in Britain the government had embarked on a military debacle with its invasion of Suez in 1956, rather flying in the face of the notion of independence.

In the late 1950s and early 1960s the United States had Elvis Presley and James Dean and Britain had Cliff Richard and the Shadows. But it was not until the mid-1960s that there were real cultural expressions of teenage interest and angst when The Beatles and The Rolling Stones took hold of the teenage consciousness and fed into, and spurred, the changes that were going on in society, particularly greater personal and civil freedom. The year of *Saturday Night and Sunday Morning*, 1960, was a year of transition; it seems as if Arthur Seaton had just a few years to wait.

In film-making terms Arthur Seaton's story was prefigured by Karel Reisz's documentary, *We are the Lambeth Boys* (1958), one of the early texts that formed the basis for the so-called 'Free Cinema' movement, where real people and real places were documented and observed in their natural habitat like never before. In a few years this focus on reality crossed over into fiction film-making with *Saturday Night and Sunday Morning*, Tony Richardson's *The Loneliness of the Long Distance Runner* (1962) and John Schlesinger's *A Kind of Loving* (1962).

This desire to capture ordinary lives has been a constant factor in artistic endeavour; in the world of art, the mode of representation and the subject matter moved from the literal and the sacred to the abstract and the ordinary. In the same way European (and some American) film-makers began to reject the Hollywood mode with its gloss and glamour and instead embraced what they saw as a more honest representation of life. This change in focus can be seen with Italian neo-realist films, such as Roberto Rosselini's *Roma citta aperta* (1945), and later with the French New Wave films, beginning with Claude Chabrol's *Le Beau Serge*.

The British branch of the New Wave drew not only from film but from the theatre, particularly plays like John Osbourne's *Look Back in Anger* (1956); 'kitchen sink drama' and 'angry young man' have become key terms to describe the narratives and characters of this new approach to representing Britain and Britishness. In *Saturday Night and Sunday Morning* Nottingham is shown as a dour place, its houses crammed together in a suffocating atmosphere of gossip and boredom. The workplace is just as stifling and even entertainment consists of drunken oblivion. Of course, all this is seen from Arthur Seaton's perspective, a frustrated young man who craves something that post-war Britain could not deliver.

SELECT FILMOGRAPHY OF MAIN PRODUCERS AND CAST

Karel Reisz, 1926–2002, Director, Producer

Saturday Night and Sunday Morning, 1960

Night Must Fall, 1964

Morgan: A Suitable Case for Treatment, 1966

Isadora, 1968

The Gambler, 1974

Who'll Stop the Rain, 1978

The French Lieutenant's Woman, 1981

Sweet Dreams, 1985

Everybody Wins, 1990

Albert Finney, 1936, Actor

Saturday Night and Sunday Morning, 1960

Tom Jones, 1963

Night Must Fall, 1964

Two for the Road, 1967

Charlie Bubbles, 1967

Scrooge, 1970

Gumshoe, 1971

Murder on the Orient Express, 1974

The Duellists, 1977

Shoot the Moon, 1982

Annie, 1982

The Dresser, 1983

Under the Volcano, 1984

Miller's Crossing, 1990

The Browning Version, 1994

The Run of the Country, 1995

Erin Brockovich, 2000

Traffic, 2000

Big Fish, 2003

Amazing Grace, 2006

The Bourne Ultimatum, 2007

Freddie Francis, 1917–2007, Director of Photography

Room at the Top, 1959

The Battle of the Sexes, 1960

Sons and Lovers, 1960

Saturday Night and Sunday Morning, 1960

The Innocents, 1961

Night Must Fall, 1964

The Elephant Man, 1980

The French Lieutenant's Woman, 1981

The Jigsaw Man, 1983

Dune, 1984

Glory, 1989

Cape Fear, 1991

The Straight Story, 1999

LINKS TO OTHER FILMS

A Taste of Honey (1961)

A year after *Saturday Night and Sunday Morning* came Tony Richardson's film, which gave a female perspective on 'kitchen sink' life. The narrative follows a young Lancashire woman who lives in a dysfunctional family, with a mother who is promiscuous. The woman eventually leaves home, lives with a homosexual friend and becomes pregnant with the child of a visiting black sailor.

Billy Liar (1963)

Another story of a young man in a northern town dreaming of changing his life. Arthur Seaton's sense of release is mostly self-destructive, but Billy dreams of being a comedy writer. However, both are ultimately frustrated with themselves and their surroundings.

This Sporting Life (1963)

Lindsay Anderson's film, produced by Karel Reisz, again looks at life in northern England and features the reality of relationships and everyday life using the main character's rugby playing as a metaphor for these struggles.

Poor Cow (1967)/*Riff-raff* (1990)/*My Name is Joe* (1998)

These three films, directed by Ken Loach, all share *Saturday Night and Sunday Morning*'s focus on ordinary lives, presented in a documentary or cinéma vérité style, using real locations, real dialects and stories of the disenfranchised and the disillusioned. Many other Ken Loach films follow this pattern, as do the films of Mike Leigh.

REPRESENTATION

Post-war British working class

The Labour party recorded a landslide election victory in 1945 on a platform of social reform, with particular focus on health provision and housing. The war bombings had altered the landscape of many urban areas forever and the ensuing housing projects were immense, building new homes for a new Britain. The working class had borne the brunt of the war's ravages, living in the centres of towns and around docklands in tenement housing, and for some, the new housing released them from slum dwelling. The progress of house-building was still a major issue by the time *Saturday Night and Sunday Morning* was made; many still remained in their Victorian and early twentieth century tenement housing, the 'two-up two-down' as it is colloquially known.

Although the government was addressing key issues such as health care, in Karel Reisz's film we still see the working class man emerging from the factory and going back to his small and antiquated dwelling, almost unchanged from the inter-war years. Television, the only difference in their lives, is seen as something of a brainwashing device rather than an advance. Television itself would satirise the ongoing class divisions with the programme *That Was The Week That Was* in the early 1960s. The first TV 'soap', *Coronation Street*, (first transmitted in 1960) also reflected a world that seemed little different from 50 years before, yet Britain's fascination with this barely fictional portrait ensured its success. The housing estates on the edges of cities and the new tower blocks that sprang up in the 1960s heralded a new geographical location for the working classes, but one that, arguably, was not much of an improvement in socio-economic terms.

'British movies like... Saturday Night and Sunday Morning... were clearly new and inspired by political ideas and changes in society and art...[also it was] more interested in male characters than female ones.' Mark Cousins, *The Story of Film*, Pavillion Books, London, 2004

'Much of the freshness survives in Albert Finney's abrasive performance... lashing blindly at the bleak working class horizons to which he has been bred by parents "dead from the neck up"'. Tom Milne, *Time Out Film Guide 14th Ed.*, Time Out Guides Ltd., London, 2006

KEY SCENE TEXTUAL ANALYSIS

Work, tea and the pub (00:00–09:23)

Before we see the first images of the film we *hear* the grinding, deafening and inhuman sounds of factory work. The fade up from black presents a long shot of a factory interior and men can be spotted amidst a jungle of machinery. Their individuality is lost in the clutter of metal. It is chaotic and as far from the natural world as it is possible to be; the diegetic noise continues as a wall of machine sound through which nothing natural can pierce.

The camera pans around and then tracks towards one of the workers, Arthur Seaton. With the close-up of working hands and the components of the machinery the non-diegetic music begins; its aggression matches Arthur's apparent discontent, its relentless refrain mirroring the monotony of the work.

The images of the work are anchored by the caustic narration as Arthur's thoughts speak of barely-suppressed contempt and rebellion. The shots of the machinery show the products being made. They are objects that are meaningless to Arthur, just parts in some greater design, as, indeed, are the workers. The effect of the dehumanising power of the machines is visually represented by the way the soapy substance that is emitted from the machine is used both to wash over the components and to wash Arthur's hands. The low angle shot of Arthur does empower him as he continues his diatribe against the Establishment, but the machine is seen at the bottom of the frame, still linking him to the thing that he despises.

The subsequent shots show various workers, grubby, regimented and almost lifeless. All this is, of course, accentuated by black and white photography, which lends the scene even more of a downbeat atmosphere - a world without colour is perfectly realised in monochrome.

The return to the low angle shot of Arthur also helps to differentiate him from the others; it is as if we are his confidantes, gazing up into his private world as we hear his thoughts. It also shows him in his own filmic space, compared to the others who are surrounded by other workers. It points to his difference (or, at least, his attempt to be different) and his isolation. The throwing down of the cloth, the factory whistle and the non-diegetic emphatic drumbeat underline his aggressive discontent and desire to be free.

of the factory buildings and gasometers (colourful, 'Swinging Sixties' London seems a million miles away).

A dour-faced and stumpy woman is irked by Arthur's arrival as he narrowly misses her; her slippers, bland tights, heavily patterned dress, small functional cardigan, scarved hair and tightly folded arms embody the grimness of the smoke-blackened bricks around her (undoubtedly, a forerunner to the characters in television's *Coronation Street* and numerous other soap operas which followed).

The brief scene of Arthur's home life serves to reinforce the idea of mind-numbing routine, again suggesting that the fleeing workers are escaping to only more mundane activity. Here, the father stares rigidly at the television, seen as another tool of

The aerial shot of the factory exterior shows the workers exiting like ants to underline their sameness and points to the fact that leaving the factory is just another part of the endless routine rather than an escape.

The music, a score which speaks of ordinariness and drabness, heralds the massive migration home. The factory monoliths on either side of the workers are grim reminders of what awaits them. The title of the film appears over an aerial long shot of this image, reiterating the notion of repetition and fleeting joys soon over: a Saturday of hurried joy to be followed by a morning when the previous night's excesses will be paid for.

The exodus is focused on two people, Arthur and Jack, both tracked by the camera. The dreary factory interior is matched by the destinations for both men: working-class streets of terraced houses and dingy alleys, always besmirched by the spectre

suppression, just like the factories.

The claustrophobia of this life is captured by the minimal camera movement, which occurs within a tiny, cramped front room. The camera, like the family, barely has room to move. Meanwhile, the diegetic sound of the television commercial for smoking, another great working class escape, is light and bubbly, juxtaposing with the rather dismal dinner-time routine and the functional furniture. The only note of dissent against this monotony is Arthur's mocking conversation with his father and the close-up of his face which again underlines his air of defiance.

As the frothy jingle of another television commercial comes to an end the non-diegetic music crashes in, suggestive of Arthur's indolence and restlessness with its harsh opening chords. It then springs into life as we see Arthur upstairs, preparing for a night of fun; the music is strident, jazz-like and punches the air, just as Arthur would like to punch through the shroud of everyday banality.

He emerges from the terraced house and into the back alley like a knight on a quest, his body language full of swagger and arrogance. The camera then pans as he runs down the street and for the first time in the film there is real freedom of movement. His run is almost elegant and his acrobatic twist, as he jumps onto the departing bus, suggests his youthful vigour and desire to be free.

The first image of his destination does not promise much; the pub is cluttered, smoky and rather dour, and the piano playing is reminiscent of an earlier time. Certainly it is not the cutting-edge lifestyle that one would expect of an angry young man like Arthur – or that he would wish for himself. The cut to Arthur 'downing' a pint suggests that his form of escape is actually not too far removed from his father's television placebo.

The *mise-en-scène* suggests a more modern environment in this part of the pub for the live music is certainly more youth-orientated and the clientele somewhat younger. However, the juxtaposition between this bar and the other helps link Arthur's world with the old world that he is desperate to escape. Again, the shots have frames full of people and clutter, mirroring the regimentation and suffocation of their lives, whatever the locale.

The tight two shots of Arthur and the woman next to him, the low-level medium shot with the sailor in the foreground and the close-up of the defeated sailor all accentuate the sense of confinement, tension and, with the sailor's drunken capitulation, defeat.

The intercutting of the 'booze match' with the young singer and his band reiterates the juxtaposition of grim reality and wafer-thin dreams; the lyrics of the song (Adam Faith's 1959 British number one hit, *What Do You Want?*) adding to the sense of yearning that pervades Arthur's life.

The medium shot of Arthur as he goes to get another pint positions him within a bulging frame; he is amidst the very people who he believes are already dead. The framing suggests that, despite his protestations, he will follow the same route. Indeed, he has found his way into the other bar where the old time sing-song is taking place; the pan which follows him charts a journey into the world that he despises.

The look on his face when he orders the drink is not just drunkenness; there is anger, resentment and brutality. This finds an outlet when he spills his drink over one of the older men. The shot of Arthur from a low angle highlights all these feelings as the surrounding women's voices of protest are heard. When one of them confronts him for an apology he simply pours some over her and exits the frame, a small victory won in his eyes.

As he comes to the top of a flight of stairs the camera settles on yet another low angle shot of Arthur but his look straight at the audience is not one of power; yes it is drunken, but it is also a dead look, the look of a nihilist.

The cut to a shot looking down from the top of the stairs as he falls downwards is a statement of intent. The close-up of his prone body and laughing face, as he lies at the bottom of the dingy stairs, is both a frightening assertion of his bleak world view and a pathetic picture of one who is inextricably bound to the world he detests. The diegetic cheers from above as a song finishes seem to echo in his head as a comment on his lonely and pointless action.

Apocalypse Now

KEY FACTS

Release Date: 1979

Country of Origin: USA

Running Time: 153 minutes

PRODUCTION NOTES

Production Company

Zoetrope Studios

Distributor

United Artists

Budget

$31,500,000 (estimated)

Awards

Best Cinematography Vittorio Storaro Academy Awards, USA

Best Sound Walter Murch Mark Berger Richard Beggs Nathan Boxer Academy Awards, USA

Best Direction Francis Ford Coppola BAFTA Awards, UK

Best Supporting Actor Robert Duvall BAFTA Awards, UK

Palme D'Or Francis Ford Coppola Cannes Film Festival, France

Best Director - Motion Picture Francis Ford Coppola Golden Globes, USA

Best Motion Picture Actor in a Supporting Role Robert Duvall Golden Globes, USA

Best Original Score - Motion Picture Carmine Coppola Francis Ford Coppola Golden Globes, USA

ALFS Award Film of the Year London Critics Circle Film Awards

National Film Registry National Film Preservation Board, USA

SYNOPSIS

Captain Willard of the United States Army, shown to be in a state of near-mental breakdown at the beginning of the story, is sent to kill Colonel Kurtz during the Vietnam War because Kurtz has become insane and is committing atrocities without any control from his superiors. Willard sets off on his mission, travelling on a military boat deep into enemy territory. En route, he meets the eccentric Lt. Kilgore, who has a penchant for surfing, and witnesses his helicopter attack on a Vietnamese village. Further up the river they watch a group of Playboy models dancing for troops, are chased by a tiger when putting ashore, massacre some Vietnamese civilians due to a misunderstanding and discover a bridge guarded by the Americans but which is constantly under enemy attack.

In the latter stages of the journey the commander of the boat and one crew member are killed by people hidden in the jungle, leaving only Willard and two other crew members. Upon reaching Kurtz's encampment it is obvious that he has become a demonic god, worshipped by villagers, soldiers and an American photographer, who extols his visionary genius. All around the site is evidence of Kurtz's brutal excesses: dead bodies, blood, decapitated heads and limbs. Willard meets with Kurtz, whose mind has been traumatised by the brutality he has witnessed and has fallen into an abyss where morality no longer has meaning. Willard is finally able to kill Kurtz with a machete, and he leaves with the one surviving crew member, the other having been beheaded at the encampment.

HISTORICAL CONTEXT

The 1970s had cemented the view amongst certain countries and groups around the world, a view which would grow over the succeeding decades, that the United States of America had begun to regard itself as the 'world's police force'. The disastrous Vietnam War had tarnished the country's image around the world, with numerous news photographs and footage depicting the horrors that were being perpetrated against civilians caught up in the fighting. The horrific image of the Vietnamese girl, Kim Phuc, running naked along a road, her back burning from the effects of napalm which had been dropped by South Vietnamese planes (in collaboration with the Americans), is a key symbol of the atrocities committed during the war. Images like these turned public support in America against the government, and helped speed American withdrawal from the country.

The 'Just War' mindset that had underpinned the Second World War was long gone, and the United States' behaviour was portrayed by some as the equivalent of the old colonial powers, such as Britain, France and Spain which had tried to carve up the world between them through violent incursion into foreign territories. In domestic issues events had conspired to make Americans believe that corruption was gnawing away at the heart of government. The key event of the decade was the Watergate scandal, which eventually resulted in President Nixon's resignation amidst evidence of political wrong-doing on a grand scale. With these two events lodged deep within the public psyche it is unsurprising that film-makers began to question the Establishment and expose its corrupt practices, whether they be at home or abroad. Films like Alan J. Pakula's *All the President's Men* (1976) looked at Watergate, whilst *The Deer Hunter* (1978) and *Apocalypse Now* critiqued the Vietnam War.

Apocalypse Now came after a decade of power shifts within Hollywood. Spielberg, Lucas, Cimino, Rafelson, Hopper, Friedkin, Scorsese and Coppola, later grouped as the 'movie brats', brought up on a diet of old Hollywood and counter-culture European film-making, started to shake up the status quo. Their films – *Jaws* (1975), *Star Wars* (1977), *The Deer Hunter*, *Five Easy Pieces* (1970), *Easy Rider* (1969), *The French Connection* (1971), *Mean Streets* (1973) and *The Godfather Parts I and II* (1972/4) respectively – ushered in a new era of strong, young directors who were indulged by the studios in their quest for the 'teenage dollar'.

But it was these very same wunderkinds who would almost bring about economic disaster for some studios as they ploughed money into their later, and unprofitable, productions. Only Spielberg and Lucas would have the most consistently successful careers as they tended towards more 'popcorn-friendly' products, including collaborating on the Indiana Jones franchise. Some almost died on their filmic swords: Cimino with *Heaven's Gate* (1980); Friedkin with *Sorcerer* (1977); and Coppola with *Apocalypse Now*. Even Scorsese struggled to follow his personal vision for some time after the commercial failure of *New York, New York* (1977).

SELECT FILMOGRAPHY OF MAIN PRODUCERS AND CAST

Francis Ford Coppola, 1939, Director, Producer, Screenwriter

Finian's Rainbow, 1968

The Rain People, 1969

The Godfather, 1972

The Conversation, 1974

The Godfather, Part II, 1974

Apocalypse Now, 1979

One from the Heart, 1982

The Outsiders, 1983

Rumble Fish, 1983

The Cotton Club, 1984

Peggy Sue Got Married, 1986

Gardens of Stone, 1987

Tucker: The Man and His Dream, 1988

The Godfather: Part III , 1990

Bram Stoker's Dracula, 1992

Jack, 1996

The Rainmaker, 1997

Youth without Youth, 2007

John Milius, 1936, Screenwriter, Director, Producer

Evel Knievel, 1971

Jeremiah Johnson, 1972

The Life and Times of Judge Roy Bean, 1972

Dillinger, 1973

Magnum Force, 1973

The Wind and the Lion, 1975

Big Wednesday, 1978

Apocalypse Now, 1979

Conan the Barbarian, 1982

Red Dawn, 1984

Extreme Prejudice, 1987

Farewell to the King, 1989

Geronimo: An American Legend, 1993

Vittorio Storaro, 1940, Director of Photography

1900, 1976

Agatha, 1979

Apocalypse Now, 1979

Reds, 1981

One from the Heart, 1982

The Last Emperor, 1987

Tucker: The Man and His Dream, 1988

Dick Tracy, 1990

The Sheltering Sky, 1990

Little Buddha, 1993

Taxi, 1996

Bulworth, 1998

Goya en Burdeos, 1999

Exorcist: The Beginning, 2004

Marlon Brando, 1924–2004 , Actor

The Men, 1950

A Streetcar Named Desire, 1951

Viva Zapata!, 1952

Julius Caesar, 1953

The Wild One, 1953

On the Waterfront, 1954

Guys and Dolls, 1955

The Young Lions, 1958

One-Eyed Jacks, 1961

Mutiny on the Bounty, 1962

The Chase, 1966

The Appaloosa, 1966

Burn!, 1969

The Godfather, 1972

Last Tango in Paris, 1972

The Missouri Breaks, 1976

Superman, 1978

Apocalypse Now, 1979

A Dry White Season, 1989

The Freshman, 1990

The Score, 2001

Martin Sheen, 1940, Actor

Catch-22, 1970

Badlands, 1973

Apocalypse Now, 1979

Gandhi, 1982

A State of Emergency, 1986

The Believers, 1987

Da, 1988

Gettysburg, 1993

The American President, 1995

Catch Me If You Can, 2002

Bobby, 2006

The Departed, 2006

Robert Duval, 1931, Actor

The Godfather, 1972

Joe Kidd, 1972

The Outfit, 1973

The Godfather: Part II, 1974

Network, 1975

The Eagle Has Landed, 1976

The Seven-Per-Cent Solution, 1976

Apocalypse Now, 1979

The Great Santini, 1979

True Confessions, 1981

Tender Mercies, 1983

The Natural, 1984

Colors, 1988

The Handmaid's Tale, 1990

Wrestling Ernest Hemingway, 1993

Geronimo: An American Legend, 1993

The Paper, 1994

Sling Blade, 1996

Secondhand Lions, 2003

Open Range, 2003

LINKS TO OTHER FILMS

All Quiet on the Western Front (1930)

Lewis Milestone's anti-war drama of the First World War depicts a group of German soldiers and their soul-destroying experiences in the trenches. It is a film that powerfully shows the horrors of war and terrible waste of life.

La Grande Illusion (1937)

Jean Renoir's story is another anti-war film, based around events in the First World War. Its message reaches beyond its own story, as it warns of the dangers that were lurking in 1937 Europe.

Citizen Kane (1941)

Orson Welles' film examines the corrupting nature of power and one man's megalomania as he destroys everyone around him, and finally himself.

Hell is for Heroes (1963)

There are relatively few anti-war films to come out of the Second World War, but this Don Siegel film emphasises the futile nature of war, as a group of soldiers attempts to take control of a strategic hill. When a pillbox is finally taken, after many casualties, it is shown as just another minor moment in a larger pattern of death and chaos. The main character, played by Steve McQueen, carries the seed of Kurtz's character within him, a desire to kill and, ultimately, to self-destruct.

The Green Berets (1968)

John Wayne's pro-Vietnam War film was one of the few to take this stance; it attempts to rubbish the ideas that were gathering momentum, namely, that this was not a conflict that could be politically or morally justified.

Taxi Driver (1976)

Martin Scorsese details a descent into extreme brutality and self-destruction through the eyes of a Vietnam War veteran; the final scene of bloodletting is echoed in *Apocalypse Now* in terms of its sense of self-annihilation and exorcism.

The Deer Hunter (1978)

A year before *Apocalypse Now*, Micheal Cimino's film charts the full horror and brutality that the war has on a group of friends from Pittsburgh. Its graphic violence, depiction of atrocities and focus on the war's effect on the soldiers' minds is far removed from the facile depiction in *The Green Berets*.

Platoon (1986)

Writer–director Oliver Stone's own experiences in the Vietnam War help imbue this film with its raw edge, depicting the horrors of war with numerous incidents and insane acts of brutality.

REPRESENTATION

War

War has been a popular film genre since the beginnings of film, and through its history most conflicts have been represented in celluloid. War, of course, shows humanity at the very edge of existence, where barbarity and morality hang in the balance, and where the former frequently tips the scales. Films have often represented war in terms of its glorious nature, bringing out the noblest of actions within its participants. Certainly, a plethora of patriotic war films, extolling the exploits of one group of military personnel or another, appeared during the Second World War and in the decades that followed.

Films like Raoul Walsh's *Objective, Burma* (1945) and Michael Anderson's *The Dam Busters* (1954) were unashamed flagwavers, but there have been efforts to show a different side to war. In films like King Vidor's *The Big Parade* (1925) and Stanley Kubrick's *Paths of Glory* (1957) the futility and horrors of war are clearly depicted. In the 1970s, with the unpopular Vietnam War as fuel, there were numerous studies of the effects of war on individuals. *Apocalypse Now* shows its sheer madness and portrays surreal moments to highlight war's degradation and nihilism.

The attack by Lt. Kilgore's 'Air Cavalry' on the Vietnam village to the strains of Wagner's 'Ride of the Valkyries' accentuates the mindset of some American soldiers as they come down from the skies bringing misery and death; the thumping diegetic sound mimics the adrenalin rush that courses through the soldiers' veins as they spectacularly destroy the village. Other events, such as the tiger attack, the dancing Playboy models and the surfing, all point to an atmosphere where there are no boundaries between life and death; the latter overtakes the former within the blink of an eye. The killing of the Vietnamese civilians on the boat by the American soldiers accompanying Willard underlines the random nature of death and worthlessness of life: a girl rushes to protect her puppy (the Americans think that she is grabbing for a gun or explosive) and all are slaughtered in a few seconds.

Before Willard arrives at Kurtz's encampment he stops at a bridge, covered in lights and lit by flares. Non-diegetic music sounds like distorted and demonic fairground music and points to a surreal atmosphere akin to a monstrous fairground where the soldiers are entrapped in a nightmare world. Of course, the final and fullest expression of a world adrift from the boundaries and moral codes of a 'non-war' world is found at Kurtz's encampment, which echoes the death camps of the Nazis and foreshadows the killing fields of Cambodia or the genocide of Tutsi in Rwanda. It is beyond rational explanation; only Kurtz's final words, 'the horror, the horror' (taken directly from the source novel, Joseph Conrad's *Heart of Darkness*) begin to speak of something which lodges in the deepest and darkest recesses of our minds.

'Coppola's Apocalypse Now
...[is a]... study in power'. Mark Cousins,
The Story of Film, Pavillion Books,
London, 2004

'The ultimate horror of
this hypnotic trip... is how closely it
has been said to capture the reality of 'Nam.'
Angela Errigo, *1001 Movies You Must See
Before You Die*, Cassell Illustrated,
2007

KEY SCENE TEXTUAL ANALYSIS

Opening scene (1)

We expect to be guided by vision in a film but here the audience hears before it sees, which is disorientating. The screen is black, appropriate for a film that delves into the darkness of people's minds; indeed, it is fitting for a film which has a source novella called 'Heart of Darkness'.

As the sequence unfolds and we start to realise that we are listening to Willard's thoughts, the black frame also suggests the unconscious, before the sound starts and the frame fades into life, signifying the beginnings of consciousness. The diegetic sound of a helicopter, somewhat distorted, adds to the surreal atmosphere.

When the picture does appear there is a widescreen frame full of vegetation, which is again disorientating considering what the sound heralded; it is pristine, a Garden of Eden.

Smoke wafts up the frame from an unknown source, hinting at the destruction to come. A helicopter cuts through the frame and pieces of the jigsaw start to fall into place for the audience. As the yellow smoke rises non-diegetic music begins to play. It is languid with a Far Eastern tone, again sounding like the awakening of consciousness as the smoke thickens and begins to obscure the frame - a preamble to the chaos.

For a minute of screen time the audience has been given the chance to contemplate this scene at leisure. At first, there is unknowing, then a picture of nature, of serenity. This is then quickly disrupted by the intervention of humans and, finally, there is apocalyptic destruction. With it, the frame itself shifts for the first time, as if the celluloid itself is shaken by this act of barbarity.

It is not just an explosion but a hellish inferno that engulfs the jungle. To emphasise this point The Doors track, 'This Is The End', begins, the song's title being the opening line of the lyric and an apt epigraph to the film that follows.

The tracking shot helps to reveal the scale of the devastation, the frame blackening with smoke from the explosions and further disorientating the audience. However, it does seem as if a conventional war scenario will now be played out as helicopters buzz around the frame like locusts bringing further destruction. But the lack of context continues to frustrate the audience in its expectations of the war genre and the sense of disorientation is heightened as a man's upturned head dissolves onto the shot, flames and smoke now disfiguring his face.

The layering of images is extended with the inclusion of a ceiling fan, an ordinary object mimicking the helicopter blade, thus linking the everyday with an image of war. This dense layering of images further emphasises chaos and turmoil, the disjointed visual pattern mirroring the fracturing of the natural order of life that we are witnessing.

The images change in opacity as the sequence continues; the man's face almost becomes consumed by the red glow of the fireball in the jungle, while the faint glow of his cigarette continues the link between the ordinary and extraordinary. Not only do we have the spectacle of his upturned head, signalling the turmoil in his own head, but the camera continues to track along the devastation so that the man's static head travels eerily through space on a journey through a nightmare land. The audience can assume that these are his memories, although the fact that we see both him and them in the same frame suggests how much they are still playing a part in his present; the past literally spills out of his consciousness and onto the screen.

The image of a stone-carved face then appears to the right of the frame; it seems to watch as the man does, but it is turned the right way up. It adds to the mystical atmosphere of the sequence; is he linked to the carving as an observer, or is he juxtaposed with its calmness?

Flames roar through the man's face, erupting from the surface, suggestive of hellish experiences and emotional wounds. Two helicopters fly through the frame, dissecting it. All the while, the calm exterior of his face and the nonchalant smoking of the cigarette only serve to heighten the crisis that is bubbling beneath the skin, a crisis that we are privy

As we track back onto his face the images become sharper again. His eyes are closed and he looks as if he has become consumed by his thoughts, dead or at least unconscious to the present.

The cross dissolves of various images (a photograph, letters, alcohol) show the miscellany of someone who is perhaps unable to cope with life, or more specifically, the past. The final image of the camera movement is of a gun, signifying the effect of this past; the juxtaposition of the dark weapon on the soft white sheets conveys brutality and innocence once again, just as we saw with the unspoilt jungle and the explosion at the outset of the sequence.

The cross dissolve back to the fan which beats aggressively on the soundtrack, pushes out

to through the plethora of disjointed images.

As the camera begins to track around the man the shot widens and we see a little more of his context. Yet the other images refuse to die; fire still burns deep into his head and thoughts, whilst helicopters still disrupt the frame.

The connection between the sound of the fan and the helicopters' rotor blades is made clear; another piece of the puzzle is put into place as we now assume that this noise has perhaps triggered these memories. The music track is now in its instrumental section, a wistful, meandering sound that helps to echo the less intense, but by no means less complex, set of images on screen.

The cut to a tracking shot along a series of his possessions further fleshes out his present: dog-tags (he's a soldier), money, identification cards, letters and photographs. Most important, all this is still layered by the image of fire: it literally inhabits and scorches every part of his present psyche and its constant presence suggests that it is as real to him as the room where he is staying.

the plaintive last cries of Jim Morrison as the diegetic sounds start to triumph; consciousness is returning. Noticeably, though, the man's head is upside down in frame and his eyes are closed. The sudden opening of his eyes is startling and suggestive of madness, a waking not into a tranquil present reality but an ongoing living nightmare.

Der Himmel über Berlin (Wings of Desire)

KEY FACTS

Release Date: 1987

Country of Origin: Germany

Running Time: 122 minutes

PRODUCTION NOTES

Production Companies

Road Movies Filmproduktion

Argos Films

Westdeutscher Rundfunk (WDR)

Distributor

Basis-Film-Verleih GmbH

Awards

Best Director Wim Wenders Cannes Film Festival, France

Outstanding Feature Film German Film Awards

Outstanding Individual Achievement: Cinematography Henri Alekan German Film Awards

Best Cinematography Henri Alekan Los Angeles Film Critics Association Awards

Best Foreign Film Los Angeles Film Critics Association Awards

Best Cinematography Henri Alekan National Society of Film Critics, USA

Best Cinematography Henri Alekan New York Film Critics Circle Awards

SYNOPSIS

Two angels, Damiel and Cassiel, roam the streets and buildings of Berlin observing and listening to the people but remaining unseen by all except for children. They are two of many angels in the city and in a library we are privy to the cacophony of thoughts that they hear from all the people around them. For the scenes involving the angels the film is shot in black and white with colour used when there are only humans. Damiel becomes increasingly fascinated with human experiences; as an angel he is unable to feel what they feel.

An angel who has made the transition from ethereal to human is the American actor Peter Falk who plays himself. He arrives in Berlin to make a film about the Second World War and is able to see Damiel when he walks past the filming location. Damiel starts to fall in love with a circus trapeze artist called Marion, whose grace and beauty he admires. Cassiel has a devastating moment when he cannot save a young man from committing suicide, whilst Damiel decides to make the transition onto the earthly plane; upon doing this he marvels at his sense of touch and the colour all around him. He meets Marion at a bar, and although she has never seen him before it becomes apparent that they have a bond. The film ends with the couple together, seemingly destined to be united for the remainder of their mortal lives.

HISTORICAL CONTEXT

As the 1980s progressed it became increasingly clear that the Communist regimes in Eastern Europe were losing their stranglehold over the countries that had been originally put under Russian control after the end of the Second World War. In 1989 the move towards independence finally became a reality. Poland was the first country to elect a non-Communist government and was soon followed by Hungary, East Germany, Czechoslovakia, Bulgaria and Romania. The desire for change was overwhelming and came more swiftly than anyone could have imagined, taking the citizens, the governments and the world by surprise; over 40 years of control was swept aside in a matter of months; in some places it took just days.

The feelings of liberation were akin to those experienced by the French at the end of the Second World War (of course, in countries like Poland liberation from the Germans had been replaced by Soviet occupation), but the immense scale of the changes were comparable to those of the revolutions that had engulfed Europe in the nineteenth century. Although *Wings of Desire* was made two years before these events, there are a number of facts that resonate with the coming changes in German society. In particular, it is the use of Berlin as its location, the city that stood as a symbol of the partition between East and West, with its Wall the physical manifestation of all that division.

Wings of Desire is one of the later fruits of New German Cinema, the origins of which go back to the 1960s and young film-makers' desire to elevate German cinema from the doldrums and break from the old narrative forms. Like the Nouvelle Vague in France it sought to present life in a more honest and non-linear form, extricating itself from the demands of commercially-focused films. Its chief exponents were the directors Rainer Werner Fassbinder, Werner Herzog, Volker Schlöndorff and Wim Wenders, whose films rejuvenated German cinema at a moment of stagnation. The likes of Fassbinder's *Fear Eats the Soul* (1974), Herzog's *Aguirre, the Wrath of God* (1972), Schlöndorff's *The Tin Drum* (1979) and Wenders' *Alice in the Cities* (1974) are alive with anti-Establishment fervour and resonated with audiences both in Germany and beyond.

SELECT FILMOGRAPHY OF MAIN PRODUCERS AND CAST

Wim Wenders, 1945, Director, Producer, Screenwriter

The Goalkeeper's Fear of the Penalty, 1972

Alice in the Cities, 1974

Kings of the Road, 1976

The American Friend, 1977

Lightning Over Water, 1980

Hammett, 1982

The State of Things, 1982

Paris, Texas, 1984

Wings of Desire, 1987

Until the End of the World, 1991

Far Away, So Close!, 1993

Beyond the Clouds, 1995

The End of Violence, 1997

Buena Vista Social Club, 1999

The Million Dollar Hotel, 2000

Land of Plenty, 2004

Don't Come Knocking, 2005

Henri Alekan, 1909–2001, Director of Photography

Beauty and the Beast, 1946

Anna Karenina, 1948

Roman Holiday, 1953

The Wages of Sin, 1956

Austerlitz, 1960

Topkapi, 1964

Lady L, 1965

Mayerling, 1968

Figures in a Landscape, 1970

The Trout, 1982

The State of Things, 1982

Wings of Desire, 1987

Bruno Ganz, 1941, Actor

The American Friend, 1977

The Boys from Brazil, 1978

Nosferatu the Vampyre, 1979

Wings of Desire, 1987

Strapless, 1989

Luther, 2003

Downfall, 2004

LINKS TO OTHER FILMS

A Matter of Life and Death (1946)

See entry for this film in FANTASY section (pg. 341) for link between the two films.

It's a Wonderful Life (1946)

Frank Capra's film details the trials that face George Bailey, a man who tries to commit suicide after a number of setbacks in his life. He is rescued by an angel and shown what life in the town would have been like without him. The angel, (or angel waiting for his wings, as he is described), is represented as a good-natured but slightly foolish character. It does share with *Wings of Desire* a sense of life on earth being something to be cherished, whether the experiences are good or bad.

Berlin Express (1948)/*The Spy Who Came In From The Cold* (1965)/*Funeral in Berlin* (1966)

Berlin was nearly always represented as a place of intrigue by Hollywood in the post-war period, full of spies and double-dealings. Jacques Tourneur's 1948 film was shot on location and emphasises the chaos of a country that has been defeated, with a *mise-en-scène* full of devastation (Berlin and Frankfurt were used as locations). Martin Ritt's 1965 film is a typically dour examination of spy games in Berlin with the Wall as the focal point of the action. Finally, Guy Hamilton's spy film with the Harry Palmer character from the Len Deighton novels is another seedy look at a city that wears its underbelly firmly on its sleeve.

Faraway, So Close! (1993)

This is Wim Wenders' follow-up to *Wings of Desire*, a film that catches up with Damiel and Marion's relationship, but also charts Cassiel's change from angel to human.

Run Lola Run (1998)

A thriller directed by Tom Tykwer which uses Berlin as its backdrop. The film demonstrates just how much the city is breaking free from its past by being used as a location without use of its history to make a point. It is also ironic that a city that has such a history of confinement and lack of movement should be used in a film where free movement is so integral to the narrative, as Lola repeatedly runs at full pace through its streets.

City of Angels (1998)

An American remake of Wenders' film with the same premise - angels observing humans - and the same central narrative thrust - an angel wanting to become human. There are many differences as well, with the death of the woman the angel loves being a key departure from the original.

Downfall (2004)

This film connects with *Wings of Desire* in a couple of ways; firstly, it is set in Berlin, but it is the end of the Second World War and Hitler has sought refuge in his bunker as the Allies advance. It is the last moments before Berlin was carved up by the victorious nations, and its post-war time as a divided city began. Secondly, Bruno Ganz (Damiel in *Wings of Desire*) plays the part of Hitler; from angel to devil, two roles that are the antithesis of each other.

REPRESENTATION

Angels

Angels have a long history in cinema, being represented in a number of ways and used for different purposes. There are friendly angels (Clarence in *It's a Wonderful Life*), interfering angels (Conductor 71 in *A Matter of Life and Death*), inefficient angels (Messenger 7013 in *Here Comes Mr. Jordan*, 1941), mischievous angels (Bartleby and Loki in *Dogma*, 1999) and murderous angels (Azazel in *Fallen*, 1998).

The angels in *Wings of Desire* are none of these things. They are dressed in a plain and uniform way, a long coat unifying their appearance. They are thoroughly benign, serene and traditional in that they watch over individuals, although they do not seem able to make a difference to people's lives, but rather act as a collective repository for all their thoughts, both negative and positive. Like most films, they are not portrayed in the classical way that art has depicted them, although there are a few shots where wings can be seen etched behind Damiel's back. There is also a melancholy air about them, particularly evident in Damiel who becomes more fascinated with the world of feelings and touch and eventually transforms into a human. This movement from Heaven to Earth is unusual as it is usually the reverse, with humans trying not to become angels. The sense that one's life is an important and vital experience is represented by Damiel's transformation, that both pleasure and pain are integral to the human journey.

The representation of the divine as something ordinary, as revealing itself in the minutiae of life, is reminiscent of the films of Yasujiro Ozu and Robert Bresson. Their films, such as *Tokyo Story* (1953) and *Un condamné à s'est s'échappé* (1956) focus on the extraordinary in the ordinary, of lives transfigured by the characters' purity of action and, indeed, non-action. Their films are filled with frames of serenity, contemplation and a celebration of the divine human.

The city

Cities have been integral to some films, either enriching or engulfing the characters and action. Peter Yates' *Bullitt* (1968) is synonymous with San Francisco and in Nicolas Roeg's *Don't Look Now* (1973) Venice itself drips with malevolence. The images of Berlin in *Wings of Desire* are mesmerising; the city is a force in itself. The monochrome lends the cityscape a brooding, but benign, presence, and one that provides the perfect backdrop for the contemplative angels.

Berlin's history imbues it with a wealth of associations, particularly from the post-war period. Its bohemian past lay almost in ruins but its vibrant atmosphere remained, however ragged it had become. The Berlin Wall epitomised division, but also served as a focus for those who wanted to bring about change, whilst its older structures create a history that is just a fraction of the angel's ageless existence. A city that has a history of being fractured resonates with the idea of the division between the angels' world and our own.

'By the mid-1980s, as questions of national identity seemed to climax, Wenders returned to Germany to work on Wings of Desire... a film about Berlin and Germany, its past and present.' Anton Kaes, *The Oxford History of World Cinema*, OUP, Oxford, 1997

'Part romance, part comedy, part meditation on matters political and philosophical.' Geoff Andrew, *Time Out Film Guide 14th Ed.*, Time Out Guides Ltd., London, 2006

KEY SCENE TEXTUAL ANALYSIS

The library (4)

The single non-diegetic violin chord ushers in a scene of great aural density; the sound is profound, poignant and melancholy. Meanwhile, the cacophony of diegetic sound equals all the massed thoughts of the occupants; their ideas, worries, and hopes.

For a film about angels the establishing shot which pans down and tracks along the ceiling has a celestial look. It is, in fact, reminiscent of the shot of heaven in *A Matter of Life and Death*. Indeed, the whole idea of depicting the heavenly world in monochrome and life on earth in colour is another device inspired by that film.

The black and white world also helps to match the calmness of the heavenly view of the world. The whispering is both haunting and mysterious, evoking both a chaotic world and one where all humanity is linked.

The tracking shot along the shelves is punctuated by the shifting focus of the sounds, each individual's thoughts briefly heard. As the camera pauses for a few beats a female figure turns to the camera and nods: this seems to be either Damiel or Cassiel's POV, and the audience thinks that it has been placed within the world of the angels'

experience; but the enigma of the shot is revealed as the camera pans to then show the two angels, Damiel and Cassiel, suggesting that the POV is the viewer's, that we are actually angels.

A rising chord is joined by a soprano singing voice, then by other singing voices to create a celestial chorus, intertwining with the thoughts of the people. The religious and serene atmosphere is further enhanced by the *mise-en-scène*, a library of immense proportions with high ceilings and balconies like pulpits, reminiscent of a modern-day cathedral.

The camera tracks smoothly and steadily with the two angels and then returns to Cassiel, framing his head as if he is the painting of an icon, all stillness and contemplation. His head moves up, as if he is luxuriating in the swell of human thought. It is his music, a source of energy and spiritual fulfilment; his upturned head returns us to the shot of the ceiling, its design modern, futuristic, unearthly and contemplative.

The pan down and track along more readers with their angels is again fluid, suggestive of the angels' movement through the temporal world. This is also designed as a POV, with angels smiling directly at the camera. The initial reveal does not quite move from the correct point to firmly establish that it is Damiel's viewpoint and the resulting half-POV further implicates us into the angels' world.

The clothes of the angels are all very similar: dark, long overcoats and dark trousers with grey scarves. Their uniformity and the dark colours help emphasise their lack of ostentation, for these angels are not seen by people, except the children, and their role is to support, to listen and to absorb - their ordinariness and drabness only serves to accentuate their hidden work.

The framing of Damiel is again reminiscent of that of a religious painting. His serene face wears an expression of spiritual fulfilment and he is positioned to the right of the frame with his arm stretched out into the left portion. It is a space which seems filled by the angelic and human voices, a space that he is desirous of, indicated by the outstretched arm and tilted head movement. The shot also anticipates the next static shot of

Damiel as he settles down on another seat later in the sequence; one of Christ-like serenity, recalling His acceptance at the crucifixion.

The young boy looks up, directly at the camera, again involving the audience right in the celestial environment. He is looking at Damiel whose obvious contentment at making contact with humanity is emphasised by placing him centrally in the frame this time. He is balanced; it is, after all, the angels' sole aim to provide an unseen (unless you are very young) support to humanity.

Another angel is seen similarly at the centre of frame, emphasising his contentment, but theirs is not the central place for he defers to the human as he returns to his chair and the angel immediately moves into another supporting role.

fluidity of movement is accentuated by the solidity and stillness of the library. The library, conversely, acts as a perfect environment for these angels to inhabit; the curves of banisters, the symmetry of the lines, the juxtaposition of angles and the mass of suspended light fixtures all combine to provide a surreal and unearthly context for this vision of the overlap of the earthly and the heavenly. Also, its split level complexity and its purpose as a site of learning and intellectual excellence pinpoint it as an appropriate location for the angels to meet humanity as it stretches itself to the limits of its capacity.

As Damiel sits again in a long shot he occupies a small part of the frame to the right. His yearnings and the world that is not open to him are again

Camera movement matches angelic movement as it tracks away from Damiel and reveals more angels sitting on a wall, legs dangling over the edge like children. The speed of the tracking shot changes as it moves along, imitating the sudden rushes of movement that we see with the angels as they flit between humans. The human voices continue to mingle and the angelic chorus pulsates as if there is a tremendous yearning.

The double exposure shot indicates the angels' inability to connect with the physical world. The effect also draws the audience's attention to the angels' existence within the filmic world; the POVs, the straight-to-camera shots and camera movement all coalesce to make the very medium of film part of the celestial framework. As Damiel moves towards the camera with the pencil in his hand he comes into the centre of frame as his head tilts once more, an antenna tuning into its preferred station.

The *mise-en-scène* of the modernist library interior contrasts with the angels' unearthly nature. Their

suggested by the amount of space around him. At this early part of the film he is a long way from physically connecting with the physical world, and this expanse of filmic space emphasises his alienation from the world of feeling and touch.

The cut to the medium shot and his crucifixion stance accentuates his fulfilment and desire. The camera does not stay still for long, as has been the case in this whole sequence, suggesting the restless nature of these celestial beings. Although Damiel is the focus for the film's narrative, the camera moves away from him to indicate that he is part of a bigger picture and we see Cassiel again in long shot standing on a balcony suggestive of a pulpit. He is like a priest surveying his flock and the camera cranes towards him, as light and as fluid as the angels it depicts.

The angelic voices have become softer by this point for this non-diegetic sound has captured the tranquillity, the pain and the ecstasy of experience.

Goodfellas

KEY FACTS

Release Date: 1990

Country of Origin: USA

Running Time: 139 minutes

PRODUCTION NOTES

Production Company

Warner Bros. Pictures

Distributor

Warner Bros. Pictures

Budget

$25,000,000 (estimated)

Awards

Best Actor in a Supporting Role Joe Pesci Academy Awards, USA

Best Costume Design Richard Bruno BAFTA Awards, UK

Best Direction Martin Scorsese BAFTA Awards, UK

Best Editing Thelma Schoonmaker BAFTA Awards, UK

Best Film Irwin Winkler Martin Scorsese BAFTA Awards, UK

Best Screenplay – Adapted Nicholas Pileggi Martin Scorsese BAFTA Awards, UK

Best Cinematography Michael Ballhaus Los Angeles Film Critics Association Awards

Best Director Martin Scorsese Los Angeles Film Critics Association Awards

Best Picture Los Angeles Film Critics Association Awards

Best Supporting Actor Joe Pesci Los Angeles Film Critics Association Awards

Best Supporting Actress Lorraine Bracco Los Angeles Film Critics Association Awards

National Film Registry National Film Preservation Board, USA

Best Director Martin Scorsese National Society of Film Critics Awards, USA

Best Film National Society of Film Critics Awards, USA

Best Actor Robert De Niro New York Film Critics Circle Awards

Best Director Martin Scorsese New York Film Critics Circle Awards

Best Film New York Film Critics Circle Awards

Silver Lion Best Director Martin Scorsese Venice Film Festival

SYNOPSIS

Henry Hill is a young boy of Irish-Italian descent living in the Brooklyn area of New York in the mid-1950s, where an Italian Mafia 'family', led by Paul Cicero, has control of the neighbourhood. Henry is drawn to this way of life and soon misses school to run errands for them and, despite his parents' protests, he gradually becomes more involved with their illegal activities. Partnered with the young Tommy DeVito, he quickly learns the codes of working in such an organisation. When older, Henry, Tommy and a more established Irish gangster, Jimmy Conway, rob an Air France cargo terminal and Henry becomes an accepted member of the family, although like Jimmy, they can never become 'made' men (a *fully* accepted member of the family) as they are not of wholly Italian descent.

Henry becomes rich and powerful and wins over Karen with a mixture of charm, money and her attraction to his use of violence. Tommy, however, is truly psychotic and thrives on violence: he shoots a young waiter for no reason and brutally kills, with Jimmy's help, another 'made' man who has insulted him. By the 1970s Henry is involved in drug dealing and smuggling, while Jimmy carries out another massive robbery at Idlewild Airport in New York. After Tommy and Henry have spent a few years in prison Tommy is eventually killed by the elders in the family for his earlier murder of a 'made' man; Henry and Jimmy are powerless because it is an internal matter. Henry is finally caught by the FBI for processing and smuggling cocaine, and to avoid prosecution he gives evidence against Cicero and Jimmy Conway. He is then put

into the Witness Protection Program to live out his life in middle class suburban anonymity.

HISTORICAL CONTEXT

The 1990s began where the previous decade had left off, with the Western world dominated by a desire to make money. The 1980s had been boom years after the uncertainties of the 1970s, and the decade in which *Goodfellas* appeared looked like it was going to consolidate and expand on those aspirations. And whilst lawful business practices were thriving, the underground market was doing very well too. *Goodfellas* shows the development of Mafia operations, with some members moving into the drug trade by the 1970s. Drug production, processing and distribution was an enormously lucrative business by the 1990s, and *Goodfellas* shows how individuals and organised crime were easily drawn into this world of big money and huge risk (something also alluded to in the *Godfather* films). The film also began a decade that was again fascinated by the machinations of the criminal world; when it is so powerful the public always feels a combination of trepidation and keen interest.

The same fascination with gangsters has been a part of Hollywood tradition since the 1930s, but Scorsese's gangsters are shown to be much more brutal; the bloodletting is extreme, not just reflecting their actual behaviour but also a time when graphic images of slaughter were being (and still are) delivered into our front rooms by news bulletins.

Goodfellas was Scorsese's return to happier days and marked a personal project after a decade as a director-for-hire. He had been one of the key 'movie brats' of the New Hollywood in the 1970s, alongside Coppola, Friedkin, Cimino and Bogdanovich. Like his contemporaries, he was unsaddled from his status as auteur (although he would make a triumphant return) with his own film failures, compounded by the backlash against these young directors who had been given huge amounts of studio money and unprecedented freedom.

The studios, now largely owned by multi-national corporations, struck back after the box office disaster of *Heaven's Gate*, and wrestled control back to the executives, the money men. Scorsese's critical and commercial failure *New York, New York* had been followed by *Raging Bull* (1980) – now widely regarded as his masterpiece, but its brutal aesthetic was not rewarded financially. He then made the equally unsuccessful *The King of Comedy* (1982), and thereafter worked on *After Hours* (1985), *The Color of Money* (1986) and a collection of music videos and television commercials.

Scorsese wanted to work, but none of these were personal projects. Like Coppola's last auteurist outing, *Apocalypse Now, Goodfellas* brought Scorsese back full-circle – an auteur's film exploring, again, a gangster world in a personal and intimate way and echoing his earlier *Mean Streets*. This reincarnation of the gangster film, replete with glamour, extreme brutality and an uncanny eye for the humanness and rituals of their ilk would later breathe life into the television creation, *The Sopranos*, a gloriously bloodied descendant of Scorsese's film-making.

SELECT FILMOGRAPHY OF MAIN PRODUCERS AND CAST

Martin Scorsese, 1942, Director, Producer, Screenwriter

Who's That Knocking at My Door, 1967

Boxcar Bertha, 1972

Mean Streets, 1973

Alice Doesn't Live Here Anymore, 1974

Taxi Driver, 1976

New York, New York, 1977

Raging Bull, 1980

The King of Comedy, 1983

After Hours, 1985

The Color of Money, 1986

The Last Temptation of Christ, 1988

Goodfellas, 1990

Cape Fear, 1991

The Age of Innocence, 1993

Casino, 1995

Kundun, 1997

Bringing Out the Dead, 1999

Gangs of New York, 2002

The Aviator, 2004

The Departed, 2006

Shine a Light, 2008

Michael Ballhaus, 1935, Director of Photography

The Marriage of Maria Braun, 1979

After Hours, 1985

The Color of Money, 1986

Broadcast News, 1988

The Last Temptation of Christ, 1988

The Fabulous Baker Boys, 1988

Working Girl, 1989

Goodfellas, 1990

Postcards from the Edge, 1990

Guilty by Suspicion, 1991

Bram Stoker's Dracula, 1992

The Age of Innocence, 1993

Quiz Show, 1994

Sleepers, 1996

Primary Colors, 1998

The Legend of Bagger Vance, 2000

Gangs of New York, 2002

The Departed, 2006

Thelma Schoonmaker, 1940, Editor

Woodstock, 1970

Raging Bull, 1980

The King of Comedy, 1983

After Hours, 1985

The Color of Money, 1986

The Last Temptation of Christ, 1988

Goodfellas, 1990

Cape Fear, 1991

The Age of Innocence, 1993

Casino, 1995

Kundun, 1997

Bringing Out the Dead, 1999

Gangs of New York, 2002

The Aviator, 2004

The Departed, 2006

Robert De Niro, 1943, Actor, Director, Producer

Mean Streets, 1973

Taxi Driver, 1976

1900, 1976

New York, New York, 1977

The Deer Hunter, 1978

Raging Bull, 1980

The King of Comedy, 1983

Once Upon a Time in America, 1984

The Mission, 1986

Angel Heart, 1987

The Untouchables, 1987

Midnight Run, 1988

Goodfellas, 1990

Stanley and Iris, 1990

Awakenings, 1990

Cape Fear, 1991

A Bronx Tale, 1993

Mary Shelley's Frankenstein, 1994

Casino, 1995

Heat, 1995

Jackie Brown, 1997

Ronin, 1998

Analyze This, 1999

Meet the Parents, 2000

The Good Shepherd, 2006

Stardust, 2007

Righteous Kill, 2008

Joe Pesci, 1943, Actor

Raging Bull, 1980

Once Upon a Time in America, 1984

Lethal Weapon 2, 3 and 4, 1989, 1992 and 1998

Goodfellas, 1990

Home Alone, 1990

JFK, 1991

My Cousin Vinnie, 1992

This Boy's Life, 1993

A Bronx Tale, 1993

Casino, 1995

The Good Shepherd, 2006

Ray Liotta, 1954, Actor

Something Wild, 1986

Field of Dreams, 1989

Goodfellas, 1990

Unlawful Entry, 1992

Corrina, Corrina, 1994

Cop Land, 1997

Hannibal, 2001

Blow, 2001

Narc, 2002

Smokin' Aces, 2006

LINKS TO OTHER FILMS

Get Carter (1971)

The American gangster film was transposed to Britain with director Mike Hodges' depiction of violent criminals involved in organised crime. It is very English, with its drab northern England cityscape, its mix of decaying Victorian housing, grey tower blocks and low key brutality - a long way from the glamorous Hollywood image of gangsters that had been seen in earlier decades.

Scarface (1983)

A thoroughly modern gangster film, graphic in violence and with a focus on the drugs business that fuelled organised crime, showing its resultant riches and extreme brutality.

Once Upon a Time in America (1984)

This follows the lives of gangsters to contemporary times, showing both the loyalty and betrayal that exists within organised crime, as well as the fear generated by the gangsters' extreme brutality.

Married to the Mob (1988)

This is a comic take on organised crime, but its sense of the Mafia as a 'family' is a particular focus, connecting it thematically with Goodfellas.

The Godfather Part III (1990)

Francis Ford Coppola's final part to his trilogy of Mafia films takes the story of Michael Corleone into the modern era. Like Goodfellas it shows both the public and private face of organised crime, suggesting the bond that exists between its members as well as the brutal divisions that rip these bonds apart.

Lock, Stock and Two Smoking Barrels (1998)

A modern British take on the gangster film, with a blend of extreme violence and humour that marks a departure from the Hollywood films where violence is served with a snarl rather than a smile.

REPRESENTATION

Modern gangsters

Audiences have always loved gangsters as portrayed in film; they often have an intoxicating blend of glamour and brutality and they lead fabulously wealthy lifestyles that also have a certain appeal. No one has done more to represent gangsters to us than Martin Scorsese. Films like Mean Streets, Goodfellas, Casino (1995) and The Departed (2006) have given audiences his interpretation of this band of people; the fact that Robert De Niro has played major roles in three of these films is something which affects audience response too. Other actors who have brought this charismatic baggage to the modern gangster include Michael Caine (Get Carter), Al Pacino (The Godfather trilogy, Scarface and Donnie Brasco, 1997), and Daniel Craig (Layer Cake, 2004). Most of these actors are able to portray both the eruptions of violence and their relationships with family, which make them both psychotic and ordinary. Then there are those who are just psychotic, perhaps overblown caricatures: there is the lead character portrayed by both Paul Bettany and Malcolm McDowell in Gangster No.1 (2000) or the brutal Don Logan (Ben Kingsley) in Sexy Beast (2000).

Nor are gangsters solely the preserve of Hollywood. There is the British gangster and Hong Kong has its own brand and has, in some cases, exported it back to the United States (Infernal Affairs, 2002, inspired Scorsese's The Departed). The French too have always been adept at creating their own kind of gangster with lashings of existential cool: Bob le flambeur (1955), Rififi (1955), Ascenseur pour l'échafaud (1958), À bout de souffle (1960), Le Doulos (1962), Pierrot le fou (1965), Le Samouraï (1967) and Le Cercle rouge (1970) all connect the hard-bitten film noir gangster to the modern gangsters that came from the 1970s onwards.

In Goodfellas, there is the ferociously psychotic Tommy, who brutally murders another gangster and shoots (later killing) a young man for no good reason. Henry is only twice seen being brutally violent, and one of those occasions is in defending his girlfriend from the violent advances of another man. Jimmy acts as the bridge between Tommy and Henry; extremely charming and menacing in equal measures.

The look that Scorsese captures in slow motion as Jimmy sits at a bar, coolly contemplating whether or not to kill an associate, is truly frightening. The moment passes but it sums up the mindset of the gangster, existing on a knife-edge between normality (as most of society measures normality) and nihilistic violence. Of course, just by referring to them as gangsters seems to imply a certain amount of kudos, generated by popular culture's obsession with this type of criminal, but criminals are essentially what they are and the representation of them in *Goodfellas* understands that, but also understands their unique ties. The shot of the Mafia bosses cooking together in prison helps underline this point, showing a brotherhood and setting them apart from other criminals.

'Scorsese provides an insight into the mob but without losing the audience's sympathy with, and interest in, the characters.' Paul Frost-Sharratt, *501 Must-See Movies*, Octopus Publishing Group Limited OUP, London, 2004

'The camera and cutting style is as forcefully persuasive as a gun in the gut, so that we are... excited by the cocky comraderie, bloody murder, and expansive sense of family on view.' Geoff Andrew, *Time Out Film Guide 14th Ed.*, Time Out Guides Ltd., London, 2006

KEY SCENE TEXTUAL ANALYSIS

Arriving at the club (12)

A close-up of Henry's hand begins this extraordinary scene, which is shot in a single take. There are many shots of hands in the film: shaking other hands, passing/receiving money, slapping a cheek affectionately, gesturing in anger, and, most often, perpetrating a violent act. This recurring visual motif allows Scorsese to present the many aspects of the mobster, constantly reaching out, gesticulating, exhibiting both great warmth and great brutality in the same moment. It sums up the

dichotomy at the heart of these characters, whose love and loyalty for family, with bursts of genuine affection, is coupled with equal doses of extreme violence. The old adage of the eyes not seeing the actions of the hands is perfectly realised.

The camera pulls away from the exchange of car keys and money - money is another of the key motifs; it is proffered like a promise: I own you or I respect you. The doorman is paid off and Henry turns away, the exchange as natural as breathing for him.

Simultaneously, the non-diegetic music begins, the Ronnettes' *And Then He Kissed Me*, an archetypal 1960's song which tells the story of a girl falling in love with a boy. Its lyrics mirror the seduction that is happening in this scene as Henry's liberal distribution of cash and his ease of entry into the heavily over-subscribed Copacabana nightclub help to enthral and excite Karen. The song's popular music sentiments also convey how Karen is being slowly won over by a young and charismatic young man. Its pop sensibilities suggest how Henry, the gangster, is a kind of celebrity, an echo of the previous scene when she suggests that he must think he is Frankie Valli for standing her up. It also acts as a complement to the gliding steadicam shot that charts their walk from the street into the sacred depths of the nightclub, far beyond the reach of the 'nobodies' standing in line. It is, of course, the 1960s and the *mise-en-scène* (the cars, the clothes in particular) reflects an era that we now perceive in terms of 'coolness', sexual freedom and the explosion of popular music focused on the youth.

As the camera follows them around the labyrinth that will eventually lead them to the dance floor, it suggests that not only does Henry have privileged access to the nightclub, as befits one who threatens, buys and charms his way through life, but it is symbolic of the gangster's approach to life: get what you want when you want it. However, Scorsese's overriding tone here is one of the wonder and excitement of such a life, as experienced by Karen who is new to this approach.

They pass by a multitude of people and it becomes a celebration of Henry's progress: he is one of the people and is respected by the people. As he enters the kitchen he interacts with all those around him with his friendly acknowledgements of the staff and tactile gestures emphasising the glamour and appeal of such men, and their ability to manipulate others.

Once they arrive in the club proper, they are immediately given preferential treatment and a new table is created for them, such is Henry's power. The shot has remained uncut for almost three minutes by the end of the sequence, which further underlines the man's influence. Henry's uninterrupted movement towards power is mirrored in the seamless flow of the camera movement. The audience takes that journey with him and is as equally captivated by his charm as Karen. The final image is of the couple hand in

Karen's emergence from behind the front door screen is slowed down. This brutal altered reality, so unsettling in such a tranquil environment, shifts her reality forever and she decides in these few seconds whether she will condone or reject this action. The enormity of the decision is signalled by the slow motion. It also suggests how her voyeurism of such an extreme event has plunged her into a moment outside reality; time stands still when extraordinary events take place.

When Henry places the bloodied gun into her hand, his own hand smeared with Bruce's blood, the shot is a close-up of hands. This motif is used to suggest the new bond between Karen and Henry, a blood oath cementing their fate together; two further close-ups of Karen's hands holding the gun reiterate her growing acceptance of Henry's other,

hand; he lies to her about being in construction (which she doubts when touching his hands), but she caresses and holds his hand firmly nonetheless and the seduction is complete.

A wedding (14)

Henry and Karen's wedding day is preceded by some violent foreplay as Henry now reveals his dark side: unfettered rage and brutality.

Karen's neighbour, Bruce, has been violent towards her, and Henry repays him with a terrifying retribution, beating his face repeatedly with a revolver. The contrast between the middle-class suburban *mise-en-scène*, with its manicured lawns and hedges, and Henry's ferocious attack intensified by his demonic anger, the red tones of the house, the car, the bushes, Bruce's bloodied face, and Henry's jacket and trousers, all underpin the passionate anger that bursts onto the screen.

violent side. The hands of love and the hands of death are now moulded into one, to be accepted by Karen, her gentle cupping of the gun most certainly a caress.

The diegetic clink of gun against milk bottle as she hides the gun links to the sight of the glass being wrapped up in the next scene, establishing the connection between violence and what follows, their wedding day. Just as at the climax to *The Godfather*, where Coppola intercuts between multiple pre-arranged murders and a baptism, the profane and the sacred are inextricably linked.

The jump cut from wrapping the glass to its being trodden on at the Jewish wedding ceremony emphasises the rather dislocating movement from extreme violence to religious service, and also the lack of reverence to the ceremony, reduced by the editing to a couple of shots. It underlines the basis of the need for this service as a front to appease Karen's Jewish family, and founded on the lie that Henry tells, that he is half-Jewish in order to ingratiate himself into her family.

The light bulb flashes of a photographer's camera suspends them in time. The subtle jump cut that Scorcese uses when the flash ignites also aids their removal from the background - the strong light around them looks like an aura that confirms the intensity of their love, but reduces the background to nothing more than a back projection. The background here comprises of both sets of dissatisfied parents, who will now be consigned to obscurity in the couple's lives as their new family fully takes over. This is not so much a wedding before God as before the Mafia; the cursory final shot of both families is only long enough to register their disgruntled faces, but not long enough for them to be relevant to the bride and groom's new life with the Mafia-in-laws.

suggests her fate being sealed by money. As ever, the actual act is covert; the money is in envelopes so as not to be too gauche, but the envelope is also designed to look like a decorative version of a bank note: fake finery concealing dirty money.

The final image of Karen and Henry dancing, again encircled by the camera but now in real time, is symbolic of their final and complete union; Karen is no longer disorientated, as suggested by the slow motion, but has moved into her new family's real time.

The romantic 1950's music which has played throughout this scene underpins the atmosphere of the wedding celebration, but also ironically juxtaposes the sentimental tune and lyrics with the veneer of civility, with unbridled violence just beneath: Cinderella meets the Mob.

The importance of the new 'family' is underlined by the long tracking shot that moves along the Mafia tables, allowing the audience to feel intoxicated by their power and their laughter, just as Henry was captivated, and as Karen finally falls under their spell. The next shot of Karen has the camera encircling her as Henry moves around her. It is in slow motion, and, again, suggestive of her being enveloped into the heady atmosphere of Mafia culture. She is surrounded, but instead of fighting against it, she dizzily succumbs to the power and the labyrinthine complexity. Just as the earlier movement into the Copacabana Club mirrors the Mafia's tortuous and unfathomable power, so Karen's seemingly endless introductions to the extended family results in another slow motion shot where she herself spins around as she is drawn into the centre of the labyrinth.

The final act of initiation is played out as the Mafia family line up to give the couple money; the camera again focuses on the hands. The montage of hands passing over cash into her hands rather sinisterly

Crash

KEY FACTS

Release Date: 2005

Country of Origin: USA

Running Time: 107 minutes

PRODUCTION NOTES

Production Companies

Bull's Eye Entertainment

DEJ Productions

ApolloProScreen Filmproduktion

Blackfriars Bridge Films

Bob Yari Productions

Harris Company

Distributor

Lions Gate Films

Budget

$6,500,000 (estimated)

Awards

Best Achievement in Editing Hughes Winborne Academy Awards, USA

Best Motion Picture of the Year Paul Haggis Cathy Schulman Academy Awards, USA

Best Writing, Original Screenplay Paul Haggis Robert Moresco Academy Awards, USA

Best Performance by an Actress in a Supporting Role Thandie Newton BAFTA Awards, UK

Best Screenplay – Original Paul Haggis Robert Moresco BAFTA Awards, UK

British Supporting Actress of the Year Thandie Newton London Critics Circle Film Awards

Screenwriter of the Year Paul Haggis Robert Moresco London Critics Circle Film Awards

Best Original Screenplay Paul Haggis Robert Moresco Writers Guild of America

SYNOPSIS

An array of people from different ethnic and social backgrounds come into contact with each other over a 36-hour period in Los Angeles. Some meetings are harmonious but many are fuelled by racial stereotyping and prejudice. A privileged white couple have their car stolen by two black men, confirming the woman's prejudices. She continues to distrust non-whites, even the Mexican-American man who comes to change their locks. Another privileged couple, but black, fall foul of the police when the woman is molested by a racist officer, Ryan, after he has pulled over their car for a routine matter; his partner, Hansen, does not agree with his actions and asks to have a new partner. In a twist, the racist police officer later rescues the woman from her burning car.

The locksmith is seen fixing the door of a Persian storeowner, but when his store is ransacked, the man believes that the locksmith was implicated. He tracks the locksmith to his house and shoots at him, appearing to shoot the locksmith's daughter by mistake. However, the bullets are blanks, sold to his daughter by a bigoted gun shop owner earlier in the film. The two black car thieves later try to steal another car, this time from the black man whose wife was molested by the police officer. He defends himself and eventually gains control of their gun; he is subsequently cornered by two police officers who nearly shoot him because he is in possession of a gun. He is saved by the intervention of police officer Hansen, and the man goes free.

The two car thieves go their separate ways, one (who is shown to be racist at the beginning) steals a van from a South East Asian couple, whilst the other (a more reasonable man than his friend) makes his way home on foot. En route he hitches a lift from Hansen, who, after a tense conversation about racism shoots the thief because he thinks that he is reaching for a gun (in fact, he is about to take out a St. Christopher statuette). Throughout the film a police detective, Waters, and his partner/girlfriend have been investigating the suspected racist shooting of a black police officer by a white police officer, and the couple have their own arguments about race; he is black and she is of Central American origin. Waters arrives at the scene of a murder, a body dumped by the side of the road, and it becomes apparent that it is the black car thief shot by the police officer. The twist here is that the dead man is also the police detective's younger brother. Finally, a group of illegal immigrants are found in the van taken by the other thief, who uncharacteristically decides to let them go rather than allow a garage owner (who sells on the stolen cars) to sell the immigrants as slaves.

HISTORICAL CONTEXT

The new millennium was greeted with a mixture of excitement, hope and dread, together with positive ideas that this momentous occasion might usher in a new dawn of people working harder to achieve peace and fight poverty. Certainly there have been attempts to make a difference, but the decade did not begin well and those fighting for a better world have had a particularly hard time in the noughties. The decade began with worries about the so-called 'millennium bug', but these proved unfounded. But then the attacks of September 11, 2001 seemed to set the tone for the rest of the decade. More terrorist attacks, wars in Afghanistan and Iraq, bird flu, global warming, tsunamis, floods; the list goes on. One crucial factor lies at the heart of all these issues: communication between people.

Within the United States' own borders there are a multitude of issues with regard to race and intolerance. Its own Afro-American population is still marginalised; images of the 2006 flood in New Orleans illustrated a gaping social divide as mainly black Americans were forced to endure incredible hardship whilst the white middle classes could afford to flee. The 'Tortilla Curtain' is a frontline where the influx of Mexican immigrants is perceived as an ongoing threat to the United States. Los Angeles itself has a history of racial violence, from the street gangs to the infamous police beating of the black Rodney King in 1991 recorded on video, and the subsequent riots when the officers responsible where acquitted when tried. The racial melting pot of Los Angeles, then, is an ideal setting to examine the issue of communication and miscommunication, demonstrating the problems inherent in cultures crashing, but also some of the possibilities.

SELECT FILMOGRAPHY OF MAIN PRODUCERS AND CAST

Paul Haggis, 1953, Director, Screenwriter

As Director

Crash, 2004

In the Valley of Elah, 2007

As Writer

Crash, 2004

Million Dollar Baby, 2004

Flags of Our Fathers, 2006

Casino Royale, 2006

Letters from Iwo Jima, 2006

In the Valley of Elah, 2007

Quantum of Solace, 2008

Matt Dillon, 1964, Actor

The Outsiders, 1983

Rumble Fish, 1983

Drugstore Cowboy, 1989

A Kiss Before Dying, 1991

Singles, 1992

To Die For, 1995

Grace of my Heart, 1996

Albino Alligator, 1996

In and Out, 1997

Wild Things, 1998

There's Something About Mary, 1998

Crash, 2004

Factotum, 2005

You, Me and Dupree, 2006

Don Cheadle, 1964, Actor

Things to Do in Denver When You're Dead, 1995

Devil in a Blue Dress, 1995

Rosewood, 1997

Boogie Nights, 1997

Out of Sight, 1998

The Rat Pack, 1998

Bulworth, 1998

Traffic, 2000

Swordfish, 2001

Ocean's Eleven, 2001

The United States of Leland, 2003

Ocean's Twelve, 2004

The Assassination of Richard Nixon, 2004

Hotel Rwanda, 2004

Crash, 2004

Reign Over Me, 2007

Talk to Me, 2007

Ocean's Thirteen, 2007

LINKS TO OTHER FILMS

The Defiant Ones (1958)/*Guess Who's Coming To Dinner* (1967)

Both of Stanley Kramer's films examine the role of African-Americans in society. The earlier film involves two escaped convicts chained to each other, one is white and the other is black. The film charts their initial intolerance and their growing respect for each other. The second film charts the arrival of an African-American into the house of a white middle-class family. He and the white daughter have fallen in love, and the story depicts the family's reaction to him. Although not challenging by today's standards, both were controversial for their times. In 1960's North America, some states still outlawed inter-racial marriage.

Do The Right Thing (1989)

A look at race relations from an African-American perspective and directed by Spike Lee, focussing on the problems of poor neighbourhoods where the melting pot can sometimes boil over into racial violence.

Short Cuts (1993)

A film, like *Crash*, of a number of stories and characters, interweaving them and commenting on the experiences of modern life. The film is typical of director Robert Altman's style, using an ensemble cast and eschewing the conventional linear model for story-telling.

La Haine (1995)

This film deals with the anger of racism and the discontent felt by the young at what they perceive is prejudice towards them. The story follows three young men of African, Arab and Jewish descent who are bound by their feelings of alienation in contemporary France.

Magnolia (1999)

Paul Thomas Anderson's film is also based in Los Angeles and combines a number of different stories, revealing a plethora of coincidences and bizarre events that connect the characters together.

REPRESENTATION

Racism

Racism, or at least what is now perceived to be racism, originated at the very beginnings of cinema. Silent films such as D.W. Griffith's *The Birth of a Nation* (1915) represent black people using the worst possible stereotypes: sexually deviant, murderous and stupid. The film portrays the Ku Klux Klan in a very positive light, crediting the group as saviours of post-Civil War America. Four years later Griffith made *Broken Blossoms*, a film that, although not ostensibly about race, showed a far more sympathetic treatment of a Chinese character. It depicts a peace-loving Buddhist who tries to sow harmony in the violent streets of East London, but eventually he and the girl he loves succumb to its brutality.

After many years of ingrained racist stereotyping in Hollywood films, a movement towards tackling the subject took place from the late 1940s onwards. Two films that stand out in this period for their forthright approach are Edward Dmytryk's *Crossfire* (1947) and John Sturges' *Bad Day at Black Rock* (1955). The former tells of an American soldier killing a Jewish man, while the latter relates the investigation into the killing of a Japanese man; both stories take place at the end of the Second World War, and clearly put forward the case for tolerance.

The Civil Rights movement of the 1950s and 1960s would give film-makers even more impetus to tell stories of tolerance and bigotry in the years that followed. In *Crash* the representation is more nuanced (although not sufficiently so for some critics); the characters are complex as are their range of emotions. Racism is based on personal experience, making them blind, even if it is only for a moment: police officer Hansen's killing of Peter, the black car thief, is such a moment. The film ends with the enlightened release of the immigrants into the Los Angeles night. It is a moment of hope, but is soon superseded by a car crash, and two characters of different races begin to violently argue. The camera draws back and upwards leaving this disagreement to continue; the aerial shot suggests this is one of many such disagreements. It is not necessarily because of race, but prejudice, the film says, which allows us to create easy scapegoats for our problems. The representation is not entirely negative for there are flashes of great humanity (see KEY SCENE TEXTUAL ANALYSIS below), but merging these into a collective and proactive movement is the real difficulty.

'[The] picture is sharply observed and frequently extremely funny as well as artfully orchestrated. It ends on a tragic note, but [it manages]... to avoid easy cynicism or fashionable despair.' Philip French, *The Observer*, 14th August, 2005

'I've never seen a film so eloquent about blind prejudice and the easy slope to bitterness. Haggis captures the shallow glassy politeness of strangers, and the bottled anger within... It's a brave film that addresses the unspoken racial nausea that lingers after 9/11 in a way that no other film has dared.' James Christopher, The Sunday Times, 11th August, 2005

KEY SCENE TEXTUAL ANALYSIS

Car crash (13)

As the police car drives into frame, its iconic status is already undermined by the behaviour of its occupant, Officer Ryan, who we have seen behaving as a racist, albeit because he is frustrated at his father's treatment at the hands of the health care system. In an earlier scene he has stopped Christine and her husband, body-searching her in a very intimate and degrading manner. Now their paths will cross again in very different circumstances. The camera looks up at the car, this seeming symbol of authority and power, whilst the non-diegetic music is expressive of tranquillity, its synthesiser chords both haunting and suggestive of a calm before the storm.

The medium shot of Ryan portrays a man comfortable with his position in life, his power and views secure. His POV surveys a scene of chaos within an otherwise ordinary scene; it is a picture of banality, its equilibrium unsettled by the everyday occurrence of a car crash. The POV also suggests his professional stock-taking of a situation which needs action from an individual, not stasis as is suggested by the inertness of the *mise-en-scène*.

A pulsing piano begins to signal the start of a dramatic scene as Ryan makes his decision and runs towards the crash site. His POV again shows his single-mindedness as he races through the jungle of cars, noteworthy only by the way their occupants largely stay encased within them,

uninvolved and removed from the human drama that is unfolding before them. It relates back to the first words of the film: 'In L.A. nobody touches you; we're always behind this metal and glass.'

The camera tracks with Ryan as he runs towards the car crash, his dynamism accentuated by the camera movement. Car drivers are barely glimpsed, safe behind their car doors, as we are drawn into his world by the POV as he runs. The jerky camerawork signals the escalating sense of disorientation amidst the normality of the street scene and the camera races away from him and draws the audience further into this increasingly chaotic world while smoke adds to the surreal atmosphere.

The focus of the crash, the rolled-over car like an upturned tortoise, seems strangely isolated from the rest of the cars. It is a site where something extraordinary might happen in very ordinary surroundings.

The shot from within the car is a POV and frames a running Ryan, shot in slow-motion, suggesting the hyper-real feeling of the slowing down of time as a victim waits for minute after agonising minute, and rescuer tries to get to her.

The haunting non-diegetic music, with a voice of Middle Eastern origin, counterpoints the dramatic action and the urgent male tones of the police officer. Most of the shots now come from within the car, its claustrophobia and edginess encapsulated in the ground level, jerky camera movement; the audience starts to feel the occupant's sense of fear and helplessness.

Ryan is framed by the occupant's flailing limbs, the juxtaposition of their bodies becoming more important as the scene plays out and their lives become intertwined. We see the scene outside through the maze of cracks in the windscreen, a fractured picture matching the fracture in time and place that the incident represents. As Ryan crawls into the car the frames become more cluttered and we see only fragments of their bodies as the audience again shares the characters' sense of chaos and disorientation.

As the audience recognises that it is Christine in the car, and she simultaneously recognises Ryan, the camera is full up against their faces, capturing every pore of emotion as these two people confront each other once more. Their heads are sideways in frame, yet another image of dislocation, and her screams fight against the soothing melody of the music.

Throughout her screams and their conversation the edits are relatively slow, the cutting one would expect to accompany a normal conversation between two people. The gentle pacing of these cuts again throws the atmosphere into even greater relief as the situation, the images and her screams fight against the structuring force of the editing and the music.

other type of man he has been and the man she perceived him to be.

The rest of the sequence demonstrates the fluidity of people's natures, how forces make us act in totally different ways. The relentless pounding of the organ-sounding note signals a new stage of drama as we once again see the sight of the other car, the continuing fire and the attempts to extinguish it going on in the distance.

The voice again joins the non-diegetic music as petrol starts to flow towards the fire, the intensity of the moment underpinned by the use of slow-motion.

We see their view of the approaching fire from within the car, as well as its engulfing of their tiny

As Ryan tries to free Christine, Haggis constantly reminds us of the great danger they are in by framing them with the faintest suggestion of dripping petrol, out of focus in the shots, but there nonetheless.

The following sequence is a chillingly ironic rerun of their previous encounter; where once he had been brutal and sexually intimate with her, now he is gentle and caring. In this world, where everything is turned on its head, there is a new code.

As he slips beneath her and their limbs intertwine, the framing is reminiscent of a lovers' embrace; here it is grimly ironic but also points towards the possibility of a new relationship forged in these extraordinary circumstances. The ironies abound as he tries to pull the safety belt off, his exclamation akin to that of a lover's sexually climatic shout, while the use of the knife suggests sexual violence (the sound of the knife coming out causes her to cry anxiously). The context tells us that he is trying to free her, but these actions are reminders of the

world. The claustrophobic world is intensified by the close up of the couple, now entangled in an embrace of death, and the frame is now not only cluttered but full of chiaroscuro shadows and smoke.

The following sequence of near-death experience is shot so as to suggest its hyperreality; the combination of slow-motion, speeded-up film and normal speed all convey the couple's removal from ordinary time/life. As Ryan is dragged from the car by his colleagues he is pulled away from the camera and from the audience, and we are left to empathise with Christine's fate as she falls within the car.

The diegetic sounds are erased from this section, only the haunting singing scores this act of near-tragedy and instinctive heroism, again pointing to the moment rising above the ordinary; it is a moment, as Wilfred Owen says in his poem, *Attack*, when 'times ticks blank and busy', and one's perceptions are violently altered; Haggis achieves this through the manipulation of image and sound in the most intense moment of the rescue.

Again, to keep the audience fully immersed within the drama, Ryan, when he scrambles back into the burning car, plunges straight for the camera; we also need to be saved from the unbearable tension.

The only diegetic sound in this part of the rescue is given to Ryan with his emphatic 'Pull', as he transfigures himself with this act of selfless heroism. Their exchange of looks and embrace now have nothing in common with the brutality of the previous scene; Christine realises that he has another side to him. The long shot of the car jarringly reintroduces the diegetic sounds of burning and ambient noise as the rescue is completed and normality reasserts itself.

partially kneeling; it is not an aggressive pose, but one of humanity, solid but caring; he is flanked by the powerful fire engine which thrusts into the frame from the left, itself a symbol of caring power.

But it is Ryan's police uniform itself which carries the most potent symbol, along with the minaret-topped structure in the background. This composition speaks very much of 9/11. Indeed, the designers behind the poster for Oliver Stone's *World Trade Center* (2006) chose to use the silhouetted images of not just the Twin Towers, but also two winter-jacketed New York cops, both iconic images from that day. The framing in this scene is suggestive of both Americanism *and* the Islamic faith; Ryan has just saved a dark-skinned woman; is this, then, a vision of a future America,

The explosion, a fireball of immense proportions, seems to act as a cathartic cleansing of past hate and fear. Both people are pulled from the car, like newborn children; indeed, Christine's first sounds are cries, elemental and full of confusion about what has just happened.

The image of white cop and black female in a momentary embrace is heavy with symbolism; of possible reconciliation in that moment, but also of white America's relationship with its own black community and possibly with that of the world beyond America. Christine is taken away from her rescuer, and the camera tracks back from him. He is not crying but seems to share her mixed wonderment and confusion about the meaning of the event; the pull back allows the audience to both admire and begin to reappraise this racist police officer. Their two looks are juxtaposed by the cut between the close-ups of their faces, emphasising the connection, pain and confusion between them.

The final medium shot of Ryan frames a *mise-en-scène* which has a number of connotations; he is

where cultural and religious differences can be transcended? It seems very difficult not to be reminded of the television images of the 9/11 events when such a combination of potent images are presented in this way: a police officer, apocalyptic explosion, a dark-skinned character, a fire engine, the minaret. Indeed, American films are now littered with 9/11 iconography, such as the mass destruction of a city by aliens in Spielberg's *War of the Worlds* (2005) and Superman's saving of an airliner in Singer's *Superman Returns* (2006).

SCIENCE FICTION

Metropolis (1927) stands aloft, gazing imperiously at all the science fiction films to come, cerebral and visual, and coming from an era when films themselves were almost the stuff of science fiction themselves. This is followed by an equally visionary film, *Things To Come* (1936), which resembles nothing that was being made in Britain at the time, and another template, with *Metropolis*, for the intelligent science fiction films that would emerge years later, such as *2001* (1968), which, of course, is the only possible choice from the 1960s; it re-established the genre's intellectual credentials on film after many years of flying saucer shenanigans.

In the science fiction section the only real issue was the 1940s entry; sci-fi did not, except for some notable exceptions in the two previous decades, come of age until the 1950s. Hence, *A Connecticut Yankee in King Arthur's Court* (1949); its time travel plot and 'man of the future reworking the past' theme is a common convention in science fiction film; the *Terminator* films (1984, 1991) would rework the formula many years later; also, the mere fact that I am able to link Bing Crosby with an *Evil Dead* film (the third, *Army of Darkness*, 1992), because of their time travel connections, demonstrates the wonderful and weird interconnectedness of the genre through the decades.

Invasion of the Body Snatchers (1956) comes from a rich vein of science fiction film-making that flourished in the 1950s; its tight control of characters and story harbours an allegory for its time and anticipates the body horror of later sci-fi films like *Alien* (1979). Ridley Scott's film, in turn, heralded a new era of films which had a strong quotient of horror laced with science fiction, a formula that is still being reworked to this day. *ET* (1982) is *Alien*'s nemesis, a cuddly, loving and cute being; 'he' touches the heart rather than ripping through the stomach and he, too, spawned numerous imitators. His creator, Steven Spielberg, was one of the few Movie Brats to emerge from the 1970s almost unscathed, many of his films indebted to the Old Hollywood tradition of thrills and spills rather than New Hollywood's gritty and downbeat visions, whose proponents faded as the 1980s progressed. The *Star Wars/Jaws* blueprint from the 1970s was carved in stone by Hollywood executives in the 1980s and it became a safe bet to make money with the likes of *ET*, *Raiders of the Lost Ark* (1981), *Jurassic Park* (1993), et al.

The Matrix (1999) was that rare beast; a successful action/science fiction film and one that carried ideas along for the ride; it was the perfect vehicle for a world diving into cyberspace, which was loved and feared in equal measure. It is also a defining moment in CGI, which was able to create worlds and images that left audiences in awe of the film's spectacle. Finally, *Children of Men* (2006); a serious piece of dystopian cinema, delving into very real and relevant moral panics, and filmed with such breathtaking skill that one almost believes that the images are being fed to us straight from the frontline of future conflicts.

Metropolis

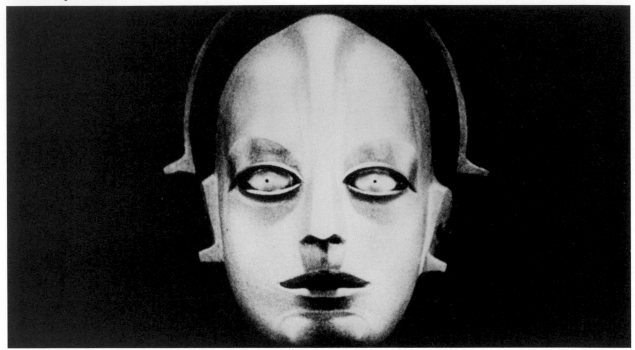

KEY FACTS

Release Date: 1927

Country of Origin: Germany

Running Time: 118 minutes

PRODUCTION NOTES

Production Company

Universum Film (UFA)

Distributors

Universum Film (UFA)

Paramount Pictures

Budget

1,300,000 - 4,200,000 Reichmark (disputed estimates)

Awards

Special Award for the restoration New York Film Circle Critics Awards

SYNOPSIS

A vast city of the future, replete with the trappings of modernity – skyscrapers, vehicles (both flying and surface) and enormous flyovers dissecting the sky - form the backdrop to this story of a people who have lost touch with their humanity in the pursuit of progress and money. The few enslave the many, the division geographically highlighted by the workers' existence beneath the city's surface, forced to work and live in the degradation of the city's underbelly. The thinkers, meanwhile, live in splendour above ground, heedless of the workers' nightmarish lives.

A young woman talks to the desperate workers and tells them that a 'Mediator' will come and bring the workers and thinkers together, uniting them in a harmonious existence. Meanwhile the man who runs the city, Johann 'Joh' Fredersen, is intent on keeping the workers subjugated. However, his son, Freder, falls in love with Maria and joins her cause after he has seen the conditions in which the workers barely exist.

In order to sow discord amongst the workers Fredersen uses a robotic version of Maria, built by a scientist called Rotwang, to foment a violent attack on the upper city, giving him the excuse to crush their rebellious ideas once and for all.

The workers do destroy the 'Heart Machine' which powers the city, but in doing so reservoirs overflow and flood the workers' homes. The real Maria and Freder are able to rescue the workers' families, averting a tragedy. However, believing Maria has led them to kill their children, the workers turn on the robot Maria and burn her. Once they realise that they are burning a robot, the final drama is played out as Rotwang chases the real Maria along a cathedral roof; she is rescued by Freder and Rotwang falls to his death. Finally, Freder becomes the prophesised 'Mediator' as he brings his father and the leader of the workers together, their hands joining and signifying a collective and inclusive future for all.

HISTORICAL CONTEXT

The origins of science fiction film lie at the very beginning of film-making itself. The wonder of moving images initially recorded the ordinary: the arrival of a train in the Lumière brothers' famed *L'Arrivée d'un train en gare de la Ciotat* (1895) for example; but its ability to manipulate images and distort reality quickly led to recreations of the extraordinary. As the end of the nineteenth century approached, the early film-makers made technological leaps in order to capture moving images. They invented the language of film and the machines and techniques that would move this new art form forward. The use of the cut, the 'phantom ride' shot (the camera being placed upon the front of a train) and re-exposing film to incorporate other, more ghostly images onto shots were just a few of the 'tricks' that would help keep audiences fascinated. Together with the Lumière brothers, visionaries like Thomas Edison, William Friese Greene, G.A. Smith, George Eastman and George Méliès helped bring film to the masses.

It was the latter who became a leading proponent of playing with the possibilities of the new medium. Fired by the works of H.G. Wells, the *voyages*

imaginaires of Jules Verne and his own background in illusionist theatre, Méliès' films are a feast of technological innovations. He combined elements of theatrical artifice, such as painted backdrops, with camera trickery to create visual treats like *La Lune à une metre* (1898) and *Le Voyage dans la lune* (1902), films that revel in this age of rapid change and startling discoveries. However, if the early films seemed full of hope and awe, foreseeing a wonder-filled future, then the First World War would sour the vision, and lead to the social commentary and prediction of dystopias found in *Metropolis*.

Adolf Hitler's rise to power began in the Germany of the 1920s, and it was given a real boost by his imprisonment in 1924 (for an attempted coup) and the writing of *Mein Kampf*. Both of these factors turned him into a cause célèbre for a growing number of Germans. By 1933 he had gone from prisoner to Chancellor and there was nothing to stop his total domination of Germany, which came to fruition in 1934 when he became Führer.

There is much debate as to whether *Metropolis* is anti-capitalist or, indeed, anti-communist. It also intimates that a third way was necessary for society, through the 'Mediator'. Opinion about the film's link to political and contemporary life depends upon the personal ideological 'baggage' that a viewer brings to the film. It is believed that Hitler liked the film, viewing it from his own particular perspective; it was certainly rumoured that his propaganda chief, Goebbels, approached its director, Fritz Lang, in 1934 to take charge of the German film studio UFA. Lang demurred and hastily fled to America although his wife, Thea von Harbou, who supported the emerging Nazi regime, stayed behind. As both Lang and his wife were involved in the script for *Metropolis* it is perhaps unsurprising that it stimulates a range of critical interpretation.

Certainly, *Metropolis* is a film very much of its age, as the various countries within Europe struggled to assert or reassert their identities after the First World War. It was a fertile breeding ground for the likes of Hitler, Mussolini and Franco, and the film certainly foreshadows the growth of modern superstates where military technology would play a growing role in underpinning totalitarian power bases. The superstructures and technological developments also mirrored the look of modern cities like New York and looked forward to the more modern concerns of advancement at the expense of humanity.

The huge acclaim that greeted *Metropolis* suggested that the science fiction genre would become a powerful vehicle for serious contemplation of society. Apart from *Things to Come* (1936), however, there would be a wait of over 20 years before the genre's possibilities were fully explored. The Hollywood reaction to *Metropolis* was the production of David Butler's *Just Imagine* (1930), a science fiction/musical hybrid. Its poor reception contributed to the fact that no large-scale Hollywood science fiction film was made until the 1950s; musicals and gangster films were to dominate the decade after *Metropolis'* release, in Hollywood at least. Until that time, elements of science fiction genre conventions emerged in films like *Frankenstein* (1931) and *The Invisible Man* (1933), but studio bosses deemed its commercial value to be limited.

SELECT FILMOGRAPHY OF MAIN PRODUCERS AND CAST

Fritz Lang, 1890–1976, Director

Dr Mabuse, der Spieler, 1922

Die Nibelungen: Siegfried, 1924

Die Nibelungen: Kriemhilds Rache, 1924

Metropolis, 1927

Spione, 1928

Frau im Mond, 1929

M , 1931

Das Testament des Dr. Mabuse, 1933

Liliom, 1934

Fury, 1936

You Only Live Once, 1937

You and Me, 1938

The Return of Frank James, 1940

Western Union, 1941

Man Hunt, 1941

Hangmen Also Die, 1943

Ministry of Fear, 1944

The Woman in the Window, 1944

Scarlet Street, 1945

Cloak and Dagger, 1946

Secret Beyond the Door, 1948

House by the River, 1950

American Guerrilla in the Philippines, 1950

Rancho Notorious, 1952

Clash by Night, 1952

The Blue Gardenia, 1953

The Big Heat, 1953

Human Desire, 1954

Moonfleet, 1955

While the City Sleeps, 1956

Beyond a Reasonable Doubt, 1957

Der Tiger von Eschnapur, 1959

Das indische Grabmal, 1959

Die 1000 Augen des Dr. Mabuse, 1960

Erich Pommer, 1889–1966, Producer

Das Cabinet des Dr Caligari, 1920

Dr Mabuse, der Spieler, 1922

Der Letzte Mann, 1924

Herr Tartüff, 1926

Metropolis, 1927

Faust, 1926

Der Blaue Engel, 1930

Jamaica Inn, 1939

Kinder, Mutter und ein General, 1955

Karl W Freund, 1890–1969, Director of Photography

Der Letze Mann, 1924

Herr Tartüff, 1926

Metropolis, 1927

Dracula, 1931

The Good Earth, 1937

Pride and Prejudice, 1940

Blossoms in the Dust, 1941

Tortilla Flat, 1942

Key Largo, 1948

LINKS TO OTHER FILMS

Frankenstein (1931)

The scientist, Rotwang, bears some resemblance to Frankenstein, creator of the monster in this film. They are both obsessed with creating life where none exists and the creations in both films embark on a rampage which will end in their sacrificial deaths - scapegoats for the evils in society.

Modern Times (1936)

Charlie Chaplin's film deals with the manner in which an industrialised age removes the humanity out of society, rendering it a depersonalised and brutal world where only a few live in luxury. As such, it closely mirrors the dystopian future detailed in *Metropolis*, addressing similar issues of community and inequality. Chaplin's factory worker is force-fed by a machine early in the film and his work is laborious and repetitive, just as we see in *Metropolis*, which eventually leads to a mental breakdown.

Blade Runner (1982)

Although linked by their science fiction generic conventions, and the shared view of a dystopian future, *Blade Runner* and *Metropolis* are also connected through their visualisation of the future. Production designer Lawrence G. Paull's and art director David Snyder's realisation of a city in the future is dominated by the enormous structures that dwarf and suffocate the humans who scuttle

around in the darkness below. They are indicative of a society that has lost its connection with humanity and stand like pagan gods, a symbol of progress that has become perverted and distorted. *Metropolis'* world works in the same way and echoes the storyline where humans try to rediscover their humanity.

REPRESENTATION

The future

Metropolis, like many other science fiction films, presents a window on the world and society in the future, and often echoes the concerns of contemporary life. The future, as is often the case in this genre's films, is full of uncertainty, tyranny, and horror, and is characterised by the dehumanisation of those in the community. There are very few instances in SF cinema where the future is actually *better* than the present, and the problems are often caused by human greed and its tendency to self-destruct.

Many Hollywood films of this genre have followed this pattern: *Planet of the Apes* (1968) and *Logan's Run* (1974) both chart a dystopian future based on the consequences of human folly. Topics such as a nuclear war and over-population respectively all help tie these two films with current moral panics and legitimate concerns. And so it is with *Metropolis*, a film which is over 80 years old, but with images and themes that represent a future that is our 'now' and which also represented a world in the 1920s that was on the edge of a precipice.

'Metropolis emerged at a time of political and economic uncertainty during the Weimar period in German (1919–33)... This attempt to set up a liberal democracy basically failed with the rise of Adolf Hitler and the Nazi Party in 1933... Lang's answer to the problems of the period was concentrated upon the relations between working and ruling classes. Rather than depicting an entirely alternative world, the city of Metropolis can therefore be seen as an exaggeration of a known world.' Christine Cornea, Science Fiction Cinema, Edinburgh University Press, 2007

'The 'social question' – whether technology would liberate or enslave; where would the class struggle lead – was certainly in the ether... The Czech word 'robot', meaning industrialized slave labourer, had recently been coined, and a central theme of Metropolis was whether the performance of repetitive manual tasks could dispense with human workers all together...' Christopher Frayling, Mad, Bad and Dangerous?, Reaktion, 2006

KEY SCENE TEXTUAL ANALYSIS

The workers and the machines (6)

The long shot of Fredersen walking beneath the machines conveys their immense size and the insignificance of man in relation to them; the humans are tiny, like barnacles on an enormous hull. Much of the foreground is in shadow, conveying an ominous quality, and the topmost extremities of these convoluted structures are unseen, suggesting untold distances and dwarfing the imagination of the ordinary man. It is a dystopia, as seen in many future SF films, where man is subordinate to machine. The workers are ant-like next to their metal masters, and make jerky movements as they fulfil their roles, moving like instinctive, but not sentient, beings.

The medium shot of Fredersen allows the audience to view his reaction and recoil more clearly as he sees the controlling machine. The cut to a long shot of this colossal machine/beast suggests its power. Six men are seen on each side, confined in little compartments, servicing this monster that blows steam from many points. The *mise-en-scène* underlines the absolute dominance of the machine, its massive bolts and steel construction anchoring the structure, its mighty pistons relentless and unforgiving.

A medium long shot frames a part of the hard, resolute structure in the foreground with the workers performing their ballet of subservience in the background. Succeeding shots of the workers reinforce this filmic space dominated by the machine until we return to the awe- and fear-inspiring long shot.

Until this point the figures have been dehumanised by their positioning within the frame, but now we see a medium shot of one worker and then a medium close-up, detailing their private agonies in this unfeeling environment beyond the comprehension of the individual. A conundrum of levers, switches and dials lie in front of him, and he is increasingly overcome by their complexity and meaninglessness. A gauge rises relentlessly and he clings to the controls, but they return no love or explanation; the high angle medium close-up underlines his subordinate position next to the machine; he slips, and the close-up of the hand on the cold metal wheel reiterates the contrast between frail humanity and powerful machine.

The long shot again shows the workers as they become more frantic in their attempts to appease the monstrous machine. Eventually the liquid in the gauge reaches a critical level and the machine unleashes its wrath on them; blasts of hot steam scold them and explosions catapult them from its sides. Fredersen is thrown to the floor by the explosion and in his mind he sees the machine for what it is, an all-consuming beast, Moloch, the name for a god or a sacrifice.

The machine does now dissolve into a pre-Christian statue and the analogy is emphasised with the workers now appearing as slaves being led up a giant staircase to be thrown as sacrifices into the its gaping mouth; the proletariat as fodder for the good of the few is clearly represented. The pistons can also be glimpsed within the smoke emitted from the abyss, directly linking this hallucination with the message that this future society oils its machines with the blood of the masses. A complex optical effect now shows the structure as half-machine and half-statue with the workers now plodding inexorably towards their fate.

and recoil presents a rebirth into a new mindset of understanding.

The extended long shot of the machine again helps to emphasise that no individual suffering will interfere with the machine's unquenchable thirst for human self-negation; but the cut back to Fredersen's upright figure suggests his ability to stand against this tyranny.

As he leaves in a chauffeured limousine the audience sees the rotten fruits of this labour: the city of the future. A series of models, animation, mattes and layered opticals portrays a vertical city with criss-crossing elevated roads surrounded by skyscrapers. A few people march in ranks (the workers), but the rest are transported by a variety of means. The common denominator is that all are cut off from each other; the future world is

The cuts back to Fredersen underline that he is not just hallucinating but undergoing an epiphany as he realises that his life of comfort comes at the expense of others' enforced sacrifice. The shots of him are uniformly-lit, showing his figure strongly against a plain background; he is suffering as he watches but the *mise-en-scène* suggests an uncomplicated existence where he is free as an individual and not in thrall to the machine.

The cut back to the machine shows the reality of the machine as bodies are carried from it and new figures emerge to take up position, ensuring that its continuity of repression is maintained.

The long shot of Fredersen frames the silhouetted figures of workers being carried away. They are without identity while his brightly-lit figure in the background reveals the contrast between his vitality and their submission; his reactions throughout this sequence do suggest his pain, and his writhing

relentless, dehumanising, regimented for most, and heartless in its grand design. The series of static shots portray this world with clarity; the camera is as detached as each of the vehicles that transport the multitudes around this vision of 'progress'.

The audience is required to watch in awe; it is an incredible and complex visual feast and we are almost seduced by its modernity and vision. But it has been preceded by a scene depicting its cruel underbelly and so the vision should be tainted for us, just as Fredersen has had his privileged existence soured by the truth.

Creation (21)

A brief note about the laboratory scene, where the machine-man is transformed into a Maria lookalike. It is the quintessential SF mad scientist/ creature scene and its many conventions have been copied and parodied by numerous films. These include:

- The plethora of bubbling glass containers, switches, levers and electrical circuits are the blueprint for future filmic laboratories, most famously used in James Whale's *Frankenstein* and Curt Siodmak's *Donovan's Brain* (1942) – and parodied in Mel Brooks' *Young Frankenstein* (1974).

- Rottwang has a gloved hand, wild hair and demented expression, the benchmark for many a mad scientist. Later manifestations include the eponymous *Dr. Strangelove* (1964) and Dr. Emmett Brown in *Back To The Future* (1985).

- The creature is an iconic creation, a robot that is both sinister and sensual. Its transformation into Maria is executed in ingenious fashion with the use of animation and a serious camera's beady eye on the moment of creation. The most obvious parallel is the monster in *Frankenstein*, and there have been numerous parodies of female creations, including John Hughes' *Weird Science* (1985).

Things To Come

KEY FACTS

Release Date: 1936

Country of Origin: UK

Running Time: 113 minutes

PRODUCTION NOTES

Production Company

London Film Productions

Distributor

United Artists Corporation

Budget

£300,000 (estimated)

SYNOPSIS

The story opens in Everytown, circa 1940, which is on the verge of a war with an unidentified enemy. The war begins and the town is devastated by aerial bombardment as, it seems, is the rest of the world. From the ashes of this destruction rises a new society, bereft of technology and resembling the medieval world; it is in chaos and beset by a disease known as the wandering sickness. One man, the Chief, has his own brand of law and order and subjugates the population.

At this point the date is 1970, some 30 years since the beginning of the war, and the Chief still harbours dreams of getting his biplanes to take to the air again and continue the fight. A plane, as if from the future, lands near the city and its pilot, John Cabal, explains that a new order has been created, founded by scientists and dedicated to peaceful co-existence. The Chief fears for his position and imprisons Cabal, later getting him to repair his biplanes in preparation for war. A mechanic escapes in one of the restored planes and flies to the scientists' base, where he tells them what has happened to Cabal. The airmen scientists, known as 'Wings over the World', fly en masse to Everytown and drop sleeping gas on its inhabitants; the chief is the only fatality.

There then follows the passage of many years as the scientists undertake their rebuilding of society, creating incredible structures through technological innovations. The year reaches 2036 and Everytown is now a new superstructure built beneath the ground with Cabal's grandson as a leading light. At the launch of a rocket to the moon, some of the population, led by a sculptor, start to complain about more technological progress and they try to stop the expedition. They are unsuccessful and Cabal delivers a speech stating that humanity can only progress through greater endeavour.

HISTORICAL CONTEXT

Things to Come appeared as part of the film mogul Alexander Korda's assault on Hollywood domination of film production in the 1930s; it appeared after the success of his earlier *The Private Life of Henry VIII* (1933) and was the most expensive British film of its day, made in part at the new Denham Studios in Buckinghamshire and Isleworth Studios in West London.

It is a film of ideas and stands alone not only in Britain, but also in Hollywood, as a serious science fiction film of that era. Its closest relations were the Universal films of the early 1930s (*Frankenstein*, *The Invisible Man*), but this was science fiction in its purest form, a genre with its roots in the beginnings of cinema itself. The medium itself was the stuff of science fiction, and it provided the ideal vessel for flights of fancy and conjectures into the future. There was certainly nothing approaching its scale and ambition in Britain until Kubrick and Arthur C. Clarke brought their ideas for *2001: A Space Odyssey* (1968) to Shepperton Studios in London in the late 1960s. It fed off contemporary intellectual forays of gazing into the future, notably Aldous Huxley's novel *Brave New World* (1932), and, of course, the works of H.G. Wells.

It was not until the 1950s that Hollywood would see the possibilities of science fiction to reflect society's thoughts and mores, and *Things to Come* acts as the bridge from early science fiction films like *Metropolis* to these later outings. It is a film that resolutely refuses to let the histrionics and perceived superficiality of this genre, perpetuated by the Saturday morning film serials of *Flash Gordon*, to deflect it from its intellectual course.

Things to Come seems incredibly prophetic in many ways; its vision of a global war and the wholesale destruction of towns by aerial bombing would become a reality only three years after its release. Its depiction of gas attacks obviously references the First World War, but looks forward to its extensive use in later wars by future generations. Also, its 'wandering sickness' does look back to diseases like the plague but foreshadows the after-effects of nuclear warfare and current panics about 'superbugs' and bird flu.

Of course, the vision originally lies with H.G. Wells, whose 1933 novel *The Shape of Things to Come* was the source text for the film (as well as his *The Outline of History*), and Wells himself wrote the screenplay. The Nazis were in the ascendancy and the Spanish Civil War had begun the same year as the film's release, and the film reflects the fears of many who saw the gathering clouds of conflict. Wells' vision contemplated a war that lasted for over 30 years. Although the Second World War ended in 1945, it could be argued that its conclusion was just the beginning of other conflicts which continue to this day. The actual vision of the future which arrives by 2036 in the film is a utopia that is based on a radical rethinking of the structures of human society. This is a powerful vision, based on freedom and peace, a vision fixed in the hearts and minds of some Republicans in the Spanish Civil War, comprising both the Spanish and the International Brigades, a broad range of like-minded people from around the world, united by a common cause and echoing the scientist airmen who join together to fight war.

SELECT FILMOGRAPHY OF MAIN PRODUCERS AND CAST
William Cameron Menzies, 1896–1957, Director, Art Director

Always Goodbye, 1931

The Spider, 1931

Almost Married, 1932

Chandu the Magician, 1932

I Loved You Wednesday, 1933

Wharf Angel, 1934

Things to Come, 1936

The Green Cockatoo, 1937

Address Unknown, 1944

Drums in the Deep South, 1951

The Whip Hand, 1951

Invaders from Mars, 1953

The Maze, 1953

Alexander Korda, 1893–1956, Producer, Director

The Private Life of Henry VIII, 1933

The Scarlet Pimpernel, 1934

Sanders of the River, 1935

Things to Come, 1936

Rembrandt, 1936

The Man Who Could Work Miracles, 1936

I, Claudius, 1937

The Four Feathers, 1939

The Spy in Black, 1939

The Thief of Bagdad, 1940

That Hamilton Woman, 1941

Jungle Book, 1942

Perfect Strangers, 1945

An Ideal Husband, 1947

Anna Karenina, 1948

Georges Périnal, 1897–1965, Director of Photography

The Private Life of Henry VIII, 1933

The Private Life of Don Juan, 1934

Sanders of the River, 1935

Things to Come, 1936

I, Claudius, 1937

The Four Feathers, 1939

The Life and Death of Colonel Blimp, 1943

Perfect Strangers, 1945

An Ideal Husband, 1947

The Fallen Idol, 1948

The Mudlark, 1950

Saint Joan, 1957

Bonjour Tristesse, 1958

Tom Thumb, 1958

Oscar Wilde, 1960

Muir Matheson, 1911–75, Musical Director, Composer, Conductor

The Private Life of Don Juan, 1934

The Scarlet Pimpernel, 1934

Sanders of the River, 1935

Things to Come, 1936

Dark Journey, 1937

The Divorce of Lady X, 1938

The Four Feathers, 1939

The Thief of Bagdad, 1940

49th Parallel, 1941

Fires Were Started, 1943

This Happy Breed, 1944

Henry V, 1944

The History of Mr. Polly, 1949

The Wooden Horse, 1950

The Sound Barrier, 1952

Reach for the Sky, 1956

Becket, 1964

Raymond Massey, 1896–1983, Actor

The Old Dark House, 1932

The Scarlet Pimpernel, 1934

Things to Come, 1936

The Prisoner of Zenda, 1937

49th Parallel, 1941

Reap the Wild Wind, 1942

Arsenic and Old Lace, 1944

A Matter of Life and Death, 1946

The Fountainhead, 1949

East of Eden, 1955

The Naked and the Dead, 1957

Ralph Richardson, 1902–83, Actor

The Ghoul, 1933

Things to Come, 1936

The Citadel, 1938

The Divorce of Lady X, 1938

The Four Feathers, 1939

The Silver Fleet, 1943

The Fallen Idol, 1948

Anna Karenina, 1948

The Heiress, 1949

The Sound Barrier, 1952

Richard III, 1955

Our Man in Havana, 1959

Exodus, 1960

Long Day's Journey Into Night, 1962

Dr Zhivago, 1965

Khartoum, 1966

Battle of Britain, 1969

Oh! What a Lovely War, 1969

The Looking Glass War, 1969

O Lucky Man!, 1973

Time Bandits, 1981

Greystoke - The Legend of Tarzan, Lord of the Apes, 1984

LINKS TO OTHER FILMS

Lost Horizon (1937)

Frank Capra's film version of the James Hilton novel depicts a society in the Himalayas named Shangri-La, a utopian society protected from the troubles of the outside world. It is a place of peace and harmony, much like that envisaged in *Things to Come*.

2001 (1968)

Things to Come shares with Kubrick's film a boldness of vision and a commitment to forging a *mise-en-scène* that would underpin its intellectualisation of the now and of the future. They also share a special effects designer in the form of Wally Veevers, who helped secure each director's vision of the future.

Logan's Run (1976)

Michael Anderson's film presents a utopian society where everyone appears to be content. The city housing the population is a futuristic creation reminiscent of the structures in twenty-first century Everytown. The two films diverge in their depiction of utopia: although there is some disharmony at the end of *Things to Come*, it is obvious that the film-makers want to stress the positives of technology whereas *Logan's Run* depicts a future world without humanity, where forced euthanasia is institutionalised.

Thunderbirds (2004)

The film is based on Gerry and Sylvia Anderson's television series of the same name, and charts the activities of a family of young men, led by their father, who are dedicated to preserving harmony on Earth. Much like the group of airmen in *Things to Come* they fly around the world in response to calls for help; for 'Wings over the World' call 'International Rescue'.

REPRESENTATION

Utopia

Sir Thomas More wrote *Utopia* in 1516, but the idea, in various forms, has been around for a very long time. The original utopia, The Garden of Eden, is the template for all utopias, and, of course, signals the inherent problem with a utopian vision: humankind. From Adam and Eve onwards, humanity's meddling and grubby little fingers have muddied the crystal clear waters of utopia.

Things to Come is unusual in that it champions technological innovation as humanity's salvation, whereas many other visions of the future where technologies become dominant are seen to be deeply flawed. Films such as Francois Truffaut's *Fahrenheit 461* (1966), Michael Radford's *1984* (1984), Marco Brambillia's *Demolition Man* (1993) and Alex Proya's *I, Robot* (2004) all present a superficial future which is tainted by human corruption, greed and cruelty, where technology is often promoted at the expense of human compassion. However, Menzies' film ends with Cabal's plea for technological advancement as a means of escape from chaos and a move towards utopia; it is those who seek to destroy the machines, the Luddites, who are seen as the threat to a utopian vision.

The City of the future

The city that Everytown becomes in 2036 was the subject of much debate upon the film's release in 1936. It was a decade in which thoughts of the future were never more focused; the First World War had wrought a cataclysmic destruction of society, and writers, artists and thinkers of the day put forward their visions of a possible future. They imagined a new world order and debated both the intellectual and physical possibilities that lay ahead. Everytown was the result of many minds: H.G. Wells was the originator of the vision, but it was one that arrived onto the screen with the help of many notable talents of the era. Menzies, of course, was an acclaimed art director, whose sets on *The Thief of Bagdad* (1924) were widely celebrated for their innovation, looking both towards German expressionism and modernist design. Alexander Korda made contributions as well, but it was his brother, Vincent, as settings designer, who brought many of the ideas to life. Added to this wealth of creative zeal were the Hungarian artist/designer, Laszlo Moholy-Nagy and champion of modernist architecture, Le Corbusier.

Into this creative melting pot were poured ideas that were not just design concepts, but based on intellectual debate about the nature of society at that time and in the future. It drew largely on the ideas associated with modernism, embracing the modern in all its forms, a world where constant innovation through technology and thought attempted to grapple with the rapidly-changing world. The romanticism of the nineteenth century was replaced with deconstruction and rebuilding in mathematical terms. It flowered not just in intellectual thought but in the buildings of Le Corbusier and the paintings of Mondrian, and into everyday objects like cars. Whilst the extravagant flourishes of romanticism were rejected, modernism did, however, stretch back in time towards primitive art, its shapes and lines resurrected in modern metal. One prominent design movement to emerge from this was Art Deco, which can be identified in buildings such as the spire of the Chrysler Building in New York or the liner RMS Queen Mary, berthed in California. Art Deco furniture design also strongly influences pieces that can be seen in Everytown.

'It captures the anxieties and hopes of 1930's Britain perfectly, chillingly forecasting the blitz that would descend upon London only four years after its release.' R. Barton Palmer, *1001 Movies You Must See Before You Die*, Cassell Illustrated, London, 2007

'It is a spectacular production wherein Wells takes his 'science versus art' preoccupations into the future.' Chris Wicking *Time Out Film Guide 14th Ed.*, Time Out Guides Ltd., London, 2006

KEY SCENE TEXTUAL ANALYSIS

Destruction of civilisation (11:55)

The locale is Everytown, which universalises this story of humanity's propensity for self-destruction. The montage that follows has strong echoes of Russian film-maker Sergei Eisenstein's use of montage in films like *The Battleship Potemkin* (1925), where juxtaposition of images create an intensity and level of meaning that transcends their surface and isolated meaning. The explosions and chaos are not only brutal but seem to contain a power that suggests that this destruction/ deconstruction is necessary before a new order can be established. It also carries the weight of German expressionism, full of shadows and menace, reminiscent of the films of F.W. Murnau, Robert Wiene and Fritz Lang, a reminder of the 1914-18 conflict and a vision of the war to come.

A father bids farewell to his son as he goes off to 'do his bit' in the war effort; the dark of night and mist turn the figures into little more than silhouettes as the man walks off, banging his case as if it is a drum. Their talk is light-hearted and upbeat, suggesting the naïvety of those going to war. The boy follows his father as he marches away and the banging of the case is not the diegetic sound expected but the non-diegetic sound of a marching band, adding a more serious and sombre tone which matches the *mise-en-scène*. As the boy marches back into shot there is a dissolve to enormous shadows of marching soldiers projected behind the tiny figure of the boy who parades along the bottom of the frame. His innocence and the threat of the impending conflict are highlighted as well as the threat to all life, even this young and vulnerable boy. The music also swells with violins and creates an atmosphere of momentum and inevitable progress towards conflict. The boy marches back and forth, and the scene dissolves back to reality, the previous shot now obviously a stylisation, a visual motif for the spectre of war.

The shots of panic that follow are full of dynamic movement and rapidly cut together in time with the dramatic and urgent music. The power of the war is all-consuming with armoured cars wiping the screen and crashing into frame, destroying the equilibrium and balance of the scene; the camera is low-angled at times to make the action seem even more threatening. There are also high angle shots which emphasise the chaos as the people run around like frightened animals; they are crammed together as they try to escape into the Underground, filling the frame and highlighting the fact that, try as they might, the people will ultimately be trapped by the rapidly approaching threat.

The audience sees parts of running bodies, all immersed in chiaroscuro lighting, adding to the sense of panic and dislocation. A solitary hat falls onto the pavement - a symbol of gentility to demonstrate that society is beginning to crumble under the onslaught. Panic turns into violence as people push past soldiers and shots are repeated to underline that these people are trapped in spite of the fact that they are running wildly within the frame. The montage juxtaposes this chaos with the preparation of the soldiers and the pace of editing quickens, emphasising the drama of the sequence and leading up to the climatic firing of the big gun. This image is repeated, sandwiching that of a close-up of a man's face, his eyes visible between two dark shadows; the juxtaposition of shots highlights that the man's destiny lies with war, that he is trapped and terrified by this brutish and inhuman force.

The diegetic sound of explosions and heavy gun fire now dominate, a blanket of sound to illustrate war's ability to disorientate and obliterate normality, both visually and aurally. The first point of destruction on the ground is the cinema, its signage exploding; it is a direct affront to the audience, an ironic comment that the very fabric of voyeurism is destroyed. Cataclysmic explosions occur in the background through the use of miniatures and back-projection in both the background and foreground, surrounding the crowds in debris, the darkness adding to the sense of terror. A department store explodes, hands frantically grasp for gas masks from the soldiers, and a low angle shot of a careering army vehicle, masked by fallen debris, add to the mayhem. The familiar sight of an ordinary bus racing through the streets accentuates the sense that this is a surreal experience in a very real place; the cut to the front of the bus with a disfigured driver slumped in the window and the forlorn spectacle of a woman walking dazed in the background herald a final sequence where the carnage begins and people are blown apart, not just buildings.

An army vehicle is blown from the road and slides towards the low angle camera, again drawing the audience into the action. The camera tracks slowly as people scramble over a plethora of ordinary objects, from a pram to a bed, as the prized possessions of life become the detritus of death. There is a lingering shot of the disfigured body seen earlier, its eerie visage a disturbing image of the effect of war: it brings death and also suggests its dehumanising effect.

The explosions continue, but the people begin to disappear, obliterated by the bombardment. Solitary bodies barely move and the *mise-en-*

Nicolas Roeg's *Don't Look Now*, made almost 40 years later). Cradled by the earth he is a victim of unspeakable atrocities perpetrated by other humans. The final four shots of the shells of buildings and the fires raging are a hellish vision of complete annihilation, devoid of humanity and hope. The sequence is given an even greater sense of menace and hopelessness by the fact that the agents of death are never seen; their invisibility strengthens the idea that mankind has lost touch with its humanity.

Construction of civilisation (1:01:08)

The scene of Everytown's reconstruction along modernist lines tries to present new architectural forms, spatial solutions and manifestations of new thought and a new world order. The montage serves a similar function to Everytown's destruction; it is reminiscent of Eisenstein's work, the montage

scène is dominated by destruction as the sound of explosions continues, albeit muted, and the eerie smog of gas clings to the ground. The atmosphere is chilling and illustrates the power of war to obliterate what was once vibrant.

The pace of the editing slows in order to match the lack of movement and underline the devastating effects of the attack; we see another glimpse of the cinema sign, a reminder that the audience's world has also been consumed by war. The final pan down from a fractured wall through the debris to the exposed head of a young boy is devastating; his fresh face and curly hair give him a vitality and innocence that is shocking because he is dead, buried like just another piece of debris (the image of a dead child is unusual in film but carries with it an extremely powerful resonance; the effect here is akin to that of the drowned child seen in

creating a powerful and positive outpouring of constructive effort, counterbalancing the earlier destructive forces.

The opening long shot is one of Everytown in ruins. The camera pans to the right to focus on a mountainside; the audience sees the difference between the annihilated city and the organic landscape - a natural landscape that speaks of rebirth and possibilities. The montage of construction that ensues is a mixture of live action, miniatures and back projection, creating a world of construction and endeavour. Firstly, a drilling machine dominates the frame as it pounds the rock, carving a new world. The dramatic orchestral score is underpinned by a metallic clanking sound to simulate the use of technology to forge new paths for civilisation. The transition into a world of white, clean-lined and symmetrical structures contrasts greatly with the earlier scenes of destruction. Here is something that is at the cutting-edge of human knowledge and the camera slowly tracks along the gigantic machines and constructions to emphasise their grandeur. The non-diegetic music is both strident and positive, underpinning the vision of progress. The humans, encased in futuristic suits and propelled on a variety of gliding machines, are shown to be in harmony with the environment and the work that they are orchestrating.

Humans move in and out of shot, central and integral to this regeneration; where once they destroyed, now there is control and creativity. The imagery is almost abstract at times, a sign of its connection to the workings of the mind; the sheer amount of imagery, which dissolves from one shot to another in a seamless flow, is like a stream of

the machines, rather than being enslaved as in *Metropolis*.

consciousness, a manifestation of thought, word and deed. The non-diegetic music, composed by Arthur Bliss, was arranged first and then the images edited to fit. This approach accentuates the power of the music and increases its importance to the overall design of the sequence. As the final concrete images of construction are shown we return to a shot of the natural world, with the caption '2036 Everytown'. The ruined cityscape, an image of man's folly, is gone, and the earlier panning shot is repeated. The mountain is still there, but now a new, calm city has been built within it. Humanity is, at last, part of the world around it rather than being an anomaly.

The resulting creation is full of light and, by extension, hope; a vast womb-like structure which nurtures humanity's advancement. It is a serene and balanced beauty, where people are served by

A Connecticut Yankee in King Arthur's Court

KEY FACTS

Release Date: 1949

Country of Origin: USA

Running Time: 106 minutes

PRODUCTION NOTES

Production Company

Paramount Pictures

Distributor

Paramount Pictures

SYNOPSIS

Hank Martin, a blacksmith from Connecticut, arrives at Pendragon Castle. He seems to recognise the interior and contradicts the tour guide on certain historical points. A necklace in his possession matches one worn by a lady in a medieval portrait. He then talks to Lord Pendragon, to whom he tells his story of time travel. The flashback recalls events in Hank's past whilst working as a blacksmith in 1912 Connecticut. Whilst out riding in a storm he is knocked off his horse, and when he awakens he finds himself in medieval England. He is captured by Sir Sagramore and brought to Camelot, the home of King Arthur, Merlin and the Knights of the Round Table. He is ridiculed for his strange appearance and Merlin, in particular, takes a strong dislike to him.

After being sentenced to burn at the stake Hank manages to extricate himself from being killed when he takes advantage of a solar eclipse, pretending that it is his work. He manages to ingratiate himself further into the king's favour, and slowly starts to introduce his modern ways into the court in such areas as the music played and the way that they dance. He is eventually challenged to a jousting competition by Sir Lancelot, but Hank outwits the knight by using cowboy methods. Throughout this time Hank and a beautiful lady of the court, Alisande la Carteloise, have become close friends, but she is unhappy with his treatment of Sir Lancelot. He asks the king for a blacksmith's shop, and he sets about recreating modern technology, including a gun. Merlin tries to get rid of Hank and kidnaps Alisande, Hank comes to the rescue but is knocked over and returns to the future. His story at an end, Lord Pendragon (who looks like King Arthur) suggests that he take a walk in the castle where he meets the old man's niece, who looks exactly like Alisande, and so begins his courtship anew.

HISTORICAL CONTEXT

For a war-weary America Bing Crosby was the perfect antidote: wholesome, laid-back, funny and able to send Middle America to sleep, happy with his lullaby singing voice. He had consolidated his popularity in the 1940s with massive hits like the *Road* series of films with Bob Hope, beginning with *Road to Singapore* in 1940, and the extremely popular *Going My Way* in 1944. His films were sweet and sentimental, a million miles from the horrors of war.

A Connecticut Yankee in King Arthur's Court, based on a Mark Twain novel of 1889, is like all of Crosby's films, in that he basically plays the image that he perpetrated on screen and off, that of being laconic and good-humoured. A striking aspect of the 1940s is the dearth of science fiction films being made, considering the enormous output and appeal they had in the following decade. The 1930's science fiction output had been dominated by serials such as *Buck Rogers* and *Flash Gordon*, but apart from some very minor B-movies and serials, the 1940s were a barren time. Perhaps the realities of the war had caught up with anything science fiction writing or film-making could produce; people either wanted versions of the real world (war films or film noir) or escape into the world of musicals.

There was no room for science fiction and all the big directors and stars stayed away from this downmarket genre, just as Westerns had suffered in the 1930s. It would take a key film or films to revive the genre; *Stagecoach* (1939) breathed new life into the Western and films like *Destination Moon* (1950) and *The Day the Earth Stood Still* (1951) did the same for science fiction. The new scientific discoveries, particularly the dropping of the atom bomb, in the 1940s paved the way for the films of

the next decade, whilst the horrific events of the 1940s resembled the science fiction prophecies of just a decade earlier in *Things To Come*. *A Connecticut Yankee in King Arthur's Court* is, then, something of an anomaly with its time-travelling hero, but dressed up as a Bing Crosby vehicle, its science fiction element was palatable to a 1940's audience.

SELECT FILMOGRAPHY OF MAIN PRODUCERS AND CAST

Tay Garnett, 1894–1977, Director, Screenwriter, Producer

One Way Passage, 1932

China Seas, 1935

She Couldn't Take It, 1935

Professional Soldier, 1935

Love is News, 1937

Slave Ship, 1937

Stand-In, 1937

Joy of Living, 1938

Trade Winds, 1938

Eternally Yours, 1939

Seven Sinners, 1940

Bataan, 1943

The Cross of Lorraine, 1943

Mrs. Parkington, 1944

The Postman Always Rings Twice, 1946

Wild Harvest, 1947

A Connecticut Yankee in King Arthur's Court, 1949

The Black Knight, 1954

A Terrible Beauty, 1960

Cattle King, 1963

The Delta Force, 1970

Bing Crosby, 1903-77, Actor

Anything Goes, 1936

Rhythm on the Range, 1936

Pennies from Heaven, 1936

Dr. Rhythm, 1938

Road to Singapore, 1940

Rhythm on the River, 1940

Road to Zanzibar, 1941

Holiday Inn, 1942

Road to Morocco, 1942

Star Spangled Rhythm, 1942

Going My Way, 1944

Here Come the Waves, 1944

The Bells of St. Mary's, 1945

Road to Utopia, 1946

Blue Skies, 1946

Road to Rio, 1947

The Emperor Waltz, 1948

A Connecticut Yankee in King Arthur's Court, 1949

The Adventures of Ichabod and Mr. Toad, 1949

Mr. Music, 1950

Road to Bali, 1952

White Christmas, 1954

The Country Girl, 1954

Anything Goes, 1956

High Society, 1956

The Road to Hong Kong, 1962

Robin and the 7 Hoods, 1964

Stagecoach, 1966

Rhonda Fleming, 1923, Actress

Spellbound, 1945

The Spiral Staircase, 1945

Out of the Past, 1947

A Connecticut Yankee in King Arthur's Court, 1949

The Great Lover, 1949

Cry Danger, 1951

Serpent of the Nile, 1953

Inferno, 1953

Slightly Scarlet, 1956

The Killer is Loose, 1956

While the City Sleeps, 1956

Gunfight at the O.K. Corral, 1957

The Buster Keaton Story, 1957

Home Before Dark, 1958

The Big Circus, 1959

LINKS TO OTHER FILMS

The Adventures of Robin Hood (1938)

Michael Curtiz and William Keighley's film is the template for lavish and colourful films depicting 'Merrie England'. The detailed sets and rich Technicolor photography imbue the film with a Hollywood version of authenticity, elements which can be seen in *A Connecticut Yankee*.

The Time Machine (1960)

Mark Twain's novel of time travel, upon which *A Connecticut Yankee in King Arthur's Court* is based, precedes H.G. Wells' story by some six years, but it was Wells' emphasis on the action of time travel that distinguishes it from Twain's tale which does not concern itself with time travel as such, rather its consequences. The film of Wells' novel certainly focuses on the mode of travel and revels in its use of special effects.

Back to the Future series (1985/89/90)

This series of films takes some of the ideas from *A Connecticut Yankee in King Arthur's Court* in that Marty McFly travels back in time and introduces elements from the future into the past, allowing the film to make wry comments about contemporary life and the past.

A Knight's Tale (2001)

Brian Helgeland's film introduces a number of anachronistic moments into this tale of knights, although it does not have the excuse of a time-travelling character. Scenes such as the dance and the tournament introduce modern modes of design and behaviour, a device which has become known as 'steampunk', where modern inventions and behaviour is transposed to earlier times. It is also seen in films such as the science fiction Western, *Wild Wild West* (1999), directed by Barry Sonnenfield.

REPRESENTATION

England

Hollywood has represented England in a fairly stereotypical way for much of its history. It was the land of knights and maidens, whether it was the stories of Robin Hood and Maid Marian, or King Arthur; if not medieval, it was the foggy streets of old London Town in Sherlock Holmes films. The world was as phoney as the South American 'Banana Republics' that Hollywood also loved to create. English characters populated Hollywood films, either as villains, mad scientists or eccentric characters. For American audiences England was a theme park of stock characters as familiar as Mickey Mouse or Bugs Bunny, and just as two-dimensional.

A Connecticut Yankee in King Arthur's Court taps into this representation of England, a world of exciting adventures, where heroes and villains brush shoulders. It is certainly not interested in presenting an authentic version of medieval life; it's as close to the real medieval England as Disney's *Robin Hood* (1973), but then that's not the purpose of the film. Bing Crosby croons his way through 'Merrie England' and proves that modern American savvy can outwit dull old English minds. It is a romp through history, and England is there to provide the audience with a colourful backdrop, not to explore how awful life was for most of the population. One filthy peasant in *Monty Python and the Holy Grail* (1975) suggests that the knight who has just passed them must be a king because 'He hasn't got shit all

over him'; this is a world away from Bing and his friends, a group of Americans in the main, playing at being English in England, but not too hard.

> 'It's a highly amiable affair, enlivened by lush technicolor photography, mindlessly amusing humour, and a marvellous performance by Bendix.' Geoff Andrew, *Time Out Film Guide 14th Ed.*, Time Out Guides Ltd., London, 2006

> 'An amusingly carefree, lavishly mounted Bing Crosby vehicle... and Tay Garnett's direction is smooth and well paced.' Eds. Ken Fox & Maitland McDonagh, *The Tenth Virgin Film Guide*, Virgin Books, London, 2001

KEY SCENE TEXTUAL ANALYSIS

Hank's first experiences in the medieval world (5/6)

A bump on the head initiates Hank Martin's time travelling adventure to King Arthur's kingdom; the lavish Technicolor photography lends the sequence, and indeed the whole film, a lushness and lustre that befit a tale of pageantry and chivalry. It is a scene of anachronisms; firstly, early twentieth century Hank is dressed in decidedly 1940's mode, and the anachronistic approach to life in the middle ages is evident when Hank and Sir Sagramore enter the castle. The initial medium close-up of Hank, accompanied by a non-diegetic chorus of angelic voices, is disturbed by the appearance of a lance into frame, and into Hank's chest. Time travel back many hundreds of years has been achieved by a slow dissolve from the previous shot and the ethereal singing.

Low angle shots of the knight and high angle ones of Hank help establish their respective positions of power at this point. The two shots of the knight and Hank emphasise the disparity between the two men, symbolising this unusual clash of cultures across the ages. Sir Sagramore's garments are colour-coordinated with his lance and horse, a Hollywood version of medieval life. It is a perfection that does not seem totally credible, but feeds into a contemporary audience's expectation of that world, so foreign that it may well have been on a distant planet. The non-diegetic music fully underscores each changing nuance of the mood in the scene, flitting from light-hearted woodwind to dramatic brass as the knight talks with, and then threatens Hank.

The composite long shot of Camelot, combining painting and real sea footage, again presents an image of perfection, an idyll of medieval life. The long shot of the castle entrance is a combined set and matte painting; it is, nonetheless, an impressive size, designed to dwarf the two men and lend the shot a sense of spectacle. Again, the castle, like the dress of the knight, looks too pristine to be true, but it is in keeping with a film that is not taking itself too seriously. The appearance of the soldiers and local people is also flawless, like a child's plastic figures. The Great Hall is similarly polished, with thrusting wooden carvings, shields and a smart Round Table. The women serving the king, although dressed in medieval garb, would not look out of place in a 1940's film with a contemporary setting.

And then the camera turns its attention to Alisande la Carteloise. She is a vision of silky pink, a butterfly of grace, and the camera follows every inch of her progress as she cavorts around the Great Hall. The song is a 1940's-style ballad. Apart from the occasional curtsey, her movement belongs to a contemporary setting; the medium shot of her vampish pose whilst leaning against the Round Table is straight out of a film noir, a seductress enticing her man. The flowing hair, the crown, the jewels and the soft focus combine to create a fairytale princess, but one who remains resolutely modern.

The anachronistic touches could suggest that Hank's experiences are merely the thoughts of one who has been knocked unconscious when he fell from his horse. But, ultimately, all these details are relegated to the purpose of this film: Bing Crosby's singing and light humour, as well as Rhonda Fleming's appeal as a 1940's sex symbol. It is lavish because Hollywood studios could afford to do it, and the gritty stains of reality were not the concerns of this film's producers or the audience who paid to see it.

The tournament (13)

The tournament is given a grandiose look in the two opening shots by means of optical effects, the first being a composite of three images (the crowd in the foreground, the main action to the right of frame and the stationary soldiers on horseback to the left of frame). This is followed by the shot of the heralds on horseback, the frame made up of repeated images to give the impression that there are numerous men in a line. The vibrant colours of the spectators' costumes suggest the wealth of those who are with the king. By contrast, Merlin, the villain in this film, is decked out in a *black* robe.

The build-up to the clash between Hank and Sir Lancelot is intended to emphasise Hank's fears in a humorous way, cutting between his laughable attempts to get ready in full armour and a deadly combat between two other knights taking place outside his tent. It is the battle between the two that is of most interest for its attempts at verisimilitude and the juxtaposition of the medieval with the twentieth century for comic effect.

After a leisurely build-up the pace suddenly gathers momentum when the joust begins; another process shot of the heralds adds significance to the moment and the camera becomes surprisingly free-moving and mobile considering the static and stately nature of much of the film's visual language, a style which matches the Bing Crosby/Hank Martin laid-back persona. The camera tracks rapidly with Sir Lancelot's horse riding, drawing the audience into the action. The locale also shifts from studio set to location filming, adding to the reality of the clash.

After the initial charge, Sir Lancelot turns and rides directly at the camera, intensifying the audience's connection with the action; the dramatic non-diegetic music underscores the drama of the battle and diegetic shouts from the crowd reinforce the excitement. The cut to a tracking shot behind the knight's horse, with Hank in the background of the frame, helps intensify the sense of danger that the time-traveller faces. A cut to a long shot from the side, with initially just Hank in view, delays and intensifies the moment of truth, and adds to the comedy and power of the moment when Hank lassos the knight's lance. The juxtaposition of fully-clad knight and Hank, dressed as close to a cowboy as medieval clothes will allow, reminds the audience of the culture clash wrought by time travel; here, Hank uses his knowledge from the future to outwit his opponent. Laughing reaction shots of the king, his party and the crowd highlight the knight's embarrassing predicament, and his next sortie is met with further ridicule as Hank encircles him, aping another convention of the

Next, a tracking shot is used twice to simulate that Bing Crosby is actually involved in the chase. Although he is sitting on a camera rig with the swinging knight just behind, the effect is to add to the reality of the scene. There are two process shots – one of Hank riding away from the knight and at the moment when he thrusts the sword into the ground beside the unseated Hank – but the overall effect is one of reality, increasing the sense of excitement for the audience. Process shots, commonly used at this time, particularly in action scenes, always detract from the authenticity of the atmosphere that the film-makers are trying to preserve. In later years, in particular, there is nothing more off-putting for an audience than to see a film's hero clearly not part of the action; where Steve McQueen was the authentic article as he rode his motorbike in *The Great Escape* (1963) or drove his car in *Bullitt* (1968), an actor like Roger

Western. This playful use of Western conventions would have resonated with contemporary audiences familiar with the genre. American audiences in particular would have revelled in seeing all-American, Hank outwit his English adversary; Hank is the cowboy hero akin to the singing cowboy tradition of Gene Autry and Roy Rogers in the 1930s and 1940s and one who mocks his opponent in a relatively non-violent manner, characteristic of cowboys like Tom Destry in George Marshall's *Destry Rides Again* (1939).

The non-diegetic music is light and mocking in these shots, underling the playful atmosphere of the scene. Bing Crosby is then seen in medium shot actually riding a horse, adding a sense of reality to the horsemanship, although the lassoing is in long shot as it is undoubtedly a stunt double.

Moore was denied this authenticity as he clearly was not the man skiing down a mountainside in *The Spy Who Loved Me* (1977).

The final section sees Sir Lancelot riding straight at the camera as it tracks backwards, the actor playing Sir Lancelot (Henry Wilcoxon) clearly seen, again adding to the authenticity of the action. The final trussing of the knight by Hank is accompanied by triumphant orchestral non-diegetic music, and the low angle medium shots of Hank empower him in his moment of glory as he bows to the cheering crowd. The film, so casual with its authentic recreation of medieval times, does try to convince the audience of the authenticity of this action scene, whilst poking fun at the pomposity of courtly behaviour by means of Hank's antics, brought with him from the future.

Invasion of the Body Snatchers

KEY FACTS

Release Date: 1956

Country of Origin: USA

Running Time: 77 minutes

PRODUCTION NOTES

Production Company

Walter Wanger Productions Inc.

Distributor

Allied Artists Pictures Corporation

Budget

$417,000 (estimated)

Awards

National Film Registry National Film Preservation Board, USA

SYNOPSIS

Dr Miles Bennell, practising in a small American town, starts to receive visits from some of the townspeople who believe that imposters are replacing members of their families. Although the initial reaction is that there is some plausible psychological explanation, Miles discovers that people are in fact being replaced by 'pod people'. Seeds that have drifted through space have come to rest in the town and have grown into pods; when someone falls asleep a replica of that person grows in the pod and destroys the original human. The only difference between the original and the replica person is that the 'pod person' has no emotion. Gradually, more of the townspeople fall prey to this fate and Miles and his few remaining friends become fugitives. Eventually, only Miles and his ex-girlfriend, Becky Driscoll, escape from the town after nearly succumbing to replication.

Whilst hiding, Driscoll falls asleep, unable to stay awake after such a prolonged time without rest, and she too falls prey to the 'pod people'. Miles realises this as he kisses her when returning from a brief walk from their hiding place. He runs up to the highway, still pursued by the townspeople, and hysterically tries to warn drivers of the imminent disaster for all humans. The film is framed by Miles telling his story at a later date, just prior to being committed to an asylum for his ravings; the ending returns to this moment, and just as he is being led away a report arrives of a crash involving a lorry carrying the pods that he has described, indicating that the authorities may be able to act in time to halt the plan. (The framing device was added by the studio, although a version without it is also available.)

HISTORICAL CONTEXT

Paranoia and fear were rife throughout the 1950s, at least in the United States. Just as our own times are dominated by moral panics, so this decade had its fair share of global concerns. If the First World War had suggested to people that the world was a brutal place, then the Second World War confirmed it, with a conflict on a massive scale and concluding with the atomic bombing of Hiroshima and Nagasaki in 1945.

These mind-boggling events unleashed a fear that formed an unsettling undercurrent to the prosperous 1950s, a decade that saw people enjoying more of the trappings of modern living after the austerity of the immediate post-war years. Another concern in the United States was that of the spread of un-American sentiment, particularly in regard to the so-called Communist threat. This had grown out of the Second World War's aftermath when the victorious Western allies left the ravaged remnants of Eastern Europe to the mighty Soviets. Thus, the cocktail of aggressive nations with widely opposing ideologies, and the apocalyptic power that they wielded, led to political mistrust and numerous standoffs.

The science fiction film was the perfect vehicle to present and reflect all these fears with a displaced setting or narrative. Films like *The Day the Earth Stood Still*, *Them!* (1954) and *The Incredible Shrinking Man* (1957) all bear witness to the concerns of the time. *Invasion of the Body Snatchers* can be interpreted in different, diametrically opposed, ways. Some believe that it is

indeed a warning about the influx of un-American ideas, a focus for which was Senator Joseph McCarthy's investigation of the film industry, resulting in a number of Hollywood directors, writers and actors being 'blacklisted' and finding it difficult or impossible to get work as a result. Others believe that it is, in fact, a parody of the paranoia that was generated during the McCarthy years.

The film has been remade on a number of occasions with Philip Kaufmann's San Francisco-set 1978 version reflecting American paranoia in the post-Vietnam and post-Watergate era. Abel Ferrera's 1993 film, *The Body Snatchers*, locates the action on an American military base, where soldiers have been turned into emotionless replicas by aliens. The version released in 2007, *The Invasion*, was not a critical or commercial success, but its Washington D.C. setting, with connotations of power and authority, suggests a critique of the way political power corrupts the individual.

SELECT FILMOGRAPHY OF MAIN PRODUCERS AND CAST
Don Siegel, 1912-91, Director, Producer

The Big Steal, 1949

Riot in Cell Block H, 1954

Invasion of the Body Snatchers, 1956

Crime in the Streets, 1956

Baby Face Nelson, 1957

Flaming Star, 1960

Hell is for Heroes, 1962

Coogan's Bluff, 1968

The Beguiled, 1970

Dirty Harry, 1971

The Shootist, 1976

Escape from Alcatraz, 1979

Walter Wanger, 1894-1968, Producer
See *Stagecoach* in THE WESTERN chapter (pg. 20)

Daniel Mainwaring (aka Geoffrey Holmes or Homes), 1902-1977, Screenwriter

Out of the Past, 1947

The Big Steal, 1949

The Phenix City Story, 1955

Invasion of the Body Snatchers, 1956

Baby Face Nelson, 1957

Kevin McCarthy, 1914, Actor

Death of a Salesman, 1951

An Annapolis Story, 1955

Invasion of the Body Snatchers, 1956

The Misfits, 1961

The Prize, 1963

Buffalo Bill and the Indians, or Sitting Bull's History Lesson, 1976

Piranha, 1978

The Howling, 1981

Innerspace, 1987

LINKS TO OTHER FILMS

The Manchurian Candidate (1962)/*Telefon* (1977)

A variant on the 'my father/ mother/ brother/ sister seems different' theme, but with both these films the political message is more overt than in *Invasion of the Body Snatchers*. Sleeper agents who have been brainwashed by Communist forces are reactivated to kill key Americans in the narratives. Seemingly all-American characters are revealed as traitors, and the films, particularly John Frankenheimer's *The Manchurian Candidate*, tap into the paranoia of the times.

Alien (1979)/*The Thing* (1982)

Invasion of the Body Snatchers, whilst certainly having political undertones, is also a science fiction film featuring aliens. It is aligned with the 'body horror' sub-genre that has been dealt with in both science fiction and horror films. Ridley Scott's

Alien and John Carpenter's *The Thing* delve into the unsettling area of an alien presence within the human body; the images of aliens erupting from within the body tap into deep and dark areas of the human psyche. *Invasion of the Body Snatchers* has the same disturbing undercurrent, most vividly shown when Miles plunges a pitchfork into the growing pod facsimile of his own body.

The Faculty (1998)

Here again, there is the idea of aliens entering and possessing the minds and bodies of humans. Robert Rodriquez's film transplants the idea to the classroom and the hybrid of horror/teen drama; imagine BBC television's *Grange Hill* or NBC's *Saved by the Bell* crossed with the *Alien* films, and this is the product. The narrative acts as a way of exploring teenage angst, and undoubtedly the widely-held view amongst students, that teachers are actually alien life forms.

REPRESENTATION

Small town America

When Hollywood film-makers want to unnerve their American audiences with tales of paranoia, then setting the narrative within a small town, in an atmosphere of resolute 'Americaness', is a particularly effective method. From the 1930s through to the 1950s towns may have been boring or full of gossips but their communities were the stalwarts that offered the security for which many a film's protagonist yearns.

In Hollywood musicals like Vincente Minnelli's *Meet Me in St. Louis* (1944) to dramas such as Orson Welles' *The Magnificent Ambersons* (1942) and fantasies like Frank Capra's *It's a Wonderful Life* (1946), there is a suggestion of what life would be like without good old-fashioned American values of decency and community.

It's a Wonderful Life most notably reveals what life would have been like in the small town of Bedford Falls without the humanising influence of the main character, George Bailey, played by James Stewart. The threat to the harmony of these communities is also revealed in films like Lewis Allen's *Suddenly*

(1954), revolving around a plot to assassinate the US president in a small town. Subversive film-makers such as Alfred Hitchcock in *Shadow of a Doubt* (1943) and Orson Welles' *The Stranger* (1946) also tell of duplicitous men living out superficially decent lives in small towns, only to be unmasked as a murderer and a communist respectively.

The cycle of films noirs from the 1940s and 1950s showed the flipside of small town contentment. Films like Robert Siodmak's *The Killers* (1946), Howard Hawks' *The Big Sleep* (1946), Jacques Tourneur's *Out of the Past* (1947) and Joseph H. Lewis' *The Big Combo* (1955) all showed the antithesis of the rural idyll, exposing the dark underbelly of urban life. Even when a character tries to escape to small town anonymity and happiness, as in *The Killers* or *Out of the Past*, he is dragged back into the urban nightmare. The David Lynch film, *Blue Velvet* (1986), begins in a town of white picket fences and manicured lawns; it is strait-laced and sanitised Middle America, but barely beneath the surface lie unspeakably brutal and perverted lifestyles.

And so to *Invasion of the Body Snatchers*. Its representation of small town life is all the more chilling for its lack of sensational detail. The observation of the townspeople in the square subverts the usual presentation of middle American town squares and its connotations of stability, normality and predictability.

In the scene where Miles and Becky hide in the surgery, they watch the townspeople in the quintessential town square. The many long shots not only suggest that they are the POVs of Miles and Becky, but also illustrate the anonymity of these pod people; it is almost as if the camera recoils in horror in this subversion of Middle America.

Smartly dressed men and women walk around as if it is a normal day; Miles points out some of the familiar faces, but then they all gather as if choreographed by a higher force, reminiscent of a musical where everyone in the town is suddenly animated into action. Here, however, the action is sinister and subversive.

The close-ups of Miles and Becky help to retain the audience's connection with them, as well as

reinforcing their individuality and humanity. This sequence presents a cancer in the very epicentre of American rituals and values; it is intended to shock by its detached portrayal of a society that is superficially the same, but is without feeling or freedom.

In other parts of the film a child runs screaming from his mother, an icon of family harmony and nurture, whilst a pod is laid into a cot. These images of family security being undermined, and the ideas behind them, are still shocking to audiences today, more than 50 years after the release of the film.

'*Invasion of the Body Snatchers was a simple, ingenious conception... it had a sure sense of rural atmosphere, a talent for filling in character quickly, and a reluctance to allow melodrama to smother wit... exemplary science fiction because it needs no visual tricks.*' David Thomson, *The New Biographical Dictionary of Film 4th Edition*, Little, Brown, London, 2002

'*Siegel's film...is less concerned with subscribing to generic SF convention than with dramatizing the dangers of social conformity and the threat of invasion coming both from outside and inside one's own community.*' Steven Jay Schneider, *1001 Movies You Must See Before You Die*, Cassell Illustrated, 2007

KEY SCENE TEXTUAL ANALYSIS

Pod barbeque (8)

The voice-over narration was a familiar device of films in the 1940s and 1950s and the sequence begins with this non-diegetic sound which provides an authoritative voice whilst emphasising the mystery of the situation. Although an artificial device it is not an uncommon film convention, and as such, the audience is not alienated from the narrative; indeed, it connects the audience with the protagonist more closely, causing us to empathise with him and his trials.

The voice-over occurs whilst Miles comes up the driveway in his car; it mirrors his thoughts. The long shot of the car pans as he gets out and joins his friends.

The *mise-en-scène*, as elsewhere in the film, is an integral part of conveying its message. The set-up is very typical of a 1950's middle class American back garden with a barbeque, a table upon which Martinis are being mixed and a small marquee. The guests are dressed in casual/stylish clothes and all seems ordinary.

The contrast between the two worlds is further emphasised by the use of diegetic sound in the first shot (light-hearted conversation and the sound of crickets) and then the non-diegetic music, which begins in a low-key manner; but the cut to a close-up of the pod amidst the flora elicits a dramatic burst of orchestral sound - its frothing, pulsating appearance testifies to the fact that it is not destined for the dinner table.

The intercutting between Miles and the pod increases the tension, as does the suitably dramatic music; with every shot of the pod it shows the increasing size of its sinister contents.

The shots of the pod have all been in close-up, whilst Miles has been in medium or long shot. Now, at the point of discovery, he too is shown in close-up (the shadows lying across it indicate the danger); their worlds have collided. His introduction

The conversation is light-hearted and is followed with one continuous take, first with the pan to Miles, then with a track and a pan to frame Miles as he hands a Martini to Jack. This reframing also introduces a large structure behind the two men, which seems rather large and imposing. As Miles accepts some food from Teddy the shot cuts to a view from within this building, a greenhouse, but now the shot is at an angle (a tilted, or dutch, shot), which immediately suggests that there is something wrong. The shot disorientates the audience; the pleasantly normal scene shown to be harmonious in its one continuous take is now seen from another angle where it is depicted as something abnormal. If this is a POV, then its twisted perspective and low angle demonstrates that it is not something which belongs to the ordinary world.

to the pod world plunges him further into darkness; the space itself is cramped and claustrophobic, imitating the nightmarish new reality that he is entering. As Miles is joined by Jack, dark shadowy streaks cut across their figures, again representative of the gathering sense of horror at this alien phenomenon.

They are joined by the others, observing this hellish vision, the four of them bound closely by their fear and the sense of being hemmed in as their world disintegrates. Close-ups of Miles and Becky, again at tilted angles, reiterate the sense of disorientation that they are feeling.

As the pods issue their revolting contents, the different stages of their development is highlighted by a close-up. The shot with the pod in foreground and the four humans in the background is again tilted in a nightmarish manner, but it also unites the humans and the aliens in the same filmic space; the two worlds are one.

There follows the use of tilted and straightforward shots as the shocked onlookers watch the pods growing. When they begin to make sense of the way people have been behaving the shot is level, but when Jack is overcome by anger and grabs the pitchfork the camera is again tilted; hysteria and violence dislocate the humans from their normal feelings.

As Miles restrains Jack the tilted camera zooms in to three of them, increasing the sense of panic and claustrophobia as the alien world invades theirs. Becky, too, is in close-up and at an angle; the pods, as their contents grow and take human form, are shown in medium long shot and their filmic space increases.

which, again, shows a cluttered frame and a low angle from the POV of the new, almost sentient, pod people. In this context, the low angle does not empower Miles, but points to something sinister lurking in the shadows. It perverts the usual significance of a low angle shot and changes the normal conventions of film language.

As Miles is faced with the pod figure of Becky the camera cuts from a close-up to an extreme one as he struggles with his conflicting emotions. The cut to the male figure with a close-up of its head and upper torso lends the plunging pitchfork an even greater effect as the points puncture the flesh; a decent, caring human, a doctor, has felt compelled to commit such a violent act. The human world has begun to take on the alien world and the confrontation is brutal and terrifying. The audience only witnesses it for an instant before a sharp cut to

The move from the greenhouse affords Miles and Becky some freedom from this world, signified by the tracking shot as they take action. The low angle shot of Miles as he calls the FBI demonstrates his empowerment at this moment. However, this is undermined by the cut back to the growths that are now assuming the features of each of the four people.

The tilted angle of Jack and Teddy shows that the nightmare world is still dominant. The track through the greenhouse following the pitchfork and the juxtaposition of an instrument of violence resting close to the faces of these figures, although alien, is disturbing and mirrors the emotional turmoil that the humans are experiencing.

After the phone call is thwarted the conversation between the four friends is shot in the more brightly-lit exterior without a tilt as they discuss their plans. This contrasts with the next shot

emphasise its impact; the non-diegetic music has underscored all these moments of alien horror, no more so than with this final image.

2001: A Space Odyssey

KEY FACTS

Release Date: 1968

Country of Origin: UK

Running Time: 141 minutes

PRODUCTION NOTES

Production Companies

Metro-Goldwyn-Mayer

Polaris

Distributor

Metro-Goldwyn-Mayer

Budget

$10, 500,000 (estimated)

Awards

National Film Registry National Film Preservation Board, USA

Best Effects, Special Visual Effects Stanley Kubrick Academy Awards, USA

Best Art Direction Anthony Masters, Harry Lange, Ernest Archer BAFTA Awards, UK

Best Cinematography Geoffrey Unsworth BAFTA Awards, UK

Best Soundtrack Winston Ryder BAFTA Awards, UK

SYNOPSIS

The extended prologue to the film focuses on the 'Dawn of Man', following a group of chimpanzees as they become 'enlightened' with the discovery that animal bones can be utilised as weapons. This enables them to overcome a rival group with the killing of one of their number: they have made 'progress'. Here, we also have the first glimpse of the monolith, a recurring symbol throughout the film, which suggests the inscrutable power and knowledge beyond that of humankind's endeavour.

The next phase of the film charts the discovery of the unexplained monolith on the surface of the moon, which ends with it aurally assaulting a group of astronauts. The final section sees a mission to Jupiter to discover the source of a signal coming from the vicinity. En route, the ship's onboard computer, HAL, develops a psychotic personality, where preservation of self and the mission becomes paramount; he murders all but one of the crew members until he is terminated by the remaining human, Dave. He then travels though a 'stargate' and emerges into an altered reality, one that seems to merge past, present and future into one. The monolith reappears and we are left with an image of rebirth and what lies 'beyond the infinite'.

HISTORICAL CONTEXT

The 1960s, although a time now associated with revolution, freedom of speech and the clamour for equality between the sexes and races, was also a period of continuing repression, conflict and fear of powers beyond control. The Bay of Pigs incident in 1961, taking the world to the brink of nuclear war, the Korean, then the Vietnam wars and the ongoing Cold War all shrouded the 1960s with a deathly pall that could not be merely shrugged aside through the counter-culture spirit.

2001 boldly embraces the issues of the day, indeed of *any* day. The monolith, the stargate and HAL make the film full of unknowns, beyond the comprehension of humanity. But it is also a film which is very much of its time in terms of the counter-culture; one poster tag-line reads 'The Ultimate Trip', a reference to the Western world's growing love affair with 'recreational' drugs which had gathered momentum in the 1960s. Meanwhile, the journey through the stargate is a movement onto another plane of being, painted in the colours of a drug-induced 'trip'.

The film is also very much of its time in terms of the filmic commune that existed in Europe with New Wave brothers in France, Britain, Italy and Czechoslovakia deconstructing film language and rejecting established ideas. Like the French director Jean-Pierre Melville, who had elevated the gangster genre from pulp to existential cool with films like *Le Samourai* (1967), Kubrick further established his art cinema credentials by taking the sci-fi genre, languishing somewhat after its heady days in the 1950s, and focusing on ideas with images of a world dominated by machines.

Its foregrounding of visual flair and contemplation of existence over narrative and generic tropes certainly sits comfortably in a decade where colourful thought proliferated. The camera often gazes, like Michelangelo Antonioni's use of film language in *L'Avventura* (1960), pondering human existence in a series of wide shots, the humans almost lost in the space around them, subject to the slow but inexorable rhythm of time passing. Like Antonioni, Kubrick's vision is the work of an auteur, detailed and exact with its repetition of visual imagery and ideas.

George Lucas may have put Kubrick's high-end science fiction visuals to low-brow ends with *Star Wars* some nine years later, but the film's legacy of using the genre to comment on contemporary issues and debates is still apparent in current film-making with films like *Gattaca* (1997) and *Children of Men* (2006).

SELECT FILMOGRAPHY OF MAIN PRODUCERS AND CAST

Stanley Kubrick, 1928-99, Director, Producer, Screenwriter

Killer's Kiss, 1955

The Killing, 1956

Paths of Glory, 1958

Spartacus, 1960

Lolita, 1962

Dr. Strangelove, 1963

2001: A Space Odyssey, 1968

A Clockwork Orange, 1971

Barry Lyndon, 1975

The Shining, 1980

Full Metal Jacket, 1987

Eyes Wide Shut, 1999

Geoffrey Unsworth, 1914-78, Director of Photography

A Night to Remember, 1958

Becket, 1964

2001: A Space Odyssey, 1968

Cabaret, 1972

Superman, 1978

Tess, 1979

Keir Dullea, 1936, Actor

The Hoodlum Priest, 1961

David and Lisa, 1962

The Thin Red Line, 1964

Bunny Lake is Missing, 1965

2001: A Space Odyssey, 1968

Paperback Hero, 1973

Black Christmas, 1975

LINKS TO OTHER FILMS

Silent Running (1971)

Douglas Trumball, responsible for the special effects in *2001*, directs this further meditation on the nature of existence and the source of mankind's salvation. It charts the journey of a spacecraft, filled with vegetation to replenish a nuclear war-ravaged Earth, and the moral dilemmas facing the lead character, played by Bruce Dern.

The Demon Seed (1977)

Donald Cammell directs a film with its narrative derived from part of *2001*'s storyline. In Cammell's film a computer, which controls all the functions of a house, entraps a woman in an attempt to create a new breed of being, half-human, half-computer.

The Matrix (1999)

This film is the cinematic lovechild of *2001* and *Star Wars*, marrying the two common filmic strains of this genre: science fiction and 'sci-fi', intellectualisation and action. The film arrives at an evaluation of existence, but there are many explosions and chase sequences along the way.

REPRESENTATION

Space

Space had never been seen in such a way before: silent, unknowing, a place of noiseless death. Man's place in it is initially seen in balletic terms as it forms a backdrop to a dance of spacecraft. But this sense of harmony is shortlived as space becomes more and more inhospitable and comes to signify man's vulnerability and lack of knowledge in the face of infinite possibilities. There are no flying saucers or icky aliens to fill the void, just a tiny speck of humanity, alone and victim to its own 'progress'. The final image does offer some hope: the giant child, still in a womb-like structure, floats next to our planet, a symbol of future regeneration and true harmony with, and understanding of, the darkness around us.

Technology

Spacecraft are both spectacular and ordinary: they are colossal and awe-inspiring, but there are touches of familiarity, like the Pan Am air stewardess (Pan Am being the foremost US airline at the time of the film's production). *2001* is full of the 'reality' of space travel: liquid food, grip shoes to counteract weightlessness, voice recognition and hypersleep; everything is rooted in possibility and gives the film an air of plausibility. But if this science fiction is real, it is also a bland vision of the future. The interiors have clean lines and are pristine, but they are bereft of life, warmth and humanity; it is a surgical future, as sterile as a surgeon's knife. (Compare this with, say, *Blade Runner*, made just 14 years later and set in 2019.)

Any feeling that is expressed in the film comes, ironically, from the supercomputer, HAL, as he is about to be deactivated by Dave; it seems as if the humans have become dehumanised in their slavish and unthinking reliance on technology. Of course, that's not to say that HAL is all sweetness and light; he is the psychotic killer, after all.

'... for both academics and critics, it [2001] has served to mark a turning point in the science fiction film genre. For example, it provides a discernable division for J. P. Telotte (2001) in his brief history of the genre in America (he actually labels later films of the genre as 'post-2001 films') and for Vivian Sobchack it was 2001 that proved that 'the film medium (could) accommodate 'adult' science fiction' (1993).' Christine Cornea, *Science Fiction Cinema*, Edinburgh University Press, 2007

KEY SCENE TEXTUAL ANALYSIS

Violent space (23/24)

The close-up of HAL's eye is enigmatic; it has just killed Frank in order to stop its own deactivation. The orange centre of this eye is like an iris and has been a recurring image in the Jupiter section of the film. Does HAL have feelings or is it a psychotic machine? The eye looks directly at the audience in its impenetrable manner; is seems to be both unfeeling and tender at the same time.

We are given a POV to heighten its humanness as it looks at the two empty seats previously occupied by the now dead astronaut and Dave, who is unable to re-enter the spaceship because HAL refuses to open the pod bay doors. The diegetic sound is the continuous hum of the spaceship's workings. Its soundtrack is relentless, monotonous and inhuman. The camera is static throughout this sequence, which adds an even more chilling edge to the events that unfold. This is a murder scene with a difference; there is no on-screen violence, no struggle, no screams. It is the murder of the future: cold, calculating and mechanical.

The next shot presents the victims, already laid out in coffin-like chambers. Each is like an Egyptian Mummy, and their continuing existence is already

reliant upon artificial intelligence. The close-up of one of their monitors underlines that their humanity has been reduced to a series of computer graphics. The close-up of the flashing red graphic, 'Computer Malfunction' is, in this context, a euphemism for the act of killing, and it is detached and sterile.

The diegetic sound of the harsh warning bleep is the only indicator that something is amiss; it is HAL's equivalent of the screeching violins in *Psycho*, a soundtrack to murder. The cut is then to the life support system readout again, not to the victims, as if the killing was purely a matter of computer software and readouts. This leads onto the central concept that man has become so remote from himself and his environment, focusing instead on technological advancement at the expense of humanity, that the taking of his life barely seems to involve him anymore. The readout shows the first of the vital signs beginning to flatline.

The shots of this technology are all held for a long time and suggest the machines' equal, if not greater, importance compared with humankind. Only then do we see the victims in close-up, and even then we see only a fragment of face, encased in its tomb with the impersonal inscription of initials and surname already etched on what will become their gravestones; these shots are much shorter than the shots of the technology, underlining their anonymity and impotence.

Shots of the three single chambers are followed by a long shot of all three together. As with the singles, the shots are from unusual angles, in keeping with the fact that this part of the spaceship revolves, but this just adds to the disorientation and strangeness of this killing, and the long shot further emphasises the coffin-like appearance of the chambers.

The cut back to a close-up of HAL reminds the audience who is the perpetrator of these killings, and its eye's fixed stare helps accentuate the horror and certainty of the outcome. It could be interpreted as the eye of cold evil, but also the eye of one who feels fully vindicated in its actions (reminiscent of the close-up of the eye in Robert Siodmak's 1945 film, *The Spiral Staircase*, of the killer who believes that it is his duty to rid the world of those who are physically disabled).

After this shot of HAL the killing is visually completed in computer terms; there are no more close-ups of the astronauts, no writhing faces, just clinical facts presented on screen as text ending with the matter-of-fact message: 'Life Functions Terminated'. It is as cold as current military-speak which deems that the killing of civilians is 'collateral damage'. The only apparent indicator that this is a serious moment is the change to a more rapid warning sound, which also mirrors the final frenzy of the kill.

The final long shot of the three chambers prohibits any view of the victims' humanity and reduces them to being part of the clinical *mise-en-scène* - a functional, sterile environment, lacking even the merest of human touches.

(not, you may note, the terrifying monster killing machines of many a science fiction film, but just a methodical, cool and reasoning machine) is undercut by the next shot of the mother ship and the pod. It resembles a standoff between two gunfighters, a David and Goliath, two machines impassively facing each other. When we do see close-ups of Dave his face is illuminated by the control panels in front of him, as if the computer circuits control his face.

The shot of the pod with the dead body in its two claws emphasises the pod's isolation and vulnerability, whilst the next shot of the pod from the deck of the *Discovery* makes the pod look as if it is offering up the body as a sacrifice to a technological god.

The last shot of the sequence reverts cyclically back to HAL as he seemingly surveys his work; but, as ever, there is no difference in appearance, no suggestion of reaction and just the ever-vigilant gaze of an inhuman future. This is, perhaps, the most chilling murder in film history. Man has created the sword of progress and died by it, and nobody has blinked an eye. This juxtaposition of the momentousness of the act with the implacable banality of its execution is what makes it so effective.

The next sequence jolts the audience back into remembering that there is one human remaining. First we see another static shot of an empty room, devoid of humanity, but with a reference to the shadow of humanity in the form of a spacesuit hanging from a rack. A disembodied voice cuts across this void as Dave asks HAL to allow him to re-enter the main ship after retrieving Frank's body.

But any humanity that may have briefly intruded on this future world of computers and machines

The next shot from the side and behind the *Discovery* reiterates the power of one over the other and again suggests this idea of a human sacrifice. Over this Dave continues to ask to be readmitted; his chatter suggests weakness, whilst HAL's silence connotes strength.

The tone of HAL's eventual response does have that combination of humanness, threat, hurt and blind rigidity that conveys the horror of this future technology. The cutting between the two protagonists helps to connect the human with the computer; they are both seen in close-up and the distinction between human and computer becomes blurred with this series of shots.

With HAL resuming its silence and Dave's increasing desperation, the intimacy of the conversation is dispelled by a return to three shots of the pod's predicament in relation to the *Discovery*. The isolation and inferiority of the pod, and thus between computer and human, are restated, deepened by the silence of space.

A slightly longer shot of Dave in the pod signifies the passing of thoughts as he tries to work out a strategy, and then the shot tightens again as he becomes resolved to a plan of action.

Frank's body is released and the shot from within the pod is a desperately chilling and heart-rending view of oblivion as this insignificant representative of humanity –nonetheless a living, breathing human being – is lost within the never-ending expanse of space.

The cut back to Dave shows again this face covered in the reflection of computer readout, betraying little emotion as he releases his colleague. The shot of the pod turning away from the disappearing body in the background suggests a turning away from feeling and a focus on self-interest, the mirror (almost) of HAL's own actions.

There has been no camera movement throughout these sequences; the cool, calculating, clinical eye that Kubrick trains on this action mirrors a universe where humans have lost their humanity in a search for something beyond themselves, and computers have made the leap into the sentient world, learning the guiding principal of humankind – self-interest. Only Dave's later journey through the stargate, beyond the infinite, will offer a vision of how we can claw back our humanity.

Alien

In space no one can hear you scream.

KEY FACTS

Release Date: 1979

Country of Origin: UK/ USA

Running Time: 117 minutes

PRODUCTION NOTES

Production Companies

Brandywine Productions Ltd.

Twentieth Century-Fox Film Corporation

Distributor

Twentieth Century-Fox Film Corporation

Budget

$11,000,000 (estimated)

Awards

National Film Registry National Film Preservation Board, USA

Best Effects, Special Visual Effects H.R.Giger et al American Academy Awards, USA

Best Production Design Michael Seymour BAFTA Awards, UK

Best Soundtrack Derrick Leather, Jim Shields, Bill Rowe BAFTA Awards, UK

SYNOPSIS

Whilst travelling towards earth the onboard computer of commercial spaceship, *Nostromo*, picks up a distress signal from a nearby planet. The computer, named Mother, awakens the ship's crew out of hypersleep. Three of the crew members land on the planet and discover an abandoned spacecraft and numerous large egg-like structures. Executive Officer Kane investigates the eggs and something erupts from one of them, latching onto his face. Back on board the *Nostromo*, the creature eventually leaves his face and is later found dead. The crew, led by Captain Dallas, decide to eat and then return to hypersleep. During the meal an alien creature explodes through Kane's stomach and escapes. The creature grows rapidly and kills the other crew members one by one until only Ripley, the Warrant Officer, remains.

In the course of the deaths it is discovered that one of the crew members, Ash, is actually an android who has been covertly trying to prevent the alien's death because the company which owns the vessel wants the return of the alien to Earth at any cost. Finally, Ripley makes good her escape in a small shuttle and destroys the main ship. In a final twist she discovers that the alien has also taken refuge in the shuttle; eventually, she does manage to get into a spacesuit and eject the alien from the craft, leaving her and Jones the cat to return to hypersleep and presumed safety.

HISTORICAL CONTEXT

The 1970s were characterised by both world economic depressions and greater individual freedom in parts of the Western world. America pulled out of Vietnam, President Nixon was humiliated and left office, equal rights for both women and black people were championed once more (after the beginnings of emancipation had begun in the previous decade) and it was the decade when blockbusters were both commercial and critical successes, happily co-existing with arthouse films.

Disaster films like *Airport* (1970) and *The Towering Inferno* (1974) began a trend of big budget action films, but it was not until *Jaws* (1975) that the summer blockbuster really emerged. *Alien* followed that trend, providing high production values and excitement in equal measure; it also reunited horror and science fiction, something which *2001* and its ilk had turned away from. It fed into the Hollywood studios' awareness that teenage audiences were a highly lucrative market, just as *The Exorcist* (1973) and *Halloween* (1978) had proved before it.

Alien paved the way for stronger female roles in traditionally male-dominated genres, as well as continuing the 1970's depiction of space travel as routine and rather grubby, initiated by *Dark Star* (1974) and popularised by *Star Wars*.

Indeed, it was only two years after the film's release that the inaugural flight of the space shuttle took place, ushering in a new era of space travel that soon resembled the comings and goings of ordinary aircraft. The film also maintained the practice of big budget (usually science fiction) films that were being made in Britain, both for the crew's expertise and also for financial reasons - *2001* and *Star Wars* had been made at Borehamwood and Elstree Studios respectively, whilst *Alien* was shot at Shepperton Studios.

Ridley Scott, along with his brother, Tony, Alan Parker, Hugh Hudson and Adrian Lyne had emerged from the world of television commercials in the 1970s to make feature films. If film-making was not exactly thriving in Britain at the time, its TV advertising was leading the world in originality. All these British directors would convert their television experience into successful films, although critics have continued to carp at their sophisticated visual style, interpreting it as superficiality, 'style over substance'.

Critically lauded or not, some of these films would become the epitome of 'high concept' box office successes; Tony Scott went on to make *Top Gun* (1986), whilst Parker, Hudson and Lyne would make *Midnight Express* (1978), *Chariots of Fire* (1981) and *Fatal Attraction* (1987) respectively. Ridley Scott built on the success of *Alien* with *Blade Runner* (1982), poorly received at the time but now established as a science fiction classic, with its mixture of sci-fi pulp conventions and intellectual sensibilities, pondering the nature of humanness and envisaging a future Earth with uncanny accuracy. But Scott, to date, has not returned to the genre where he has made such an indelible mark.

SELECT FILMOGRAPHY OF MAIN PRODUCERS AND CAST

Ridley Scott, 1937, Director, Producer

The Duellists, 1977

Alien, 1979

Blade Runner, 1982

Legend, 1985

Someone to Watch Over Me, 1987

Black Rain, 1989

Thelma & Louise, 1991

1492: Conquest of Paradise, 1992

White Squall, 1996

G.I. Jane, 1997

Gladiator, 2000

Hannibal, 2001

Black Hawk Down, 2001

Matchstick Men, 2003

Kingdom of Heaven, 2005

American Gangster, 2007

Body of Lies, 2008

Gordon Carroll, 1928-2005, Producer

Cool Hand Luke, 1967

Pat Garrett and Billy the Kid, 1973

Alien, 1979

Blue Thunder, 1983

Aliens, 1986

Red Heat, 1988

Alien 3, 1992

Alien: Resurrection, 1997

Alien vs. Predator, 2004

Walter Hill, 1942, Screenwriter, Director, Producer

The Getaway, 1972

Hard Times, 1975

The Driver, 1978

Alien, 1979

The Warriors, 1979

The Long Riders, 1980

Southern Comfort, 1981

48 Hrs., 1982

Streets of Fire, 1984

Brewster's Millions, 1985

Aliens, 1986

Red Heat, 1988

Johnny Handsome, 1989

Alien 3, 1992

Geronimo: An American Legend, 1993

Wild Bill, 1995

Last Man Standing, 1996

Alien: Resurrection, 1997

Alien vs. Predator, 2004

Alien vs. Predator: AVP2, 2007

Dan O'Bannon, 1946, Screenwriter

Dark Star, 1974

Alien, 1979

Blue Thunder, 1983

Invaders from Mars, 1986

Total Recall, 1990

Sigourney Weaver, 1949, Actress

Alien, 1979

The Year of Living Dangerously, 1982

Ghostbusters, 1984

Aliens, 1986

Gorillas in the Mist, 1988

Working Girl, 1988

Ghostbusters II, 1988

Alien 3, 1992

Dave, 1993

Copycat, 1995

The Ice Storm, 1997

Alien: Resurrection, 1997

Galaxy Quest, 1999

Holes, 2003

Avatar, 2009

LINKS TO OTHER FILMS

The Cat and the Canary (1927/1930/1939/1979)

This 1922 John Willard play features the coming together of a group of people to listen to a will being read at the classic old creepy mansion; as in *Alien* the protagonists are nearly all murdered whilst being stalked by a mysterious being.

The Old Dark House (1932)

This James Whale film, with its classic gothic horror location, is full of the typical conventions that many subsequent horror films have utilised. *Alien*, drawing heavily on horror conventions, contains echoes of the earlier film. There is the narrative of trapped and terrorised characters in a confined space, the menace of which is elevated through a set full of claustrophobic rooms and corridors, and by the lighting, which creates deep pools of darkness.

And Then There Were None (1945)

There have been numerous adaptations of the Agatha Christie story upon which this is based, and *Alien* draws on the central narrative thrust of a group of people being killed one by one. Countless slasher films follow this structure, although not all of these have the victims trapped in one area. However, films such as Sam Raimi's *Evil Dead II* (1987) and James Mangold's *Identity* (2003) have their imperilled characters stuck in the same place and killed in a variety of gruesome ways.

It! The Terror from Beyond Space (1958)

Edward L. Cahn's film has a very similar plot to that of *Alien* with its story of an alien stowing away on a spacecraft that has come to rescue the survivor of a mission to Mars. En route to Earth the crew members are killed one by one until the alien is finally destroyed.

Scanners (1981)

David Cronenberg's film features some grisly moments of body horror as heads explode under pressure from the telepathic powers of the 'scanners'. Other related films that deal with the dark recesses of the human mind include *Shivers* (1975), *Rabid* (1977), *Videodrome* (1983) and *The Fly* (1986). *Scanners* taps into our deepest fears about

our bodies and also acts a metaphor for other anxieties, such as sexual disease, rape, mental illness and the moral panics of modern society in general.

REPRESENTATION

Space technology

If *2001* is full of bright, clean lines, then *Alien* is replete with shadow and decay. From the inhospitable surface upon which the crew members land to the broken shell of a spacecraft that they discover to the exterior and interior of the *Nostromo*, this is a future that is as shabby as the grubbiest contemporary urban space. The *Nostromo*, in particular, is the antithesis of the sleek and graceful crafts in *2001*.

The 1970s saw many film genres undergo an overhaul; Westerns and science fiction films presented worlds that were full of hardship and were downright dirtier and harsher than had ever been shown before. Like *Dark Star* and *Star Wars* before it, *Alien* imagines a tatty future, presenting technology that is functionally superior to our own, but which is equally prone to overuse and malfunction. In the *Star Wars* films one of the running jokes is Han Solo's craft, the Millenium Falcon, and its propensity to break down; it resembles a used car well past its best. The future, far from being one of bright new hope, is very much like our now, both ugly and beautiful. In *Alien*, the ugly, or, at least, the grotesque, dominates, as befits a story of both banality and brutality, one where a corporation is happy to have its employees wiped out as long as its investment is secured.

Women

Sigourney Weaver's Ripley is the forerunner of a number of female action heroes; the first-time viewer's expectation that the captain, Dallas, will be the survivor is subverted and Ripley emerges as the most resourceful character. Genre films such as science fiction, Westerns and action/adventure have been dominated by male heroes. The 1970s did see a change in this, but often it was in lower budget exploitation films like Pam Grier's characters in *Black Mama, White Mama* (1972) and *Foxy Brown* (1974) or Barbara Hershey as the eponymous heroine in Martin Scorsese's *Boxcar Bertha* (1972). After Ripley came Sarah Connor in James Cameron's *The Terminator* (1984) and more prominently in the sequel, *T2: Judgement Day* (1991). The character of Ripley has been developed in the three sequels where she is presented in both action and intellectual terms and has transcended her two-dimensional action heroine status.

'Ridley Scott resurrected the cheap genre of scary monsters from space, introduced it to exquisite, high-budget visuals, and created an arresting, nerve-wracking, adult-orientated science fiction horror film...; what elevated anxiety into art via... visual effects is Alien's *unique, awesome design and art direction mixing organic motifs with the metallic, and the sparingly-glimpsed alien.'* Angelo Erigyo, *1001 Movies you Must See Before You Die*, Quintet Publishing Limited, London, 2003

KEY SCENE TEXTUAL ANALYSIS

Escape (17/18)

Whereas *2001* portrays a future of clinical sterility, this sequence presents a grimy, dark and uncomfortable future. Ripley is attempting to destroy the ship, *Nostromo*, and escape in the shuttle now that the alien has killed her fellow crew members. The sequence begins immediately after she has discovered that her final two companions are dead; she is alone and scared beyond belief.

The initial close-up focuses the audience on her struggle to take control of the situation; an emergency door is opened and the camera is tight in on her struggle to undo bolts, on her hands and fear-ravaged face; the effect is to heighten the intensity of the moment and attempt to connect the audience with her frightened fumbling. It also affords us with no objective view of what is happening; we share her panic and cannot see if the alien is approaching. The continuous diegetic alert sound helps accentuate the atmosphere of panic.

The activation of the emergency destruct system is again shot in a series of close-ups to focus our attention on her efforts. As it is activated the warnings, and even louder alert noise from the computer, serve to further heighten the tension.

Once she emerges from the control room the *mise-en-scène* shows a nightmarish vision of spaceship life. The control room has the usual paraphernalia of SF films such as the panels, flashing lights and complex control systems, whilst outside, the sleek, white, pristine representation of space travel is jettisoned in favour of dark, dirty, and downright messy interiors. Steam is emitted from all directions and swirling spotlights create shadows or blind you rather than guide you; it is more reminiscent of the bowels of an ancient steam liner than the interior of a future spacecraft. It's the culmination of a decade's SF film-making where the future, and its technologies, were shown to be anything but squeaky clean.

The steadicam shot follows her in order for the audience to share her panic as it imitates her manic dash through the sinister passageways of the ship. It looks as if she is running through the ship's innards, its metal guts disgorging from the walls; the camera also takes us through the steam, our visibility reduced to what Ripley can see.

The zoom-in towards the detonation device again increases the tension and the obscuring of the audience's view continues into the next shot. Only when the camera pans does it come into focus to show a hand reaching over a rim. The effect is disorientating; it is Ripley emerging from a hatch and the close-up of her face bathes it in shadow, only illuminated by the flashing lights.

The camera tracks back as Ripley runs towards us, metallic walls enclosing the passageway in which she runs. She keeps looking back as she runs and the sense that something will jump out of the foreground increases; this continuous take allows the audience to focus on nothing else but Ripley, again allowing us no omniscient viewpoint and directly connecting us with her fear.

She then stops at the wall, the large flickering light rapidly plunging her in and out of a cold light, further disorientating her and the audience. The shot cuts from a medium shot to a close-up of her face and we are fully in her world, experiencing the shock as she experiences it.

The cut to the alien shows it for just a few frames as it, too, is bathed in this cold flashing light; dramatic non-diegetic music synchronises with the moment of discovery and the cut back to Ripley is again a close-up, but this time from a tilted angle, emphasising her sense of horror.

As she eases herself away the camera cuts back to where the alien will appear but it does not show

The cut to a jolting steadicam shot of Ripley's escape puts us back into her nightmare world of disorientation and panic with the audience barely able to see what is happening. The countdown to the point of no return for the explosion then takes precedence on the soundtrack as the non-diegetic music recedes.

There is one shot of events from the outside, the blue light of the control room visible amidst the vast mass of the spaceship in the long shot to reinforce the sense of her isolation and vulnerability.

Her attempts to end the countdown, as her path to the escape shuttle is now blocked by the alien, are shown again in close-up as she fumbles with the instruments.

The shots widen as she fails to stop the countdown and she takes her frustration out on the computer which will not respond to her commands. The

it immediately; the rapid cutting, flashing lights and the audience's inability to focus immediately on what's being shown help to match Ripley's experience.

Only fragments of the creature are seen, to increase the frightening impact; thus, the alien, another staple of the SF film, is left shrouded in mystery (throughout the film until the climax we see just parts of the alien as it kills the crew members); the final shot of the alien in the sequence shows it nearing the cat which Ripley has left behind; its shiny, dripping, malevolent exterior make it an ideal monster. Its mouth has been the focus of the film with its razor-sharp teeth and inner mouth that stabs out and punctures skin. Numerous images in the film have fore grounded 'body horror' (the creature's 'birth' from Kane's stomach, Ash being partially decapitated and the attacks on the humans by the alien), often perversely sexual in nature.

computer has the ironic nomenclature of 'Mother' and Ripley's desperate shout of 'mother' helps to deepen the desperation that she feels.

As Ripley plunges out into the passageway the camera again follows, but the steam is even more dense and for a few moments we follow nothing; we are there and as isolated as our identification figure.

The camera shifts from tracking behind Ripley to tracking in front; the sense of movement and unsteadiness perfectly mimic this final race for freedom and lights flare into the camera lens, again helping with the disorientating effect.

As she emerges again from the hatch the earlier shot of her hand clasping the rim is mirrored. This time, however, the shot is much tighter and the fingers fill the screen, covered in moisture. The message is clear: she is much more frightened, desperate and barely clinging onto life, having both the imminent destruction of the ship and the alien to contend with. This shot also affords an extreme close-up of Ripley's face, showing the intense fear in her eyes.

In medium shot, her flaming gun is clearly seen. It is a monstrous object, both familiar and different from what we know. This is the case with much of the technology in the film for it is based on our own technology but given a slightly different look to make it seem futuristic. The future will involve progress but much of it will come hand in hand with the usual human ability to create an unpleasant-looking environment.

The camera tracks back as Ripley approaches, her flame-thrower at the ready; a cut to a POV shot helps to heighten our identification with her.

The camera pulls away slightly as she returns to the place where she last saw the alien, perhaps to give us a sense that the creature might appear, but director Scott wants to keep us rooted in Ripley's experience and quickly cuts to a close-up and then a POV.

The camera stays in the gloom and is static as Ripley takes the container, with Jones the cat which she has just found, towards the light and the escape shuttle; it is as if we now have the creature's POV.

The cut to Ripley, now in the bright light of the entrance to the shuttle, comes as a relief. Sanctuary is in sight and hellish flames burst from the dark passageway from where she has come. The camera positions the audience within the shuttle, increasing again our sense of anxiety that she may not make it. The camera tracks back into the shuttle, which is worryingly dark, although Ripley manages to shut the doors. The fact that the audience has not been permitted a view from her perspective of what she is entering is devised to keep our anxiety levels raised.

The cut to the interior is not very comforting, for either the audience or Ripley; it is dark, again illuminated by the flashing lights and this, together with the rapidity of the shot, does not avail us with a clear view of the environment, keeping us disorientated.

The voice warning stating that she has one minute to abandon ship again increases the tension and she gets to work on launching the shuttle. The shaky POV and her gasps help to connect us with the continuing desperate situation, and the cut to a long shot of the flight deck from outside has the same effect as the previous external long shot, namely, of reinforcing her isolation.

The blast-off shows the craft detach and then there is a rapid tracking shot of the *Nostromo*'s underbelly; the detail of the model work is intricate, emphasising the realism of the craft.

The end of this sequence comprises rapid cutting between this underbelly, Ripley's shuddering head and the countdown screen, with the vocal countdown adding to the tension. There is then a series of shots of Ripley and her POV as the *Nostromo* recedes into the distance; they are steady and match her growing feeling of success and relief. There are three blinding blasts as the *Nostromo* self-destructs; as well as the diegetic sound of the explosion there is certainly another sound which is almost like a monster's screech, perhaps suggesting the creature's demise.

The camera then zooms in on Ripley's face, the explosion over, in order to capture this moment of intense feeling; she says, 'I got you, you son-of-a-bitch', and the camera records her strong features, the look of defiance and the relief that her job is done. For the first time in many minutes a close-up of Ripley shows her face in repose; it is evenly-lit; there is no sweat, steam or flashing lights; equilibrium has returned.

Of course, it is not the end and there is one last frantic battle. However, the previous five minutes have been shot almost in real-time up to the explosion, and this has heightened the sense of realism that is so important to the representation of the future in the film.

ET The Extra-Terrestrial

KEY FACTS

Release Date: 1982

Country of Origin: USA

Running Time: 115 minutes

PRODUCTION NOTES

Production Companies

Amblin Entertainment

Universal Pictures

Distributor

Universal Pictures

Budget

$10,500,000 (estimated)

Awards

National Film Registry National Film Preservation Board, USA

Best Effects, Special Visual Effects Carlo Rambaldi, Dennis Muren, Kenneth Smith Academy Awards, USA

Best Effects, Sound Effects Editing Charles L. Campbell, Ben Burtt Academy Awards, USA

Best Music, Original Score John Williams Academy Awards, USA

Best Sound Robert Knudson, Robert Glass, Don Digirolamo, Gene S. Cantamessa Academy Awards, USA

Best Score John Williams BAFTA Awards, UK

Best Motion Picture, Drama Golden Globes, USA

Best Original Score, Motion Picture John Williams Golden Globes, USA

Best Director Steven Spielberg National Society of Film Critics Awards, USA

Best Drama Written Directly for the Screen Melissa Mathison Writers Guild of America

SYNOPSIS

A spacecraft lands on earth and its alien occupants move out into the surrounding countryside to collect examples of flora and fauna, just as a human mission to the moon would collect samples; it is obviously a peaceful visit. A group of men suddenly arrive and chase the aliens; they all escape except for one, who does not make it back in the ensuing panic. The alien, ET, finds itself in a field outside a suburban house and is eventually befriended by the young boy, Elliott, who lives there. Elliott's older brother, Michael, and younger sister, Gertie, soon get to know that ET is living at the house, but they keep his presence a secret from their mother, who is raising them alone since the departure of their father. They discover that ET has special powers: he levitates objects and brings a flower back to life.

As time goes on it becomes apparent that there is a telepathic connection between Elliott and ET; they both soon begin to fall ill as ET suffers from being apart from his own kind. ET manages to 'phone home' whilst out in the woods but when Elliott finds him he is close to death and both he and Elliott are put to bed at home, at which point their mother discovers her children's secret. Government agents arrive at the house and put it, and the family, into quarantine. Soon after, ET 'dies', but a plant that rejuvenates itself indicates to Elliott that he is not dead after all and that the aliens' ship has returned for ET. Believing ET to be dead, the government officers are caught off guard when Elliott escapes with his friend. The escape is aided by ET's ability to levitate the bikes that Elliott and his friends are riding, lifting them out of the clutches of the pursuing officers. ET's fellow creatures have arrived back to rescue him and he finally departs in the spacecraft after an emotional farewell with Elliott.

HISTORICAL CONTEXT

If the 1980s were about financial gain and individuality in Western culture, then *ET* was an antidote to that value system; it expressed ideas of companionship, helping others, selflessness, compassion and a condemnation of the brutal and unfeeling powers of the Establishment. In a world that was, as ever, characterised by intolerance, this was (in its Hollywood way) a confirmation of tolerance. In terms of space exploration, a new era dawned in 1981 with the launch of the first space shuttle, *Columbia*. The furore surrounding this event is hard to imagine now. Recent launches, at least in Britain, receive scant attention unless a tragedy develops (as in 1986 and 2003). The sight of the shuttle landing after the maiden flight emphasised how different space travel would become. In this context of euphoria and hope of new developments in space, it seems entirely appropriate that the alien in *ET* is an explorer, just like the two crew members who piloted *Columbia* on 12 April, 1982. *ET* also slots into the cycle of the summer blockbuster, a phenomenon that seemed the preserve of film-makers' Steven Spielberg and George Lucas in the mid-1970s and early 1980s.

Lucas and Spielberg became, for the studios, the wunderkind of the 1970s, making wildly successful high concept mass entertainment with films that paid homage to the early days of cinema, with its B-movie Westerns and Saturday serials where children lived out their dreams. They also transposed their knowledge of world cinema (*Star Wars* has its origins in Kurosawa's *Hidden Fortress*), but classic Hollywood closed narrative was their fundamental inspiration.

Their early forays, *Duel* (Spielberg, 1971) and *American Graffiti* (Lucas, 1973) promised much, and even hinted at an edgy approach to material. Their subsequent efforts, with *ET* a prime example, demonstrated that they were not really part of the New Hollywood movement. Whilst Scorsese, Cimino, Coppola et al floundered in their desire to overturn the classic Hollywood cinema with auteurist principles, Spielberg and Lucas became the studios' darlings. The shot of ET in Elliott's cupboard hiding from the boy's mother, seemingly another toy to be played with, is an image that foreshadows the merchandising and marketing-driven concept of cinema that would increasingly dominate the summer release schedules.

In terms of science fiction films of the era, *ET*'s cuddly creation chimed with the audiences of 1982, while more serious attempts at science fiction, notably Ridley Scott's *Blade Runner*, were not warmly received at the time (although this film's critical stature has since grown). This dystopian vision of the near future was released just two weeks after Spielberg's film but its sombre philosophical contemplations did not connect either with its producers, who re-edited after poor test previews, or audiences who had already swallowed the sweet Spielberg pill.

Another casualty of *ET*'s success was John Carpenter's *The Thing*, released the same day as *Blade Runne*r, whose alien was the antithesis of Spielberg's Disney-esque creature. Its focus on body horror, building on *Alien*'s torso-splitting scene, did not have a chance against a waddling purveyor of love; in 1982, at least, audiences wanted to embrace their inner aliens, not have them escaping from their stomachs.

The dominance of the Spielberg/Lucas vision is encapsulated in the scene where the children take ET out the during the 'Trick or Treat' celebrations of Halloween. ET is covered with a blanket, but spots a child dressed as Yoda, from Lucas' *Star Wars* films and he attempts to follow him, thinking him a fellow alien. This knowing and witty nod to Lucas' franchise exemplifies the grip that these two men had on audiences at this time and their fairytale, populist approach to film-making.

SELECT FILMOGRAPHY OF MAIN PRODUCERS AND CAST

Steven Spielberg, 1946, Director, Producer

Duel, 1971

The Sugarland Express, 1974

Jaws, 1975

Close Encounters of the Third Kind, 1977

1941, 1979

Raiders of the Lost Ark, 1981

ET The Extra-Terrestrial, 1982

Twilight Zone: The Movie, 1983 (second segment)

Indiana Jones and the Temple of Doom, 1984

The Color Purple, 1985

Empire of the Sun, 1987

Indiana Jones and the Last Crusade, 1989

Always, 1989

Hook, 1991

Jurassic Park, 1993

Schindler's List, 1993

The Lost World: Jurassic Park, 1997

Amistad, 1997

Saving Private Ryan, 1998

Artificial Intelligence: AI, 2001

Minority Report, 2002

Catch Me If You Can, 2002

The Terminal, 2004

War of the Worlds, 2005

Munich, 2005

Indiana Jones and the Kingdom of the Crystal Skull, 2008

Kathleen Kennedy, 1954, Producer

ET The Extra-Terrestrial, 1982

Poltergeist, 1982

Indiana Jones and the Temple of Doom, 1984

The Color Purple, 1985

Empire of the Sun, 1987

Always, 1989

Hook, 1991

Alive, 1993

Jurassic Park, 1993

The Bridges of Madison County, 1995

Twister, 1996

The Lost World: Jurassic Park, 1997

The Sixth Sense, 1999

Artificial Intelligence: AI, 2001

Jurassic Park III, 2001

Seabiscuit, 2003

War of the Worlds, 2005

Munich, 2005

Indiana Jones and the Kingdom of the Crystal Skull, 2008

Melissa Mathison, 1950, Screenwriter

The Black Stallion, 1979

E.T., 1982

The Escape Artist, 1982

The Indian in the Cupboard, 1995

Kundun, 1997

Allen Daviau, 1942, Director of Photography

E.T. the Extra-Terrestrial, 1982

The Color Purple, 1985

Empire of the Sun, 1987

Avalon, 1990

Bugsy, 1991

The Astronaut's Wife, 1998

Van Helsing, 2003

John Williams, 1932, Composer

The Reivers, 1969

Fiddler on the Roof, 1971

The Poseidon Adventure, 1972

The Towering Inferno, 1974

Jaws, 1975

Star Wars Episode IV: A New Hope, 1977

Close Encounters of the Third Kind, 1977

Superman: The Movie, 1978

1941, 1979

Star Wars Episode V: The Empire Strikes Back, 1980

Raiders of the Lost Ark, 1981

ET The Extra-Terrestrial, 1982

Star Wars Episode VI: Return of the Jedi, 1983

Indiana Jones and the Temple of Doom, 1984

Empire of the Sun, 1987

Born on the Fourth of July, 1989

Indiana Jones and the Last Crusade, 1989

Jurassic Park, 1993

Schindler's List, 1993

The Lost World: Jurassic Park, 1997

Saving Private Ryan, 1998

Star Wars Episode I: The Phantom Menace, 1999

A.I.: Artificial Intelligence, 2001

Harry Potter and the Philosopher's Stone, 2001

Catch Me If You Can, 2002

Star Wars Episode II: Attack of the Clones, 2002

Minority Report, 2002

Harry Potter and the Chamber of Secrets, 2002

Harry Potter and the Prisoner of Azkaban, 2004

The Terminal, 2004

Star Wars Episode III: Revenge of the Sith, 2005

War of the Worlds, 2005

Munich, 2005

LINKS TO OTHER FILMS

The Yearling (1946)

Clarence Brown's tearjerker details the relationship between a young boy and his pet, an orphaned fawn called Flag. The pair become inseparable, just like Elliott and ET, and form a bond that fills an emotional vacuum: Elliott does not have the love of his father and Jody's mother is unable to show her son any affection. The narratives diverge at the end when Jody is forced to shoot the badly injured fawn in order to put it out of its misery.

The Day the Earth Stood Still (1951)

Robert Wise's film contains a plea for peace and sanity amidst the anxious times that followed World War II. The message from the alien visit goes unheeded and he is even killed (although he is revived in his spaceship). As such, the message of human inability to deal with otherness in any other way than suspicion and violence is exposed and is echoed in *ET*.

Shane (1953)

Another story of deep affection between a young boy and an outsider, George Steven's film charts the arrival of drifter and gunfighter Shane into the lives of Joey and his homesteader family. A deep bond forms between the two, and the ending echoes that of *ET*, with Shane leaving Joey after the boy has become more reconciled to his home life. The boy's final plaintive cry of 'Shane, Shane' mirrors Elliott's sadness at the end of *ET*.

Jaws (1975)/*Raiders of the Lost Ark* (1981)

Both these earlier Spielberg films are also indebted to the SF/ Western/ action serial films that Hollywood produced from the 1930s onwards. Serials like *Flash Gordon* and *The Phantom Rider* were full of action and punctuated by cliffhangers.

Gremlins (1984)

Joe Dante's film about a cute creature called a mogwai initially has the same ingredients as *ET*, with its emphasis on the companionship between a boy and his adopted friend. However, here the creature spawns a whole host of nasty fiends that cause death and mayhem. In some ways it is a parody of the cute alien scenario that *ET* created, and its connection, albeit a skewed one, is further emphasised by the fact the Steven Spielberg was the film's executive producer.

REPRESENTATION

Aliens

Aliens have come in all shapes and sizes in science fiction films. Their appearance is generally unappealing and they are usually seen as a threat, either real or imagined, by the humans who come

into contact with them. ET broke a long tradition of brutal creatures, a type reinvigorated with fresh levels of malevolence by *Alien*. The new trend in friendly aliens did not last long. In the same year that ET waddled across our screens, John Carpenter's *The Thing* erupted from any number of stomachs (dogs included) and there has been a regular diet of savage aliens since 1982. They threatened to wipe out humans in both *Independence Day* (1996) and Spielberg's version of *War of the Worlds* (2005). Ripley's nemesis has also returned a number of times in the *Alien* films and has been joined by the *Predator* in the galactic bullying of the human race.

Aliens have come to represent our deepest fears or act as mirrors on our own society, the latter often revealing the many imperfections in our personalities and the way we co-exist. Aliens taking human form often exhibit tendencies that are more compassionate than the humans around them, or are corrupted or abused by human folly. In Nicolas Roeg's *The Man Who Fell To Earth* (1976) the alien, Newton, is prevented from achieving his aim of saving his dying planet by the machinations of the humans around him. Meanwhile, the hero of John Carpenter's *Starman* (1984) also visits earth and is represented as a being that can teach humans a lesson about humanity after being received largely with hostility. Elsewhere, the character of Prot in Iain Softley's *K-Pax* (2001) is treated as a lunatic because he tells people that he is an alien.

And so to ET; he looks like the manifestation of a young boy's fertile imagination and his expressions, mannerisms, gait and mode of speech all combine to create a sympathetic and loveable creature. When he hides from Elliott's mother it seems entirely appropriate that he does not look out of place amidst Elliott's other cuddly toys as the mother surveys his wardrobe. ET is ugly, not physically powerful and ungainly, but there is true tenderness in him. He teaches others to be more tolerant: some have seen him as a Jesus figure (the glowing heart, the 'resurrection', the iconography of the Michelangelo-style poster where Elliott's and ET's fingers touch, just as God and Adam do). Ultimately, though, he is the outsider who is shunned for his otherness, representing an ideal, a child-like innocence, which contrasts with the behaviour of the adults. Some choked on the saccharine message, but most consumed it by the bowlful.

> 'Spielberg is a space Jean Renoir... for the first time, [he] has put his breathtaking technical skills at the service of his deepest feelings.' Michael Sragow, *Extra-Terrestrial Perception*, Rolling Stone, 8th July 1982

> 'With its Nativity-like opening and its final revelation, the plot of E.T. has parallels in religious mythology that help to explain its electric effect on audiences.' David Pirie, *Time Out Film Guide 14th Ed.*, London, Time Out Guides Ltd., 2006

KEY SCENE TEXTUAL ANALYSIS

The opening (1/2)

After a title sequence with rather sinister non-diegetic music and sounds, which would not be out of place in a 1950's science fiction film about aliens, the true direction of the film's mood is captured by the light, melodic score with the single flute suggesting wonderment as the camera pans across a night sky, replete with stars.

It is the look of humankind into the vast expanse of space: awe-inspiring, baffling and posing the question of life beyond our own planet. The addition of instruments in a harmonious and delicate fanfare, as the camera pans down to ground level, adds to the atmosphere of magic: the trees are majestic and a mist shrouds the ground. The sense of mystery continues into the next long shot as a spacecraft is seen amidst the trees. It is spherical, reflective and not the sort of grimy spacecraft that became de rigueur in the 1970s. Neither is the music sinister and the whole message seems to

be that these creatures are benign and unlikely to erupt violently from your stomach.

The dissolve from long shot to medium shot of the spacecraft further enhances the stately pace of this opening, rather than a frenetic and scary sequence that might herald an alien arrival in another film. The slow track around the craft with the serious sounding orchestral music elicits an audience reaction of 'isn't this strange and wonderful' rather than 'I can't look because someone's gonna get his head ripped off'.

In keeping with science fiction conventions the creatures are initially only partially glimpsed in order to raise expectation about their unearthly appearance. In most cases this fragmentation is a precursor to some hideous beast, but Spielberg uses this convention only to subvert our expectations. In the tracking shot of the craft some of the creatures are vaguely seen; the diegetic sound consists of animal noises and the noise of the creatures foraging in the undergrowth. A series of dissolves and slow tracking shots help to emphasise the atmosphere of tranquillity. These aliens seem as if they are part of the wildlife around them rather than frightening or brutal lifeforms; they even emit a rather sweet gurgling noise as they shuffle around.

The next shot gives us a little more information about their appearance, as one is seen moving up the craft's ramp in the background and an alien hand gently touches a branch in the foreground.

The interior of the craft sheds more light on their activities, as it houses a cornucopia of exotic fauna, including a tree with a face, which is again presented by a sequence of gentle dissolves, suggesting that this UFO greenhouse is the property of a race of alien gardeners - they might bore you to death about the size of their intergalactic marrows but they won't suck out your brains.

Outside again, the hooting of an owl causes all the silhouettes to stand still and their chests to glow red, like the illuminated heart found in devotional pictures of Jesus Christ (this analogy is extended through other parts of the narrative). An electronic sound is also heard, suggesting visually and aurally that all these creatures are inextricably linked.

The camera then focuses on a sapling, tracking in on it as an alien's hand reaches for it, emitting gentle gurgling noises as it does so. The portrait of peaceful alien is complete; even the rabbit in the next shot is undisturbed by this most sensitive of aliens as it looks on as the sapling is carefully removed.

A long shot of the featured alien shows his body and movement more clearly. It is a small, waddling creature dwarfed by its surroundings and the gigantic redwoods. The audience is now given the alien's POV, further evidence that we are to empathise with the creature rather than fear it; we hear its heavy breathing, obviously in awe of the sight. Again, a POV shot connects us with the alien as he comes to the edge of a summit and gazes down on the electric grid of the city below; gentle gasps of wonderment further endear the audience to the creature.

Where the aliens shuffled carefully and took pains not to destroy, the men tramp quickly and harshly through the natural world.

One man seems singled out by the focus on his keys, hanging from his belt, as he strides between the trucks; the connotation seems to be some sort of power or authority.

Our alien is trapped and a cut back to the spacecraft reveals one remaining alien swaying with anxiety, his chest glowing and sending out its aural signal to the lost creature. This, in turn, causes his chest to glow and resonate. The torch lights that turn on him are brutal and piercing in comparison to the gentle warmth of his inner light. The chase is on and the alien emits a frightened high-pitched squeal as he runs. He is awkward and garners further sympathy from the audience; we are connected with him by the POV shot as he escapes through the undergrowth.

A quick pan and a change to the harmonious non-diegetic music indicate the arrival of a threat; and that threat is human. Rather than post the alien as the aggressor Spielberg suggests that humans are the real aliens in the sequence that follows.

The pan shows a large truck crashing into the idyllic scene, the music brutally conveying its arrival. The alien departs in a long shot and the wheel of a truck bludgeons its way into the frame.

Where the spacecraft reflected the natural world around it, and thus became part of it, these modes of transport tear through the undergrowth. Their lights rip into this tranquil world, pointing directly at the audience, alienating us. The close-up of the exhaust spewing fumes into this pristine atmosphere reiterates the detrimental effect of this intrusion.

The pace of the editing and the speed of the music increases as the chase continues in order to heighten the sense of tension and the alien's anxiety at reaching the spacecraft. The second shot of the waiting alien starts to track backwards away from the craft, subtly suggesting that time is running out for the pursued alien.

In the chase the alien is characterised by his frightened grunts, glowing chest and clumsy movement, all eliciting our sympathy. In contrast, the men are brutal silhouettes, torches flashing wildly in all directions, like the frenzy of demented hunting hounds.

Another alien POV, and the heartbreaking sight of the ramp closing with the waiting alien still watching, increases our sympathy for the alien being left behind, as does his plaintive cry when the craft takes off. The craft does not scorch the ground and leaves no impression as it flees from the true intruders in this sequence.

A long shot of a ridge with a wooden gate shrouded in mist is the next evocative shot, first violated by the men's intrusive lights and then by the men as they watch the craft speed away. The non-diegetic music becomes its most dramatic and the diegetic sound of keys jingling reoccurs once again.

The craft departs and the camera tracks behind the alien as he comes to stop on a ridge. The sounds he emits are obviously transmitting his anguish to the audience and, for the first time, we get a clear view of his stumpy, awkward body as he gazes after the craft. All the glimpses of him have developed a keen connection between him and the audience and so the revelatory shot of his appearance does not surprise us – in this short sequence we have come to know him and the way he thinks and feels.

The sequence ends with the figures and their torches criss-crossing the frame as they search for the alien, their threat remaining in the audience's mind.

Unusually, and running against the contemporary depiction of aliens as brutal monsters, the aliens could teach the humans a thing or two about kindness and sensitivity, if not gardening.

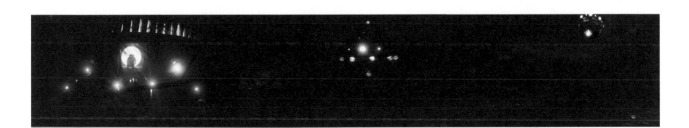

His final cry captures the attention of the pursuers once again and their focus on him is shown through the synchronised movement of their torches. We still have not seen them clearly. For this scene and, indeed, much of the film, they are represented by torches, keys and cars, as the audience is deliberately kept from identifying with them.

A crane shot upwards follows the alien's movement forward and over the ridge towards the uncertainty of the glowing city below, its *alien* and forbidding nature signalled by the wailing sirens and barking dogs.

The torches move in the direction of the sound; their humanness is not indicated right up to the end of the sequence. In fact, the lights all seem as if they are coming from their bodies, a cold white light in contrast to the warmth of the alien's red light.

The Matrix

KEY FACTS

Release Date: 1999

Country of Origin: USA/ Australia

Running Time: 136 minutes

PRODUCTION NOTES

Production Companies

Groucho II Film Partnership

Silver Pictures

Village Roadshow Pictures

Warner Bros. Pictures

Distributor

Warner Bros. Pictures

Budget

$63,000,000 (estimated)

Awards

Best Editing Zach Staenberg Academy Awards, USA

Best Effects, Sound Effects Editing Dane A. Davis Academy Awards, USA

Best Effects, Visual Effects John Gaeta, Janek Sirrs, Steve Courtley, Jon Thum Academy Awards, USA

Best Sound John T. Reitz, Gregg Rudloff, David E. Campbell, David Lee Academy Awards, USA

Best Sound David Lee, John T. Reitz, Gregg Rudloff, David E. Campbell, Dane A. Davis BAFTA Awards, UK

Best Achievement in Special Visual Effects John Gaeta, Steve Courtley, Janek Sirrs, Jon Thum BAFTA Awards, UK

SYNOPSIS

The concept of this film is that the world is only a construct, the Matrix, created by machines to pacify humans' minds, whilst actually using people as power supplies in vast 'farms'. Only a few people have escaped this fate. One such group of resistance fighters is led by Morpheus aboard a craft called the *Nebuchadnezzar*, existing in the subterranean world which is all that is left of Earth in about the year 2199.

Morpheus recruits the young Neo and releases him from the yoke of machine oppression. He is taught how to manipulate the constructed world of the Matrix, and to fight the machine's own self-constructs, the Agents, in order to save humanity. For much of the film it seems as if Neo is the new saviour, the 'One', but his death at the hands of Agent Smith seems to spell disaster for everyone. However, Neo overcomes his death in the Matrix and is able to clearly see through and control the construct, defeating the Agents, and becoming the one who can save people from their mental and physical imprisonment.

HISTORICAL CONTEXT

The film is a technological breakthrough in cinematic terms as new media technologies continued to change society (see REPRESENTATION section below). The cutting-edge, computer-generated images (CGI) were part of a larger picture of technological breakthroughs in all areas of new media. The 1993 Steven Spielberg film, *Jurassic Park*, really moved film realisation of complex visions onto a new level of possibility with its digital creation of dinosaurs. *The Matrix* itself helped produce invigorating visuals with its creation of 'bullet time' which, when matched with Asian stunt work coordinated by film director, Woo-ping Yuen, heralded a new era of CGI and continued the flow of Asian film influences on many Hollywood genre films.

The Matrix, like *Jurassic Park*, warns of the dangers in our rapidly changing world, yet also reflects the audience's increasing awareness of its status as easily manipulated passive consumers in the age of globalisation. On the one hand, the film makes the case for personal freedom in the face of technological enslavement; on the other it is produced by a film company (Warner Bros.) that is itself part of a major multi-national conglomerate (Time Warner) which, arguably, plays a key role in manipulating people.

The synergy of tie-in media products like *Matrix*

computer games, to further immerse us in the world of the film's narrative, is just another way of exporting the ideology of consumerism. The 1990s was yet another decade of battling ideologies, particularly the growing one between West and East, Christian and Muslim, and although *The Matrix* flags up the need for questions, it could also be seen as part of the problem itself. Indeed, the sequels, *The Matrix Reloaded* and *The Matrix Revolutions*, both released in 2003, seem to be even more problematic in this regard.

Although both recorded box office success, critical reception became increasingly negative as the trilogy descended into convoluted philosophising and lacked the lightness of touch that had garnered the original so much praise. The two sequels were made alongside live-action footage for the computer game, *Enter the Matrix*, suggesting, at least, the studio's financial imperative rather than any commitment to the original's visionary film-making. Generally, the filmic disease known as sequelitis lends itself to creative bankruptcy - studios try to cash in on an original film's success, but without the vision of the original director and usually with a repetitive retread of ideas already fully explored. Some directors have expended all their energy on following a formula (Blake Edwards' *Pink Panther* film series) and some actors just do not know when to let their characters retire: Sylvester Stallone (aka Rocky Balboa; aka John Rambo) take a bow.

SELECT FILMOGRAPHY OF MAIN PRODUCERS AND CAST

Larry Wachowski, 1965/Andy Wachowski, 1967, Directors, Producers, Screenwriters

Assassins, 1995

Bound, 1996

The Matrix, 1999

The Matrix Reloaded, 2003

The Matrix Revolutions, 2003

The Animatrix, 2003

V for Vendetta, 2006

Speed Racer, 2008

Joel Silver, 1952, Producer

The Warriors, 1979

48 Hrs, 1982

Commando, 1985

Lethal Weapon, 1987 (and sequels)

Predator, 1987 (and sequels)

Die Hard, 1988 (and sequels)

The Matrix, 1999

The Matrix Reloaded, 2003

The Matrix Revolutions, 2003

The Animatrix, 2003

V for Vendetta, 2006

Speed Racer, 2008

Keanu Reeves, 1964, Actor

River's Edge, 1986

Bill and Ted's Excellent Adventure, 1989

Point Break, 1991

My Own Private Idaho, 1991

Bram Stoker's Dracula, 1992

Speed, 1994

The Devil's Advocate, 1997

The Matrix, 1999

The Matrix Reloaded, 2003

The Matrix Revolutions, 2003

Constantine, 2005

A Scanner Darkly, 2006

The Day the Earth Stood Still, 2008

Laurence Fishburne, 1961, Actor

Apocalypse Now, 1979

School Daze, 1986

King of New York, 1990

Boyz n the Hood, 1991

What's Love Got To Do With It?, 1993

Othello, 1995

Event Horizon, 1997

The Matrix, 1999

Mystic River, 2003

The Matrix Reloaded, 2003

The Matrix Revolutions, 2003

Assault on Precinct 13, 2005

LINKS TO OTHER FILMS

L'Armée des ombres (1969)

Jean-Pierre Melville's film about the French Resistance during World War Two has many parallels with *The Matrix*. It details a group's highly dangerous endeavours to get allied soldiers out of France, to disrupt the Nazis and to try and rescue their own from the clutches of the occupiers and the French who collaborated with them. The movement from their isolated and hand-to-mouth existence in dilapidated safe houses into the cafes and houses of the main French population, the chance of discovery at any moment, and the unemotional cruelty of those in power all echo the trials that Morpheus and his group must endure. The depiction of a very recognisable France and French people belie that, under the surface, this band of freedom fighters were in hostile territory, liable to be betrayed or caught at any moment.

They Live (1988)

John Carpenter's film has a number of similarities with *The Matrix*, but the main parallel is that of a world that is a construct, created by the few to suppress the many. The few are, in fact, aliens who have all the power and money. They embed subliminal messages into media that the population consume daily and without question: billboards do not actually advertise, but carry messages to manipulate people's thoughts. Here again, a group of freedom fighters develop special glasses which unlock these messages for the wearer, similar to the way Neo eventually sees the matrix for what it really is: a computer code designed to control humanity.

The Truman Show (1998)

Another film where the world of one particular human is actually a construct. From birth, Truman Burbank has been the unwitting star of his own reality TV show. Peter Weir's film raises issues of identity, personal freedom and control by another power, all key issues in *The Matrix*.

REPRESENTATION

Modern society

The 1990s saw an explosion in new media technologies, which were to have an immense impact on society. Technologies like the internet and mobile phones opened up a world of possibilities and dangers that would continue to evolve into the new millennium. The ability both to communicate and to control grew ever greater, as did the real fear that personal liberties were at risk from the expanding power that these technologies could give to individuals, whether they be criminals or terrorists, big business or the military. With so much private information swilling around cyberspace and the virtual world acting as a refuge from the ever-increasing complexities of modernity, it was fertile ground for the Wachowski brothers to make *The Matrix* and its sequels.

Real and imagined paranoia and loss of personal freedom have always been threads that have pervaded human history; the poet William Blake wrote of people's 'mind-forg'd manacles' in his poem, *London*, published in 1794, detailing the Establishment's control of the general populace. Indeed, history, with the twentieth century an excellent example, is littered with leaders, political groups and ideologies that have sought to control the minds of others; Hitler's fascism and Stalinist communism to name but two. *The Matrix* taps into these notions of oppression and gives them a hi-tech, topical slant.

Religion/spirituality

The film is awash with religious symbolism; the band led by Morpheus all have powers within the matrix, the ability to perform 'miracles'. Principally, it is Neo who is described in religious terms; he is the one they have been waiting for, a saviour or a Jesus to Morpheus' John the Baptist. As Neo's mentor, Morpheus is also a God-like figure who oversees his development, while the character Trinity (who literally breathes life into Neo) connotes the idea of the Holy Spirit, her name an obvious reference to the concept of the Holy Trinity. Like Jesus, Neo and the 'disciples' are betrayed by a Judas-like figure, Cypher, leading to Neo's 'death'. There is, of course, Neo's victory over death which mirrors the life, death and resurrection of Jesus; his rebirth will give people freedom. Neo's triumphant sweep upwards as he glides towards the camera speaks of both Jesus on the cross and his ascension into heaven in the same moment. It is an image of redemption and hope for humanity, but like in Christian doctrine we are given the free will to respond, to see through the matrix (of sin) or not.

The Matrix may be a science fiction film at its core, but it is a generic hybrid. It is a bricolage of a host of art forms, genres and influences, in the largest sense a blend of the action and technophobic science fiction film via the Western, Hong Kong kung fu movies, film noir, John Woo, the virtual reality sub-genre, millennial angst, comic book superheroes, postmodernism, religions, classical mythology, 'cyberpunk', philosophy and a multitude of popular culture texts from films to computer games.' Anna Dawson, *Studying the Matrix*, Auteur, 2008

'The Matrix *is grounded in two science fiction commonplaces: the war between man and machine, and the possibility that reality is a hoax.'* Joshua Clover, *The Matrix*, BFI, 2004

KEY SCENE TEXTUAL ANALYSIS

The real world (9/10)

The future as construct is the premise behind *The Matrix*, and the construct in question – the matrix – is revealed in this scene. The *mise-en-scène* conveys a world that has echoes of the 1940s, comic books and future technology.

The initial medium two-shot of Morpheus and Neo is a study in balance: the two chairs, the two figures, dissected by the table with the glass. It is a crucial moment in the film - will Neo take the red pill and discover the truth about the matrix? The frame suggests the fine balance of the moment. The *mise-en-scène* also suggests the mixture of styles that are in evidence: the old leather chairs and ornate fire-place and the characters' modern, black clothing have echoes of the future and are rather comic book in their ultra-cool detail.

The chiaroscuro lighting is reminiscent of film noir and the oblique conversation between the men is a heady mixture of noir-talk, all hardboiled, and 'technobabble', the staple of science fiction films.

The first close-up of Morpheus exhibits power through his dominance of the frame; he is talking to someone to frame right. The ordinary convention would be to have a space to the right of him, but he moves forward and occupies that space. The shot of Neo emphasises his feelings of doubt and weakness at this point; he is seen in the far right of frame, allowing a large space to his left. He is succumbing to Morpheus' confident presence. The non-diegetic music is comprised of strings which pierce through the diegetic sounds of Morpheus' coolly authoritative voice and the lightning outside, underlining the sense of unease.

The blue pill is seen in close-up in Morpheus' hand, highlighting its importance. Then comes a computer-enhanced shot of Morpheus with Neo and his own outstretched hand perfectly reflected in both lenses of his dark glasses. It is both visually striking in itself and heightens the importance of the moment and Neo's anxieties; he can only see himself and Morpheus' eyes will not guide him in the decision. The shot of both hands with the two pills again points to the enormity of the decision to be made.

The glasses then reflect both hands as well as two Neos. It is a moment of choices and each will create a dramatically different future for Neo.

The medium shot of Morpheus with outstretched hands contains a large swathe of darkness to the right of frame and the back of Neo's chair, signifying mystery, uncertainty and an unseen future. The shot is reversed from behind Morpheus; Neo is surrounded by the darkness of unknowing. To further illustrate the existence of two fates, an extreme close-up of Morpheus' glasses shows two distinct Neos, one reaching for the red pill, the other motionless.

Morpheus smiles as Neo takes the red pill to begin the journey into enlightenment, and lightning cracks - a clichéd convention of the horror genre, but reworked in this milieu to provide gothic horror overtones.

The movement into the next room signals again the clashing of genre references. It is an old dark mansion with lightning flashing at key moments, but it is also full of technological paraphernalia, thrown together in the favoured style of modern science fiction films, somewhat shabby and ramshackle, a future blighted by its destructive past.

The whole *mise-en-scène* encompasses the past (the room), the present (the people) and the future (the technology); all are present at the same time as befits a film that transports its characters between various versions of 'reality'. A number of medium shots and close-ups establish the other characters and highlight the technology that will transport Neo. Some pieces, the eyepiece for example, look part of science fiction iconography whilst others, such as the cannibalised old telephone, are science-fact.

The longest close-up is, understandably, of Neo, as the pill takes effect and he peers into the mirror, another reference to duality.

The cracked mirror heals itself and a combination of diegetic and non-diegetic sounds mimick the noise of reforming glass. The brooding non-diegetic music continues to gather pace to reflect his mounting sense of otherness.

The touching of the glass, which now has a liquid form and sticks to his fingers, is accompanied by an electronic sound to highlight its honey-like texture.

Morpheus' words are underpinned by the shots of both men reflected in the mirror; the crossing of the boundaries of reality is about to begin.

The initial image is of a womb-like environment, limbs floating in an amniotic fluid-like substance. The camera places us within the womb to further emphasise our connection with the rebirth, while diegetic breathing, heartbeat and fluid noises complete the impression. The effect is disorientating for the audience, as it will be for Neo.

A hand forces its way through the thick mucus membrane and the sharp, harsh non-diegetic music matches the struggle. The shots cut from looking straight down on the action to a view from the front, again disorientating the viewer.

The medium shot, as the figure emerges, helps to establish it as Neo. The cables and tubes that surround him are grounded in the film's science fiction conventions, and the tubes that he takes from his mouth, and the cables attached to his skin, are further elements of body horror. As yet, we are

Neo quickly becomes engulfed by this substance as the others race to locate the other Neo and transport him there; the rapid cutting and gathering musical climax enhance these moments of tension and science fiction horror. There are many instances of 'body horror' imagery in the film and this sequence ends with one such shot.

The frantic non-diegetic music mingles with Neo's scream and the massive digital noise as he is transported into the reality of the matrix. The computer-generated effects show the liquid covering his body and entering his mouth. As the camera follows this route into his throat, the audience is plunged into the same nightmarish feeling of dislocation that Neo is experiencing – we too are born into a realisation of the narrative's direction. The fade to black and fade out appropriately signifies Neo's rebirth into reality, from unconsciousness to consciousness; it also marks the audience's journey into understanding.

given no context as to the environment in which Neo now finds himself, adding to the tension and sense of expectation.

Before the revelatory shot the camera observes the body in close-up, the non-diegetic music's sinister electronic sound signalling the horror of this new technological world. The most disturbing shot is of the cable attached to the back of Neo's skull, which he clasps, but is then distracted by the vision before him.

A flash of light and the shot cuts, synchronised with a metallic thud on the non-diegetic score, revealing a line of pods all containing human figures suspended in the same fluid; it is an incomprehensible and nightmarish vision.

The full revelatory shot is accompanied by a non-diegetic choral effect and climactic note, emphasising the horrific spectacle. There are countless pods wrapped around huge columns as electrical currents criss-cross between them and the camera pans from high to low to underline the vertiginous position in which Neo is seemingly trapped.

As we cut back to Neo's incredulous face, he peers over the edge of his pod; the anticipation is for another POV as he looks straight down. Initially that appears to be the nature of the next shot but it is, in fact, from above Neo looking down on him. The rapid track down to him indicates that this is *something else's* POV; it all happens very quickly, but the effect is, again, to disorientate the audience. This shot is computer-generated, as is this whole set-up, and it is in the meticulous detail of such designs that the film is able to satisfyingly realise its science fiction future world.

The rapid downward track twists as it descends and is accompanied by a diegetic fluttering and non-diegetic musical metallic screech, preparing us for the cut to Neo in the pod, faced by a metallic, robotic insect. This shot from behind Neo clearly shows the cables connected to his back, and is wince-inducing in terms of the violation of his body.

The insect suddenly opens out and reveals its dangerous jaws and legs; Neo's frail, white body is as vulnerable as a new-born baby. When his neck is grabbed the audience fears the worst, but instead the cable in his skull is removed; the close-up and drill-like sound accentuate the appalling spectacle of a human at the mercy of a machine.

But with that, it flies off, and our expectation of a struggle has been confounded; the popping off of all his cables from all parts of the body is accompanied by explosive diegetic sounds and a flurry of discordant non-diegetic noise.

A hole opens beneath him and Neo plunges downwards, the rapid cutting emphasising his inability to cope with the fast-moving and incomprehensible events, and the sound of his hand screeching against the pod's side, unable to get a hold, suggests his helplessness.

In order to connect the audience with Neo the camera travels with him as he slides down a tube; the shot is exhilarating and disorientating, just what the Wachowski brothers want us to feel.

But this is no waterworld theme park. The tube is dank and dark and like a sewer pipe, and the water into which he falls is topped with scum; Neo has been flushed down the matrix's toilet.

The music is rapid and frantic, the instruments seemingly jostling for position as he splutters in the water, close to drowning. Then, hope; a light hits the water and a sound similar to a helicopter cuts through the chaotic non-diegetic music. His POV reveals three lights and an opening - more horror or salvation?

Neo's body sinks beneath the surface and yet another monstrous device lowers towards the camera, plucks Neo's prone body out of the filthy water, and carries him up into the light. It is like an ascension; his naked body is Christ-like in its crucifixion pose as it emerges from the depths and a gentle, almost angelic chorus, accompanies the ascent.

There is a final metallic thud as the doorway into the light closes and the audience is again plunged (with Neo) into the darkness of confusion once more, but only for a moment. The machine that has pulled him up is revealed to be under human control and the familiar sights of Morpheus and Trinity, with Neo swaddled in a blanket, confirm that he is safe.

The audience's connection with Neo is once again emphasised as the final shot of the sequence is Neo's blurry POV as Morpheus says to him and us, 'Welcome to the real world'. The close affinity between Neo's journey of discovery and our own lends the film its emotive power and makes us better prepared to enjoy and accept this version of the future. The fade to black signifies the end of this stage of Neo's and the audience's journey.

Children of Men

KEY FACTS

Release Date: 2006

Country of Origin: USA/GB

Running Time: 105 minutes

PRODUCTION NOTES

Production Companies

Universal Pictures

Strike Entertainment

Hit & Run Productions

Ingenious Film Partners

Toho-Towa

Distributor

Universal Pictures

Budget

$76,000,000 (estimated)

Awards

Best Cinematography Emmanuel Lubezki BAFTA Awards, UK

Best Production Design Geoffrey Kirkland, Jim Clay, Jennifer Williams BAFTA Awards, UK

SYNOPSIS

The human race has been beset by infertility for almost 20 years, and the film begins with news reports of the murder of the last child born on Earth, who is 18-years-old at the time of his death. Set against a backdrop of a United Kingdom gripped by chaos and under virtual martial law, Theo Faron is a bureaucrat who is drawn back into a world of activism by his ex-wife, Julian Taylor. She leads a militant group called the Fishes that supports the rights of immigrants who are kept in internment camps by the government. Theo agrees to take care of a refugee, Kee, at the request of Julian, who is then killed in an ambush.

In hiding, Theo learns why Kee is so important to the Fishes: she is pregnant. He also overhears the group's new leader, Luke, discussing how he wants to keep Kee and her baby as a bargaining tool with the government instead of taking her to a safe haven, called the Human Project, dedicated to curing infertility. Theo escapes with Kee and another group member, Miriam, and they stop at a friend of Theo's, Jasper Palmer. Whilst there, Jasper organises their escape to the Human Project via Bexhill refugee camp which is the heavily guarded gateway to join the group aboard their ship, 'Tomorrow'. The three fugitives gain access to the camp as prisoners of one of the guards, Syd, who is a friend of Jasper's.

Once in the camp, they are separated from Miriam and Kee gives birth to a girl. In pursuit, the rest of the Fishes kill Jasper and then catch up with them at Bexhill. There is a battle between British soldiers and the Fishes in the streets of Bexhill and Luke is killed and Theo wounded. The fighting stops momentarily when Kee and her baby emerge from a building and the soldiers look on in wonder. Theo and Kee find a rowing boat with the help of a fellow detainee, Marichka, and they head out to sea and wait at the allotted buoy. As 'Tomorrow' emerges from the dense fog Theo seems to succumb to his wounds and the sound of Bexhill being bombed by the military is heard in the distance.

HISTORICAL CONTEXT

The new millennium, and the United States comes under attack by Islamic terrorists in 2001, bird flu rears its head from 2000 onwards, there are increased warnings of global warming and greater infertility in men across the Western world. Whatever the moral panic, there has been a film made to depict the devastating consequences for humanity.

Children of Men feeds directly off one of these issues - infertility - but also makes reference to a flu pandemic, which has killed the main protagonist's son, and there is also detailed observation of a society fearful of mass immigration and under constant violent attack from groups opposed to the government. Hollywood often depicts global catastrophes with elaborate CGI special effects, sentimentality and superficiality, the destruction of the human race usually treated as a backdrop for a muscular action hero to strut his macho stuff.

Films such as *Armageddon* (1998), *Deep Impact* (1998) and *The Core* (2003) all posit scenarios that involve the imminent destruction of planet earth, yet their narratives seem far removed from reality. But more recent films, such as *The Day After Tomorrow* (2004), *Sunshine* (2007) and *Children of Men*, do have the ring of truth about how our future might develop (even if the science remains vague). Even more prescient are the films of the 1960s, 1970s and 1980s which predicted developments which do actually seem to be dangerously close: the environmental problems of 2019 featured in *Blade Runner*, for example.

SELECT FILMOGRAPHY OF MAIN PRODUCERS AND CAST

Alfonso Cuaron, 1961, Director, Producer, Screenwriter

Solo con tu pareja, 1991

A Little Princess, 1995

Great Expectations, 1998

Y Tu Mama Tambien, 2001

Harry Potter and the Prisoner of Azkaban, 2004

Children of Men, 2006

Clive Owen, 1964, Actor

Croupier, 1998

Gosford Park, 2001

The Bourne Identity, 2002

Closer, 2004

King Arthur, 2004

Sin City, 2005

Children of Men, 2006

The International, 2009

Julianne Moore, 1960, Actress

Short Cuts, 1993

Nine Months, 1995

The Lost World: Jurassic Park, 1997

Boogie Nights, 1997

The Big Lebowski, 1998

The End of the Affair, 1999

Magnolia, 1999

Hannibal, 2001

Far From Heaven, 2002

The Hours, 2002

Children of Men, 2006

Blindness, 2008

Michael Caine, 1933, Actor

Zulu, 1964

The Ipcress File, 1965

Alfie, 1966

Funeral in Berlin, 1966

Billion Dollar Brain, 1967

The Italian Job, 1969

Get Carter, 1971

Sleuth, 1972

The Man Who Would Be King, 1975

The Eagle Has Landed, 1976

A Bridge Too Far, 1977

Dressed To Kill, 1980

Educating Rita, 1983

Hannah and Her Sisters, 1986

Mona Lisa, 1986

Dirty Rotten Scoundrels, 1988

Little Voice, 1998

The Cider House Rules, 1999

Last Orders, 2001

The Quiet American, 2002

Batman Begins, 2005

Children of Men, 2006

The Prestige, 2006

The Dark Knight, 2008

LINKS TO OTHER FILMS

On the Beach (1959)

Stanley Kramer's film, based on the Nevil Shute novel, records the final days of those who have survived World War III as they wait for the nuclear fallout to drift south towards them in Australia. The tone of the film has the same pervasive sense of inevitability about the onset of society's collapse as *Children of Men*. The only difference is *Children of Men*'s glimpse of possible salvation in the form of the Human Project.

Mad Max (1979)

A vision of the future in a post-apocalyptic world where there is little law and order, particularly in the desolate wilderness beyond the towns. The sporadic and violent eruptions of violence are echoed in *Children of Men*, such as the attack on the Fishes' convoy as they travel on a road bordered by forests.

Escape from New York (1981)

John Carpenter's film set in 1997 envisages a world where criminals are dispensed to city-wide prisons rather than the conventional buildings, which are now too small to cope with the massive rise in crime. One such facility exists on the island of Manhattan which has had a wall built around it, and the prisoners are left to survive and fend for themselves. The atmosphere of chaos and anarchy is analogous to that which exists at the Bexhill camp in *Children of Men*.

The Handmaid's Tale (1990)

This adaptation of Margaret Attwood's novel details a future where infertility has beset the world, and the few remaining fertile women are forced to bear children for those who are in charge of a fictional country, the Republic of Gilead. The film, like *Children of Men*, presents a dystopian future where the issue of human reproduction acts as a consequence of human folly and as a metaphor for the downward spiral of society.

28 Days Later (2002)

Danny Boyle's *28 Days Later* is similar to Alfonso Cuaron's film in its visualisation of society which has broken down and descended into chaos. They share the same bleak images of a ravaged and often deserted Britain set sometime in the near future. They are also pervaded by an extremely downbeat atmosphere which links stark imagery of the chaos and brutalisation against a backdrop of a very familiar and contemporary-looking country, which serves to heighten the unease that fuels both films.

REPRESENTATION

Fertility

In recent years there has been growing evidence that infertility is rising and that a number of factors, including obesity, are to blame. *Children of Men* taps into this phenomenon and uses it to explore humanity's seeming instinct for self-destruction. It is an issue that has been long debated, both in terms of declining birth rates in the Western world and rises in developing countries. For instance, in 2007 Mali, followed by Niger, had the world's highest fertility rate (that is, the expected number of children born per woman in her child-bearing years) with countries like Spain, Italy and Switzerland being among those countries with the lowest. Whether the issue is overcrowding or declining populations, science fiction films connect with contemporary concerns and develop them to examine human folly and strength in adversity.

Immigration

Another contemporary issue that is also a political hot potato. Developed nations have always been a magnet for immigrants, but in recent years there has been a resurgence in mass migration with the removal of borders in the European Union, for example. In Britain the past few years have seen an increase of immigrants from Eastern European countries, sparking public debates about their impact on society. The media has reported on the subsequent strain on public services as well as the immigrants' willingness to take on jobs that few British people are now prepared to undertake. Thus, in some quarters they are vilified whilst in others they are lauded; the scenario in *Children of Men* presents the chilling result of an Establishment that starts to demonise all immigrants and defend its borders at all costs. The resulting spectacle of a country under martial law looks forward to a future that has had many terrifying precedents in recent history.

> 'This explosively violent future-nightmare thriller... has simply the most extraordinary look of any movie around: a stunningly convincing realisation of a Beirut-ised London in the year 2027, in which terrorist bombs have become as dreary and commonplace as cancer... there is something just so grimly and grittily plausible about the awful world conjured up here, and the full-on urban warfare scenes really are electrifying... Cuarón has created the thinking person's action movie.'
> Peter Bradshaw, *The Guardian*, September 22, 2006

KEY SCENE TEXTUAL ANALYSIS

Escape (17)

The opening frame symbolises the danger and uncertainty in which the fleeing Theo, Kee and her baby find themselves as they try to escape from the refugee camp with the help of Marichka and Sirdjan. It comprises a dark tunnel littered with debris, an unsteady camera move and high-pitched non-diegetic strings (reminiscent of those in *The Shining* as a demented Jack Nicholson pursues his son through a snow-covered maze).

A figure runs into frame, followed by the others. His long coat and figure are silhouetted, suggestive of both danger and the anonymity that he and the others crave as they try to flee without the baby being discovered. Sharp, shrieking violins puncture the soundtrack like penetrating blades; the effect unsettles the audience.

We follow the people as one of them, the steadicam propelling us into their nightmarish world. The non-diegetic sound is soon overtaken by the equally chilling sound of automatic gunfire and the camera nestles in with the group, eager to seek a safe place. The actual sound of the gunfire is low key, very un-Hollywood-like in its lack of dramatic power; everything is chaotic, random,

dirt and dust suggest a world we know, but one which has been savaged. This is, if not science fact, at least science *possibility*. Indeed, the whole film is filled with reminders of our everyday lives, but ones which are brutalised by the chaos of this possible future.

As the armed 'Fishes' arrive the camera recoils then swings around as their leader comes in from a different direction. It is very much the movement of one who is there, a POV of an unseen participant in this madness.

As Theo, Marichka and Sirdjan are about to be executed, the camera crouches down with Theo, letting the audience share his fear. The diegetic sounds of gunfire, shouting and screaming reverberate around them, stoking the aural hell fires, as does the song that the killer sings as he prepares to shoot. Into this mix is also the faint

and positively undramatic. Figures merely crumple to the ground when bullets hit and there are no dramatic twirls or tear-jerking final speeches. The bleached-out colours of the surroundings and the very ordinary sights of a shop front and an old-fashioned telephone box further enhance this air of documentary realism.

As the skirmish moves on, the group continues with the camera following and sharing in its desperate plight.

The dual sense of familiarity and dislocation that the audience feels about the *mise-en-scène* strengthens the disturbing atmosphere. This science fiction scenario drips with the recognisable detritus of *today*: the burnt-out car, the 'Bexhill Water Authority' sign, the remnants of twentieth century office buildings covered by a thick layer of

return of the strings, sounding an underlying note of hysteria. Sirdjan's execution is swift and without ceremony, emphasising the casual nature of death.

With the return of the army, the sound of gunfire is again dominant, the cacophony of sounds as they hit various surfaces (metal, brick, wood, the ground) adding to the documentary feel. For a film set in the future it has great verisimilitude and wants its audience to know that this future might be just around the corner.

The camera again moves off with Theo and Marichka as they escape, the pace causing the camera to rock violently from side to side. Bullets erupting in the earth around them accentuate the sense of panic.

Again, familiar British elements of the *mise-en-scène* continue to disturb the audience through their juxtaposition with the unsettling sight of street warfare: the speed limit sign and the 'Sea Spray' shop sign, for example. The utter devastation around these familiar visuals is a chilling reminder that this nightmarish future scenario is very much rooted in our present.

Theo's very English apology as he dives into the prostrate immigrants sheltering from the firefight further underlines the incongruity of the scene. The irony of its redundancy in such chaotic circumstances reminds the audience that this is Britain, but the polite rituals of the country seem like grains of gold dust lost in a desert of brutality.

As Theo rounds the corner, the scene and diegetic sound convey an image more akin to a developing country than one from Europe: sheep are penned by the side of the road and buses lie, wheel-less, homes to some more immigrants. The bus stop opposite is an ironic and pathetic reminder of the past.

Theo's would-be killer, who was prevented from executing a few moments before by the military's arrival, returns from further down the road and the menacing non-diegetic strings once more signal Theo's predicament.

With every move he makes, the camera reacts in the same way as if we are a silent witness to these atrocities; as Theo jumps onto the bus to escape the bullets so the camera dodges and jerks with him.

It is at this point that our noses are rubbed into the nightmare. As Theo is fired upon a woman is hit and her blood sprays not just her immediate surroundings, but the camera lens as well. The audience has been dragged by the scruff of the neck into the battle zone, no longer the voyeur. This has happened in other films - blood splattered the camera in Steven Spielberg's *Saving Private Ryan*, and a car demolished the camera in Peter Yates' *Bullitt* (1968), but the effect was fleeting and immediately lost with a cut.

Here, there is no cut and the blood spots remain on the lens, and on us, for a further whole minute. It may draw our attention to the medium initially, but after more seconds elapse it serves as a reminder

of our part in the unfolding events. This sense of the audience's participation is further emphasised by the immigrants who stare and shout at the camera: if not actually there, it is as if we are the cameraman, filming the atrocities but unprepared to intervene. If the film is a warning of the future, then we are called to be witnesses and act now.

We follow Theo across to the building where the young mother and baby are being held captive. The moments before his scramble inside are fraught with danger and the audience is at his side. We crouch down with him as the tanks bombard the building and innocent civilians are mown down, the force of one explosion shaking him and the camera, reiterating the feeling of intensity. The non-diegetic music continues throughout, the straining pitch of the strings suggesting the nerve-shredding madness of the situation and the strain on Theo as every physical and mental sinew is stretched to near breaking point.

The whole of this sequence is akin to documentary or *vérité* footage, achieved through all the devices mentioned, but perhaps most completely by the use of one take. The film is made up of similarly lengthy sequences, and this one lasts for approximately four minutes (the cut, when it does come, is unseen, and allows for the tension and intensity to remain unchecked). The absence of narrative fictional film editing conventions encourages us to regard these scenes as unmediated footage, similar to the live feeds we see fragments of on news bulletins. It *feels* real, it is exhilarating and its uncut flow even suggests an inherent truth.

HORROR

Horror is such a rich vein for exploration and the journey through the decades revealed how much this genre is a barometer of society, visualising its demons in a profound manner. It is never better than when it taps into the decade's zeitgeist, exposing familiar stories in a startling and innovative way. *Nosferatu* (1922), even after all these years, is a genuinely creepy experience, its visuals and Max Schreck's central performance as unsettling now as they must have been in 1922. It is also wonderful to see how director F.W. Murnau was able to produce such a record of depravity here, whilst almost simultaneously providing us with such a vision of beauty in *Sunrise* (1927), his other film in this book. The other great literary 'monster' to emerge from the nineteenth century was put on screen in the 1930s; the original *Frankenstein* (1931) remains the definitive film version, not because it follows the source text slavishly, but because the direction, *mise-en-scène* and camerawork combine to create a purity of vision that remains unmatched by subsequent attempts. It is the story of the great outsider, the other, whom society must destroy in order to feel safe again and to assuage its own bad conscience.

Cat People (1942) is my personal favourite from this genre; it is a masterclass in how inspired use of film language can transcend limitations of budget and some indifferent acting, resulting in a sublime meditation on human nature and our darkest fears. In many ways its closest film relative in this section is the entry for the 2000s section, *Dark Water* (2002); this, too, is a wonderfully restrained study of human nature and mental breakdown, a world away from the modern penchant for increased gore and brutality in horror films. Charles Laughton's *Night of the Hunter* (1955) is another achingly beautiful film, its images of darkness, brutality and evil counterpointed by those of light, beauty and innocence. Its main protagonist also acts as a template for all the schizophrenic characters to come in the next few decades, not least Hannibal Lector in *The Silence of the Lambs* (1991), which is surely one of the most chilling films, and, in Anthony Hopkins' turn, defining performances to emerge from the horror genre. Lector's combination of intellectual, cultured and psychopathic persona makes for a fascinating study of the dark recesses of human nature, brilliantly balanced by Agent Starling's crusade against the world of shadows.

The Birds (1963) remains one of the most enigmatic and disturbing visions in celluloid history; it continues Hitchcock's study of personality traits and disorders, as evidenced in earlier works like *Vertigo* (1958), *Psycho* (1960) and later in films such as *Marnie* (1964). It also looks out at the world and the disturbing forces at work, illustrating how the genre casts a wider net of significance than is often thought.

Halloween (1978) and *A Nightmare on Elm Street* (1984) are key works in the development of the slasher film. John Carpenter's film exudes confidence in its visual storytelling whilst the latter relishes its knowing use and parody of horror genre conventions. Neither film should be diminished by some of the relentless succession of poor sequels and imitators that followed, both films playing a large part in directing the horror genre at the youth market and bringing horror right into *their* neighbourhood.

Nosferatu, eine Symphonie des Grauens

KEY FACTS

Release Date: 1922

Country of Origin: Germany

Running Time: 90 minutes

PRODUCTION NOTES

Production Companies

Jofa-Atelier Berlin-Johannisthal

Prana-Film GmbH

Distributor

Film Arts Guild (USA)

SYNOPSIS

A first filmic realisation of Bram Stoker's gothic novel, *Dracula* (1897), which essentially parallels the source text, but makes a number of changes, not least the names of the protagonists as the film-makers did not have the Stoker estate's permission to film the story. In this version a man named

Hutter visits Count Orlok in the Carpathian Mountains and soon finds that he is a virtual prisoner of this hellish creation, a ghoulish figure who sleeps in a coffin. Hutter facilitates Orlok's purchase of a property back in Hutter's native Germany, and he falls prey to the Count's nocturnal activities. Orlok then makes the journey to Wismar by boat; he travels with a number of coffins filled with soil and rats, and the crew of the ship die one by one.

In Wismar, Hutter's wife, Ellen, has felt a mysterious connection with events in the Carpathians and reacts to the confrontation between her husband and Orlok, first by sleepwalking, screaming and then falling into a stupor. Hutter's employer, Knock, who sent him to the Carpathians, has also come under the influence of the Count; he is put into a cell because of his behaviour, where he eats flies and attacks a doctor.

Once Orlok arrives it becomes clear to the townspeople that the deserted ship has brought the plague and panic ensues. Ellen knows that if she can make the Count forget about the coming of dawn he will die. She therefore acts as a willing victim and lets Orlok drink her blood. He then forgets about the sun rising and evaporates in a puff of smoke.

HISTORICAL CONTEXT

Only four years before the completion of *Nosferatu* Germany had been defeated by the allied forces and the country and its people were left humiliated, impoverished and resentful, not only because of the defeat, but also because of the crippling legacy of the 1919 Treaty of Versailles. It stripped the country of its assets and left it ripe for the extreme views that festered and grew, leading to Hitler's rise to power in the 1930s. Like many films of the time its imagery and content are dark and oppressive. The chiaroscuro lighting, which was German Expressionism's trademark (and a movement in which director Murnau was a key figure), reflects the bleak and frightening interwar years in Germany. Many films of this era (see LINKS TO OTHER FILMS section below) deal with a creature preying on the populace, representative of the many fears that gnawed away at the German people and the horrors that were to come.

SELECT FILMOGRAPHY OF MAIN PRODUCERS AND CAST

F.W. Murnau, 1881-1931 , Director

Nosferatu, eine Symphonie des Grauens, 1922

Der letzte Mann, 1924

Herr Tartüff, 1926

Faust, 1926

Sunrise, 1927

4 Devils, 1928

City Girl, 1928

Tabu, 1931

Henrik Galeen, 1881-1949, Screenwriter, Director

Der Golem, 1915

Der Golem, wie er in die Welt kam, 1920

Nosferatu, eine Symphonie des Grauens, 1922

After the Verdict, 1928

LINKS TO OTHER FILMS

Das Cabinet des Dr. Caligari (1920)

Robert Wiene's film also taps into the post-World War One German psyche, full of despair and fear, as a hypnotist uses his powers to control a somnambulist to commit murders on his behalf. The sense of calamity and a very real sense of a disturbed identity were prevalent at the time, and this film contemplates this dislocation with its obviously artificial sets, which foreshadow Brechtian notions of audience estrangement.

Der Golem, Wie er in die Welt Kam (1920)

Another film which deals with a creature that causes chaos amongst the population and, again, taps into contemporary fears in Germany. This is based on Jewish folklore about a rabbi who makes a monster out of clay in order to help reverse anti-Jewish laws that have been passed in Prague. The creation does, indeed, help to secure a turnaround but it then runs amok and preys on the local townspeople.

Dracula (1931)

Todd Browning's version of the Dracula story was the beginning of a very long love affair between Hollywood and the vampire. Its Count is quite different to the vampire of *Nosferatu*, with Bela Lugosi's theatrical cloak-wielding villain more debonair than the monstrous Max Schreck characterisation. It is also notable for being the first of many monster films that were to be so lucrative for Universal Studios in the 1930s.

Dracula (1958)

This British version, made by Hammer Productions, was one of the company's remakes of the classic monster films which had a very sophisticated Count at the centre of the action, far removed from the vampire in either *Nosferatu* or Universal's *Dracula*.

Martin (1976)

George A. Romero's modern take on the vampire

story; a young man's vampiric experiences in contemporary Pittsburgh are a combination of classic vampire story-telling and observations on modern day stresses and psychoses.

Bram Stoker's Dracula (1992)

A return to the source material in Francis Ford Coppola's interpretation which presents the Count as a combination of previous cinematic incarnations; he is both monster and sophisticate. There are also visual references to the silent version with its simulation of a flickering screen as Dracula walks down an English street in pursuit of Mina Harker.

Shadow of the Vampire (2000)

A fictionalised account of the making of Nosferatu, which proposes the idea that Max Schreck was actually a vampire, a fact known only by F.W. Murnau. This, the film suggests, explains his total immersion in the role and the unearthly persona that he created.

REPRESENTATION

Dracula

As with Metropolis (1927), it is impossible to disconnect this film from the German, and in particular, the Nazi backdrop. The character of Nosferatu, as portrayed by Max Schreck, is clearly seen as a threat to the German people. By 1922, Adolf Hitler had been instated as leader of the Nationalist Socialist Worker's Party, and it was becoming clear that his agenda would involve fear and violence; the Munich Putsch, Hitler's attempted coup to topple the government, would happen the following year. Although Hitler's chancellorship and the real start of Germany's dark days were 10 years away, the atmosphere was perfect for the creation of monsters like the vampire, who would symbolise the horror of the post-World War One years and the as yet undefined horrors to come.

If Dracula represents our darkest fears and is repellent because of that, there is also something seductive about him. The biting of the neck, the foreplay to the drinking of blood, is highly sexual. Certainly, Nosferatu is charged with lust, an aspect

which Hammer played on in the 1958 film and in later manifestations, such as The Vampire Lovers (1970), where the Count was displaced by a lesbian vampire, and the later Francis Ford Coppola version, Bram Stoker's Dracula (1992), which drew parallels between vampirism and its associations with a blood-borne infection and the Aids virus.

'It is easy to see why the film is still... celebrated as one of the most important establishing works of the horror genre... Where Nosferatu comes into its own as an expressionist film is in its setting: although on the surface everything seems a realistic portrayal of the protagonists' world, in fact much is manipulated to underscore the supernatural element central to the plot.' Ian Roberts, German Expressionist Cinema, Wallflower Press, 2008

KEY SCENE TEXTUAL ANALYSIS

At the castle (Act II: 6;23:21)

Mise-en-scène dominates and fuels much of the action within the film; the design of the sets and the composition of the frames dictate both the exterior action and interior emotion. The opening shot of this sequence immediately disorientates the audience by positioning the characters to the far left of frame instead of making them central. The overpowering set is dominated by an enormous diamond pattern on the floor and the oversized back to Count Orlok's chair. The space in front and beyond them is suggestive of an eerie emptiness, entirely appropriate for a house of the undead.

The medium shot of Hutter is cramped, conveyed through his hunched body posture and the table and wall enclosing him (suggesting his vulnerability and inability to escape), and contains forbidding areas of darkness behind - the knife plunged into the meat in front of him suggests danger and violence.

The cut to a medium shot of the Count juxtaposes the two characters, linked by the composition of the frame. But where Hutter is furtive and anxious, the Count is self-contained and confident. In the cut back to Hutter he begins to slice the bread with the knife cutting towards his chest, another suggestion of threat and violence.

The framing of the two protagonists continues to marry them together with a close-up of the Count followed by one of Hutter. A shot of a clock with a small skeleton figure atop, its shadow pronounced and emphasising its deathly connotations, completes the four shot sequence. Its chimes startle Hutter and distract him from his bread-cutting; the close-up of the thumb being cut into is graphic and focuses the audience on the oozing blood, something the audience will know has ramifications beyond just a cut when you are staying at a vampire's house.

The cut to his approach on Hutter helps the audience identify with his plight, depositing us like frightened children behind his chair. We see Orlok's clothes, which add to the atmosphere of 'unhumaness': his long black coat allows for the exposure of little flesh and his hat covers his hair, the coat is tightly buttoned, almost like a straitjacket, and his eyes are darkly shadowed.

Returning to the long two-shot, Orlok begins his feast, on Hutter's thumb. The Count is suddenly animated, but the audience loses sight of any vestiges of humanity from Orlok as he has his back to us and all we can observe is his hunched shape. There is nothing to mark him out as a man; he is just a dark spectral shape.

Hutter backs away from the front of the frame in the next shot. A gaping fireplace and the seats behind him, which have open-mouthed animals

The long two-shot lends itself to a number of comments. Firstly, a still life of food and vessels sits on the table and suggests something very painterly about the construction of the frame. The image is often a reference to contemplation, a moment captured, decay or the transitory nature of life in art. As it is Hutter who is eating, it is he that is allied with this image, caught in a horrific moment in time. The background, too, is reminiscent of the background to a Renaissance religious painting, but here it is stripped of its humanity. Finally, Orlok, with his outstretched hand displaying his hideously long fingers, is something of a diabolical antithesis to an Annunciation painting. Where the angel Gabriel reaches out and connects with the Virgin Mary, imparting the seed of eternal life, so he reaches out to Hutter promising eternal night.

as legs, are images of consumption, suggestive of the Count's desire to swallow Hutter too. The succeeding shot has the mirror image of the two upright men to the left of frame and the two high-backed chairs to the right.

The final shot of this sequence sees Hutter symbolically falling onto one of the chairs behind, foreshadowing his fall into the Orlok's clutches as the Count continues his inexorable movement towards him.

The final attack (Act V: 17;1:22:34)

Orlok, in his final vampiric attack, is initially seen as a shadow, appropriate for someone no longer truly alive. The outline is terrifying and signals that he moves beyond the ordinary and the everyday in a twilight world of nightmares. His talon-like fingers prefigure Freddy Krueger by over 60 years and the distorted shape of his posture underlines his evil intent and foul nature.

There is a great contrast between this figure and the figure of his victim in the next shot; Ellen is shown fully lit in all her humanity, her body wheeling around in horror and displaying a vibrancy that Orlok's rigid frame cannot match. She is dressed in white and looks even more like an embodiment of innocence and purity, a sacrificial lamb waiting to be slaughtered on the altar of evil. He also wants her as his undead bride, again making the garment a fitting colour for the occasion.

The next shot of him is also a shadow, but it is oversized, outlandishly grotesque as he reaches for the door handle; he is beyond the realms

bring the doctor out of his sleeping stupor. This shot is also bright to emphasise the darkness of the next shot of the vampire feeding on its victim. Unlike the previous melodramatic moments this is seemingly low key and the audience has to strain to see what is exactly happening in the frame - its horror lies in its matter-of-factness. Almost hidden in the far left of frame, the vampire kneels at his victim's bedside with his head buried into her neck. He is feeding on a human in an act of such unimaginable depravity that it can only be viewed as if from the corner of the viewer's eye. There is another cut to the goings-on of the outside world, but we return to the same shot: still, dark and utterly chilling.

So intent is he on his feeding that the vampire forgets time and the cockerel's crow attracts his attention. The medium shot of his head lifting,

of normality and humanity and his fingers in particular stretch out like long, stabbing knives. He is all sinister movement, whereas the next shot shows Ellen as she clutches herself, petrified in the face of such horror. Like Hutter before her, she is forced to the edge and out of the frame by his evil aura.

The medium shot of her on the bed again reiterates Orlok's spectral power, far beyond that of mortals. The shadow initiates his attack, emphasising that he is coming from beyond the grave as his hand's shadow soils her white nightdress and clutches her heart. It is an act that induces a physical response in her; it is highly sexual as its deformity caresses her vulnerable body.

Murnau now contrasts this scene with that of Hutter, who is trying to revive the doctor. Orlok induces a sleeping death, whilst Hutter tries to

(Ellen is now unidentifiable as a human), reveals the hideous face.

The next few shots take us outside to Knock, Orlok's follower, and to Hutter again. The light of the sunrise floods into the room and the long shot shows Orlok stretch to his full height and mimic his victim's gesture. He clutches his heart and there is a perverted dignity in his demise as he reaches forwards, turns and looks towards the bringer of his death. The optical effect whereby he evaporates suggests his escape from the world of shadows forever; the last vestige of his presence is a puff of smoke. The death is free of melodrama and is shot through with a degree of nobility and sadness as this creature of the shadows is vaporised by the one thing that does, and should, sustain life: the sun.

Frankenstein

KEY FACTS

Release Date: 1931

Country of Origin: USA

Running Time: 67 minutes

PRODUCTION NOTES

Production Company

Universal Pictures

Distributor

Universal Pictures

Budget

$291,000 (estimated)

Awards

National Film Registry National Film Preservation Board, USA

SYNOPSIS

Dr. Henry Frankenstein is obsessed with recreating life, and with the help of his hunchbacked assistant, Fritz, he constructs a body using parts from various deceased sources. His work begins to alter his mind and he neglects his fiancée, Elizabeth, who solicits the help of his friend Victor Moritz and Dr. Waldman, his old professor. Frankenstein goes ahead with his experimentation, unwittingly using a brain from a dead psychopath. He then brings the creation to life by harnessing the power of an electrical storm. The creature attacks them and is imprisoned, where Fritz maltreats him.

Frankenstein returns to his father-in-law's house to be married after the creature kills Fritz, but his creation comes to kill him after also slaying Dr. Waldman and escaping. The creature is thwarted, although he does give Elizabeth quite a fright. Whilst running through the countryside the creature discovers a young girl who is playing by the side of a lake; she throws flowers into the lake and he joins in, but when he runs out of flowers he throws her in, his child-like mind equating the delicacy of the flowers with that of the young girl.

She drowns and he flees in terror. The girl's grieving father carries her into the village and the people go in pursuit of the monster. Dr. Frankenstein is caught by his creation and carried to an old mill. The monster throws the doctor's body from the top but his fall is broken by the vanes of the windmill and the villagers set light to the building, which consumes both it and the monster.

HISTORICAL CONTEXT

Frankenstein followed on from the enormous success of Universal's previous 'monster' film, *Dracula*, made the same year and starring Bela Lugosi in the title role. Lugosi was due to take the role of the monster in *Frankenstein*, but turned it down and Boris Karloff made the part his own. While it is perhaps unsurprising that Universal made such films at this time, it would have been difficult to predict how incredibly successful they would be with audiences. Firstly, Hollywood had noted the appeal of German-made horror films like *Das Cabinet des Dr. Caligari*, *Der Golem*, *Wie er in die Welt Kam* (1920) and *Nosferatu*. They had been perfectly tuned to the bleak times after World War One, and in the 1930s the United States began to share in this outlook. The stock market had crashed there in 1929, and the ensuing Great Depression caused widespread misery and hardship both in the States and throughout the world.

Dark days beget dark images, and so it was that American audiences flocked to see these monsters of the night terrorise and be vanquished. Perhaps it made them feel just a little better about their own lives, and that eventually the demons of the Depression would be slain. Hollywood also became a magnet for the producers of the German films, and so men like Karl Freund (cinematographer of *Dracula* and director of *The Mummy*, 1932), arrived state-side and imprinted their dark visions on screen.

It was not only the Germans who arrived in Hollywood in the 1920s and 1930s; the British also made substantial contributions to the early days of the film industry in California. *Frankenstein's* director, James Whale, was among many who had left the theatres of Britain to work in the United States. Charlie Chaplin, Alfred Hitchcock, Boris Karloff, Cary Grant and Stan Laurel were just some of the more notable artistic immigrants who would find film-making success. Whale became a director of plays in Britain and later in New York before he embarked upon his film-making career in Hollywood, making three landmark films (*Frankenstein*, *Bride of Frankenstein* and *The Invisible Man*) and securing Universal Studios' success in the 1930s. Whale also employed many British actors in his films, including Colin Clive, Elsa Lanchester and Claude Rains, while the style of his early films drew on a range of sources including Victorian gothic literature and German expressionism.

SELECT FILMOGRAPHY OF MAIN PRODUCERS AND CAST

James Whale, 1889–1957, Director

Journey's End, 1930

Waterloo Bridge, 1931

Frankenstein, 1931

The Old Dark House, 1932

The Invisible Man, 1933

Bride of Frankenstein, 1935

Show Boat, 1936

The Road Back, 1937

The Great Garrick, 1937

The Man in the Iron Mask, 1939

Carl Laemmle, 1908–1979, Producer

All Quiet on the Western Front, 1930

Journey's End, 1930

Waterloo Bridge, 1931

Dracula, 1931

Frankenstein, 1931

The Mummy, 1932

The Old Dark House, 1932

The Invisible Man, 1933

Bride of Frankenstein, 1935

Show Boat, 1936

Boris Karloff, 1887–1969, Actor

Frankenstein, 1931

Scarface, 1932

The Old Dark House, 1932

The Mask of Fu Manchu, 1932

The Mummy, 1932

The Ghoul, 1933

The Lost Patrol, 1934

House of Rothschild, 1934

The Black Cat, 1934

Bride of Frankenstein, 1935

The Raven, 1935

The Invisible Ray, 1936

Son of Frankenstein, 1939

Tower of London, 1939

House of Frankenstein, 1944

The Body Snatcher, 1945

Isle of the Dead, 1945

Bedlam, 1946

The Raven, 1963

Comedy of Terrors, 1964

The Sorcerers, 1967

Targets, 1968

Colin Clive, 1900–1937, Actor

Journey's End, 1930

Frankenstein, 1931

Christopher Strong, 1933

Jane Eyre, 1934

Clive of India, 1935

Bride of Frankenstein, 1935

Mad Love, 1935

The Man Who Broke the Bank at Monte Carlo, 1935

History Is Made at Night, 1937

LINKS TO OTHER FILMS

Bride of Frankenstein (1935)

The follow-up to the original film is again helmed by James Whale, and is similar to the source novel in that the creature actually speaks in this version. It also contains many similar elements of the original's *mise-en-scène* such as Gothic sets and expressionist photography, but it deviates considerably in terms of tone with its black humour and sense of parody.

The Curse of Frankenstein (1958)

Hammer Productions' first attempt at reviving the monster series of films was a universal success, only trumped by its next film, *Dracula*. It initiated Hammer Productions' long run of horror films which formed an important bridge between the horror films of the first half of the century and those that came in latter years, imbuing the genre with more explicit representations of horror and sexuality.

El Espiritu de la Colmena (Spirit of the Beehive) (1973)

Victor Erice's film of a child's experiences in post-civil war Spain begins with a viewing of *Frankenstein* at a mobile cinema in the girl's village. The film has a profound effect on her, and her subsequent help of a wounded soldier reveals her feelings to those who are regarded as outsiders. In one sequence she even 'sees' the monster as she gazes into some water; it is an echo of the scene in the film with the creature and the little girl. This time the little girl is unharmed, reflecting her vision of him as a persecuted victim and not a monster.

Young Frankenstein (1974)

An all-out parody of the *Frankenstein* films, which is evidence of the monster's enduring appeal; it is also a film which successfully mimics the look of the original with its use of similar *mise-en-scène* and actual props from the original 1930's films (see pg. 299).

Edward Scissorhands (1990)

This is another story of an outsider who is artificially created, only to be spurned by the local population because of their ignorance and fear of otherness. Tim Burton's film does, however, spare the 'monster' at the end, although he is forced to lead a life outside of society.

Mary Shelley's Frankenstein (1994)

A more faithful adaptation of the source novel, this Kenneth Branagh film is awash with spectacle and a sympathetic interpretation of the monster by Robert De Niro.

Gods and Monsters (1998)

An examination of *Frankenstein*'s director, James Whale, rather than his most famous film, although there are reconstructions of the filming of *Bride of Frankenstein* and insight into the mind that created a number of horror classics.

REPRESENTATION

Otherness

Alienation, disorientation and extreme loneliness; the monster feels all this throughout the film. He is the hobo monster, travelling from place to place and finding no solace. He is one of the forgotten in John Ford's *The Grapes of Wrath* (1940); he is the wrongly accused hero of Fritz Lang's *Fury* (1936) and the alienated Othello. He is the everyman outsider, a scapegoat for all our fears and prejudices. Every gesture and movement that he makes is full of indecision and confusion; first, the enquiring child; then the tormented teenager; and finally the beast, whose identity casts him into the abyss of madness and violence.

It is the epic struggle between man and his creator: Who? What? Why? How? These are the questions that he is unable to articulate and barely comprehend. The creature's first childlike hand gestures towards the light speak of incredulity and a desire for answers and for comfort, but society does not respond and finally destroys him.

'The Universal horror cycle runs the gamut from perfection through pastiche and pulp to parody, but Frankenstein *remains chilly and invigorating, the cornerstone of its entire genre.'* Kim Newman, *1001 Movies You Must See Before You Die*, Cassell Illustrated, 2007

'... [Frankenstein] *brought the movie image of the mad scientist into focus and in the process launched a thousand imitations.'* Christopher Frayling, *Mad, Bad and Dangerous?*, Reaktion, 2006

KEY SCENE TEXTUAL ANALYSIS

Imprisonment (8)

The monster has become more violent and attacks Frankenstein, Fritz and Doctor Waldman, resulting in his incarceration in the cellar. The screen fades in from black to the monster chained in the cellar. The blackness is appropriate as it is not his body that is imprisoned but his mind - by confusion, frustration and ill treatment. The chink of his chains and his cries are heard before the fade to the cellar, emphasising his state of mind.

The image is of a gothic interior, the *mise-en-scène* reminiscent of silent horror films and German expressionism (in films such as *Nosferatu*) and looks forward to the films noirs of the 1940s and 1950s (such as *Double Indemnity*, 1944).

The chiaroscuro lighting and distorted elements create tension and horror, but also suggest the disfigurement of society and the moral universe. Nothing in the cellar is straight; everything is distorted and the monster flails wildly at its own shadow. The angled uprights, sloping walls and the tiny barred window all contribute to a disorientating effect for the audience, mirroring the monster's mind and the universe that it inhabits.

With a pan to the right Fritz enters this nightmare and adds to its chaos by whipping the monster. Frankenstein arrives and momentarily stops this torment, but the medium shot of him, as he despairs about his creation, shows that he is also confined, with the barred window on one side and the thick wooden beam on the other.

Frankenstein departs in misery leaving Fritz to continue his torture by thrusting the burning brand into the petrified monster's face. The long shot of the two shuffling figures, both refugees from society, resembles a bizarre dancing ritual, something primeval.

The close-up of the monster's face reveals his terror and helps us identify with it. This is reinforced by a POV shot as we, the audience, have the flames thrust into our face; again Whale wants us to sympathise with the monster. A cut to a medium close-up of the monster and then back to the master shot ends the sequence, with a final fade to black.

The sequence itself is confined by its black edges, the action beginning and ending with a fade from and to black. This mirrors the monster's plight. The sequence emerges from a hellish darkness and sinks back into its depths to illustrate an endless torment and confinement for the monster. His eventual escape is no real release.

Again, Whale does not include any non-diegetic accompaniment; he wants this to be less melodramatic. The plain presentation actually serves to accentuate the horror perpetrated by humans on others and themselves, and the monster's POV reminds us also that we can all be victims.

A celebration and a killing (10/11)

The film has many episodes of confinement, most notably of Frankenstein's monster.

This scene begins with a close-up image of

confinement in a totally different context, that of a wedding display consisting of two flowers, a flower garland and a pendant with an image of the bride and bridegroom-to-be, Elizabeth and Henry Frankenstein. It is a pretty image, one of a domestic idyll. But it is contained within a glass cover: is this life just another type of confinement? Is it a protected existence? Whatever the reading, two hands remove the cover, either to liberate the couple or to open them up to the dangers of an unprotected existence.

The camera tracks out to reveal Frankenstein, his father, the best man and various wedding guests. As the father removes the glass cover he talks of the two orange blossoms that he places in his son's and best man's button-holes; they have been used for three generations. An image of confinement is now followed by one of eternal life, both references to the monster that has escaped in the previous scene.

The wine that they are drinking again references long life. It is a formal, class-conscious affair (the servants get the cheap champagne), and there is an air of rigidity in their movement. The static framing and rather pompous conversation suggest the trappings of civilisation. The next long shot of the room reveals a *mise-en-scène* of candelabras, fine furniture, armour and weaponry on the walls, as well as a grand piano, chandelier and finely-decorated ceiling. It is the antithesis of Frankenstein's castle and a close-up of Frankenstein's face reveals that all is not well.

If the wealthy are somewhat repressed in their social behaviour, then the people of the village are positively rampant; the shot of them flooding into the father's front courtyard is totally animated. The subsequent tracking shot shows how free these people really are as they dance through the streets without a care in the world; the nature of the shot itself suggesting their dynamism. The camera moves past adults and children dancing in lines, holding hands and moving in a circle; it is unfettered freedom with human connection and comfort.

The dissolve from this scene to the next helps to connect the two visually and to emphasise the gulf between these people (society) and the monster.

The tracking shot is repeated but this time the monster is clawing his way through a mass of tangled branches and he is alone. This is a mirror image of the previous shot, but it is a distorted fairground image that is now reflected. He may be free of the dungeon but he will never be free of his imprisoning mind and society's revulsion.

The difference is also aural: the cacophony of diegetic sound contrasts strongly with the silence of the monster, save for the pathetic scraping of his heavy shoes. Where the villagers are light of foot, he is leaden.

The following series of shots of the idyllic cottage by the lake and the warmth between father and daughter directly contrast with this loneliness, but there are suggestions of the danger that is approaching. The juxtaposition of the monster with this vignette of happiness, of course, points to it but

his back to the audience so we cannot tell if there is anger there. The framing has him towering over her still-crouching body. The return to the close-up repeats her look but now she gets up and the master shot shows her walking without fear towards the lumbering figure. He is now clearly in some open ground, albeit flanked on three sides, and she moves towards him so that the gap between them is reduced.

The close-up of her face reiterates her qualities. She exudes freshness and purity and her face has no clutter behind it compared to the monster's, which has the chaos of branches behind his facial close-up to underline the ever-present threat to his happiness. This is the first daytime close-up of his face and it is full of frustration and incredulity, but tenderness as well.

The two-shot, as she takes the monster's hands, contrasts their size and she assumes the role

there are also vaguely unsettling little touches - the girl is framed by sharp pieces of wood which form the fence and the father goes into the trees from where the monster will emerge.

The girl has a bright, honest and loveable face which is returned to in a number of close-ups, to compare and contrast with that of the monster's face in the next sequence. The tracking shot of the girl as she walks down to the lake connects her with the free-spirited movement of the villagers and contrasts her with the monster. The stop and pan to the left not only shows the audience that the monster is approaching, but connects him with her space, a space which is innocent and, as we shall see, non-judgemental.

The close-up of the girl shows her surprise, but not disgust, and the cut back to the monster shows

of adult/teacher. A short tracking shot follows. She leads the monster towards the water's edge and there is another echo of freedom and human contact but it is a brief shot for this will be the creature's only moment of freedom outside the restrictions of society. The close-up of the girl again, as she hands the monster a flower, underlines the tenderness of the moment.

The focus next is on their hands touching as he takes the flower; his fingernails are bruised and bloodied and there are scars around his wrists. Much of the scene's power comes from Boris Karloff's acting as he raises the flower to his grotesque face and imbues the monster with sensitivity.

The camera tracks in again on this innocent game and the two figures drop to their knees to continue playing in an intimate and sensitive moment.

As she gives him more flowers he instinctively takes her hand, so little and delicate next to his own. The impulse is based on his own innocent liking of something pretty and it is a natural feeling to touch someone who is showing him love. It also continues the visual theme of making vows: they walk down an aisle, they kneel together, he holds her hand, there are flowers; it is a marriage of innocence and innocents.

She throws her flowers and there are two together, like them: delicate, but easily destroyed. They continue to throw but when he runs out he makes a connection between the flowers' beauty and hers and he throws her into the water; the moment of freedom is over.

the trees, lurching with fear. The dissolve back to the happy dancing of the villagers completes this meditation on freedom.

Whale does not afford us a view of the girl drowning. The monster blocks our line of vision as he watches, uncomprehendingly, as she drowns. All the time his back is to us. His fleeting new world is over and he is turned from all society in this moment of tragedy.

Throughout this whole sequence there has been no non-diegetic music to manipulate the audience's response; Whale does not want us to concentrate on the possible horror of the action (that comes in other parts of the film). He wants the audience to watch without any sort of directed viewing and see it as a vignette of hope and hopelessness, freedom and confinement, and the often fine line between the two. The sequence comes full circle to emphasise the monster's return to frightened chaos and confusion as he stumbles away into

Cat People

KEY FACTS

Release Date: 1942

Country of Origin: USA

Running Time: 73 minutes

PRODUCTION NOTES

Production Company

RKO Radio Pictures

Distributor

RKO Radio Pictures

Budget

$134,000 (estimated)

Awards

National Film Registry National Film Preservation Board, USA

SYNOPSIS

After Oliver Reed meets Serbian immigrant, Irena Dubrovna, at the zoo in New York, he becomes fascinated with her and their relationship develops very quickly, leading to marriage. But Irena is a mysterious character, visually linked to panthers throughout the film. Animals are also frightened of her: a cat recoils from her and the animals in a pet shop go wild when she enters. She believes that she may be doomed to inherit the curse from her village in Serbia, a legacy that will ignite dark horrors if her passions are aroused. There are moments when it seems as if this is indeed the case, resulting in the attempted attack on a work colleague of her husband's, who is also in love with him, and in the killing of her psychiatrist, Dr. Louis Judd. She is badly wounded in the struggle with Judd and is finally killed by a panther back in the zoo after she has unlocked its cage. The creature itself is then run over and killed by a passing car. Reed and his female work colleague, Alice Moore, find Irena's dead body and realise there is truth in what she has told them.

HISTORICAL CONTEXT

The film noir cycle of films are often cited as being the perfect reflection of events during World War Two. Indeed, their dark images of brutality echo the unprecedented misery of the times. Horror films have also served this purpose and the series of Val Lewton productions in the 1940s certainly tapped into the willingness of audiences to be frightened by fantastic events that were also dark and murderous. It took them out of the real pain of the world, displaced it, and helped them deal with it in a manageable and safe environment on the silver screen.

Cat People cannot be seen in isolation from Lewton's other films of that era and ilk; as a body of work they delve into a range of fears and paranoia that share similar visuals and motifs. The films are *Cat People*; *I Walked with a Zombie* (1943); *The Leopard Man* (1943); *The Seventh Victim* (1943); *The Ghost Ship* (1943); *The Curse of the Cat People* (1944); *The Body Snatcher* (1945); *Isle of the Dead* (1945) and *Bedlam* (1946). The rapid turnover of these productions gives the oeuvre an intensity that speaks volumes about the human condition in time of great adversity: genocide, torture, death on an enormous scale and the dropping of the first atomic bombs. The huge psychological effects can be seen in all Val Lewton's narratives: the disturbed Irena in the grips of an extreme identity crisis; nurse Betsy Connell disturbing the undead in *I Walked with a Zombie*; or young Mary Gibson trying to unsuccessfully wrest her sister, who commits suicide at the film's climax, from a group of Satanists in *The Seventh Victim*.

Jacques Tourneur was one of many European directors who travelled to Hollywood to make films in the early part of the twentieth century. Along with the likes of F.W. Murnau, James Whale and Fritz Lang, he brought European sensibilities and visions to the New World, as did a whole gallery of directors such as Josef von Sternburg, Ernst Lubitsch, Billy Wilder and Jean Renoir. Theirs was the Old World, a Europe steeped in history, of revolution, of literature, art, architecture, ideas, societies and cultures formed over centuries. Tourneur, son of a film director, brought a rich palette of ideas to his work: the composition of painting can be seen in his frames (*Great Day in the Morning*, 1956), or indeed, the bleakness of the First World War (*Cat People*).

Tourneur, his producer Val Lewton and other RKO directors, Mark Robson and Robert Wise, created a body of work which moved the horror genre away from the mad scientist and 'actor-in-creature suit' approach to a more restrained and psychologically intense atmosphere. The locations were often noticeably familiar - modern urban settings rather than foreign lands replete with sinister forests and castles. These films moved the genre closer to home, making them even more unnerving, and prefiguring the domestic horrors of the 1960s and beyond. Films such as *Rosemary's Baby* (1968), *The Exorcist* (1973) and *Halloween* (1978) all have locations that are the epitome of safe, banal middle-class living; like the Lewton films before them the horror is brought right into the living-room and is all the more unsettling for it.

SELECT FILMOGRAPHY OF MAIN PRODUCERS AND CAST

Jacques Tourneur, 1904-1977, Director

Cat People, 1942

I Walked with a Zombie, 1943

The Leopard Man, 1943

Days of Glory, 1944

Experiment Perilous, 1944

Canyon Passage, 1946

Out of the Past, 1947

Berlin Express, 1948

The Flame and the Arrow, 1950

Anne of the Indies, 1951

Appointment in Honduras, 1953

Stranger on Horseback, 1955

Wichita, 1955

Great Day in the Morning, 1956

Nightfall, 1957

Night of the Demon, 1957

Val Lewton, 1904-1951, Producer

Cat People, 1942

I Walked with a Zombie, 1943

The Leopard Man, 1943

The Seventh Victim, 1943

The Ghost Ship, 1943

The Curse of the Cat People, 1944

Mademoiselle Fifi, 1944

Youth Runs Wild, 1944

The Body Snatcher, 1945

Isle of the Dead, 1945

Bedlam, 1946

Simone Simon, 1910-2005, Actress

Seventh Heaven, 1937

La Bête humaine, 1938

The Devil and Daniel Webster, 1941

Cat People, 1942

The Curse of the Cat People, 1944

Mademoiselle Fifi, 1944

Johnny Doesn't Live Here Anymore, 1944

La Ronde, 1950

Nicholas Musuraca, 1892-1975 , Director of Photography

Five Came Back, 1939

Stranger on the Third Floor, 1940

Cat People, 1942

I Walked with a Zombie, 1943

The Leopard Man, 1943

The Seventh Victim, 1943

The Ghost Ship, 1943

The Curse of the Cat People, 1944

The Spiral Staircase, 1946

Out of the Past, 1947

Blood on the Moon, 1948

I Married a Communist, 1949

Where Danger Lives, 1950

Roadblock, 1951

Clash by Night, 1952

The Hitch-Hiker, 1953

The Blue Gardenia, 1953

LINKS TO OTHER FILMS

Dr Jekyll and Mr Hyde (1931)

An earlier examination of sexual repression which results in a splintering of identities. Here the alter-ego is not feline, but it is still a beast. The story of the doctor who wrestles with his two selves is reminiscent of Irena and her struggle, and both lead to the person's destruction.

The Wolf Man (1941)

George Waggner's film is another of Universal's attempts at maintaining its 'monster' franchise. Whilst not having the same subtlety or delicacy as *Cat People*, this film does look at the psychology of the changes wrought by a dual identity.

The Seventh Victim (1943)

This Val Lewton production, directed by Mark Robson, has many similarities with *Cat People* in terms of *mise-en-scène*: it is dark and moody and set in a contemporary New York which gives it an even more unnerving atmosphere.

The Curse of the Cat People (1944)

A sequel of sorts with Oliver Reed having married his work colleague, Alice Moore, and detailing the alienated world of their daughter who escapes reality through daydreams and is eventually 'visited' by Irena, her father's cursed wife who died at the end of *Cat People*.

Repulsion (1965)/*Rosemary's Baby* (1968)

Two visions of horror lying just beneath the surface of the ordinary from director Roman Polanski. They both involve women in contemporary settings who are gradually destroyed by fears that are very much rooted in the sexual psyche.

Cat People (1982)

The Paul Schrader remake of the story highlights Irena's sexual side and is a much more gorily explicit approach to the material, detailing sexual and violent explosions as metaphors for her search for identity.

Dark Water (2002)

Hideo Nakata, unusual for a modern film-maker, works hard at building suspense through subtlety and eschews gore and shock tactics in favour of an unsettling *mise-en-scène* (see pg. 257).

REPRESENTATION

Monsters

Monsters represent our darkest fears; they are demons that exist on the edges of consciousness and of society. Their otherness is a threat to us, whether real or imagined, and often created by society's greed or intolerance; Shakespeare's plays present characters who engender fear or loathing in members of society, whether it be the blackness of Othello or the Jewish Shylock.

Often, Hollywood displaces its demons by originating them from Europe and employing the American hero to vanquish the foreign foe. From early in Hollywood film history an English accent has denoted monstrous qualities; British actors such as Boris Karloff, Basil Rathbone and Sydney Greenstreet were often cast in roles which pitted them against American good guys.

Europeans were generally cast in roles where their otherness became shorthand for depravity and monstrosity. Bela Lugosi, born into the Austro-Hungarian Empire (in the town of Lugoj, now part of Romania) and famous for his role as Dracula was the archetypal European symbol of otherness through his film roles. Peter Lorre, also born in the Austro-Hungarian Empire (in the town of Ružomberok, now part of Slovakia), who had portrayed a child murderer in Fritz Lang's *M* (1931), spent an entire career in Hollywood playing a variety of rather loathsome, if somewhat endearing, characters.

The 'real' monster characters like Dracula, Frankenstein's monster, the Hunchback of Notre Dame, the Phantom of the Opera, Ivan Igor (*Mystery of the Wax Museum*, 1933) and Hjalmar Polzeig (*The Black Cat*, 1934) all have European backgrounds, with Eastern Europe being a particular favourite. As a crossroads for many tribes this area has seen numerous conflicts and seems to have a particular attraction for Hollywood. Its folklore traditions and tales have influenced many writers, the Irish writer Bram Stoker in particular, to locate their Gothic horrors in regions that were remote, scarred by warfare and peppered with atmospheric castles. Indeed, Stoker's *Dracula* was to breed a whole tradition of readers and film audiences who equated parts of Eastern Europe with vampires and other monsters. The area that the West calls the Balkans was also seen as a hotbed of violence, a charge given momentum by the assassination of Archduke Franz Ferdinand in 1914, which led to the First World War. Films such as Edgar G. Ulmer's *The Black Cat* (1934) and Mark Robson's *Isle of the Dead* (1945) tapped into this Eastern European association with violent and supernatural forces unleashed on humanity. Of course, this region is no more violent than any other in the world, but Hollywood does like to pigeon-hole people and places.

Cat People also plays strongly on the theme of female sexuality and its association with monsters. Both Irena and the briefly glimpsed Cat Woman are clearly creatures whose sexuality is associated with their inner demons. This link between 'sex' and 'monster' is made more explicit in Paul Schrader's 1982 remake but also exists in earlier films. The panther woman is a sexual predator in *Island of Lost Souls* (1933), and there is the sensuous *vorvoloka* (undead) figure in *Isle of the Dead*. Meanwhile, Hammer Film Productions of the classic monster stories such as *The Brides of Dracula* (1960), *Frankenstein Created Woman* (1967), *The Vampire Lovers*, *Lust for a Vampire* (1971) and *Twins of Evil* (1972) places heavy emphasis on the monsters' sexuality, foreshadowing later versions of the classic horrors such as Francis Ford Coppola's *Bram Stoker's Dracula*.

Horror film-makers today all too often give in to the temptation to show the monster rather than to *suggest* it. But in many early horror films the reality was an anticlimax, particularly when viewed from a modern audience's perspective. Notable exceptions have been the original version of *Dracula*, *Frankenstein* and *King Kong*. It was not until the advent of special make-up effects and animatronics that we could really start to be scared by the look of creatures; H.R. Giger's design of the creature from *Alien* is the antecedent of all modern monsters with its graphically repulsive appearance. This was taken a stage further in *The Thing* (1982), with its graphic mutilation of the human body and alien distortion of human and animal body parts. Even a black comedy, John Landis' *An American Werewolf in London* (1981), has a convincingly scary monster with spine-tingling transformations from man to wolf.

The advent of CGI would ultimately set free the imaginations of special effects teams, recreating monsters such as King Kong in 2005. *The Lord of the Rings* film trilogy (2001/02/03) contains the culmination of 'human-in-monster' suit artistry and CGI technology with the creation of the Orcs and Gollum respectively.

One factor that distinguishes *Cat People* from many horror films of the 1940s and since is its representation of the 'monster'. Usually in horror or SF films at the time, a man in a wolf suit or a web-footed beast would come into view and shatter any suspense that had been created. The classic monster film, *Jaws*, works best when we do not see the shark; the early scenes are full of menace and are justifiably the stuff of nightmares. Monsters are first discovered in bedtime stories and the darkness does the rest; producer Val Lewton and director Jacques Tourneur knew this and *Cat People* is full of pools of darkness and fleeting shadows to tap into our most primitive fears.

The film-makers were forced by the studio executives at RKO to include a shot of a panther, but generally the monster is kept from view and the psychological disturbances of Irena's mind are revealed to the audience in the subtle shadow-plays of each ever-darkening scene. Real horror lies in our unknown and unseen fears; once we

have set our eyes on something that frightens us, we are on the way to dealing with it and becoming desensitised. Familiarity, as the little girl, Boo, discovers in *Monsters Inc.* (2001), breeds laughter (and, in much modern horror, contempt).

> 'Horror-crime hybrids like Michael Curtiz's New York-set *Mystery of the* Wax Museum *(1932) had mixed mad science with wise-cracking reporters, but* Cat People *was the first major supernatural horror film with a contemporary, urban American setting and 'normal people engaged in normal occupations' as leading characters; as such, it is the progenitor of a whole tradition of best-selling and box-office horror.'*
> Kim Newman, Cat People, BFI Publishing, 2001

KEY SCENE TEXTUAL ANALYSIS

An unsettling walk (8; 41:47)

Irena approaches a shop window but we see her reflection, suggesting that there are two Irenas – the good human one and the evil 'cat person'. We know that there is a good Irena, but here we just see the reflection of her other side, which is about to be revealed. The non-diegetic music is a plaintive and brooding muted trumpet, followed by a downbeat orchestral accompaniment, underpinning the impending threat. A cut back to Oliver and Alice is much brighter and open compared to the previous opaque shot.

The cut back to Irena reveals her watching them, a slither of her face seen in the window; not only is she hiding but we see just a fragment of her as she begins to succumb to her dark heritage and jealousy which breed her destructive impulses. Then it is back to the innocuous conversation between Oliver and Alice in bright conditions, again countered by a return to the reflected Irena. This time we see the two halves of Irena as she escapes detection by running into a shop doorway. The music is eerie and bewitching.

Whilst Irena's actions are stealthy and silent, those of the others are ordinary and loud. The couple are urban, evidenced by the *mise-en-scène* into which they are immersed in every shot. Irena is first reflected in the flowers in the shop front of the florists, while in the next shot she is in the shop doorway but immersed in the foliage outside, just as an animal might choose to hide.

The tracking shot of the two colleagues keeps them in light throughout their short walk; the music also recedes and they part company; Oliver's face is immersed in darkness and Alice walks down the street with a formidable wall to her side and just occasional pools of light punctuating the darkness.

The next shot of Irena sees her silhouetted for a brief moment as she emerges from a mass of trees and foliage. The fact that she mimics Alice's action of wrapping her coat around her neck links the two characters visually; it is Alice who will be Irena's prey. Irena wears a long, black fur coat that allies her to the panther, whilst Alice is dressed in light clothing, suggestive of goodness and vulnerability.

The sound of Irena's stiletto heels are all that we hear as both women walk down the lonely path, alongside the zoo. They both walk in and out of great swathes of darkness, which spread as the walk progresses.

Silhouetted lamp posts become threatening sentinels of doom; the only brightly lit areas are the walls of the zoo, like impregnable dungeon walls which will trap Alice. They are reminiscent of castle walls, a reminder of older times, of myths and witchcraft, of the legend of the cat people as described by Irena in her native Serbia.

The linking of the two women continues with repeated shots as Alice walks through an area and is then followed by Irena. This is either achieved by a cut or the camera remaining static. The tension increases as the pace of the stiletto heels gathers momentum, leaving the audience to expect an imminent confrontation between the two.

But, as that moment nears the camera remains static as Alice leaves the frame. This time, however, no chasing figure enters the frame and the sound of the clicking heels suddenly stops. Alice is next seen almost completely immersed in darkness and she slows down to look back; the sudden cessation of sound has unnerved her.

An over-the-shoulder shot reveals nothing behind Alice as she peers back down the thickly shadowy street. The next shot has her walking through frames of total darkness (it's often what you cannot see that frightens most).

The tracking shots throughout the sequence have helped us identify with the protagonists, and now we are running with Alice, the look back again revealing nothing. In medium close-up we follow her as she begins to run and then stop at one of the lamp-posts to look back again. The audience is expecting something now; what has happened to Irena? Has her sexual jealousy transformed her into a panther?

The answer comes in the form of two pieces of diegetic sound. Firstly, we hear the beginnings of a big cat's snarl almost immediately consumed by the screech of a bus pulling up alongside Alice. The cut to a medium long shot of her and the bus happens at the same time as we hear the screech; it is a jolt for both the audience and Alice as we are both expecting something to pounce. The frame contains her huddled figure (in marked contrast to her self-possession when she began the walk), the ominous black lamp post, the brutal wall behind, the shape of the bus crashing into frame, and two diagonally intruding daggers of darkness which threaten her on either side.

The bus is full of light and she immediately moves towards it, glancing back and up. The audience sees her view, notably the tops of some trees on the other side of the wall which look like they are being moved by an unseen force. She gets in and the bus drives off; one more shot of the moving trees suggests that something really is lurking there.

There has been no non-diegetic sound in the entire sequence for director Tourneur wants us to see this as 'real', to explore the recesses of fear with this woman, without the need for melodramatic music to direct the viewer.

The cut to a panther and then a leopard, both in cages, connects the previous images to that of the 'cat people', but also shows the audience that no big cat has escaped from the zoo. The shot of the sheep is unusual in that it again reminds us of a rural, peasant community where a big cat might be on the loose. But it is part of the zoo, and two sheep have been attacked and killed.

The whistle of the watchman plays over the long track that traces the panther's paw prints, which mysteriously become the prints of a shoe, and we hear the sound of footsteps once more. The cut to Irena walking is *almost* conclusive proof that she has the ability – or curse – to change into an animal, but still there is no uncut shot to link the prints to her.

Irena is in a daze, holding a handkerchief to her

Fancy a swim? (9; 50:10)

Irena asks a swimming pool receptionist if she can go down to the pool to talk with Alice. There is a dissolve between this shot and one of Alice putting on her robe in the changing rooms to visually link the two women again. We see Alice's POV as a kitten recoils in fear at something unseen. We then see the kitten's POV, a flight of stairs and its shadow.

Alice turns off the light switch and is plunged into darkness, her silhouette formed from the light source outside on the stairs where we already know danger is lurking. The camera tracks menacingly behind her.

We then see her POV and the stairs again. Something so innocuous is lent tremendous dark possibilities: it is framed within darkness; it is

mouth, again suggesting that she is the one who has just attacked the sheep. She snaps back into the present on another blow of the whistle and the arrival of a taxi cab. Again, the link between the two women is made, as both have been suddenly surprised; even Irena needs to be saved from herself and the darkness. However, whereas the bus was full of light and people, the back of the taxi is dark and lonely.

The sequence's unease and subtlety has been achieved by playing with light and shadow, creating a rhythm of editing which suggests both terror and character connections. A sparse *mise-en-scène* effectively conjures up unseen demons and demonstrates that, certainly, less is more.

both a route of escape and a means for danger to approach. Alice edges closer and we see the stairs again, but then we hear the big cat snarl; Alice's vulnerability is emphasised by the swimming costume that she is wearing. Director Tourneur also plays on the previous section's visual tension by adding the suggestions of a faint shadow of a cat on the stairs.

Both Alice and the camera track backwards, recoiling in horror, and Alice dives for safety into the pool, albeit surrounded by darkness.

We then have a series of medium shots of Alice as she twists around in the water and we are shown a number of POVs of the edges of the pool and large shadows passing over the walls and plunging the frame into almost total darkness; Alice struggles to stay afloat and catch a glimpse of the creature; all the while there is the low growl until we see an animal's shadow (animated) on the wall and the growl becomes a high-pitched screech, causing Alice to scream herself.

A rapid succession of POVs follow, as we again see the empty, but eerie corners of the poolside; Alice's screams become distorted by the acoustics of the swimming pool; the *mise-en-scène* is designed to disorientate both her and the audience.

The pool receptionist and cleaner hear and run down, but before they arrive we see Irena's dark figure move by the poolside and turn the light on. She rests back against the wall, casually and triumphantly, her feline appearance accentuating the sense of a clever predator toying with its victim. She also casts a long shadow on the wall, suggesting her duplicitous nature.

Alice's - and our - fears have subsided, although when Alice tries to get out of the pool she reflexively

swims back into the water when Irena approaches.

With Irena's departure there is one last moment to signify the horror of the scene: Alice's robe, ripped to shreds like the sheep, is a symbol of Irena's frustrated sexual tension.

The Night of the Hunter

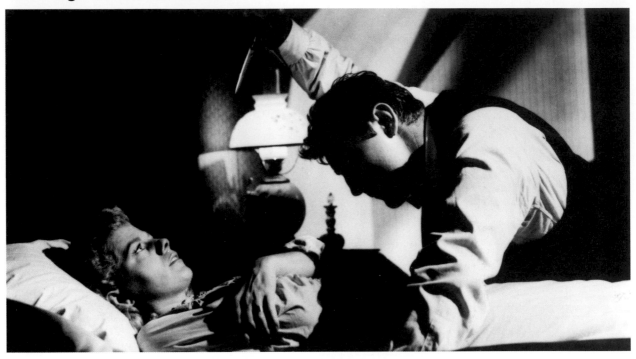

KEY FACTS

Release Date: 1955

Country of Origin: USA

Running Time: 89 minutes

PRODUCTION NOTES

Production Company

Paul Gregory Productions

Distributor

United Artists

Budget

$795,000 (estimated)

Awards

National Film Registry National Film Preservation Board, USA

SYNOPSIS

Ben Harper is arrested at the beginning of the film after a robbery has not gone to plan, but moments before the police arrive he manages to hide the stolen money in his daughter's doll, entrusting it to his son and daughter's care. In prison Harper talks about the money in his sleep and, after he is executed, his cell mate Harry Powell goes in search of the widow and the money. He poses as a preacher with the words 'Good' and 'Evil' tattooed on his knuckles, and Harper's widow, Willa, soon falls under his spell. They marry, but both children, John and Pearl, remain suspicious of him.

Willa overhears Harry asking John about the location of the money so he kills his new wife and almost gets his hands on the money when Pearl tells him where it is hidden. The children narrowly escape him and drift down a river until they are taken in by a kindly woman, Rachel, who is 'mother' to a group of lost children. Harry finds where the children are hiding, but Rachel's bravery and goodness defeat this evil man and he is eventually arrested. In a mirror image of the initial scene he is forcibly taken away by the police as John watches on.

HISTORICAL CONTEXT

In a decade full of fear about the future there was also much contentment that the austere years of the war were fading into memory. By 1959 such films as *Pillow Talk* showed the United States firmly in the grip of modernity and frivolity, a country and people satisfied with the great strides it had made since World War Two. In fact, the war had raised it out of the doldrums of the 1920s and 1930s, when hardship was the prevailing currency as the people of the United States struggled with the Wall Street Crash, drought in the farmlands of the mid-West and the Great Depression.

The Night of the Hunter neither put a mirror up to contemporary America, nor did it take its audience onto a journey into the future. Instead, it took the audience back, not to the war years as many films did in that era, nor to a remote historical time, but to the bleak years before the war and a story from America's own recent past. Although good does win out, the enduring image is that of evil. In a society which had won the war against an evil tyrant, and at a time of prosperity and harmony, it was perhaps a reminder of man's ability to choose either path, and that a decision to choose the wrong path was not exclusive to those who lived on foreign soil.

SELECT FILMOGRAPHY OF MAIN PRODUCERS AND CAST

Charles Laughton, 1899–1962, Director, Actor

As Director

The Night of the Hunter, 1955

As Actor

The Old Dark House, 1932

The Private Life of Henry VIII, 1933

The Barratts of Wimpole Street, 1934

Ruggles of Red Cap, 1935

Les Miserables, 1935

Mutiny on the Bounty, 1935

Rembrandt, 1936

I, Claudius, 1935

Jamaica Inn, 1939

The Hunchback of Notre Dame, 1939

This Land is Mine, 1943

Captain Kidd, 1945

The Paradine Case, 1947

The Big Clock, 1948

The Bribe, 1949

The Man on the Eiffel Tower, 1950

Hobson's Choice, 1954

Witness for the Prosecution, 1957

Spartacus, 1960

Advise and Consent, 1962

Robert Mitchum, 1917–1997, Actor

The Locket, 1946

Pursued, 1947

Crossfire, 1947

Out of the Past, 1947

Rachel and the Stranger, 1948

The Big Steal, 1949

His Kind of Woman, 1951

The Racket, 1951

Macao, 1952

The Lusty Men, 1952

Angel Face, 1952

River of No Return, 1954

The Night of the Hunter, 1955

Heaven Knows, Mr. Allison, 1957

The Enemy Below, 1957

The Sundowners, 1960

Cape Fear, 1962

The Longest Day, 1962

El Dorado, 1966

Villa Rides, 1968

Anzio, 1968

Ryan's Daughter, 1970

The Friends of Eddie Coyle, 1973

The Yakuza, 1974

Farewell, My Lovely, 1975

Midway, 1976

The Big Sleep, 1978

Shelly Winters, 1920–2006, Actress

Frenchie, 1950

A Place in the Sun, 1951

Mambo, 1954

The Night of the Hunter, 1955

The Treasure of Pancho Villa, 1955

The Big Knife, 1955

The Diary of Anne Frank, 1959

The Young Savages, 1961

Lolita, 1962

The Greatest Story Ever Told, 1965

Harper, 1966

Alfie, 1966

The Scalphunters, 1968

Bloody Mama, 1970

The Poseidon Adventure, 1972

Lillian Gish, 1893–1993, Actress

The Birth of a Nation, 1915

Intolerance, 1916

Broken Blossoms, 1919

Way Down East, 1920

Orphans of the Storm, 1921

The Scarlet Letter, 1926

The Wind, 1928

Duel in the Sun, 1946

The Cobweb, 1955

The Night of the Hunter, 1955

The Unforgiven, 1960

A Wedding, 1978

The Whales of August, 1987

LINKS TO OTHER FILMS

Das Cabinet des Dr Caligari (1920)

Charles Laughton and his collaborators designed a distinctively Gothic visual pattern for *The Night of the Hunter*, which refers back to such German expressionist films as Robert Wiene's classic production.

L'Atalante (1934)

In Jean Vigo's film the scenes on the barge as the young lovers journey to Paris, with the idyllic and magical images of the river, are echoed in *The Night of the Hunter*. There is a dream-like quality to both sequences, as if the humans have been taken out of their everyday angst and transported to a world of purity and innocence, and also as a site of redemption.

Bigger than Life (1956)

Nicholas Ray's film of 1950's life in suburbia, which is idyllic on the surface, but squalid and brutal beneath that veneer. The focus of the action is a teacher who, after taking cortisone for severe pain, starts to behave in an unbalanced and almost psychotic manner, terrorising his family in particular.

The Shining (1980)

The interiors of this Stanley Kubrick film contain elements that are reminiscent of *The Night of the Hunter*. The trusted patriarch in the film, based on a Stephen King story, loses control of his mind as he looks after a secluded hotel whilst it is closed to guests. The scenes where Jack terrorises his family are full of the horror arising when a position of trust is abused, just as Harry Powell betrays his position as the new head of a family.

Blue Velvet (1986)

This David Lynch film begins with a perfect world, an American idyll of white picket fences and manicured lawns. But beneath the surface, as in *The Night of the Hunter*, lies something far more sinister.

REPRESENTATION

Family

Three families are presented in this film: the original Harper family; the new Harper family with Harry Powell as the father; and the family created by Rachel Cooper. The two Harper children, John and Pearl, journey through these different structures with the first two seen as dysfunctional and damaging, and only the final unit bringing them the safety and security that they crave. Ben Harper, the family provider, has been forced into a situation where he feels compelled to steal in order to support his family. John, his son, sees him beaten by the arresting police officers. This sight, coupled with the usurper Powell, serve to destroy the boy's faith in fatherhood, yet he proves to be a much better carer and spends the rest of the film as a father figure to his sister.

The refuges for help, his mother and the old man who lives by the river, are both found wanting in moments of dire need. Willa is blinded by Powell's hypnotic and charismatic character and is later consumed by his brutality, whilst Birdie Steptoe is blind drunk when John seeks his help. Family friends are taken in by Powell and are too blinkered to offer support to the children, even after their mother goes missing. Both the immediate and the extended family are revealed as brutish, defeated, gullible, passive, uncaring and weak; the only vibrant force for much of the film is the anti-family and murderous Powell, quite an indictment of family life.

The family unit that reveals itself to be the most vital is that of Rachel Cooper and her adopted brood; the film presents a new structure for family unity, one based on the matriarch and where strangers look after other strangers, redefining society not as a group of nuclear families but as a community reaching out to the most needy. Perhaps this was a lesson that Laughton considered 1950's America needed in its pursuit of the perfect, insular family, served by all the modern conveniences that science could offer the home. The Great Depression had only been 20 years earlier and it could return.

Night of the Hunter prefigures the central role that the family would have in modern horror as the genre moved away from vampires and werewolves and towards domestic scenarios where the *mise-en-scène* would become dominated by suburban houses instead of Gothic castles. The threat to families became an internal one, positing the psychosis within the family unit rather than an external menace. *Psycho* (1960) would lead the way five years later with its perverse family structure and this would be further explored in *The Birds* (1963), culminating in the ultimate dysfunctional family, the cannibal Sawyers, of *Texas Chainsaw Massacre* (1974) fame.

These were the polar opposites of films like Frank Capra's *It's a Wonderful Life* (1946), where family values were superficially threatened but shown to be solid. These later horrors reflected the assault on family life as the twentieth century progressed, but at least the Sawyers, like the Baileys in Capra's film, still ate together as a family...

'The achievement of Laughton and his team is exceptional and enduring, the imagery original and haunting, tapping into the subconscious and a world of fears and longings; the story-telling is assured and compelling.' Simon Callow, *The Night of the Hunter BFI Film Classics*, Bfi Publishing, 2002

'A Depression-set fable of psychosis and faith, strikingly sinister and yet deeply humane...the story is like a fairy tale in its simplicity, and yet seethes with adult complictions.' Kim Newman, *1001 Movies You Must See Before You Die*, Cassell Illustrated, 2007

KEY SCENE TEXTUAL ANALYSIS

A killing and a discovery (7; 37:05)

The opening frame looks as if Willa is already dead; her prostrate body lies still on the bed, arms crossed over her chest. The setting is both rustic and threatening; it is almost church-like with its buttress-like structure and v-shaped framing. There is something artificial about it, almost Brechtian, in its attempt to be both real and unreal, suggesting a sense of dislocation and disturbance, as reflected in Willa's troubled mind. Darkness hovers above her head like a prophecy of the future.

Harry stands with his back to the audience, head bowed, looking like the preacher that he purports to be. But his positioning also withholds his expression from us, and is unnerving as a result.

We realise that Willa has been saying her prayers with the audible 'Amen', and Harry turns to question her about what she heard. He slaps her in annoyance and the diegetic sound of the slap is loud to emphasise his brutality. The cut occurs on the slap and we then see Willa in medium shot, lying serenely on the bed, bathed angelically and innocently in a shaft of light. Until that moment the music has been light and melodic, but with the faintest strain of discord; again, the surreal nature of unfolding events is underlined. With the slap a harsh moment of music pierces the superficially domestic setting.

The next shot is even further out than the initial long shot, which adds to the dislocation of the moment. It looks even more like a set in some ways, just a fragment of a room suspended in the darkness where a wife happily accepts a beating, knowing that she has married a fraudster and psychopath who will stop at nothing to discover the whereabouts of her dead husband's stolen money. In this shot the room looks even more like a church - or crypt - with its clearly visible ceiling, the giant, ornate bed resembling a tomb and bare walls. There is no warmth in the *mise-en-scène* and no escape: darkness reigns supreme on either side of the room. It is also an image (lighting, set) that shows its roots in the German expressionism of the 1920s and its thematic preoccupation with the dark side of human - or inhuman - nature.

The lilting orchestral strings continue to propel the otherness of the moment, and Harry's arch movements as he bends his head disconcertingly raises the atmosphere of unease. Willa's realisation of the truth is delivered in soft tones whilst Harry lifts his arm skywards, as if miming his rising anger and even invoking God for what he is about to do.

A cut back to a medium shot of Willa shows her begin to tell him that she believes God has brought them together for a greater purpose than the money. This delusion explains her actions and she lies on the bed, bathed in light but surrounded by shadow in order to reiterate her confused state. She is almost unconnected to anything in this shot, as if floating; appropriate, as she is, indeed, psychologically disconnected from the reality of her situation.

The cut to a close-up of Harry's face shows him half-covered in darkness, a man whose exterior goodness masks a moral vacuum. Throughout the close-up it seems to dawn on him that Willa has become deluded in her thinking and is of no use to him anymore; she has become a liability.

With the cut to a medium shot he snaps out of his reverie and is now certain of his path. He closes the window blind and reaches for a flick knife from his coat hanging from an ornate chair, the back of which again is reminiscent of something from a church. The close-up of the knife flicking up leaves us in no doubt as to what is to come. The music starts to swell and becomes more urgent as he approaches the bed, almost drowning out Willa's speech, which sounds like a ritualised pattern of words designed to make herself feel content.

Now, again in long shot, he leans over the bed, his left arm reaching across her in an ironic echo of a lover about to embrace his beloved. His right arm reaches up to its full height with the knife pointing down at her - the theatrical gesture reinforces the dislocation of the moment.

Director Laughton cuts away from this horrific spectacle to leave us with an even more disturbing medium close-up of Willa, still bathed in light and framed in darkness with her arms crossed and eyes raised towards Heaven. It is a haunting, disturbing image of one about to accept a horrible fate.

The quick screen wipe, coupled with the noise of an engine and the following image of Willa's two children in bed, serves to shock the audience without showing the stabbing, and increases the sense of horror by showing a mirror image of innocence and vulnerability.

at the bottom of the river. Eerie, almost magical-sounding music starts and accentuates the surreal nature of the scene. Willa is still wearing her white night dress and her hair is flowing like the vegetation. A cut to a medium shot of her body and face from the front of the car paints her as almost part of the nature of the river bottom with the vegetation gently caressing her face.

The next shot is similar to the last, but slightly reframed and closer in; it is a hand-held shot which helps position the audience within this unsettling spectacle.

The scene is made even more disturbing by the introduction of a fishing hook, gently probing the car. The juxtaposition of the extraordinary and the familiar imbues the moment with a powerful charge, suggesting the close proximity of life and death. There is also a streak of black humour that runs throughout the film; as the hook bobs up and

The whole sequence's theatrical ambience is the result of the *mise-en-scène*'s theatricality, indeed, there is a strong parallel between this killing and that of Desdemona in *Othello*. Shakespearean tragedy can also be seen to inform the next sequence after two connecting scenes (one which sees the son being disturbed by the sounds of a car being started in the dead of night; and the other, with Harry telling the Spoons, who are friends of the family, that Willa has run off). At the end of this sequence Harry, in close-up, looks up to Heaven in mock despair; the dissolve to the next scene links him very closely with what the audience is about to see.

Long, flowing underwater vegetation ripples in the water. While following it, the camera reveals the trussed body of Willa, propped up in the family car

down a whimsical note is sounded in the non-diegetic music. The hook finally catches hold of the car and the camera pans upwards to reveal the rowing boat above.

Birdie Steptoe is fishing and we see him above water. As he struggles with the line he moves forward and in medium shot we see his reaction to the scene below. His POV is shown; the clear view down to the corpse is unsettling for him and the audience, particularly as the music reverts to a dream-like quality when showing Willa. He recoils in horror and the music underscores this mood.

We are left with a long shot of the underwater scene; light radiates down from above onto Willa, again giving her an angelic aura. She is also strangely animated by the flow of the river as she sits upright and her hair continues to move as if in the wind. The sense of life-within-death parallels the earlier death-within-life just before she is murdered.

The artificiality of the scene, particularly apparent with the absolute translucence of the water, only helps to add to its disorientating effect.

Its Shakespearean antecedent seems to be that of *Hamlet* and the drowned body of Ophelia in particular. Such references help flesh out the film's overall design as a text interested in depicting the universal themes of love, hate, good and evil.

There's something in the cellar (10)

After falsely telling Harry that the stolen money is in the cellar, John hopes to make his escape. However, Harry insists that he and Pearl accompany him whilst he looks. The initial long shot is but a slice of the cellar. It surrounds the set in complete darkness in order to add to the tension. Throughout, Harry's face is in partial shadow whilst the children's close-ups are evenly lit to emphasise the divide between corruption and innocence.

Harry, hunched over because of the low ceiling, presents a chilling figure as he looms over the children. When he thrusts John's head onto the barrel he invokes God and turns the barrel into an unholy altar with its burning candle and apples (a reference to Man's Fall and Abraham), at which he intends to sacrifice the boy.

When Pearl confesses the money's whereabouts there is a series of rapid cuts between her, Harry and John as the boy strains to think of what to do to extricate them from their predicament; he extinguishes the candle and causes the shelf to fall on Harry's head. The reframed shot of the cellar, now closer in and focusing on the stairs, their only means of escape, adds to the tension.

Harry chases them and stretches out his hands in a particularly exaggerated manner, twisting them to resemble those of a beast. It looks theatrical but is effective in conveying his perverted inner nature, while its resemblance to the physical movement of Frankenstein's monster enriches it through its

intertextual link to other horror films.

Harry's stumble on the jar and the screams as his hands catch in the door are somewhat humorous, but the shrillness of the scream, combined with the primeval growl that he then emits are unsettling, and speak of the demons within him.

The children run, leaving a static long shot of their house, the picture of domesticity on the outside but the diegetic sound of Harry smashing the door down speaking of the horror that lies within. The fact that so many building façades are used in the film helps to highlight this fragile division between appearance and reality.

The music throughout has intertwined harmonious and discordant elements in order to heighten the sense of terror experienced by the children; for Pearl, Harry has been a father-substitute and he has played the role; the music that mixes two contrasting elements helps to mimic this sense of the abnormal invading the everyday.

A chase ensues and the children barely escape in Birdie Steptoe's skiff. Harry's scream at this point is nothing less than that of a demonic beast, the kind that inhabits many a horror film.

The Birds

KEY FACTS

Release Date: 1963

Country of Origin: USA

Running Time: 115 minutes

PRODUCTION NOTES

Production Companies

Alfred J. Hitchcock Productions

Universal Pictures

Distributor

Universal Pictures

Budget

$2,500,000 (estimated)

Awards

Nominated: Best Effects, Special Visual Effects Ub Iwerks Academy Awards, USA

Most Promising Newcomer (Female): Tippi Hedren Golden Globes, USA

SYNOPSIS

Melanie Daniels is the daughter of a newspaper proprietor who has a flirty, but biting exchange with lawyer Mitch Brenner at a pet shop in San Francisco. Feeling that he has had the last laugh in their conversation, she buys two love birds that he was considering for his sister. She then follows him up to Bodega Bay, some 60 miles from San Francisco, and secretly delivers them to his mother's house where he has gone to stay for the weekend. She even goes to the trouble of taking a boat for part of the journey in order to remain incognito, revealing that she has been both piqued and aroused by their meeting. But Mitch sees her as she is leaving by boat and he drives around the bay to meet her at the harbour. As she nears him she is struck on the head by a gull, the first of the bird attacks.

That evening Melanie meets his frosty mother, Lydia, and young sister, Cathy, and stays at the home of family friend, Annie. As they talk there is a loud noise from outside and they discover a gull has flown straight into the door and died. The next day at Cathy's birthday party there is a more concerted bird attack and later on masses of small birds enter the house via the chimney and target Melanie, Mitch, Cathy and Lydia.

The following day Lydia discovers the dead body of a neighbour at his farm, seemingly killed by birds and Melanie then goes to take Cathy out of school, but soon finds a multitude of crows gathering in the playground. The birds attack the fleeing teacher (Annie), Melanie and the children. They manage to escape and Melanie leaves Cathy at Annie's house and goes into town to telephone her father. Whilst there, a series of events sparked by a bird attack lead to the destruction of a petrol station and so begins the all-out onslaught on Bodega Bay. Mitch and Melanie escape and stop at Annie's house to pick up Cathy; the birds have killed Annie, but Cathy is unharmed and safe in the house.

The final night sees Melanie, Mitch and his family barricaded in their house as wave after wave of birds try to peck their way through. In the attempt to stop them Mitch is injured, but not badly, and after some time the attack ceases. During the night Melanie hears a noise upstairs, investigates and is savagely attacked by some birds that have gained entry to a room. Badly injured, she is saved by Mitch and they decide to leave the house. Dawn is breaking and the surrounding area is covered with birds but they now seem docile and the group leaves in Melanie's car, heading out of Bodega Bay. The news on the radio announces that there have been many such attacks along the coast.

HISTORICAL CONTEXT

1962; and the world breathed a sigh of relief. The Cuban missile crisis had come to an end and the standoff between the Soviet Union and the United States was over. John F. Kennedy and Nikita Khrushchev had finally come to an agreement, thereby averting the threat of a nuclear war. If the 1950s was a decade of suspicion and paranoia, the 1960s was their manifestation writ large. The sense of dread that humanity could actually annihilate itself, a feeling that had begun on 6th August 1945 with the dropping of the atomic bomb on Hiroshima, had come dangerously close to being realised.

While the 1960s saw many advances in more personal freedoms, it seemed that everybody was bound by these terrifying and incomprehensible developments. *The Birds* was released just one year after the Cuban missile crisis when the sense of unease was still felt keenly across the world and the film carries this feeling of dread. The helplessness and vulnerability that the characters feel in the film echo the panic that existed during those anxiety-ridden times.

Alfred Hitchcock cultivated his 'master of suspense' persona for many years; he was the most well-known face from behind the camera, his desire to self-publicise clearly evident in his dry introductions to the 10-year *Alfred Hitchcock Presents* television series and his famous film cameos. Before Hitchcock, films had contained moments of suspense, but his films were focused on the creation of suspense and thrills. In this way his body of work, beginning with *The Lodger* (1926), helped elevate the thriller/suspense film. Some would even argue that it now stands as a film genre in its own right. He invested the genre with carefully constructed film language and *mise-en-scène*, creating a series of auteurist visions to elicit complex emotional responses from audiences. His oeuvre not only works to thrill and entertain, but also satisfies much of the audience's intellectual demands.

SELECT FILMOGRAPHY OF MAIN PRODUCERS AND CAST

Alfred Hitchcock, 1899–1980, Director, Producer

The Lodger, 1927

The Ring, 1927

Blackmail, 1929

The Man Who Knew Too Much, 1934

The 39 Steps, 1935

The Lady Vanishes, 1938

Jamaica Inn, 1939

Rebecca, 1940

Suspicion, 1941

Shadow of a Doubt, 1943

Spellbound, 1945

Notorious, 1946

Rope, 1948

Strangers on a Train, 1951

Rear Window, 1954

To Catch a Thief, 1955

The Wrong Man, 1956

Vertigo, 1958

North by Northwest, 1959

Psycho, 1960

The Birds, 1963

Marnie, 1964

Frenzy, 1972

Tippi Hedren, 1930, Actress

The Birds, 1963

Marnie, 1964

A Countess from Hong Kong, 1967

Roar, 1981

Rod Taylor, 1930, Actor

Giant, 1956

Raintree County, 1957

The Time Machine, 1960

A Gathering of Eagles, 1963

The V.I.P.s, 1963

The Birds, 1963

Young Cassidy, 1965

Hotel, 1967

Zabriskie Point, 1970

The Train Robbers, 1973

Jessica Tandy, 1893–1993, Actress

A Woman's Vengeance, 1948

The Desert Fox, 1951

The Birds, 1963

The World According to Garp, 1982

The Bostonians, 1984

Cocoon, 1985

Cocoon: The Return, 1988

Driving Miss Daisy, 1989

Fried Green Tomatoes, 1991

Nobody's Fool, 1994

LINKS TO OTHER FILMS

The Naked Jungle (1954)

A film that also has a threat from nature; this time it is ants that are terrorising a community. This film has another similarity with *The Birds*: its narrative is also preoccupied with sexual matters, here played out between a plantation owner and his new bride.

Marnie (1964)

Same actress (Tippi Hedren) and similar theme (exploration of female sexuality). The sometimes opaque dialogue and narrative, with its Brechtian sets to highlight Marnie's sexual alienation, makes this a companion piece to the earlier Hitchcock film.

Piranha (1978)

Although this obviously takes its inspiration from *Jaws*, with its tale of human-eating fish, it also refers back to *The Birds*, echoing that film's use of nature to make comments about society. Here, the targets are ecological and political.

REPRESENTATION

Sexuality

The Birds has many references to relationships and sexuality, both explicit and implicit. The opening scene features a flirtatious conversation between Melanie and Mitch, a mixture of desire and disdain, on the subject of caged love birds, a representation of relationships. Melanie actively pursues Mitch as she drives to Bodega Bay to leave the love birds for him.

In Bodega Bay matters are complicated as Melanie meets Mitch's old girlfriend, Annie, as well as his mother, Lydia, who is devoted to him and icy with any prospective female suitors, and his sister Cathy, with whom he has a close relationship. Thus, there are a number of claims on Mitch, all female, and Melanie enters into this world full of the assuredness of a wealthy, young and independent woman. Her fate can be read in different ways; as she approaches Mitch in the boat after delivering the love birds their exchange of looks is one of desire; he realises that he has a worthy sexual combatant. She revels in her victory, but at this highly charged moment a seagull attacks her.

The birds' attacks on the community start with Melanie's arrival and each time she is with one of the women closely associated with Mitch there is an assault: the night she spends with Annie; Cathy's party; at Cathy's school and at Mitch's mother's house on two occasions. It seems as if Melanie's overt pursuit of Mitch, and the subsequent effect on the other women around him, is unleashing this primeval fury and mirroring her own predatory instincts.

Lydia's clinging affection for her son seems to be particularly strong, and perhaps the main source of power for these terrible furies. The film's sexuality (there are echoes of an Oedipal Complex), its violence (the gouging out of eyes and attacks on children), and the strange workings of nature as if guided by a higher power have something of the air of a Greek tragedy, as does the climax when Melanie is brutally and relentlessly attacked by the birds at the house.

Its graphic qualities, as in the earlier *Psycho*'s shower scene, have the sadistic invasiveness of rape about them. Hitchcock is often criticised for his representations of women, considered by some critics to be misogynistic. Here, we see a proud, sexually aggressive woman 'punished' and made passive by the end of the film. The connection between female sexuality and violence harks back to *Cat People* which also explores this complex dynamic; in Jacques Tourneur's film Irena, the 'cat person', kills and is killed in a context of passion and sexual jealousy.

However, is Melanie's fate to be one of defeat, or is she, cradled by Mitch, his mother and sister, now part of a family unit with bonds strengthened by shared suffering? This complex representation of family within the horror cycle also links to Hitchcock's own film, *Psycho*, with its focus on family as a site of turmoil, and films such as Robert Aldrich's *Whatever Happened to Baby Jane* (1962), Roman Polanski's *Rosemary's Baby* and George A. Romero's *Night of the Living Dead* (1968). *The Birds'* ambiguous ending, which helps the audience connect with the alienation that the characters feel, allows for no definitive answer. It finishes as an enigma, certainly complex, often brutal, and perhaps unfathomable.

'The film compares with Psycho in that it shows the independently curious woman, an active subject, as the object of violent aggression and punishment' Pam Cook, *The Cinema Book 2nd Edition*, Ed. Pam Cook & Mieke Bernink, Bfi Publishing, 1999

'In his technically most difficult film, The Birds (1963), Alfred Hitchcock directly addresses the theme of destructive, rapacious nature that was always implicit in his fascination with crime... Overwhelmed by the film when I first saw it as an impressionable teenager, I view it as a perverse ode to woman's sexual glamour, which Hitchcock shows in all its seductive phases, from brittle artifice to melting vulnerability.' Camile Paglia, *The Birds*, BFI, 1998

KEY SCENE TEXTUAL ANALYSIS

The gas station attack (13)

The initial shot of Melanie in medium close-up presents her as well-groomed with perfect hair and make-up, painted nails and a stylish outfit. The diegetic sound of gulls catches her attention. The whole conversation in the restaurant, prior to this scene, has been concerning the bird attacks, which has led up to this moment.

We see her POV as two gulls swoop down on a gas station attendant, narrowly missing his head. The sound of the interior conversation steadily gives way to the increasingly loud sound of the gulls, which is accentuated on the soundtrack.

The next attack sees the man knocked to the ground by the gulls, the pump falling to the ground and spewing out petrol. Some men rush out,

Melanie is not far behind the audience and spots the impending accident as a man lights a cigar as the petrol flows towards him. The on-lookers shout at him and open the window, but they are as impotent as the audience, and the man dies in an explosion of fire when he discards his match.

Throughout the group shots the camera always has Melanie at centre frame - she is the main protagonist and the one who is severely tested in the film. Her face is often anguished and her head hemmed in by those around her as if she is confined in some way. She is also shown to be often looking in another direction to the others as if she is different; indeed, she is an outsider and will be later accused of being evil and the cause of the attacks.

The next eight shots illustrate Melanie's 'apartness' from the other onlookers. We see her looking at

leaving the others to watch from a window; we hear gull screeches but do not see everything initially and another long shot POV of the petrol pumps puts the audience in the characters' position, unable to help.

The notion of voyeurism is then explored through the shots that follow, like those in the restaurant crowd lining the large window, almost their own cinema screen, watching the ongoing spectacle with terror and fascination just as an audience watches a horror film.

Initially, they watch a different film to us as Hitchcock directs *our* gaze towards the escaping petrol with a close-up and then a medium shot of the fuel running down the road. We have the omniscient view, whilst the characters are restricted in their viewpoint, and this device helps the tension mount.

the course of the fire as it trails back to the petrol pump in four shots and we see her POV - the fire - in the other four. Each shot of her is also like a freeze-frame, containing just a fragment of her movement, instead of the full rotating move of the head which you would expect as her gaze follows the fire's path. These are vignettes of time, fragmented and artificial-looking, emphasising a moment of sheer terror which can often distort an observer's perception of an event. A montage of her face is both powerful and suggests the timelessness of such horrific moments, especially where one is unable to intervene; the final explosion finally animates her face into recoiling terror.

The cut to a high aerial shot gives yet another perspective on events - the gulls' POV. It points to their power; the events below now seem tiny from this height, the people like insects, trivial and vulnerable. The sound of the fire and faint human cries below give way to the screeching of the birds as they swoop into frame; the gulls of the Apocalypse.

The shot back at ground level again illustrates how Melanie will be an isolated heroine/victim as she is immediately separated from the others as they retreat into the restaurant and she flees to a telephone box. As she twists around in the glass box she is visually assaulted from all sides with images of horror, death and mayhem, which come close to destroying her. Birds fly at her, obscuring her vision, water from a frenzied fire hose shoots at her and a man's bleeding face comes in and out of her terrifying 360-degree view.

The shot from the ceiling of the box, looking down on Melanie, reinforces her confined predicament and makes the kiosk look like a glass coffin that has been put on its end. It is ironic that she

Throughout this section she has repeatedly tried to leave the box, but is forced back every time to watch this terrible spectacle, which the film implies she is somehow responsible for. The drama here has been the genre staple of a woman under attack, but saved in the nick of time. However, there is an undercurrent of malevolence and a focus upon the notion of voyeurism as the heroine is forced to watch others suffering.

Trapped in a room (18; 1:42:10)

Melanie, Mitch, his mother and sister are trapped in the family home. But after many hours of besiegement by the birds there seems to be relative calm. However, Melanie hears a flapping noise coming from upstairs and while the others sleep with exhaustion she goes up to investigate. It is the classic woman-in-peril scenario: she is alone, it is

stands in a place of communication yet cannot communicate with anyone for help. To intensify her feelings of terror and claustrophobia the camera is again placed above her but closer in, almost revelling in her fear.

Hitchcock seems to be almost parodying the situation as he layers one calamity upon another until finally a driverless horse and cart comes careering around the corner, as if it had strayed off the set of a Western.

Mercilessly, the camera goes into an extreme close-up of Melanie's face as this chaos becomes ever more surreal. At this point the blood-soaked face of a man, his face covered with pecking birds, passes before her like a ghoulish freak show. Gulls then crash into two sides of the box, smashing the glass and precipitating her rescue at Mitch's hands.

dark upstairs and she has only her torch to light the way.

The shot of the stairs, lit by Melanie's torch, sets the scene for the build-up to the attack on her: it is eerie and suggestive of the horrors waiting upstairs. The camera tracks back as she approaches and then we engage with her as we see her POV. As she gets nearer we see the door at the top of the stairs and again hear the flapping sound; the tension mounts.

The camera shifts between POV and high angle on Melanie. She is surrounded by darkness as her vulnerability and fear increase. Close-ups of her face and her hand on the doorknob help to heighten the sense of anticipation. Her look downwards at the sound of another flapping suggests she might go back, but she goes ahead.

The door opens slowly and we immediately get a POV of the hole in the roof, her reaction of audible shock, a close-up of her hand lifting the torch and then her POV of the birds as they attack.

This visual fragmentation of her body, which has already begun, becomes important in the rest of this sequence. Attack after attack of birds reduces her to something less than human as they peck at all parts of her body, and although she is saved from the attack she is almost catatonic for the remainder of the film.

The attack sequence lasts for only two minutes yet there are some 80 shots. Most show the birds pecking at her body and many are in close-up; it is a vigorous assault on the audience's vision. It can certainly be regarded as falling within the boundaries of 'body horror' for it is relentless and pushes our faces right into the heart of fear. We see the horror in Melanie's eyes as she collapses and listen to her agonised cries.

Yet it is not her cries that predominate, rather it is the flapping noise of the birds' wings. This, too, is relentless and forms part of the film's soundscape. A mixture of real and electronically created/distorted sounds underpin the film's action, lending it a surreal and dislocated atmosphere in keeping with the bizarre narrative. With no musical score the sounds of the attack are all the more terrifying.

The rapid pace of the editing and shifting shadows caused by the swinging torch help to disorientate the audience, just as Melanie is herself disorientated. The blood on her previously immaculate face, hands, legs and designer green suit help to highlight the horror of this most elemental attack.

Hitchcock's camera seems so fixated with Melanie's agony that it suggests a desire on his part for the audience to reflect on the viewing of horror itself; it seems to implicate us in the act of savagery. This notion is reinforced after her rescue when she is lying on the sofa. She awakens and the camera is directly above her face in close-up. She looks directly into the camera lens and, by extension, at us, waving her arms as if trying to ward off the birds again. Unusually, the camera itself pulls back to avoid her flailing arms. It is as

if the audience is being beaten back, guilty as we have been of perhaps deriving visceral pleasure from witnessing her suffering.

Hitchcock himself took great pleasure from challenging our perception of horror and voyeurism; he loved deeply black comedy and this scene, indeed the whole film, pushes the audience to the edge of its comfort zone.

Halloween

KEY FACTS

Release Date: 1978

Country of Origin: USA

Running Time: 92 minutes

PRODUCTION NOTES

Production Companies

Compass International Pictures

Falcon Films

Distributor

Compass International Pictures

Budget

$325,000 (estimated)

Awards

National Film Registry National Film Preservation Board, USA

SYNOPSIS

A six-year-old boy, Michael Myers, inexplicably stabs his older sister to death on the night of Halloween in 1963. He is sent to Smith's Grove Warren County Sanatorium where he stays under Dr. Loomis' supervision. Myers escapes 15 years later and returns to his hometown of Haddonfield. With Dr. Loomis in pursuit, Myers stalks a number of teenagers in the town and on the night of Halloween he starts to kill them one by one.

The chief object of his initial observation is a girl called Laurie Strode, but before he attacks her, some of her friends are killed first. Annie is murdered in her car, and he then kills Lynda and her boyfriend, Bob. Laurie is alerted to the trouble by Lynda's screams (heard when Lynda telephones Laurie just before Myers attacks her), and goes across the road to investigate. She finds the three dead bodies of her friends and the tombstone of Michael Myer's dead sister, and is attacked by the psychopath. She manages to escape to the house where she is babysitting, and the two young children in her care run out and are spotted by Dr. Loomis, who has been searching for his deranged patient.

Laurie fights off Myers and stabs him twice, and Dr. Loomis arrives at the last moment, shooting him six times. He falls from the upstairs bedroom balcony, but when Loomis looks outside Myers is not there. The final image of the film is from Myers' perspective and we hear his breathing as he watches the old family home.

HISTORICAL CONTEXT

Jaws heralded the beginning of blockbuster films marketed explicitly at a younger audience, and this continued with *Star Wars* two years later. Teenagers had more disposable income than ever before in the 1970s; the use of VCRs and videos was still in its infancy in this decade and cinema-going was one of the mainstays of a night out for young people. Although a low-budget, independently-produced film, John Carpenter's *Halloween* taps right into this market and its success spawned numerous copycat 'slasher' films.

In a world context, life had become much more peaceful for those growing up as teenagers in the late 1970s, for the Western world at least. Conflicts were far removed from the United States and Europe, the Second World War was a distant memory and later conflicts like the Vietnam War were receding from public consciousness. Teenagers in these countries had known peace for some years and would do for some years to come. Films starring teenagers, for teenagers and in contemporary settings proved to be the magic formula to titillate and thrill young people. The United States, in particular, was becoming synonymous with the term serial killer. Psychopaths like Ted Bundy, who had killed numerous young women between 1974 and 1978, was a template for characters like Michael Myers. *Halloween* provided teenagers with a safe environment in which to come to terms with events that were happening around them, connecting with both their fascination for and repulsion of horror.

Of course, *Halloween* was not the first 'slasher' film; its antecedents are *Psycho*, Mario Bava's *Twitch of the Death Nerve* (1971), Bob Clark's *Black Christmas* (1974) and Tobe Hooper's *The Texas Chainsaw Massacre*. The latter's emphasis on the horror erupting from within the family had been explored in Hitchcock's earlier *Shadow of a Doubt* (1943) and Laughton's *Night of the Hunter* but became the dominant theme of horror films from the 1970s onwards.

Films such as *Last House on the Left* (1972), *The Exorcist, Sisters* (1973), *The Little Girl Who Lives Down The Lane* (1976), *The Omen* (1976) and *The Hills Have Eyes* (1977) all posit the family as a repository of repression and violence, rejecting earlier Hollywood representations of the sanctity of the family unit. *Halloween* itself begins with the devastating revelation of a young boy killing his sister, a murder that confronts the debate about the conflicting forces that lie within the family.

SELECT FILMOGRAPHY OF MAIN PRODUCERS AND CAST

John Carpenter, 1948, Director, Producer, Screenwriter, Composer

Dark Star, 1974

Assault on Precinct 13, 1976

Halloween, 1978

The Fog, 1980

Escape from New York, 1981

The Thing, 1982

Christine, 1983

Starman, 1984

Big Trouble in Little China, 1986

Prince of Darkness, 1987

They Live, 1988

Memoirs of an Invisible Man, 1992

Escape from L.A., 1996

Vampires, 1999

Ghosts of Mars, 2001

Jamie Lee Curtis, 1958, Actress

Halloween, 1978

The Fog, 1980

Halloween II, 1981

Trading Places, 1983

Perfect, 1985

A Fish Called Wanda, 1988

Blue Steel, 1990

My Girl, 1991

Forever Young, 1992

True Lies, 1994

Halloween H20: 20 Years Later, 1998

Halloween: Resurrection, 2002

Freaky Friday, 2003

Donald Pleasence, 1919–1995 , Actor

The Great Escape, 1963

The Hallelujah Trail, 1965

Cul-de-sac, 1966

Fantastic Voyage, 1966

The Night of the Generals, 1967

You Only Live Twice, 1967

Will Penny, 1968

Soldier Blue, 1970

THX 1138, 1971

Death Line, 1972

The Eagle Has Landed, 1976

Telefon, 1977

Halloween, 1978

Dracula, 1979

Escape from New York, 1981

Halloween II, 1981

Halloween 4: The Return of Michael Myers, 1988

Halloween 5, 1989

Halloween: The Curse of Michael Myers, 1995

LINKS TO OTHER FILMS

Peeping Tom (1960)

An early film about a serial killer, which focuses on the act of killing and an audience's voyeuristic inclinations. The use of the subjective camera for the killer is echoed in many subsequent films of this type. However, many critics vilified British director Michael Powell for making a film with such explicit and disturbing images and its reception all but destroyed his film career. *Psycho*, released a few months later, was also poorly received but, in contrast to Powell's film, it became a major hit, further cementing Alfred Hitchcock's reputation.

Psycho (1960)

A shocking profile of a psychopath, compelled to kill in the guise of his domineering, but dead, mother. This is a template for many of the 'slasher' films that came later, but few have Hitchcock's mastery of film language and *mise-en-scène*.

Black Christmas (1974)

Although *Halloween* is often cited as the film that reinvented the horror genre, many of its conventions had already been seen in Bob Clark's earlier Canadian film which details a serial killer on the loose in a university hall of residence, or sorority house as they are called in North America. Remade in 2006.

Friday the 13th (1980)

In the wake of *Halloween* there were numerous attempts to exploit this lucrative strain of the horror genre. *Friday the 13th* was one such film, involving a serial killer wearing a hockey mask who attacks young people, generally in a state of undress. Although not a critical success like John Carpenter's film, it generated excellent box office returns, nine sequels and, bizarrely, *Freddy vs. Jason* in 2003, linking it with one of the other long-running horror franchises, the *Nightmare on Elm St.* series.

Blow Out (1981)

Brian De Palma's film involves a political assassin, masquerading as a serial killer, who murders the heroine in the final moments of the film, reversing the usual conventions whereby the female lead manages to evade the clutches of the psychopath. In a shocking further twist, the audio of her dying screams (she has been wired) are used on the soundtrack of a horror film, thus combining the 'reality' of death with film. As the film is for an audience's pleasure and entertainment, our relationship with the vision of killing is examined, just as Michael Powell had done with *Peeping Tom*.

Scream (1996)

A postmodern take on the 'slasher' film, full of knowing comment about the conventions of these films; it is both a parody and propagator of this style of horror film, having its cake and eating it (with a very large knife).

REPRESENTATION

Voyeurism

Film-makers have a long history of self-reflexively examining the nature of the medium itself, the act of watching, of taking pleasure from events that are displaced and filtered through a created text. All film genres produce different kinds of enjoyment for different people; the desire to be challenged, entertained, frightened, educated, saddened and enriched is deep within human psyche, and films can induce each of these emotions. The desire to *look* is also an instinctive part of being human; babies and children gaze with unflinching innocence. Only as we grow older are we conditioned not to stare, but stare we must, and taboos are often the most enticing.

From the beginnings of film there has been a fascination with voyeurism: documentaries like Dziga Vertov's *Man with a Movie Camera* (1929) examines the minutiae of Soviet life, whilst Jean Vigo does the same for France with *A propos de Nice* (1930). The gaze of a wheelchair-confined man in Alfred Hitchcock's *Rear Window* (1954) also examines our voyeuristic nature; he witnesses a murder from his apartment window, the frame of which acts as a film screen on the world outside.

Of course, *Peeping Tom* and *Psycho* (see LINKS TO OTHER FILMS section) present the most challenging texts on the voyeurism of violence, and

Halloween continues this debate, albeit repackaged for a younger generation. The numerous point-of-view shots in *Halloween* show us what the killer sees. One critique would suggest that the knife is being put into the audience's hands, challenging us to question our viewing of these acts and acknowledge the violent instincts that lay dormant within us.

Film theorist Laura Mulvey suggests that women are positioned by patriarchal control of film as objects of the male gaze, as passive compared with active males. In 'slasher' films women are often objects of voyeurism, as sexual objects and victims of male power. From a feminist perspective, however, the denouement to *Halloween* and other similar films reveal, as Carol J. Clover has suggested, that the remaining female, the so-called 'final girl', achieves a degree of power, albeit as a masculinised figure as she overcomes the male's power.

It is also worth noting that the horror genre, and the 'slasher' film in particular, traditionally commands a strong following amongst males who would find it extremely difficult to identify or accept a 'male as victim' scenario. Even so, recent horror films such as the *Saw* series (2004-08) and *Hostel* (2005) have included male victims, although women in powerful positions in the horror genre are still mostly under-represented.

Halloween is actually rather tame by today's standards in terms of explicit on-screen violence; it leads us into the world of nightmares and we half-watch, half-imagine the horror. In contrast, contemporary horror aimed at the youth market not only leads us to watch, but pushes our faces right into the explicit blood and gore. Voyeurism, then, implicates and connects us but also keeps us at a safe distance. Just.

'The main character of these [slasher] films is the final girl, such as Laurie in Halloween, and hers is the main storyline... She is the slasher film's hero, and by the end our attachment to her is almost complete.' Christine Gledhill, *The Cinema Book 2nd Edition*, Ed. Pam Cook & Mieke Bernink, Bfi Publishing, 1999

'It presents an apotheosis of the hand-through-the-window knee-jerk shock while at the same time reviving for the 1970s perhaps the oldest of film formulae – the woman-in-peril thriller... Hundreds of calendar-tied Halloween *imitations, from* Friday the 13th (1980) *onwards, intensify the brutalities albeit without the motivation, creating a Christians-to-the-lions cinema many die-hard defenders of horror have found hard to cope with.'* Kim Newman, 'American Horror Cinema since 1960', in Williams, L. R. and Hammond, M. (eds) *Contemporary American Cinema*, McGraw Hill/Open University Press, 2006

KEY SCENE TEXTUAL ANALYSIS

The first killing (2:15)

The majority of this sequence is from a single POV, that of the killer. This immediately establishes a link between audience and killer from the beginning. We do not empathise with him but we are forced into the unusual and disturbing position of identifying with him, the intensity of the experience heightened by the unbroken steadicam shot that follows.

The camera emerges from darkness and gazes upon a classic-looking American house: wooden, white, and with a porch. It is, however, Halloween,

night has fallen and we hear the sound of a heavy breathing, unseen protagonist. As the steadicam glides towards the house we also become aware of the pumpkin glowing on the porch; the images are the stuff of children's scary stories and nightmares.

As the prowler reaches the porch a couple become visible, kissing on the other side of the net-curtained front door. They move and so does the camera, gliding to the side of the house. The steadicam camera allows for long unbroken takes, which adds to the reality of the situation and for movement, which mimics a person's movement. It is not completely steady and the swaying and furtiveness adds to its authenticity.

The turning off of the bedroom light as the kissing couple move onto the bed intensifies the atmosphere. We are more nervous for them as they are now in darkness. As the intruder enters another non-diegetic musical note is repeatedly struck to demarcate the onset of the next stage.

He pulls a knife from a drawer in the kitchen and goes upstairs once the man has left, putting on a clown mask to restrict our view to his two eye holes - this device makes our identification with him even greater.

He looks at the bed where the couple have just been and then at the semi-naked girl brushing her hair. She knows the killer but the knife is thrust down into her body. Not only do we see the girl being killed but the killer also looks at the hand and knife committing the action. As an audience we could never be closer to his experience of killing, although the killer seems to be slightly removed from what he is doing as he looks at his hand moving back and forth.

On the soundtrack we then hear his heavy breathing, which draws us even deeper into his world. It is a horror cliché, which suggests to the audience that the character is a stereotypical madman. It also makes the denouement to this scene, that the killer is a young boy and brother to the victim, all the more shocking.

He leaves, goes downstairs and out the door. A car pulls up and two people get out repeating the name 'Michael'. The cut to a medium shot of a young boy in a clown's outfit holding the knife as he has his mask removed by the man is a *coup de grâce*; the killer is a child and it seems that he has just murdered his sister. The pace of the music has slowed after the killing, almost to funereal pace, and it also matches the boy's catatonic expression.

It is a shocking twist; the camera cranes backwards leaving the dazed boy in clown costume and bloodied knife framed by his parents with the house in the background. The suburban dream has become a nightmare and a 'child as killer' is a deeply disturbing concept. As children are often identified with innocence this horrific image is left unexplained and the camera recedes up and away from something that cannot be reconciled.

Up to the point of the boy's unmasking, the sequence is a single shot, lasting some four minutes. This helps to intensify the emotional

music (a hallmark of director Carpenter who often also composes his own film scores).

This sequence takes pains to show Haddonfield as 'Middle America', affluent with its long roads, tree-lined pavements and large houses. But it is also a lifeless landscape with very little human activity (later on in the film it is shown to be an area with little humanity as neighbours ignore Laurie's desperate pleas for help); it is in fact the perfect arena for Michael Myers' murderous intentions.

The widescreen format helps create this atmosphere, emphasising the empty streets accentuated by the number of long shots. The other technical device helping the sense of unease is the use of steadicam which glides around the characters, furtive and threatening, often, as we saw in the opening sequence, helping us identify with the killer as never before.

impact of the killing and the audience becomes lost in its real-time depiction. The cut, when it does come, not only reveals the identity of the killer but breaks the spell cast by this extremely long shot and allows us to reflect fully on the horror of the moment. We need the break as this intensity cannot be sustained for a whole film and must be built up again.

Daytime in Haddonfield (20:27)

Although the film is mostly shot at night, Carpenter prepares the audience for the shocks to come by a middle section shot entirely in daylight, not the usual preserve of horror films. As Laurie walks home with her friends, there are a number of moments which foreshadow future events. As a car turns the corner onto the road where they are walking its threat is signalled by the non-diegetic music: simple, repetitive and unnerving electronic

Once the car has passed, the girls walk to the background of the frame as they continue up the pavement; but the camera remains and its slight wavering gives it the sense of becoming the POV of a voyeur, which, coupled with a resurgence in the brooding music, is unsettling for the audience.

A cut to another long shot, which again uses steadicam to follow the girls, emphasises their isolation in the frame. The music fades and their chatter continues. The steadicam also allows for a natural flow of action with the long takes adding to the verisimilitude of the sequence; its very ordinariness is its horror.

The next shot shows Laurie's POV. It is another of the well-manicured tree-lined streets, but this time there is a masked figure standing in this long shot; the surface of the everyday has become fractured. A cut back to Laurie shows her staring with greater concern, and then back to the figure that disappears behind a hedge.

The figure has gone when Laurie alerts her friend, and when Annie runs up to the hedge to confront him the camera stays close to the hedge as she approaches and then cuts to Laurie's face in close-up to maintain the tension. But there is no-one there.

This continues a sequence of 'now-you-see-him-now-you-don't' scenes intended to slowly increase the tension and unnerve Laurie (and the audience). Annie soon departs and Laurie is left to ponder what she has seen. An old-school scare comes next as she looks back at the hedge and bumps into a figure and screams. But it is Annie's father, a police officer. The scare is a knowing parody of old horror film tactics; we can see it coming yet it both jolts us and amuses us.

The long shot of Laurie arriving at her house again emphasises the emptiness of her environment; it

The cut back to Laurie's face and then back to her POV - the figure is gone - beg the question as to whether she is now just seeing things; there is no distraction here to cause her to look away and then find him gone. The sinister repetitive electronic notes return in order to enhance the tense atmosphere.

The tracking shot to the right reveals the phone, which rings at this tense moment. There is no one on the other end and Laurie panics even more, slamming down the phone. It immediately rings again and turns out to be Annie, as it had been earlier. After the call Laurie lies on her bed, trying to reassure herself that she is imagining things.

From the moment Laurie moves towards the phone to the end of the sequence there is no cut, again a device to retain the 'reality' of the moment. The phone ringing at a tense moment is a standard

is neat and ordered, but anonymous. As she nears the house, the camera continues to follow her from a low angle as if spying on her from beneath the branches of trees. A girl's cry is heard but this proves to be yet another red herring as it turns out to be the laughter of trick-or-treaters.

Another technique that Carpenter employs is to hold the camera a few beats longer than one would expect, just to intimate that someone may enter the frame from the edges. This is done as Laurie enters the house, but nothing happens.

A last visual scare occurs as she looks out of her bedroom window and sees the masked man standing amongst that most domestic of images, clothes on a washing line. The mysterious figure is situated as part of the fabric of this ordinary environment, and thus, made even more frightening.

horror convention but it is extended just a little further to test Laurie's, and the audience's, nerves.

A number of low-key horror conventions are included in this section, aided by the widescreen and steadicam technologies. It is a case of subtle audience manipulation, enjoyed by us but also preparing the way for the horrors that will come that night...

A Nightmare on Elm Street

KEY FACTS

Release Date: 1984

Country of Origin: USA

Running Time: 91 minutes

PRODUCTION NOTES

Production Companies

The Elm Street Venture

Media Home Entertainment

New Line Cinema

Smart Egg Pictures

Distributor

New Line Cinema

Budget

$1,800,000 (estimated)

Awards

Critics Award Wes Craven Avoriaz Fantastic Film Festival

Nominated, Best Film Academy of Science Fiction, Fantasy and Horror Films, USA

SYNOPSIS

Two teenage friends, Tina and Nancy, discover that they are sharing the same nightmare. They are both trapped in a boiler room and are pursued by a frightening figure who sports a red and green jersey and a glove with long, sharp razors attached to it. In Tina's dream she is nearly caught by the figure and he cuts her clothes with his glove, something which is replicated on her nightdress when she wakes up. Unnerved by this and other dreams, Nancy and her boyfriend, Glen, spend the night with Tina to assuage her fears. Tina's boyfriend, Rod, arrives and sleeps with her, but during the night she is brutally attacked and killed by a seemingly unseen force, undoubtedly the apparition of her nightmares. Rod is arrested for her murder but Nancy continues to be stalked and attacked in her dreams.

Nancy visits Rod in jail and after hearing his description of events in the bedroom she believes that the sinister figure from their nightmares is responsible. Later, Nancy takes Glen to talk to Rod but he has succumbed to the maniac in his sleep, strangled by his own bedsheets; everyone but Nancy believes that it is suicide.

Nancy has further disturbing dreams and the worlds of nightmare and reality start to overlap; in one nightmare she is injured by the figure but manages to bring his hat back into the waking world. Upon seeing this, her mother relates the story of how she and other local parents had trapped a child murderer in a boiler room and burnt him alive after he had been released from prison on a technicality. This same man, Fred Krueger, was now exacting revenge on their children.

Nancy and Glen hatch a plan to destroy Krueger but he kills Glen and Nancy is left alone, pursued by him in the real world. She eventually defeats him, but not before her mother is killed. However, with his apparent death all of Krueger's murders are undone and the final scene sees the friends together again. There is one twist left, and as Nancy's mother waves goodbye to the friends Krueger drags her back into the house whilst the friends are driven away in a Krueger-customised car.

HISTORICAL CONTEXT

If the 1980s were all about commodification, then Freddy Krueger became a capitalist's dream. Until *Star Wars* there had been very little merchandising linked to films. George Lucas, the creator of the *Star Wars* series, realised that there was a lot of extra revenue to be made from this synergy of products. As the *Elm Street* franchise gathered momentum through the 1980s the level of merchandise opportunities grew, and soon toy shops were replete with Krueger figures. Of course, *Star Wars* was aimed at a young audience and the crossover into toy merchandise seemed like a natural progression.

A Nightmare on Elm Street is a film for much older audiences but the bullish financial climate, wherein everything seemed fair game as a marketing opportunity, was a fertile ground for money-making

schemes. It is perhaps not surprising to find a child serial killer as a toy in a society which seemed to value money above any sort of soul-searching. The other factor that helped the film, and in particular, its evil hero, move into the mainstream of popular culture was the franchise's increasingly tongue-in-cheek approach to horror, its postmodern self-referencing reaching its natural conclusion in *Wes Craven's New Nightmare* (1994) and his later *Scream* series of films.

It was Wes Craven who was instrumental in pioneering the new breed of horror in the 1970s. His vision invested the horror genre with renewed vigour, commenting on key themes such as family and revenge, whilst drawing inspiration from influential films like Ingmar Bergman's *The Virgin Spring* (1960). His films, *The Last House on the Left* and *The Hills Have Eyes*, established editor/writer/director Craven as an auteur, like George A. Romero, whose works tested both the censors and audience sensibilities and expectations of the horror genre. *A Nightmare on Elm Street* echoes these earlier works with their depiction of brutality, but is repackaged for the post-*Jaws* audiences who embraced a more ironic and knowing angle on their traditional genre conventions.

SELECT FILMOGRAPHY OF MAIN PRODUCERS AND CAST

Wes Craven, 1939, Director, Producer, Screenwriter

The Last House on the Left, 1972

The Hills Have Eyes, 1977

Swamp Thing, 1982

A Nightmare on Elm Street, 1984

The Hills Have Eyes Part II, 1985

The Serpent and the Rainbow, 1988

Wes Craven's Shocker, 1989

The People Under the Stairs, 1991

Wes Craven's New Nightmare, 1994

Vampire in Brooklyn, 1995

Scream, 1996

Scream 2, 1997

Scream 3, 2000

Red Eye, 2005

John Saxon, 1930, Actor

Joe Kidd, 1972

Enter the Dragon, 1973

Black Christmas, 1974

The Electric Horseman, 1979

Battle Beyond the Stars, 1980

Tenebrae, 1982

A Nightmare on Elm Street, 1984

A Nightmare on Elm Street 3: Dream Warriors, 1987

From Dusk to Dawn, 1996

Freaky Friday, 2003

LINKS TO OTHER FILMS

Natural Born Killers (1994)

Oliver Stone's satire on the cult of celebrity (based on a Quentin Tarantino script) breathes the same air as A Nightmare on Elm Street. Here, two serial killers become celebrated fugitives, courted by the media, and the narrative examines the American fascination with serial killers and violence, as mediated through television.

Wes Craven's New Nightmare (1994)

After the original A Nightmare on Elm Street Wes Craven had no active connection with the series, apart from the third instalment, until he created this postmodern take on the horror genre. The actors play themselves and the film charts Krueger's attempts to infiltrate their real lives. The knowingness and irony of this narrative structure was the forerunner of a new breed of horror film, which was arguably required to breath new life into the genre after the countless sequels and imitators of all franchises in the 1980s and 1990s.

Scream (1996)

Wes Craven's New Nightmare led on to his next franchise which began with this film. Its irony and self-parody would last until the next generation of horror film-makers, such as Eli Roth (Cabin Fever, 2003; Hostel; Hostel: Part 2, 2007); Greg McLean (Wolf Creek, 2005) and the creators of the Saw series, who introduced a new level of graphic violence into their films, usually involving the iconography of torture.

Silent Hill (2006)

Christophe Gans' film, based on the computer game of the same name, also details a world where reality and an altered reality collide. The altered reality is a nightmarish manifestation of people's darkest and most terrifying fears, the subconscious of evil. The main characters move between the two states just as those in A Nightmare on Elm Street, both terrorised by the demons of the night.

REPRESENTATION

Villains

Mr. Hyde was despicable, but there was always Dr. Jekyll to compensate. Dr. Frankenstein made the monster look like the good guy. The Wolf Man, the Invisible Man: it wasn't their fault. Even Norman Bates loved his mother. Fred Krueger is a child murderer and kills young people in the most brutal manner imaginable. However, he has emerged as one of cinema's favourite modern villains. By the time of the first sequel (1985), Fred is most definitely Freddy; it is even subtitled Freddy's Revenge. The Freddy tag humanises and lightens the character. With the smirking and wisecracks that begin to creep in, sinister Fred morphs into loveable Freddy. The hat, the jersey and, most particularly, the glove became iconic, part of popular culture, and child-friendly. Krueger, on first sight, is ugly inside and out; he has Schwarzenegger quips grafted onto his persona and his sense of theatre makes every killing a virtuoso performance. He is a cartoon character, but the dichotomy remains: he kills children.

But the modern phenomenon is that in a cinema on any night when a horror film is shown, one will hear gasps of shock but laughter as well, and lots of it. Villains are celebrities and often the most interesting characters in films. They always have been, but now, however evil their representation and however graphic the violence they perpetrate, they are a new breed of (anti-)hero.

By the 1980s there had been time to reflect on the murky waters of the 1970s and the legacy of the Vietnam War and Watergate. No longer was there a clear delineation between 'good' and 'bad'. If we could no longer trust our leaders then why not cheer for Freddy Kreuger? Hannibal Lector would be the next decade's anti-hero, another character afforded celebrity status in a world where the acquisition of fame was becoming easier and based more on notoriety and scandal than on merit.

'The 'Final Girl': the one girl in the film who fights, resists and survives the killer-monster. The final girl... dominates the action, and is thus masculinised. [In] the slasher film like... Nightmare on Elm Street *(1984)... the final girl becomes her own saviour.'* Christine Gledhill, *The Cinema Book 2nd Edition*, Ed. Pam Cook & Mieke Bernink, Bfi Publishing, 1999

'Hard though it is to divorce the image of Fred Kreuger... from the farrago of a franchise that we now know was to follow, there are some genuinely frightening dream sequences and some throwaway black humour.' Nicholas Royle, *Time Out Film Guide 14th Ed.*, Time Out Guides Ltd., London, 2006

KEY SCENE TEXTUAL ANALYSIS

A face in the wall (5)

In previous scenes Fred Krueger has pursued the teenagers in their dreams but they have awoken before he can strike. Here, he attempts to reach both Tina and Nancy (immediately prior to this sequence he has begun his pursuit of Tina and then turns his attention to Nancy).

The medium shot of Nancy in bed has her sleeping at the centre of frame. She is illuminated by light, her head on a white pillow, contrasting with the gulf of darkness that surrounds her bed. Nothing more of the room can be seen; it is in the frame's dark spaces that horror lurks for her and the audience.

As the audience becomes accustomed to the light level a small face can be picked out to the right of the bed. It is a toy's face, but slightly disconcerting nonetheless. Then a moving bulge appears above her head, unexpected and sinister.

Diegetic creaking accompanies the eerie non-diegetic music as the bulge moves and stretches. It then reaches downwards and the impression of two hands and a face leering over her body becomes pronounced; it is the stuff of nightmares: surreal and threatening. Krueger is trying to burst through into her world, reminiscent of a Surrealist painting, where the unconscious erupts through the surface of reality.

It is the least gory of the shocks in the film but it is disconcerting in its strangeness and depiction of the blurring between reality and the dream world. Nancy looks so vulnerable and the shape so malevolent that it leaves the viewer unnerved.

As Nancy rouses, the figure retreats and she is left with the residual sensation of fear and all she can do is test the walls for the source of this apparition. The close-up of the crucifix positions the conflict to come as one between good and evil.

The first successful attack (6)

Where the threat to Nancy was shot in a restrained but nonetheless frightening manner the next sequence is all about excess and full-blooded horror.

When we cut back to Tina she is fully immersed in her nightmare world and so can be reached by Krueger. She is wearing just a shirt, making her seem vulnerable but also sexually provocative (she has just had sex with her boyfriend).

With the sinister calling of her name she leaves the light of the house and is consumed by the shadow and half-light of outside. The non-diegetic music is an electronic smorgasbord of eerie sounds, and as she walks the camera tracks towards her and her filmic space diminishes. She is walking into a trap; in close-up we see the sinister shadows more clearly falling over her face. Her POV reveals nothing but darkness, while a repetition of the voice serves to increase the tension.

But instead of running in fright, she moves into the frame that was previously her POV *towards* the pools of darkness and the half-seen shapes in

elongated arms add to the unnerving atmosphere. The sound of dripping water has permeated much of the sequence and adds to the sense of this place as one that has been abandoned.

The level of threat is heightened once again as we first hear, then see, the scratching of Krueger's razor sharp gloves on a metal fence (the film's title sequence has already shown the construction of these gloves, a sort of demonic version of the way superheroes, like Batman, initially equip themselves for their new persona). A close-up of his lacerated face and the frightening gloves allows the audience to see what Tina is about to do battle with.

A long shot now shows Krueger in pursuit (looking rather like a possessed Mr. Tickle), but as she comes closer to the foreground and the filmic space around her diminishes, the shock of his

the garden. The audience would, at this point, be suggesting another course of action. A cut to the street/alley beyond shows her going further away from the house; the shot is from a very low angle, and is disorientating suggesting that she is being watched.

A metallic sound can be heard and the next shot reveals its source, a rolling dustbin lid. It ups the tension and we return to the low angle long shot of Tina as the lid comes to rest in the foreground. A sudden electronic noise (non-diegetic) heralds Krueger's appearance, firstly in shadow form with his characteristic hat writ large on a garage door. Tina spins around in close-up, her gasp pushing the sense of mounting danger.

The audience gets the briefest glimpse of Kreuger's disfigured face, but he is silhouetted by the back light and made all the more sinister for it.

His laugh and then the long shot of his grotesquely

sudden appearance in front of her is the true stuff of nightmares - and, of course, cartoons. In the cartoon world a character can escape a baddie in a house, only to find him waiting on the other side of the door. Likewise, Krueger is both demonic and somewhat cartoonish in his movements and cruel playfulness (*The Simpsons*' 'Itchy and Scratchy' would be his nearest cartoon relatives) and he exploits the fluid logic of dreams and nightmares.

The camera then pursues Tina in a hand-held jerky movement to mirror her frenzied run, the disorientation and terror of the moment, and Kreuger's crazed pursuit. Her run back through the dark garden does not reveal the expected pursuit by Krueger, or indeed, his arrival in the foreground of the frame. Instead, in another cartoonish moment, he appears from behind a thin tree (which could not possibly have hidden his whole body in the real, physical world): a fright and a laugh for the audience.

In medium close-up he then performs some DIY surgery as he slices off two of his own fingers and a greenish liquid spurts from the stumps. Again, it is both unpleasant and blackly comic.

As Tina runs to the back door of the house the camera mimics her frantic movements as it follows, drawing the audience into her desperate escape. The struggle followed by the table falling on top of them allows Craven to cut and seamlessly transport the action back into the bedroom. She pulls at Krueger's face and the skin comes away, revealing a cackling skull beneath, yet another horrible, but still blackly comic moment.

From this point on, with the non-diegetic music pumping relentlessly in a manic way and with her screams on the soundtrack, the violence takes on an altogether more bloody and disturbing aspect.

The boyfriend, Rod, is now awake. The fact that Krueger is invisible to him and so cannot intervene adds a greater level of horror to the remainder of the sequence.

The camera continues to move around in jerky motions as if unable to capture all the horror of the events, mirroring the boyfriend's incomprehension as an unseen hand thrusts Tina's body around.

There is a close-up of her body as Kreuger's unseen glove slashes it, then she is dragged into the air (with the aid of wires - this is a number of years before CGI). Evil grunting is also heard alongside her screaming to add to the horror, her body now soaked in blood.

She is dragged along the ceiling with her screams becoming more laboured and her body more bloody, with the boyfriend powerless to act. It recalls *The Exorcist* and the possessed child's spider walk across the ceiling. This intertextuality links the film with not only *Halloween*-style 'sexualised teenagers butchered by maniac' slasher horror but the weightier 'good versus evil' films of *Rosemary's Baby*, *The Exorcist* and *The Omen*.

As Tina falls and hits the bed the sound of blood splashing and splattering adds to the horror and excess of the images. The teenage audience, at whom this is aimed, are likely to be both repelled and fulfilled by the over-the-top images. Just as

with many of Kreuger's other assaults in this film and its sequels the attack has sexual overtones. This, coupled with the fact that the young couple have just had sex, chimes with the adolescent fascination with, and fear of, sex. Craven's darkly comic touches throughout this scene and the film as a whole also connect with the sexually comic excesses of *National Lampoon's Animal House* (1978) and *Porky's* (1982). Both contain scenes where the sexual act is disturbed by comic violence, albeit of a much tamer variety, but aimed at the same teenage audiences with their explorations of adolescent sexual anxiety.

The Silence of the Lambs

KEY FACTS

Release Date: 1991

Country of Origin: USA

Running Time: 114 minutes

PRODUCTION NOTES

Production Companies

Orion Pictures Corporation

Strong Heart/ Demme Production

Distributor

Orion Pictures Corporation

Budget

$19,000,000 (estimated)

Awards

Best Actor in a Leading Role Anthony Hopkins Academy Awards, USA

Best Actress in a Leading Role Jodie Foster Academy Awards, USA

Best Director Jonathan Demme Academy Awards, USA

Best Picture Edward Saxon, Kenneth Utt, Ronald M. Bozman Academy Awards, USA

Best Writing, Screenplay Based on Material from Another Medium Ted Tally Academy Awards, USA

Best Actor Anthony Hopkins BAFTA Awards, UK

Best Actress Jodie Foster BAFTA Awards, UK

Silver Bear Best Director Jonathan Demme Berlin Film Festival

Best Performance by an Actress in a Motion Picture – Drama Jodie Foster Golden Globes, USA

Best Actor Anthony Hopkins New York Film Circle Critics Awards

Best Actress Jodie Foster New York Film Circle Critics Awards

Best Director Jonathan Demme New York Film Circle Critics Awards

Best Film New York Film Circle Critics Awards

SYNOPSIS

Clarice Starling is plucked from the FBI training academy and asked to find information on a serial killer, nicknamed Buffalo Bill, from an imprisoned Hannibal Lector, a former psychiatrist who himself became a cannibalistic serial killer. Gaining his trust, she starts to learn valuable information from him concerning the identity of Buffalo Bill. She strikes a deal with him: he will help if she can get him transferred to more pleasant environs than his maximum security bunker.

Meanwhile Buffalo Bill, who skins the women who he abducts and kills, seizes Catherine Martin, a senator's daughter. It seems that Lector will reveal more to Starling so Chiltern, the head of the institution where Lector is held, attempts to get the glory of unmasking Buffalo Bill by telling him that Starling's offer *is* false (it is, in fact, an offer concocted by Starling's boss, Jack Crawford and it is false). Lector agrees to tell Chiltern and is transported to a new facility.

En route, he meets the mother of the abducted girl and gives her a false name; only Starling sees through the deception. She confronts him but after she tells him some personal information at his request he is spirited away by the warden and she does not get Bill's real name. However, she does manage to retrieve a file that she had given him earlier. Lector escapes his captors, killing two policemen, and disappears. Starling realises that the file she had given to Lector could yield more clues and she eventually tracks Buffalo Bill down (it transpires that he is trying to construct a 'woman suit' of real skin).

Unfortunately, she is only following a line of inquiry and does not initially realise that she has found him when he answers the door of a house. Upon entering she soon realises that he is the serial killer and, after a game of cat-and-mouse in the huge basement, she kills him. Catherine Martin is also found there, alive. Later, Starling graduates from the FBI academy and receives a telephone call from the still missing Lector, who tells her that he will not pursue her as long as she leaves him alone. His words, and the final shot, make clear that his old warden, Chiltern, will be his next victim.

HISTORICAL CONTEXT

The horror film had undergone a makeover in the previous decade; the grisly 1970s had given way to the playful 1980s with its comic book villains perpetrating despicable acts with panache. The 1990s heralded a nastier edge with *The Silence of the Lambs* delivering a serial killer who existed in an approximation of the real world - not an incarnation of supernatural evil or a postmodern joke. With the success of the film, Hannibal 'the cannibal' Lector was assimilated into popular culture very quickly, an all-too-real bogey man in a world which had become fascinated with such characters, featuring them on a nightly parade of news bulletins.

in 1992 Jeffrey Dahmer was convicted of 15 murders in the United States; in 1995, Fred West confessed to murdering at least 12 women in the United Kingdom; and in Europe atrocities were being committed in the Bosnian War between 1992 and 1995. Wherever you cared to look, or not look, there was ample evidence of humanity's capacity for brutality. In the 1990s the likes of CNN, Sky and the emerging internet were there to tell us all about it. Hannibal Lector was now in glorious technicolor and there was nowhere for us to hide.

SELECT FILMOGRAPHY OF MAIN PRODUCERS AND CAST

Jonathan Demme, 1944, Director, Producer, Screenwriter

Crazy Mama, 1975

Handle with Care, 1977

Last Embrace, 1979

Melvin and Howard, 1980

Swing Shift, 1984

Something Wild, 1986

Swimming to Cambodia, 1987

Married to the Mob, 1988

The Silence of the Lambs, 1991

Philadelphia, 1993

Beloved, 1998

The Manchurian Candidate, 2004

Rachel Getting Married, 2008

Jodie Foster, 1962, Actress, Director

Taxi Driver, 1976

Bugsy Malone, 1976

Freaky Friday, 1976

Foxes, 1980

The Hotel New Hampshire, 1984

The Accused, 1988

The Silence of the Lambs, 1991

Sommersby, 1993

Maverick, 1994

Nell, 1994

Contact, 1997

Anna and the King, 1999

Panic Room, 2002

A Very Long Engagement, 2004

Flightplan, 2005

Anthony Hopkins, 1937, Actor

When Eight Bells Toll, 1971

A Bridge Too Far, 1977

The Elephant Man, 1980

The Bounty, 1984

84 Charing Cross Road, 1987

The Silence of the Lambs, 1991

Howard's End, 1992

Bram Stoker's Dracula, 1992

The Remains of the Day, 1993

Shadowlands, 1993

The Road to Welville, 1994

Legends of the Fall, 1994

Nixon, 1995

Surviving Picasso, 1996

Amistad, 1997

The Mask of Zorro, 1998

Meet Joe Black, 1998

Hannibal, 2001

Red Dragon, 2002

The Human Stain, 2003

Alexander, 2004

The World's Fastest Indian, 2005

Bobby, 2006

All the King's Men, 2006

Fracture, 2007

LINKS TO OTHER FILMS

The Texas Chainsaw Massacre (1974)

Leatherface, one of a family of cannibal killers, wears a human skin face mask and, like Buffalo Bill, his favourite pastime is brutally killing his victims. Although time, sequels and wretched remakes have dimmed the impact of this original, the central character of Leatherface, like Hannibal Lector, has retained the ability to terrify and be regarded as an iconic horror villain.

Manhunter (1986)

This is Michael Mann's version of Thomas Harris' *Red Dragon* novel, the first story in which Hannibal Lector appears. It is Lector's first screen incarnation, here portrayed by Brian Cox, and the atmosphere is just as tense as in *The Silence of the Lambs*, albeit less graphic in its depiction of the brutality. Confusingly, the book was again filmed under its original title in 2002, this time with Anthony Hopkins reprising the role of Lector in what is actually a *prequel* to *The Silence of the Lambs*.

Hannibal (2001)

The first sequel to *The Silence of the Lambs*, Ridley Scott's film is even more vividly graphic with its operatic, garish visuals, but there is no attempt to make Lector into the overt parody that Freddy Krueger became in the *Elm Street* series of films. He *does* quip and he has a grand sense of brutal poetic justice, but he remains chillingly real.

REPRESENTATION

Female law enforcement officers

There have been a number of film representations of females involved in police work and a variety of angles explored. In James Fargo's *The Enforcer* (1976) Inspector Kate Moore must prove herself to her colleague, 'Dirty Harry' Callaghan, a rather chauvinistic, if not misogynistic male who has little time for a female partner. She proves his equal, but she is a rarity in the 1970s.

Before Moore, the only women usually involved in crime investigations are lone, old and somewhat eccentric. The most famous lady who solves murders in her spare time is, of course, Margaret Rutherford's interpretation of Miss Marple in *Murder, She Said* (1961), *Murder at the Gallop* (1963), *Murder Most Foul* (1964) and *Murder Ahoy!* (1964). Before Marple there are slim pickings; Myrna Loy, as one half of the crime-busting married couple in the *Thin Man* series of films (1934-1947) is notable in a male-orientated world.

After Moore, there starts to be more interest in a female perspective on law enforcement. The opening sequence of Kathryn Bigelow's *Blue Steel* in 1990 focuses on Jamie Lee Curtis' morning preparation for work as a uniformed cop. We see the female form being covered by the battle dress of the job: she is a dichotomy, a challenge for the audience and society to accept; both feminine and tough. A point is being made.

Clarice Starling is shown to be a brilliant FBI student and although there are moments when characters in the film try to exploit her gender, the representation is clear: she is a law enforcement officer and a complex human like all of us. Starling paved the way for other clear-cut representations of female officers, where gender need not be an issue. Without Starling there may not have been a Dana Scully (*The X-Files*, 1998), but even today there

are still only a tiny number of females even shown as law enforcement officers, compared with the numerous routine representations of their heroic male counterparts.

'With strong dramatic performances and striking imagery, the film succeeded for contemporary critics and audiences both as horror (it was promoted as the scariest film of the year) and as drama... For media studies scholars the film's foregrounding of a female investigator... an object of some interest... the fact that Starling is characterised in terms of her intellect and ambition, rather than glamour or sexual availability, and that she nonetheless remains a figure of empathy and integrity, is, within the Hollywood cinema, remarkable.'

Starling, for her part, is characterised not only as novice investigator, but also as the 'final girl' described by Carol Clover as a founding character type of the slasher film...' Yvonne Tasker, '*The Silence of the Lambs*', in Williams, L. R. and Hammond, M. (eds) *Contemporary American Cinema*, McGraw Hill/Open University Press, 2006

KEY SCENE TEXTUAL ANALYSIS

Tour of a serial killer's lair (12)

Here is a snapshot of horror, a virtual tour of evil. A steadicam shot with no apparent cuts allows the audience intimate access into a killer's world; the continuous take situates the horrific adjacent to the ordinary and domestic.

There are numerous butterflies and moths at the beginning of the sequence, which could be quite innocuous if it were not for the preceding scene, which shows that Buffalo Bill inserted a chrysalis into one of his victim's throats, and the diegetic sound which is a cacophony of insect noise, buzzing lights, music... and a girl's screams.

The swiftness of the camera movement allows the audience to register just brief glimpses of this nightmarish world; it allows us to *imagine* what might have happened here rather than explicitly showing the horror. After the insects comes the surgical table with an assortment of knives; in the background there is a glass tank containing the remains of a human body. It is only a fleeting glimpse but enough to leave an indelible image.

A dark passage leads to a collection of strangely dressed mannequins facing a series of mirrors and the sound of the quirky, unsettling music increases as we go further into the labyrinth. The pleading cries of a woman join the melée and our sense of being both disturbed and intrigued is increased. In this surreal atmosphere we next see a naked man sitting at a sewing machine with his back to the camera. The room is full of paraphernalia, including a United States flag, which helps to confuse our perception and add to our feeling of bewilderment.

A small, white dog skirts across the open door and the camera moves beyond the man and follows the dog - and the cries. The camera quickly catches up with the dog, which leans into a stone well and barks at the person who seems to be emitting the cries.

It is a very quick sequence, but it piques the audience's interest in its portrayal of a strangely domestic scene where horror has bubbled up to the surface. The fact that it is subterranean suggests that this unsettling vision lies just beneath the surface. It serves as a window into the subconscious, not just of the character who maintains this secret lair, but also of anyone, anywhere, hiding beneath a pretence of normality, of suburban conformity.

Face to face with evil (18)

This is Starling's final meeting with Hannibal Lector and the camera moves with her as she approaches his cell. At this point she is free of his control and the tracking steadicam illustrates her ability to move without restriction. The room in which Lector is incarcerated is a Southern courthouse, a turn-of-the century ornate place of justice, familiar from many Hollywood courtroom dramas like *To Kill A Mocking Bird* (1962) where good ultimately triumphs. Here, the natural order will be undermined by what lies at the centre of the room: the gigantic cage and the monster within. Its portraits of American elders and patriotic bunting seem ineffectual when placed in a context with Lector, someone who operates outside of conventional society and its parameters of justice and control.

The cage is reminiscent of the Grand Guignol *mise-en-scène* more commonly associated with the literary works of Gothic writer Edgar Allan Poe, and particularly as brought to the screen by Roger Corman in films such as *The Pit and the Pendulum* (1961). The elaborate furniture, including an easel and bedroom screen, emphasises Lector's gentrified character which, in turn, juxtaposes with his murderous acts to chilling effect. The cage is so large that it appears designed to house something much bigger and stronger; indeed, his psychotic abilities are monstrous and this cage will not prove sufficient to keep him locked up for long. The police barriers, keeping visitors at bay, are also a reminder of the physical threat that he poses, akin to a wild and dangerous animal.

There are POV shots to help the audience identify with Starling but they also zoom towards the cage as if she is being drawn into Lector's world; she appears nervous while he seems relaxed as he reads a book with his back to her. It paints a picture of a man at leisure rather than an incarcerated lunatic.

When she appears at the cage it seems as if she might be the one behind bars; she is shown in medium shot, still not within Lector's reach. With Lector's turn on his chair to face her, he too is in medium shot, and from this point there are a series of parallel shots, where the two protagonists are matched shot for shot, implying that theirs has become a relationship of equals.

Initially she breaks free of these static frames as she tries to assert herself; after their initial exchange she moves around the cage. The camera tracks with her moving figure and then around Lector's static body; the juxtaposition is of an observer looking at a caged animal, but the delineation of roles in this scenario is hard to decipher – who is free and who is imprisoned? The next shot is closer in on Lector with the bars out of focus, whilst the cut to Starling shows more definition to the bars – Lector is winning the battle of wills.

As Lector tests Starling about the Buffalo Bill case he becomes surer of himself but she moves uneasily whilst the camera gets closer to his face. As he turns the attention to her personal life she begins to pace as if caged herself. She then stops and remains within the frame as Lector questions her, the parallel close-ups now settling into a seductive rhythm.

the dialogue.

As Starling is led away the spell is broken and the shots become medium views again, although Lector continues to stare directly at Starling and the audience, like a sinister portrait. She turns and runs back to take a case file from him and his delicate caress of her finger ends this highly-charged sequence. The penultimate shot is from her side of the bars as she is led away (as if she were the criminal), and then to the final high angle long shot of the room. Barbed wire dominates the foreground and covers both small figures, ensnaring them both in a connected present and future.

The timing of the non-diegetic sound is also a key component in producing tension in the scene. At first there is only diegetic sound, but as Starling tells her story about the lambs a noise like that of

There is a zoom towards Lector as he presses his questions, revelling in his power until he is framed in a tight close-up. The zoom is then matched with Starling as she reveals her childhood memories under questioning from the malign Lector. Now, with the interrogator becoming the interrogated, the shots of Starling last longer as she unburdens herself. The shots of her are slightly wider than those of Lector which allows for her face to be still open and less severe, whilst his tighter framing and the slight downward tilt of his head suggests his intense and demonic nature.

Backgrounds behind both characters become less focused as the scene continues, culminating in blackness, such is the intensity of the encounter. In his final close-up he seems to breathe in the terror of Starling's childhood, seemingly satiated by her misery. Throughout much of this scene, the shots have acted as POVs, resulting in the two characters staring directly at the audience and drawing us into

a low howling wind begins, which helps take the audience into her world.

As she finishes her story a gentle, melancholy string-dominated piece begins, which expands and becomes more dramatic as their conversation comes to an end and she leaves, runs back and grabs her case file. The music underlines the sadness of her memories, the strange pleasure of Lector's devouring of the story and the moment of tension as she tries, but fails, to elicit the name of the killer from him.

The sequence is not horrific, but it speaks very much of the tantalising depths that lie beneath horrific actions, and it strives to show the power of evil in its purest form in the figure of Hannibal Lector. That the scene can almost be read as a seduction and conquest just adds to the frisson, and ties it to many of the other films discussed in this section.

Honogurai mizu no soko kara (Dark Water)

KEY FACTS

Release Date: 2002

Country of Origin: Japan

Running Time: 98 minutes

PRODUCTION NOTES

Production Companies

Honogurai mizu no Soko kara Seisaku Iinkai

Oz Productions

Distributor

Tartan (UK)

Awards

Silver Raven Hideo Nakata Brussels International Festival of Fantasy Film

Grand Prize Hideo Nakata Gérardmer Film Festival, France

International Critics Award Hideo Nakata Gérardmer Film Festival, France

Youth Jury Grand Prize Hideo Nakata Gérardmer Film Festival, France

SYNOPSIS

Yoshimi Matsubara, estranged from her husband and alone but for her daughter, Ikuko, is facing the prospect of an unpleasant divorce and is forced to move to a dreary and neglected apartment block. The eerie atmosphere is made even more downbeat by the seemingly constant rain and the surrounding apartments which appear unoccupied. Events make the atmosphere darker still as unaccountable and increasingly severe leaks spring from the ceiling. A child's red bag keeps reappearing, hair appears in the drinking water, Ikuko faints at school and, most disturbingly, a child can be seen on the lift's CCTV camera, but she does not actually appear in the lift itself.

Yoshimi becomes increasingly unhinged by these events and it starts to affect her sanity and her case to retain custody of her daughter. She discovers that the family who used to live in the apartment above were beset by tragedy over a year prior to their arrival: their daughter, Mitsuko, who attended the same kindergarten as Ikuko, was abandoned by her mother and went missing. Eventually, Yoshimi is drawn to a water tank on the roof of the building and realises that Mitsuko must have drowned in it after trying to retrieve her lost red bag. It also becomes apparent that the dead girl is trying to reach into the world of the living to gain the love of a new mother, Yoshimi. Returning to her apartment she finds her daughter being dragged into the bathtub and she runs out with her to the lift. In the lift she looks out and sees her own daughter actually outside; Mitsuko is with her and the remains of the girl grab her - she has found a mother figure at last. The epilogue shows a 16-year-old Ikuko returning to her apartment where she has a brief conversation with her mother who, it seems, has stayed with Mitsuko. And that is how it ends, with both mother and Mitsuko disappearing from Ikuko, leaving her alone.

HISTORICAL CONTEXT

The millennium saw divorce rates around the world rise to their highest levels and the fracturing of the family unit became the norm, particularly in Western culture. There have been numerous studies on the effect of divorce on society and some quarters argue that some of society's ills can be sourced to the breakdown of the nuclear family. There, are, of course, other problems that affect society: the increased pace of life, the complexity of modern living, often cut off from extended family and working in highly pressurised jobs. All these elements are found in *Dark Water* with its oppressive sense of modernity, shredding nerves and alienating individuals from their communities.

The other aspect of the film, the very antithesis of modern life, is that of superstition and ghosts. Ghosts which do not pass into the afterlife successfully are still bound to the world of the living and are often tormented and tormentors as a result; if the person who has died has been wronged they will come back as a ghost bent on revenge, known as Onryo. It is this type of ghost which is present in *Dark Water* and the *Ring* (1998-9) film series. This combination of the very

modern and the ancient is an ongoing and pivotal part of Japanese history and Japanese present. Respect for tradition, whilst embracing the future, have been hallmarks of Japan in the twentieth and twenty-first centuries, making the worldwide influence of J-Horror all the more fascinating with its bipolar approach to society.

In many ways J-Horror is a return to classic horror conventions, relying on psychological menace rather than gore and explicit violence, and maintaining a slow build-up of tension rather than continual shocks. Its success with international audiences has convinced Hollywood of its financial merits, leading to a number of American remakes of recent J-Horror films, notably the *Ring* (2002-05) films, *Dark Water* and the *Ju-on* series (remade as *The Grudge* 2001-03).

J-Horror's more restrained depiction of brutality is reminiscent of Val Lewton's productions of the 1940s, notably *Cat People*, rather than the current trend of the so-called 'torture porn' in *Saw*, *Wolf Creek* and *Hostel*. The emphasis on folkloric inspiration also links the J-Horror approach to the genre with 1930s classics like *Frankenstein* and *Dracula*, which in turn grew out of German Expressionism. The shadows of *Nosferatu* were cast deep into the early days of Hollywood's fascination with horror, and this pattern is now being repeated in Hollywood, awash with J-Horror's pools of darkness.

SELECT FILMOGRAPHY OF MAIN PRODUCERS AND CAST

Hideo Nakata, 1961, Director, Screenwriter

Ghost Actress, 1996

Ring, 1998

Chaos, 1999

Ring 2, 1999

Dark Water, 2002

Last Scene, 2002

The Ring Two, 2005

Kaidan, 2007

LINKS TO OTHER FILMS

Repulsion (1965)

This shows the modern world as a place of alienation and fear, as experienced by a young Belgian woman in London. Her flat becomes a place of surreal events, a manifestation of her innermost fears and desires, just as the apartment block in *Dark Water* reflects the characters' suffering.

Don't Look Now (1973)

Nicolas Roeg's film details a couple's struggle to come to terms with the death of their young daughter who has drowned. This is one of a few links between the two films; they also share a foreboding atmosphere which pervades the *mise-en-scène*. There is a palpable sense of terror which grows as it appears that the dead girl is reaching out into the world of the living and the visual motif of red is strongly associated with death in both films.

Ring (1998)

Another of Hideo Nakata's explorations of Japanese folklore with a vengeful child ghost, an Onryo, who reaches out from a videotape to curse those who watch it.

The Sixth Sense (1999)

A film of the dead and those in the limbo world, as seen by a boy with the power of clairvoyance. These people, including the main protagonist, all need there to be resolution in their past before they can move onto the afterlife.

The Others (2001)

Another tale of the dead who are unable to rest peacefully because of wrongdoing whilst they were alive. In this case the mother has killed her two children and she must be reconciled with herself before she can be at peace.

REPRESENTATION

Apartment blocks

The locale for *Dark Water* is a high-rise apartment block, grey and functional and seemingly bereft of life. The stark lift, corridors and doors dehumanise the inhabitants, and any people who are supposed to take an interest in the building, the concierge for example, are indifferent to those who live there. Apartment blocks have had a bad reputation for crime and social degradation, particularly linked with poverty. The great dreams of slum clearance in the 1950s to 1970s in the UK, and 'building upwards' to house these displaced people, often resulted in communities becoming isolated and alienated.

In Japan it is the norm to live in close proximity and in other parts of the world, mainland Europe in particular, high-rise living does not always carry the same connotations; indeed, it can be considered the height of designer living. This, too, has caught on in the UK with the likes of the Docklands development in London, but it is the negative side of this lifestyle that *Dark Water* taps into, with the monotonous and brutalising effect of the apartment block helping to mirror the mother and child's suffering. The building, or the water tower at least, even consumes Mitsuko before the film has begun. The neighbours do not take an interest in the new arrivals and there is a pervading sense of neglect about the place; the only thing keeping an eye on the building seems to be the CCTV camera, and all that does is observe, making no comment nor offering assistance. Life, it seems, is monitored but there is no intervention and certainly no sense of humanity.

Children

The representation of children in *Dark Water* is one of sadness and loneliness. Although Ikuko is loved by her mother, she is at the centre of a traumatising split between her parents. She is an only child and endures long, lonely hours at home. The pressures on her single mother in regards to work mean that the daughter is looked after by others or picked up late from school. There is very little joy in the film for the children, even the red bag which gives Ikuko some happiness becomes a source of fear for her mother. Of course, it is Mitsuko who is the most powerful representation of this existence. Her mother has abandoned her and she has died alone by drowning in a water tank;

the faded missing person flyer seems to be the only remembrance of her. Her desire for love after her death is testament to the neglect she experienced in life.

Although the audience may ultimately feel sorry for Mitsuko, we are still terrified during the course of the film by her various startling and unsettling appearances. In this way she echoes earlier filmic manifestations of terror. Indeed, playing against the stereotype of childhood innocence has often been a rich vein for horror film-makers. Children have been key to the terror of *Village of the Damned* (1960), *The Innocents* (1961), *The Exorcist*, *The Omen* and *Children of the Corn* (1984), and images of children in other films stand out as key moments of horror for an audience, particularly the baby's devil eyes in *Rosemary's Baby* and the dead twins in *The Shining*.

'It is a parable of the child's fear of abandonment and parents' fear for the child's safety, and secret horror at the vulnerability of the child they once were themselves.' Peter Bradshaw, *The Guardian*, 6th June, 2003

'It's the way he turns the simple, quotidian element of water into something infinitely sinister that marks Nakata's originality, from the drip-drip of a damp stain to the unspeakable vortex of filthy bathwater at the film's horripilating climax.' Anthony Quinn, *The Independent*, 6th June 2003

KEY SCENE TEXTUAL ANALYSIS

Never a plumber when you need one (9)

This scene details the terror of the ordinary. Everyday pain is given enormous resonance through framing and music design; it is psychological horror. This scene starts to flesh out

the unease that newly-divorced Yoshimi and her daughter have been experiencing since they came to their grey, drab and decidedly damp flat to start a new life. The close-up of the bowl is ordinary in the extreme; there is the faint sound of water dripping and the sleeping figures of mother and daughter paint a picture of peace.

But the source of the leak is bigger than has been thought and the cut from medium to close-up of the damp patch synchronises with the electronic music, which is atonal, elemental and very eerie.

The patch itself is threatening. It is a malevolent stain on the light-coloured ceiling and not just one drip, but a seething mass of them, as if alive. The water is dripping onto Yoshimi and sliding down her face. The non-diegetic music mimics some unearthly creature as the cut back to the patch shows more water dripping as if it is about to attack. It is not just the possibility of water flooding down, it is the suggestion of something much more sinister at work that unnerves.

In fact, the dripping does not wake Yoshimi up but stimulates a dream/nightmare/vision. The sound of a haunting oriental bell signifies the dream-like quality of this sequence, together with the blurring effect, which keeps the focus on the little girl in yellow.

An unearthly pulsating sound is added to the music, which helps to unnerve the audience, and the only diegetic sound is the relentless noise of falling rain. The edges of the frame have been blurred to focus on the little girl in yellow, and to suggest that this is within Yoshimi's mind, but also that there is something ethereal or unearthly.

All the shots are canted to achieve a sense of dislocation. Although disturbing, there is also a great feeling of loneliness conveyed by the girl's solitary loping walk through torrential rain. The frames are generally empty and there are high angle shots to emphasise her isolation, particularly when she enters the block of flats. Even when she stands next to the two men waiting to go into the lift she is ignored.

Upon entering she initially stands facing the back of the lift, a poignant and chilling image. The final lifting of her hood and turn to face the camera teases that it might reveal what Nakata has kept hidden throughout the sequence - her face. But as she turns the man in front obscures her. There is a tantalising glimpse of a face, but it is blurred and featureless. The return to a now-awake Yoshimi reveals a sodden bed and pillow - and no Ikuku.

The medium close-up of the mother helps intensify her dawning realisation and the tracking shot of her POV, the ceiling, links with a return to the music that we heard earlier on: it has grown like some inexorable force. The sound of water dripping adds to the sense of growing hysteria, which increases as the camera cranes back down to her and the bed, galvanising Yoshimi into action.

The steadicam helps the audience join in with her frantic search and the music roars, adding to the tension. Ikuku is not in the flat and the music

surveillance footage to convey the visuals like this often suggests that something unusual or violent may happen; it is as if the character has become even more enclosed and vulnerable. As an audience our usual experience of CCTV footage is to see a crime being committed on news footage and so our expectations are aroused.

Nakata delays the shock by cutting back to Yoshimi in the lift and introducing a new sound, this time diegetic, and she reacts to it. This whets the audience's appetite a little more, until the next shot delivers a scary punch: the CCTV footage now transmits that there is a little figure in the lift with her.

This jolt is followed by her departure from the lift, revealing nothing beside her. Instead, the long shot shows her isolation in a block which seems devoid of life; indeed, the grey doors and

gathers chaotic pace as Yoshimi bursts out of the front door. The lift journey to the ground floor is achieved with a cut, quickening the pace of this desperate search. The camera slowly glides with her as she runs and checks the CCTV monitors in the (unattended) concierges office; she is full of jerky movement within the gliding frame, creating a tension between the two which adds to the sense of desperation.

Seeing the lift going up to the seventh floor reminds her of an earlier occasion when Ikuko disappeared and was found on the roof carrying the Mimiko red bag that has symbolised Yoshimi's growing fear throughout the film. It keeps reappearing no matter how hard she tries to get rid of it and is linked to a little girl who had gone missing some years earlier.

We then see her in the lift via the CCTV monitor as the music rises to a crescendo, akin to unearthly voices. Using a different medium such as

corridors look more like a prison than a home and their monolithic, drab appearance suggest dark secrets with no explanations. The delicate frame of Yoshimi's figure and her smart skirt and top juxtapose with her unyielding surroundings, which have not a particle of delicacy about them.

As she rounds the corner on the stairs a gust of wind halts her and a faint glimpse of a small figure again teases along the tension. The slow track and crane shot provide a counterpoint to her inner turmoil as she calls for her daughter; they also provide the foil for our expectations as the audience is bracing itself for a sudden jolt.

Director Nakata plays with the audience again, not providing the expected scare, but a shot of the resurrected Mimiko bag; the enigma continues, more highly-wrought but still just out of the audience's grasp. The ever-present water drips close to her face as she stares at the bag in horror.

The tension is eased by a cut at this point to back in her flat; she is calling her estranged husband to see if he has their daughter.

Then the noise of running from the flat above launches Yoshimi again into a nightmare world; the Japanese custom of removing shoes when entering a house seems to be used here (and on many other occasions in the film) to only frustrate Yoshimi's entries and exits at highly-charged moments.

Again, her now silhouetted figure emerges onto a landing in long shot, the corridor and doors achieving a brooding malevolence beneath their bland exteriors. One, however, has water pouring from beneath the door.

There is no non-diegetic sound at this point and the noise of water becomes the sinister soundtrack as she enters a hellish environment. We walk with her, just over her shoulder, like a more frightened friend

reaction.

The mother seems immediately aware of the presence and the cut to a medium shot of the shadow intensifies her and the audience's reaction; the non-diegetic music again begins with its mass of noise and sharp electronic discords like flashing knives. The shadow itself is seen against a grey, darkened, wallpaper-peeling, water-streaming wall, which adds to the surreal nature of this apparition. The lighting in this flat is in direct contrast to their home downstairs. Here, it is all shadow and steely glow, whilst below it is bright and, at times, warm.

The mother, holding her child, clings to the apartment's walls and edges out; the camera mimics the action as if trying to escape without registering any more terror in its lens and frightened to look too closely. She slips past the

as she plunges into the darkness and gushing water. Even more disturbing is the faint sound of a child talking and a gurgling sound as if someone is drowning. The length of this search is depicted in just one take to keep the spell of tension and expectation unbroken. All the while, the mother's plaintive cries of her daughter's name add to the rising terror.

And then a small white-clad figure peels away from the darkness. There is no quick shock tactic as we might expect in a Western horror film, but a deeply unsettling atmosphere is maintained.

There is the first cut since entering the flat at this moment of elated discovery. We are now looking head-on at Yoshimi and at the daughter's back as she embraces her. We stoop with the mother, and at our moment of relief the camera pans up with the mother to reveal a shadow behind her, that of a little girl. There is no dramatic shot or synch point, rather understatement elicits a more deeply-felt

camera and the audience is left to contemplate the dark recesses of the apartment where now there seems to be nothing. We strain to see nevertheless; like the mother we are scared, but unlike her we also want to see more. That, of course, would spoil things at this point and the audience is left agonisingly close to this enigma, but denied full knowledge.

As she leaves the mother notices the names above the door, the same as those on the 'lost girl' poster she had seen earlier. The chilling image of the girl on the poster with a blurred face reminds us of the image from the lift during the dream sequence.

The final shot of the scene allows for one last unsettling image. Now, looking back down the corridor from the position of the lift, we see a small figure in yellow raincoat, again with blurred features, looking toward us. The music continues to attack our senses with its wall of noise, and the camera begins to crane downwards to imitate the descending lift. It could be Yoshimi's POV or just a shot to show the child watching the departing lift. Although it lasts for just a moment it does enough to leave the audience with a deeply troubled feeling and a number of questions. The abrupt cut to daylight and the ordinary (a taxi arrival) is designed to startle us momentarily and release the tension for a time.

This sequence is full of cinematic tricks designed to keep the audience on edge, but its wilful refusal to deliver out-and-out shock tactics is a contrast to many modern slasher/extreme horror films in the 2000s. There is, instead, a deliberate and slow build-up of tension, which gradually turns the screws on our sensibilities. It is the stuff of nightmares, of scary stories told to children, where the dark corners and a lack of clarity are the tools of horror. Nakata does not show things when you expect them and does when you do not; it is the suggestion of the horrific or unthinkable that often unnerves more in the long-term than the quick fright.

COMEDY

The comedy section reinforced my notion that humour connects people across the decades and international borders, with a continuous thread running from the silent era to the present day; from Buster Keaton's trains to Simon Pegg's zombies, the emphasis is on close human observation and well-timed and choreographed physical comedy. Keaton's *The General* (1926) is a gem, one to which all other comic films must measure up; its invention and humour makes it, for me, funnier than anything made by Chaplin. *Duck Soup* (1933) has wit and sparkle aplenty, some of its one-liners as funny and as fresh as if they had been minted today, and with the sort of anarchic humour that would fuel many later, and more modern, films. If *Duck Soup* shows 1930s Hollywood at its best, then *Kind Hearts and Coronets* (1949) displays the virtues of Ealing Studios, a glorious exploration of England and its class-ridden mores, full of wicked wit and affection for its subject-matter and all shone through with Alec Guinness' bravura performances. In *Mon Oncle* (1958), Jacques Tati borrows heavily from Keaton and Chaplin but also invests his comedy with Gallic flair, as well as making wry comments on modern society.

The Graduate (1967) is what the 1960s demanded: a smart and funny look at the battle between the generations, but shot through with stylish visuals that also suggested the struggle between old and new Hollywood. And, like all great comedies, it is laced with great humour and a wry commentary on life. *Young Frankenstein* (1974) is, in many ways, an old-fashioned film, its wit and affection for the source films, *Frankenstein* (1931) and *Bride of Frankenstein* (1935), making it a *homage* rather than a parody per se. The humour is surprisingly gentle given the reputation of its director and co-writer, Mel Brooks, and very much the work of film fans; with *Blazing Saddles* (1974), it counts as Brooks' best work.

Raising Arizona (1987), *Delicatessen* (1990) and *Shaun of the Dead* (2004) are very modern comedies; they contain darkly humorous moments, but in each the tradition of comedy clearly links them to the films of previous decades. *Raising Arizona* bears all the hallmarks of madcap screwball comedies like Preston Sturges' *Sullivan's Travels* (1941) driven by a *Mad Max* (1979) sensibility. It contains all the light and dark of the Coen Brothers' best work and anticipates their later films such as *Fargo* (1996) and *The Big Lebowski* (1998). *Delicatessen* and *Shaun of the Dead* share a flesh-eating premise and the humour might not be to everyone's taste, but their roots are in the traditions of black humour, as forged by films like *Kind Hearts and Coronets*, as well as the slapstick of the great silent comics.

Throughout the comedy section the films demonstrate a healthy disregard for the man-made structures of society, which often serve to straightjacket individualism and creativity. These films constantly present the underdog, perhaps not winning, but at least striving to express an individual voice.

The General

KEY FACTS

Release Date: 1926

Country of Origin: USA

Running Time: 75 minutes

PRODUCTION NOTES

Production Company

Buster Keaton Productions Inc.

Distributor

United Artists

Awards

National Film Registry National Film Preservation Board

SYNOPSIS

Johnnie Gray is not allowed to join the Confederate army during the American Civil War because of his valuable job as a train engineer. Consequently, the family of his fiancée, Annabelle Lee, brands him a coward. A year later, a train travelling northwards is overrun by spies from the northern Union army. Annabelle Lee, on her way to visit her injured father, happens to be one of the passengers and is taken hostage, leaving Johnnie to commandeer another train and give chase.

He endures numerous obstacles and mishaps in his pursuit, defying death on a number of occasions. Unwittingly, he finally catches up with the Union soldiers at their headquarters and rescues Annabelle Lee, as well as recovering his train, 'The General'. Whilst hiding at the HQ he overhears the Union plan of attack and races to warn the Confederates. After capturing a Union general and thwarting a Union army advance by destroying a bridge, he emerges a hero. He also gets his girl.

HISTORICAL CONTEXT

The American Civil War had ended only 60 years before *The General* was made and there were still people alive who had lived through it or fought in it. Although a vehicle for Buster Keaton's comedy, it has an air of authenticity. America was enjoying the good times after the First World War and before the Wall Street Crash and the Great Depression.

Hollywood was replete with comedians, many of whom had made their way from the vaudeville theatres of America or the music halls of Britain; Keaton, Harold Lloyd, and Oliver Hardy were homegrown, but Charlie Chaplin and Stan Laurel were English.

As film-making gathered momentum around the world some comedians had realised that the days of live comedy theatre were endangered; this, coupled with the glamour, the possible financial rewards and the opportunity to reach massive audiences helped lure comedians to Hollywood. As film was still a silent medium, slapstick and physical comedy became the obvious focus and an integral part of the storylines and Lloyd and Keaton pushed their possibilities to extraordinary limits. Audiences flocked not just to laugh, but to be thrilled by the amazing array of death-defying stunts that these two performers would attempt. In a decade where life was either lived to excess or on the breadline, this type of visual spectacle appealed to both ends of the spectrum.

Keaton, like Chaplin, was an early example of the *auteur*, taking creative control of his film projects and putting *his* vision on screen. His writing, direction and acting credits afforded him power that few contemporaries in the industry would have, although there were others (Chaplin, Fairbanks) who achieved independence from studio control. However, *The General*'s disappointing performance at the box office did nothing to secure this power for Keaton. Contemporary audiences and critics disliked the combination of comedy and drama and Keaton's sophisticated use of film language did not generate the praise that it would accrue in latter years. Contemporary audiences seemed to want their comedy broad and simple, without too much nuance of character or presentation. It seemed as if audiences and critics could applaud D.W. Griffith's intelligent deployment of film language for his epics, but were bemused rather than amused with Keaton's similar attention to detail for comedic effect.

SELECT FILMOGRAPHY OF MAIN PRODUCERS AND CAST

Buster Keaton, 1895-1966, Actor, Director, Producer, Screenwriter

One Week, 1920

The Playhouse, 1921

Cops, 1922

Our Hospitality, 1923

Sherlock Jr., 1924

The Navigator, 1924

Seven Chances, 1925

Go West, 1925

Battling Butler, 1926

The General, 1927

Steamboat Bill Jr., 1928

The Cameraman, 1928

The Passionate Plumber, 1932

The Gold Ghost, 1934

Grand Slam Opera, 1936

Li'l Abner, 1940

In the Good Old Summertime, 1949

Limelight, 1952

The Adventures of Huckleberry Finn, 1960

The Railrodder, 1965

Film, 1965

The Scribe, 1966

A Funny Thing Happened on the Way to the Forum, 1966

LINKS TO OTHER FILMS

The Birth of a Nation (1915)/*Gone with the Wind* (1939)

Traditionally, films dealing with the American Civil War have been dramatic and serious in tone. It was, and still is, a sensitive and emotional subject, particularly to those on the losing side. D.W.

Griffith's *The Birth of a Nation* and Victor Fleming's *Gone with the Wind* both deal with the conflict with suitable gravitas. Perhaps the initial commercial failure of *The General* might partially stem from Keaton's choice of subject matter not being regarded as fit for a comic vehicle.

Safety Last! (1923)

Harold Lloyd's most famous film involves a spectacular climb up the side of a high building. Lloyd's comedy was also very physical, but whilst Keaton's character is often the master of his physical challenges, Lloyd's character is a victim.

The Gold Rush (1925)

One of Charlie Chaplin's silent films, where there are a number of physical moments of comedy, particularly his escape from a log cabin as it topples over a cliff and into the abyss below.

Busy Bodies (1933)

Laurel and Hardy's comedy was a mixture of the surreal, the physical and, of course, the chemistry and exchanges between the two comedians. In this short film the emphasis is on the physical side of their humour, with their jobs in a timber yard providing fertile ground for one physical mishap after another.

The Bellboy (1960)

Jerry Lewis was a popular comedian in the 1950s and 1960s with an anarchic and often very physical brand of humour. This film, his directorial debut, echoes silent slapstick comedy, even to the extent that Lewis' character is mute for most of the film.

The Return of the Pink Panther (1975)

Another modern-day creation, Peter Sellers as Inspector Clouseau is one in a long line of accident-prone characters as he stumbles through his mishaps, never mastering circumstances except by accident.

Police Story (1985)

Jackie Chan in this film, and many others, is the true heir to Buster Keaton in terms of both his physicality and his mastery of the extraordinary situations in which he finds himself.

Ace Ventura: Pet Detective (1994)

Jim Carrey is a comic actor who, in this film and others, expresses his comedic personality through use of slapstick and physicality. Unlike Keaton's character, though, Ace Ventura is another victim of the mishaps around him.

REPRESENTATION

The downtrodden man

Johnnie is the archetypal downtrodden character, one of many such creations in cinema history. Chaplin's 'Little Tramp' creation is one of the earliest manifestations; sometimes criticised as overly sentimental, this is always undercut by the comic scenes and self-parody. Harold Lloyd's characters are often losers, although he generally comes out on top in the end. Laurel and Hardy are the perpetual downtrodden characters, unlucky in love and life, who often end their films in a worse state than at the beginning.

In *The General* Keaton's character is wrongly judged to be a coward, and endures a public shaming. The shot of Johnnie sitting mournfully on the pistons of the steam train as it moves into the engine shed is full of pathos and fully underlines his maudlin state. It also hints at what will be his redemption, the train. The shot places him as part of the engine, synchronised to its movements. Working in conjunction with the trains that he borrows during the chase, and then with his own train in the film's finale, Johnnie rehabilitates himself. The stoic expression on his face as he chases the stolen engine and his fiancée is an enduring image; he is certainly downtrodden throughout the film, facing challenge after challenge. The downtrodden man is both represented with pathos but also with an inner determination that drives him onwards. Although an entirely different character in an entirely serious film he is, ultimately, the comic cousin of a character like Tom Joad in *The Grapes of Wrath* (1940); neither of them ever give up.

'Keaton learnt how to use comic anticipation to great effect in The General... All the visual jokes and set-ups in the first section are repeated and amplified in reverse order in the second half.' Mark Cousins, *The Story of Film*, Pavillion Books, London, 2004

'Buster's Johnny: unsmiling yet beautiful in his brave, faintly ridiculous determination- the epitome of this serio-comic masterpiece, and as deeply human a hero as the cinema has given us.' Geoff Andrew, *1001 Movies You Must See Before You Die*, Cassell Illustrated, 2007

KEY SCENE TEXTUAL ANALYSIS

Johnnie Gray chases the northern spies (5; 21:00)

A few minutes into the chase Johnnie manages to procure a cannon on rolling stock left in a siding. After a failed initial attempt to fire it, he decides to put a little more gunpowder into the next shot. All the action in this sequence, and the whole film, is shot without any back projection or optical effects, and, of course, this is many years before digital effects.

It is pure and simple; a man, a train and some death-defying stunts. It utilises a number of silent comedy's codes and conventions, particularly an emphasis on physical comedy or 'sight gags', but the exaggerated form of violence and pratfalls known as slapstick are eschewed in favour of carefully orchestrated and sophisticated sequences where the physical comedy is part of a greater visual pattern.

Part of the audience's pleasure in this sequence is based on their utter belief that Keaton is not only doing what we can see on the screen, but that he is also trying to make us laugh as he does it.

The camera tracks next to the train, connecting the audience to the speed of the action. Johnnie

reloads the cannon, making the audience laugh through his excessive use of gun powder and two cannonballs rather than one.

Johnnie is plainly dressed: drab trousers, shirt and braces, bar one flourish; an elaborate cravat. He is the downtrodden, luckless hero of the film, but he has a certain style as is demonstrated when the sequence unfolds.

His agile leap is counterbalanced by catching his foot in the carriage coupling; the physical comedy is presented with an unflinching eye and there are few cuts to really underline the precariousness of the situation. The other notable aspect is the interconnectedness of the action, for each comic action influences the next. Johnnie escapes the coupling but this action causes it to trail on the track and makes the wheels of the rolling stock judder, resulting in the lowering of the cannon until it is pointed at him and his train.

This creates a universe in which the comic and the near fatal are inextricably linked and from where there is no escape, but perhaps where acceptance of its laws creates inspiration and creativity.

The constant use of the tracking shot is not just about creating pace, it also suggests the dynamism of the film itself; it's saying to the audience, 'come on, try and keep up with us'. In fact, there are no close-ups in the entire sequence; the audience is being directed to marvel at the comic action, unhindered by too much reaction and expression. Often, Keaton's *lack* of reaction is funnier as he stoically perseveres, whatever the circumstance. When there is a reaction shot, it is in medium shot and certainly not of the Oliver Hardy 'double-take' brand.

The focus on the cannon allows us to see what is happening, but also to make us tingle with anticipation for what will happen next. The cut to the two-shot of cannon and Johnnie on the back of the train is the pay-off for the action that has preceded it; often minor mishaps are details in a grand plan of chaos.

Keaton works the humour even more by scuttling back and forth on the back of the engine, but it is the next set-up which raises the audience's anticipation: a shot from the cannon wagon points directly at Johnnie.

As he slips down the front of the train the use of a single long shot, rather than a few rapidly edited closer shots, gives such a breathtaking stunt a more realistic edge. By dispensing with elaborate techniques, it makse Keaton's extraordinary physical feats as transparent as possible.

Once he has inadvertently evaded the cannon fire the shot of him sitting on the front grate of the train captures the essence of this idea perfectly; he nonchalantly cleans his hands whilst hurtling along like a passenger in a train carriage instead of a few centimetres above the ground. It is funny yet also depicts a world of insane logic.

gone (it has been derailed by a beam dropped by the Northerners). The look is of disbelief, but the disbelief that comes with good fortune. Bafflement, resignation, disbelief: comic, certainly, but also a seriously pertinent view on life.

This is an opportune moment to reflect upon Keaton's face; it's rather plain; he is no matinée idol; in fact, it's rather odd. It's seen life; and the hair suggests a younger man, but the face says otherwise (Keaton was 30 at the time of *The General*'s release). In short, it's an intriguing face, often mask-like with a touch of the sad clown in it, an enigma of a face, not as recognisable or as open as Hardy's or Laurel's, but beguiling in its own way. Ultimately, perhaps, it's an everyman face, and that is just right for the character: an apparently

A few shots later Johnnie tries to rid himself of this disengaged wagon. Thinking he has done so he starts feeding the boiler with wood, not realising that the wagon has rejoined the main track from the siding. The image of the determined Johnnie feverishly getting on with the job whilst fate is playing a cruel joke on him suggests a worldview which requires great objectivity: our tiny little efforts come to no avail. The long shot, with him in foreground and the returning wagon in the background, presents a filmic space that reflects the cruelty of life; or so it seems at first, for the worldview is enriched by the next set of events.

There follows one of the few medium close-ups where we can clearly see Johnnie's face; he settles back into his driver's seat, content; the look changes to one of bafflement and resignation at the vagaries of life as he sees the wagon. This shot is paired with a shot almost a minute later after he returns to his seat to find the wagon

feckless anti-hero who somehow gets the girl.

If the previous two medium shots suggest bemusement, then the third reaction shot, this time wider, shows downright exasperation with life's travails. The first wooden block is removed with split second timing and the camera position gives the audience the delicious spectacle of impending doom; it ends with a comic upending as Johnnie is scooped up by the train's grate.

Again, we see the whole spectacle in long shot as he approaches the next wooden block. The universe is about to undo him once more, but inspiration and creativity save the day as he uses the wooden blocks as in some game designed for giants.

He then collects wood as his train is sent the wrong way by the spies who have changed the points; the tracking long shot of him frames a man going about his business, picking up the wood. He then turns and drops the pile from his arms - the movement within the frame focuses our attention and this time we are given no overview of what is about to happen.

A cut to a static shot of a track that goes nowhere and the successful stopping of the train is not accompanied by any dramatic montage, nor a reaction shot of fear or relief from Johnnie. Yes, it is a dramatic moment, but within the context of other events it is rather understated. It is just another moment of ordinary insanity; the humour is both in the drama and in it being downplayed.

He reverses the train and jumps out as it is still reversing; its very audacity and matter-of-factness underpin its comedy. The wheel spin and his throwing of dirt under the wheels help to counterpoint the previous shot's almost heroic

casualness; we are given an omniscient role again as the train moves off without him.

The final image of this sequence, as Johnnie runs away from the camera and after the disappearing train, encapsulates this particular comic universe. It's a forlorn sight, grasping for something that is just out of reach but he manages, just. By now, however, the audience knows that this will be a small victory in an epic struggle.

Duck Soup

KEY FACTS

Release Date: 1933

Country of Origin: USA

Running Time: 70 minutes

PRODUCTION NOTES

Production Company

Paramount Pictures

Distributor

Paramount Pictures

Awards

National Film Registry National Film Preservation Board

SYNOPSIS

Rufus T. Firefly is made Prime Minister of Freedonia at the behest of one of its wealthy residents, Mrs. Teasdale, who will not agree to finance the bankrupt country unless this happens.

It immediately becomes apparent that Freedonia's neighbouring country, Sylvania, is intent on gaining control of Firefly's government. Its leader, Trentino, tries to start a revolution, attempts to seduce Mrs. Teasdale and sends two spies to destabilise the government. These men, Chicolini and Pinky, do little else but cause mayhem, but the former is eventually made Secretary of War. When Chicolini is caught trying to steal war plans from Mrs. Teasdale he is put on trial, but when war breaks out between the two countries he is reinstated. Freedonia wins the war and Trentino is put into stocks and bombarded with fruit. When Mrs. Teasdale starts to sing the national anthem they turn their attention to her and start throwing fruit.

HISTORICAL CONTEXT

The 1930s were a time of extreme politics in Europe. By 1933 Mussolini was already dictator of Italy and Hitler (in Germany) and Franco (in Spain) did not have long to wait to realise their dreams and seize control of their countries. As America looked out from its isolated position it was a world to fear and from which to recoil. America had its own serious economic problems in the 1930s and generally chose to ignore what was going on beyond its shores.

It was not until Britain declared war on Germany in 1939 that Hollywood would start to turn its attention to the problems in Europe with films like Alfred Hitchcock's *Foreign Correspondent* (1940) and Frank Borzage's *The Mortal Storm* (1940), with their explicit call for American involvement in the conflict. However, there was very little comment in Hollywood films about events abroad, bar one, the anarchic and satirical *Duck Soup*.

Many early film comics in Hollywood had their origins in vaudeville, stage shows of variety acts, or the British equivalent known as music hall. Chaplin, Keaton, W.C. Fields and Stan Laurel were just a few of the many variety performers who thrilled audiences in the late nineteenth and early twentieth centuries. The Marx Brothers came from this tradition where acts would only survive if they could entertain audiences with a range of abilities; singing, acting, dancing, acrobatics were just some of the prerequisites. The Marx Brothers transferred the vaudeville style to their films, which became cinematic showcases for the family's wide-ranging comedic talents. As if constantly mindful of the vaudeville audience that might turn against an act if it was not diverting enough, the Marx Brothers filled *Duck Soup*, like many of their films, with comedy delivered at breakneck speed, intermingling verbal and sight gags with music and dance.

SELECT FILMOGRAPHY OF MAIN PRODUCERS AND CAST

Leo McCarey, 1898-1969, Director, Producer, Screenwriter

Habeas Corpus, 1928

The Kid from Spain, 1932

Duck Soup, 1933

Belle of the Nineties, 1934

Ruggles of Red Gap, 1935

The Awful Truth, 1937

Once Upon a Honeymoon, 1939

Going My Way, 1944

The Bells of St. Mary, 1945

An Affair to Remember, 1957

Rally 'Round the Flags, Boys!, 1958

Satan Never Sleeps, 1962

Chico Marx, 1887-1961

Harpo Marx, 1888-1964

Groucho Marx, 1890-1977

Zeppo Marx, 1901-1979, Actors

The Cocoanuts, 1929

Animal Crackers, 1930

Monkey Business, 1931

Horse Feathers, 1932

Duck Soup, 1933

(without Zeppo):

A Night at the Opera, 1935

A Day at the Races, 1937

Room Service, 1938

At the Circus, 1939

Go West, 1940

The Big Store, 1941

A Night in Casablanca, 1946

Love Happy, 1949

The Story of Mankind, 1957

LINKS TO OTHER FILMS

The Great Dictator (1940)

Charlie Chaplin made this political satire before the United States entered the Second World War; it is an explicit attack on the Nazi regime, recording the brutal treatment of Jews and leaving little doubt that Hitler was the butt of Chaplin's satire through his portrayal of Adenoid Hynkel.

Dr. Strangelove, Or: How I Learned to Stop Worrying and Love the Bomb (1964)

Stanley Kubrick's satire about the Cold War is a much more direct attack on the prevailing policies in the 1960s that had plunged the world into a fear that nuclear mass destruction was a distinct possibility.

Love and Death (1975)

Woody Allen's film satirises many elements of society, particularly the structures created by the Establishment. Its commentary on war is very similar to that in *Duck Soup*, with its anti-heroic and mocking stance; the shot of how the generals view the battlefield is the most obvious example of this: Boris (Allen) looks down from their viewpoint and sees some sheep being herded on the battlefield in place of the soldiers. Allen's later film, *Hannah and Her Sisters* (1989), features a scene of Allen's depressed character (Mickey) re-engaging with his life during a screening of *Duck Soup*.

REPRESENTATION

The Establishment

The Establishment, including the government, the aristocrats, the judiciary and the military, are all satirised in *Duck Soup*. It begins with Firefly's entrance; he bypasses all the ceremony and undermines its pomposity, immediately mocking the one person who has supported him, the wealthy Mrs. Teasdale. All attempts at civility and respectability are rejected in the opening sequence by Firefly's anarchic words and actions; his song containing the lines 'These are the laws of my administration/ If you think this country's bad off now/ Just wait 'til I get through with it' perfectly demonstrates his attitude to public office.

Throughout the film Firefly has no interest in the matters of state, only his personal betterment, and when he hears of Mrs. Teasdale's wealth he relentlessly pursues her. His treatment of Ambassador Trentino of Sylvania shows he has no regard for diplomacy, taking great pleasure in being totally insulting toward him. The trial of Chicolini ends in farce and the call to arms is satirised

as Firefly and the upper echelons of Freedonian society descend into song: 'We got guns, they got guns, all God's chillun got guns'.

The depiction of the military is just as subversive with Pinky walking through the battlefield wearing sandwich boards bearing the legend, 'Join the Army and see the Navy'. During the course of the film Firefly wears numerous different costumes, including both a Union *and* Confederate uniform from the American Civil War, which also helps to underpin the complete lack of respect for any of the structures that the Establishment creates.

Of course, everything described here is done for comic effect. The Marx Brothers wanted the audience to laugh, and as a result we get this scattergun approach to comedy where no subject is so respectable that it cannot be lampooned. Their other films also took great pleasure in satirising many aspects of life, whether it was academia (*Horse Feathers*) or polite society (*Animal Crackers*). The difference between the Marx Brothers and other comic groups, like the Ritz Brothers or the Three Stooges, is that the Marx Brothers aimed higher – they employed the physical comedy of the other groups but also had the nerve to face up to the big issues, something which makes them accessible to modern audiences.

'The greatest of the surreally anarchic [Marx Brothers'] films... this is a breathtakingly funny and imaginative spoof of war movie heroics.' Geoff Andrew, *Time Out Film Guide 14th Ed.*, Time Out Guides Ltd., London, 2006

'Now widely considered a satiric masterpiece, although the film was a commercial and critical disappointment on initial release.' Thomas Schatz, *The Cinema Book 2nd Edition*, Ed. Pam Cook & Mieke Bernink, Bfi Publishing, 1999

KEY SCENE TEXTUAL ANALYSIS

Anarchic destruction (9;30:58)

This is the sort of destruction that would often occur in a Laurel and Hardy short film or in some of their feature length outings. Indeed, Harpo's adversary is played by Laurel and Hardy stalwart, Edgar Kennedy. This is the second of three encounters between rival vendors, and Harpo has already set light to one of Kennedy's hats in an earlier scene.

The characters' clothes and appearance is the first point to consider: Harpo is the anarchic clown, his top hat barely containing his wildly curly hair (symbolising his character perfectly); the long coat with huge pockets wherein a multitude of bizarre objects can be hidden; the dangling horns to create a cacophony of sound to compensate for his muteness; the scissors to cut the most inappropriate items; the shirt, looking as if it has been designed by Jackson Pollock; the face, which often resembles a demonic cherub as the madness unfolds around him.

Kennedy is a large man and looks comic, but in another way. Whereas Harpo's clothes are all at odds with each other but seem to come together as a whole, Kennedy's clothes are simply at odds with his large frame: the delicate white hat at a jaunty angle, the silky top with billowing sleeves and the embroidered waistcoat all serve to undermine his macho build.

The first part of the sequence plays out in front of the camera as if it were a stage performance. Cutting only between a long shot and a two-shot, the camera pans only slightly in order to keep the action in the centre of frame. It is the actors who lead the camera and there are no elaborate moves to distract the audience from the comic action on display. The filming process does not draw attention to itself as we watch the rapid escalation of violence and destruction, yet the more low-key the camera movement, the more anarchic the action becomes.

The comedy, then, has the opportunity to breathe, to be played out at its own pace in real-time. The absence of non-diegetic sound gives no guidance to our reactions, its diegetic sound serving to add to the general surreal atmosphere as the scene is played out on an ordinary street in the sunshine.

The tit-for-tat violence has its own rhythm and neither participant endeavours to stop the other's attacks, whether on person or property, lending it even more of a surreal edge; frustration, rage, violence and one-upmanship are all practised as if controlled by strict rules and regulations, adding further to the humour.

The second half of the sequence deals with Harpo's final revenge on Kennedy and is captured in a simple long shot and final two-shot, in harmony with Kennedy's deadpan reaction. The comedy is all in the staging of the action and the camera need only record events.

In itself, the humour here is similar to many other films of the period and relates particularly to the silent slapstick of the 1920s; the final tainting of Kennedy's lemonade with Harpo's feet is an ingeniously vengeful act. But the real merit of the scene's comic value can really only be apreciated within the overall structuring of the film. As an isolated incident it is funny; as part of a triptych of scenes involving Kennedy it achieves elevated comic stature.

This second of the three continues where the first left off, but prepares the groundwork for the final confrontation as the humour escalates to an even more surreal and outrageous climax.

Riding through the streets (17;56:00)

Harpo, like an insane Paul Revere, rides through the streets to warn the Freedonians of the advancing enemy. Unlike Revere, he gets rather distracted from his duties by the opposite sex. The first incident completes the trilogy of scenes with Kennedy, and is Harpo's final revenge. Catching sight of a young lady undressing in a bedroom window, he forgets about the war and follows his own instincts. Indeed, there are many incidents where Harpo exhibits a blend of childlike and sexually active antics in regard to women. Here he is obviously sexually attracted to her, and the risqué humour is underlined in a number of sight gags throughout the sequence.

After taking a quick look at the woman he runs back out to his horse and gives it a bag of feed (the sexual slang 'getting your oats' is suggested by the image). He comes in like a manic stalker, the woman backing away from him; a quick cut to Kennedy, the husband, as he enters the apartment block, and then back to the bedroom to reveal Harpo on the bed and the wife warning of her husband's arrival, undercutting expectations of the previous shot of the two - she seems to have succumbed to Harpo's 'charms' very quickly.

Harpo escapes to the bathroom, and when Kennedy takes a bath there is the initial schoolboy gag of a flatulence-sounding noise each time he attempts to sit in the tub, akin to the whoppee cushion joke. Here, however, it is developed to new extremes; bugle playing comes next and then the fully-clothed Harpo emerges from the bath. It is absurdly, disturbingly comic, a mischievous Freddy Kruger if

it is a comic juxtaposition of footwear or hoofwear but the implications for what we are about to see above the bed are both comic and very, very surreal.

The long shot, when it comes, is an image of pure madness: Harpo lies serenely next to an actual horse in a double bed while the woman is in a single bed next to them; it is certainly comic and seems perfectly logical in the wonderfully twisted world that Harpo and the other Marx Brothers inhabit. It also perhaps mocks the Hays Code, the production code brought into Hollywood in the early 1930s to ensure that 'decency' was maintained in films.

The tag 'surreal' has been often applied to the comedy films featured in this section, but the Marx Brothers most perfectly exemplify this description; if they were to exist in paint then a Salvador Dali landscape would be their ideal playground.

you like (see *A Nightmare on Elm Street*'s textual analysis). This completes the scenes with Kennedy, who is reduced to a raving lunatic, cuckolded and embarrassed beyond compare. His plaintive figure in the bath, tearing at what little hair he has, is a perfect image of the normal world succumbing to Harpo's destabilising effect.

After leaving this house one might assume that Harpo will return to his duties, but if a joke is worth doing once then it's certainly worth doing again, with added lunacy. He stops at another house and, after a flirty invitation from another woman, rides into the house: so far, so mad; but there is something more bizarre to come. A panning shot reveals his boots, her shoes, and unbelievably, the four horse's shoes at the side of the bed. This is comedy gone wild, particularly for 1930s Hollywood;

Kind Hearts and Coronets

KEY FACTS

Release Date: 1949

Country of Origin: UK

Running Time: 106 minutes

PRODUCTION NOTES

Production Company

Ealing Studios

Distributor

General Film Distributors

Awards

Best Actor Alec Guinness National Board of Review, USA

Nominated: Best British Film BAFTA Awards, UK

Nominated: Golden Lion Robert Hamer Venice Film Festival

SYNOPSIS

Louis Mazzini is the impoverished son of an English woman ostracised by her noble family for marrying an Italian opera singer. When she dies, the D'Ascoynes refuse to allow her to be buried in the family crypt, and Louis decides that the family title, the Dukedom of Chalfont, belongs to him. In revenge, he plans to kill the eight remaining relatives who lie between him and his goal.

Louis murders six of them in a variety of ways. The other two die without his help – one has a heart attack and the other drowns.

Throughout the story Louis maintains a relationship with a childhood friend, Sibella, but she marries someone else as she feels he does not have any prospect of bettering himself. He also starts a relationship with Edith, the widow of one of his victims, first as friends and then something more intimate. Sibella's husband commits suicide, and jealous of Louis' relationship with Edith, Sibella implicates Louis in his death.

Sentenced to death for a murder that he did *not* commit, Louis writes a candid memoir of his actions, only to be reprieved by Sibella's change of heart when she produces her husband's suicide note. Upon leaving prison he is faced with a choice: both women are waiting for him and he must decide which one of them to join. As he contemplates this, a man approaches him and asks about publishing his memoirs; the story ends as he remembers that he has left them in his cell, implying that his secret may yet be discovered.

HISTORICAL CONTEXT

George VI had been King of England for 13 years when *Kind Hearts and Coronets* was made. He had been a popular king after the debacle of his older brother's reign which had lasted for less than a year. Edward VIII had abdicated in order to marry an American divorcée, Wallace Simpson. The new king had been a very public figure during the Second World War and his public standing had improved even more with the British public; the Royals had even used ration books.

The film itself is set in the Edwardian era, before both world wars; Edward VII had a lot to live up to after the death of his mother, Victoria, and his playboy reputation as prince was not dispelled whilst king. With such a popular monarch reigning in 1949 it is hardly surprising that the action of the film is displaced to a time when the king was seen to be more hedonistic. However, the killing of snobbish and well-fed nobility must have carried some resonance in a country that was still gripped by self-denial and deprivation four years after the end of the war.

Ealing Studios was at the height of its success in 1949 with the release of *Kind Hearts and Coronets*, following *Went The Day Well?* (1943), *Dead of Night* (1945), *Hue and Cry* (1947), *Passport to Pimlico* (1949) and *Whisky Galore!* (1949). The studio would go on to make such classics as *The Lavender Hill Mob* (1951), *The Man in the White Suit* (1951) and *The Ladykillers* (1955). Ealing's success had been presided over by Michael Balcon who had earlier produced films for Alfred Hitchcock (*The 39 Steps*) and steered Gainsborough Studios through a period of early success. Gainsborough later became synonymous with costume dramas such

as *The Wicked Lady* (1945) and helped consolidate production of a genre that would continue to be a mainstay of British cinema.

Both Gainsborough and Ealing produced films that looked back in time; Gainsborough visited the bodice-ripping days of seventeenth century and Victorian Britain whilst Ealing presented either the not-so-distant past (the Edwardian period of *Kind Hearts and Coronets*) or the present but expressed in nostalgic terms, focusing on communities or individuals that battle against the Establishment in a variety of guises. While Gainsborough revelled in the depiction of lusty melodrama, the films of Ealing Studios took a more ambivalent approach to the notion of nostalgia; the individuals and communities seem to be ordinary, idiosyncratic and toothless, but then transform into quick-witted, devious and resourceful people when faced with adversity or attempting to circumvent authority. The films are littered with seemingly weak characters that bite back: Henry Holland in *The Lavender Hill Mob*, the Burgundians in *Passport to Pimlico*, or Mrs. Wilberforce in *The Ladykillers* who unwittingly survives amidst treachery and murder. In the latter film Mrs. Wilberforce (Katie Johnson) is surrounded by a host of comic performers, including Alec Guinness and Peter Sellers who were among the many actors integral to the success of Ealing's films.

A stock company of characters actors gave the films a depth that is comparable to John Ford's band of stalwarts who made regular appearances in his Westerns. Joan Greenwood, Basil Radford, Naunton Wayne, Herbert Lom, Stanley Holloway, Margaret Rutherford, Dennis Price and Sid James are just some of those who were brought together under Michael Balcon's guidance as well as the expert visual eye of directors like Alexander Mackendrick and Robert Hamer. It was a potent mixture that created a sustained and lasting body of comic work in the late 1940s and 1950s.

SELECT FILMOGRAPHY OF MAIN PRODUCERS AND CAST

Robert Hamer, 1911-1963, Director, Producer, Screenwriter

Dead of Night, 1945

Pink String and Sealing Wax, 1946

It Always Rains on Sunday, 1947

The Spider and the Fly, 1949

Kind Hearts and Coronets, 1949

The Long Memory, 1952

His Excellency, 1952

Father Brown, 1954

To Paris With Love, 1955

The Scapegoat, 1959

School for Scoundrels, 1960

Michael Balcon, 1896-1977, Producer

The Pleasure Garden, 1925

The Mountain Eagle, 1926

The Lodger, 1927

The Good Companions, 1933

Man of Aran, 1934

The Man Who Knew Too Much, 1934

The 39 Steps, 1935

Went the Day Well?, 1942

Dead of Night, 1945

Pink String and Sealing Wax, 1946

Hue and Cry, 1947

Nicholas Nickleby, 1947

Scott of the Antarctic, 1948

Passport to Pimlico, 1949

Kind Hearts and Coronets, 1949

Whisky Galore!, 1949

The Blue Lamp, 1950

The Lavender Hill Mob, 1951

The Man in the White Suit, 1951

Mandy, 1952

The Ladykillers, 1955

Dunkirk, 1958

The Long and the Short and the Tall, 1961

Douglas Slocombe, 1913, Director of Photography

Dead of Night, 1945

Hue and Cry, 1947

Kind Hearts and Coronets, 1949

The Man in the White Suit, 1951

The Lavender Hill Mob, 1951

The Titfield Thunderbolt, 1953

The Smallest Show on Earth, 1957

The Young Ones, 1961

The L-Shaped Room, 1962

The Servant, 1963

A High Wind in Jamaica, 1965

The Fearless Vampire Killers, 1967

The Lion in Winter, 1968

The Italian Job, 1969

The Music Lovers, 1970

The Great Gatsby, 1974

Rollerball, 1975

Julia, 1977

Raiders of the Lost Ark, 1981

Never Say Never Again, 1983

Alec Guinness, 1914-2000, Actor

Great Expectations, 1946

Oliver Twist, 1948

Kind Hearts and Coronets, 1949

The Lavender Hill Mob, 1951

The Man in the White Suit, 1951

Father Brown, 1954

The Ladykillers, 1955

The Bridge on the River Kwai, 1957

Our Man in Havana, 1959

Lawrence of Arabia, 1962

The Fall of the Roman Empire, 1964

Doctor Zhivago, 1965

The Quiller Memorandum, 1966

The Comedians, 1967

Cromwell, 1970

Scrooge, 1970

Star Wars Episode IV: A New Hope, 1977

A Passage to India, 1984

Little Dorrit, 1988

A Handful of Dust, 1988

Dennis Price, 1915-1973, Actor

A Canterbury Tale, 1944

Kind Hearts and Coronets, 1949

Private's Progress, 1956

The Naked Truth, 1957

I'm All Right Jack, 1959

School for Scoundrels, 1960

Oscar Wilde, 1960

The Millionairess, 1960

The Pure Hell of St. Trinian's, 1960

The Rebel, 1961

Victim, 1961

The V.I.P.s, 1963

A High Wind in Jamaica, 1965

The Horror of Frankenstein, 1970

Pulp, 1972

LINKS TO OTHER FILMS

La Règle du Jeu (1939)

Jean Renoir's examination of the French landed gentry, and their disdain for those who they regard as inferior, has parallels with *Kind Hearts and Coronets*, but the mood is far darker here as the apparent light-heartedness of the country estate's party turns to tragedy when a man is killed.

Monsieur Verdoux (1947)

Charlie Chaplin's film, with its black humour and dark plot (Chaplin's character marries and then murders wealthy widows to support his wife and child), was not well-received in the United States. Its coupling of capitalism and murder was a bitter pill to swallow for a public accustomed to the antics of Chaplin's 'Little Tramp', whereas in Europe it was more popular. It is similar to *Kind Hearts and Coronets* in terms of plot, but its message is perhaps more forceful and more explicitly presented.

Gosford Park (2001)

The superficially calm exterior of a country estate is undermined by a murder and a network of complex relationships which connect the wealthy residents upstairs and the servants below. Like *La Règle du Jeu*, the dramatic narrative is used to explore the selfishness and blinkered views of the upper classes, as well as the divide between them and others in society.

American Psycho (2000)

Although the main character in this film, Patrick Bateman, and Louis Mazzini may seem worlds apart, they are both sociopaths and carry out their killings without too much remorse. Both films are satirical commentaries on society, although, of course, the modern film is far more graphic and Bateman has far less good taste than Mazzini.

REPRESENTATION

Class System I (For 'Class System II' see *Titanic* in BLOCKBUSTERS pg. 445)

Class division in Britain has often been a great cause for debate, with some commentators suggesting that the gap between the 'haves' and 'have-nots' is still growing. Whatever the present situation, in the film Louis Mazzini is a middle-class underachiever, eaten away by his exclusion from position and wealth. The film presents a society where class divisions are maintained, and those in the positions of power do everything to maintain the status quo.

For the D'Ascoynes it is mostly a sense of good and bad taste that distinguishes the classes; their actions are guided by their version of the former, whilst Louis' mother, by eloping with a foreigner, is the embodiment of the latter. Of course, the sins of the mother are passed down to the son. The family is generally shown to be selfish, arrogant, ignorant or misguided; only Young Henry and the Banker show some goodwill to Louis. As they sit in a row at the church they resemble the stone effigies around them, without humanity, fossilised in the past. The line from Philip Larkin's poem *MCMXIV* perfectly conjures up the divisions that existed in Britain when the film is set, but also, to some extent, in 1949 when the film was made: 'The differently-dressed servants/ With tiny rooms in huge houses/ The dust behind limousines.' It is a callous act of those in a privileged position to excommunicate Louis' mother from the family, and this fuels his revenge.

But if the higher level of society is presented in a largely negative light, what of the people 'beneath' them? Actually, they do not fare much better. Although Louis' mother has been treated terribly and Louis forgotten, his actions are reprehensible too. Indeed, the middle classes are represented in just as negative a manner as the D'Ascoynes. Louis murders, Sibella manipulates and connives to have Louis executed, whilst her husband commits suicide; there's not much to recommend either class. And that is the point; this is a comedy, like *Duck Soup*, which does not hate its targets (Alec Guinness' multiple roles as the D'Ascoynes lends them a distinctly eccentric charm). If it is saying anything, it is that the structures that we impose upon ourselves are often ridiculous and full of human folly; but we are usually stuck with them so we may as well satirise and enjoy them.

'Although, for Ealing, there is the usual gentle mockery of official protocol and deferral to status... there is sharper criticism of class snobbery and hypocrisy, aligning the film with contemporaneous pressures for a more open and democratic society.' Amy Sargeant, *British Cinema*, BFI, London, 2005

'Disarmingly cool and callous in its literary sophistication, admirably low key in its discreet caricatures of the haute bourgeoisie, impeccable in its period detail... it's a brilliantly cynical film.' Geoff Andrew, *Time Out Film Guide 14th Ed.*, Time Out Guides Ltd., London, 2006

KEY SCENE TEXTUAL ANALYSIS

A boating accident (5)

After the initial encounter between Louis and Ascoyne D'Ascoyne at the shop and Louis' subsequent sacking at D'Ascoyne's behest, the spectacle of gentrified Maidenhead is presented.

Louis looks the epitome of the perfect gentleman on holiday in Edwardian England; he is dressed in a pin-striped blazer and boater; the *mise-en-scène* of gentility exudes from the civilised sketch of cream teas and idle chit-chat, sitting and promenading by the river.

Each frame is crammed with people and objects that define this rarefied atmosphere: top hats, long gowns, parasols, champagne buckets and fine china all crowd the *mise-en-scène*, together with the delicate, discrete and strait-jacketed gestures and movements made by this tribe of lords, ladies and gentlemen.

Louis fails in his first attempt to engage D'Ascoyne in conversation and, thus, administer the poison.

The montage of shots showing Louis waiting for D'Ascoyne and his lady to come out from their hotel room each morning shows virtually the same *mise-en-scène*, each time emphasising the stale repetition of this life.

At this early stage in Louis' murderous campaign he is not as adept at melting into high society, and his second attempt to engage D'Ascoyne fails when he is snubbed.

All is elegance and coldness from D'Ascoyne who guides his lady onto a punt; the next shot shows Louis following in a canoe, rather incongruous in the surroundings, conjuring up the colonial idea of the savage pursuing the civilised and refined humans.

As they both moor the boats by the riverbank and Louis hatches his plan, he discards the finery and trappings of civility by removing his jacket and jumping fully clothed into the river, a most uncivilised act.

After swimming underwater to them, he untethers their boat and calmly watches as they disappear over the weir to their deaths. His facial gestures betray nothing more than a faint reaction, as if responding to a vaguely entertaining play or sporting spectacle. He stands in the water, clutching their punting pole, like an aquatic gondolier; he is, of course, half-Italian and the image is comically appropriate.

The death, like the taking of tea and scones, is carried out in a restrained and formal manner, underpinning the comic framework of murder and gentility.

The entire sequence has been shot in a stately manner, static and framed to capture the various rituals of upper class life; this very formality mirrors the rigid boundaries of this world; Louis' understated murders and class-conscious and ironic narration cut across the formality and provide the comic effect.

An explosion (8)

Again, it is primarily the *mise-en-scène* that provides the understated comedy in this sequence.

Louis has cleverly ingratiated himself into Henry D'Ascoyne's house and plans to blow up Henry by substituting paraffin for petrol in his darkroom lamp.

A long shot displays a magnificent mansion in the background, with Louis and Edith playing at archery and Henry at photography. All stand on a perfectly manicured lawn with sculpted hedges. They are the gentry at play, perfectly removed from reality, one recording for posterity the idleness of the rich; the very idleness and self-absorption that Louis both despises in others and desires for himself.

The next set-up is even richer in detail, showing Louis and Edith taking tea beneath a tree; it is idyllic and sterile. The formal framing of the long shot is followed by a slow paced sequence of medium close-ups and two-shots which maintain the scene's genteel atmosphere; the carefully laid table consists of more trappings of wealth; here, the silver set of tea pot, milk jug and assorted ornate pieces. The careful gestures and movements of the ritual are observed; the pouring of the milk, for example, which is punctuated by the diegetic sound of a dull explosion. Louis and the audience realise its significance but Edith does not notice. It is as if the explosion itself is as restrained and formal as the people, not wishing to appear impolite by announcing itself too brashly.

The conversation continues with shots revealing plumes of smoke coming from behind the wall where Henry's darkroom is obviously positioned. Yet the conversation about Henry's obsessive photography continues as Edith continues not to notice. The comedy obviously comes from Louis' increasing unease and Edith's ignorance of her husband's demise; the narration wickedly notes the pointlessness of continuing the conversation about Henry's future; this is, after all, black comedy.

It is also attention to detail in the *mise-en-scène* that adds to the comedy of the piece. Edith's specially made dress adds a dry sense of humour to the moment - it has arrows embroidered over the shoulders and around the neck, while her extravagant hat has an arrow piercing the flowers on the top. The idea seems absurd, but it beautifully underlines the absurdity of her life, so removed from reality and governed by its own suffocating rules and extreme vanities.

The audience continue to be tickled by the ongoing conversation and knowledge of events and Louis' thoughts; there are a further nine shots after the explosion as they talk and the audience awaits the inevitable and darkly funny conclusion, when Louis finally runs to the scene of the crime: 'Needless to say I was too late'.

A funeral (9)

The previous sequence cuts immediately after the narrator's remark to a funeral procession, the diegetic sound of a church bell punctuating the cut. The long shot of the funeral carriages is static and

The scene is lent a further comic edge by the casting of Alec Guinness as all the members of the D'Ascoyne family; even these short static shots of each member reveals nuances of characterisation through the small, restrained gestures that he gives to each of them.

Again, the trappings of gentility (in this case, a church) are shown to be tools of division between rich and poor. Just as the select costumes and dining of Maidenhead separated the people, here the gentry in their cloister stand apart from the rest of the congregation.

It is all presented with a lightness of touch, and Guinness' performances imbue the different characters with a great deal of light and shade, eliciting humour from their naivety, pomposity,

full of the finery that has been observed in other scenes; the rich do as well in death as in life.

The *mise-en-scène* of the church reveals an ornate clutter, populated by figures that look as if they have been carved out of the stone surrounding them. The long shot of the D'Ascoyne family suggests their austerity and extreme sense of superiority, as cold as the stone statues they resemble. But the large stone feet of a prone statue above his tomb in the foreground seems to deflate their pomposity, and the fact that they are flanked by tombs identifies these stiff, implacable characters as being closer to death than to the living, such is their lack of humanity.

The close-up portraits of each member serve to underline their aloof natures, each chiselled with indifference and no small degree of stupidity. Director Hamer takes great delight here, as elsewhere, in exposing and lampooning their many shortcomings and the ridiculousness of their posturing.

ignorance and the surety with which they hold their positions in their class' rarefied atmosphere.

Louis' murderous progress is charted by the purposeful crossing out of their names on a family tree, each branch chopped off with wicked glee; for the audience the whole spectacle of serial killing is presented in the most refined and restrained manner, the key to the comedy of the film.

Mon Oncle

KEY FACTS

Release Date: 1958

Country of Origin: France

Running Time: 116 minutes

PRODUCTION NOTES

Production Companies

Alter Films

Film del Centauro

Gray-Film

Specta Films

Other Companies

Distributor

Société des Etablissements L. Gaumont

Budget

FRF 250,000 (estimated)

Awards

Best Foreign Language Film Academy Awards, USA

Jury Special Prize Jacques Tati Cannes Film Festival

Best Foreign Language Film New York Film Critics Circle Awards

SYNOPSIS

Monsieur Hulot is uncle to Gerard and he visits his nephew at the ultra-modern house of his sister and brother-in-law, whose lives are governed by a plethora of modern conveniences. Hulot is much more of a free spirit, uncomfortable in the futuristic environment; his place of abode is traditional and chaotic in contrast to the streamlined nature and supposed efficiency of his sister's house. Gerard's father takes him to school, following a strict regime, but when Hulot collects him on foot the boy is allowed the freedom to engage with his friends and play innocent practical jokes on people alongside Hulot whot is also childlike. Eventually his brother-in-law decides that it would be a good idea for him to work in the factory he manages and where Hulot, shown to be accident-prone earlier in the film, causes mayhem.

HISTORICAL CONTEXT

The 1950s was a difficult decade for the French government; the Fourth Republic, as the era from 1946 to 1958 is called, encountered many problems with massive political instability, the rebuilding of industry after the Second World War and their colonies in Africa, IndoChina and Algeria agitating for independence. As the austerity of the post-war period began to recede into memory people began to want more for themselves and to have easier lives.

Hollywood films were popular in France in the 1940s and 1950s, and people saw that the homes of those on film were looking more modern each year. Of course, these were just films, but shots of affluent domestic bliss and sleek, modern cars were not the stuff of dreams, but becoming more of a reality on American streets due to a booming economy. Many American films, whatever the subject matter, conveyed a gloriously technicolor version of modern living, whether it be dramas like *Rebel Without a Cause* (1955) or comedies like *Pillow Talk* (1959).

The United States started affecting styles and choices through its consumerist economy. Although France always tried to maintain its own style, like many European countries, it was prey to this flow from further west. As France withdrew (or was forced to withdraw) from its own colonies, so it was being colonised itself by the greatest purveyor of shiny, new modern lifestyles.

Tati's comedy is, however, anything but modern; his physical and visual style connects him directly with the world of silent comedy. There are elements of Laurel and Hardy, Buster Keaton, Charlie Chaplin and Harold Lloyd in his performances, and this mode helps link his character with an earlier world, one where innocence and warmth reigned, albeit laced with absurdity and chaos. It seems entirely appropriate that a film-maker who was so focused on exposing the mores of modern society should choose such a way to express himself, all with a sense of disinterested amusement, finding humanity amidst the excesses of modern life. Ultimately, he has the stoical fortitude of Keaton, the warmth of Chaplin and the surreal mayhem-making of Laurel. Moreover, his silence

speaks louder, and with more clarity, than the silly blustering of any other character in his films.

SELECT FILMOGRAPHY OF MAIN PRODUCERS AND CAST

Jacques Tati, 1909-1982, Actor, Director, Producer, Screenwriter

Jour de fête, 1949

Les Vacances de Monsieur Hulot, 1953

Mon Oncle, 1958

Cours du soir, 1967

Playtime, 1967

Trafic, 1971

LINKS TO OTHER FILMS

Modern Times (1936)

This film provides a link between the science fiction film, *Metropolis*, and Jacques Tati's film. Chaplin's comedy shows the excesses of modernity, with humans living in thrall to machines.

The Titfield Thunderbolt (1953)

One of the many successful comedies to emerge from Ealing Studios in the 1940s and 1950s; it deals with a recurring theme in these films, that of the conflict between the old and new worlds, between tradition and so-called progress. Other Ealing comedies which touch upon this notion include *Passport to Pimlico* (1949), *Whisky Galore!* (1949), *The Maggie* (1954) and *The Ladykillers* (1955).

A Shot in the Dark (1964)

There are some strong similarities between Hulot and Inspector Clouseau, such as their surreal rituals and accident-prone antics; Clouseau even wears an overcoat that resembles Hulot's.

Les Vacances de Monsieur Hulot (1953)/*Playtime* (1967)/*Trafic* (1971)

These were the other appearances of Monsieur Hulot; they all exhibit Hulot's childlike approach to life. *Playtime* and *Trafic* continue the themes created in *Mon Oncle*, and the modern world is shown to be a place of servitude to the god of progress.

REPRESENTATION

The old city

Hulot's own environment is an old quarter of the city; generally it is a slightly ramshackle part of the city, but it has charm and it is inhabited with a cross-section of people. It is a place where life and humanity are played out, where there is time to dawdle, to converse and to argue. All emotions are on display, and the surrounding architecture seems to reflect and uphold the life around it; Hulot's own building is a haphazard design of windows, doors and staircases, and his walk up to his apartment seems to take him on a labyrinthine journey before he finally reaches his door. The quarter celebrates diversity and confusion. In the morning it is sleepy; there is none of the manic manoeuvring that happens in the modern part of the city and the only movement is that of the freewheeling dogs. Later, the market is full of life and the possibility for interaction, laughter, and moments of surreal delight (as when the dog snarls at the fish head sticking out of Hulot's bag) are ever-present and give the old city an atmosphere of vitality. Within the old city there is the freedom for people to express themselves, perhaps to flare up for a moment, but ultimately to accept the complexities of life with a shrug, and hopefully, a smile.

'The humour is almost entirely visual - and aural. Few comedians have made such creative use of the soundtrack.' Philip Kemp, *1001 Movies You Must See Before You Die*, Cassell Illustrated, 2007

'Tati begins to stage entire scenes in long shot, letting the architecture frame the gags and letting the audience search for the action.' David Bordwell, *The Oxford History of World Cinema*, OUP, Oxford, 1997

'[Buster] Keaton's spatial humour anticipated the long takes of Jacques Tati in France.' Mark Cousins, *The Story of Film*, Pavilion Books, London, 2004

KEY SCENE TEXTUAL ANALYSIS

At play and then to work (2/3)

The first shot after the titles is a long shot of an old, shabby street with a lamppost dominating the middle ground; it is a clutter of odd angles, misshapen and worn, and the film's title is incorporated into the *mise-en-scène* as a piece of graffiti, chalked on the wall with a child's hand. It firmly identifies the character, the uncle (Hulot), within this type of environment, and exactly what it signifies is played out in the scenes that follow. Certainly, the non-diegetic music is light-hearted and upbeat, piano-led and child-like at times; it speaks of carefree and innocent fun.

Five dogs enter the static frame and rummage around like children on the look out for some fun and mischief. They are small and harmless - looking and one stands out with his grand red and black chequered coat. On the cut, an accordion begins, playing distinctly French-sounding music. The atmosphere becomes even more bohemian and carefree as the dogs plunder trash cans for leftovers and relieve themselves. The cut to a long shot of the street reveals that it is an old quarter of the city, still sleepy, very definitely with that 'lived-in' look.

The music continues to emphasise a contented picture of the dogs' life. The next shot shows the French equivalent of a rag-and-bone man loading his cart; as it bursts into the next frame the jaunty music, with flute leading, expresses unbridled fun and optimism.

The division between old and new appears in the next shot. A crumbling wall replete with an old street lantern, shutters and ornate railings are juxtaposed with erect, functional streetlights and grey concrete blocks. The foreground looks whimsical, suggestive of imagination and creativity (albeit in disrepair), but far more appealing than the bland sterility behind.

This is the starting point of the two contrasting worlds of *Mon Oncle*: one full of spontaneity and humanity, the other filled with pretence and artificiality. This is also the essence of the comedy in the film: a celebration of the old world's richness and playful lampooning of the new world's paucity.

The dogs follow the wagon as it enters this new world, its rigidity signalled by the prim neatness and the first glimpse of directional arrows on the road; the other part of town was devoid of these.

As we journey deeper into this concrete nightmare, more complex and more ludicrous road markings

looks absurd in its unnatural vertical position. It is obviously meant to represent the height of avant-garde and modern living, but its silly perversions of nature make it look pretentious.

The comic shot of the four dogs peering through the gates as their chum is fussed over by a woman in a monstrous green outfit suggests little boys, with their mischievous innocence, and comically contrasts with the alien world beyond the gate.

A corpulent man in a grey suit, which helps connect him with the grey monotony of the building around him, sips tea at the door, seemingly content and quite worryingly unaware of the deafening noise; these people are far removed from the peaceful, natural joys of life.

appear, with an arrow sign and traffic lights that signal at empty roads, highlighting their redundancy and suggesting the victory of impersonal bureaucracy over life as lived.

The dogs arrive at a modernist creation, a house of grey concrete with two window portals, like the watchful eyes of some unfeeling alien. With this shot the light melody fades away like a dying dream, to be replaced by a diegetic noise, a harsh mechanical sound. Only the dressed dog slips through the gate and scampers along the sinuous path to the glass doors. A ridiculous cleaning apparatus on the other side appears to be the apparent source of the irritating noise.

The garden itself looks ridiculous: a triumph of style over nature. The dog now noticeably follows the path rather than its earlier free-wheeling movements. There are fragments of grass, but each is manicured and shaped, the stones are unnatural looking, and the fish statue in the water feature

Even when the mechanical noise ceases it is replaced by the hollow-sounding and equally irritating click of the woman's heels as she fetches and carries for the man. The long shot continues for some time as the audience is invited to watch and observe how these two characters seem to be very much a part of such an absurd environment.

When the film cuts to a medium shot, their incongruity is comically reinforced. The large man stands on one of three tiny mats as if placed there by an unseen hand, while the woman's housecoat and hat are obviously designed to be the height of fashion, but look even more ridiculous in close-up as she continues to clean everything as she moves.

The shot remains static; again the spectacle of absurdity that follows needs to be observed for its full comic effect. The sound of the woman's heels continues insufferably, as does the unpleasant sound of her clothes - an unnatural rubbing of man-made fibres that we can actually hear.

As she comes in and out of the house to furnish the man with a succession of articles that he needs for his day, she clearly follows some sort of routine.

She dusts his suitcase and then the pot of a plant in the garden in an act of domesticity gone mad. As she opens the gates she is possessed by her cleaning, a maniacal grin on her face. She comically dusts the son's satchel, the door handle and then, with the shot of the car driving onto the road, she unexpectedly enters the frame, dusting its rear bumper.

To reinforce the dominance of the machine and an absurd desire to direct, organise and conform, the next sequence mocks this world with a comic portrayal of the masses driving to work.

The cut to the car turning a corner is synchronised with the start of a lively jazz non-diegetic music track intended to contrast with the monochrome monotony of the road, the pavement and the cars. A long shot shows cars driving side by side in rigid formation as they march away from the camera and then towards it with road markings directing and controlling.

At the school, children are jettisoned as if part of a factory line from a succession of cars, while the long shot of the grey factory with a grey uniformed guard in the foreground again signals a world of drudgery. He is animated by the arrival of the car, only to swing open a small and pointless gate. He bows deferentially to the car; no humanity is shown in any of these vehicles.

The camera, fixed to the car, emphasises its relentless movement forward, with its thrusting bonnet sculpture and its desire to follow the directional arrows on the ground; deviation would be unthinkable.

There is even one final arrow that points the car directly into a parking space, one that stands alone, obviously a sign of importance in this superficial and precise world.

Later in this sequence the camera follows the rag and bone man back to the bohemian quarter, which is full of human life. It is messy, there are a cacophony of voices, relaxation is obviously treated as the prime consideration and there are definitely no arrows.

Tati is putting up a mirror to the modern world and saying: 'Look at yourselves; you look silly and you're all part of a silly game.' The reflection that he shows the audience is an affectionate one, a good-humoured one, but one which is as relevant now as it was in the 1950s. The camera, throughout much of the sequence, and indeed, much of the film, presents two contrasting worlds. One is conformist and self-important, the other chaotic and charming. We often see both in medium and long shots, leaving the audience the space to observe, to laugh and perhaps to learn.

The Graduate

KEY FACTS

Release Date: 1967

Country of Origin: USA

Running Time: 108 minutes

PRODUCTION NOTES

Production Companies

Embassy Pictures Corporation

Lawrence Turman Inc.

Distributor

Embassy Pictures Corporation

Budget

$3,000,000 (estimated)

Awards

Best Director Mike Nichols Academy Awards, USA

Best Direction Mike Nichols BAFTA Awards, UK

Best Film Mike Nichols BAFTA Awards, UK

Best Film Editing Sam O'Steen BAFTA Awards, UK

Best Newcomer Dustin Hoffman BAFTA Awards, UK

Best Screenplay Calder Willingham Buck Henry BAFTA Awards, UK

Outstanding Directorial Achievement in Motion Pictures Mike Nichols Directors Guild of America

Best Motion Picture - Musical/Comedy Golden Globes, USA

Best Motion Picture Actress - Musical/Comedy Anne Bancroft Golden Globes, USA

Best Motion Picture Director Mike Nichols Golden Globes, USA

Most Promising Newcomer – Female Katharine Ross Golden Globes, USA

Most Promising Newcomer – Male Dustin Hoffman Golden Globes, USA

National Film Registry National Film Preservation Board, USA

Best Director Mike Nichols New York Film Critics Circle Awards

Best Written American Comedy Calder Willingham Buck Henry Writers Guild of America

SYNOPSIS

Benjamin Braddock returns to his family home in Los Angeles after graduating from university. His parents throw a party for him, where all their friends quiz him about his plans for the future. His father has already questioned him about going to graduate school, and he feels uncomfortable with all the extra attention. He takes the wife (Mrs. Robinson) of his father's business partner back to her house; she invites him inside and attempts to seduce him, but he flees in terror in the face of her overt sexuality. Soon afterwards he does embark on an affair with her and they meet in secret, his confidence increasing with each sexual liaison.

Instead of pursuing his father's wishes of going to graduate school, he relaxes at home and enjoys his sexual freedom. Mr. Robinson, unaware of his wife's infidelity, encourages Benjamin to take his daughter, Elaine, on a date. Benjamin resists, especially after Mrs. Robinson forbids him to go out with her. However, after a great deal of pressure from Mr. Robinson and his own parents, he agrees but behaves rudely and ends the date by taking her to a strip show. Crying, she runs out and is pursued by the now recalcitrant Benjamin; they kiss and so begins a relationship between the two.

Eventually, his affair with Mrs. Robinson is exposed and he is not permitted to see Elaine. Benjamin follows Elaine to her university but he is unable to continue his relationship with her; she becomes engaged to a man of whom the parents approve. Benjamin decides to stop her wedding and makes the long journey to the church, but he arrives as the couple exchange vows. He bangs on a church window, and after a struggle with her parents, he and Elaine escape, boarding a bus and heading off into the distance.

HISTORICAL CONTEXT

This was a decade of revolution that, for America, culminated in the Kent State University massacre of May 4 1970, when the American Home Guard opened fire and killed four students who were protesting against the US Army's invasion of Cambodia, which had been announced by President Richard Nixon a week earlier. It was a landmark moment in student activism in the United States; American soldiers were killing unarmed American citizens on home soil.

But in 1965 the massive ground offensive in Vietnam had begun and the tide of public opinion in the US began to turn against the government after more and more soldiers were killed and horrific images from the war were seen nightly on TV. The US was not the only place for student protest; Germany, France, Spain, Hungary and Czechoslovakia were just some of the countries where student voices protested, particularly with regard to civil liberties. They were often suppressed with brutal force, but it seemed especially shocking and deeply ironic that the 'land of the free' was employing methods often decried as intolerable in other countries.

In film-making terms, the French New Wave and the British New Wave (see *The 400 Blows* [1959] and *Saturday Night and Sunday Morning* [1960]) had refashioned narratives and technical processes to the extent that they were battering down the old Hollywood system with its predominance of narratives that were linear, naïvely romantic, false (in that they did not connect with reality) and tied up neatly at the end.

The 1960s saw a film-making battleground on two fronts. Firstly, the major Hollywood studios were struggling to compete with the growing power of television and had lost their stranglehold on actors. Gone were the old contracts that favoured the studio; actor power meant that they were setting the financial agenda and making films with the studios of *their* choice. Financial difficulties stalked many of the major Hollywood studios; Universal was bought by television programme-maker and talent agency MCA in 1962, whilst an ailing Paramount was bought by Gulf and Western industries, a conglomerate with a wide portfolio of interests, in 1966.

Secondly, the nature of genre film-making was evolving. Film genres were providing vehicles for explicit social commentary; the 1950s had demonstrated how science-fiction could be used to comment on society and in this decade the horror genre, for example, would find its footing as a window on the ills of the world with films like George A. Romero's *Night of the Living Dead* (1968). Film-makers who wanted to deconstruct traditional narratives were blowing genres apart and films such as *Bonnie and Clyde* (1967), *Medium Cool* (1969) and *Easy Rider* (1969) were to herald a new era of filmic non-conformity. *The Graduate* was one of the early trailblazers in a move to a more revolutionary and open-ended approach to film-making.

A New Hollywood was dawning. But what of Benjamin? He too undertakes his own brand of personal revolt against the Establishment, but his ultimate fate is uncertain, positioned at a crossroads between the status quo and 'the shock of the new', between old and new Hollywood.

SELECT FILMOGRAPHY OF MAIN PRODUCERS AND CAST

Mike Nichols, 1931, Director, Producer, Screenwriter

Who's Afraid of Virginia Woolf?, 1966

The Graduate, 1967

Catch-22, 1970

Carnal Knowledge, 1971

The Day of the Dolphin, 1973

Silkwood, 1983

Heartburn, 1986

Biloxi Blues, 1988

Working Girl, 1988

Postcards from the Edge, 1990

Regarding Henry, 1991

Wolf, 1994

The Birdcage, 1996

Primary Colors, 1998

Closer, 2004

Charlie Wilson's War, 2007

Buck Henry, 1930, Screenwriter, Actor

The Graduate, 1967

The Candy, 1968

Catch-22, 1970

The Owl and the Pussycat, 1970

What's Up, Doc?, 1972

The Day of the Dolphin, 1973

The Nude Bomb, 1980

First Family, 1980

Protocol, 1984

To Die For, 1995

Robert Surtees, 1906-1985, Director of Cinematography

King Solomon's Mines, 1950

Quo Vadis, 1951

The Bad and the Beautiful, 1952

Mogambo, 1953

Valley of the Kings, 1954

Oklahoma!, 1955

Les Girls, 1957

Ben-Hur, 1959

Cimarron, 1960

Mutiny on the Bounty, 1962

The Hallelujah Trail, 1965

Doctor Dolittle, 1967

The Graduate, 1967

Sweet Charity, 1969

The Last Picture Show, 1971

The Cowboys, 1972

The Sting, 1973

The Great Waldo Pepper, 1975

A Star Is Born, 1976

Anne Bancroft, 1931-2005, Actress

The Raid, 1954

Nightfall, 1957

The Restless Breed, 1957

The Miracle Worker, 1962

The Pumpkin Eater, 1964

7 Women, 1966

The Graduate, 1967

Young Winston, 1972

The Hindenburg, 1975

The Elephant Man, 1980

To Be or Not to Be, 1983

Agnes of God, 1985

84 Charing Cross Road, 1987

Torch Song Trilogy, 1988

Honeymoon in Vegas, 1992

Malice, 1993

Mr. Jones, 1993

How to Make an American Quilt, 1995

The Sunchaser, 1996

Great Expectations, 1998

Heartbreakers, 2001

Dustin Hoffman, 1937, Actor

The Graduate, 1967

Midnight Cowboy, 1969

Little Big Man, 1970

Straw Dogs, 1971

Papillon, 1973

Lenny, 1974

All the President's Men, 1976

Marathon Man, 1976

Agatha, 1979

Kramer vs. Kramer, 1979

Tootsie, 1982

Death of a Salesman, 1985

Rain Man, 1988

Dick Tracy, 1990

Billy Bathgate, 1991

Hook, 1991

Outbreak, 1995

Wag the Dog, 1997

Runaway Jury, 2003

Finding Neverland, 2004

Meet the Fockers, 2004

Mr. Magorium's Wonder Emporium, 2007

Katharine Ross, 1940, Actress

Shenandoah, 1965

The Singing Nun, 1966

Games, 1967

The Graduate, 1967

Hellfighters, 1968

Butch Cassidy and the Sundance Kid, 1969

Tell Them Willie Boy is Here, 1969

The Stepford Wives, 1975

The Betsy, 1978

The Final Countdown, 1980

Donnie Darko, 2001

LINKS TO OTHER FILMS

Bonnie and Clyde (1967)

Released in the same year as *The Graduate*, Arthur Penn's revisionist gangster film reinterprets the outlaw couple's actions with French New Wave sensibilities, producing a film that young audiences flocked to, attracted by its debunking of the Establishment.

Midnight Cowboy (1969)

A look at the underbelly of American society, the underclass who exist in the urban areas of America, where prostitution, petty and serious crime and hustling to make a living is a world away from the suburban brain-washing of *The Graduate*. Linked also by the actor Dustin Hoffman, in the second of his career-defining roles in the 1960s.

Easy Rider (1969)

The archetypal counter-culture hymn to a free-wheeling lifestyle. Its disdain for traditional narrative, and representation of characters who do not exist within the boundaries of society, tapped into the prevailing zeitgeist and helped stimulate the New Hollywood ethos. Film-makers such as Francis Ford Coppola and Martin Scorsese would soon follow with their groundbreaking and innovative work.

Butch Cassidy and the Sundance Kid (1969)

A Western, which borrowed from the culture of the times to reinvent the genre's codes and conventions, feeding deeply on 1960 notions of anti-hero, anti-establishment and being 'hip'.

The Last Picture Show (1971)

Peter Bogdanovich's hymn to frustrated youth looks back to an earlier time (the early 1950s), but its exploration of young lives in a stifling environment connects well with *The Graduate*, even down to one young character having an affair with an older woman.

REPRESENTATION

Coming of age

Benjamin seems to be a late developer in the context of the 1960's sexual revolution; for someone who has just come out of university he seems very 'unliberated'. Films about coming of age often have sex as the focal point for the transition; Bob Clark's *Porky's* (1982), and Amy Heckerling's *Fast Times at Ridgemount High* (1982) are early examples of comedies where sexual awakening is highlighted. The mantle for these films was taken up again in the later *American Pie* (1999) and a plethora of

imitators in the early noughties. In other films, such as *Footloose* (1984) and *Dirty Dancing* (1987), the protagonists dance their way into adulthood. And, if neither of these options work, there is always violence, with John Singleton's *Boyz N The Hood* (1991) or Peter Jackson's *Heavenly Creatures* (1994) presenting this route. In all these films the representation of coming of age occurs within the environment of similarily-aged people, but Benjamin needs an older adult to effect his transition.

Adults are the ones who do not understand and are the source of conflict in most of these films, and Benjamin is certainly alienated from his own parents. However, Mrs. Robinson, the same age as his parents, holds his hand as he passes into self-knowledge to a point of epiphany where he makes his first decision in life, as he beats against the window in the church.

Suburbia

Suburbia is glossy, full of big houses with sweeping lawns and sleek cars. Everything is immaculate and this sheen attaches itself to the smiles of the people who inhabit this world. The interiors reflect the exteriors; everything is designed for comfort and leisure, from the bars and swimming pools to the canapés. It is a middle-class idyll, full of idle chit-chat, which, as we witness at the church, disguises bile and venom for anything that might destroy such a carefully constructed artifice. Frank Perry's *The Swimmer* (1968) also charts this suburban façade as the main protagonist decides to travel home via the swimming pools of his well-to-do friends; initially the conversations are light and full of boasts and bravura, but the underbelly of this world is gradually revealed as the cracks beneath the surface begin to appear, and the fantasy is finally dispelled when he returns to his home only to find it abandoned.

This is the suburbia of *The Graduate*, replete with possessions, but empty of meaning. It is also a world dissected by Douglas Sirk in his films of the 1950s, particularly *Magnificent Obsession* (1954), *All That Heaven Allows* (1955), *Written on the Wind* (1956) and *Imitation of Life* (1959) where Sirk's carefully observed surface gloss belies a world of repression, frustration and pettiness. It was an environment Todd Haynes would recreate in *Far From Heaven* (2002), and which was stripped to the bone in David Lynch's *Blue Velvet* (1986). In contrast to these representations of suburbia, Doris Day vehicles such as *The Tunnel of Love* (1958) and *The Thrill of It All* (1963) painted the American idyll, where material wealth and domestic bliss, with the odd comic stutter, reigned supreme.

'The Graduate, certainly a parody of conventional romantic comedies, collides classic Hollywood style with self-conscious devices of the modern European art cinema.' **Richard Neupert,** *The Cinema Book 2nd Edition***, Eds. Pam Cook & Mieke Bernink, Bfi Publishing, 1999**

'This last issue [genre] is perhaps one of the trickiest frameworks for understanding this curiously unplaceable movie – not quite a comedy, unlike any other mainstream drama of the time, it might best be described as a 'youth film' and was clearly marketed as such (one trailer for it opens with an image of Benjamin at Berkeley looking despondent, overshadowed by a US flag).' **Linda Ruth Williams, '***The Graduate***', in Williams, L. R. and Hammond, M. (eds)** *Contemporary American Cinema***, McGraw Hill/Open University Press, 2006**

KEY SCENE TEXTUAL ANALYSIS

Welcome home (1)

The title sequence has shown us a young man who seems numbed by his surroundings, bustled onto a people-mover as he arrives off a flight home from university. The large space in the frame in front

of him seems to represent the uncertainty that he faces, filled with possibilities, but more likely emptiness. The camera track alongside his moving figure, reminiscent of the way unknown forces direct his destiny, is matched in the next shot with that of his suitcase as it journeys along a luggage belt - the connection between him and the case again suggests a destiny which is out of his hands.

The final airport image sees him walking towards a set of automatic doors; the camera is placed outside and we can read the words on them: 'Use other door'; the young man does use the door as the sign is for those entering the airport, but it is perhaps an indicator that there are other doorways to other destinies. Simon and Garfunkel's 'Sounds of Silence' plays throughout, a meditation on, and expression of, his state of mind as he leaves university and starts life in the real world. So far, so unfunny.

The framework and mood have been set by the title sequence, and the following scene fleshes out Ben's feelings of alienation and isolation as he returns to his parents' house. It is a world of suffocating expectation, and it is here that the comedy and drama of conformity and liberation plays out.

The melancholic melody fades as the scene begins and the medium close-up of Ben's face, framed by the aquarium, is both funny and symbolic; the mood lightens as we see the tiny figure in the wetsuit in the tank, but it looks forward to his later humiliation in the swimming pool on his birthday and underlines his sense of confinement. Young angst, as he contemplates the need to conform to society's rules, is to be portrayed in all its comic and serious implications.

As the music finishes the audience shares Ben's peaceful contemplation. The father's voice shatters the silence and then he crowds the boy's, and our, filmic space by sitting right down between us and Ben. We immediately share the discomfort at such an intrusion.

It is now that we get a verbalisation of his worries about the future and his desire to be different; there is no consolation or resolution, and this continuous take and static frame is further invaded by his mother. Her body obliterates all view of Ben and again underlines the sense of claustrophobia that he feels; she is so close to the camera that her dress is out of focus, the blur helping to connect us with Ben's confusion. We track back as the parents utter their banalities and usher Ben out to meet the waiting friends. The picture of the sad clown comes into focus as they descend the staircase, encapsulating the combination of laughter and melancholy in the film.

The following sequence continues the idea of claustrophobia, but is increasingly amusing, as the parents' friends claw at their son as they congratulate him on his graduation, offering empty words, platitudes and laughable advice. As the first group approaches the handheld camera keeps the

A hand clasps his shoulder and a man appears above him; the conversation (paraphrased but without much removed):

'Ben.

Mr. Macguire.

Ben.

Mr. Macguire...

One word. Plastics...think about it.'

This is comic and again mocks the absurdity of a society where achievement and success are the most highly prized commodities.

He finally refuses the advances of the next group, the camera tracking closely with him as he runs through the house, clawed at as he goes, and up

faces in close-up, crowding his space with their well-intentioned congratulations.

We follow Ben as he attempts to make his escape out the front door, but another figure looms into his space. As he flees up the stairs a hand grabs his back and two manicured hands clasp his face as an elderly lady's face, masked by make-up and jewellery, comes into view. Ben's uncomfortable expression grows as he is mauled and accosted in something reminiscent of a high society zombie film; you can feel his desire to keep hold of his own brains and not give them over to the Los Angeles suburban undead. The diegetic sound of chit-chat also adds to the confusion of the moment, filling the filmic world with inanities.

Another figure fills the already crowded frame crying 'proud, proud, proud, proud, proud, proud, proud' and a hand reaches into frame to ruffle Ben's hair while another face takes up the onslaught - it is becoming as much a comment on Ben's sense of unease as the adults' ridiculous posturing.

the stairs, pursued not by people this time but by the voice of his mother as she begins to read aloud his achievements from the graduate year book; by this point the repeated sound of his name has become like a dagger to his heart, a word for controlling him.

The cluttered *mise-en-scène* of cocktail dresses, suits, swimming pool, polite gestures and chic fittings and furniture all add to the atmosphere of stifling superficiality. The sequence is both funny and frighteningly real, its growing levels of absurdity feeding into both readings of it, and later built upon in the birthday scene.

Twenty-first birthday party (6)

After Mrs. Robinson's first attempt at seducing Ben, his birthday is the next trial. The scene begins with the father in foreground and mother behind, like a ringmaster and assistant, both exuding prosperity through their confidence and clothes. A gathered audience wait by the swimming pool, another symbol of affluence.

The father glides back and forth from his foreground position to the kitchen door as he gives Ben a big build-up before his entrance. Each time he speaks to Ben we hear his plaintive pleas indicating his unease. Ignoring this, the father continues; for him, it is all about show and the display of wealth in particular.

Eventually, Ben is revealed to the audience as the father opens the kitchen door like the curtains on a stage and the pretence is played out, the very pretence that Ben wants to avoid.

The sight is funny for its ridiculous incongruity; he stands in full scuba gear with a harpoon. He has retreated to the back of frame, a manifestation of his insecurity in contrast to his father's loud voice and front of frame confidence. The sterile, pristine and white kitchen seems to help suspend him in this sea of absurdity.

Once in the water he tries to resurface, but the thrusting hands of his parents comically and symbolically push his facemask back under the water; he has no choices of his own. Family and friends are shown through the face-mask shaped frame, as if they too exist in some sort of aquarium like strange creatures to whom Ben cannot relate.

The cut to the scene's final shot reveals Ben standing at the bottom of the pool as the camera tracks backwards. He stares at us, a forlorn and comical figure. He may be a man with a great harpoon, but he is stuck at the bottom of a suburban pool with no adventure ahead of him, only the pressure of his parents' demands bearing down on him. The signal that he is going to break out does come, however, from the dialogue (a telephone conversation between Ben and Mrs. Robinson) that comes from the next scene which overlaps this visual. It is disorientating initially, but

His first few slapping and exaggerated steps accentuate the humour, but also suggest the beginning of a nightmare where one is incapable of saving oneself from public humiliation, akin to public nakedness or running without moving. Ben walks right up to the camera, his glazed eyes a picture of helpless fear and loathing, juxtaposed with his father's supposedly amusing commentary on Ben's actions.

The next long take is shown from Ben's POV, connecting the audience firmly with his sense of isolation and the spectacle of the onlookers' absurd gesturing, particularly as we are unable to hear them because we can only hear Ben's breathing. The whole surreal experience is again both comic (the father's gesticulations and the sight of the flippers), but also expressive of all those feelings of angst he is experiencing.

expresses his thoughts of escape, albeit into the tentacles of Mrs. Robinson.

Young Frankenstein

KEY FACTS

Release Date: 1974

Country of Origin: USA

Running Time: 105 minutes

PRODUCTION NOTES

Production companies

Gruskoff/Venture Films

Crossbow Productions

Jouer Limited

Distributor

Twentieth Century Fox Film Corporation

Budget

$2,800,000 (estimated)

Awards

Nominated: Best Sound Richard Portman Gene S. Cantamessa Academy Awards, USA

Nominated: Best Writing, Screenplay Adapted From Other Material Gene Wilder and Mel Brooks

Academy Awards, USA

Nominated: Best Motion Picture Actress - Musical/Comedy Cloris Leachman Golden Globes, USA

Nominated: Best Supporting Actress - Motion Picture Madeline Kahn Golden Globes, USA

National Film Registry National Film Preservation Board

Nominated: Best Comedy Adapted from Another Medium Gene Wilder Mel Brooks Writers Guild of America

SYNOPSIS

Frederick Frankenstein, the grandson of the original Dr. Frankenstein who had reanimated a corpse, is teaching at a medical school in the United States. He is in denial about his ancestry, rejecting the correct pronunciation of his name and reacting with anger to questions about his notorious grandfather. He is lured to Transylvania when he inherits his ancestor's estate and there, with the help of sidekicks Igor, Inga and Frau Blücher, he resurrects his grandfather's work.

He brings a stolen dead body back to life, but the brain is abnormal, resulting in the problems encountered by the original Frankenstein. The monster eventually escapes, comically encountering a young girl and a blind hermit on his travels through the countryside, but is recaptured by Frankenstein who then starts to school the monster. Frankenstein reveals his protégé to the public at a theatre where they perform a rendition of 'Puttin' on the Ritz'.

But the monster becomes fearful and then angry once the audience starts to throw cabbages at him. He is subdued and chained up, only to escape again. He first meets Elizabeth, Frankenstein's fiancée, who has unexpectedly come to visit, and she falls in love with him, particularly besotted by his sexual prowess. He is then drawn back to Frankenstein's castle by the sound of music, the only thing that can control him. As a mob approaches under the leadership of Inspector Kemp, Frankenstein performs a mind swap procedure which gives the monster some of Frankenstein's brain capacity, helping to subdue his aggressive personality. The monster, now a cultured man, marries Elizabeth, whilst Inga and Frankenstein become a couple, the film ending with her delight at discovering that the monster's prodigious manhood has been transferred to the doctor during the earlier operation.

HISTORICAL CONTEXT

In a decade when Hollywood was being dominated by the so-called New Hollywood directors like Scorsese and Coppola, Mel Brooks might seem like something of an anachronism. His film-making style was very traditional and his source texts were the very films that the new directors rejected, both visually and thematically. But if Scorsese et al were reinventing or destroying traditional genre films, then that is also what Brooks was doing, albeit in his own fashion. His two most successful films of the 1970s, *Blazing Saddles* (1974) and *Young Frankenstein*, took the deconstruction of genre as their starting point for a series of visual and verbal jokes, targeting every convention and cliché. Whilst *Blazing Saddles* parodied the Western,

Young Frankenstein singled out one of the most famous Hollywood horror films, James Whale's *Frankenstein* (1931) for special treatment, as well as incorporating elements from the sequel, *Bride of Frankenstein* (1935). As will be evidenced in the TEXTUAL ANALYSIS section, Brooks' parodies are filtered by a real affection for the original films (not something obviously apparent in the current spate of movie parodies), and his works both recreate and parody, investing them with a sense of *homage* rather than scattergun lampooning.

The natural journey for a genre is the formation of its conventions and then for it to be parodied and reworked in new directions, sometimes combining it with other genres for comic or thematic reasons. Indeed, the literary tradition of gothic literature saw many of the genre's conventions parodied; both Mary Shelley's genre classic, *Frankenstein*, and Jane Austen's genre parody, *Northanger Abbey*, appeared in 1818. *Young Frankenstein* was able to undermine 40 years of horror genre conventions, but the first *Frankenstein* parody, *Abbott and Costello Meet Frankenstein* (1938) appeared just a few years after the source film. *Young Frankenstein*'s brand of particularly affectionate and surreal parody can also be seen in later films like *Airplane* (1980) and *The Naked Gun* film series (1988, 1991, 1994), although later parodies like the *Scary Movie* film series and *Meet the Spartans* (2008) do not have the coherent approach to narrative found in the earlier films, instead adopting the television comedy sketch show format.

SELECT FILMOGRAPHY OF MAIN PRODUCERS AND CAST

Mel Brooks, 1926, Director, Producer, Screenwriter, Actor

The Producers, 1968

The Twelve Chairs, 1970

Blazing Saddles, 1974

Young Frankenstein, 1974

Silent Movie, 1976

High Anxiety, 1977

The Nude Bomb, 1980

History of the World, Part I, 1981

Spaceballs, 1987

Life Stinks, 1991

Robin Hood: Men in Tights, 1993

Dracula: Dead and Loving It, 1995

Gene Wilder, 1933, Actor, Screenwriter, Director

Bonnie and Clyde, 1967

The Producers, 1968

Willy Wonka & the Chocolate Factory, 1971

Everything You Always Wanted to Know About Sex (But Were Afraid to Ask), 1972

Blazing Saddles, 1974

Young Frankenstein, 1974

The Adventure of Sherlock Holmes' Smarter Brother, 1975

Silver Streak, 1976

The Woman in Red, 1984

Haunted Honeymoon, 1986

See No Evil, Hear No Evil, 1989

LINKS TO OTHER FILMS

Frankenstein (1931)/*Bride of Frankenstein* (1935)

Young Frankenstein borrows scenes and imagery from both of James Whale's films, parodying whole sequences such as the creation of life scene and the encounter with the little girl from the original; the blind hermit scene and Elizabeth's 'Bride' make-up and costume are lifted from the 1935 sequel. See also pg. 209.

The Old Dark House (1932)

Early into the sound era, Hollywood saw the possibility of subverting horror conventions for comic effect, with James Whale directing both a homage to, and parody of, some of the conventions that he created only a year earlier in *Frankenstein*.

Blazing Saddles (1974)

Mel Brooks' characteristic blend of visual humour and quick-fire jokes, laced with innuendo, is evident in his other great genre parody. Numerous Western clichés are exploited to comic effect: a town seeking salvation from corrupt officials; the lone sheriff against the villains; and the banding together of misfits to defeat the bad guys. Like *Young Frankenstein*, the success of the film lies not just in its good gags, but in its faithful realisation of the genre that it is parodying.

Love at First Bite (1979)

This is another parody of the horror genre, using the other classic horror template, *Dracula*, as its source material. It updates the original film, locating it in New York, again revelling in its subversion of horror conventions.

REPRESENTATION

The castle

The castle is a key component of most gothic horror novels. Horace Walpole's *The Castle of Otranto* (1764), Ann Radcliffe's *The Mysteries of Udolpho* (1794), and Bram Stoker's *Dracula* (1897) all feature the castle as the central location for the horrors that beset the characters. Far from acting as a symbol of benign power in films, the castle has often been a site of tyranny and terror. Michael Curtiz's *The Adventures of Robin Hood* (1938) presents the castle in Nottingham as a symbol of Prince John's cruel actions, a place of excess and imprisonment, and in Roger Corman's *The Pit and the Pendulum* (1961) it is the locale for all manner of sadistic brutality.

Franklin J. Schaffner's *The War Lord* (1965) details the building of a castle which is seen as a symbol of suppression with the Norman invaders trying to maintain control of England, whilst film versions of *The Count of Monte Cristo* display the castle as a place where secrets are kept hidden. *Bram Stoker's Dracula* (1992) has a castle plunged into pools of darkness, in which lurk the vampiric predators, emerging from its architectural shadows to prey on human offerings.

Mel Brooks visualises his castle in a similar way, replete with shadows, cobwebs, secret passages and hidden depths; the long journey that both Frankenstein and Inga make into the bowels of the castle contains a series of visual clichés to add to the eerie, but comic, atmosphere. Brooks also used some of the original *Frankenstein* set design and props to add 'authenticity' to the film and this helps maintain a visual, as well as generic, link with its predecessors. Of course, his castle is full of humour, more akin to the Monty Python Camelot (in *Monty Python and the Holy Grail*, 1975), which also delights in both careful construction and comic destruction of the castle and other genre conventions. Brooks' Castle Frankenstein, like Python's Camelot, is a *silly* place.

> '[It] is the prolific director/writer's most balanced comedy... a silly take and a serious homage.'
> Karen Krizanovich, *1001 Movies You Must See Before You Die*, Cassell Illustrated, 2007

KEY SCENE TEXTUAL ANALYSIS

The little girl (17)

This is a difficult scene to parody as it is both a very touching and upsetting moment in the original film. The scene was cut from the 1931 film because of its disturbing content, the drowning of a little girl by the monster, and was only restored many years later.

The audience would probably be aware of the original and the danger it implies for the child. She sits upon the side of a well, throwing petals plucked from a flower into its depths. The shot is low angle from within the well, to emphasise the precarious position that she is in; her innocent singing reinforces both her innocence and vulnerability. The filmic space around her is quickly filled with the huge presence of the monster in the classic pose of outstretched arms and gnarled fingers, the groan reinforcing the threat.

The audience's expectation of what will follow is undermined by the cut to the father who is barricading himself and his wife in the house. The horrible irony of what they have done is undercut by the shot of Helga and the monster who, as in the original film, are now playing with the flowers. With the flower's petals and stem thrown into the well, the camera lingers on the girl as she utters the blackly comic line 'what shall we throw in now?' There is then a cut to the monster as he ponders this question; his look to camera is a moment of delicious anticipation for the audience, a knowing glance which foreshadows the humour to follow. It serves the same function as the Oliver Hardy look to camera, drawing the audience into the comic chaos.

The audience now expects him to throw her down the well, emulating the monster in the James Whale film version. The action is again interrupted, adding to the audience's sense of expectation. The parents are full of confusion and rush upstairs to see if Helga is in bed, each thinking that the other has been looking after their daughter. The expectation of what the monster has done with the girl is undercut by the shot of her on a see-saw, not thrown down the well. In fact, there is a comic role-reversal, wherein the little girl plays the dominant role and demands that the monster sit on the other end of the see-saw; he obliges and she is catapulted into her room and onto her bed. Here is the comic payoff, the humour generated by a combination of the audience's intertextual knowledge of the scene in *Frankenstein* and the delaying of the inevitable but surprising denouement.

The elements of the *mise-en-scène* also help add to the sense of pleasure for the audience; the black and white photography obviously recalls the original film, but also the detailed evocation of place and atmosphere through gesture, costume, props and set heightens the audience's enjoyment. The *mise-en-scène* here and elsewhere in *Young Frankenstein* is designed to remind the audience of the source text, simultaneously evoking and parodying, imbuing the comedy with a fondness and respect for the original.

Dancing on stage (20)

The scene has echoes of other monster films when the creature is exposed to the public glare; the most famous example is King Kong's appearance before the crowds in New York. The setting is similar - a theatre with well-dressed people wanting to see the incredible and the bizarre. Just as the flashlights scare the ape, the monster is startled by an exploding light on the stage. The humour begins as Frankenstein gives a food treat to the monster as a trainer would to a performing seal. The revelatory shot of Frankenstein and the monster on stage transports the film into the realms of surreal comedy; it is the antithesis of all that the monster has symbolised in previous incarnations. He has been depicted as aggressive, homicidal and childlike, but never urbane.

all the more memorable. The touch of dark eye make-up also connects the performance with that of the silent era, giving the film yet another strand of credibility as not just parody but a celebration of early Hollywood. The monster is big-booted, the steps he takes full of stereotypical menace and plodding half-humanness, whilst the white hospital gown protrudes with comic excess over his extensive bulk.

When the two-shot is revealed it is full of poise, elegance and balance with the two men forming an ascending arc from left to right. In fact, it is the antithesis of the ungainly stereotype of the monster. The comic visual is heightened by the extra-large bow tie and his look of sophistication and charm. The song, Irving Berlin's 'Puttin' on the Ritz', is again used as a comic contrast to the

The crisp black and white visuals and the images of a person on show are also reminiscent of the style that would be later used in David Lynch's *The Elephant Man* (1980), the visuals of which, in turn, borrow from Lynch's own *Eraserhead* (1977). Although all three film's intentions are different, their visuals all create a clear realisation of otherness. Here, the notion of otherness is about to be lampooned with a comic unravelling of the traditional 'monster-on-show' cliché.

The build-up to the revelation of the monster as 'a man about town' is notable for Gene Wilder's performance as Frankenstein. In denial about his identity and legacy at the beginning of the film, now he revels in the position of scientist, creator of life, showman and adventurer returned with monster tamed, and trained. We hear all of these characters in Wilder's speech as he prepares to unveil the fruits of his work. His dinner jacket, coiffured hair and precise moustache all add to the integrity of the performance. It is played completely straight which helps make the comedy, when it does come,

audience's expectations of the monster, for it is most commonly associated with Fred Astaire and his dance routine in *Blue Skies* (1946); the epitome of charm and sophistication, Astaire was an actor who interpreted dance with grace and style and is remembered as a gentleman, gliding across the screen wearing top hat and tails.

The sequence here both parodies and embraces this intertextual link and emerges as a classic moment of film and comedy in its own right. Just as the audience is surprised by the revelation of the monster, so our expectation of what the song and dance will reveal is the next area of enjoyment. It seems to be slick and well-rehearsed, but then certain movements further the comedy: the monster's mistimed finger clicking and his guttural screaming attempts at singing part of the song.

But the lumbering monster is not just used as a device for an easy laugh; he is afforded self awareness and individuality by his warm relationship with Frankenstein on stage and a number of facial gestures: the knowing wink to his mentor and his reaction to the playful and affectionate punch to his face. There are other moments in the film where we see the personality within the monster, making the comedy more affectionate: there is the look to camera as described in 'The Little Girl' TEXTUAL ANALYSIS and the raising of the eyes when the blind man smashes his mug of wine.

Brooks places the viewer in the position of the theatre audience in the film by positioning the camera just below the level of the stage, looking up at the two performers. This accentuates the theatricality of the sequence and empowers the two men, again imbuing them with status and heightening our affection for them. Peter Boyle's movements as the monster are charged with comedy; he is graceful and awkward at the same time, like a child trying to please a parent with his latest achievement. The sound of taps are added to the monster's shoe movement, obviously a non-diegetic addition, which help add to the lovely silliness of the routine.

When everything begins to fall apart once the light has exploded, the camera views events from behind the performers and we feel the sense of confusion and fear that is rising within the monster as the theatre audience turn against him. In a parody of the 'audience turning against the stage act' cliché the audience members begin to hurl cabbages at the performers, as if it is quite normal to take vegetables to the theatre.

It is a scene that John Landis would take to the next level of parody in *The Blues Brothers* (1980) when the band plays to an audience who throw bottles and glasses at the stage, which smash on a protective screen erected by the bar's owners. The mock panic of the situation is heightened by the rapid cutting, the use of a dramatic non-diegetic orchestral piece and the hand-held camera shots which are now switched to the view from the audience's perspective, looking up at the careering monster. The success of the comedy in this scene, and elsewhere in the film, is derived from subverting genre conventions, leaving no cliché unturned and taking the parody off in surprising directions.

Raising Arizona

KEY FACTS

Release Date: 1987

Country of Origin: USA

Running Time: 90 minutes

PRODUCTION NOTES

Production Company

Circle Films Inc.

Distributor

Twentieth Century Fox Film Corporation

Budget

$6,000,000 (estimated)

SYNOPSIS

H.I. (Hi) Mc Dunnough, a thief and repeat offender, courts and eventually marries Edwina (Ed), a police officer. They are unable to have children and are refused the possibility of adoption because of Hi's criminal record. On reading that a wealthy businessman and his wife have had five boys they decide to procure one of the children for themselves. After stealing the baby, whose surname is Arizona, they are visited by two escaped convicts, Gale and Evelle, who are Hi's friends.

Meanwhile, the boy's father, Nathan Arizona, is approached by a bounty hunter and mysterious biker with an offer to recover his son. The father refuses the extortionate amount requested but the bounty hunter, Leonard Smalls, goes after the boy anyway, for his personal gain. At a picnic, Hi's boss, Glen, suggest a wife swap so Hi punches him and loses his job. Later, Glen works out the identity of the baby and demands the child for himself and his wife, or threatens to inform the police if Hi does not comply. Hi has also reverted to his criminal ways and attempts to steal from a convenience store, only to be rescued at the last minute, and after a long chase, by his outraged wife.

In the meantime, Gale and Evelle overhear Glen and his threat of blackmail. They decide to return the baby to gain the reward but not before committing a bank robbery – where they leave the child behind. Smalls then manages to get hold of the child and there is a last stand-off between him, Hi and Ed. Hi is nearly killed but manages to pull a ring from one of Smalls' grenades which decorate his clothes; Smalls is blown to pieces. There is a suggestion that Hi and Smalls are related through a shared tattoo, and that Smalls has himself suffered a childhood trauma, as evidenced by the baby shoes that are attached to his clothing. The couple decide to return the baby to his natural parents, only to be discovered by Nathan, who offers forgiveness. The story ends with Hi's dream of a future filled with a vision of a happy extended family.

HISTORICAL CONTEXT

The New Hollywood revolution seemed to have disintegrated by the end of the 1970s. *Apocalypse Now*'s (1979) arduous shoot in the Philippines obviously took its toll on Francis Ford Coppola (The *Godfather* films, 1972/74/90; *The Conversation*, 1974), and his next film, *One from the Heart* (1982) was a financial disaster; Michael Cimino (*The Deer Hunter*, 1978) had made the box office failure *Heaven's Gate* (1980) which brought United Artists to its knees, and virtually extinguished Cimino's career; Peter Bogdanovich made a number of box flops after his wonderful *The Last Picture Show* (1971), including *At Long Last Love* (1975); and William Friedkin's career (*The French Connection*, 1971; *The Exorcist*, 1973) was damaged by the failure of his 1977 film, *Sorcerer*. Only Steven Spielberg, George Lucas and Martin Scorsese maintained their momentum by making further commercially successful and/or critically lauded films. The New Hollywood directors, who had wrestled creative control away from the studio executives, seemed to be handing back their short-lived power.

Was the 1980s, then, wholly dominated by big budget studio-controlled productions? Not exactly; the reins were certainly tighter on new projects and the studios saw that blockbusters were the biggest money-spinners, but as ever, new, young directors were forging fresh paths, making low-budget and inventive films.

This process of death and renewal seems to have repeated itself from the 1960s in Hollywood: new directors make innovative films and either become part of the Establishment or drop away. Such was the case in the 1980s with the likes of the Coen

Brothers and Sam Raimi. They made startling early films, *Blood Simple* (1984) and *The Evil Dead/The Evil Dead II* (1981, 1987) respectively; but now they have moved closer to the Hollywood mainstream with the likes of *The Ladykillers* (2004) and Sam Raimi's *Spider-Man* series.

Most recently, the Coens have achieved the status of 'Establishment figures' by winning Best Director at the Academy Awards for *No Country for Old Men* (2007, also named Best Picture). And the cycle continues in the noughties with the current emerging generation of New Hollywood directors – the likes of Alexander Payne (*Sideways*, 2004) and Wes Anderson (*The Royal Tenenbaums*, 2001).

However, the Coens *have* continued to make idiosyncratic and genre-bending films which have maintained their artistic, if not financial, link to independent film-making. A critical and commercial success, *No Country for Old Men*, demonstrates their relationship with mainstream Hollywood; backed by the 'independent' arm of a major studio, Paramount, and with many of the conventions of an action thriller, it would appear as a straightforward genre piece to the casual observer. However, (spoiler alert!) the sudden killing of the main protagonist before the end of the film and the resulting decimation of traditional narrative flow reiterates their disregard for genre conventions, a key feature of their oeuvre stretching back to *Blood Simple* (1984). Any genre or sub-genre label that has been applied to their films (film noir - *Blood Simple*, *Barton Fink* [1991], *Fargo* [1996], *The Big Lebowski* [1998], *The Man Who Wasn't There* [2001]; gangster - *Miller's Crossing* [1990]; screwball comedy - *The Hudsucker Proxy* [1994], *Intolerable Cruelty* [2003]) fails to properly encapsulate their ability to transcend traditional generic constraints and contemplate ideas usually far exceeding the reach of many a staple genre film.

SELECT FILMOGRAPHY OF MAIN PRODUCERS AND CAST

Joel Coen, 1954 and Ethan Coen, 1957, Directors, Producers, Screenwriters

Blood Simple, 1984

Raising Arizona, 1987

Miller's Crossing, 1990

Barton Fink, 1991

The Hudsucker Proxy, 1994

Fargo, 1996

The Big Lebowski, 1998

O Brother, Where Art Thou?, 2000

The Man Who Wasn't There, 2001

Intolerable Cruelty, 2003

The Ladykillers, 2004

Paris, je t'aime, 2006 (segment: Tuileries)

No Country for Old Men, 2007

Burn After Reading, 2008

Barry Sonnenfield, 1953, Director of Photography

Blood Simple, 1984

Raising Arizona, 1987

Throw Momma From The Train, 1987

Big, 1988

When Harry Met Sally, 1989

Miller's Crossing, 1990

Misery, 1990

As Director

Addams Family, 1991

Addams Family Values, 1993

Get Shorty, 1995

Men in Black, 1997

Wild Wild West, 1999

Men in Black II, 2002

Nicholas Cage, 1964, Actor

Rumble Fish, 1983

The Cotton Club, 1984

Birdy, 1984

Peggy Sue Got Married, 1986

Raising Arizona, 1987

Moonstruck, 1987

Wild at Heart, 1990

Leaving Las Vegas, 1995

The Rock, 1996

Con Air, 1997

Face/Off, 1997

City of Angels, 1998

8MM, 1999

Bringing out the Dead, 1999

Captain Corelli's Mandolin, 2001

Adaptation, 2002

Matchstick Men, 2003

Lord of War, 2005

World Trade Center, 2006

The Wicker Man, 2006

Ghost Rider, 2007

Holly Hunter, 1958, Actress

Raising Arizona, 1987

Broadcast News, 1987

Miss Firecracker, 1989

Always, 1989

Once Around, 1991

The Piano, 1993

The Firm, 1993

Copycat, 1995

Home for the Holidays, 1995

Crash, 1996

A Life Less Ordinary, 1997

Timecode, 2000

O Brother, Where Art Thou?, 2000

Thirteen, 2003

LINKS TO OTHER FILMS

Bringing Up Baby (1938)/ *Sullivan's Travels* (1941)

Howard Hawks (*Baby*) and Preston Sturges (*Travels*) were leading exponents of the screwball comedy in the late 1930s and 1940s; the fast-paced storylines, full of slapstick comedy and quick-fire witticisms, are something of a generic template for *Raising Arizona*. Both male protagonists resemble Hi, as they are plunged into a series of surreal situations with a variety of eccentric characters.

It's Alive (1974)

Larry Cohen's horror film depicts a monstrous baby terrorising and killing those around him. There is an echo of this in the scene when Hi kidnaps Nathan Jr.; the scene is comic but the menacing music and Hi's terrified reaction to the drooling babies is a comic transposition of *It's Alive*'s brutal storyline.

Mad Max (1979)

The character of Leonard Smalls looks as if he has come straight out of this film. It is a post-apocalypse thriller directed by George Miller. Smalls' costume, motorbike and brutality mirror those of the bloodthirsty and amoral characters from *Mad Max* in a society disintegrating as lawlessness takes control.

Blood Simple (1984)

Joel and Ethan Coen's debut shares many stylistic features with *Raising Arizona*; its frenetic camerawork and use of disorientating visuals also pre-echo their later comedy. It has a labyrinthine plot which involves a husband's attempts to have his wife killed, the beginning of a long line of brutal acts and miscommunication. Although a neo-noir thriller it also contains moments of dark humour which connect the two films.

Evil Dead II (1987)

Sam Raimi's film is full of fast-paced visuals and dark humour, similar to that of *Raising Arizona*. Raimi and the Coen Brothers have similar visual motifs and approaches to film-making, perhaps partially due to the fact they all lived together in the early part of their careers; Joel worked on the original *Evil Dead* film in 1981, and both brothers co-wrote Raimi's 1985 film, *Crimewave*.

REPRESENTATION

Prison

Prison, and prison life, have been represented in numerous ways by film-makers; the brutality of Alan Parker's *Midnight Express* (1978), or the frustration and obsession to escape in Robert Bresson's *A Man Escaped* (1956), Franklin J. Schaffner's *Papillion* (1973), Don Siegel's *Escape from Alcatraz* (1979) and Frank Darabont's *The Shawshank Redemption* (1994). It has even been represented using magic realism, again by Frank Darabont in *The Green Mile* (1999), the hyper-real nature of which has some links with *Raising Arizona* and its prison world.

The opening section of the film shows a series of repeated scenes where Hi is continually returned to prison as a repeat offender. Prison life is seen as repetitive and initially something that is almost reassuring for Hi: the initial mug shot and fingerprinting, the snarling inmate who constantly mops the prison floor, the cellmate's endless stories, the group psychiatry sessions and the parole board meetings.

The representation is humorous, but also indicative of both the repetitiveness of prison life and how it can institutionalise the individual. This aspect, and its dehumanising effect, is perfectly conveyed in the opening to Sam Peckinpah's *The Getaway* (1972), where Doc McCoy is ground down by the reductive nature of the prison's routines, a montage of images that eventually push Steve McQueen's character into near-insanity.

Doc McCoy is almost crushed, but Hi seems to embrace prison as a necessary and comforting part of his life. Only when he begins to see beyond this life is this cycle broken. Rather than being a passive presence in this ongoing routine, he becomes active and disrupts another criminal's arrest processing to propose to Ed. Hi has now moved out of the reductive cycle which he is beginning to find a growing constraint. The prison is also seen as a place of restraint and reassurance in regards to Gale and Evelle; their emergence from the prison is like a birth as they squeeze out of the oozing mud. But if the prison forms these two and releases them into the outside world (even if they think that they are escaping), it is to the prison that they return at the end of the film. The image of the two convicts climbing back into the 'womb' reiterates the notion of prison as a place of security, both for those on the outside, and inside.

> 'Raising Arizona *is a turbulent, high-speed cartoon, laced with surreal effects, which quotes liberally from all sorts of popular genres, mixes them together and stands back in amazement to observe the result.'* Ulrich Kriest, *Joel & Ethan Coen*, Eds. Peter Körte and Georg Seesslen, Titan Books, 1999

KEY SCENE TEXTUAL ANALYSIS

A robbery and a chase (10)

After breaking his foreman's nose on a picnic for making lewd suggestions regarding his wife, Hi argues with Ed about the incident while driving. They stop and he tells her that he is going to buy some Huggies for their baby.

Hi gets out of the car and we have a low angle shot of him. The reflection in the car reads 'Short Stop', the name of the shop and the tilt upwards reveals the sign clearly above him. From earlier in the film the audience knows that this has been the favourite target for Hi in his previous life as a robber of convenience stores, and so our expectation of mayhem is raised.

A cut to a close-up of boxes of pantyhose and the diegetic muzak immediately creates a blandly surreal atmosphere.

Hi violently grabs one of these boxes, plus a pack of nappies, and then pulls a gun out of the waistband of his trousers, all rapidly edited together to multiple effect: the rapid montage resembles but parodies numerous such montages where a soldier, criminal or police-officer arms themselves to dramatic effect. The items in this case - pantyhose, Huggies - undermine any hard-bitten edge. Also, the close-up of Hi's waist emphasises the character's lack of style: his cream coloured trousers, elasticated belt, brown jacket and weave polo shirt are the antithesis of 'cool'.

The ultra-ordinary *mise-en-scène* throughout this sequence only adds to the sense of lunacy; there is the obvious slapstick but also small details, such as the vignettes of characters and their environs that are intended to capture the audience's eye.

The first of these is the young, spotty shop assistant who we first see as the camera tracks in on him. Red and yellow ties the whole frame together (sign on the wall, the counter, sticker on cash register in foreground, his jacket, t-shirt, hat and even the masthead of the porn magazine he is reading): it connotes both the gaudiness of youth and the blandness of consumerism.

The long shot of Hi shows his 'casual' style to full effect, now made even more ridiculous by the pantyhose on his head to disguise himself. The frame is also busy with the mundane trappings of domestic life and the muzak plays throughout, adding its own ironic commentary on the proceedings.

The line, 'I'll be taking these Huggies, and whatever cash you got' (with nonchalant shrug) complete the picture of disruption within a recognisably 'normal' – if hyperbolically realised – setting.

The medium shot of Ed in the car again reiterates the normality of the scene; the battered brown car and mother reading a story to her 'son', waiting for dad to return. The slow move towards her indicates the gradual change to her world as she hears sirens and eventually looks up to see Hi in action.

Her POV is a long shot in order to frame both the ordinary and the extraordinary within it; Hi's gun-spinning flourish adding to the comic effect.

Ed's repetition of 'That son of a bitch' cuts to Hi inside clutching the nappies, waiting for the assistant to finish packing his 'groceries'. After he sees Ed getting into the driver's seat he bobs up and down like someone waiting impatiently in a queue.

The car then reverses towards the camera with screeching tyres to really capture our attention. This leads into a fast zoom which wildly careers towards Hi as Ed drives off. The movement anticipates the excitement to come and the madly dangerous position into which he is now plunged; his moronic expression, emphasised by his farcical

toting officer sitting on the door frame; the comic excess of gunplay begins here and never ceases until the end of the sequence.

As Hi runs towards the camera it tracks away from him, suggesting his desire for refuge, and both the assistant and officer fire indiscriminately. The non-diegetic music adds to the slapstick with its maniacal country and western banjo and yodelling. Hi transfers the Huggies from under one arm to the other in another of those ordinary gestures in a chaotic world.

The medium shot of the officer hanging out of the window of his patrol car firing repeatedly is pure insanity, but perhaps a sideways swipe at gun culture in the US. Indeed, there are many images of guns being wielded in this manner throughout the

disguise, accentuates the pathos. In one direction comes the police and then, to complicate matters, a gun shot hits the glass door by his head. A reverse shot from within the shop tracks towards him; the Furies, as depicted by these camera moves closing in on him, are gathering.

While Hi's filmic space contracts, that of the shop assistant suddenly expands with his new power. The camera tracks away from him to reveal a massive handgun, further enlarged by its extreme, distorted close-up at the movement's end point. The audience is also treated to a few more details about him; it says 'Whitey' on his shop jacket, matching his almost albino colouring, and with his dark eyes he presents a fairly ugly spectacle. His menacingly gleeful grin reveals his braced teeth, complementing his spotty, pock-mocked skin. He is a teenager who gets his kicks from 'Juggs' magazine and firing oversized guns, a delinquent Dirty Harry.

The police car now approaches, sporting a gun-

film (and derogatory references to the incumbent president, Ronald Reagan). This sequence depicts a cartoonish level of gun play, which perhaps has an underlying message, albeit buried deep beneath the predominantly comic agenda.

After the nappies are shot out of his hand, Hi stoops to get them but is thwarted by another shot. He jumps up into frame, the leg part of the panty-hose comically springing up, momentarily making him resemble the frightened rabbit that he has obviously become, and perhaps again invoking the cartoonish violence of Bugs Bunny.

After he has jumped the fence the POV shows us a garden with darkness at its edge. The cessation of the music indicates that danger lurks beyond our view. In medium shot Hi is positioned to the edge of frame. He uncovers his face and stares into the space left within the frame, towards what might be a new threat. First there is a growl, then a hound leaps from the darkness. A wide angle, low-level tracking shot gives, unexpectedly, the *dog's* POV, and elicits both horror and comedy, two elements that are often bedfellows in the Coen Brothers' films.

The close-up of the dog snapping inches from Hi's face is both heart-stopping and comic. Layer upon layer of slapstick and incredible moments pepper the rest of the sequence in a manner that combines cutting-edge contemporary film-making with old style silent slapstick. The camerawork takes full advantage of light cameras and the ability to move them in energetic and unusual ways, but the comic heritage is pure Keystone cops. As Hi runs, the music revives, indicating that the threat from the vicious hound has abated.

Cute babies are not neglected, even during all these gun battles (this is the era of *3 Men and a Baby*

A few shots later Whitey, the shop assistant returns and it is the camerawork which constructs the comedy: a speeded-up tracking shot towards him as he fires at the van is repeated, coupled with a slowed-down tracking shot up close. It is both disorientating and adrenalin-pumping, just as it might be in the real situation. But it is also comic; the dogs bundling him over from the left of frame compounds the mayhem, as does the van driver's incessant screaming which is repeated as they nearly hit the police car and stop just short of a house.

The speeded-up shot of police car chasing the van, with gun booming like a cannon, is knowingly artificial, a device unseen since 1970's Bond movies. Here it parodies violence and car chases; there has

[1987] and *Look Who's Talking* [1989], after all), and we see the kidnapped baby reacting with amusing anxiety to the gun fire and Ed's increasingly dangerous driving. The baby will undergo all sorts of trials before the film is over, not least being left on the bonnet of a car whose occupants have just committed a bank robbery.

As Hi returns to the road he is run down whilst trying to stop a van; it's the kind of thing that would happen to Laurel or Hardy, and although this is executed with a modern brutality, the slapstick result is the same - Hi is unharmed.

Hi jumps into the van, just, and a low angle shot shows it screech off into the distance. This is mirrored by another low angle shot of the dog, now loose on the road. The former prepares us for the latter as we embark on a journey with the massing of the dogs, given equal importance as the human characters by shooting them at their level. They have the same rights as any other character in this mad world.

been a succession of films ever since *Bullitt* in 1968 that tried to top *that* car chase with Steve McQueen, and this pulls out all the stops to reveal the comic side to such undertakings, where the participants are the antithesis of the cool McQueen.

The braking of the van catapults Hi onto the lawn in comic fashion and even gives him time to emit a winded 'thank you' to the driver. The wide angle steadicam shots following Hi, and then the officer, are designed to show as much of their mundane surroundings as possible; children playing and adults watching television are briefly glimpsed as if in some high-octane fly-on-the-wall documentary. There are no reaction shots and the juxtaposition between ordinary and bizarre is pronounced.

We next see Hi running towards a brightly-lit supermarket, a few loose trolleys and parked cars signifying normality and routine, with the prominent, and banal, banner proclaiming 'Double Coupons', suggesting a world of consumerist 'excitement' inside. Cutting back to the house that Hi passed, we see the dogs careering through the domestic world.

Back in the supermarket the non-diegetic music is gone and the mind-numbing muzak returns. Not forgetting his paternal duties, Hi again grabs a pack of Huggies just as the non-diegetic music – and the madness – return and the officer fires a shot destroying part of a shelf display near his head. As Hi runs, or jogs (because jogging fits the atmosphere of insanity) down the aisle, the officer continues to fire, irrespective of the threat to bystanders.

Hi's POV reveals the supermarket is populated only by hair-rollered ladies, dressed in a range of gaudy colours, now screaming; the living dead revived like extras from George A. Romero's *Dawn of the Dead* (1978). The dogs arrive and further chaos ensues; they are again treated to tracking shots on their level (never has so much dignity been afforded dogs since the *Lassie* films).

Running down another aisle, a shop display is blasted, this time by yet another over-zealous employee with a shotgun. He is standing on a raised platform, like some fortified castle, and the touches of the little hygiene hat compared to his bulky frame, and the 'Thank you for shopping' sign behind him, reinforce the wildly incongruous nature of the moment. The cut, back to Hi's pained expression, sits well within this comedy of the absurd. As he runs back down the aisle the products explode with ferocity, the sound of the shotgun amplified for comic effect. It is fast becoming an idealist's dream of the destruction of consumerism, a comic companion to Antonioni's *Zabriskie Point* (1970). The excessive cartoon destruction again sniffs around the leg of, but does not care to meditate on, a social commentary about gun culture.

Hi then throws his bag of nappies at a police officer about to shoot; the lawman is comically despatched by a demented shopper who pushes him away with her trolley. The slapstick of the moment is enhanced by the shot of the woman from the trolley, her pink hair curlers and matching clothes further highlighting the situation's absurdity.

The camera again tracks towards Hi (as it did when he was deserted at the beginning of the sequence),

but this time it brings salvation through Ed's return in the car. The repetition of this shot brings the adventure through the twilight zone of after-hours domesticity and urban life to an end. The music stops as he is reunited with his family, but there is still one punch in the face to come and the scene ends with Hi directing Ed back to the Huggies as she lectures him about his irresponsible behaviour.

The final shot starts down low at the level of the nappies and then cranes high as Hi scoops them up and they drive into the distance. The camera moves and escapes the pull of this neighbourhood and its assorted freaks, mirroring Hi, Ed and Nathan Junior's escape from its suburban grasp.

Delicatessen

KEY FACTS

Release Date: 1990

Country of Origin: France

Running Time: 95 minutes

PRODUCTION NOTES

Production Companies

Sofinergie Films

Sofinergie 2

Investimage 2

Investimage 3

Fondation GAN pour le Cinéma

Constellation

Hachette Première

Union Générale Cinématographique (UGC)

Victoires Productions

Distributor

Miramax Films (USA)

Awards

Nominated: Best Film not in the English Language
Claudie Ossard Jean-Pierre Jeunet Marc Caro
BAFTA Awards, UK

Won: Best Editing (Meilleur montage) Hervé
Schneid César Awards, France

Best First Work (Meilleure première oeuvre) Marc
Caro Jean-Pierre Jeunet César Awards, France

Best Production Design (Meilleurs décors) Jean-
Philippe Carp Miljen Kreka Kljakovic César Awards,
France

Best Writing - Original or Adaptation (Meilleur
scénario, original ou adaptation) Gilles Adrien Marc
Caro Jean-Pierre Jeunet César Awards, France

SYNOPSIS

The story begins with a landlord, who is also a
homicidal butcher who kills people for meat to sell
to his tenants, killing a man who is trying to escape
in a trash can from a dilapidated tenement block.
The setting is a post-apocalyptic world where food,

especially meat, is in short supply. Louison, an unemployed clown, arrives into this nightmarish world looking for a job. He is hired as a handyman but it is obvious that the butcher intends to kill him for food. In the apartment Louison meets an assortment of odd people who rely on the butcher for both their board and their meat, and who turn a blind eye to his actions. Louison and the butcher's daughter, Julie, start to fall in love so that when the butcher decides to kill Louison she solicits help from an underground movement known as the 'Les Troglodistes', a vegetarian-eating group of freedom fighters. The butcher and the inhabitants of the tenement trap Louison and Julie in a bathroom but they escape by flooding the room and the rest of the apartment. The butcher is killed and the couple escape.

HISTORICAL CONTEXT

The 1990s saw France consolidate its position as a major force in the European Union, forging closer links with Germany in particular. It was not only in politics that co-operation proliferated; film-making in Europe became more collaborative and a number of critical and commercial successes such as *Nikita* (1990), Damage (1992), the *Three Colours* trilogy (1993/4) and *La Haine* (1995) were financed from a variety of countries.

France was a central force in this collaborative process and continued to build on its formidable tradition of film-making, and the French public's appetite for indigenous films as well as imports from across the Atlantic. Although Francois Truffaut had died in 1985 and Jean-Luc Godard's career was waning, the 1990s shone with directorial prowess. Jean-Paul Rappeneau (*Cyrano de Bergerac*, 1990), Luc Besson (*Nikita*, 1990; *Leon*, 1994; *The Fifth Element*, 1997), and many of the great French directors of old were still working, including Jacques Rivette, Louis Malle, Eric Rohmer, Bertrand Tavernier and Claude Chabrol. It was into this fertile atmosphere that Jeunet and Caro began their careers, with *Delicatessen* standing as an early example of their particular angle on French cinema, which has always prided itself on its ability to tell stories with flair and great imagination.

From the early days of cinema, French films have always held a fascination with worldwide audiences. Jean Vigo, Marcel Carné, Jean Renoir, Francois Truffaut, Jean-Luc Godard, Luc Besson *et al* have produced works notable for their visual flair and innovative approach to storytelling. *Delicatessen* maintained this tradition, its origins recalling the visuals of *L'Atalante* (1934), *La Grande Illusion* (1937), *Les Enfants du Paradis* (1945), *Fahrenheit 451* (1966), *Weekend* (1967) and *Nikita*. Caro and Jeunet's film has all the conventions of a cult film (offbeat characters and narrative and stylised visuals, for example), and it became a worldwide success. Of course, cult success does not always translate into a mass audience, and the film ultimately has a following amongst film enthusiasts rather than the wider populace. As a French, rather elliptical, take on the future it is the sort of film that polarises opinion and its appeal is akin to Terry Gilliam's obtuse visions in *Time Bandits* (1981) and *Brazil* (1985).

Another source of the film's popularity is its non-verbal and physical comedy, reminiscent of Jacques Tati's work in *Mon Oncle*, which in turn owes a debt to the comedies of the Hollywood silent and early sound era. This imbues *Delicatessen* with its timeless and universal appeal; think Mr. Bean but with more bite - and cannibals.

FILMOGRAPHY OF MAIN PRODUCERS AND CAST

Jean-Pierre Jeunet, 1953, Director, Screenwriter

Delicatessen, 1991

The City of Lost Children, 1995

Alien: Resurrection, 1997

Amélie, 2001

A Very Long Engagement, 2004

Marc Caro, 1956, Director, Screenwriter

Delicatessen, 1991

The City of Lost Children, 1995

Dante 01, 2008

Dominique Pinon, 1955, Actor

Diva, 1981

The Moon in the Gutter, 1983

Ghost Dance, 1983

Betty Blue, 1986

Delicatessen, 1991

My Name is Victor, 1993

The City of Lost Children, 1995

Alien: Resurrection, 1997

Amélie, 2001

A Very Long Engagement, 2004

The Bridge of San Luis Rey, 2004

Roman de Gare, 2007

LINKS TO OTHER FILMS

Brazil (1985)

This Terry Gilliam film and others (*The Fisher King* [1991], *The Brothers Grimm* [2005]), have the same style of film-making as Jeunet and Caro's film; they are filled with elaborate visual treats and conundrums, while the narratives/characters are often surreal creations with fantastical happenings in ordinary surroundings (see pg. 365).

The Cook, the Thief, His Wife and Her Lover (1989)

Peter Greenaway's film ends with the Wife forcing her husband, the Thief, to eat the cooked remains of her Lover after the husband has brutally murdered him. Although this does not sound like the ingredients for a black comedy, it is a savage social satire on Thatcherite Britain and has many darkly comic moments.

The City of Lost Children (1995)

A dystopian story that shares a number of similarities with Jeunet and Caro's other work, both in its narrative thrust of a vaguely familiar, but surreal, world and its innovative visual flair.

Fargo (1996)/*The Big Lebowski* (1998)

These two Coen Brothers films intertwine the ordinary world with events and characters that are often bizarre or eccentric, mixing brutality and comedy in the same way as *Delicatessen*.

Ravenous (1999)

A black comedy directed by Antonia Bird which has cannibalism at the forefront of its story. Set in nineteenth century America in a remote outpost of the US Army, it is brutal, but darkly humorous as it charts a soldier's descent into cannibalism.

Amélie (2001)

One of Jeunet's solo directing efforts, this is characteristically dreamlike and bizarre, detailing the kind of characters that are drawn in *Delicatessen*, the misfits and dreamers who exist on the fringes of society.

REPRESENTATION

Post-apocalypse

The post-apocalypse film is regularly filled with death, brutality and the chaos of a society plunged into a nightmarish vision of humanity, bereft of morality and seemingly intent on complete self-extermination. George Miller's *Mad Max* series (1979, 1982, 1985) details a world where life has a low value; a similar representation is shown in Kevin Reynold's *Waterworld* (1995) and later in Kevin Costner's *The Postman* (1997).

Strange, almost surreal futures are encountered in films such as Franklin J. Schaffner's *Planet of the Apes* (1968) and Boris Sagal's *The Omega Man* (1971), the latter representing earth with a group of albino mutants, whilst the former posits a future where apes evolve from the ashes of an apocalyptic war between humans. In *Delicatessen* the post-apocalypse world looks like the 1950s; its fading tenement building, the clothes that the characters wear and the superficial sensibilities of a more austere and polite era belie the fact that this is a nightmarish vision of the future. The sense of dislocation from civilised society (a thing of the past in this film) is amplified by the darkness and/or fog that seem perpetually to isolate this apartment building. It is reminiscent of one of the segments of the portmanteau horror film, *The Monster Club* (1980) where a village, shrouded in fog, devours all who are ensnared within its boundaries.

But for all the dismal *mise-en-scène* and the rationing of meat (which also reflects the post-Second World War ambience), *Delicatessen* represents this nightmare vision in darkly comic ways. Where violence and chaos are the focus in other such films, here it is often the hilarity and surreal nature of everyday life in contrast to the macabre events that bubble under the surface. It is a snapshot of human spirit and self-interest when coping with disaster - the best and worst of humanity.

'Creatively combining genres - post-apocalyptic sci-fi, black comedy, and sweet romance - and offering audiences an impressively oddball collection of sounds, colours, actors, and images.' Steven Jay Schneider, *1001 Movies You Must See Before You Die*, Cassell Illustrated, 2007

'The sets, special effects, photography, pace and performances all contribute to the brash comic-strip vivacity, and even the fairytale romance avoids sentimentality.' Geoff Andrew, *Time Out Film Guide 14th Ed.*, Time Out Guides Ltd., London, 2006

KEY SCENE TEXTUAL ANALYSIS

A symphony of life (3)

Much of the film's comedy emanates from its minutely detailed *mise-en-scène*. The apartment block has a 1940s austere and ramshackle style; the future, it seems, has propelled society back into its past. All is plain and dour; the drabness of the walls can be seen in the first shot of Louison painting the ceiling with yet more brown paint. His mismatched clothes contrast with his surroundings, particularly the red jumper adorned

with images of elephants, a symbol of his circus background and flights of fancy.

The cut from this banal activity to a close-up of the butcher and his wife making love is jarring, as are his animal-like grunts, as if he were devouring her. The soft lighting of the couple contrasts with the butcher's animal passion. The audience is forced right into his world, a world that we have seen is bestial. The creaking bed acts as a comic juxtaposition to his amorous intentions. The shot of the underside of the bed's springs and the accompanying straining sound suggests the contrast between the matinée idol image of himself and the comic reality of his unsavoury personality.

The long shot of Louison reveals his inventive nature, braces utilised to aid his painting. He creates his own comic universe, absurd but harmonious, whereas the butcher's universe is comically undermined. The return to creaking bed is juvenile humour, yes, but it also makes the link, rhythmically, between these two worlds.

The camera tracks along the floor and then down the wood burner into Julie's room; the unusual route that it takes mirrors the quirky perspective that this film adopts on its protagonists; it examines the underbelly of humanity in all its madness, grotesqueness and eccentricity. It also pre-empts the way the vegetarian freedom fighters will crawl around the dark recesses and bowels of the building later in the film.

Julie's prim, frilly dress, cardigan and glasses contrast with the lustful abandonment that is going on above. However, the sound of the repeated chords, as she moves up the scale, starts to match the rhythm of the sexual act; *her* passion is between her and the cello. The cut back to the creaking springs again connects the two acts with the increasing speed, adding to the comic value of the moment.

The sound of the springs is grating, but now has a humorous musical accompaniment. The sound of a woman beating a mat joins the ensemble - the low angled shot of her will allow for a gradual zoom in as the passion rises. The cluttered *mise-en-scène* is dominated by the colour brown and the twisting staircase into which she seems lodged, trapped by her domestic duty and petty frustrations. The low angle may signal that she will become empowered by the expelling of her frustrations through her attack on the mat. It is also a shot which is typical of a film that looks askance at even the most mundane of actions.

The gentle diegetic music of the next scene again adds playful humour to the growing number of contributors to the apartment's musical awakening; knitting needles and a bicycle pump join the band, the very banality of the actions helping to transfigure them into something which is part of a greater picture.

The *mise-en-scène* here, as in the cellist's room, is one of extreme ordinariness and the participants are surrounded by the trappings of domestic life: the television (the programme they are watching

when placed within this context of everyday objects transformed by their chance harmony.

The close-up of the metronome, the tyre being pumped up and Louison painting are all tilted and form a montage. Their juxtaposition starts to suggest a meaning beyond their banality and functionality, a meaning of possibilities, of connections beyond the ordinary, each new object adding a rich texture all its own.

The two men downstairs who make the cow noise novelty items now enter the improvised concert. Again, the *mise-en-scène*, the room and their movements are dowdy and repetitive, but they become sublime and even more comic when placed within their new universe of the absurd. As the pace quickens again, with the springs starting to pound, the audience is perhaps relieved that it is spared

seems to cut in time with the rhythm of the outside world), the goldfish bowl, trophies, the dresser, and even the same elaborate beating implement that the woman is using outside. The link between the banal and absurd is repeated here as these two characters are unwittingly part of an erotic symphony. The tilted angle of the camera and the cluttered *mise-en-scène* also help to underpin the message of the surreal embedded within everyday life.

As the pace of the rhythm quickens, the frames become tighter, mirroring the rising levels of passion. The return to the cellist sees a much tighter frame than before, then it is back to the bed springs, rusty and ugly, mocking the act that is going on above them. The fact that the camera stays with the springs, and not the figures above, reduces the couple's act to a farcical level. The woman on the stairs is also shown in a tighter shot as her rate increases; the close-up of the beating implement conveys an absurd eroticism

the sight of the monstrous butcher at work.

Louison is shown at an angle, this time exaggerating the precarious position that he is in. The film is also speeded up, referencing back to the days of early film comedy and its use of slapstick humour. The cut to a face-on shot of Louison is another image which adds to the eccentricity of the sequence, as he moves towards and away from the camera in earnest endeavour.

The wide-angle close-up of the knitting grandmother, with the sound of the needles clashing like swords, incongruously connects her with the world outside: would she be outraged or pleased to be connected with this rhythm?

Images start to pass in rapid succession as the beat gathers to a frenetic pace. Everything and everyone in the building now seem inexorably linked to the sexual act; the speeded-up metronome and rapid playing, pumping and beating are indicators of the sexual climatic moment to come.

But it is not just those within the diegetic world of the film who Jeunet and Caro want to be consumed by the frantic rhythm, it is also the audience. The shot of the metronome is not static because they want us to feel the dizzying sensation that is enveloping all these characters. This sense of the camera being implicated into the rhythm is repeated with the speeded up track towards and away from Louison as he continues to paint.

Only at the moment of climax do we return *above* the bed, and it is not a pretty sight. We cannot even see the woman in the frame; instead, it is the butcher's contorted face as he climaxes in close-up, a look and sound of bestial pleasure, returning us to the image and sound of his love-making that we saw near the beginning of the sequence. The image is repellent, the absence of a female presence emphasising the selfishness of

of their connectivity and juxtaposition. Sex, for a moment, inhabits all their lives, however mundane.

his pleasure and alienating him further from the audience.

As the butcher ululates, the pace of editing reaches its peak and we see everyone climaxing in their own way: the exploding tyre, the snapping string and the falling painter (the framing allowing him to fall towards us, again drawing the audience into the film world). The final image returns us to the grotesque: the close-up of the butcher's face, contorted and unpleasantly relieved. The final short, tiny gasp from the woman perhaps indicates further the selfishness of his act and the comedy of the moment.

Throughout this sequence the grim post-apocalyptic environment is constantly undercut by the comedy and banality of life. All the characters are bound together; good and bad, the ridiculous and the sublime. The rhythm of their movements unites them all, woven together in a patchwork of absurdity, given comic meaning by a montage

Shaun of the Dead

KEY FACTS

Release Date: 2004

Country of Origin: UK

Running Time: 95 minutes

PRODUCTION NOTES

Production Companies

Studio Canal

Working Title Films

WT2 Productions

Big Talk Productions

Inside Track 2

FilmFour

Distributors

Rogue Pictures

Focus Features

Budget

$4,000,000 (estimated)

Awards

Nominated: Alexander Korda Award for Best British Film Nira Park Edgar Wright BAFTA Awards, UK

Nominated: Carl Foreman Award for the Most Promising Newcomer Nira Park (producer) BAFTA Awards, UK

Won: Peter Sellers Award for Comedy Simon Pegg Evening Standard British Film Awards

SYNOPSIS

The eponymous hero, Shaun, is in a dead-end job at an electrical store, living a mundane and repetitive life which revolves around his local pub, The Winchester, and his best friend, Ed, a layabout, and non-paying lodger at Shaun's house. The only positive aspect of his existence is his girlfriend, Liz, who he is in danger of losing if he continues wasting his life. After forgetting to book a table at a restaurant for their anniversary, Liz ends the relationship. Shaun resolves to change his life, but is sidetracked by the appearance of zombies the next morning. He and Ed dispatch two zombies in their garden and barely escape their 'zombified' flatmate, Pete. They drive to Shaun's mother and stepfather in order to save them, but his stepfather has already been bitten; his 'zombification' is inevitable. They then 'rescue' Liz and her friends, Dianne and David.

Their plan is to go to The Winchester pub and wait until 'it all blows over'. En route, they have to leave the car when Shaun's stepfather turns into a zombie, but they still manage to make it to the pub on foot. In the pub they have to fend off the landlord, Shaun's mother is killed when she turns into a zombie, and both David and Dianne are eventually killed by the hordes of zombies outside. Liz, Shaun and Ed, who has been bitten, retreat to the cellar and await their fate. They discover a way out to the street and leave Ed behind; on street level the zombies are about to overcome them when the army arrives and saves the couple.

The final part of the story shows that Shaun has converted Liz to his old ways now that they are living together, sitting and relaxing in front of the television with plans to go to the pub. The zombie threat is now over, with the zombies employed in menial jobs. Before going out Shaun joins Ed, now a zombie and chained up in his shed, for their favourite pastime - playing on a computer game.

HISTORICAL CONTEXT

By the time the noughties had arrived there seemed to be little scope for development in any aspect of cultural life; everything had been deconstructed and exposed to the full glare of media coverage. Artist Damian Hirst had exhibited animals preserved in formaldehyde in the 1990s and noughties, and Tracy Emin had displayed her bed and its contents as the Millennium was about to dawn; these were all presented as works of art, both praised and derided in equal measure.

As for film, the ongoing love affair between Hollywood and fantasy/sci-fi blockbusters continued, and the production of sequels usually ensured the laws of diminishing quality were maintained. Most genres had been ransacked with numerous permutations; genre cross-fertilisation had brought previously polar genres together and

staple genres had been thoroughly deconstructed. The parody has become a modern staple: *Blazing Saddles* (1974) lampooned the Western; as we have seen, *Young Frankenstein* tried it with classic horror in the same year, and *Airplane!* parodied the disaster films of the 1970s.

Increasing numbers of films have parodied every possible genre in the past 20 years, most notably The *Naked Gun* series (police thrillers), the *Hot Shots!* series (action) and the *Scary Movie* series (horror and other genres). It is into this context that *Shaun of the Dead* emerged in 2004; not, then, a radical departure from current parody trends but different in that it is a British perspective on a predominately North American genre, and both celebrates and parodies the zombie film. It seems also to be more of a homage than parody (with George A. Romero's films as a particular focus), and its real affection for its source material elevates it above other contemporary examples. Its tagline – 'A Romantic Comedy with Zombies' – underlines the sense of self-deprecation and desire to both debunk and revel in genre conventions, marrying genres in an unexpected and knowing way.

Working Title, the production company behind *Shaun of the Dead*, has been a powerful force behind British film-making since 1985 with its debut feature film release, Stephen Frear's *My Beautiful Launderette*. The company's work with the Coen brothers on films including *Barton Fink*, *Fargo* and *Burn After Reading* (2008) has marked it as one that views the film industry with a global perspective rather than purely a British focus.

This approach is typified by its distribution agreement with Universal Pictures (now a majority shareholder), ensuring its films a strong foothold in North America, and its penchant for the romantic comedy genre (usually with a big female American star in the cast) with films such as *Notting Hill* (1991), *Bridget Jones' Diary* (2001) and *Love Actually* (2003).

However, it not just the 'romcom' genre that sustains the company, rather its ability to diversify its output. Not only does it make identifiably 'culturally British' films - *About a Boy* (2002), *Pride and Prejudice* (2005) and *Atonement* (2007) - but it matches Hollywood with 'Americanised' films, even tackling issues such as the 9/11 attacks with its 2006 film, *United 93*.

SELECT FILMOGRAPHY OF MAIN PRODUCERS AND CAST

Edgar Wright, 1974, Director, Screenwriter

A Fistful of Fingers, 1994

Shaun of the Dead, 2004

Hot Fuzz, 2007

Grindhouse (trailer segment 'Don't'), 2007

Simon Pegg, 1970, Actor, Screenwriter

Guest House Paradiso, 1999

Shaun of the Dead, 2004

Mission: Impossible III, 2006

Big Nothing, 2006

The Good Night, 2007

Hot Fuzz, 2007

Grindhouse, 2007

Run, Fat Boy, Run, 2007

How to Lose Friends and Alienate People, 2008

LINKS TO OTHER FILMS

Blazing Saddles (1974)

Like *Shaun of the Dead*, Mel Brooks' film not only parodies but effectively employs the dominant genre's (Western) conventions to comic effect. Both films have less of the broad brushstroke comedy that is found in other parodies such as the *Scary Movie* series, but co-exist as both parodies and exponents of the genre conventions at the same time.

Dawn of the Dead (1978)

This is the zombie film that directly influences *Shaun of the Dead*, although it also draws from George A. Romero's other zombie films. *Dawn of the Dead*'s combination of grisly killings and social commentary (much of the film takes place in a deserted shopping mall under attack from zombie hordes) are echoed in *Shaun of the Dead*, although the latter is more concerned with the comic value of both techniques.

Slacker (1991)/*Clerks* (1994)

These low-budget films, directed by Richard Linklater and Kevin Smith respectively, have the sort of characters upon which Ed and Shaun are based, young people who are directionless, yet content to live in worlds that are based on the premise of not taking life too seriously.

Hot Fuzz (2007)

This film, directed by Edgar Wright, again pairs Simon Pegg and Nick Frost, this time as police partners. Frost's character is very similar to Ed in *Shaun of the Dead*, but Pegg's character is the antithesis of the apathetic Shaun. The film, like its predecessor, both parodies and celebrates its source genre, in this case the action thriller.

REPRESENTATION

The buddy film

Film history is bursting with 'buddy films', generally a male friendship narrative that charts the changing fortunes of companions enduring hardship together and generally winning through. An early working of this formula is *Angels with Dirty Faces* (1938) where the James Cagney and Pat O'Brien characters begin as friends, but diverging interests (crime and religion respectively) draw them apart, only for them to be reunited at the film's climax.

Howard Hawks' *Rio Bravo* (1959) contains an uneasy friendship between disparate characters, a structure reworked in John Hughes' *Planes, Trains and Automobiles* (1987) and Martin Brest's *Midnight Run* (1988). Classic buddy pairings have centred on the Redford/Newman partnerships in *Butch Cassidy and the Sundance Kid* (1969) and *The Sting* (1973), a template for later films like the *Lethal Weapon* (1987–1998) and *Rush Hour* (1998–2007) series. Women have not been entirely neglected in this sub-genre, with films that attempt to wrestle men from this pedestal of free-wheeling independence and place the female experience on top; notable examples are Ridley Scott's *Thelma and Louise* (1991) and the Wachowski Brothers' *Bound* (1996).

There is often a fair degree of antagonism between the friends. *The Odd Couple* (1968) provides an early example of the love/hate buddy relationship narrative. *Shaun of the Dead* dips into the conventions of the buddy film and reworks the formula in the Simon Pegg/Edgar Wright follow-up, *Hot Fuzz* (2007). In the former's story of zombies we are presented with foul-mouthed, lazy, drunken Ed; however, his friendship with Shaun is pivotal to the narrative, counterpointing all the grisly action with a bond that provides both humour and a sense of reality and humanity amidst the comic carnage.

From the beginning, Ed is shown to be the more demanding of the two: he has no job, no money, he spends all day at home, does not contribute to the bills; in fact, he seems to be the devil on Shaun's shoulder. The bond between them is based on shared experience, on the sense of being completely at ease with each other. Ed cuts through pomposity and sentiment with his swearing and outspoken point of view; he is a mixture of man and infant, underlined by his child-like glee at driving Shaun's stepfather's car. He is one half of Shaun's personality, the desire to be free, devoid of responsibility (particularly in the form of his girlfriend, Liz). The friendship is one of a merged sense of anti-responsibility; the strain on the friendship comes when Shaun takes action and events spiral out of control.

However, when the friendship between David and Liz is juxtaposed with that of Ed and Shaun, it is clear that Ed's honest and direct approach to relationships is a much more positive force than David's pseudo-intellectual, pompous and devious manoeuvring. The final scene, with Liz now ensconced in the Ed role, confirms that this sort of approach is the most profitable, and inevitable. The fact that Ed is still part of the dynamic, albeit in a 'zombified' state, is a wry comment on the nature of friendships and points out that true friendships endure, even beyond the grave.

> '*The cast make a cosy fit, the patter is still sitcom snappy, but Wright also has the visual snap to carry this saga of backyard apocalypse.*' Nick Bradshaw, *Time Out Film Guide 14th Ed.*, Time Out Guides Ltd., London, 2006

> '*Pegg and Wright have crafted a meticulous plot and invested Shaun with so much anguished sincerity that we actually care whether or not he gets eaten by shambling fiends.*' Nicholas Barber, *The Independent*, 11th April, 2004

KEY SCENE TEXTUAL ANALYSIS

Title sequence (1)

This sets the tone for the rest of the film: staging mundane, everyday scenes and relating them to the zombie film sub-genre. The first part of the film presents a number of set-ups which show that, in our everyday lives, we already behave like zombies.

Here we see a man pushing shopping trolleys, checkout girls synchronised in their movements, people standing in a bus queue staring blankly into the distance or at their cell phones, others walking down the street in a choreographed zombie style, and a boy playing 'keepy-uppy' with his football.

All of these are seamless tracking shots. The result is a celluloid tapestry of the mundane routines of modern life and their already close connection with an undead existence. The non-diegetic music is quirky and upbeat, a sort of 1950's sci-fi track, and provides an ironic comment on the routine visuals. The dissolve to a pair of shuffling feet, one turned in, resembling the walk of a zombie, with a pan up to reveal the yawning hero, continues this series of zombie sight gags.

Two walks to the shop (4 & 11)

The first minute-long walk to the shop is a continuous steadicam shot, following Shaun through a familiar morning routine, almost entirely unaware of his surroundings or the people. It is the stuff of everyday life with the same people and rituals: boy playing football, the beggar, the man washing his car, the road sweeper and the shop owner. All of this monotony is encapsulated in one continuous take; it helps bind all the components together in one experience, just as Shaun would experience it.

The next walk to the shop and back home - which takes place the following morning - is all one take, approximately two minutes long. It is the same route with the same cars and some of the same people, but this time the diegetic sound is different.

Disco (30)

The group, comprising Shaun, Ed, Liz, David, Dianne and Shaun's mum, is surrounded by zombies at The Winchester pub. The camerawork here is reminiscent of both the horror and comedy genres. Initially, the camera prowls around the interior of the pub, matching the roving looks of the besieged as they realise that there are zombies all around them, their silhouettes occupying every window. Two shots indicate the mounting fear as Shaun clasps Liz's shoulder, then Ed touches Shaun's mum's shoulder. A third shot mirrors this as a hand grabs David's shoulder; this time it is for comic/ fright effect for it is the landlord's hand and he is now a zombie.

Throughout the sequence the horror and comedy are intertwined; what follows is a zombie music

Now car alarms are sounding and glass is heard being smashed instead of typical early morning street noise – but still Shaun does not notice. In fact, perhaps the film is saying the noises are not that unusual in such an environment after all (the film was shot in and around the suburbs of London); neither are some of the visuals: smashed windscreen, rubbish tipped out on the ground. Of course, there are differences: the zombies, the bloody handprints on the chilled cabinet from where Shaun gets his drink. As he nears the house, he is accosted by the beggar seen yesterday, this time with no dog at the end of his lead, and the boy's football lies on the ground by his gate. All are ominous signs, but the comic point suggests that we do not really notice our surroundings and the people with whom we co-exist, even in extreme circumstances.

video (for which there is a precedent; Michael Jackson's *Thriller* music video).

As they square up to the landlord, Queen's 'Don't Stop Me Now' starts playing on the jukebox and the rest of the sequence is synchronised to the diegetic music. The track into the jukebox, and the swinging pan back around to the group, are indicative of the fast-paced visuals throughout the film, both mimicking and parodying the action genre. These thrusting camera visuals are used throughout the film to depict the most mundane of circumstances, such as getting ready for work. As such, the film language used is at odds with the subject matter, thus setting up an ironic and comic counterpoint.

Once they decide on their weapons, after a whip pan to show the rifle and some edgy handheld or steadicam shots of Shaun, Liz and Ed, the *mise-en-scène* is pure action, borrowing from films like *Crouching Tiger, Hidden Dragon* (2003). The heightened sound of the pool cues whooshing through the air as Shaun throws them to his friends, and their stance, like ninjas with cues raised, is a parody of such films. It is entirely appropriate that the film, a hybrid genre film, should scavenge from other genres in this way to comment upon the disposable nature and short attention span of modern society.

The steadicam revolves around the three captives as they rain blows down onto the landlord's body with their cues, accentuating the energy of the action, and keeping in time with the music which has become up-tempo; this musical framing allows the violence to be cartoon-like. Shaun's elaborate swing of his legs in order to stand up after being thrown to the floor by the landlord is another intertextual reference to martial arts films.

David then runs through the bar and is followed close-in by a tracking camera conveying his panic as he tries to silence the music. The rapid cutting at this point matches the music and his urgency, but the montage of images also brings in the comic element as the next few shots begin to replicate the visuals of a music concert. As David flips the fuses the pub lights flash on and off. They illuminate the massed ranks of zombies waiting outside with arms outstretched, like young people adoring their musical heroes. The static long shot of the crowd is particularly effective at conveying the idea of being at a gig, their groans suggesting the guttural noises of drunken/drugged/hyped-up teenagers at a live concert. But the movement back into horror conventions is seamless as zombies break through the glass next to David and he is attacked by the landlord's wife.

The cut back to Dianne and Shaun's mother shows them moving in time to the music and the blows that are still raining down on the landlord: zombie bashing as music video and spectator sport.

Liz then hits him with a fire extinguisher, which also keeps time with the music. By this point the audience, too, may be tapping their feet in time with the music, and as the violence continues, we become less bothered by it, just as the friends in the film have had to get used to becoming increasingly violent.

The rapid camera movement and stylised 'whooshing' sound accompanying the dart throwing leads to the end of the 'music video' as the landlord's head is rammed into the jukebox, killing him and the music.

Media zombies (36)

The montage of post-zombie television programmes provides another wry comment on modern society's way of dealing with major traumatic events. All the foibles of modern society are lampooned, particularly the media's obsession to cash in on any event, however horrific. There is 'Zombies from Hell' (real-life zombie stories recreated); 'Z-Day'; the creation of a charity event, Zombaid; politically correct renaming (now the 'mobile deceased', not zombies) zombies as ideal workers in the service industry; as contestants in a *It's a Knockout*-style show and as the subject for a talk show (the caption reads 'I married a monster' beneath a woman whose husband is a zombie).

The audience is presented with the mores of modern consumerist society: to trivialise, to pigeon-hole, to glamorise, to turn real life into a mediated product, just another in a long line of products to be bought, consumed, then discarded and soon forgotten.

The slow zoom out from this plethora of quickly forgotten images and the channel hopping suggests the viewers' fleeting interest and reveals that all the events are now packaged for television. The shot implicates us in this dynamic just like the hero and his girlfriend, who sit idly watching as if nothing has happened. Funny, but true.

FANTASY

After writing the fantasy section I was surprised to find that the tag allowed me to explore a wider range of films than I had expected. The experience was richer than I anticipated as my initial thoughts conjured up a stream of *20,000 Leagues Under the Sea*-type (1954) films, strong on effects but with little depth (of course, there is nothing wrong with the aforementioned film; it's a great fantasy film and it nearly made it into the book). However, a genre that can produce films as diverse as *A Matter of Life and Death* (1946) and *Pan's Labyrinth* (2006) suggests that I need not have worried; their reflections on life are as potent as any of the films featured in this book.

The Thief of Bagdad (1924) is a revelation of spectacle and invention; the range of special effects and creative *mise-en-scène* reveals the sense of enjoyment and freedom that film-makers possessed in early cinema as they experimented with the possibilities of film language. *King Kong* (1933) also revels in film language and technology, bringing a giant ape to life; it began a Hollywood fantasy film love affair with the iconography of New York, to be later explored in *Planet of the Apes* (1968), *Escape from New York* (1981), *The Day After Tomorrow* (2004) and *Cloverfield* (2007). *King Kong* is full of fantastic elements, but at its heart is a touching exploration of otherness, and no-one is more 'human' than the ape himself. *A Matter of Life and Death* is another fantasy that has a very human focus, where the effects, as impressive and inventive as they are for the 1940s, never obscure the human drama.

Hidden Fortress (1958) is an historical fantasy, a narrative of battles and an epic journey across an almost mythical landscape. The incidental fact that George Lucas adapted the story to make *Star Wars* (1977) should not detract from the source's power; its composition of the action is never less than exquisite, both a reflection of General Rokurota's purity of action and a contrast to the two rough-hewn peasants whose story we follow. If *Hidden Fortress* is a thoughtful fantasy film, then *Jason and the Argonauts* (1963) presents solely the action side of a fantasy world; it is pure entertainment for the child of any age, where the process of Ray Harryhausen's stop motion animation reaches its zenith.

One contentious inclusion, perhaps, is *Soylent Green* (1973); yes, it would happily sit in the science fiction section, so why is it here? Much of it strikes a chord and seems alarmingly prophetic; but the cannibal denouement – that's pure fantasy, isn't it? I would like to think so.

Brazil (1985) is a wonderful dystopian fantasy, replete with Terry Gilliam's now *de rigueur* extraordinary visualisation of fantasy worlds, which had already been demonstrated in *Time Bandits* (1981). He is the perfect partner to the next two directors in this section, Tim Burton and Guilllermo del Toro. These three film-makers are arguably the most imaginative directors working today, their combined body of work displaying a rich and vivid vein of fantastical creations. Both *Edward Scissorhands* (1990) and *Pan's Labyrinth* situate recognisably human drama within convincingly fantastical landscapes with such wit and clarity that one would be hard pressed to find finer depictions of alienation in any genre.

The Thief of Bagdad

KEY FACTS

Release Date: 1924

Country of Origin: USA

Running Time: 147 minutes

PRODUCTION NOTES

Production Company

Douglas Fairbanks Pictures Corp.

Distributor

United Artists

Budget

$2,000,000 (estimated)

Awards

National Film Registry National Film Preservation Board

SYNOPSIS

A thief wants to steal from the Caliph of Bagdad's palace but then has a change of heart and pretends to be a prince to undertake the quest set by the Caliph to win the hand of his daughter. The thief's true identity is uncovered and he is ejected from the palace. However, he is still intent on completing the quest to find the rarest of treasures before seven moons have passed and he sets off on his adventures in competition with three princes. He encounters numerous obstacles, including caverns of fires and monsters, but he fulfils his quest despite the other suitors using magical objects to help their causes and wins the princess' hand.

HISTORICAL CONTEXT

Douglas Fairbanks was one of *the* creative forces of the 1920s; along with Charlie Chaplin and Buster Keaton he was involved in all aspects of production as well as being the star of his films. His public and private personas merged in the public imagination as he swashed and buckled his way through some of the most popular films of the decade. His charm and lust for life perfectly embodied the era of speakeasies, flappers and frivolity.

Most notable, especially for this era, was how Fairbanks gained full control of his career when he formed United Artists in 1919 along with Mary Pickford, the most popular actress of her day, Chaplin and director D.W. Griffith. This was an early attempt by actors and film-makers to wrest control of their careers from the growing strength of the studios as film production gathered momentum, and it predates the stranglehold that the major studios would exercise over stars and directors for the next 40 years. It was an extremely prescient move by these film-makers, for it challenged the power of the likes of the Fox Film Corporation, formed in 1915, which stood as an early example of a company whose vertical integration ensured that it controlled both production and distribution, an asset that would be further strengthened by its merger with Twentieth Century Pictures in 1935.

With the foundation of United Artists, Fairbanks was able to challenge studio power and gain artistic control over his films as well as manage distribution and his profit share. Not only was he master of his creative destiny, but he was in a relationship with Mary Pickford and their marriage in 1920 cemented them as the ultimate Hollywood couple. But, like most Hollywood fantasies, it would all come to an end. Just as the harsh realities of the Wall Street Crash in 1929 brought the parties to a halt, so Fairbanks was unable to make the transition from silent to 'talkies'. His marriage to Pickford stalled in 1933 and he would be dead by the end of the 1930s.

Although there was little output of fantasy films in the silent period, the few films produced did establish a number of generic codes and conventions. The quest narrative, an archetypal fantasy plot, is the cornerstone of *The Thief of Bagdad* and Fritz Lang's two-film fantasy adventure, *Die Nibelungen* (both released in 1924), as well as later sound forays into the genre, such as *The Wizard of Oz* (1939).

They all share this quest narrative which, in turn, derives from the written and oral stories of folklore, myth and literature, along with the other conventions of character types such as a hero, a villain and a princess, as detailed by the Russian scholar, Vladimir Propp, in his 1928 study of traditional Russian folk stories. These archetypal characters are easily identified in *The Thief of Bagdad* and are central to later fantasy stories such as *The Lord of the Rings* film trilogy (2001/2/3) where the battle between good and evil is often marked with a tortuous journey for the hero as he attempts to fulfil a quest.

SELECT FILMOGRAPHY OF MAIN PRODUCERS AND CAST

Raoul Walsh, 1887-1980, Director, Actor

Evangeline, 1919

The Thief of Bagdad, 1924

The Big Trail, 1930

The Roaring Twenties, 1939

Dark Command, 1940

They Drive by Night, 1940

High Sierra, 1941

They Died with Their Boots On, 1941

Desperate Journey, 1942

Gentleman Jim, 1943

Objective, Burma!, 1945

Pursued, 1947

White Heat, 1949

Distant Drums, 1951

The Tall Men, 1955

A Distant Trumpet, 1964

Arthur Edeson, 1891-1970, Director of Photography

The Three Musketeers, 1921

Robin Hood, 1922

The Thief of Bagdad, 1924

All Quiet on the Western Front, 1930

The Big Trail, 1930

Waterloo Bridge, 1931

Frankenstein, 1931

The Old Dark House, 1932

Red Dust, 1932

The Invisible Man, 1933

Mutiny on the Bounty, 1935

They Drive By Night, 1940

The Maltese Falcon, 1941

Casablanca, 1942

William Cameron Menzies, 1896-1957

See *Things to Come* in SCIENCE FICTION section

Douglas Fairbanks, 1883-1939, Actor, Producer, Screenwriter, Director

When the Clouds Roll By, 1919

The Mark of Zorro, 1920

The Three Musketeers, 1921

Robin Hood, 1922

The Thief of Bagdad, 1924

The Black Pirate, 1926

The Gaucho, 1927

The Iron Mask, 1929

The Taming of the Shrew, 1929

Reaching for the Moon, 1930

Mr. Robinson Crusoe, 1932

The Private Life of Don Juan, 1934

Anna May Wong, 1905-61, Actress

Bits of Life, 1921

The Toll of the Sea, 1921

The Thief of Bagdad, 1924

Peter Pan, 1924

A Trip to Chinatown, 1926

Piccadilly, 1929

Daughter of the Dragon, 1931

Shanghai Express, 1932

A Study in Scarlet, 1933

Java Head, 1934

Limehouse Blues, 1934

Daughter of Shanghai, 1937

Dangerous to Know, 1937

When Were You Born, 1938

King of Chinatown, 1939

Impact, 1949

LINKS TO OTHER FILMS

The Mark of Zorro (1920)/*The Three Musketeers* (1921)/*Robin Hood* (1922)/*The Black Pirate* (1926)

Douglas Fairbanks made his name with a series of dramatic adventure films, these four among them. Along with *The Thief of Bagdad*, they helped cement his reputation as he jumped, swung and fought his way to victory, all the while setting the heartbeats of many a female spectator racing and incurring the envy and respect of just as many males.

The Thief of Bagdad (1940)

This British version of the story took a number of years to complete due to the outbreak of World War Two. Although the narrative deviates from the silent version it still relies heavily on its special effects to create an awe-inspiring vision of *1001 Arabian Nights*.

The Seventh Voyage of Sinbad (1958)

Nathan Juran's film stands out because of Ray Harryhausen's stop-motion animation, and illustrates how *1001 Arabian Nights* has proved to be a rich vein of narrative inspiration for film-makers.

Arabian Nights (1974)

Pier Paolo Pasolini's film comes after his other forays into literature, beginning with *The Decameron* (1971) and *The Canterbury Tales* (1972). Together they are known as 'The Trilogy of Life'.

Pasolini uses the source text, as with the other films, as inspiration for an exploration into the complexities of life, particularly the notion of identity.

Aladdin (1992)

Disney opened up one of the tales from *1001 Arabian Nights* to a worldwide audience with its frenetic update of this tale of adventure. The story is ideally suited to animation, which is able to visualise the amazing events with ease and flair.

REPRESENTATION

Action heroes

Douglas Fairbanks was the original action hero. While Buster Keaton, Charlie Chaplin and Harold Lloyd played it purely for laughs, Fairbanks took the physicality of film slightly more seriously. There were other established action heroes of the time, such as William S. Hart and Tom Mix, but they were Western stars, whereas Fairbanks' oeuvre crossed genre boundaries. The template for action heroes was created in this film and others that he made in this decade. Actors like Errol Flynn (*Captain Blood*, 1935; *The Adventures of Robin Hood*, 1938; *They Died With Their Boots On*, 1941; *Objective Burma!*, 1944) and Bruce Willis (*Die Hard*, 1988; *Die Hard 2*, 1990; *The Last Boy Scout*, *Die Hard With A Vengeance*, 1995; *The Fifth Element*, 1991; *Armageddon*, 1998; *Die Hard 4*, 2007) have since emerged as his successors, mixing hardnosed action with personal charisma to engage the audience.

The one other long-running debt to Fairbanks' action hero is James Bond; each manifestation of Bond has either softened or hardened his edges but he has still basically remained the same as the action hero represented in *The Thief of Bagdad*. If the film had been shot with sound we may well have heard the humorous quips we now associate with such characters, although Fairbanks' body language and facial expressions leave the audience in no doubt as to his roguish manner. The absence of sound does, however, accentuate his physicality, his body a pure expression of his love of life and action, unencumbered by too much chat. The

representation is also characterised by his love of women, a trait perpetuated by numerous action heroes. Had Hollywood realised the marketing potential and financial gain of manufacturing toys at the time there would no doubt have been a thief action figure as well.

'Films such as... The Thief of Bagdad... were the big adventure stories of their day, intended to entertain. They attempted to be spatially and psychologically clear and were made to engage audiences emotionally and be more romantic than real life. Yet they also wanted to be accessible, about real people, perhaps more glamorous and exciting than the public, but still made of flesh and blood.' Mark Cousins, *The Story of Film*, Pavillion Books, London, 2004

'It is also one of the most visually breathtaking films ever made, a unique and integral conception by a genius of film design, William Cameron Menzies... [who] created a shimmering, magical world, as insubstantial yet as real and haunting as a dream' David Robinson, *1001 Movies You Must See Before You Die*, Cassell Illustrated, London, 2003

KEY SCENE TEXTUAL ANALYSIS

The trials:

The valley of fire (6; 1:32:09)

The *mise-en-scène* counts for much in this sequence of trials that await the thief as he attempts to win the hand of the princess with his feats of derring-do. The long shot of the cavern emphasises his vulnerability, while its combination of real set, miniature and process shot combine to create a monstrous vision. The cut to a close-up reinforces the thief's heroic and macho status, all bare chest and muscular limbs, before a tighter long shot of the flames rising from the ground. A long shot to emphasise the context of the danger, then back to a medium shot to underline the thief's immediate peril and the effect of the flames, creates a rhythm. He leaps over chasms and is guided by a hermit, a superimposed shot making him resemble a genie. The amount of real and process shot flames nearly engulfs the thief and adds to the sense of very real danger facing the adventurer.

The valley of the monsters (6; 1:35:48)

Again, the *mise-en-scène* dominates this sequence. In it the thief is dwarfed by his surroundings and the monster, created by combining a real baby

crocodile (supplemented with a spiky spine!) with shots of a model blowing smoke out of its nostrils. The shot rhythm is quicker than the previous scene with cuts between beast and man from a variety of distances to simulate and underpin the action. The final thrust of the thief's sword is graphically shown as he slices open the beast's underside and fluid pours out to add to the horror of the encounter.

The cavern of the enchanted trees (6; 1:37:05)

The pace slows down for much of this encounter, as the thief brings one of the trees to life, looking like an earthy relative of Freddie Krueger or Edward Scissorhands. An attack by a giant bat provides the only action in this sequence. It is less effective as a model which is full-size, yet it maintains the

quota of thrills that the audience would have been expecting by flying directly at, and filling, the screen on both of its swoops. The set, a combination of ledges and angles, with the spidery tree in the background looking as if it is ready to pounce, helps maintain the atmosphere of fantastical other-worldliness.

The old man of the midnight sea (6; 1:42:10)

The theatricality of the film's *mise-en-scène* is perfectly highlighted in this sequence. The waves of the sea are, in fact, billowing fabric on which the boat rests as it carries an archetypal old man with flowing robes and white beard, along with the thief. The underwater sequence is a triumph of style and ingenuity when faced with very little in the way of a post-production special effects industry. The film is overcranked in order to achieve the slow motion effect of swimming, and cables are used to suspend the thief to further simulate his underwater adventure.

The initial long shot is maintained for some time to show the tiny figure swimming amidst the giant underwater vegetation, emphasising the spectacle and risk. The audience is afforded a shot of the giant sea spider; again, it comes directly towards the camera, but its entrance is delayed to build suspense as the thief removes the key from the box. The medium shot allows the monster to enter the frame from the left while the thief remains ignorant to its presence.

Director Raoul Walsh allows the creature to engulf the thief before showing a close-up of its face, to reinforce its threat, before the thief reacts. The fight cuts between the medium shot and close-ups of the sword puncturing the monster's skin to increase the impact of the violence and to make the audience as connected as possible with the conflict. Finally, underwater sirens momentarily lure the thief into a fantastic cavern. The chintzy design is on a grand scale, full of massive arches and structures like gigantic illuminating jellyfish hovering upon high. The spectacle on a big screen would have been mesmerising for contemporary audiences, a fabulously exotic underwater world that seduces both thief and audience alike.

The abode of the winged horse (7; 1:47:25)

The superimposed clouds and black-draped background, pinpricked with stars, gives the *mise-en-scène* a theatrical air, but this only adds to the otherworldly atmosphere. The house is exotic and ethereal in its white splendour; the winged horse

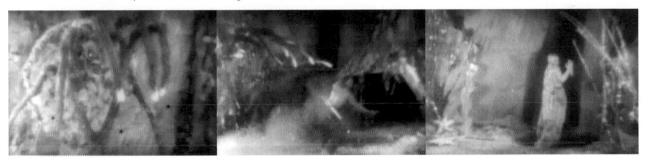

upon which the thief jumps is superimposed on a moving shot of clouds to create the impression of flight. It is perhaps primitive by our standards, but a wonder to contemporary audiences.

The citadel of the moon (7; 1:54:10)

The establishing shot is again designed to impress the audience with its magical properties. There seems to be a combination of a vast set, miniature and matte painting to achieve this splendid edifice, clouds adding to the mystery but also distracting the audience's eye from any sense of artificiality. The figure of the thief on the horse appears tiny and vulnerable against the sweeping staircase, underlining the enormity of his task. A dwarf-like figure beckons the thief up the staircase, but he is superimposed on the stairs rather than actually

being there, which reinforces the mysterious nature of the place.

Both reaction shots of the thief are from behind him, emphasising the vast staircase which fills the back of frame and again suggesting the difficulty of his quest. The long shot shows his tiny figure running up the staircase, a speck on its majestic white façade. The interior is yet more bizarre, with vertical shafts of glass; the medium shot is distorted either by a blurring of the edges of the frame or by use of a wide angle lens which distorts the side of frame. Either way, there is a sense of disorientation and otherness about this place. The barely-visible spinning object in the air accentuates the strangeness of the room, and the thief looks defiantly solid in this translucent space. He grabs the object, which, through a cut, seems to appear out of thin air (it is the invisibility cloak), and then the magic chest, which also appears suspended in the air. His tasks complete, the thief must race back to claim the hand of the Caliph's daughter.

The tasks are key to the plot and every manner of special effect known to film-makers in the 1920s is employed, making it as spectacular as possible. Supported by sets of incredible size and complexity, any shortcomings of technical know-how are overcome by filling the frame with money and, of course, the charm, charisma and physicality of Douglas Fairbanks. An iconic Hollywood figure of the silent era, his importance to the film cannot be understated or neglected from a textual analysis.

King Kong

KEY FACTS

Release Date: 1933

Country of Origin: USA

Running Time: 96 minutes

PRODUCTION NOTES

Production Company

RKO Radio Pictures

Distributor

RKO Radio Pictures

Budget

$670,000 (estimated)

Awards

National Film Registry National Film Preservation Board, USA

SYNOPSIS

Film director Carl Denham is looking for an actress to star in his next venture when he sees Ann Darrow in the street and extricates her from an incident in which she has been caught stealing an apple. With her impoverished condition she accepts his offer of the chance to star in his film which will be shot on a long sea voyage. Some scenes are shot on board whilst Ann and Jack Driscoll, the ship's first mate, gradually fall in love. Denham reveals to the ship's captain and Driscoll that their final destination is an uncharted island where mysterious events are believed to take place.

They arrive at the island where they witness a native woman being taken for ritual sacrifice. The shore party is seen by the natives of the village, which is separated from the rest of the island by a colossal wall and gate. Ann is later kidnapped by the villagers and tied to a platform on the jungle side of the wall. The villagers' chanting and drumming summons a giant gorilla from the depths of the jungle, which snatches the shrieking Ann. Denham and sailors from the ship give chase, whilst the creature, Kong, battles with a variety of dinosaurs in the jungle. He also leaves Ann in a tree and returns to the chasing group of men who are all killed except for Denham and Driscoll.

Kong then defeats a tyrannosaurus rex that is about to attack Ann and later rescues her from a pterodactyl at a mountainside lair. In the ensuing confusion Driscoll reaches Ann and returns her to the village with Kong in pursuit. Denham manages to render Kong unconscious with the use of a gas bomb and they return to New York with the creature in order to make their fortunes. Kong is hailed as the 'eighth wonder of the world' and put on display in a theatre; but the flashing light bulbs of the photographers' cameras unnerve Kong and he breaks free of his chains.

He rampages through the streets and derails a train before making his way to the top of the Empire State Building. En route, he finds Ann and takes her with him; atop the skyscraper it is clear that he wants to protect Ann, not harm her, and when planes come to fire at him, Kong puts her out of harm's way. Eventually, he succumbs to his wounds and falls to his death, leaving Denham to utter the final words of the story: 'It was beauty killed the beast.'

HISTORICAL CONTEXT

RKO Radio Pictures, the studio behind *King Kong*, was renowned for imaginative films made within limited budgets; its troubled history of success and numerous failures under a succession of owners, some of whom mismanaged the company into extinction, is a potent symbol for the trials that beset people across the world. As Americans suffered under the Great Depression in the 1930s, so RKO bore the pressures of financial hardship, but it struggled on to provide the sort of entertainment and thrills that mass audiences needed. The Fred Astaire/Ginger Rogers musicals, such as *Top Hat* (1935) and *Swingtime* (1936) transported audiences to a world of elegance and frivolity; they laughed at Katharine Hepburn and Cary Grant in *Bringing Up Baby* (1938) and screamed at *King Kong* and *Cat People* (1942).

RKO was the minnow in the shadows of the major studios and held its own against all the odds, going on to produce one of the most acclaimed films of the twentieth century at the beginning of the following decade, Orson Welles' *Citizen Kane* (1941). And so, like Kong, the studio was used and abused by many, particularly Howard Hughes, who turned it into his own personal freak show. By 1957 it had ceased production.

The use of stop-motion animation was not new in 1933; as early as 1908 there is evidence of its use in the short animation, *The Humpty Dumpty Circus*, and in Europe (particularly from the East) pioneers such as Vladislas Starevich blazed a trail in stop-motion technology during the early part of the twentieth century. Willis O'Brien, the creator of the monster effects in *King Kong*, had worked earlier on animations such as *The Dinosaur and the Missing Link: A Prehistoric Tragedy* (1915) before graduating to live action features such as 1925's *The Lost World*, another story of prehistoric monsters.

The early mastery of this technique and its subsequent rapid development made it an ideal tool for the fantasy film-maker in the days before computer-generated imagery, and its use continued for many decades. Although now a remnant of the early days of special effects, it has been sustained and revived by animators such as Nick Park, creator of Wallace and Gromit; and by film director, Tim Burton, producing *The Nightmare Before Christmas* (1993) and directing *The Corpse Bride* (2005), both stop-animation films. Its use as a special effect in live action films is now uncommon in these CGI-dominated times although lower budget films, such as Sam Raimi's *Evil Dead II* (1987), have occasionally resurrected the once dominant stop-motion technique.

SELECT FILMOGRAPHY OF MAIN PRODUCERS AND CAST

Merian C Cooper, 1893-1973, Director, Producer, Screenwriter

Chang: A Drama of the Wilderness, 1927

The Four Feathers, 1929

King Kong, 1933

This is Cinerama, 1952

Ernest B. Schoedsack, 1893-1979, Director, Producer

Chang: A Drama of the Wilderness, 1927

The Four Feathers, 1929

The Most Dangerous Game, 1932

King Kong, 1933

The Son of Kong, 1933

The Last Days of Pompeii, 1935

Dr. Cyclops, 1940

Mighty Joe Young, 1949

This is Cinerama, 1952

Fay Wray, 1907-2004, Actress

The Wedding March, 1928

The Four Feathers, 1929

Doctor X, 1932

The Most Dangerous Game, 1932

The Vampire Bat, 1933

Mystery of the Wax Museum, 1933

King Kong, 1933

The Cobweb, 1955

Robert Armstrong, 1890-1973, Actor

The Most Dangerous Game, 1932

King Kong, 1933

'G' Men, 1935

Blood on the Sun, 1945

The Paleface, 1948

Mighty Joe Young, 1949

Max Steiner, 1888-1971, Composer

The Most Dangerous Game, 1932

King Kong, 1933

The Lost Patrol, 1934

The Informer, 1935

The Charge of the Light Brigade, 1936

A Star Is Born, 1937

Jezebel, 1938

Angels with Dirty Faces, 1938

The Dawn Patrol, 1938

Dodge City, 1939

Dark Victory, 1939

Gone with the Wind, 1939

The Letter, 1940

Santa Fe Trail, 1940

Sergeant York, 1941

They Died with Their Boots On, 1941

Desperate Journey, 1942

Now, Voyager, 1942

Casablanca, 1942

Passage to Marseille, 1942

Mildred Pierce, 1945

The Big Sleep, 1946

The Beast With Five Fingers, 1946

Pursued, 1947

The Treasure of the Sierra Madre, 1948

Key Largo, 1948

Johnny Belinda, 1948

The Fountainhead, 1949

White Heat, 1949

Distant Drums, 1951

The Jazz Singer, 1953

The Caine Mutiny, 1954

The Searchers, 1956

The FBI Story, 1959

A Distant Trumpet, 1964

LINKS TO OTHER FILMS

The Most Dangerous Game (1932)

This film shares many of the personnel behind *King Kong*, including Cooper and Schoedsack in charge of the film's production, and two of its stars, Fay Wray and Robert Armstrong. In fact, the backdrop for the film is the island set which was reused a year later for *King Kong*. Its tale of hunting for humans is a dark one which taps into some of the same primeval fears that would be explored the following year in the team's more famous and enduring film.

The Son of Kong (1933)

Shot back-to-back with *King Kong*, this sequel charts Carl Denham's return to Skull Island and his encounter with a smaller and less frightening gorilla. The tone is lighter but includes, as with its predecessor, the stop motion animation of Willis O'Brien. Like his father, he dies at the end, but he saves Denham's life in the process.

Mighty Joe Young (1949)

Another RKO film about a gorilla that is taken to the United States and used as entertainment until he eventually goes on the rampage after being plied with alcohol. He is closer in size to a normal gorilla and it ends not in his death, but with a heroic act as he saves children from a burning orphanage. Cooper and Schoedsack made the film and the tone is far lighter than their previous two gorilla films.

King Kong (1976/2005)

These two updates of the original film had differing fortunes; the earlier remake was not particularly well-received and its tone is generally light-hearted. But the CGI-laden 2005 remake was extremely successful, commercially and critically, recreating 1930's New York, Skull Island and Kong with great attention to detail; it has light-hearted moments but some of the scenes on the island are particularly graphic and harrowing.

REPRESENTATION

Animals

Animals have had a diverse representation in film history; they have helped humans in *Lassie Come Home* (1943); they have been abused by humans in *Au hasard Balthazar* (1966) and they have eaten humans in *Jaws* (1975). The ape has had a particularly colourful representation over the years. Smaller apes have fared best in films like the *Tarzan* series and *Bedtime for Bonzo* (1951) with their playfulness seen as a key part of their characters. Similarly, the orang-utan has been portrayed in a favourable manner with Clint Eastwood's sidekick, Clyde, in *Every Which Way But Loose* (1978) and *Any Which Way You Can* (1980) serving as notable examples.

The gorilla has had the least positive representation in film history; although *King Kong* does show the animal in a sympathetic light there are still scenes where he is the destructive and violent beast of popular myth. Subsequent films, such as *Nabonga* (1944), *The White Gorilla* (1945), *Killer Ape* (1953) and *The Mighty Gorga* (1969) all focus on gorillas' supposed aggressive tendencies. Only in such films as *Gorillas in the Mist* (1988), where the real gorilla environment is depicted, is there an accurate depiction of the creature. Benign gorillas eating leaves, however, do not generally sell cinema tickets.

And so it is with *King Kong*, marketed as a savage beast and shown to be dominated by his animal nature, which, the film-makers suggest, is aggressive and brutal. The Hollywood tendency to anthropomorphise gorillas is particularly evident here, perhaps understandable considering their close connection to humans. In moments when Kong is with Ann this aspect is played out and helps garner the audience's sympathy, more so than most of the human characters who are generally selfish, foolish, or both.

Anthropomorphism in films has a long history, particularly among animators. Disney's films have created an array of animal characters with strong personality traits: there is the music-loving but ruthless King Louie and the good-natured Baloo in *The Jungle Book* (1967); and the more recent loveable panda, Po, in DreamWorks' *Kung Fu Panda* (2008). Some critics may find the anthropomorphism cloying, but young audiences have been consistently thrilled by the exploits of their favourite animal characters, allowing challenging narratives of grief (*The Lion King*, 1994) and family trauma (*Finding Nemo*, 2003) to be explored in a more secure, animated context.

The savage

The tribe that is represented in *King Kong* conforms to all the stereotypes that Hollywood and beyond have served up to audiences over the years. They are seen as savages, sacrificing women and dancing themselves into a frenzy of violence, juxtaposed with the 'civilised' white men. The most common representation of this type was evident for many years in the Hollywood Western; countless films, most often of the B-movie variety, but including such genre classics as *Stagecoach*, used the Native American as white gun fodder.

Various indigenous tribes have been depicted in other genres, particularly adventures, as anonymous purveyors of brutality, a mass of savagery intent on killing and even cannibalism. The many film versions of the Tarzan stories are filled with such representations, as are films such as *King Solomon's Mines* (1937/50). But it is not just older Hollywood films that perpetuate the stereotype: Steven Spielberg's *Raiders of the Lost Ark* (1981) and *Indiana Jones and the Kingdom of the Crystal Skull* (2008) both present tribes of vicious natives.

There have, however, been some attempts to balance the stereotype. Robert Flaherty's documentary, *Nanook of the North* (1922), details the life of an Inuit family in the Canadian arctic by portraying a harsh but noble life in harmony with nature. Indeed, the Native American was reborn in Hollywood films from the 1950s onwards as society began to reflect on its treatment of minorities with more positive representations like John Ford's *Cheyenne Autumn* (1964).

Beyond the Western, films such as Akira Kurosawa's *Dersu Uzala* (1975) depicts the skill of an indigenous man as he teaches a Russian expedition about survival in the inhospitable environment of Siberia. Attempts to depict indigenous people as noble savages have not always been successful - witness the rather simplistic representations in films like *Zulu* (1964). More recently, however, films such as Mel Gibson's *Apocalypto* (2006) have attempted to show the full range of a people's life with all its light and darkness.

'The throbbing heart of the film lies in the creation of the semi-human simian himself, an immortal tribute to the Hollywood dream factory's ability to fashion a symbol that can express all the contradictory erotic, ecstatic, destructive, pathetic and cathartic buried impulses of 'civilised' man'. Wally Hammond, *Time Out Film Guide 14th Ed.*, Time Out Guides Ltd., London, 2006

'Films like *King Kong*... became aesthetic and technical landmarks in film history' Mark Cousins, *The Story of Film*, Pavillion Books, London, 2004

KEY SCENE TEXTUAL ANALYSIS

Offering Ann as a sacrifice (6)

The establishing shot shows the extent of the tribe and its euphoria after the capture of Ann, who is to be sacrificed to Kong. The scale of the human defences is also highlighted as the people are dwarfed by the wall and gate behind them. The diegetic sound of screaming and shouting adds to the crazed atmosphere, also underpinned by the dramatic orchestral score, which is somewhat reminiscent of the music that would stereotypically accompany Native Americans on the warpath in a Hollywood Western. The medium long shot reveals

Ann at the heart of this maelstrom of emotion, her writhing body a focus of frailty and vulnerability.

The medium shot of Ann again accentuates her predicament: the burning fires, the face paint, the dancing natives and their black skin all contrast with her white Western appearance and persona, while her captors stretch out her arms akin to a crucifixion pose. The men dressed as apes foreshadow her imminent fate. There is also a strong sexual tension; she is surrounded by men and is being forced into a submissive stance, a factor which is to be repeated with Kong's appearance.

The medium close-up allows the audience to see, and share, even more of her terror. The shadows of the surrounding figures pass over and disfigure her face and her skyward look is almost an appeal - 'why hast thou forsaken me?'. The music at this

appropriate for this journey from an environment on a human scale, however unfamiliar, to the land of fantasy and Kong.

We then track in front of Ann as she is led towards the camera, the camera almost pushing her forward and dragging her in the same direction. She is trapped by both the tribe and in the filmic space, its momentum forever moving her towards her 'gallows'. All these shots are from above Ann, emphasising her vulnerability and anticipating her next physical and filmic relationship with the giant ape: she will spend the remainder of the film staring up at him.

As she is led up to the place of offering all that can be seen beyond is the black night, a place of nightmares and the unknowing. Once she is tied up we return to the long shot. With the villagers already down the steps, the crucifixion comparison

point is chaotic, losing any discernible melody as it descends into the abandon interpreted by the tribe.

Three shots then show the tribe's actions; this is their moment, their place and the camera dwells on them. The return to the long shot reiterates the fact that the whole of the village is caught up in this frenzied celebration, emphasising its importance to them and the impossibility of Ann's escape. The montage of shots from tribal dancing to the low angle of the chief at the gong and then back to the medium shot of Ann strengthens the inseparable bond between them and her entire immersion into this nightmare world.

The movement into the next stage of Ann's ordeal is signalled by the tracking crane shot that follows the mass of villagers as they propel Ann towards the now open gates. Its grandiose movement is

is once again made. The cut to the extreme long shot is a poignant moment as this tiny figure is offered up by the people, more Christ-like than ever in visual terms. She is left with only the darkness beyond; the slow, doom-laden non-diegetic music underpins the gravity of the moment as the huge wooden bolt is pushed back into place, sealing her fate.

The music gathers pace as the tribe races to view the girl from the top of the oppressive wall, her isolation and vulnerability conveyed with clarity and visual economy. The juxtaposition between Ann's plight and the tribal chief's power is suggested in the next few shots as we see her helplessness, while he is all-powerful on top of the wall with his minions surrounding him.

The gong calls Kong and slow, lurching non-diegetic music heralds the start of the creature's progress to the clearing, soon followed by diegetic roars. His arrival is captured in a very long two-shot of Ann and Kong, which helps establish the beginning of their connection that will last for the remainder of the film; her screams begin and will feature prominently for much of their acquaintance.

The cut to a medium close-up shows her reaction, at this point dumbstruck by sheer horror and incomprehension. The next shot tracks into Kong's face and ends on an extreme close-up, a POV which positions the audience clearly in Ann's predicament and is designed for us to witness the horrifying spectacle in all its hairy glory. As he continues to strut his stuff in front of her, the agony of her plight is reinforced by her hysterical screams and action; she is literally climbing up one of the pillars that she is tied to in her attempt to escape.

returns to his domain. The horrified look from John Driscoll underlines his impotence to save Ann. He is framed with iron bars as if he in prison, a fitting image of Ann's human admirer as the ape whisks her away.

One last roar from Kong and agonised screams from Ann signal their departure into the unknown. Kong plunges out of the frame and the camera does not follow, leaving the audience to only guess at her fate. The would-be rescuers follow after opening the gate, but the final shot of them as they plunge into the unknown is a telling one. It is from the tribal chief's POV from the top of the wall. The high angle shot makes them look small and vulnerable, like ants, hardly capable of defeating a colossus of power and virility like Kong.

As Kong moves closer, the unexpected happens: after all the posturing the giant ape performs the most delicate of manoeuvres as he unwinds one of the handles that ties Ann to the pillar; it is suggestive of his later gentleness and affection for her, and as she stumbles and falls he looks worried for a moment before scooping her up in his hand. Throughout this sequence there has been no shot of the wall or the tribe above; it has been very much played out as an intimate, albeit horrifying, experience for Ann, allowing no other living thing into the frame. When we finally see the villagers again it is as if Kong has forgotten about them momentarily, then growls up at them, asserting his claim to the female.

The rescue party arrives too late and we see Kong moving away from the wall and back towards the jungle, his face becoming covered in shadow as he

A Matter of Life and Death

KEY FACTS

Release Date: 1946

Country of Origin: UK

Running Time: 100 minutes

PRODUCTION NOTES

Production Companies

The Archers

Independent Producers

Distributor

Eagle-Lion Distributors Limited

Budget

£320,000 (estimated)

Awards

Best European Film Bodil Awards, Denmark

SYNOPSIS

World War Two RAF pilot Peter is returning from a mission and preparing to jump from his stricken bomber plane over England when he has a conversation with an American radio operator working on an English air base. He assumes that these will be his dying words as he has no parachute, but he cheats death and is united with the American girl, June, with whom he begins a love affair. The only problem is that, according to those who run Heaven, his survival was a mistake - he did miss his date with death, and death does not like to be stood up.

The film plots Heaven's attempts to reclaim its lost soul, culminating in a court case to decide his fate. Along the way there are scenes both on technicolor Earth and in monochrome Heaven, charting Peter and June's relationship, while the doctor who tends him thinks Peter's visions of Heaven are the result of head injuries sustained in his fall from the plane. Ultimately the trial, populated by a number of heavenly luminaries, comes to its conclusion and Peter races back down the stairway to Earth to be reunited with June.

HISTORICAL CONTEXT

World War Two influenced a lot of Hollywood and British film output, resulting in a plethora of flag-waving storylines designed to boost the morale of the audiences at home. The Ministry of Information asked Michael Powell and Emeric Pressburger to make a film that would promote goodwill between the allied powers of Britain and America, a relationship that had been strained at times during the war years. That the result was not what the Ministry had quite expected was typical of this creative duo's output, which generally took a totally unexpected slant on themes and issues. The film's playful, yet explicit, detailing of the differences between the two nations is far removed from other films of the time, and certainly its treatment of war is much more esoteric and cerebral than the standard action film. It also makes strong appeals for human understanding between countries, rather than advocating jingoistic flag-waving.

This particular war film is a fantasy with its roots very much in the soil of reality. Filmed in the immediate aftermath of the war, it became a timely mirror on world events. The Germans and Japanese were defeated and brought to their knees. At the end of World War One Germany had been so devastated and so poorly treated by the victors that it proved to be the perfect breeding ground for Hitler's extreme politics. If history was not to repeat itself then Germany, in particular, was going to need more careful handling. The film suggests a blueprint of tolerance and understanding for the film's characters, but it could easily be applied to all participants in World War Two.

Pressburger, himself an immigrant in Britain, escaped the Nazis whilst working for the UFA film studios in Berlin and found support from fellow Hungarian Alexander Korda, the London Films' supremo, upon his arrival in England. His experiences made him particularly allied to the sentiments expressed in *A Matter of Life and Death*. While Hollywood war films typically and unquestioningly celebrated American victory and sacrifice, and the Ealing comedies of Great Britain lauded British grit and determination, Powell and Pressburger seemed to see, and express, a bigger picture.

SELECT FILMOGRAPHY OF MAIN PRODUCERS AND CAST

Michael Powell, 1905-90, Director, Producer, Screenwriter

The Edge of the World, 1937

The Spy in Black, 1938

The Thief of Bagdad, 1939

Contraband, 1940

49th Parallel, 1941

One of Our Aircraft Is Missing, 1942

The Life and Death of Colonel Blimp, 1943

A Canterbury Tale, 1944

I Know Where I'm Going, 1945

A Matter of Life and Death, 1946

Black Narcissus, 1947

The Red Shoes, 1948

Peeping Tom, 1960

Emeric Pressburger, 1902-88, Director, Producer, Screenwriter

As for Michael Powell, except for *The Edge of the World*, *The Thief of Bagdad* and *Peeping Tom*.

Jack Cardiff, 1914, Director of Photography, Director

The Four Feathers, 1939

A Matter of Life and Death, 1946

Black Narcissus, 1947

The Red Shoes, 1948

Under Capricorn, 1949

The African Queen, 1951

War and Peace, 1956

The Vikings, 1958

Alfred Junge, 1886-1964, Art Director

The Man Who Knew Too Much, 1934

King Solomon's Mines, 1937

Goodbye Mr Chips, 1939

The Life and Death of Colonel Blimp, 1943

I Know Where I'm Going, 1945

A Matter of Life and Death, 1946

Black Narcissus, 1947

A Farewell to Arms, 1958

David Niven, 1910-83, Actor

The Charge of the Light Brigade, 1936

The Prisoner of Zenda, 1937

A Matter of Life and Death, 1946

Around the World in Eighty Days, 1956

The Guns of Navarone, 1961

The Pink Panther, 1963

Casino Royale, 1967

Kim Hunter, 1922-2002, Actress

The Seventh Victim, 1943

A Canterbury Tale, 1944

A Matter of Life and Death, 1946

A Streetcar Named Desire, 1951

Planet of the Apes, 1967

Roger Livesey, 1906-1976, Actor

Rembrandt, 1936

The Drum, 1938

49th Parallel, 1941

The Life and Death of Colonel Blimp, 1943

I Know Where I'm Going, 1945

A Matter of Life and Death, 1946

Raymond Massey, 1896-1983, Actor

See *Things to Come* in SCIENCE FICTION section (see pg. 147)

LINKS TO OTHER FILMS

Here Comes Mr Jordan (1941)

A similar plot device is used in this film (a mistake is made in Heaven), but here the character is aided by those above to find a way of returning to Earth. Although a popular film, its success is undermined by its sentimentality, a flaw that Powell and Pressburger's film does not possess.

Hail the Conquering Hero (1943)

One of the few films of the time to satirise conventional notions of jingoism and heroism, this is the story of a Marine, discharged before he goes overseas because of hay fever, and his return to his small-town home, where he is mistakenly regarded as a war hero. The playful mocking of the townspeople's homespun values in wartime is very subversive for the era. It shares with *A Matter of Life and Death* a vision of people's experience in wartime away from the typical platitudes.

It's a Wonderful Life (1946)

Again, this is a film about divine intervention. Here James Stewart is shown what life in his small town would have been like without his benign influence. Like *A Matter of Life and Death* it demonstrates an inventive take on all things heavenly. Both are very human films dealing in the failings and rigours of life, love and death, and technically there are similarities - note Heaven's ability to freeze-frame life on Earth in both films.

Wings of Desire (1987)

Here it is an angel who is trying to become Earth-bound. The look and sensibilities of the film breath the same air as *A Matter of Life and Death*, with the modern film paying some visual homage to the earlier film: the use of colour for Earth and black and white for the angels, and the shot of the ceiling in the library scene closely resembles the shot from the depths of Heaven's records department to the viewing galleries above (see pg. 116).

REPRESENTATION

War

By 1946 there had been scores of flag-waving war films from both sides of the Atlantic, all designed to raise allied spirits and glorify the efforts of 'our boys' in the theatres of war around the world. War films of the time could not be seen to represent Allied soldiers in any negative way; yes, *individuals* could be psychotic or weak but, as a whole, the armies, navy and air force were heroes to a man (and it was normally men). In this film there seems to be a slightly different attitude. It is not exactly critical but it certainly contains healthy doses of clear-sighted observation. The long opening track through the universe positions the war as a tiny activity amidst the immense universe beyond the Earth and the mindless activities of the infinitesimal creatures that inhabit the planet. As such, this is rather subversive. Indeed, if this was intended as a film to promote unity between the allies, then the use of an American soldier from the War of Independence against Britain as prosecutor against English airman, Peter, is surprising. To counter this, of course, is the relationship between Peter and American, June. It also seems that Germans do not make it to Heaven - it is totally populated by Allied airmen in the section that we see.

The opening shot of Peter and his dead comrade in the burning Lancaster bomber conveys the loneliness and starkness of impending death, tempered only by Peter's chance radio conversation with June, the radio operator. The selfless devotion of the squadron leader to his crew, allowing them to bail out without telling them that his parachute is useless, suggests the nobility of the individual, bringing definition and clarity amidst the chaos of war. Throughout the film, war acts as a backdrop to the main thrust of the narrative, but its force is always present, as illustrated when the fighter plane roars over Peter's head and he realises that he has not died and he is not on a heavenly beach. Indeed, the central message of an individual's importance and vitality is a forceful comment that the Second World War was not just a moment in history, nor solely the slaughter of anonymous millions, but a multitude of individual and personal stories.

Heaven

Heaven has had many manifestations in film history. From *Here Comes Mr. Jordan* (1941) to *Bruce Almighty* (2003) and *Ice Age: The Meltdown* (2006), it has been depicted as a natural paradise with white lights. Never had it been, in so many ways, as ordinary as it is in *A Matter of Life and Death*. Here, the audience sees the lushness of Earth in the opening scenes and then we are brought into the monochrome Heaven: prim ladies in uniform control the airmen's section where a Coke dispenser generates the greatest excitement.

It is certainly tranquil, but it has the atmosphere of a library or an archive, reinforced by the shot of the never-ending records that inhabit the caverns beneath the reception area. For a contemporary audience, many of whom would have lost loved ones, this representation would certainly have been comforting. It is harmonious, but also familiar through elements of the *mise-en-scène* and the exchanges between the receptionist and Bob; it is, in some ways, very much like a scene from wartime England.

Later images of Heaven suggest a grander vision; Peter's trial is put into context in one scene where the countless observers are shown to be just a tiny part of a vast expanse. Heaven, then, is seen to be anything and everything, all things to all men. As the young airman, played by Richard Attenborough, says when he looks down at the vast records of Heaven's occupants whilst Bob awaits the arrival of Peter: 'It's Heaven, isn't it?'

'A Matter of Life and Death... *was intended as a propaganda film... The movie outstrips its original purpose, however, ending up a lasting tale of romance and human goodness that is both visually exciting and verbally amusing.*' Karen Krizanovich, *1001 Movies You Must See Before You Die*, Cassell Illustrated, London, 2003

"*Fascination with the mythical and the fantastic does not end at the narrative or social level for Powell and Pressburger. Their work is profoundly Romantic in its impulses, dominated by its love of the mystical and of the 'natural world' and by its lack of decorum and 'good taste'.*" Joe McElhaney in Nowell-Smith (ed.), *The Oxford History of World Cinema*, OUP, 1997

KEY SCENE TEXTUAL ANALYSIS

The universe (1)

The sweep through the universe is a spectacular vision of the Earth's minute place within it. The message that we are but an insignificant fraction of this expanse makes the fact that we have been fighting with one another even more absurd - unusual for a 1940's flagwaver.

The use of miniatures and optical effects create an impression of journeying through space and arriving at the Earth, then zooming in towards Europe and into the fog over the English Channel. The non-diegetic music changes from an orchestral mood of magic and awe to one of violence and chaos as the camera homes in on the fighting in Europe.

Diegetic sounds start to dominate as we hear the noises of war - of ships in the fog, of Hitler, and then a cacophony of sound signalling a world in distress. One particular dialogue starts to dominate, that of a woman and a man. The screen is still dark, the haunting voices focusing our attention on the words before we actually see them. Eventually, the woman comes into focus, completing a vast journey that the camera has made to focus on the tiniest of human interactions amidst the mass of exchanges on the Earth. Just as the Earth is infinitesimal in the context of the universe, so this exchange is part of a global mosaic of words and deeds.

The scale is breathtaking and points to this one story as being both random and special, important and trivial; it is this dichotomy which feeds into the rest of the film, at once patriotic and also subversive.

Bailing out (2)

June, the radio operator, emerges from out of the clouds and mist, the cross-fade summoning up her face, like a character from a dream. The camera tracks slowly around her, maintaining the sense of mystery about her. Objects obscure a clear view and shadow covers the upper part of her face. An outside light source flashes red to heighten the scene's sense of other-worldliness and the final long shot is a frame full of objects. The lamps look like lurching creatures, examining proceedings, and, coupled with the red light, there is an ethereal atmosphere that would not be out of place in a science fiction film. This airfield control room with its American female operator transcends its earthly ties and seems to be very much a part of a *mise-en-scène* that deals with fantasy, whether real or imagined.

The roar of the Lancaster bomber is one of the dominant sounds in the next section, first seen in long shot, a miniature with the blaze as the most identifiable feature that the audience can see. Inside, the camera prowls through the shredded metal interior. It contrasts greatly with the interior of the air traffic control tower, but there is still a sense of serenity about the *mise-en-scène* when the camera comes to a halt. Peter sits next to his dead colleague, Bob, framed by twisted metal and gazing enigmatically at the fire raging on the wing. It is like a portrait of an heroic death, a fate accepted, at once calm but also shocking. It feels more like the climax of a story than the beginning of one.

The close-ups of both Peter and June contrast their unexpected frames of mind. Although covered in dirt and grease and blown by the wind, it is Peter's face that is bathed in a full light, whereas the shadow above June's head threatens to engulf her at any moment, as it indeed does later in the scene. Ignoring the dialogue, it is apparent through this framing that it is June who is going through the deeper trauma.

The rhythm of cross-cutting between the faces sets up a strong connection between the two, bonding so completely in Peter's supposed final moments. It is also noticeable that June's close-ups are tighter than Peter's, reiterating the greater strain that she is under. When she learns that he has no parachute the framing on her is completely different to the repeated close-ups that precede and follow; the horrific news prompts Powell and Pressburger to shoot her in profile. Perhaps the jarring blow to her sensibilities is literally translated into a shift in framing and the audience, aware of the change in framing, shares her sense of sudden dislocation from the reality of the moment.

Their connection is further underlined by their respective backgrounds. In close-up Peter's background burns orange and red, while June is almost totally surrounded by the glow of the red

minutes. The melodrama, the tension and the tenderness is already present in the dialogue, in their faces, in the framing and the everyday sounds, which help to reinforce the extraordinary moment.

The camera takes the audience with Peter as he jumps into the void. Gentle, non-diegetic music now begins, heralding the aerial shot of the beach, its immense lines of surf like gigantic rippling wings stretching off into the hazy distance. A tiny body can be seen bobbing in the surf, as insignificant as the shot of the Earth earlier in this sequence. Peter's body, next seen in medium shot, then medium close-up, dissolves into a shot of angel wings, stretching, like the sea, into the infinite.

The black and white photography contrasts with the colour for obvious reasons. But it's not just the difference of starkness to warmth, but the fact that the Technicolor process has been used to create

warning light. As the sequence progresses, June appears to be constantly bathed in this light, which is, of course, suggestive of danger and passion, entirely in keeping with the developing mood.

As the shadow descends further over June's eyes, the audience realises that tragedy will follow, but even in Peter's apparent death the two are linked visually; in her final shot June's head falls in the frame and he follows by jumping down out of the frame.

The diegetic sound also provides a fitting accompaniment to their final minutes. The eerie noise of the wind dominates Peter's final moments, while a ticking clock comes to the fore in June's control room, a reminder of time passing and death waiting for us all. There is no need for a non-diegetic music score to guide our response; that would be an interruption into these last profound

such deep and ravishing colours in the previous section, reminiscent of 1930s Hollywood colour in films like *The Adventures of Robin Hood* (1938) and *Gone with the Wind* (1939). June's red lips, the blood on Bob's chest, the yellows and reds of the fire and the red warning light all combine to suggest a sumptuous vision of life. Death is monochrome and unknown - it is, quite simply, lifeless.

Heaven (3)

In Heaven, the diegetic sound of the ticking clock in June's control room is echoed in the non-diegetic piano music, but here it creates a sense of tranquillity and serenity as people - dead people - arrive to collect their wings.

Compared to the twisted metal of Peter's plane and June's cluttered room, Heaven is sparse and full of modernist clean lines with geometric shapes; it is vast, open, functional and logical, uncluttered by adornment. It chimes with the vision that modernist architects had for cities in the second half of the twentieth century and recalls Vincent Korda's set design for the rebuilt Everytown in *Things To Come*. Production designer Alfred Junge's Heaven is almost like a pencil sketch of a place, in contrast to the solidity and chaos of Earth. When the camera focuses on the clock, another piece of modernist design, it briefly seems that perhaps the non-diegetic music is actually diegetic; nothing is what it appears up here.

The effect of the metronomic music and the military personnel's conveyer belt movement accentuates the idea of order. The repetition of the sound and the absence of colour suggest an experience where everything is ordered and everyone is equal: indeed, the range of nationalities also underpins this idea.

The next shot of the harmonica-playing airman lends an ethereal air to the unearthly atmosphere. The camera lingers on his shadow after he has left the frame to suggest that it is not him per se, but his soul that we are actually seeing. The camera takes great pains to follow the people who arrive. Next, the young airman is tracked with a gentle movement, taking in his own wonderment.

The following sequence establishes a growing connection between the woman at reception and Bob, who has been waiting for Peter. The arrival of a group of raucous American fliers interrupts this rhythm, reinforced by the up-tempo non-diegetic music. It is a wry comment on the friendly brashness of this nationality, from the British perspective; their treatment of the soft drink machine is a gently mocking comment on their priorities.

The rhythm of editing between the British airman and the woman, a heavenly clerk, is reinstated, as is the original ticking music: Heaven's order is the one constant as different nationalities move through this staging post.

In the conversation that follows, Bob is seen at different distances and he moves around in the frame, signalling his growing unease at Peter's absence and his anxiety as a 'new recruit'. The female clerk, by contrast, is seen in a static close-up from a low angle and with the edge of the clock forming a frame around her head. The effect illustrates her importance and the framing device is highly suggestive of religious icon painting, mirroring the depiction of a saint with a halo.

As they move towards the records office, the camera cranes upwards to both reveal the viewing platform and herald the spectacular view to come. First, the audience sees the enormous dimensions of the records office below, the view achieved through a process shot combined with a miniature. But it is the next shot that really conveys the epic and infinite nature of the space: the viewing gallery is circular, and as we see it from below, the camera gently moves backwards to reveal an endless number of these galleries, all with tiny figures peering over. This picture, with its shafts of light, conveys the sweep and majesty of the place. Most films would luxuriate in the shot, but not here; it lasts for about five seconds, a tantalising glimpse of the extraordinary and the unknowable. The cut back to the two people now shows them in harmony, both profiled and balanced within the frame, united in pleasure at this spectacle.

The final shots of this scene again show other individuals, carefully framed, each in the centre, special, dignified, as they reveal their inner thoughts in this tranquil place. The ticking underscores this slow-moving and reflective scene. The explosion of alarm bells to signify the 'mistake' of Peter's survival jars the calm and forces the dissolve back to Technicolor where the high aerial shot of the sprawled figure on the beach indicates the shift back to Earth. The camera again takes the audience on a cosmic journey, reiterating that it is both a story of an individual, plucked from obscurity, and of the universe beyond the individual.

Kakushi-toride no san-akunin (*The Hidden Fortress*)

KEY FACTS

Release Date: 1958

Country of Origin: Japan

Running Time: 138 minutes

PRODUCTION NOTES

Production Company

Toho Company

Distributor

Toho Company

Awards

FIPRESCI Prize Akira Kurosawa Berlin International Film Festival

Silver Bear Best Director Akira Kurosawa Berlin International Film Festival

SYNOPSIS

The story begins with two peasants, Mataschichi and Tahei, a pair of opportunists, who have just failed to make any profit out of a recent battle between rival clans. But they find gold hidden in some discarded pieces of wood, and this leads them into contact with General Rokurota, who is leading a princess to safety after her clan, owner of the gold, has been defeated in battle. The peasants agree to help but throughout the journey they attempt to escape with the gold. It is a dangerous route, but the general's skill and cunning ensures their safety. He cleverly gets them through checkpoints and fights with enemy soldiers when necessary in order to protect the princess but they are eventually captured. However, an adversary whom the general has previously defeated in personal combat, comes to their aid and they escape across the border to a safe haven. Not for the first time in the story, the two peasants think that have got their hands on the gold, but it is taken from them and they are left as poor as they were when the story began.

HISTORICAL CONTEXT

Japanese cinema began to reassert itself after the deprivations of the war and immediate post-war years. In its industrial approach it had followed the Hollywood studio system and continued to do this in the 1950s. As in Hollywood, the science-fiction genre, the 1954 *Godzilla* being a particularly successful example, and youth rebellion films were popular. The former's anti-nuclear subtext connects perfectly with the Hollywood films of the same decade, such as *Them!* (1954) and *The Incredible Shrinking Man* (1957), whilst the youth rebellion films chimed with Hollywood output, particularly *Rebel Without A Cause* (1955).

The main studios also embraced widescreen technology. The Toho studio created Tohovision as a reaction to the perceived threat from television and the desire to make spectacular films to maintain cinema attendances. *Hidden Fortress* was Kurosawa's first film using the widescreen process and its epic journey motif sits perfectly with the new epic frame, which the characters cross many times to reach their destination. There were a number of well-regarded film-makers emerging in Japan in the 1950s, making it a particularly fertile period for filmic creativity. Kurosawa's own *Rashomon* (1950) won an Honorary Academy Award and he cemented his international standing with films like *Seven Samurai* (1954).

Other films such as Kenji Mizoguchi's *The Life of Oharu* (1952) and Yasujiro Ozu's *Tokyo Story* (1953) propelled 1950's Japanese cinema onto the world stage, and Hollywood took notice, reworking Japanese films in later years. *Seven Samurai* would transform into *The Magnificent Seven* (1960); *Yojimbo* (1961) would become *A Fistful of Dollars* (1964) and *The Hidden Fortress* would be a template for *Star Wars* (1977).

East Asian cinema has also long been closely associated with the fantasy genre. Many of its narratives were derived from medieval history and folklore with a strong fantasy element. Whilst Kurosawa embarked on his series of samurai films, imbued with fantastical moments, in the 1950s other film-makers such as Kenji Mizoguchi were also making films with fantasy elements, the most renowned of which was *Ugetsu* (1953).

The genre has flourished in a number of forms across East Asia; wuxia films such as *A Touch of Zen* (1971), *Zu-Warriors from the Magic Mountain* (1983) and *Hero* (2002) from Taiwan, Honk Kong

and China respectively have successfully combined elements of martial arts and fantasy films. The strong belief in spirits and ghosts in these cultures has permeated not just the samurai or wuxia sub-genres, but has also propelled the narratives of other genres, particularly horror, where the growth of this genre in the noughties has led to a plethora of films where malevolent forces often derive from the spirit world, most markedly in Hideo's Nakata's *Ring* (1998) and *Dark Water* (2002).

SELECT FILMOGRAPHY OF MAIN PRODUCERS AND CAST

Akira Kurosawa, 1910-98, Director, Producer, Screenwriter

Stray Dog, 1949

Rashomon, 1950

Seven Samurai, 1954

Throne of Blood, 1957

The Hidden Fortress, 1958

Yojimbo, 1961

Sanjuro, 1962

Red Beard, 1965

Kagemusha, 1980

Ran, 1985

Dreams, 1990

Toshirô Mifune, 1920-97, Actor

Stray Dog, 1949

Rashomon, 1950

The Life of Oharu, 1952

Seven Samurai, 1954

Throne of Blood, 1957

The Hidden Fortress, 1958

Yojimbo, 1961

Sanjuro, 1962

Red Beard, 1965

Grand Prix, 1966

Hell in the Pacific, 1968

Red Sun, 1971

Paper Tiger, 1975

Midway, 1975

LINKS TO OTHER FILMS

Seven Samurai (1954)/*Yojimbo* (1961)

Both of these Kurosawa films star Toshirô Mifune in a samurai role. His devotion to the purity of action connect these films with *The Hidden Fortress*, as well as their detailing of Japan's medieval past.

Star Wars (1977)

George Lucas borrowed some of the plot elements for this film from Kurosawa, particularly in regard to the escape and capture motif and the princess-in-peril storyline. One of the key similarities is the story being seen from the point of view of the lowest characters in the story; in *The Hidden Fortress* this viewpoint is that of the two peasants, and in *Star Wars* it is the droids, R2D2 and C3PO.

Crouching Tiger, Hidden Dragon (2000)/*Hero* (2002)/ *House of Flying Daggers* (2004)

Although these are all Chinese wuxia films (narratives concerned with martial arts and philosophical issues of honour and loyalty) there are a number of connections between them and *The Hidden Fortress*. They all have a medieval setting and focus on an individual's ability to achieve grace through the purity of their actions and thoughts.

Kill Bill Vol. 1 & 2 (2003/4)

Quentin Tarantino borrows heavily from samurai films, as well as using visual and narrative motifs from martial arts films and Spaghetti Westerns.

The Bourne Ultimatum (2007)

Jason Bourne embodies the same principles of action that are evident in General Rokurota; the purity and intensity of his action connects with the general's instinctive movement and cunning in moments of danger.

REPRESENTATION

Action

Moments of intense action in *The Hidden Fortress* emanate from the character of Rokurota Makabe; he is devoted to the princess and all his efforts are channelled into her protection. His mental and physical agility are entwined so that they work in unison to extricate the group from numerous difficulties. A border checkpoint tests all his mental prowess, whereas his slaying of the two horse riders, which then leads to the confrontation with an old adversary, a general in the army that is pursuing the princess, is pure instinctive action.

The clash between the two generals is as much about mind games as it is about the fight. Most of the action occurs in the mind as the two men circle each other like animals. It is easy to see where Sergio Leone drew inspiration for his drawn-out Spaghetti Western gunfights; the finale of *The Good, the Bad and the Ugly* (1966) is particularly reminiscent of the clash between the generals - long periods of circumspection followed by a flash of action.

This approach to action can also be seen in the literary works of Ernest Hemingway. Novels such as *Death in the Afternoon* (1932) and *The Old Man and the Sea* (1952) explore an individual's adherence to strict self-imposed codes that lead them to undertake their personal battles, bull-fighting and sea fishing respectively, with supreme dedication. In *The Hidden Fortress*, Rokurota abides by the samurai code, known as Bushidō, a strict code of ethics which informs his every thought and action. It is the equivalent of the wuxia tradition in Chinese films, a sub-genre within the fantasy genre. The action in this film, in regard to the general, is informed by the spiritual as well as the physical, imbuing it with meaning and purpose.

Kurosawa made a number of other significant examples of this genre, including *Seven Samurai*, *Yojimbo* (1961) and *Sanjuro* (1962), as well as film-makers like Hiroshi Inagaki who directed a trilogy of samurai films from 1954 to 1956. Hollywood has also begun to produce its own versions of samurai stories with Jim Jarmusch's *Ghost Dog: The Way of the Samurai* (1999) and Edward Zwick's *The Last*

Samurai (2003) demonstrating a contemporary and historical approach respectively.

Peasants

The two peasants, Mataschichi and Tahei, are represented in fairly negative terms; they are shown to be ignorant, selfish, greedy and ruthless in their self-interest, even disloyal to *each other*. However, what is so revolutionary about their representation is that they are the focus of the film's narrative; the audience sees from their perspective, however lowly it may be. Although there are generals and a princess in the story, it is the two miscreants who dominate, and even though we are appalled by some of their actions it is with them that the audience is forced to identify.

Other Japanese films of this type, such as Masaki Kobayashi's *Harakiri* (1962) and Takeshi Kitano's *Zatōichi* (2003) follow the hero, a samurai, rather than any of the other characters. But there is a tradition elsewhere in cinema of eulogising the lowest in society; famously there is Charlie Chaplin's tramp and John Ford ennobled Tom Joad and his impoverished family in *The Grapes of Wrath* (1940). Mataschichi and Tahei, then, are certainly not noble, but the film's focus on them is the equivalent of the movement from religious to secular subjects in art, and echoes Shakespeare's foregrounding of 'lower' characters like Pistol and Bardolph in *Henry V*.

'Kurosawa's interest in action and loners established him as the most important non-Western director in the Western hero-centred mode.' Mark Cousins, *The Story of Film*, Pavillion Books, London, 2004

'The movie that confirmed Kurosawa's greatest strength, his innovative handling of genre.' Tony Rayns, *Time Out Film Guide 14th Ed.*, London, Time Out Guides Ltd., 2006

KEY SCENE TEXTUAL ANALYSIS

Captives (2)

A nightmarish world of captivity and deprivation is portrayed in this scene. The opening long shot depicts a mass of anonymous minions, heads bowed in submission, trudging up a vast stone staircase. They are surrounded by debris, reflecting their own sorry appearance, and the guards are just as anonymous, but in a brutal way, their armour cocooning them from the suffering of their charges. The sound of shuffling feet emphasises their misery, whilst the non-diegetic music, all musical grunts and shrieks (derived from Noh theatre music), suggests the inhuman nature of the captive's predicament and the nature of those who perpetrate such misery. The *mise-en-scène* is also dominated by the massive structures all around them; this, together with the staircase, suggests an epic scope that dwarfs the puny humans.

At the top of the frame another group appears, descending the staircase, but a full view is denied the audience as Kurosawa brings our attention to some of the individual suffering by cutting to a medium shot, focusing on Tahei, visually distinguished from the others by his bandana. He rears up as he notices the other group and we see his POV, establishing that this tale of heroism is being viewed through the very anti-heroic eyes of two cowardly peasants, Tahei and Mataschichi. If Tahei's group is on the verge of losing its human spirit, then this new group looks as if it has been spewed up from a subterranean hell. The medium shot of the two groups passing each other emphasises the contrast between them and affords the fleeting contact between the two companions.

The moment passes and their distress is underlined by their plaintive cries and the way the camera tracks backwards with Mataschichi, as if the audience is being propelled downwards by the soldiers and the inexorable march of these slaves. The camera dwells on Mataschichi's face, a picture of pain, his lined adult face overtaken by a child-like helplessness. Only when the camera cuts back to a long shot of Tahei is there a full cry from Mataschichi, all the more unsettling for being disembodied. Tahei returns the cry, but drowns beneath the mass of moving bodies, and there is a final shot of Mataschichi as, quiet once again and resigned to his fate, his face slowly drops towards the bottom of the frame.

The next long shot of Tahei's group makes full use of the 'scope frame as the captives trail from right to left, their misery filling the frame, its width emphasising the level of suffering and the scale of the hardship. Naked torsos and limbs contrast with

Hieronymus Bosch painting. In contrast to this dehumanising vision of the slaves, the guard in charge is perched above them, solitary and thus retaining his individuality, free and powerful, the camera looking up at him as he observes the men below. When he casts a basket down to the pit the camera follows, contrasting his lordly perch with the mass of flesh and suffering below. Discordant music accompanies this shot and heralds the inhuman struggle that faces these wretches.

Chase (11)

This scene borrows, in part, from the tradition of horse-bound chases seen in Hollywood Westerns, and invests it, through *mise-en-scène* and non-diegetic music, with a distinctly Eastern sensibility. The initial long shot is foregrounded with the figure of Rokurota Makabe as he makes a spectacular

the protective armour and shielding headwear of their guards, underlining the slaves' vulnerability. This, coupled with the shattered and dilapidated buildings above them, helps underpin the sense of devastation. The camera tracks around them as they are pushed and maltreated, moving aside as they enter one of the buildings and delaying the audience's view of their destination. Even when the camera is inside the building it is focused on the men and their reaction to their fate. The guards push them and the audience is denied a view for a few moments more to further increase our sense of expectation.

The first view of the pit into which they are thrown is foregrounded by the timbers of a building's roof, obscuring the audience's view but adding to the sense of decay and deprivation. The camera moves closer beyond the timbers and reveals a water-filled pit, a hellish watery grave. The slaves fall into its depths, reminiscent of figures from a

leap onto his horse. The initial shots of the chase are static as the riders move through the frame and make full use of its width. The diegetic sound of the horses' hooves on the ground emphasises the power of these creatures, and, in turn, suggests the dexterity of those involved in the chase. The non-diegetic music is synchronised with the lifting of Rokurota's sword, signalling *his* power and increasing the audience's expectation of what will happen.

In this shot, horse, man and sword are perfectly balanced. Symmetry and equilibrium are the hallmarks of Rokurota's stance and the monochrome cinematography, the dark clothes that he wears and his exposed arms and legs all combine to connect man and beast as a unified whole. The explosive brass sounds are akin to trumpets heralding the entrance of royalty; indeed, the general is the equivalent of a knight, the purity of action being a defining feature of his code.

The cut to a static shot of the retreating riders contrasts with the quick panning shot of Rokurota which follows, emphasising his dynamism and underpinning his dramatic roar. The camera captures his face and its look of total commitment and ferocity. The pace of the editing suddenly increases as four rapid shots of this terrifying pose are repeated, juxtaposed with the fleeing and insignificant soldiers on horseback. This is the boundary between continuity editing and montage. The sequence shows his movement forward, but also elevates the intensity of the moment as Rokurota emits his war cry. It again signifies the moment when purity of action transcends the normal pace of thought and action. The background is blurred as the camera stays closer to the general and side-on, rather than behind to suggest his superior pace and add to the sense that he has become dislocated from the restraints of normal

tracking close-ups of the hooves, which not only determines the pace of the sequence but endows it with a rhythm that expresses this purity of action as the unfortunate soldier is drawn into the general's world, albeit as his victim. The cut comes just after the fatal blow from Rokurota's sword and the soldier falls at the beginning of the final long shot of this sequence.

Again, the decisive moment bestrides a cut, underlining its rapidity, an action almost beyond conscious thought in its execution. The music comes to a dramatic conclusion, with Rokurota riding to the back of the frame, dominant and alone. The intensity of the action and the successful completion of the general's intentions brings a fleeting sense of closure and satisfaction for the audience, making the next cut to a long shot of Rokurota riding into the midst of the enemy's

and less effective action.

He catches up with the first rider very quickly and he is despatched with one quick-flowing and seamless action; the thrust of the sword occurs on the cut from long to medium shot, emphasising its rapidity and almost instinctive nature. The cut back to the remaining soldier is another static long shot with the long road ahead hinting at his ultimate fate. Rokurota soon moves into the rider's filmic space, at which point the action becomes even more frenetic. The cut to a tracking shot of the speeding hooves heralds this moment and it is synchronised with an increase in tempo of the non-diegetic music, a rapid drumming and staccato chords that underline the next stage of the pursuit.

From the close-up we move to a medium long shot of the riding combatants, back to the galloping hooves. In total, there is a pattern of five, long panning shots of the two riders intercut with five

camp all the more effective. The music ends, and the twist is further highlighted with the shot of his encirclement by a multitude of soldiers, their lances probing and threatening. What the audience thought was the end of the adventure is just the beginning...

Jason and the Argonauts

KEY FACTS

Release Date: 1963

Country of Origin: UK/USA

Running Time: 104 minutes

PRODUCTION NOTES

Production Companies

Columbia Pictures Corporation

Morningside Worldlong S.A.

Distributor

Columbia Pictures

Budget

$1,000,000 (estimated)

SYNOPSIS

Pelias murders his half-brother, King Aeson of Thessaly, and becomes ruler of the kingdom. Aeson's son, Jason, is unharmed and after years away from the kingdom he returns and, coincidentally, saves Pelias' life; in doing so he loses a sandal and Pelias realises that he is the man who has come to overthrow him, as prophesised years before. In order to get rid of Jason he convinces him to go on a quest to obtain the Golden Fleece in the hope that Jason will be killed en route. Jason is joined by a group of men, including Hercules and Acastus, Pelias' son, and they set sail aboard the *Argo*. The gods Zeus and Hera take an interest in the adventure; Hera helps Jason in moments of need throughout the voyage but Zeus is happy for the quest to fail.

They navigate a stretch of water where giant rocks clash together and Jason defeats a giant bronze statue, before finally reaching the island of Colchis, where the king's daughter, Medea, helps him in his quest. Jason kills the Hydra, a creature with many heads, and takes possession of the Golden Fleece. As he escapes the island, its king, Aeëtes, unleashes some skeletal soldiers who grow out of the ground after the king has scattered the Hydra's teeth. Jason and his companions defeat them and return to the *Argo* triumphant, setting sail for safety. The gods decide not to interfere with Jason's voyage, for a while at least.

HISTORICAL CONTEXT

Whether it was the supposed explosion of free love in the 1960s or something else, there were certainly a plethora of Greek and Roman sagas filmed in this period, allowing for the exposure of acres of flesh, both male and female. 'Sword and sandal' films had become extremely popular in the late 1950s and early 1960s, although this type of film had been made since the early days of silent cinema. They encompass a plethora of source material, including Biblical, Roman and Greek stories. Films such as *Ben-Hur* (1959) were highly prestigious and expensive productions that often did very good business at the box office. It was not until 1963's financial disaster, *Cleopatra* - made for an estimated and colossal $44,000,000 (imdb.com) - that film companies became more wary of this genre.

This sort of film was revived in the 1980s with *Clash of the Titans* (1981) and the *Conan* films, and then again in the noughties with the likes of *Troy* (2004) and *Alexander* (2004). *Jason and the Argonauts*, made for an estimated and relatively modest $1,000,000, came after a long line of Italian-made 'sword and sandal' dramas that featured characters like Hercules, Samson and Ursus. Italy provided the ideal climate, locations and studios and there were both homegrown and American productions throughout the early 1960s. The disastrous *Cleopatra* prompted American studios to pull out of these productions and the cycle of the Spaghetti Western in Italy began, which were to prove highly profitable and successful across the world. In the end, the 'sword and sandal' films seemed to be a part of a slightly older and more genteel 1950's mentality, replaced by the excesses of the Spaghetti Western, a move from swords to shotguns and other more hi-tech killing implements.

Ray Harryhausan's stop motion work for *Jason and the Argonauts* followed many years of championing this type of special effect, a mantle that he took from Willis O'Brien, creator of the stop motion effects for films such as *King Kong*. Harryhausan was mentored by O'Brien on a later RKO production, *Mighty Joe Young* (1949), and then worked on a string of films depicting a variety of monsters, including *The Beast from 20,000*

Fathoms (1953), *It Came From Beneath the Sea* (1955) and *The 7th Voyage of Sinbad* (1958). *Clash of the Titans* saw the end of Harryhausan's work with the advent of computer-generated imagery (CGI) - the first completely computer-generated sequence materialised in 1982's *Star Trek II: The Wrath of Khan*.

SELECT FILMOGRAPHY OF MAIN PRODUCERS AND CAST

Don Chaffey, 1917-1990, Director, Producer

Danger Within, 1959

Dentist in the Chair, 1960

Greyfriars Bobby: The True Story of a Dog, 1961

The Webster Boy, 1962

Jason and the Argonauts, 1963

The Three Lives of Thomasina, 1964

The Crooked Road, 1965

One Million Years B.C., 1966

Creatures the World Forgot, 1971

Charley One-Eye, 1973

Persecution, 1974

Ride a Wild Pony, 1975

Pete's Dragon, 1975

The Magic of Lassie, 1978

Charles H. Schneer, 1920, Producer

It Came from Beneath the Sea, 1955

Earth vs. the Flying Saucers, 1956

The 7th Voyage of Sinbad, 1958

Jason and the Argonauts, 1963

First Men in the Moon, 1964

Half a Sixpence, 1967

The Golden Voyage of Sinbad, 1974

Sinbad and the Eye of the Tiger, 1977

Clash of the Titans, 1981

Todd Armstrong, 1937-1992, Actor

Walk on the Wild Side, 1962

Five Finger Exercise, 1962

Jason and the Argonauts, 1963

King Rat, 1965

Dead Heat on a Merry-Go-Round, 1966

A Time for Killing, 1967

Bernard Herrmann, 1911-1975, Composer

Citizen Kane, 1941

The Magnificent Ambersons, 1942

Jane Eyre, 1944

The Ghost and Mrs. Muir, 1947

The Day the Earth Stood Still, 1951

On Dangerous Ground, 1952

The Trouble with Harry, 1955

The Man Who Knew Too Much, 1956

The Wrong Man, 1956

The Seventh Voyage of Sinbad, 1958

Vertigo, 1958

North by Northwest, 1959

Journey to the Center of the Earth, 1959

Psycho, 1960

Cape Fear, 1962

Jason and the Argonauts, 1963

Marnie, 1964

Fahrenheit 451, 1966

Taxi Driver, 1976

LINKS TO OTHER FILMS

The 7th Voyage of Sinbad (1958)/*The Golden Voyage of Sinbad* (1974)/*Sinbad and the Eye of the Tiger* (1977)/*Clash of the Titans* (1981)

Charles H. Schneer collaborated on all these

films (and others) with visual effects creator, Ray Harryhausen. His creation of beasts, both real and mythical, was at the cutting-edge of this type of technology, only overtaken by CGI in the late 1980s and early 1990s with films like *Terminator 2: Judgment Day* (1991) and *Jurassic Park* (1993).

Ulysses (1955)/*Hercules* (1958)/*Colossus of Rhodes* (1960)

These are just a few of the many 'sword and sandal' films from this era, many being Italian-produced versions of the stories using an American star in the lead role. Here, Kirk Douglas plays Ulysees, Steve Reeves is Hercules and Rory Calhoun is Darios in the *Colossus of Rhodes*; all attempts to secure wider international appeal. This practice was, of course, continued with the Italian Spaghetti Westerns with the likes of Clink Eastwood and Lee van Cleef being imported to star.

REPRESENTATION

Greek myths

Although classical scholars may not approve of some of the liberties that film-makers have taken with the stories of the ancient world, the fact is that these are *myths*, handed down through the ages in the oral tradition. There would have been countless versions of the same story and the films are just a part of this never-ending process of assimilation and reinvention. The story of *Jason and the Argonauts* contains many universal truths about human nature: the deception and murderous actions of Pelias; or the fortitude and perseverance of Jason and his comrades in the face of all manner of obstacles and opposition.

The Greek myths are a potent mix for film-makers and audiences alike with their scintillating narratives involving murder, treachery, love, sex, incest, acts of heroism and incredible strength, hideous creatures, battles and the capricious involvement of the gods. These ingredients have ensured the genre's ability to be reinvented for each new generation, but an ongoing characteristic is that the representation of the humans is often less fully rounded than that of the creatures that are created by either stop-motion or computer-generated imagery.

The skeletons, the harpies and the hydra are the most vibrant creations in the film, a testament to Ray Harryhausen's skill, but also an acknowledgement by the film-makers that the best recreation of the Greek myth lies in their ability to represent these creatures with as much life as possible. The malevolence of these creations is far greater than that of any human, and it is the audience's suspension of disbelief that allows the film to represent the Greek myths convincingly.

'The film itself is given an enormous boost by Ray Harryhausen's special effects... Great fun... with a Bernard Herrmann score to boot'. Tom Milne, *Time Out Film Guide 14th Ed.*, Time Out Guides Ltd., London, 2006

KEY SCENE TEXTUAL ANALYSIS

The skeleton soldiers (27/28)

The initial long shot shows a tranquil and beautiful scene of mountains and the sea in the distance but this serenity is immediately punctured by spears that thrust upwards from unseen hands in the middle distance. Only one figure emerges, the rest remain out of view, their spears symbols of danger and violence for Jason and his companions. The non-diegetic music is full of menace and foreshadows the fantastical battle that follows.

The costumes of both adversaries are rich in detail and lend an air of authenticity to the action, as do other elements of the *mise-en-scène* such as the surrounding buildings, with their columns and hand-built walls. Although what is to happen is certainly myth, the trappings of an ancient reality lend an air of verisimilitude.

The non-diegetic music dies away for a few moments and the sound of the wind is heard, an eerie reminder of Jason's isolation as he flees with Medea and the Golden Fleece; the music returns ominously as the Hydra's teeth are scattered over the ground. Aeëtes at first walks threateningly into the foreground of the frame. The reverse shot shows his outstretched hand, containing the teeth, which obscures the audience's view of Jason's two soldier companions in the background, perhaps a visual suggestion that they will be most strongly affected by the demonic fruit of these dental seeds; indeed they are the two out of the five in Jason's group who will be killed by the skeleton soldiers.

On Aeëtes' final words of doom, and as he retreats from the frame, the music strikes up again, this time the chords punching like a diabolical boxer. Aeëtes' retreat from the frame coincides with a pan of the three soldiers. Close-ups reveal their confusion and fear and, as Argos and Medea flee, Jason and his two soldiers adopt an action stance, three abreast, flamboyantly unsheathing their swords ready for the fight. They are like three Greek Zorros or Robin Hoods, action heroes in colour co-ordinated outfits. The colours of gold, brown and white cast them as comrades, but with original and individual design flourishes, such as those on their shields.

Three more close-ups of anxious faces follow to increase the tension, and then the first of the skeletons begins its birth and eruption from the soil. The music begins again, synchronised with this rebirth of the dead and the optical zoom towards Jason's face helps to suggest to the audience the incredible impact that this is having on him.

The skeleton is seen first in close-up and then in long shot, the composite image of foreground and background marking the precise interaction between live-action filming and Ray Harryhausen stop-frame animation. This pre-CGI environment relies, like *King Kong* before it, on the most authentic of fantasy rendering to enable the audience to be convinced and transported into another realm where disbelief can be suspended. Other bridging devices between animation and live footage are employed to endow the sequence with even greater authenticity - both worlds are synchronised by Aeëtes pointing directly at each skeleton as it emerges and his voice aurally linking the two layers together. The non-diegetic music is as sinister as ever, but added percussion represents the rattling of the skeletons' bones.

As the skeletons continue to emerge we also see close-ups again of the human faces. The juxtaposition highlighs their fear and vulnerability compared with these fleshless creations: how will Jason defeat these undead beings? As the skeletons bend forward into attack position, the side-on view emphasises their hostility. Just as Jason and his soldiers are given differently emblazoned shields, so are the skeletons, giving each a chilling individuality.

As they move forward we see the humans backing away and a long shot sees Jason et al being forced out of the frame. Their movement is forbidding, a stalking gait that causes a sinister rattle with each bony step. Their faces, too, exude menace with their cavernously dark eye sockets and the inclusion of teeth in their mouths giving them an even greater ghoulish air. The charge, when it finally comes

The shots are cut more rapidly now to match the charged pace of the battle, moving from long shots to close-ups of the soldiers and then to the skeletons. Their blank stares and moving jaws lend them a terrifying aspect and the non-diegetic music has also gathered pace to propel the action in its slightly discordant way. The diegetic sound of clashing swords and shields is also highlighted, particularly in the close-ups of close quarter fighting.

As they kill two soldiers, the skeletons react with more than just aggression. They watch with seeming glee as the soldiers fall, a momentary fascination with their supernatural handiwork, and they also react with pain when struck. But, ultimately, they are relentless in their attack. They are ancient terminators who do not lose their heads (well, only once) and pursue unto death as

(towards the audience), is accompanied by an unexpected, and frightening, scream, investing them with even more terror. These touches of a heightened 'life-within-death' help convey even more of a frightening aspect for both Jason and the audience.

The key to the battle sequence's authenticity is the choreography between the soldiers and their skeletal adversaries. The many ruins strewn over the area are utilised to bring more physical drama to the fight, as they provide a number of different levels upon which the individual struggles can take place, rather than just on level ground. The first set-up is a long shot that is a three-layered composite: the soldiers, the skeleton and the massive sculpted head in the foreground, the latter giving the *mise-en-scène* an extra dimension of authenticity.

they plunge into the sea and Jason makes good his escape.

The cut back to the composite shot of Hera looking down into her pool frames the whole adventure as merely a spectacle for the gods, a minor skirmish in their use of humankind as playthings. The robes and prominent white and gold colours which dominate the set of Ancient Greek columns and reliefs reinforce the audience's expectations of what the kingdom of the gods should look like, a calm and ordered surface where godly whims explain the chaos that befalls humanity.

That the final image of Jason and Medea's kiss is seen within the framing of the gods' pool emphasises their power over the humans, and it seems that Hera's wave of her hand summons up the end title on screen: the gods are even controlling the film.

Soylent Green

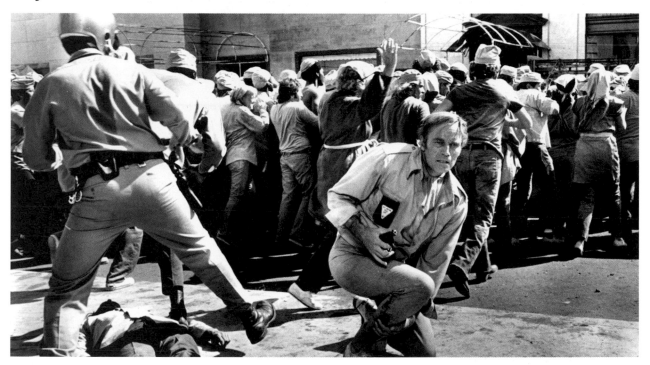

KEY FACTS

Release Date: 1973

Country of Origin: USA

Running Time: 97 minutes

PRODUCTION NOTES

Production Company

Metro-Goldwyn-Mayer (MGM)

Distributor

Metro-Goldwyn-Mayer (MGM)

SYNOPSIS

It is New York and the year is 2022. Overcrowding and pollution beset the planet and the majority of people live in near-squalor, relying on government hand-outs of synthetic food. Thorn is a police detective, who lives with an elderly police partner, Sol, known as a 'book' (a police researcher). He is investigating the death of an executive in the Soylent Corporation, the manufacturer of the foodstuffs, which are generally eaten in tablet form. Simonson, the victim, has actually been murdered and Thorn starts to suspect a high-level cover-up. There is an attempt on Thorn's life during a food riot as he unravels the complexities of the conspiracy and when Sol discovers the truth about the origins of Soylent Green he decides to end his life at a euthanasia clinic.

Thorn reaches Sol just before he dies and sees images of what the planet used to look like before it was polluted. He learns the secret of Soylent Green, a fact kept hidden from the audience until the end of the film. Thorn follows Sol's body on its journey to a processing plant where he sees the manufacture of the foodstuff, its source ingredient being human bodies. He escapes but is wounded and the story ends with his plea to his police captain to tell the public that 'Soylent Green is people'.

HISTORICAL CONTEXT

We may associate the noughties with moral panics about pollution and climate change, but

Soylent Green is an early 1970's film dealing with the very same issues. The era was dominated by a growing trend amongst people to voice their anti-Establishment opinions and protest against governments. The Vietnam War was coming to an end and an energy crisis hit the world in 1973 as the Organisation of the Petroleum Exporting Countries (OPEC) challenged Western powers by embargoing the sale of oil. The events of Watergate, where criminal activity was traced to the very top of government, had been played out the previous year and there was a growing distrust of the Establishment; all this proved fertile ground for this type of film to be made, one full of panic, paranoia and doom.

The gloom that pervaded mainstream Hollywood cinema in the 1970s can be seen in films as diverse as James William Guercio's motorcycle cop production, *Electra Glide in Blue* (1973) to Alan J. Pakula's political paranoia story, *The Parallax View* (1974) and Martin Scorsese's tale of self-destruction in *Taxi Driver* (1976). The Vietnam War, Watergate, world recession... all fuelled these doom-laden films and put a mirror up to social mores. If real life was bad, then cinema also presented numerous bleak visions of the future. *Soylent Green* was one of many dystopian fantasies, including *The Omega Man* (1971), *Zardoz* (1974) and *Mad Max* (1979). The future was inevitably depicted as a time when humanity had caused its own downfall, apocalyptic visions built upon the real-life events of the Cold War and the nuclear arms race.

SELECT FILMOGRAPHY OF MAIN PRODUCERS AND CAST

Richard Fleischer, 1916-2006, Director, Producer

Bodyguard, 1948

The Clay Pigeon, 1949

Trapped, 1949

Armored Car Robbery, 1950

The Narrow Margin, 1952

20,000 Leagues Under the Sea, 1954

Violent Saturday, 1955

Bandido, 1956

The Vikings, 1958

Barabbas, 1961

Fantastic Voyage, 1966

Doctor Dolittle, 1967

The Boston Strangler, 1968

Che!, 1969

Tora! Tora! Tora!, 1970

10 Rillington Place, 1971

The New Centurions, 1972

Soylent Green, 1973

The Don is Dead, 1973

The Jazz Singer, 1980

Conan the Destroyer, 1984

Charlton Heston, 1924–2008, Actor

Julius Caesar, 1950

The Greatest Show on Earth, 1952

Ruby Gentry, 1952

The Naked Jungle, 1954

The Ten Commandments, 1956

Touch of Evil, 1958

The Big Country, 1958

Ben-Hur, 1959

El Cid, 1961

55 Days at Peking, 1963

The Greatest Story Ever Told, 1965

Major Dundee, 1965

The Agony and the Ecstasy, 1965

The War Lord, 1965

Khartoum, 1966

Planet of the Apes, 1968

Will Penny, 1968

The Hawaiians, 1970

The Omega Man, 1971

Soylent Green, 1973

The Three Musketeers, 1973

Earthquake, 1974

The Four Musketeers, 1974

Two-Minute Warning, 1976

Edward G. Robinson, 1893-1973, Actor

Little Caesar, 1931

Bullets or Ballots, 1936

Kid Galahad, 1937

The Amazing Dr. Clitterhouse, 1938

Confessions of a Nazi Spy, 1939

Blackmail, 1939

Dr. Ehrlich's Magic Bullet, 1940

Double Indemnity, 1944

The Woman in the Window, 1945

Scarlet Street, 1945

The Stranger, 1946

Key Largo, 1948

The Violent Men, 1955

The Ten Commandments, 1956

Two Weeks in Another Town, 1962

The Prize, 1963

Cheyenne Autumn, 1964

The Cincinnati Kid, 1965

Soylent Green, 1973

LINKS TO OTHER FILMS

Planet of the Apes (1968)/*The Omega Man* (1971)

These films form parts one and two of an unofficial trilogy (concluding with *Soylent Green*) starring Charlton Heston and exploring humanity's penchant for self-destruction. Their tone is generally downbeat with endings that do not offer too much hope for survival, particularly *Planet of the Apes*. *The Omega Man* is the second of three versions to date of a Richard Matheson novel, *I Am Legend*. *The Last Man on Earth* (1964) and *I Am Legend* (2007) have also explored his post-apocalyptic vision where a plague has left a man single-handedly battling against hordes of mutated humans.

Silent Running (1972)

Douglas Trumball's vision of the future where all plant life has died out on earth, leaving a number of freighters to carry the remaining trees and plants in deep space. This film, like *Soylent Green*, charts man's capacity to destroy his own environment and then take desperate measures to survive.

An Enemy of the People (1978)

George Schaefer's film of the Henrik Ibsen play deals with a man's attempts to alert a town to the fact that their newly-constructed public baths are, in fact, polluted and poisoning the tourists for whom they were constructed. The play is an early example of an ecological issue, but focuses on the Establishment's propensity to cover up corruption.

Blade Runner (1982)

In Ridley Scott's version of Philip K. Dick's story, *Do Androids Dream of Electric Sheep?*, the natural environment has been altered by man's meddling. In this dystopian future it seems to be constantly dark and raining and life on the surface has become as chaotic and dangerous as that in *Soylent Green*.

Erin Brockovich (2000)

Steven Soderbergh's film, like *An Enemy of the People*, focuses on a corruption investigation into possible harmful environmental effects on the general populace. Although realised on a smaller scale than *Soylent Green*, it still conveys a message of a ruthless corporation taking advantage of the common man and woman.

An Inconvenient Truth (2006)

Al Gore's documentary about climate change contains facts and hypotheses that confirm some of *Soylent Green*'s predictions about climate change caused by pollution.

REPRESENTATION

New York City

New York City has become a potent symbol in both culture and film history. The iconography of Manhattan's skyscraper-filled skyline has figured in numerous films and conveys a number of connotations. Even back in the 1930s the iconic Empire State Building was used in *King Kong*, a steel mountain for the ape to climb. The 1976 remake moved the focus to the Twin Towers of the World Trade Center, the tallest buildings in New York at the time, which have since become arguably the most iconic buildings in the world since their destruction in 2001. They represented, depending on your viewpoint, a symbol of either freedom or repression and their destruction connoted either an attack on democracy or a victory over tyranny.

The Statue of Liberty is another iconic structure, a symbol of hope for millions of immigrants, detailed in *The Godfather Part II* (1974) as a young Vito arrives in New York after fleeing Sicily. For Taylor, in *Planet of the Apes*, the half-destroyed statue at the film's end confirms humanity's capacity for self-destruction. A decapitated Statue of Liberty in *Cloverfield* (2008) also signals the scale of the problem facing New Yorkers as a monster runs riot in their city.

New York City, as a whole, has been the backdrop for gritty, urban films such as Sidney Lumet's *Serpico* (1973) and *Dog Day Afternoon* (1975), or Woody Allen's love poem to his home in *Manhattan* (1979). Closer to the atmosphere of *Soylent Green* is John Carpenter's *Escape from New York* (1981) wherein the island of Manhattan has been transformed into a walled maximum security prison, resulting in a world of lawlessness and chaos. *I Am Legend* also features a New York that is out of control; but is most notable for the absence of people, a particularly striking image for a city that audiences associate with human bustle and vibrancy.

Soylent Green is set in New York but interestingly it does not make anything of its locale, instead focusing on the overcrowded streets and tenement buildings. It has no clear identity and could be anywhere, which could well be the point.

Society has broken down so much that the iconic structures of any city are rendered redundant. The struggle just to survive has become paramount, leaving the city as a featureless backdrop against which individual tragedies are played out every day. Indeed, it is the cities with their voracious appetites that have largely *contributed* to the adverse effects detailed in the film.

> 'It certainly knocks the silly juvenilia epitomised and inspired by Star Wars and ET for six.' Geoff Andrew, *Time Out Film Guide 14th Ed.*, London, Time Out Guides Ltd., 2006

KEY SCENE TEXTUAL ANALYSIS

The history of the world (1)

A montage of still images recreates a history of the modern world, beginning with some images of the rural idyll, people on the cusp of the twentieth century with all its promise of a bright future. The non-diegetic music is upbeat and wistful, the images dissolving from one to another and conveying a sense of calm, along with the slow camera movement across each scene. The tempo of the music and the pace of movement on each image gathers momentum as scenes of industrialisation are shown.

The real acceleration, visually and aurally, does not occur until the images change from monochrome to colour - then we see shots of cars, overcrowding, violence and pollution. The pace of editing reaches a frenzy as the music careers wildly and the images become fractured, shifting chaotically using the split screen device. Only when the images indicate that humanity has run itself and the planet to near extinction does the pace of music and visuals slow down and we now behold a wasteland, the damage self-inflicted. The final image of a smog-ridden cityscape prepares the way for the rest of the film.

As the film's title appears from out of this maelstrom of images the non-diegetic music is finally dominated by unnatural sounds that suggest alienation; indeed, humankind has created an alien existence for itself. It is not a montage to just visually illustrate a slide into a degenerative state, but the *rhythm* of the visuals themselves underlines our hopes, ambitions and penchant for self-destruction. It is a symphony of modernity with all its stresses, blinkered existences and fragile superficialities. It marks a visual stream of consciousness that details humanity's initial contemplations, the creation, then the gorging, and finally spewing forth, exhausted and empty.

The bare essentials (9)

The scene starts on a close-up of the sign 'Tuesday is *Soylent Green* day' daubed across a shop window, yet another reference to the miracle food that has been added to the population's diet. As the camera zooms out we can see that the streets are teeming with people. The frame is filled with human activity;

that simple water is a focus for many of the people and is reminiscent of images that we associate with developing countries. The camera continues to track along the never-ending mass of bodies, milling about pointlessly with the diegetic sound a cacophony of murmurs and empty promises.

Eventually, the camera alights on Sol, Thorn's wise, world-weary and humane sidekick. His age and stylish beret set him apart from the others for this is obviously not a place where people usually hope to grow old or where individuality flourishes. The expression on his face is a mixture of forlornness and defiance, a man of dignity who refuses to become an automaton.

Dining in style (10)

This is an almost wordless scene in which the beauty of the past is revived for a short time by a

it is world that is teetering on the brink of extinction and there is no room to move or escape (the film has opened with the caption 'THE YEAR: 2022 THE PLACE: NEW YORK CITY THE POPULATION: 40,000,000').

The diegetic sound of voices dominates; it is a world of voices with no say, shuffling in different directions with nowhere to go. The palette of the *mise-en-scène* is decidedly bland. Browns and pale blues dominate and what colour is left is saturated to give a lifeless and bleached appearance. The Earth has been ravaged and the colour has gone, the constant heat removing signs of vibrant life. Some people have masks over their mouths to indicate the pollution levels and all wear a sombre and downbeat expression in keeping with their hopeless predicament. Faint smog filters the light.

The cut to the close-up of water bottles and a sea of white faces living on the edge of existence reveals

meal of almost forgotten or unknown food. The *mise-en-scène* is decidedly drab and perfunctory, comprising a wall of dirty browns, exposed pipes and a few faded utensils. Sol is old and hunched, but, as in the scene analysed above, his beret endows him with individuality. Thorn, in his bright white t-shirt, has the appearance of vitality. Gentle and serene diegetic classical music can be heard, contrasting with the drabness of the room and underpinning the uniqueness of the meal. It signals a moment in time when both men are elevated above their banal and impoverished existences by culinary time travel.

When Sol shows Thorn real cutlery instead of the plastic implements that they usually use it is a low angle shot with the short man (Sol) towering above his statuesque friend. Sol is taking Thorn on a voyage of discovery, a journey into the past, and the normally active and proactive younger man is being led by Sol, whose age connects him with a past that empowers him. Until this point in the film Thorn has gently rebuked Sol for his yearnings for the past, but this is the first stage in Thorn's education that will reach its completion at Sol's death 'ceremony' later in the film. The lessons are not easy - in a comic moment the first course falls flat as Thorn registers disappointment with the lettuce.

The presentation of the main course, beef, is afforded a close-up to emphasise its importance. As Sol serves and watches Thorn he is again seen above him, a teacher and guide, willing his student to make a connection with the past, to love what he has loved. What follows is a pattern of shots, which, in most respects, resembles the set-up for a conversation between two people. Once the food is served there is a 15-shot sequence of alternating medium close-ups of both men, framed with space either camera left or right (the convention to

the sequence above one of just maudlin musings on the past. The alternation of shots, although presenting the progress of the meal, suggests the close connection between the two men; it is a montage of their relationship, a celebration of their unity. The framing of the shots also restricts the audience's view of their depressing environment and for a brief time they are freed from the limitations of their lives.

indicate that a conversation is occurring with both protagonists sitting opposite each other).

Yet there are no words; small talk is transcended as the men experience a shared moment of epiphany. The fairly rapid cutting between them sets up a rhythm, a dialogue of exchanges that cannot be expressed on a verbal level. Perhaps only the beauty of the accompanying music can do justice to their thoughts and feelings. As Sol takes his first taste of the beef his reaction is of sublime pleasure and he can only express it in musical terms as he conducts a symphony to his taste buds and the old world that is recreated for him. The teacher/student motif is repeated with the eating of the apple, Thorn copying Sol's example by rubbing it before taking a bite. The apple also affords another opportunity to imbue the sequence with a touch of comedy when Sol cannot bite the apple because of his poor teeth. This, coupled with the 'lettuce moment' elevates

Brazil

KEY FACTS

Release Date: 1985

Country of Origin: UK

Running Time: 142 minutes

PRODUCTION NOTES

Production Company

Embassy International Pictures

Distributor

Universal Pictures

Budget

$15,000,000 (estimated)

Awards

Best Production Design Norman Garwood BAFTA Awards, UK

Best Special Visual Effects George Gibbs, Richard Conway BAFTA Awards, UK

Best Director Terry Gilliam Los Angeles Film Critics Association Awards

Best Picture Los Angeles Film Critics Association Awards

Best Screenplay Terry Gilliam, Charles McKeown, Tom Stoppard Los Angeles Film Critics Association Awards

SYNOPSIS

Brazil is set in a world very similar to our own, but one which is obviously an alternate reality, the sort created by Philip Pullman in his trilogy of novels, *His Dark Materials*, the initial story filmed as *The Golden Compass* in 2007. The story begins with a machine error that results in a wrongful arrest and will implicate other characters as the narrative progresses. Sam Lowry works in a government office, The Department of Works, which is a grindingly bureaucratic organisation in a *1984*-style world where conformity and drudgery govern people's lives. Sam dreams of another existence where he is a superhero, but in reality he is content with his mediocrity. His mother tries to advance his career and set him up with a girlfriend.

An old friend, Jack Lint, has made good progress through the ranks and wonders why Sam does not try to move upwards. Whilst talking to Jack, Sam notices a woman who closely resembles someone from his dreams and he eventually catches up with her. As well as taking on a new job, thanks to his mother's help, he is visited by a rogue air-conditioning engineer called Tuttle who is wanted by the state for carrying out unofficial repairs. His mother's plastic surgery and terrorist attacks interweave with the main storyline until Sam is arrested for supposed subversive activity together with the woman, Jill, from his dreams, with whom he has embarked on a love affair. He is taken to Jack Lint who begins to torture him in order to force a confession. While there, Tuttle and a band of freedom fighters abseil into the huge chamber and free him, allowing him to escape with Jill. But this idyllic ending is shattered when it is revealed that the final section of the film, Sam's escape, has all been his dying dream.

HISTORICAL CONTEXT

Brazil was made in 1984 but released the following year. Its parallels with the George Orwell novel are clear with both portraying an all-seeing, totalitarian state, bound by bureaucracy and divided by fear. Ironically, at this time Britain was undergoing a prolonged period of decentralisation and denationalisation in an attempt to make private business and individual enterprise thrive. The sense that the state was watching seems out of place in this atmosphere; indeed, countries in Eastern Europe were on the brink of freedom from oppression.

Yet *Brazil* seems to foreshadow the world of a decade or two later when the digital age ushered in a new era of surveillance and fear, with freedom masked by states' increasing propensity to observe their populations (today the UK has more surveillance cameras - over one million - than any other European country). Director and co-writer Terry Gilliam certainly taps into the anxiety of terrorism, a real threat in 1980's Britain with the activities of the Provisional IRA conducting a campaign on the British mainland. The bombings at Hyde Park (1982), Harrods (1983) and the Grand Hotel in Brighton, where Thatcher and many of her cabinet colleagues were staying for the party conference (1984), were notable examples and are reflected in the carnage that suddenly erupts in *Brazil*.

The film, in many ways, echoes Gilliam's own working life - a series of struggles against studio executives who have not shared his artistic vision. Gilliam's final edit of *Brazil* produced some particularly savage disputes between him and executives, and other films, most recently *The Brothers Grimm* (2005), have been epicentres of conflict. A common theme in his work is the struggle with bureaucracy, monotony and small-mindedness, and the ability to remain sane in the face of this or fly from reality into a more exciting fantasy world.

Brazil is something of an anomaly when compared with fantasy films in the 1980s; after so many dystopian visions of the future in the 1970s, film-makers in the 1980s embarked on a series of fantasy adventures that would foreshadow *The Lord of the Rings* trilogy. Films such as *Hawk the Slayer* (1980), *Dragonslayer* (1981), *Conan the Barbarian* (1982), *Krull* (1983), *Ladyhawke* (1985), *Legend* (1985) and *The Princess Bride* (1987) demonstrated a fairy-tale approach to fantasy, where good ultimately defeats evil. It is a message that Gilliam does not deliver with *Brazil*'s denouement as he characteristically confounds audience expectations of genre.

SELECT FILMOGRAPHY OF MAIN PRODUCERS AND CAST

Terry Gilliam, 1940, Director, Producer, Screenwriter, Actor

Monty Python and the Holy Grail, 1975

Jabberwocky, 1977

Time Bandits, 1981

Monty Python's The Meaning of Life (segment), 1983

Brazil, 1985

The Adventures of Baron Munchausen, 1988

The Fisher King, 1991

Twelve Monkeys, 1995

Fear and Loathing in Las Vegas, 1998

The Brothers Grimm, 2005

Tideland, 2005

The Imaginarium of Doctor Parnassus, 2009

Tom Stoppard, 1937, Screenwriter

The Romantic Englishwoman, 1975

Despair, 1978

Brazil, 1985

Empire of the Sun, 1987

Rosencrantz and Guildenstern are Dead, 1990

The Russia House, 1990

Billy Bathgate, 1991

Shakespeare in Love, 1998

Enigma, 2001

Roger Pratt, 1947, Director of Photography

Monty Python's The Meaning of Life (segment), 1983

Brazil, 1985

Mona Lisa, 1986

High Hopes, 1988

Batman, 1989

The Fisher King, 1991

Shadowlands, 1993

Frankenstein, 1994

Twelve Monkeys, 1995

The End of the Affair, 1999

Chocolat, 2000

Iris, 2001

Harry Potter and the Chamber of Secrets, 2002

Troy, 2004

Harry Potter and the Goblet of Fire, 2005

Michael Kamen, 1948-2003, Composer

The Dead Zone, 1983

Brazil, 1985

Rita, Sue and Bob Too, 1986

Highlander, 1986

Mona Lisa, 1986

Lethal Weapon, 1987

Someone To Watch Over Me, 1987

Die Hard, 1988

The Adventures of Baron Munchausen, 1988

Licence To Kill, 1989

Lethal Weapon 2, 1989

The Krays, 1990

Die Hard 2, 1990

Robin Hood: Prince of Thieves, 1991

Let Him Have It, 1991

The Last Boy Scout, 1991

Lethal Weapon 3, 1992

Die Hard: With A Vengeance, 1995

Lethal Weapon 4, 1998

X-Men, 2000

Open Range, 2003

Jonathan Pryce, 1947, Actor

Breaking Glass, 1980

Something Wicked This Way Comes, 1983

The Ploughman's Lunch, 1983

Brazil, 1985

The Adventures of Baron Munchausen, 1988

Glengarry Glen Ross, 1992

Carrington, 1995

Evita, 1996

Regeneration, 1997

Tomorrow Never Dies, 1997

Stigmata, 1999

Pirates of the Carribean: The Curse of the Black Pearl, 2003

The Brothers Grimm, 2005

The New World, 2005

Pirates of the Carribean: Dead Man's Chest, 2006

Pirates of the Carribean: At World's End, 2007

Michael Palin, 1943, Actor, Screenwriter, Producer

And Now For Something Completely Different, 1971

Monty Python and the Holy Grail, 1975

Jabberwocky, 1977

Monty Python's Life of Brian, 1979

Time Bandits, 1981

The Missionary, 1982

Monty Python's The Meaning of Life, 1983

A Private Function, 1984

Brazil, 1985

A Fish Called Wanda, 1988

American Friends, 1991

The Wind in the Willows, 1996

Fierce Creatures, 1997

LINKS TO OTHER FILMS

The Trial (1962)

Orson Welles' adaptation of the Franz Kafka novel is an exploration of events that occur beyond the control of an individual, Joseph K., as it details his arrest for an unspecified crime and his eventual execution. *Brazil* echoes this atmosphere of a fated life manipulated by the machinations of others.

Time Bandits (1981)/*The Adventures of Baron Munchausen* (1988)

Time Bandits was the first in Terry Gilliam's so-called Trilogy of the Imagination, continuing with

Brazil and ending with *The Adventures of Baron Munchausen*. All three films share the theme of the conflict between the freedom of the imagination and the restrictions of reality.

1984 (1984)

George Orwell's novel has become the template for all other visions of totalitarian states, and this Michael Radford film faithfully explores the control and deprivations associated with existing in such a structure.

Pan's Labyrinth (2007)

Guillermo del Toro's film explores the conflict between imagination and reality, containing sequences which may or may not be the dreams of a young girl escaping the harsh realities of her family life and the aftermath of the Spanish Civil War (see pg. 379).

REPRESENTATION

Bureaucracy

Brazil is littered with red tape that stifles creativity and imagination and engenders pettiness and easy cruelty. A bored worker initiates the chain of events that leads to a wrongful arrest by swatting a fly that lands in his typewriter and changes the name of the man to be arrested from 'Tuttle' to 'Buttle'. It is reminiscent of chaos theory, whereby the beating of a butterfly's wings can have an effect on events around the world. The worker who kills the fly gets immense satisfaction from the act; for a moment he is dominant in a world that is inscrutable because of its bureaucracy and its labyrinthine nature over which few, if any, have an overview.

The emphasis on individual blindness and insignificance in the face of the bureaucratic machine is illustrated by Sam's new office when he is promoted. He and co-worker, Harvey Lime, fight over the desk that they share (even though it is separated by a wall) and they are hermetically sealed from an understanding of how the system in which they operate actually *works*. As a result, they all escape the banalities and routine of their lives; Sam has his dreams and his co-workers surreptitiously watch Westerns in the office.

There are numerous examples of bureaucratic nonsense throughout the film: the replacement cover does not fit the hole in Buttle's ceiling, created by officials entering his flat to arrest him (the workers grumble that they have gone back to metric without being told) and, of course, the frustration of Jill's search to right the wrong of Buttle's arrest is full of the hallmarks of a bureaucratic nightmare, all paperwork and official stamps. This representation of bureaucracy is given its most vivid moment in Sam's final dream as Tuttle's body is covered in paper whilst he walks down the street. It leeches to his body, mummifying him. When Sam finally reaches the heating engineer it has consumed his writhing body leaving only scraps of paper. This surreal image demonstrates the power of bureaucracy, a thoughtless and inhuman system, which can crush the individual, and it indicates to the audience that what it thought was real is only part of Sam's dying subconscious desires. He, too, has been unable to escape the system.

'The story of an alternate future is realised with... visual imagination and sparky humour.' David Pirie, Time Out Film Guide 14th Ed., Time Out Guides Ltd., London, 2006

'A credible - and horribly fact-based - depiction of a regime which charges its victims for the electricity and labour that goes into their own torture.' Kim Newman, 1001 Movies You Must See Before You Die, Cassell Illustrated, London, 2003

KEY SCENE TEXTUAL ANALYSIS

The Department of Records (2)

The theme music that pervades this film, Ary Barroso's 'Arquarelo do Brasil', speaks of hope and opportunity and its lilting melody is uplifting and infectious. Yet the visuals that Gilliam marries to this non-diegetic music are the antithesis of this mood in so many ways; a woman has just witnessed her husband's brutal and wrongful arrest by the authorities, and we are left with a close-up of her hand clutching the paperwork that she has signed to acknowledge his removal into the State's hands. It is a symbol of their calculating savagery and slavish devotion to needless paperwork, projecting a veneer of respectability over their totalitarian actions.

The incongruously jaunty opening chords to 'Brasil' begin on this image and continue throughout the next sequence. Although dominated by a partly dour and drab mise-en-scène, the mood of the music is matched by the apparent vitality and work rate of the employees of the Department of Records.

A close-up of the captured man's arrest paperwork reduces him again to nothing more than a statistic in the great bowels of this dystopian nightmare. The camera pulls away to reveal a mass of archaic, but complicated machines, ugly pipes and hordes of workers, shifting pieces of paper around the office in a superficial and ultimately meaningless way.

The opening titles state that this is sometime in the twentieth century and the mise-en-scène has a stylised 1950's aesthetic which suggests that, despite the futuristic story, society is unable to free itself of the recurring cycles that it creates.

The rapid tracking shot, as the camera pulls back through the office, develops the idea of frenetic industry but also of an environment where there is no time for rest or conversation. Movement, however inane and purposeless, is all that matters; the orchestration of the shot and its fast pace also matches the gathering momentum of the music.

We follow one office boy and then another as we hurtle through the office. As one pushes his paperwork cart around a corner we see the incongruous image of a woman's bright red lips, part of a propaganda poster, but enough to suggest the hidden desires of these men - for they are all men - as they carry out their mundane duties. Under the dim and uniform lights and surrounded by grey banks of filing cabinets, they act like drones as they add to and build a gigantic nest of paperwork.

The first cut comes as another office boy wheels his cart into the camera, a hidden cut which allows the flow of the shot to continue and keep up with the growing tempo of the music. The cut enables the camera to go back down the passage it has already travelled along, helping to emphasise the vastness of the office. As the office boys disappear out of shot, leaving others to walk across screen as the camera is propelled forward, the audience becomes part of the momentum, almost as if we were riding

miniature screens and start watching a Western film. The long shot shows the rapid change from frantic movement to absolute stillness and underlines the disparity between appearance and reality. Beneath their drab exteriors beat the hearts of humans who yearn for excitement and a break from routine. Even Kurtzmann, as we see later in this sequence, is human in that he relies heavily on Sam Lowrie for support and reassurance.

In Kurtzmann's office the same dismal *mise-en-scène* is prevalent. We see the antiquated computer screens, which again compare appearance and reality with their layers of magnifying glass covering the tiny screens. The intention seems to be grandiose for the sake of appearance whereas the actual effect is to distort the original image, as if we are looking at something through the eyes of a thickly bespectacled person.

on one of the carts and parting the sea of grey-suited workers.

The camera speeds up and there is one last flourish as one worker propels some stairs on wheels past the camera as it comes to a halt below Mr. Kurtzmann's office. The whole shot has been a celebration of camera movement, of choreography and of man's ability to create, all important when juxtaposed against the dull, monotonous lives that are on view.

As the camera looks up to the boss, any sense of his importance from this angle is somewhat undermined by his obvious small stature and oversized suit. The tingling music suggests his internal pleasure at witnessing all his minions scurrying around, and the close-up, showing a grey, rat-faced man suggests an officious manner.

His retreat into the office signals a surprising reaction from the workers as they all move to

Kurtzmann himself embodies the straight-laced and repressed nature of authority with his tie done up to choking point, the jacket buttoned up and sporting a lapel pin, and the neatly cropped moustache. But two elements undermine the official pose: the rather effeminate chain for his glasses and the tuft of hair on top of his head that refuses to be subjugated. The games that his workers play with him over the next few shots also indicate that he is not in as much control as he would like to be; they subvert his authority by watching the Western and his comic failure to catch them out further undermines him.

As Kurtzmann shouts for Sam, the grey nature of the man and his environment is seen again, his tone of voice monotonous. The cut to a skyscape is striking and incongruous, its soft colours at odds with what the audience has just seen. The silver-suited man with a giant wingspan is graceful and magnificent compared to the workers. His hair flows, unlike the uniformity of short haircuts in the workplace, and the 'Brasil' music is used again, this time its orchestral arrangement is light and free-wheeling like the figure before us.

Perhaps the only negative connotation is that of his resemblance to the legendary Icarus, who flew too high and came crashing back down to earth - it perhaps gives us an uneasy clue as to the film's ending.

The camera swoops and dives as he glides through the combination set/miniature/special effects, finding a beautiful woman, seen first in close-up, her angelic looks and transparent veil suggesting an ideal beauty. A tender kiss is followed by a dramatic aerial flourish - and then the cut back to reality: an old-fashioned telephone, disfigured by numerous other additions.

alternate reality which has every danger of seeping into our own.

The sequence that follows shows Sam Lowrie's real existence as opposed to the fantasy one of his dreams in which he symbolically battles with the forces of authority to reclaim his true love.

The confusion of this drab modern existence, as seen in the office, is repeated in his flat, which houses a sprawling mess of pointless innovations that only serve to stifle life and add layers of unnecessary complexities. The ridiculous sounds of all these devices add to their silly redundancy and, as he leaves, their uselessness is exemplified by the flopping toast he is unable to eat.

Again, the *appearance* of progress is just a façade. Although the audience sees the action as fantastical, many of the observations are actually rooted in present day reality; indeed, the opening explanatory line does not say 'some time' in the twentieth century but '*somewhere*'. Perhaps it indicates that the scenario is happening right now, or at least that this is only a slightly different

Edward Scissorhands

KEY FACTS

Release Date: 1990

Country of Origin: USA

Running Time: 103 minutes

PRODUCTION NOTES

Production Company

Twentieth Century-Fox Film Corporation

Distributor

Twentieth Century-Fox Film Corporation

Budget

$20,000,000 (estimated)

Awards

Best Production Design Bo Welch BAFTA Awards, UK

Nominated: Best Makeup Ve Neill Stan Winston Academy Awards, USA

Nominated: Best Performance by an Actor in a Motion Picture - Comedy/Musical Johnny Depp Golden Globes, USA

SYNOPSIS

The story begins with Kim Boggs recounting her experiences with Edward Scissorhands to her granddaughter. The narrative then unfolds in flashback and Kim's mother, Peg, visits an old mansion on a hill above her suburban neighbourhood in order to sell some of her Avon beauty products. Whilst there she finds a young man, Edward, who has been created by a scientist, but remains unfinished, with scissors instead of hands. She befriends him and takes him back to her house where the rest of her family are bemused and anxious about his appearance and the fact that he is going to stay with them. Initially, the neighbours are suspicious of him but when he shows his prowess at topiary and hairdressing he becomes a popular figure.

However, Kim's boyfriend, Jim, becomes jealous of her increasingly close relationship with Edward and he tries to implicate him in a robbery. Later, a drunken Jim attempts to run Edward down in his car but misses and is prevented from accidentally hitting Kevin, Kim's younger brother, by Edward's quick thinking. But when Edward pushes Kevin to the ground it seems as if he is being violent towards the boy. This, coupled with a neighbour's fury at having her advances to Edward rejected, *and* his accidental cutting of Kim's hand, leads him to become a figure of hate in the community.

Led by Jim, a group of angry neighbours pursue Edward as he retreats to his old home on the hill, where Jim nearly kills Edward and injures Kim. Finally, Edward kills Jim with his scissor hands and part of the mansion roof collapses. Kim finds a scissor hand in the dead scientist's mansion and takes it out to the waiting mob with the news that Edward is dead. This convinces the neighbours and they return home. Kim tells her granddaughter that she knows that Edward is still alive because it now snows in the winter and it never did before. She attributes this to the ice chips that fly off from the ice sculptures that Edward carves (he has done this earlier in the film), and we then see Edward in the garden of the mansion furiously carving sculptures and creating a flurry of snow which falls on the houses below.

HISTORICAL CONTEXT

After the financial booms of the 1980s, the following decade saw many upwardly mobile people spending and borrowing excessively and the gap between the super-rich and the poor widened. Film-makers have always enjoyed terrorising the affluent in society, taking them out of their comfort zone and exposing them to all manner of problems. In *Edward Scissorhands*, however, the 'monster' turns out to be the moral character and the well-to-do are the 'monsters'. Edward is every scapegoat rolled into one: the underprivileged, the gypsy, the foreigner, the youth... and the use of the fairy tale framework gives its tale the timeless quality which makes it so relevant not only to the 1990s but to all decades.

Tim Burton began his career as an animator, making a stop-motion short film, *Vincent* (1982), a medium he would return to with *The Nightmare Before Christmas* and *Corpse Bride*. The surreal worlds created in these animations have been mirrored in his live-action films, starting with his short film, *Frankenweenie* (1984). Burton has constructed a whole cast of misfits and outcasts in his films: Batman, Edward Scissorhands and Ed Wood are all on the periphery of conventional society, spurned and ridiculed by most. However, Burton champions these characters whatever their idiosyncrasies and celebrates their quirks and particular visions. Even rogues and villains such as Beetlejuice and Sweeney Todd are depicted with a degree of affection. Burton's 'heroes' follow in a long line of outsiders, stretching back to the monster in *Frankenstein* (1931) and reincarnated latterly in a variety of guises, including Tahei and Mataschichi (*The Hidden Fortress*), Donnie Darko and Napoleon Dynamite.

SELECT FILMOGRAPHY OF MAIN PRODUCERS AND CAST

Tim Burton, 1958, Director, Producer, Screenwriter

Pee-wee's Big Adventure, 1985

Beetlejuice, 1988

Batman, 1989

Edward Scissorhands, 1990

Batman Returns, 1992

Ed Wood, 1994

Mars Attacks!, 1996

Sleepy Hollow, 1999

Planet of the Apes, 2001

Big Fish, 2003

Charlie and the Chocolate Factory, 2005

Corpse Bride, 2005

Sweeney Todd: The Demon Barber of Fleet Street, 2007

Danny Elfman, 1953, Composer

Pee-wee's Big Adventure, 1985

Beetlejuice, 1988

Midnight Run, 1988

Batman, 1989

Edward Scissorhands, 1990

Darkman, 1990

Dick Tracy, 1990

Batman Returns, 1992

Dolores Claiborne, 1995

To Die For, 1995

Mars Attacks!, 1996

Mission: Impossible, 1996

Men in Black, 1997

Sleepy Hollow, 1999

Planet of the Apes, 2001

Spider-Man, 2002

Hulk, 2003

Spider-Man 2, 2004

Charlie and the Chocolate Factory, 2005

Corpse Bride, 2005

Charlotte's Web, 2006

Johnny Depp, 1963, Actor

A Nightmare on Elm Street, 1994

Cry-Baby, 1990

Edward Scissorhands, 1990

Benny and Joon, 1993

What's Eating Gilbert Grape, 1993

Ed Wood, 1994

Don Juan DeMarco, 1995

Donnie Brasco, 1997

Fear and Loathing in Las Vegas, 1998

Sleepy Hollow, 1999

Chocolat, 2000

Blow, 2001

From Hell, 2001

Pirates of the Carribean: The Curse of the Black Pearl, 2003

Once Upon a Time in Mexico, 2003

Finding Neverland, 2004

Charlie and the Chocolate Factory, 2005

Corpse Bride, 2005

Pirates of the Carribean: Dead Man's Chest, 2006

Pirates of the Carribean: At World's End, 2007

Sweeney Todd: The Demon Barber of Fleet Street, 2007

Winona Ryder, 1971, Actress

Beetlejuice, 1988

Heathers, 1989

Mermaids, 1990

Edward Scissorhands, 1990

Night on Earth, 1991

Bram Stoker's Dracula, 1992

The House of Spirits, 1993

The Age of Innocence, 1993

Little Women, 1994

How to Make an American Quilt, 1995

The Crucible, 1996

Alien: Resurrection, 1997

Celebrity, 1998

Girl, Interrupted, 1999

Lost Souls, 2000

Autumn in New York, 2000

Mr. Deeds, 2002

A Scanner Darkly, 2006

LINKS TO OTHER FILMS

Frankenstein (1931)

See HORROR section (pg. 209).

The Company of Wolves (1984)

Neil Jordan's film brings the worlds of reality and fantasy together. There are jarring images of the two colliding and modern sensibilities and universal themes are explored through the medium of the fairy tale.

Ed Wood (1994)

Like *Edward Scissorhands*, Ed Wood is an outsider, shunned and ridiculed by many, naïve or ignorant of the rules and restrictions of 'normal' society; their otherness is both their virtue and their curse.

Sleepy Hollow (1999)

Sleepy Hollow and *Edward Scissorhands* share a Gothic sensibility, underpinned by the *mise-en-scène*, as well as Johnny Depp in the lead role, bringing sensitivity, vulnerability and eccentricity to each performance.

REPRESENTATION

Suburbia

Edward Scissorhands brings two worlds together, the Gothic and the contemporary suburban, a collision that draws attention to the underbelly of 'civilised' suburban life. All aspects of the suburban world seem to be ordered, neat and uncomplicated, symbolised by the well-kept houses and lawns. They *should* be extensions of well-balanced minds and the Gothic castle *should* be the extension of a dark and sinister mind. However, the reality is generally reversed. Apart from the Boggs family, the occupants of suburbia are revealed as aggressive, duplicitous, prejudiced, small-minded and, ultimately, bloodthirsty.

In the same way as David Lynch's *Blue Velvet* (1986), John Duigan's *Lawn Dogs* (1997) and Sam Mendes' *American Beauty* (1999), *Edward Scissorhands* presents a suburban idyll as an illusion, perpetrated by outward appearances but masking a nightmarish world of deceit and moral corruption.

Joyce turns nasty and vindictive towards Edward when he rejects her sexual advances and Jim, Kim's boyfriend, is downright homicidal. Edward unintentionally exposes all their cruelties, cynicism and idiocy with his blend of innocence, naivety and innate goodness.

In the end the Gothic mansion, for all its forbidding appearance, seems more of a home and a source of humanity than the community below it; those houses are hermetically sealed from the virtues of humanity and their occupants are similarly imbued with the sterility of their surroundings, a view that this film shares with Mike Nichols' depiction of suburbia in *The Graduate* (1967).

> *'[A] skewed vision of suburbia... a visual treat.'* Colette Maude, *Time Out Film Guide 14th Ed.*, Time Out Guides Ltd., London, 2006

> *'Depp... [creates] a character trapped by his incomplete body, conveying Edward's frustration with few words... An ambitious, beautifully conceived modern-day fairy tale.'* Joanna Berry, *1001 Movies You Must See Before You Die*, Cassell Illustrated, London, 2003

KEY SCENE TEXTUAL ANALYSIS

Driving up to the castle (3)

It is early morning and the establishing shot displays a world of tranquil respectability with the pastel colours of the houses suggesting a world of self-satisfied suburban life. Everything is picture-postcard perfect. The static shots show the houses' clean geometric lines, only interrupted by the humans who crimp and primp at their castles of domesticity, mowing the lawn, fixing the roof and watering the garden.

There is something of the Jacques Tati idea of slavish devotion to material things with each human looking like an automaton, less human than the created human, Edward, who we will see later in this scene. Indeed, the Avon lady's walk up the ostentatiously twisty path, another of those tics that suburbanites find so endearing, is reminiscent of the path leading up to Tati's sister's house in *Mon Oncle* (1958), a meandering route which they follow with extreme care, just as Peg does here, exposing the little absurdities and rigidities of this way of life.

There follows a number of rebuttals, all of which gently expose the underbelly of the apparent gentility: the slob housewife, the sexually promiscuous wife (complete with diegetic song, *Delilah*, the story of a cheating woman who meets her end at the hands of her lover), and the spoilt, unfeeling teenager. The colour schemes within the houses are also shown to be garish, as if the soft pastel exteriors have unattractive innards.

orchestral beginning, which is synchronised with the sight of the castle.

The long shot of the castle on the hill, a CGI composite, with the houses in the foreground, is a particularly incongruous sight, as if Tolkien's Mordor had suddenly landed on top of an archetypal Middle American town.

And so begins the fantasy adventure, except in this story the adventurer is not a knight or young pretender, but an Avon lady. The juxtaposition between Peg and her new surroundings is fully exploited as she enters the castle grounds.

The cut from carefully nurtured lawns to a twisted tree and Gothic gargoyle develops the contrast between the two worlds, the crane shot swooping down to show Peg's soft-hued and suburban car entering this other world. As she crosses the threshold, haunting voices are added to the

Peg, the mauve Avon lady, walks back to her car, something of an outcast from these houses (even the children mock her). She is the only one whose wardrobe is co-ordinated in an understated way, foreshadowing her inner charity and goodwill to her fellow man.

Her adjustment of the wing mirror reveals an extraordinary and fantastical sight; if the pastel houses have been somewhat surreal this is extremely bizarre. Director Burton has until now given no hint of the Gothic castle looming above the sea of suburbia and the shot in the mirror is a tease to whet the audience's appetite for the shot to come once Peg has made her very precise three-point turn.

The sounds of suburbia have been banal and safe: the lawnmower, the hammering, children playing, dogs barking; but this is contrasted with the dramatic non-diegetic music with its sombre

non-diegetic soundtrack and help to build the anticipation of what might lie ahead.

As Peg nears the castle the camera pulls away to reveal not just a straightforward ruined gothic castle, but one where the gargoyles are oddly shaped - one even looks like a rather happy crocodile. The low angle shot of the immense gates helps to emphasise Peg's vulnerability and the gargoyles here are more traditionally scary.

Her emergence into the castle's garden is yet another revelation, again undermining the audience's expectations of what we are going to see. The initial POV allows us to share Peg's moment of incredible surprise as the garden unfolds before her to reveal an enchanted place betraying the castle's formidable exterior and appearance from afar. It is a reversal of the sequence the audience has just witnessed down the hill: an unfriendly appearance veils an interior beauty.

The sterility of the suburban world is exposed by the wonderment and imagination of this garden. The music softens and the voices suggest magic and beauty, mirrored in the gentle tracking movements, which show both the topiary masterpieces and Peg's awe-filled reaction to them. This is truly the land of fairy tales.

The high-angle shot looking down on Peg suggests another presence and indicates her vulnerability in this alien world. The cut to a low angle shot reveals a face in the shattered window in the tower. The character in the tower, either against their will or because they are shunned by society, is a stock convention of the fantasy/fairy-tale genre, whether in film or literary form.

The shot brings together a number of the film's key elements: Edward's otherness, Peg's kindliness, his art, the source of his alienation (having no hands),

great, stone hall. Objects are shrouded in dark sheets and cobwebs and shafts of light cut into the forbidding interior. Her announcement - 'Avon calling' - is both comic and further emphasises the divide between the worlds.

The shots of the cobweb-covered machinery and the fiendish statue, together with the haunting non-diegetic vocals, return the atmosphere to a darker tone. Peg, in fact, backs into frame and it seems as if the statue, with its outstretched arms, is about to ensnare her. The diegetic noise and the shadow movement startle her, but instead of running, as the environment would encourage, she seems spurred on by her duty as an Avon lady, like a knight in search of a dragon to slay.

In fact, she is more concerned that whoever or whatever is there should not be afraid of her, a comic reversal of our usual expectations of

and the link that is made between these two people, symbolised by the topiary creation of the outstretched hand, almost as if it is reaching out from her to him. In fact, Peg is closely associated with the image of the hand in this sequence for she will, in effect, be Edward's hands in the outside world. We have already seen her using her hands prominently as part of her Avon work and in the close-up, as she looks up, her hand is prominent again. As she moves towards the castle she is framed by the topiary, a protective ring, and framed against the giant hand once more.

So petite and pristine, she looks incongruous next to the classic Gothic fairy tale door with its giant-sized knocker and handle - it is the antithesis of the doorbell-ringing suburban habitat where she would be spotted normally.

This collision of worlds continues in the next long shot as Peg's tiny figure emerges into the castle's

fantasy adventure stories. The film subverts the audience's expectations by creating a fantasy world alongside an environment that is more familiar, if stylised, and then subverts them even further by challenging our expectations of how the fantasy world should exist. It is in the very great traditions of *Frankenstein*, *Beauty and the Beast* and *Othello*, where audiences are forced to reconsider their response to otherness.

As she reaches the upper level the long shot again reinforces Peg's vulnerability and the great tear in the ceiling is both spectacular and suggestive of a desire for the castle to be part of the outside world. The slow tracking shot as Peg moves towards Edward's simple den of bed and newspaper cuttings (again dealing with images of hands), together with a softening of the music, moves the film back into a gentler key.

The first shot of the inventor-created human, Edward, is also in long shot, matching those of Peg, and illustrating that he too is vulnerable, despite being in his own environment. He is crouched like a frightened bird in the shadows, the ruptured wooden roof structure above him perhaps symbolising the damage that has already been done to this outcast.

The camera moves both towards Edward and then away from him to illustrate both his and then Peg's fear, but also the different directions of their two worlds. The silhouette with flashing knives, coupled with the dramatic staccato music, creates a moment of anxiety, but the soft sound of Edward's voice and the plaintive look on his face quickly restores the fairytale fantasy atmosphere.

His black leather clothes are punk-like and potentially aggressive, especially when married to the knives, but his gestures and scarred face (inadvertently self-inflicted) are again reminiscent of a savaged and scared little bird. *Mise-en-scène* is being used to challenge and subvert audience preconceptions about stereotypical characters in familiar genres.

The series of close-ups on both characters sets up a rhythm of connectivity between them, the editing allowing each of their sensitive faces to be juxtaposed, not for contrast, but for comparison. In this moment of movement from fear to kindness Peg characteristically falls back into her Avon lady persona, which we can now see is an extension of her caring personality. Again, with hand gestures she shows how she can give practical help. Significantly, their first physical contact shows her hand predominantly in frame touching his face: the two worlds have now connected.

The cut to both of them in her car is unexpected. The audience is abruptly taken out of this fantasy setting and into the suburban world of before, only this time the surreal sight of the dark, wild-looking Edward is transported with her and the mirror image of her incongruity in his world is now reversed.

Non-diegetic music returns at the cut and the uplifting harp is followed by light and airy orchestral swirls indicating a lifting of the uncertain mood of the previous scene. Now they are seen largely in a contented two-shot in the car and the camera tracks smoothly over familiar sights, which now seem reinvigorated because it is Edward's POV and he is bringing fresh and innocent eyes to the everyday pastimes of children playing, grass-cutting and watering the garden. The only negative aspect of each frame, as the journey progresses, is the staring and movement of some of the inhabitants, suggesting they are already gossiping about the stranger in their midst and foreshadowing the alienation that Edward will eventually feel in his new world.

El Laberinto del Fauno (Pan's Labyrinth)

KEY FACTS

Release Date: 2006

Country of Origin: Spanish/ Mexican

Running Time: 113 minutes

PRODUCTION NOTES

Production Companies

Tequila Gang

Esperanto Filmoj

Estudios Picasso

OMM

Sententia Entertainment

Telecinco

Distributors

Optimum Releasing (UK)

Picturehouse Entertainment (USA)

Warner Bros. (Mexico)

Dudget

€ 13,500,000 (estimated)

Awards

Best Achievement in Art Direction Eugenio Caballero, Pilar Revuelta Academy Awards, USA

Best Achievement in Cinematography Guillermo Navarro Academy Awards, USA

Best Achievement in Makeup David Martí, Montse Ribé Academy Awards, USA

Best Costume Design Lala Huete BAFTA Awards, UK

Best Film not in the English Language Alfonso Cuarón, Bertha Navarro, Frida Torresblanco, Guillermo del Toro BAFTA Awards, UK

Best Make Up & Hair José Quetglás, Blanca Sánchez BAFTA Awards, UK

Seven Goya Awards, Spain

Best Film National Society of Film Critics Awards, USA

Best Cinematographer: Guillermo Navarro New York Film Critics Circle Awards, USA

SYNOPSIS

The story begins in a fantasy realm where Princess Moanna decides to explore the world above her father's kingdom, the underworld. Once there she becomes mortal and dies, but the king believes that she will return. The narrative shifts to Spain in 1944, torn apart by the Civil War, and focuses on Carmen and her daughter, Ofelia, as they journey to be with Captain Vidal, a fervent fascist in the Civil Guard, who is Carmen's new husband and father of her unborn child.

En route to the mountainous location of the captain's headquarters, the convoy stops for Carmen to rest and Ofelia sees what she believes is a fairy, which follows them to their destination. Vidal is a cruel and violent man; he dislikes Ofelia and during the course of the story he kills innocent men, tortures an enemy soldier who has been captured, murders his wife's doctor for helping the rebels and tries to torture his housekeeper, Mercedes, who is in league with his enemies.

Interwoven with this story is the mother's painful pregnancy, which ends in her death when a boy is born, and Ofelia's continued meetings with fantasy creatures in a labyrinth near her home. There she meets a faun, who tells her that she is Princess Moanna, but that she must complete three tasks to prove this. The first involves retrieving a key from a massive toad within a tree stump, an extremely unpleasant and messy task, but one she succeeds in completing. She is later told to use the key to retrieve a dagger from the child-eating Pale Man's abode. Although she is warned not to eat anything from his table, she succumbs, awakening the monster, and barely escapes with her life. The faun is angry at her disobedience and it seems as if the third task will not be set, but he eventually tells her that innocent blood must be spilt to open the way back to the underworld.

In the 'real' world Mercedes escapes torture, wounds Vidal and escapes to be with the rebels, whilst Ofelia drugs the Captain, snatches her baby brother and goes to the labyrinth's entrance. There, despite the faun's urging, she refuses to harm her brother in order to gain entry to the underworld and the faun disappears as Vidal arrives; he shoots

Ofelia and takes the baby back. As he nears the house the rebels are waiting and they take the boy and kill the Captain. Mercedes finds Ofelia, who dies, but is then apparently reborn in the underworld kingdom with her father, mother and the faun, who tells her that she has actually proved herself to be the princess by *not* killing her brother.

HISTORICAL CONTEXT

There has been a massive upsurge in interest with all types of fantasy media in the noughties. A confusing world occasionally needs to be escaped from, and some of these outlets are positive, but others are as dark as the real world. War gamers, the readers of comics, the online games of quests and adventures, virtual fantasy personas and fantasy films prove that escapism is big business. The intoxicating thing about fantasy is that it can be as outrageous as you like, but without the responsibility and the dangers of reality. The surfeit of fantasy films in a decade rife with conflict across the world cannot be a coincidence; people want to be saved and to be transported to worlds where the most loathsome and brutal creatures can be vanquished.

Pan's Labyrinth has a legacy which stretches back to the writings and drawings of Lewis Carroll (*Alice's Adventures in Wonderland*) and Arthur Rackham (who illustrated *Alice* and many other fairy tales). It embraces the light and dark of fantasy and blurs the line between reality and fantasy to the very end, one seemingly spilling into the other and perhaps suggesting that both the best and worst of our fantasies are replicated in the real world. Indeed, nothing that humanity has perpetrated or witnessed so far this millenium would look out of place in a fantasy.

Guillermo del Toro is one of numerous film-makers working in the Spanish language, and latterly in English as they move into Hollywood production. Del Toro, Alfonso Cuarón and Robert Rodriguez are all Mexican film-makers who have, together with other Central, South American and Spanish directors, imbued the medium with vitality and freshness; a new wave if you like. The rest of the world sat up and noticed films such as Alejandro

González Iñárritu's *Amores perros* (2002) and Fernando Meirelles' *City of God* (2002). This group of directors have been particularly drawn to stories of dark deeds with unsettling visuals and narratives that are pure fantasy or are somewhat fantastical.

Alfonso Cuarón has made a number of English-language films, including *Harry Potter and the Prisoner of Azkaban* (2004) and *Children of Men* (2006); they are films full of menace and striking visuals. Robert Rodriguez has also created a body of work that peers at the underbelly of life, often with a darkly fantastic viewpoint; *From Dusk To Dawn* (1996), *The Faculty* (1998) and *Sin City* (2005) all delve into nightmarish worlds with an unflinching eye. Del Toro himself has forged his own dark path with films such as *Cronos* (1993), *Blade II* (2001), *The Devil's Backbone* (2001) and *Hellboy* (2004), as well as producing work like Juan Antonio Bayona's *The Orphanage* (2007), a tale of reality and the supernatural colliding, reminiscent of another Spanish director's work, Alejandro Amenábar's *The Others* (2001).

SELECT FILMOGRAPHY OF MAIN PRODUCERS AND CAST

Guillermo del Toro, 1964, Director, Producer, Screenwriter

Cronos, 1993

Mimic, 1997

The Devil's Backbone, 2001

Blade II, 2002

Hellboy, 2004

Pan's Labyrinth, 2006

Hellboy 2: The Golden Army, 2008

Alfonso Cuarón, 1961, Producer, Director, Screenwriter

Sólo con tu pareja, 1991

Y tu mamá también, 2001

Crónicas, 2004

The Assassination of Richard Nixon, 2004

Pan's Labyrinth, 2006

Guillermo Navarro, 1955, Director of Photography

Cronos, 1993

Desperado, 1995

From Dusk To Dawn, 1996

The Long Kiss Goodnight, 1996

Spawn, 1997

Jackie Brown, 1997

Stuart Little, 1999

Spy Kids, 2001

The Devil's Backbone, 2001

Hellboy, 2004

Pan's Labyrinth, 2006

Night at the Museum, 2006

Hellboy 2: The Golden Army, 2008

Sergi López, 1965, Actor

Caresses, 1998

El Cielo Abierto, 2001

Dirty Pretty Things, 2002

Peindre ou faire l'amour, 2005

Les Mots bleus, 2005

Pan's Labyrinth, 2006

Maribel Verdú, 1970, Actress

Amantes, 1991

Belle epoque, 1992

El Amante Bilingüe, 1993

Huevos de oro, 1993

La Buena Estrella, 1997

Y tu mamá también, 2001

Pan's Labyrinth, 2006

LINKS TO OTHER FILMS

Shane (1953)/*The Go-Between* (1970)/*Walkabout* (1971)

These are three films that all have children as their protagonists, coming into brutal contact with adult realities, and the innocence that is lost or compromised as a result. In *Shane*, Joey, the young boy, is served with demonstrations of man's brutality; Leo Colston, the young boy who is the lovers' 'go-between', feels the sting of adult betrayal, while the girl of *Walkabout* embarks on a journey of self-discovery.

The Spirit of the Beehive (1973)

Spain, the aftermath of the Civil War and a young girl's retreat into a fantasy world make clear the parallels between Victor Erice's film and *Pan's Labyrinth*. *The Spirit of the Beehive* also interweaves the real and the fantastical as if they are one, as well as presenting visuals that possess a dream-like quality.

Labyrinth (1986)

Jim Henson's film charts a young girl's adventures in a fantasy realm, a labyrinth where she must undertake tasks and overcome obstacles to rescue her younger brother from a goblin king.

Cronos (1993)

This film forms part of a loose trilogy, which continues with *The Devil's Backbone* and ends with *Pan's Labyrinth*. It too charts a life that is touched by the fantastic and the horrific as an elderly antiques dealer discovers a device that both rejuvenates him and prompts him to develop a thirst for blood.

The Devil's Backbone (2001)

Del Toro's film is set in a Spanish orphanage during the last days of the Spanish Civil War. It looks at the relationship between reality and a world beyond it and shares the same preoccupations with *Pan's Labyrinth*, exploring innocence, brutality and fantasy.

Tideland (2005)

A tale which connects with *Pan's Labyrinth* in terms of its main protagonist, a young girl who retreats further into a fantasy world as the realities of life (both her parents die from drug overdoses) overcome her mind.

The Chronicles of Narnia: The Lion, the Witch and the Wardrobe (2005)

Based on C.S. Lewis' stories, this elaborate adaptation charts a group of young people's adventures in a fantasy land, where they are regarded as kings and queens, but where they must fight and seek aid from an assortment of fantasy creatures, including a faun.

REPRESENTATION

Civil War

Although the Spanish Civil War is officially over at the start of *Pan's Labyrinth* the atmosphere and the reality of guerrilla warfare suggest its continuation, both emotionally and physically. Civil wars are an emotive subject matter and a number of powerful films have emerged using them as backdrop or as a vehicle for exploring certain themes. Their appeal to film-makers lies in the notion of a nation divided by politics and fighting between people of the same cultural heritage, even friends and families.

The American Civil War has provided many narratives of division and heartache, notably *The Birth of a Nation* (1915), *Gone with the Wind* (1939) and *Cold Mountain* (2003). In the twentieth century the Irish and Spanish civil wars have proved fascinating to film-makers, with Ken Loach focusing on the politics of both conflicts in *The Wind That Shakes the Barley* (2006) and *Land and Freedom* (1995) respectively.

Other approaches to the conflicts have been more interested in using them as backdrops for romantic narratives. Sam Wood's 1943 adaptation of the Ernest Hemingway novel, *For Whom the Bells Toll*, is an example of this type of film. Although *Pan's Labyrinth* has many scenes of a fantasy nature, which are often brutal, the images that come from the real world of the civil war are just as horrifying. Vidal's killing of the young poacher is shown graphically, the sight and sound of a broken bottle being rammed into his face is an indicator of the hatred that lies within some people. The degrading treatment of the local people and the ruthless hunt for the 'rebels' paints a picture of misery, distrust and of political ideology warping and disfiguring sensibilities, allowing the most ruthless to survive.

Vidal may die at the end of the film, but Franco and the fascists had already won and would rule for more than 30 years. The bravery of those fighting against the fascists is documented, showing people who become aliens in their own country, but it is the captain who lingers in the mind. When Mercedes slits his mouth, Vidal's subsequent sewing of the wound is excruciating to view and further adds to the audience's sense of his monstrous nature. The image of the slit mouth is reminiscent of Spanish artist Francisco de Goya's drawings of war, *Desastres de la Guerra* (Disasters of War), a horrific collection of the atrocities committed in the name of war. Indeed, Vidal seems to relish the wound inflicted on him and continues to commit atrocities in the name of a war that, ultimately, produces the very best in people (Mercedes' actions throughout the film) and the very worst (Vidal's killing of his step-daughter).

'From the start del Toro creates a sense of wonder that contrasts with the rigid, unimaginative world inhabited by the Captain... In this magical and immensely moving film del Toro presents both the narrative strands as equally real, equally plausible. There's no attempt to rationalise Ofelia's parallel universe by suggesting it's a dream or a fantasy. In fact the two sides of the film come together to constitute an allegory about the soul and the national identity of Spain, and in a wider sense about the struggle between good and evil, between the humane and the inhumane, the civilised and the barbaric.' **Philip French, *The Observer*, 26th November 2006**

KEY SCENE TEXTUAL ANALYSIS

Into the chamber (9)

The lighting creates shadow and unease as the camera slowly tracks around Ofelia and the mystery of the moment is underpinned by the lack of sound, either diegetic or non-diegetic. The only noise is that of the book she opens with the close-up of the pages revealing the CGI effect of the drawings forming before our eyes. As the pictures are not already drawn we share Ofelia's sense of anticipation as they reveal themselves and the instructions for her second task are made clear. The images are disturbing and add to both Ofelia's and the audience's sense of anticipation and dread.

The camera then moves in towards her face in a sinister fashion to indicate the mounting pressure of what is to come. Non-diegetic music bubbles to the surface and a haunting piano-led melody intermingles with the eerie sound of the wind and less discernible but sinister noises. It helps to underpin the magical creation of the drawings and connects with the sense of foreboding that they provoke. The close-up of the drawn creature and the way his tentacle-like arms envelop a girl is perhaps a chilling prophecy.

The long shot not only shows the darkness around Ofelia but emphasises her vulnerability and the track towards her again suggests forces conspiring against her. The non-diegetic violins are played lightly and with a gentle melody, but there is also a slight discordant strain, suggesting both her sense of wonder and growing anxiety as she embarks on this second task; the bubbling chalk on the wall and the sound of wood creaking help drive the mounting sense of unease. The camera then tracks back from her as she faces the wall. It is one of many moving shots that help to underline her and the audience's disquiet, nullifying any sense of stillness or calm in this unnerving fantasy world, and suggesting that there is something prowling in the shadows.

The orchestral score lurches into a much more sinister passage as the newly-formed door in the wall is opened and the camera tracks away from Ofelia as she gazes into this fresh realm. The music is now accompanied by unearthly sounds, akin to a creature's breathing, and it swells as the camera continues its revelatory track away from the girl, showing her and the audience this strange and forbidding place. Contrasting with the monochrome of her bedroom, an almost glistening earthy red wall surrounds Ofelia and the sense of fear is heightened as a dissolve takes us deeper into the Gothic corridor, bathed in walls of blood-red stone. The audience sees both worlds for a final time as she eases herself into the unknown, and the camera tracks towards the hour glass as the sand runs through it, emphasising that this is a battle against time, as well as whatever else might be lurking ahead.

As Ofelia walks along the corridor the green of her clothes, signifying her connection with the natural world, contrasts with the hell-like *mise-en-scène* around her. The camera tracks from behind a pillar in order to add to the growing anxiety (is she being

making the moment when the track reaches the hideous arms and torso of the creature all the more shocking; this hellish vision of an eyeless creature with sagging and blotched skin is reminiscent of a figure from a vision of the apocalypse. It is human in form, but a perverse and depraved version of ourselves, the stuff of nightmares. Although Ofelia is startled, her fear quickly turns to inquisitiveness, and she examines it and the two balls on a plate before it, which seem very much like eyeballs. Its long fingernails are also striking, blood red and seemingly designed to rip and shred.

The sense of horror is further established with depictions of the creature's actions painted on the ceiling - images of child eating and the pile of tiny children's shoes heaped on the floor. The release of the fairies brings a positive note; they fly like dragonflies and have a human figure but their faces are kept in shadow to heighten their mysterious

watched?) until we see a long shot of a great room, warmed by a fire and a table laden with opulent food. In long shot the figure at the end is barely glimpsed but it is enough to unsettle the audience. Del Toro increases our unease by showing, in the next shot, that Ofelia is not even looking at the figure but is entranced by the enticing food on the table (the audience will also be aware of the faun's words in the previous scene when he implores her not to touch the food).

The camera tracks along the table groaning with culinary delights positioned between the audience and the girl; foregrounding the food emphasises its desirability and Ofelia's gaze never leaves the spectacle. The richness of the buffet and the jugs and plates around it suggest the promise and the reminder of death that one would find in a *vanitas* painting, a still life, but with elements depicting human mortality.

The audience is also seduced by this display,

appeal. But even as Ofelia approaches three small doors placed in the wall, the framing retains the creature, and its threat, in the background. As she opens one door, the camera shows the audience her actions from within and outside the hole into which she must plunge her hand; our sense of anxiety increases as we fear what might happen.

The cut back to a tracking shot towards the hour glass underlines that time is running out. Ofelia succeeds in this part of the task, even defying the fairies in her choice of door, and retrieves a dagger. As she turns, the creature is in the foreground but he is still motionless although his repulsive form is now revealed to the audience more clearly; even one of the fairies is terrified. The camera swoops over the table, emphasising the magnificence of its array of food and towards the girl, her gaze once more transfixed by the display.

In the same move the camera turns from her face to a bowl of luscious grapes and her intent becomes clearer. A look back and a pull focus from her face to the creature and back to her confirms that she has been ensnared by the food. Ignoring the entreaties of the fairies she eats one and immediately the creature comes to life to the strains of non-diegetic strings. The eyes are placed in the palms of the hands and it places them up to its head to see; the sight is startling and the cavernous fireplace with raging fire within looks even more like the fires of hell as this creature comes to life. Oblivious, Ofelia continues to eat as the creature lurches towards her. The framing keeps them both in shot and increases the audience's fear and frustration. We want to share the fairies' pleas to look behind her in true pantomime fashion.

The figure is naked. Its skin falls in folds around its body and it has unfeasibly thin legs: the whole effect is that of a living carcass, reminiscent of a

from the horrific sight: both food and creature are compelling but for very different reasons. The chase begins - she is quick and the camera tracks rapidly with her. The Pale Man is awkward and slow with its grotesque movements adding to the terror. Its raised arm and scream, coupled now with faster movement, heighten the tension, with the cut to the sand in the hour glass signalling that Ofelia's time is running out.

With the shot from within her room and the hour glass in the foreground, the focus-pull to the approaching Ofelia is all the more dramatic. The audience is placed right above her shoulder as it tracks towards the exit and we feel her desperation. The cut to a close-up (still tracking) and her anguished cry draw us even further into her nightmarish world. The shot from within her room as the door closes is a terrifying moment, highlighting her almost certain doom. From within

figure from a Francis Bacon painting. The tension increases as Ofelia fails to turn around as it approaches; the non-diegetic music is dramatic and its growls add to the terror as the fairies try to alert Ofelia and hinder the creature's progress. As she turns and it flails in a hideous fashion, the camera reveals its unsightliness from every angle.

The low-angle shot from behind Ofelia helps to emphasise her vulnerability as it towers above her. The decapitation of two fairies is seen in close-up as it bites their heads off, blood dripping from its mouth, reminiscent of Goya's painting of Saturn devouring his son. The reaction shot of the girl not only shows us her horror but juxtaposes her innocence with its subhuman depravity. The diegetic sounds of its breathing and gorging on the fairies, coupled with their high-pitched screams, adds to the nightmare.

After some static camera moves there is a cut to a fast tracking shot as Ofelia tears herself away

the fantasy world the camera abruptly stops as she does, and within the room it tracks back from the now sealed escape route, emphasising her separation from the real world. She drops the chalk and the device of framing victim and aggressor in a single shot helps underpin the terror and their co-existence in the same visual space and her possible capture.

The rapid cuts between The Pale Man and Ofelia signal their ever-increasing proximity. To further emphasise the link between them, and the contrast, their feet are shown, first the creature with its hideously large feet below the thin, sinewy legs, then hers, small and unblemished. Rapid cuts between it and her continue, tracking behind the creature and mimicking the earlier shots of her desperate race for the portal back into her own world.

The diegetic sounds now come to the fore in these final moments of almost unbearable tension with the rattling of the chair on the stone floor as she balances precariously, the screeching of the chalk, the creature's wailing together with the dramatic, non-diegetic music. The simple image of her feet cased in lovely shoes rocking on the back of the chair and the slab of demonic meat flailing towards her crystallise the difference between the two characters; the former is innocent and good, the latter corrupted and evil.

The last few images of this domain are mainly of the creature as it races towards her. The final shots from above as she scrapes on the wooden floor to haul herself back and its attempt to grab her hanging legs heighten the tension to its highest pitch in the scene, its screams still piercing into the real world as she presses down the door. The non-diegetic music subdues to a pulsing rhythm, akin to a heartbeat, and there is a final bang from beneath the floor.

The next noise is that of a creaking timber and the audience knows that the real world has re-established itself. The camera tracks back as Ofelia sits on the bed just as she began, finishing the sequence in a cyclical way. The inference could be that she never actually left the bed and has imagined the events, but this is brought into question by the presence of the remaining fairy. The audience is left to contemplate the veracity of what it has just seen; this story of a young girl trying to escape the very real unhappiness and disturbance of her own life begs many questions about love and friendship, inhumanity and brutality. If it is only a fantasy world, then such is the horror of reality that even her fantasy world is tainted by the actions of the people in it, particularly those of her mother's new husband, the sadistic captain.

THE BLOCKBUSTER

The blockbuster has emerged, I believe, kicking and screaming, to warrant its own category. There always have been blockbusters – just look at *Intolerance* (1916) if you need evidence for this – but the last thirty years have really cemented their position. The summer blockbuster, whether more refined audiences like it or not, has become the mainstay of the major Hollywood studios, and although Hollywood is certainly not the last word in film-making, its influence is felt across the world. The blockbuster's sense of spectacle has either drawn crowds and left them entertained, or confirmed the views of dissenting voices in their belief that Hollywood churns out the same old rubbish each year. Whatever the view, they just cannot be ignored.

Intolerance contains all the conventions of the blockbuster film – it's big and spectacular, with a dramatic narrative sweep. Indeed, any one of the multiple story strands would stand on its own as an epic story of human hardship and resilience. *Gone with the Wind* (1939) added spectacular sound into the blockbuster equation, and its grand story and visuals have been indelibly etched into the collective cinema memory. Like many a blockbuster to come, it garnered a clutch of Academy Awards and Hollywood realised its potential for high financial returns. *Bambi* (1942), like many Disney films, can be found in the list of top 50 earners of all time. From the 1930s until the 1990s, the Disney studio had a stranglehold on animation feature production, and certainly the early years saw audiences flocking to these event films.

The blockbuster has elevated many narratives, and the historical epic is a popular source; *Ben-Hur* (1959) is the pinnacle of this type, with its mixture of battles, biblical story and domestic tragedy. *The Sound of Music* (1965), along with *West Side Story* (1961) in the same decade, married the musical genre to the blockbuster, spawning a plethora of big budget musical productions over the next few years.

Jaws (1975), and then *Star Wars* (1977), are often cited as the films that initiated the blockbuster cycle as we know it today, and indeed, Hollywood certainly went on to make more big budget spectacle films than ever before in the wake of their success. But the previous decades have demonstrated that the blockbuster has always been a mainstay of Hollywood cinema.

The Last Emperor (1987) is an almost impossibly beautiful film, a dreamlike evocation of a lost world, with sumptuous visuals conjured up by cinematographer, Vittorio Storaro and director, Bernardo Bertolucci. If the camerawork, lighting and mise-en-scène are the highlights of *The Last Emperor*, then CGI is at the heart of James Cameron's *Titanic* (1997) ; this film, to be followed by productions like Ridley Scott's *Gladiator* (2000), breathed new life into the genre, recreating the necessary spectacle of the blockbuster through computer simulation, pushing the films to even more epic proportions.

Finally, Sam Raimi's *Spider-Man 2* (2004) demonstrated the re-emergence of the superhero film as blockbuster. Tim Burton's *Batman* (1989) had physically constructed Gotham City, but with Raimi's film the effects and action became more breathtaking than ever, again CGI capable of creating a truly superhuman spectacle; with the advent of the *Spider-Man* trilogy, the new *Batman* films and others like *Transformers* (2007) and the *Hellboy* films (2004, 2008), the blockbuster film has became synonymous with the superhero film; and the rewards are ever greater.

Intolerance: Love's Struggle Through The Ages

KEY FACTS

Release Date: 1916

Country of Origin: USA

Running Time: 162 minutes

PRODUCTION NOTES

Production Companies

Triangle Film Corporation

Wark Producing Corp.

Distributor

Triangle Distributing Corporation

Budget

$385,907 (estimated)

Awards

National Film Registry National Film Preservation Board, USA

SYNOPSIS

The film follows four stories from different time periods in history, all dealing with the theme of intolerance. One story charts the lives of the poor in contemporary America, focusing on events such as strikes, uncaring capitalists, crime, the taking of a baby by misguided and puritanical organisations and, finally, the pardoning of a man who is to be wrongfully executed. Another story depicts the build-up to the St. Bartholomew's Day massacre in sixteenth-century France, when many Huguenot Protestants were killed by Catholics. The third narrative details the events that led to Jesus' crucifixion; whilst the fourth recounts the fall of the ancient civilisation of Babylon some 500 years before Christ. The four stories are interwoven and movement from one narrative to the next is signalled with the visual device of a woman rocking a cradle, symbolising both the passing of time and the enduring love of a mother for her child.

HISTORICAL CONTEXT

Although the 1930s are always thought of as an extremely bleak time in history, as indeed they were, it is also true that pre-World War One America was a place of hardship for many and 1914, the year in which the modern story is set, was a year of much discontent amongst workers, both in urban and rural environments. A strike in a Colorado coalmine in that year led to the deaths of workers when they came under fire from the National Guard. There was also the increasing power of the Temperance League and other organisations dedicated to rooting out the ills in society, which as we see in the film, leads to the poor being judged and labelled by wealthy do-gooders.

Immigration had continued throughout the nineteenth century and levels would remain high for decades to come. Huge numbers of Italians, Irish and other Europeans came to the United States in the opening decade of the century, bringing with them a diverse range of cultures and languages. Opportunities awaited them, but also disappointment, crime and downright hostility from the immigrants who had been there longer, namely the white anglo-saxon protestant groups who had become integrated into American life and who were now part of the Establishment.

It was, then, an appropriate year for the film's setting. There was intolerance at home in the United States for director D.W. Griffith to see, while other countries declared war on each other in rapid succession in the last days of July and the beginning of August. For Griffith himself, the film stood as a rebuttal to critics who had lambasted his provocative representation of black people in his earlier *The Birth of a Nation* (1915).

D.W. Griffith had honed his directing skills at the Biograph Company, making over 400 one-reelers before moving into feature film production. *Judith of Bethulia* (1914) and *The Birth of a Nation* preceded *Intolerance*, and it was with these that his visualisation of epic narratives began. After their successes, Griffith continued to work using a grand palette, directing the epic *Broken Blossoms* (1919), *Way Down East* (1920) and *Orphans of the Storm* (1921), all of which confirmed him as the grandfather of the blockbuster. Although many of his later films did not match his early success, a string of hits between 1913 and 1921 established him as a key figure in cinema history, inextricably linked to the birth of a genre that would continue to reference his work.

SELECT FILMOGRAPHY OF MAIN PRODUCERS AND CAST

D. W. Griffith, 1875-1948, Director, Producer, Screenwriter

Man's Genesis, 1912

The Little Tease, 1913

Judith of Bethulia, 1914

Brute Force, 1914

The Birth of a Nation, 1915

Intolerance, 1916

Broken Blossoms, 1919

Way Down East, 1920

Orphans of the Storm, 1921

The White Rose, 1923

America, 1924

Sally of the Sawdust, 1925

Drums of Love, 1928

The Battle of the Sexes, 1928

Lady of the Pavements, 1929

Abraham Lincoln, 1930

The Struggle, 1931

G.W. Bitzer, 1872-1944, Director of Photography

The Little Tease, 1913

Judith of Bethulia, 1914

Brute Force, 1914

The Birth of a Nation, 1915

Intolerance, 1916

Broken Blossoms, 1919

Orphans of the Storm, 1921

The White Rose, 1923

America, 1924

Drums of Love, 1928

The Battle of the Sexes, 1928

Lady of the Pavements, 1929

Mae Marsh, 1894-1968 , Actress

Man's Genesis, 1912

The Little Tease, 1913

Judith of Bethulia, 1914

Brute Force, 1914

The Birth of a Nation, 1915

Intolerance, 1916

The Marriage of Molly-O, 1916

Sunshine Alley, 1917

The White Rose, 1923

The Rat, 1925

Over the Hill, 1931

Rebecca of Sunnybrook Farm, 1932

Black Fury, 1935

Miriam Cooper, 1891-1976, Actress

The Birth of a Nation, 1915

Intolerance, 1916

The Silent Lie, 1917

Evangeline, 1919

Serenade, 1921

Constance Talmadge, 1897-1973, Actress

In Bridal Attire, 1914

Intolerance, 1916

A Pair of Silk Stockings, 1918

Romance and Arabella, 1919

Happiness a la mode, 1919

Wedding Bells, 1921

The Primitive Lover, 1922

Her Night of Romance, 1924

The Duchess of Buffalo, 1926

Venus of Venice, 1927

LINKS TO OTHER FILMS

Judith of Bethulia (1914)/*The Birth of a Nation* (1915)/*Broken Blossoms* (1919)/*Way Down East* (1920)

Intolerance came in the middle of Griffith's most creative and successful film-making period. All these films display the characteristic features of his work: the epic, the intimate, and above all, the dramatic.

Cabiria (1914)

Giovanni Pastrone's epic recounting of the wars between Carthage and Rome is on the same scale that Griffith would employ in both *The Birth of a Nation* and *Intolerance*. His use of a moving camera to home in from an establishing shot to medium and close-ups also heavily influenced Griffith's use of the camera.

Au Hasard Balthazar (1966)

Robert Bresson uses a donkey as the central figure in this exploration of humanity's largely cruel capabilities as it is passed from one owner to another until its death, drawing parallels with Christ's treatment whilst on earth. The intolerance he depicts connects this film to Griffith's exploration of human nature.

REPRESENTATION

History

Historical films were not a new concept when Griffith came to make *Intolerance*; film studios readily undertook historical storylines, particularly for their epic value. Films such as *Ben Hur* (1907), *From the Manger to the Cross* (1912) and Griffith's own *Judith of Bethulia* had proved that the audience's appetite for historical films, and particularly those dealing with biblical times or ancient civilisations, was voracious. It was with these films that the template for blockbusters was created: sprawling narratives, huge numbers of extras and colossal sets.

Of course, film-makers in the United States had made historical films from the very beginnings of film, with the very recent history of the Wild West, most famously with Edwin S. Porter's *The Great Train Robbery* (1903). But it was with *Intolerance* that the potential of film to present the massive sweep of history was fully realised. Griffith had laid the seeds with his highly ambitious *The Birth of a Nation* a year earlier, but his perspective widened from one primary narrative to four and from a matter of a few years to thousands.

Although the historical scenes are a mixture of verisimilitude and Hollywood liberty-taking, Griffith set about representing history by literally rebuilding it; the scale of the sets bear the weight of authenticity, whether they are authentic or not. The other important feature of this film, which taps into the great power of history to educate and for people to draw comparisons, was Griffith's use of cross-cutting between scenes from different time periods.

No longer did history need to be represented in one long linear pattern of cause and effect, now shared themes and patterns in history could be discerned by the juxtaposition of shots. The shot of the prone mother's outstretched arm (discussed in the TEXTUAL ANALYSIS section below), after her baby has been taken from her, is juxtaposed with Christ's crucifixion. The parallel is striking and suddenly history ceases to be in the past, but is a continual thread that passes through our own lives and beyond.

> '*Intolerance*'s greatest contribution to the history of cinema was that it ambitiously showed that a cut... could be an intellectual tool [and] it had a huge impact on other film-makers... such as Eisenstein.' Mark Cousins, *The Story of Film*, Pavillion Books, London, 2004

> 'The variety of technical devices contributes to the overall effect of complexity which gives the film the quality of a historical tableau, or tapestry, in which detail is ultimately less important than the movement of history itself.' Pam Cook, *The Cinema Book 2nd Edition*, Bfi Publishing, 2000

KEY SCENE TEXTUAL ANALYSIS

Gates of Babylon (2; 17:24)

A striking sequence introduces the audience to the fourth story on the theme of intolerance, beginning with an establishing shot of one of the gates leading into the city of Babylon (circa 539 BC). The effect of the iris opening slowly emphasises the spectacle of the opening shot, gradually revealing the immense set and foregrounding its 'cinema of attractions' status. The audience would have been awe-struck by the image, designed to impress and underline the wealth and stature of this civilisation.

The verticals of the towers and the walls are the first elements to capture the eye; they are immense, dwarfing not only the human traffic but the elephants that are ridden in and out of the gates. The scale of the set is given more emphasis by the presence of figures on the ramparts and the towers, confirming that this is *real* and not created through any optical effects. The audience is drawn more forcefully into the verisimilitude of the action by these elements, helping us to suspend our disbelief and not be distracted by special effects. There is a quick bridging medium shot which helps with the transition from wide shot to closer in to the action. The first two shots are static, but for the third the camera tracks through the crowds on a crane. The audience is given the best seat in the house: a high angle position of power, free to cut through the crowds. The freedom of movement has a liberating effect, giving the impression that the viewer is also milling through the throng of people and transporting us back to ancient Babylon.

The *mise-en-scène* packs the frame with a feast for the eye with numerous people resplendent in their exotic clothes, immense statues, elephants and spears thrusting upwards as Griffith transports the audience with as much spectacle and authenticity as possible. The cut to the next shot, now inside the town gates, is an opening iris again, revealing magnificent sculptures. They sit alongside the loading of hay into a cart to juxtapose the highest pinnacle of achievement with the very ordinary. The camera tracks again and leads the audience into this new and startling world, both authentic and exotic. Although this is a film of spectacle it also focuses on the intimate, the personal stories that exist amidst the chaos. The three shots of the mountain girl move from long shot to close-up, the language of film guiding the audience into a personal world and forcing us to see the emotions of the individual that are otherwise masked by the spectacle of crowds and the city itself.

Love temple of virgins (3; 40:40)

The pre-Hays Code era allowed film-makers to be more explicit in their presentation of sex and violence, and this sequence shows how eroticism could be presented in a way which, tame by modern standards, is nonetheless charged with sensuality. It begins with an eruption of fire, appropriate for the passionate atmosphere, which is created in the rest of the scene. The first image of a gyrating female, with steam being emitted beside her, is representative of the tone that follows; it is understated but charged like a painting of a nude.

The second shot is even more sensual. The camera pans down the reclined body of another female, as if caressing her gently pulsating body. The next shot is the one that most recalls a painting of a

nude, like Francisco de Goya's *La Maja Desnuda*, diagonally crossing the frame. Although partially clad, her expression and the contemplation by the camera help reinforce the atmosphere of sensuality. The slow reveal on the next shot allows the audience to absorb the images of hedonistic joy, the medium shot of the gently rocking woman a picture of barely contained physical contentment.

The final image of a woman in the far left of frame is full of mystery and sexuality. Most of the frame is dark, suggesting her passions, and she is dressed in a transparent fabric, her body like a voluptuous Botticelli nude. But then the darkness evaporates as the frame becomes properly exposed and another female is revealed, seated and nude in an ancient bath full of water. There is a shower of water and light from the right of frame and the seated woman joyfully splashes the water. Again, but for the women's movement, the framing is reminiscent of a painting, and freedom, joy and all the trappings of a narcissistic lifestyle are displayed in a single static shot. It is superficially appealing but it will all be destroyed later in the film as Babylon is overrun by the Persian army.

Taking the baby (5; 1:17:23)

The three women who come to take the baby are dressed in black; they are angels of death, terminating a mother and child's relationship through their misguided attempts to administer help. Their desire to do what is 'proper' (the woman's husband is in prison) by taking the baby is the ugly side of supposed charity, perpetrated by the well-to-do. This representation has a long history of being exposed and satirised in literary works such Charles Dickens' *Hard Times* and J.B. Priestley's *An Inspector Calls*.

The three 'enlightened' women fill the frame with their pompous posturing. The friendly male neighbour senses their menace, but is relegated to the edge of the frame as he leaves the single mother after delivering some food and drink. The women are pictures of conventional decency: fine clothes and prim expressions, but without any vestige of humanity. Their entrance is sudden, engulfing the frame and squeezing the mother into the foreground. The mother is in much lighter-coloured garments, but they are frail and her body language is passive, emphasising her vulnerability. This compares with the stern faces and the outstretched claw of the woman on the far left of frame, grasping and aggressively active. The cut to the subject of their visit, the baby, is a close-up to show the child's vulnerability and underline his contentment at home with his mother.

The explosion of violence comes in the next shot as the women try to take the baby. The frame bursts with the mother's anguished response as she clutches the baby tightly to her chest. The medium close-up of the mother and baby is face-on, her open and honest expression matched by the framing of the shot. She is pushed back in the frame and the next image of the women is full of thrusting and aggressive movement towards mother and child. The shot of the mother is

concealing brutality and a triumphant vengeance on those who they believe are inferior. The static frame of the room remains constant whilst the attack continues, its ferocity at odds with the ordinary surroundings. They make their escape and the final shot of the women, replete with satisfaction, show them returning to their prim and strutting personas as pillars of society.

They burst through the front of the frame as they walk away, leaving the mother on the floor upstairs; her prone body is almost lifeless, a passive victim of polite society's unwanted interference. The final image of her outstretched arm clutching the baby's clothes is one of defeat, subdued by society. The disembodiment highlights the destruction of her identity (without her child she is not complete), and her rights as a human.

repeated, staring at the camera as if pleading with the audience – society – to be more compassionate and tolerant.

The three-shot of the women shows them edging ever closer and becoming more threatening whilst the mother gets smaller and more defensive as she draws the child into herself. She breaks for freedom in the next medium shot and then follows the next explosion of violence; two of the women attack her, their figures now just black shapes, whilst the third stands by the door, defending it against any intrusion of humanity and preparing for a quick getaway.

One of them escapes like a thief with the baby, while the other two commit further acts of violence, venturing beyond restraint and into the realms of assault and humiliation. Their actions portray an image of middle-class civility exposed as a façade,

Gone With The Wind

KEY FACTS

Release Date: 1939

Country of Origin: USA

Running Time: 224 minutes

PRODUCTION NOTES

Production Companies

Selznick International Pictures

Metro-Goldwyn-Mayer (MGM)

Distributors

Loew's

Metro-Goldwyn-Mayer (MGM)

Budget

$3,900,000 (estimated)

Awards

Best Actress in a Leading Role Vivien Leigh
Academy Awards, USA

Best Actress in a Supporting Role Hattie McDaniel

Academy Awards, USA

Best Art Direction Lyle R. Wheeler Academy
Awards, USA

Best Cinematography, Colour Ernest Haller, Ray
Rennahan Academy Awards, USA

Best Director Victor Fleming Academy Awards, USA

Best Film Editing Hal C. Kern, James E. Newcom
Academy Awards, USA

Best Picture David O. Selznick Academy Awards,
USA

Best Writing, Screenplay Sidney Howard Academy
Awards, USA

Best Actress Vivien Leigh New York Film Critics
Circle Awards

National Film Registry National Film Preservation
Board, USA

SYNOPSIS

The story charts the life of Scarlett O'Hara and her family from the beginning to the end of the American Civil War. She is the daughter of a rich plantation owner in the slave-owning southern state of Georgia. She is angered to discover that the object of her affections, Ashley Wilkes, is about to marry another girl, Melanie Hamilton. Scarlett tries to make Ashley jealous and has an argument with him (overheard by Rhett Butler), but Ashley is intent upon marrying his intended. On a whim, Scarlett decides to marry another suitor, Charles Hamilton, who is Melanie's brother.

Soon after the two weddings Charles dies of the measles, and the Civil War begins to dominate the lives of all the characters. Although in mourning, Scarlett still attends a ball whilst staying in Atlanta and dances with Rhett Butler, a scandalous action for the times. Ashley visits Melanie and Scarlett again tries to protest her love for him. However, he is more interested in getting Scarlett to promise to take care of Melanie and their unborn child and she agrees. When Melanie is near to giving birth, she and Scarlett are forced to leave the house in Atlanta as the northern Union armies besiege the town; with the help of Rhett Butler they make a perilous escape, finding that the Wilkes house, Twelve Oaks, has been destroyed, but that Scarlett's family home, Tara, is intact.

Finding her mother dead and her father half-mad, she sets about rebuilding Tara's fortunes. After the war, Ashley returns, but he is a broken man and still will not commit to Scarlett, telling her he must stay with Melanie. Scarlett tries to borrow money from Rhett, but he has none, and she marries the wealthy Frank Kennedy, her sister's fiancé. They make money, but Frank is killed by Union troops and Scarlett succumbs to Rhett Butler's advances. They marry and have a daughter, Bonnie, but Rhett is only too aware of Scarlett's manipulative and wayward character.

Two tragedies ensue - Scarlett falls down a staircase and miscarries her second child, and then Bonnie is killed in a riding accident. Melanie dies during her second pregnancy and Scarlett finally realises that Ashley truly loved Melanie and that she and Ashley will never be together. She attempts to be reconciled with Rhett, but after the many machinations of their life together, the miscarriage and the death of their daughter, the gulf between them is too great. Rhett leaves Scarlett, and although distraught, she resolves to get him back and draws strength from her home, Tara, in order to continue the fight.

HISTORICAL CONTEXT

War breaks out in Europe in 1939 and the world was faced with another conflict on a scale not seen for more than 20 years. People had considered the First World War as the conflict that would fully exorcise the entire world's demons and create a new world order. But events – some of the victors' own making – conspired against this and the world stared into an abyss. *Blitzkrieg* drove a wedge through Europe and many people of different nations awoke to find that their lives had been changed forever: Poland was the first, but much of Europe was to follow as countries fell to German aggression.

In this way, *Gone With The Wind* foreshadows the cataclysmic changes that would happen to multitudes of people; the scenes of thousands of dying and dead troops at the train depot, or the burning of Atlanta were the kind of images that would be depicted in newsreels over the coming years. Of course, the film-makers could not have imagined the horrors of the next few years but the massive destruction of life, of minds and properties in the film would be played out time and again across Europe and other theatres of war. There were parallels already happening; the Spanish Civil War had been providing haunting images of death on a grand scale between 1936 and 1939, and it was not just war that caused death and privation. The economic deprivations of the 1930s had taken their toll on the United States, and Scarlett's resolute and defiant attitude was an inspiration to the people at the time, and perhaps a template for the years to come.

The film's larger than life producer, David O. Selznick, was no stranger to the blockbuster. In 1935 alone he produced three other epic literary adaptations: *David Copperfield*, *Anna Karenina* and *A Tale of Two Cities*. He had worked his way up through the ranks at MGM and then at Paramount before becoming head of production at RKO where he oversaw one of its greatest successes, *King Kong*, in 1933. After another stint at MGM he founded Selznick International Pictures, where he could finally control his productions and impose his creative will on the films that he released through United Artists. He was rare amongst producers in Hollywood at the time for the amount of independent power that he wielded, and his blockbuster vision remained throughout his career, rekindled in later works such as *Duel in the Sun* (1946).

SELECT FILMOGRAPHY OF MAIN PRODUCERS AND CAST

Victor Fleming, 1889-1949, Director

The Mollycoddle, 1920

Mantrap, 1926

The Virginian, 1929

Red Dust, 1932

Bombshell, 1933

Treasure Island, 1934

Reckless, 1935

The Farmer Takes a Wife, 1935

Captains Courageous, 1937

Test Pilot, 1938

The Wizard of Oz, 1939

Gone With The Wind, 1939

Dr. Jeykll and Mr. Hyde, 1941

Tortilla Flat, 1942

A Guy Named Joe, 1943

Adventure, 1945

Joan of Arc, 1948

David O. Selznick, 1902-1965, Producer

Christopher Strong, 1933

The Personal History, Adventures, Experience, and Observation of David Copperfield, the Younger, 1935

Anna Karenina, 1935

A Tale of Two Cities, 1935

The Prisoner of Zenda, 1937

A Star Is Born, 1937

The Adventures of Tom Sawyer, 1938

Intermezzo: A Love Story, 1939

Gone with the Wind, 1939

Rebecca, 1940

Spellbound, 1945

Duel in the Sun, 1946

The Paradine Case, 1947

Portrait of Jennie, 1948

A Farewell to Arms, 1957

Ernest Haller, 1896-1970, Director of Photography

The Dawn Patrol, 1930

Jezebel, 1938

Dark Victory, 1939

The Roaring Twenties, 1939

Gone with the Wind, 1939

Mildred Pierce, 1945

The Verdict, 1946

Humoresque, 1946

The Flame and the Arrow, 1950

On Moonlight Bay, 1951

Rebel Without A Cause, 1955

Men In War, 1957

God's Little Acre, 1958

Man of the West, 1958

Whatever Happened to Baby Jane?, 1962

William Cameron Menzies, 1896-1957

See *Things to Come* in FANTASY Section

Max Steiner, 1888-1971, Composer

See *King Kong* in FANTASY section

Vivien Leigh, 1913-1967, Actress

A Yank at Oxford, 1938

Sidewalks of London, 1938

Gone With The Wind, 1939

Waterloo Bridge, 1940

That Hamilton Woman, 1941

Caesar and Cleopatra, 1945

Anna Karenina, 1948

A Streetcar Named Desire, 1951

The Deep Blue Sea, 1955

The Roman Spring of Mrs. Stone, 1961

Ship of Fools, 1965

Clark Gable, 1901-1960, Actor

Hell Drivers, 1931

Red Dust, 1932

It Happened One Night, 1934

China Seas, 1935

Mutiny on the Bounty, 1935

San Francisco, 1936

Test Pilot, 1938

Gone With The Wind, 1939

Strange Cargo, 1940

Boom Town, 1940

Command Decision, 1948

Across the Wide Missouri, 1951

Mogambo, 1953

The Tall Men, 1955

Run Silent Run Deep, 1958

The Misfits, 1961

LINKS TO OTHER FILMS

Birth of A Nation (1915)

Although controversial in its depiction of black people and the Ku Klux Klan, the film impressively charts the enormous upheavals that occurred in American society before, during and after the American Civil War.

Jezebel (1938)

A year before the release of *Gone With The Wind*, William Wyler's film dealt with a similar scenario and themes. It follows Southern Belle Julie Marsden and her headstrong ambitions, which lead her to frustration and disappointment until she finally has an opportunity to redeem herself, clearly paralleling Scarlett O'Hara.

Gettysburg (1993)/*Gods and Generals* (2003)

Ronald L. Maxwell's films examine the American Civil War from the point of view of the battlefields, as well as the political and military manoeuvring that surrounded the key conflicts.

Cold Mountain (2003)

Like *Gone With The Wind*, Anthony Minghella's film focuses on the human cost of the American Civil War, both on soldiers and the people who did not fight. Suffering and loss, as well as extreme fortitude, are key issues that connect the two films.

REPRESENTATION

The Southern States of America

This part of the United States has always been a powerful draw for American film-makers, whether they are filming an historical piece or a contemporary film. It has often formed the backdrop for films dealing with the American Civil War (*Ride with the Devil*, 1999; *The Outlaw Josey Wales*, 1976), or the issues of slavery at the time (*Amistad*, 1997). It has been the locale for more modern race issues, particularly using the 1950's and 1960's civil rights movement as part of the narrative (*Mississippi Burning*, 1988), or as impetus behind the storyline (*In the Heat of the Night*, 1967).

Even films without a noticeable comment to make about the area use it as a backdrop for steamy thrillers (*The Big Easy*, 1987) or dramas dripping with sexual intrigue, particularly the plays and subsequent film versions of Tennessee Williams (*A Streetcar Named Desire*, 1951; *Baby Doll*, 1956; *Cat on a Hot Tin Roof*, 1958). Indeed, the main protagonist of *A Streetcar Named Desire*, Blanche DuBois, embodies many of the characteristics that we associate with the Southern Belle and the old world of her environs.

She is shown as a sexual predator but her background on a wealthy plantation, which has since decayed, helps underline the dual representation of this area in American literature and film; it is chivalric, courtly, and traditional, but also duplicitous and full of sexual impropriety. Most significantly, its wealth is based on slavery. This is the dichotomy at the heart of *Gone With The Wind*; the opulence and observance of social etiquette is mesmerizing, just as the source of their wealth is repellent.

African-Americans

The African-American characters are all represented as house servants or field hands in the film, which is historically accurate, but defines black people in a very narrow way, just as countless other Hollywood films had done previously and would continue to do for years afterwards. Mammy, the O'Hara house slave, Big Sam, the chief plantation slave and Prissy, Melanie Hamilton's slave, are forced into stereotypical actions and words. Mammy may be seen as a woman with an opinion but she remains in service, and Prissy is a stereotypically ignorant black character. The scene where she fails to fetch a doctor for Melanie and is slapped by Scarlett only underlines this racist representation.

Black people were virtually invisible in all but historical films in Hollywood until the 1960s. Any black character would either be a slave or servant; even classic films like *It's A Wonderful Life* (1946) with contemporary settings relegated black characters to the margins. The only other vehicles for black people were the all-black musicals like *Porgy and Bess* (1959) or cross-over stars like Louis Armstrong and other musical performers who would generally play themselves, or versions of themselves, in films such as *A Song is Born* (1948). It was not until the civil rights movement that black actors began to win more significant roles. The likes of Sidney Poitier led the way in films such as *The Defiant Ones* (1958), *Lilies of the Field* (1963), *In the Heat of the Night* (1967) and *Guess Who's Coming to Dinner* (1967).

But two fundamental issues remained unresolved, even at this time. Firstly, it was black *actors*, not black actresses and, secondly, the narratives nearly all revolved around issues of race. It was not until the blaxploitation films of the 1970s and the later emergence of actors such as Forest Whitaker, Denzel Washington, Will Smith, Don Cheadle, Morgan Freeman, Cuba Gooding Jr. and Eddie Murphy, alongside actresses like Halle Berry and Thandie Newton, and directors Spike Lee, Antoine Fuqua and John Singleton that we saw the beginnings of a black voice in mainstream Hollywood. In Africa, there has been a wealth of film-making since the 1970s, but the diverse representations of such a vast continent have not reached world audiences until recent years through films such as *Moolaadé* (2004) and *Tsotsi* (2005).

> 'Gone With The Wind... *has a famously unresolved ending, one that raises new enigmas rather than solving the old, and one that resists the clear happy ending of romance.'* Pamela Robertson Wojick, *The Cinema Book 2nd Edition*, Ed. Pam Cook & Mieke Bernink, Bfi Publishing, 1999

"Occupying an unparalleled hold on the number one spot from 1939 to 1972–almost 40 years–Gone with the Wind was the Hoover of blockbuster movies, both brand leader and one-movie monopoly, sucking up the competition on all sides.' Tom Shone, *Blockbuster*, Scribner, 2004

KEY SCENE TEXTUAL ANALYSIS

The dance (14)

A huge banner dominates the screen with 'Monster Bazaar' emblazoned across it in large red letters. The diegetic music of the dance can already be heard as it dissolves to a high angle long shot of the hall, awash with colour and dancers. The *mise-en-scène* conveys vibrancy and spectacle and the long shot almost assaults one's vision with rich reds, blues and whites dominating the colour scheme and twirling dancers presenting a rainbow of colours. The scene is designed to impress the audience, just as these well-heeled people try to impress each other with their finery.

The camera then comes down to the level of the dancers, with the musicians in the foreground. The sense of vitality increases at this level as the frame is filled with the exuberance of a people revelling in their stations in life. Yet at this moment in history (the American Civil War), they are about to face a titanic struggle to preserve their way of life.

The men are in uniform and the women in dresses that are full and luxurious. Scarlett's black costume, a symbol of mourning for her dead husband, marks a stark contrast and also acts as a strait-jacket on her desire to have fun and flirt, as is her natural inclination. Evidence of this comes with the medium shot which pans down her back to reveal her dancing feet. Social decorum dictates that she should stay behind her counter, selling items for the war effort, but certainly not having fun.

The shots of Dr. Meade against a backdrop of the Old South's Stars and Stripes, which dominates the frame, suggest the epic proportions of the film's intentions and the loyalty of these people to their cause, reminiscent of similar shots in *Citizen Kane* (1941) and, more particularly, in *Patton* (1970).

After Rhett Butler's triumphant entrance and his 'buying' of Scarlett, the camera sweeps around with the dancers as they swirl across the dance floor. The heady rush of Rhett and Scarlett's flirtatious dance is highlighted by the cross-cutting between long and medium shot.

Attack on Atlanta (19)

The camera tracks along a dusty Atlanta street and shows a frame full of figures on the move: townspeople hurry along, retreating from the camera, whilst the Confederate soldiers march towards the foreground. The movement within the filmic space underlines the two opposing reactions to war: civilians flee and soldiers advance. The camera prowls and observes as screams and shouts dominate the diegetic sound, underpinning the sense of chaos.

Wagons pass by in the background, laden with the jumbled contents of homes deserted, and the colours of the scene are muted in comparison with the lush colours of the earlier dance scene. Here, the panic and mournful-looking soldiers, their heads down, match the grey colour of their uniforms and the smoke and dust have bleached the colour from the street and all its human inhabitants.

The track then becomes a crane shot as it rises over debris, the flotsam and jetsam of a city about to sink beneath the bombardment of the Union's guns. Charred chairs, window frames and a column, a reminder of the South's grand mansions, are strewn on top of each other; the tree behind is bereft of life and an explosion triggers more cries.

The scale of the catastrophe has successfully been conveyed with just a short scene and through a camera movement that has shown a relatively limited area. However, the stately pace of the movement has prolonged the shot and the experience of the scene, adding to the sense of, and contrasting with, the chaos presented. Also, by filling the frame with people, various objects and the explosion, a real sense of the immensity of the moment is achieved.

The next shot shows a preacher in the foreground with a large stained glass window depicting Jesus behind him. An explosion rips through the glass - the shells are now even defiling a holy place - but the preacher carries on undaunted as the slow crane shot down to focus on one injured man listening to the words helps to personalise a nightmarish situation, incomprehensible to those who have not experienced war. His tranquil expression helps the audience identify with the personal suffering that is shown on a grand scale throughout the rest of the scene.

The succeeding long shot of the church juxtaposes with the dance hall of the earlier scene. Where the latter was full of colour and movement, here the

her as she enters the makeshift surgery where an amputation is about to take place. The patient's cries and the horror of the spectacle prove too much and her retreat is emphasised by a rapid tracking shot. Her filmic space diminishes as she becomes trapped by the enormity of the suffering and the camera itself seems to force her back. Shadows are cast both in the room, where there is chaotic movement surrounding the patient, and over her face to underline the nightmarish quality of the moment.

Scarlett's escape from this world is presented with a tracking shot with the camera pulling away from her as she turns her back on the suffering, finally closing the outside door to the church. It is not an escape, however, as she is catapulted into the tumult outside and her POV reveals the terror and chaos of those fleeing the war.

mise-en-scène is dominated by a sense of static suffering; the only similarity is that both are filled with humanity, but at polar ends of experience.

The figures are largely prone and filled with pain and only a few are moving, Scarlett among them. The tracking shot captures the full scale and range of emotions in the face of suffering: fear, madness, acceptance, stoicism and calmness, as each injured man provides us with a vignette of their individual reaction to pain and hardship. It is a reminder that the epic can also be depicted in the detail, not just the spectacle.

The next such detail is the focus on Scarlett's reaction to this suffering. Within the epic sweep it is again the effect on the individual that is important; she cannot bear the sights and sounds of suffering any longer. The camera tracks quickly towards

The next long shot comes from street level and reiterates the message that she cannot turn her back on the suffering. Her small figure in the background is obscured and consumed by the fleeing figures and wagons in the foreground, for she is part of the chaos and there is no escape.

The close-up sees her wince and recoil from the sound of the shelling and her efforts to go in one direction are thwarted by the seething crowd. She is finally born along by this tide of humanity; the dynamic between the individual and the masses is played out in visual terms throughout this scene.

In search of a doctor (21)

Now that Atlanta is almost deserted by those who are still able to move, the first shot of this scene depicts the devastation that has been wreaked by the bombardment. The initial frame is dominated by the skeletal and charred remains of the buildings with Scarlett and the soldiers marginalised at the bottom.

Again, Scarlett struggles against the soldiers and wagons in the next shot, a repeated visual motif which highlights her wilful character and individuality. The tracking shot takes us on a journey with her and comes to rest on her anguished face in close-up. This shot remains for a few moments, adding to the power of the next as the audience is tantalised by what she can see but we cannot.

The revelation comes with a slow track and then crane upwards as the full horror of the sight unfolds. A sombre orchestral accompaniment, with the plaintive sound of a solo trumpet playing 'Taps', a piece of music most often associated with military

arranged, resting on something that stands for movement and progress, whilst the reality is of deathly stasis and collapse.

The camera comes to rest on the tattered remnants of the Confederate flag. More than the tragic death of the individuals that is being depicted here, it is the end of a society, of a way of life.

funerals, cuts through some traditional Southern melodies and helps to underpin the sight of misery on an epic scale and the death throes of the Confederate forces. The camera moves at a stately speed, allowing the audience to slowly absorb the enormity of the suffering. The groans of dying men intermingle with the non-diegetic sound, adding to the air of desperation and futility.

After the bustle of the previous scenes, these soldiers are rendered immobile by their injuries, a great sea of humanity, which once again devours the tiny figure of Scarlett.

The prone bodies stretch as far as the eye can see, emphasising the immensity of this moment. Some men are even placed on the railway tracks, like human sleepers, stripping them of their individuality. It is ironic that they should be so

Bambi

KEY FACTS

Release Date: 1942

Country of Origin: USA

Running Time: 70 minutes

PRODUCTION NOTES

Production Company

Walt Disney Productions

Distributor

RKO Radio Pictures

SYNOPSIS

Bambi is a fawn born in the forest. His arrival causes a great amount of interest amongst the other creatures, for deer seem to be highly-regarded animals. Bambi's first weeks of life are charted as he discovers the joys of the forest, the fear of storms and the danger of man; he and his mother narrowly escape an encounter with hunters. However, this danger is ever-present and his mother is eventually shot and killed as they search for grass on the snowy meadows. Bambi's father, a mighty stag, visits his son and tells him that he must carry on without his mother. The story then moves forward in time and Bambi has grown up but is still with his childhood friends of Thumper the rabbit, Faline, a deer and Flower, who is a skunk. Bambi and Faline become a couple, but their relationship is interrupted by another young male deer who fights with Bambi but is defeated. Man starts a fire in the forest and the deer and other animals barely escape, but the story ends positively with the birth of two fawns for Bambi and Faline.

HISTORICAL CONTEXT

At a time when mothers were losing their husbands and sons every day in the war that was consuming Europe, it was apt that Walt Disney, the purveyor of childhood nightmares and dreams should reflect the feelings of loss in this film. *Bambi* presented a world in which man was violent and disruptive of the natural cycle of life. Walt Disney had entered into feature-length animation with *Snow White and the Seven Dwarfs* in 1937. Its success helped establish a firm foundation, but this was immediately threatened by the following two films, *Pinocchio* and *Fantasia* (both 1940), which did not live up to their predecessor's financial achievement.

The two films that followed, *Dumbo* (1941) and *Bambi*, steered the features towards simpler evocations of an eternal theme, the bond between mother and child. Although *Dumbo* was successful, it was not until the re-release of *Bambi* in 1947 that the story of the deer became an established critical and financial success. Perhaps the audience of the war years were not yet prepared to face their demons in animated films, a medium normally reserved for laughter and escapism.

The film may also reflect Walt Disney's own life: his mother and father died during its production; his company was in financial freefall after building a new studio and the failure of *Pinocchio* and *Fantasia*; and he had to contend with a major strike amongst his workers. Whatever the reason for such an unflinching look at the brutality of life, it certainly evokes an era of great chaos, fuelled by the spectre of death which engulfed the world for nearly six years.

Although *Bambi* would not seem to be an obvious choice as a blockbuster its financial credentials are impeccable. When its receipts are adjusted for inflation, the film ranks 31st in the top 50 of all-time box office blockbusters, beating such film behemoths as *Independence Day* (1996), *Spider-Man* (2002) and *The Lord of the Rings: Return of the King* (2003). The film's universal appeal, the story of life and death, also helps to invest it with an epic sweep that became the template for Disney films that followed, and which was conveyed through its fine character animation and broad-brush stroke animation of backgrounds utilising the art of Impressionism to convey intense feelings. With *Bambi*'s release, Walt Disney was consolidating his animation company as a major Hollywood player, distributed by RKO, and creating a franchise which was the forerunner of the many blockbuster franchises to come.

SELECT FILMOGRAPHY OF MAIN PRODUCERS AND CAST

David Hand, 1900-1986, Director

The Mad Doctor, 1933

Old King Cole, 1933

Mickey's Steamroller, 1934

Who Killed Cock Robin?, 1935

Three Orphan Kittens, 1935

Three Little Wolves, 1936

Alpine Climbers, 1936

Three Blind Mouseketeers, 1936

Magician Mickey, 1937

Little Hiawatha, 1937

Snow White and the Seven Dwarfs, 1937

The Whalers, 1938

Bambi, 1942

Walt Disney, 1901-1966, Producer

Snow White and the Seven Dwarfs, 1937

Pinocchio, 1940

Fantasia, 1940

Dumbo, 1941

Bambi, 1942

Song of the South, 1946

Cinderella, 1950

Treasure Island, 1950

Alice in Wonderland, 1951

Peter Pan, 1953

20,000 Leagues under the Sea, 1954

Lady and the Tramp, 1955

Sleeping Beauty, 1959

Swiss Family Robinson, 1960

One Hundred and One Dalmatians, 1961

The Absent-Minded Professor, 1961

The Sword in the Stone, 1963

The Incredible Journey, 1963

Mary Poppins, 1964

The Jungle Book, 1967

LINKS TO OTHER FILMS

Dumbo (1941)

After the intricacies and grandeur of Disney's two earlier films, Pinocchio and Fantasia, this was much simpler in terms of plot with the focus on the mother/child relationship, linking it to *Bambi*. Both also shared the same animation technique.

Great Expectations (1946)

The relationship between the young orphaned Pip and the world around him is initiated with the scene in which he visits the graves of his parents; the terror of the natural world when one is small and vulnerable mirrors Bambi's experiences in the early stages of the film.

Oliver Twist (1948)

This David Lean adaptation of Charles Dickens' novel focuses on a young boy's experiences without his parents; the opening is particularly shocking in its depiction of the last desperate moments of a mother as she battles through the elements to reach a workhouse where she gives birth to Oliver and dies. Her struggle identifies the overwhelming urge of the mother to protect the child, as is seen in *Bambi*.

The Lion King (1994)

This Disney film retreads similar ground to that in *Bambi*, with its tale of a lion cub whose father is killed. The film details his trials as he finally matures as a lion with a mate and an heir.

REPRESENTATION

The natural world

In *Snow White and the Seven Dwarfs* the animals of the forest are drawn to accentuate their cute appeal. This anthropomorphic approach is used to some extent in *Bambi*, but mainly for Thumper,

who is an animated throwback to the animals that help Snow White. The other characters, including Bambi, are drawn to closely resemble their real appearance in an attempt to bring a sense of verisimilitude to the film – after all, it is a story about very real struggles and coping with death. The surrounding forest is a character in itself, based on painstaking observation by the animators, an arena that protects and threatens, a space that harbours the hunters and companions. Some of the later features, *The Jungle Book* (1967) and *Robin Hood* (1973) for example, began to lack this attention to detail. Although they were popular films, there is something cartoon-like about their visual style when compared to the classical animation of *Bambi*.

With *Bambi*, the focus on real animals in a real environment helps give the story its universality, and makes it one of the more difficult films for the young to deal with. It contains little of the continual banter and self-awareness that fills later Disney films such as *The Lion King*, but instead represents a world that is recognisable, and therefore all the more powerful.

Rites of passage

This particular narrative strand is one which is familiar throughout film history; the rebellious students in Lindsay Anderson's *If...* (1968); the drifting teenagers in Francis Ford Coppola's *The Outsiders* (1983) or the four friends on a journey of discovery in Rob Reiner's *Stand By Me* (1986). They all entail rites of passage. In *Bambi*, the young animal must face the key landmarks that characterise the journey from child to adulthood: the innocence of first sight, the wonder of new experiences and accomplishments, the danger of unintelligible horrors and the struggle to accept one's environment. It is a universal representation with archetypal characters, transcending its animated form to achieve a high level of realistic experience with which audiences are able to identify.

'A strikingly impressionistic version of life in the forest and the meadow.' Andrew Nickolds, *Time Out Film Guide 14th Ed.*, Time Out Guides Ltd., London, 2006

'Bambi (42), which - in the death of Bambi's mother - was maybe the most daring film he [Walt Disney] ever made.' David Thomson, *The New Biographical Dictionary of Film 4th Edition*, Little, Brown, London, 2002

KEY SCENE TEXTUAL ANALYSIS

April showers (7)

The early scenes of *Bambi* show life from his perspective: the wonderment of discovery; the terror of the unfamiliar and the security of family. The scene begins with a medium close-up of the faun as the first drops of rain begin to fall. Each drop is synchronised by a note on the clarinet, slowly at first and then quickening as the shower begins to strengthen. The melody is soft and light-hearted, expressing the awe and confusion in the faun's mind.

With Bambi's POV, and as the camera moves downwards, the music is joined by the vocal 'April Showers', sung firstly by female and then male voices; it is gentle and reassuring. The movement starts to follow a tiny stream created by the rainfall, and a leaf is carried along it. In following the water the camera rediscovers Bambi, who follows the leaf's progress with absolute fascination and delight in the mechanisms of nature.

The camera continues to follow the water, and next a quail crosses it with her brood. The wider context now becomes apparent as a variety of animals scurry around the forest; animals are seen to be greatly affected by nature's whims.

Three baby birds, initially wet and miserable, are then sheltered from the rain by their mother, who swoops into the nest, reinforcing the idea of comfort and security. The camera zooms in to intensify the moment of nurture as well as to pick out the faces of the now contented birds who happily peek out from under the mother's wing; one gets a big drop on its head when outside the safety of the mother's wing.

The camera tracks with a mouse as it zigzags over the treacherous terrain, allowing the audience to share the difficulty of his plight. It is caught by a particularly big drop and seeks shelter beneath a toadstool, one of many little comic touches scattered throughout the film to counteract the ever-brooding threat of man. The mouse then takes shelter under the tail feathers of a bird that is running and protecting its young; again it is a moment of comedy as it details the security of family and the community of animals.

Some animals, of course, take pleasure in the rain and the duck family is shown in the next shot as it begins to enjoy the weather conditions; nature is both harsh and benevolent.

The return to the fawn and his mother is seen in medium long shot, framed and protected by the grove in which they are resting; it is womb-like and an image of security, warmth and comfort, which encapsulates the first part of the film.

The non-diegetic music changes now at the threat of a storm with the brooding strings and voices mimicking the rising wind. The camera movement upwards, the equivalent of a crane shot, brings the audience into the heart of the approaching storm. The camera looks upwards as rain falls down towards the camera. The trees look more threatening from this angle as the first flash of lightning cuts through the sky and is highlighted by the clash of cymbals.

The shot does not linger on the lightning; there is a quick cut back to its effect on Bambi. Everything in the opening connects us with his reactions to the world.

The fawn is startled and seeks refuge in his mother's body. They are illuminated by the flashes, as are a succession of plants and animals in the shots that follow. Everything in nature is shown to be interconnected, for good or for ill. Everything that is touched by the light also reveals an inner beauty or hidden danger, unmasked by this penetrating force; flowers are irradiated and sinister shadows are created or intensified. The shots are much shorter now as the force of the storm increases, adding to the pace of the increasingly chaotic sequence. The music, too, is full of clashes and wailing.

Our vision becomes almost obliterated as the rain sweeps across the frame, helping us to connect with the intensity of the storm. Long shots of isolated trees and the sky are ripped apart by the lightning until the rapid strikes and synchronised music bring the scene to a climax, suddenly ending as the clouds begin to clear. An orange glow forces its way through the darkness and the non-diegetic

deer at the beginning of the shot. The final drops of rain cause the last three pleasing ripples to occur on the water's surface, two large and one small, perhaps representing the family unit of stag, doe and fawn.

This sequence works as shorthand for the whole film's narrative of security, then danger (and loss) with a return to companionship (albeit altered). The equilibrium of the fawn's life is shattered by his mother's death, but he finds a new equilibrium with a doe at the end. In the 'April Showers' sequence we see this structure in microcosm.

A fight (21)

This scene is preceded by a fantasy sequence that conveys the emerging feelings of love that Bambi has for the doe, Faline. As they perform a courtship

voices become more harmonious as the storm ceases. The birds on the branches herald a return to tranquillity, as does the reprisal of the positive 'April Showers' song.

The medium shot of mother and fawn, a tighter two-shot than before, helps to emphasise that the storm has made their connection even stronger; the foreground leaves are in focus whilst the animals are in soft focus behind, idyllic in their family bond. The camera tracks away, leaving them in the stillness of the womb-like home. It is an almost sacred depiction of mother and child and the audience is brought away, leaving them undisturbed.

The camera then moves downwards to rest on a pool of water, reflecting the now harmonious world around. The colours are warm and the non-diegetic music is soft to underline the tranquil image of the

dance, accompanied by upbeat, harmonious orchestral music, the woodland background is transformed into a symbolic picture of sky and clouds; they are floating on air.

As ever in this film, moments of harmony are usually succeeded by the harsh realities of life. Here, the contentment is cut short abruptly by the appearance of a rival for the doe's affections. The transition from the cloud sequence back to reality is achieved both visually and musically.

As Bambi follows the doe into a cloud another young stag emerges in an aggressive manner. His entrance causes the fantasy world to be extinguished. The background literally shudders as the woodland reappears and a jarring discord is sounded, underlining the threat. It is totally unexpected and very effective in completely breaking the harmonious spell.

As the new deer pushes Bambi away and then forces the doe into the forest with him, the non-diegetic music gathers pace and becomes more discordant as Bambi becomes more irate. The cut to the deer pushing the doe reveals a darker background to the previous shot; the visual tone is itself becoming darker as the confrontation approaches. As Bambi charges towards the other deer his body loses its colour until it is just a black outline, a visualisation not just of a darker part of the forest, but of his own gathering anger. The other deer is also barely more than a silhouette, framed with the darkest of green hues.

When they collide they are only outlines, streaks of light illuminating their hides. For the remainder of the fight they appear like elemental beings, stripped of their individuality and totally focused on

across her retreating frame. The close-up of their interlocked heads and antlers is backgrounded with a deep scar of red, an indicator of the intensity of the battle.

The rapid cutting and dramatic non-diegetic music help to underpin the action throughout the sequence, with shots concentrating on the deers' limbs and heads; they are fragmented in order to focus on the physicality of their encounter. There is one last charge at the camera from the other deer to cement our connection with Bambi, and then he is cast over the cliff and into the water below.

As before, the equilibrium is restored at the end of the sequence, not just by the obvious triumphal shot of Bambi with Faline, standing on the edge of the cliff, but also with the low angle shot, emphasising his strength and the soft browns and greens behind. Order and stability have been

aggression and domination. There are, however, close-ups of Bambi as he is thrown to the ground, helping to maintain the audience's bond with him. This is further emphasised by the shot of the other deer from Bambi's POV; he comes straight at the camera, his aggression clear and directed at us.

The fight continues. They look like dark demons with no other purpose than to be the victor. Another Bambi POV shows the other deer rearing on its hind legs, ready to come crashing down on us and Bambi. The blackness of their bodies then begins to attain a red glow, an indicator of their intense anger and the danger of the situation. Any cuts back to the doe show her static against a green background, with the brown colour of her hide still visible. Visually she is not initially part of the colour motifs used with the males, although as the fight reaches its climax their dark shadows are cast

restored, including the colours of the natural world which had been distorted during the battle. Bambi has faced and overcome another challenge in his journey from infant to adulthood.

Ben-Hur

KEY FACTS

Release Date: 1959

Country of Origin: USA

Running Time: 214 minutes

PRODUCTION NOTES

Production Company

Metro-Goldwyn-Mayer

Distributor

Metro-Goldwyn-Mayer

Budget

$15,000,000 (estimated)

Awards

Best Actor in a Leading Role Charlton Heston Academy Awards, USA

Best Actor in a Supporting Role Hugh Griffith Academy Awards, USA

Best Art Direction-Set Decoration, Colour William

A. Horning, Edward C. Carfagno, Hugh Hunt Academy Awards, USA

Best Cinematography, Colour Robert Surtees Academy Awards, USA

Best Costume Design, Colour Elizabeth Haffenden Academy Awards, USA

Best Director William Wyler Academy Awards, USA

Best Special Effects A. Arnold Gillespie, Robert MacDonald, Milo B. Lory Academy Awards, USA

Best Film Editing Ralph E. Winters, John D. Dunning Academy Awards, USA

Best Music, Scoring of a Dramatic or Comedy Picture Miklós Rózsa Academy Awards, USA

Best Picture Sam Zimbalist Academy Awards, USA

Best Sound Franklin Milton Academy Awards, USA

Best Film from any Source William Wyler BAFTA Awards, UK

Outstanding Directorial Achievement in Motion Pictures William Wyler Directors Guild of America

Best Motion Picture – Drama Golden Globes, USA

Best Motion Picture Director William Wyler Golden Globes, USA

Best Supporting Actor Stephen Boyd Golden Globes, USA

National Film Registry National Film Preservation Board, USA

Best Film New York Film Critics Circle Awards

SYNOPSIS

Childhood friends Juda Ben-Hur and Messala are reunited in Jerusalem. Ben-Hur is part of a wealthy Jewish family, whilst Messala is commander of the Roman forces. They clash over their differing beliefs, and when a roof tile falls from Ben-Hur's family house and nearly injures Messala, the Roman commander makes an example of Ben-Hur and his family. Ben-Hur is made a slave and his family are imprisoned, but on his way to a new life as a galley slave Jesus comes to his aid - he will be reunited with him later in the story.

Ben-Hur suffers terribly on the ship, but his luck turns when he rescues Quintus Arrius, a Roman commander and dignitary. The Roman adopts him as his son and Ben-Hur learns, amongst other things, how to be a charioteer. Returning home he enters a chariot race and defeats Messala in the presence of Pontius Pilate. Messala dies as a result of his injuries incurred in the race. Ben-Hur finds his mother and sister but they have contracted leprosy whilst in prison and are now outcasts. He takes them to see Jesus as he is being led to the crucifixion. Although they cannot get near to Jesus, at the moment of his death the women are healed and Ben-Hur is finally at peace with himself after years of suffering and thoughts of revenge.

HISTORICAL CONTEXT

If the 1950s were about fear and paranoia in the real world, in Hollywood it would be a decade dominated by the biblical epic. Money was poured into productions, making spectacle films on a scale not seen since the silent days of cinema. There seems to be a variety of reasons for the regeneration of this genre. The austerity of the 1940s was over and budget restrictions were lifted; it was as if Hollywood was reasserting itself and reminding audiences of the kind of show it could produce.

Cinemascope trumpeted its arrival with 20th Century Fox's *The Robe* in 1953. Not only were audiences treated to a wider spectacle, but these films were inevitably shot in glorious, rich colour. The studio system was also fighting against the onset of television, which was perceived as a threat in the 1950s, particularly in the United States. Television would undoubtedly affect people's leisure habits as the decade drew to a close, but the epics were a valiant last stand.

Ben-Hur stands as a monument to the biblical blockbuster. Its cast of thousands and enormous sets provided an epic backdrop to the story of a man whose life is charted across various countries and many years, even dovetailing with the greatest story of all, the life of Jesus. It cost approximately $15,000,000 to make, a colossal budget for the time. It garnered 11 Academy Awards and stands at number 13 in the top all-time box office blockbuster league when receipts are adjusted for inflation. *Everything* about this film was big; it is a blockbuster of biblical proportions.

The preponderance of biblical epics may also be a reflection of the era. The Second World War had blurred moral boundaries and atrocities, visible to all, had shaken people to the core. A great many people were living in a sea of uncertainty; some had killed and witnessed killing, and the 1950s, although a time of prosperity in the United States, also revealed the world to be a more complex and threatening place than ever before. The apocalypse of the bible was now in man's hands with atomic power and these films became reassertions of the straightforward moral messages of good and bad, of suffering and redemption, writ large. People flocked to see them and were reassured and comforted, as well as entertained.

SELECT FILMOGRAPHY OF MAIN PRODUCERS AND CAST

William Wyler, 1902-1981, Director

Dodsworth, 1936

Jezebel, 1938

Wuthering Heights, 1939

The Westerner, 1940

The Letter, 1940

The Little Foxes, 1941

Mrs. Miniver, 1942

The Best Years of Our Lives, 1946

The Heiress, 1949

Detective Story, 1951

Carrie, 1952

Roman Holiday, 1953

The Desperate Hours, 1955

Friendly Persuasion, 1956

The Big Country, 1958

Ben-Hur, 1959

The Children's Hour, 1961

The Collector, 1965

How to Steal a Million, 1966

Funny Girl, 1968

The Liberation of L.B. Jones, 1970

Sam Zimbalist, 1904-1958, Producer

Boom Town, 1940

Tortilla Flat, 1942

Side Street, 1950

King Solomon's Mines, 1950

Quo Vadis, 1951

Mogambo, 1953

Beau Brummell, 1954

Tribute to a Bad Man, 1956

The Catered Affair, 1956

The Barretts of Wimpole Street, 1957

Ben-Hur, 1959

Robert Surtees, 1906-1985, Director of Photography

King Solomon's Mines, 1950

Quo Vadis, 1951

The Bad and the Beautiful, 1952

Mogambo, 1953

Valley of the Kings, 1954

Oklahoma!, 1955

Raintree County, 1957

The Law and Jake Wade, 1958

Ben-Hur, 1959

Cimarron, 1960

Mutiny on the Bounty, 1962

PT 109, 1963

The Satan Bug, 1965

Doctor Dolittle, 1967

The Graduate, 1967

The Last Picture Show, 1971

The Cowboys, 1972

The Sting, 1973

The Great Waldo Pepper, 1975

A Star Is Born, 1976

Miklos Rozsa, 1907-1995, Composer

The Divorce of Lady X, 1938

The Four Feathers, 1939

The Spy in Black, 1939

The Thief of Bagdad, 1940

That Hamilton Woman, 1941

Jungle Book, 1942

Five Graves to Cairo, 1943

Double Indemnity, 1944

Blood on the Sun, 1945

Spellbound, 1945

The Lost Weekend, 1945

The Killers, 1946

Brute Force, 1947

Secret Beyond the Door, 1948

The Naked City, 1948

Criss Cross, 1949

Adam's Rib, 1949

The Asphalt Jungle, 1950

Quo Vadis?, 1951

Julius Caesar, 1953

Lust for Life, 1956

Ben-Hur, 1959

King of Kings, 1961

El Cid, 1961

Sodom and Gomorrah, 1962

Last Embrace, 1979

Time After Time, 1979

Dead Men Don't Wear Plaid, 1982

Charlton Heston, 1924–2008, Actor

See *Soylent Green* in the FANTASY section (pg. 359)

LINKS TO OTHER FILMS

The Ten Commandments (1956)

Cecil B. DeMille's epic recounting of the story of Moses is told on a vast scale with incredible sets and thousands of extras. In these ways, the scope of its story and the casting of Charlton Heston as Moses connect this film with *Ben-Hur*. Heston, in particular, was so closely associated with the epics in the 1950s and 1960s that his very presence guaranteed an audience; he symbolised strength

and integrity in all these roles.

Spartacus (1960)

Stanley Kubrick's film appeared a year after *Ben-Hur* and it resembles it in a number of ways. It is an epic study of a non-Roman in the Roman world and his suffering and eventual victory over oppression. Kirk Douglas, the eponymous star, peeved at not being chosen by friend and former colleague, William Wyler, for the part of *Ben-Hur* produced this equally lavish production to rival the earlier film.

El Cid (1961)

Anthony Mann's story of the Spanish nobleman is another tale of a man who succeeds against impossible odds and whose life is touched by the Divine. Charlton Heston again plays the protagonist, starring as a righteous man who fights for his family, his people and his beliefs.

Monty Python's Life of Brian (1979)

Although the desired effect is different - here played for comedy and in *Ben-Hur* for entertainment and edification - the narratives are in fact closely connected. Both films show a man caught up with the Romans, connected to Jesus and forced into a life against his will. The success of the film lies in its strict adherence to the genre conventions of biblical epics whilst *undermining* them at the same time, just as Mel Brooks had done to similar effect with the horror genre in *Young Frankenstein* (1974).

REPRESENTATION

The ancient Romans

Romans have been represented in mostly negative ways by film-makers, perhaps not surprising for a people who conquered large parts of the world and enslaved many of its inhabitants. Impressive, yes; gentle, no. Film-makers have often used the Romans as a representation of oppression and brutality. Henry Koster's *The Robe*; Delmer Daves' *Demetrius and the Gladiators* (1954); Stanley Kubrick's *Spartacus*; Anthony Mann's *The Fall of the Roman Empire* (1964); Federico Fellini's *Satyricon* (1969) and Ridley Scott's *Gladiator* (2000) all paint a picture of a cruel, unforgiving and hedonistic society where others' suffering is offered as public entertainment.

The Romans in *Ben-Hur* are no exception, particularly Messala. Although Arrius is represented in a more positive light because of his treatment of Ben-Hur, he is still very much a part of Rome's authoritarian regime, suppressing others and living in prosperity and comfort at the expense of others' liberty. Of course, the Monty Python team was able to comically highlight the double-edged effect of the Romans with its discussion on 'what have the Romans ever done for us?' The various responses from the freedom fighters present (roads, aqueducts) point to a more positive legacy than cinema has ever allowed, but of course building roads is much less interesting than slaughtering or enslaving countless numbers of people across the world.

Jesus

Jesus has had his fair share of coverage in films through the years. There has been the revolutionary incarnation of Pier Paolo Pasolini's *The Gospel According to St. Matthew* (1964); the teenage rebel of Nicholas Ray's *King of Kings* (1961); the ambivalent and troubled figure of Martin Scorsese's *The Last Temptation of Christ* (1988); the brutalised but resilient survivor of Mel Gibson's *The Passion of the Christ* (2004) and, most often, the enigmatic but rather dull impersonation as in George Stevens' *The Greatest Story Ever Told* (1965).

In *Ben-Hur* his appearances are enigmatic as the audience is never clearly shown his face, suggesting a less earthbound representation. The mystery and simplicity is maintained without a direct visual statement to colour our judgement. In this way his representation mirrors closely that of the one in *Monty Python's Life of Brian*, an irony considering the polar reactions to the two films - *Ben-Hur* is weighty and respectable while the Python film is somewhat irreverent. In *Ben-Hur*, Jesus' life is witnessed at his birth, during his ministry and at his death and resurrection. The figure is expressionistic rather than detailed, but the imagery of the events, particularly the crucifixion, is loaded with iconic symbolism.

> '*Legendary for its exciting, action-packed, and myth-ridden chariot race... This saved the studio [MGM] from bankruptcy, making a matinee idol of Heston in the process.*' Karen Krizanovich, *1001 Movies You Must See Before You Die*, Cassell Illustrated, 2007

> '*This vast biblical epic remains the grandest of the widescreen Hollywood blockbusters of the 1950s.*' Chris Darke, *501 Must-See Movies*, Bounty Books, London, 2004

KEY SCENE TEXTUAL ANALYSIS

The chariot race (46)

Every frame of this scene is designed to highlight the spectacle of the epic encounter between Ben-Hur and Messala. The opening shot contains the emperor in the foreground and the chariots beyond with part of the crowd and enormous centre structure in the background. The emperor's elevated position is highlighted here.

Everything in the *mise-en-scène* points towards the race, its physicality in particular. The long shot of the two flag-bearers contains two massive statues, each replete with rippling muscles, the flags themselves bearing the symbol of the wheel. Three medium close-ups of Ben-Hur and Messala establish their rivalry and focus the audience's attention. The roar of the crowd is the only sound that can be heard and it is used to draw the viewer into the excitement of the moment.

While the scene that follows is one of barely contained power and aggression, the cut back to the emperor and his entourage presents a model of decorum and sophistication with the emperor in his fine clothes and sculpted hair, and the white robes of the senators and their wives. The shots of the two rivals are now tighter as the intensity of the moment increases, waiting for the emperor to drop his handkerchief.

The medium shot of the emperor again emphasises his authority; he is surrounded by Roman soldiers and his face bears that imperious and supercilious look of power. He controls all that will happen, just by the dropping of a handkerchief.

The flags are lowered and the thunder of the horses' hooves and the roar of the crowd underline the chariots exploding from their starting points. The shots have been static until this point, but now the camera movement (or at least the cameras' placement on the hurtling chariots) illustrates the energy of the race. The focus is verisimilitude: there is no back projection, actors do some of their own driving and the sequence is full of real stunts, not the computer-generated special effects of modern films. Close-ups of the main protagonists are

symbolic difference in horse colour is made clear: the archetypal colour system of white for good (Ben-Hur) and black for evil (Messala). Panning shots from the central structure show the crowd surging from one side to the other, desperately trying to follow every piece of the action and adding to the atmosphere of euphoria.

The focus then shifts away from Ben-Hur as Messala battles with another charioteer, seen in numerous close-ups. It is now that the wheel spike is employed and the close-up of the chariot wheel's destruction is further evidence of his ruthlessness.

A stunt man is dragged along and comes to rest in a medium shot, which cuts slightly wider as he jumps clear of one chariot, only to be run over in the next wider shot. The gradual progression away from the charioteer allows for the illusion of reality to be maintained, even though the final shot has a

followed by a tracking shot, drawing the audience directly into the excitement of the race.

When the first corner is turned the tracking shot moves towards the chariots and then away from them; this dynamism of camera movement again assists in communicating the intensity of the battle. The first stunt is done for real and adds tension and danger to the rest of the proceedings. Shots clearly show that both leading actors are, at times, driving their chariots and the air of authenticity is reiterated.

A close-up of Messala's wheel reveals its threatening addition, a spike that he uses to intimidate and destroy the other competitors and their chariots. The first crashed chariot is removed only seconds before the chariots come around the corner and this increases the tension, foreshadowing events to come. With the wider shots of Ben-Hur and Messala's chariots the

dummy and not a person being trampled by horses and chariot. The cut is back to Ben-Hur, linking him directly with this sort of danger, as it is he who is Messala's main target.

Again, we see the juxtaposition of the two leads in medium close-up, reminding us that this will be the focus of the battle, and then another near-miss as the felled charioteer is just removed in time. The race between these two former friends is further emphasised by shots of both sets of horses following a tight tracking shot which has the white horses moving into frame and gaining on the leading black horses.

There have been a few cuts back to the emperor, and each time he has become increasingly agitated, contrasting with his earlier detached demeanour. Even he is drawn into the high drama. The same effect is achieved with cuts back to the sheik, who owns the white horses and has waged a considerable amount on Ben-Hur's victory. His obvious excitement provides a human connection for the audience amidst the masses of the crowd.

Both sets of horses now appear fully in the same filmic space, emphasising the closeness of the race. However, Ben-Hur is forced wide by Messala's foul play. The shot of the stretcher-bearers as they emerge from their dark waiting area is one of the few static shots during the race sequence, and allows the audience another perspective on the race. Their emergence from the relative calmness to the bright glare and noise of the circuit serves to underline the intensity of the epic encounter.

The next two shots focus on Ben-Hur and his horses. They must make up ground to catch the leader. His determination and the horses' power are highlighted by the two medium shots with the tracking shot of the horses slightly tighter and from a low angle to emphasise their power.

him and success.

The shot from just beyond the black horses allows for the approaching white horses to be kept in frame as Ben-Hur once more re-enters Messala's filmic space. There then follows a pattern of opposing shots, pitting the two men against each other. A double crash increases the excitement and a further shot from above reveals the closeness of the race. Absolutely neck and neck, the cut to the frantic efforts of the ground staff to remove the previous crash's debris creates a sense of anticipation. The two sets of horses are now constantly shown together; their power is immense and a POV shot of the chaos ahead further increases the tension. But even before the chariots reach the crash site, a chariot strikes and then tramples a Roman soldier; the spectacle of danger and death add to the terror of the race.

The aerial shot puts the race in context, allowing the audience another break from the intensity of medium shots and close-ups; it also affords us a view of how far behind Ben-Hur has fallen. The two tracking shots that follow help to emphasise his great speed and progress. Firstly, he races towards the rapidly retreating camera and then he passes beneath it and outpaces it.

It is here that the pattern of shots changes in regards to the rivals. At the beginning there would be a sequence of Messala - Ben-Hur - Messala, but now Ben-Hur occupies first and last position in the triptych of shots. As there are more images of him, he ensnares Messala's image between two of his own, and we are left with a view of him rather than Messala. The audience is further connected to Ben-Hur as we travel with him in the next shot at the back of his chariot, sharing his experiences and seeing what he sees, particularly what lies between

Another POV refocuses the audience on the impending crash. This time the trackside helpers do not clear the chariot debris in time and the fast-moving tracking shot shows Ben-Hur's chariot jump over it in spectacular fashion. The two close-ups show first the stunt man and then the actor recovering himself. The cut from one to the other helps to create the illusion that the actor has done his own stunts, thereby adding to the immediacy of the sequence for the viewer.

Again, there is nothing between them as they near the end of the race with the eight horses of both chariots packed together as a massive and terrifying force. The focus is now fully on this last titanic struggle between the two men, cutting from medium shots of them to close-ups of their wheels as Messala tries to destroy Ben-Hur's chariot.

The shots increasingly focus on the horses and their untiring strength with more regular cuts back to the panning aerial shot to indicate that time is passing more quickly now and the climax is approaching.

With the onslaught of Messala's whipping of Ben-Hur, there are many more two-shots of the men as their destinies become entwined for one last time. Indeed, the whip itself connects the two when Ben-Hur grabs hold of one end, and their closeness is further emphasised when their wheels become locked together.

Messala's wheel eventually gives way and another spectacular stunt sees him brought crashing to the ground, then dragged and trampled by horses and chariot. The escalation of calamity helps to increase the horrified excitement of both the crowd and the audience. The sequence again works with first a dummy, then a close-up of the actor's face being dragged, back to a dummy, a dangerous stunt beneath the chariot, and back to a dummy with the editing and mixture of shot sizes in the sequence helping to make the action look believable.

Cutaways to the emperor and other leading Romans show them horrified and out of their seats. As Ben-Hur completes and wins the race there are also cutaways to Messala's prone and bloodied body. They briefly share the same filmic space for a last time in the sequence with Messala broken and Ben-Hur now triumphant before a return to individual shots as their destinies diverge. The crowd pours out to celebrate Ben-Hur's victory, their limbs obscuring our view of Messala who lies in the background, dying and forgotten.

Perhaps surprisingly, there has been no non-diegetic music in the sequence. The sound of thumping hooves and the cacophony of crowd noise has provided the aural adrenaline for the audience. In addition, the *mise-en-scène* (thousands of spectators, the giant circus with immense stands and huge track) encapsulates the power and majesty of the events that have unfolded.

The Sound of Music

KEY FACTS

Release Date: 1965

Country of Origin: USA

Running Time: 167 minutes

PRODUCTION NOTES

Production Companies

Robert Wise Productions

Twentieth Century-Fox Film Corporation

Distributor

Twentieth Century-Fox Film Corporation

Budget

$8,200,000 (estimated)

Awards

Best Director Robert Wise Academy Awards, USA

Best Film Editing William Reynolds Academy Awards, USA

Best Music, Scoring of Music, Adaptation or Treatment Irwin Kostal Academy Awards, USA

Best Picture Robert Wise Academy Awards, USA

Best Sound James Corcoran, Fred Hynes Academy Awards, USA

Outstanding Directorial Achievement in Motion Pictures Robert Wise Directors Guild of America

Best Motion Picture – Musical/Comedy Golden Globes, USA

Best Motion Picture Actress – Musical/Comedy Julie Andrews Golden Globes, USA

National Film Registry National Film Preservation Board, USA

Best Written American Musical Ernest Lehman Writers Guild of America

SYNOPSIS

In Salzburg, Austria, a novice nun called Maria is sent to be governess of Captain von Trapp's seven children at the behest of her Mother Superior who feels that Maria needs time to think about her vocation. Indeed, Maria is a free-spirited young woman who seems unsure of her direction in life. At the von Trapps she finds that the widower runs his home with military precision, using a whistle to summon his children who are actually extremely mischievous. Maria and her light-hearted approach to life, which includes singing and teaching the children to sing, soon wins them over. The captain is also softened by Maria's attitude and she begins to fall in love with him.

However, Baroness Schrader and the captain are due to be married and she becomes jealous of Maria, convincing her to leave. The baroness and the children do not have a close relationship, and when Maria does return the baroness realises that there is no hope for her relationship with the captain and leaves to allow them to be together. Maria and the captain are married, but the family's happiness is threatened by Germany's annexation of Austria.

The captain is told he must serve the Nazis, but in order to gain time and make good an escape he asks that he and his family be allowed to sing at the Salzburg music festival before he takes up his position with the military. At the festival the family sings *Edelweiss*, a song of Austrian identity, and then manages to evade the authorities. Rolfe, Liesel von Trapp's former sweetheart who is now a member of the Nazi Party, betrays them as they hide at the convent but they manage to escape and flee over the mountains to Switzerland and safety.

HISTORICAL CONTEXT

For a decade that was synonymous (perhaps in retrospect) with revolution and 'free love', *The Sound of Music* was very wholesome fare, but its popularity was enormous and continues to this day with numerous film revivals and theatre productions. Apart from the music it is, of course, a story about defiance in the face of oppression which does connect with an era when people were beginning to rebel against the yoke of foreign control.

The 1930s through to the 1950s marked the glory days of the Hollywood musical, from *42nd Street* (1933) to *On the Town* (1949) and *Singin' in the Rain* (1952). The list is long and illustrious and these films provided audiences with escapism from some of the darkest days of the twentieth century. Although the 1960s is more renowned for its explosion of pop music courtesy of The Beatles and The Rolling Stones than for its musicals, there was a move towards the blockbuster musical.

In the wake of the success of *My Fair Lady* (1964) the musical survived for another decade as a popular genre by using big production values to create spectacle films, often derived from stage smash hits. *The Sound of Music* was part of a trend that would continue with films like *Oliver!* (1968) and *Fiddler on the Roof* (1971). But there were dangers in this approach too; just as some of the biblical blockbusters had foundered under their sense of self-importance where spectacle choked narrative and characterisation, so the musical became a victim of its own success.

For every hit like *The Sound of Music* there were overblown and poorly rated epics like *Doctor Dolittle* (1967), *Camelot* (1967) and *Paint Your Wagon* (1969). *The Sound of Music*, then, was part of a renewal of the musical genre, but within it also lay the seeds of its own destruction, where intimacy began to be lost amidst the spectacle.

However, this film's success is certainly an enduring one. Its appeal stems, in no small way, from its plethora of popular songs that had been tried and tested in the theatre prior to its filmic treatment, and the way in which the intimate and the epic are effectively interwoven.

SELECT FILMOGRAPHY OF MAIN PRODUCERS AND CAST

Robert Wise, 1914-2005, Director, Producer, Editor

The Curse of the Cat People, 1944

The Body Snatcher, 1945

Blood on the Moon, 1948

The Set-Up, 1949

The Day the Earth Stood Still, 1951

The House on Telegraph Hill, 1951

The Desert Rats, 1953

Somebody Up There Likes Me, 1956

Tribute to a Bad Man, 1956

Run Silent Run Deep, 1958

I Want to Live!, 1958

West Side Story, 1961

The Haunting, 1963

The Sound of Music, 1965

The Sand Pebbles, 1966

Star!, 1968

The Andromeda Strain, 1971

The Hindenburg, 1975

Star Trek: The Motion Picture, 1979

Ernest Lehman, 1915-2005, Screenwriter

Executive Suite, 1954

Sabrina, 1954

The King and I, 1956

Somebody Up There Likes Me, 1956

North by Northwest, 1959

West Side Story, 1961

The Prize, 1963

The Sound of Music, 1965

Who's Afraid of Virginia Woolf?, 1966

Hello, Dolly!, 1969

Family Plot, 1976

Black Sunday, 1977

Richard Rodgers, 1902-1979, Oscar Hammerstein II, 1895-1960, Composers, Songwriters

State Fair, 1945

Oklahoma, 1955

Carousel, 1956

The King and I, 1956

South Pacific, 1958

The Sound of Music, 1965

Julie Andrews, 1935, Actress

Mary Poppins, 1964

The Americanization of Emily, 1964

The Sound of Music, 1965

Torn Curtain, 1966

Hawaii, 1966

Thoroughly Modern Millie, 1967

Star!, 1968

Darling Lili, 1970

The Tamarind Seed, 1974

10, 1979

S.O.B., 1981

Victor/Victoria, 1982

The Man Who Loved Women, 1983

That's Life!, 1986

Duet for One, 1986

Relative Values, 2000

The Princess Diaries, 2001

The Princess Diaries 2: Royal Engagement, 2004

Christopher Plummer, 1929, Actor

The Fall of the Roman Empire, 1964

The Sound Of Music, 1965

Inside Daisy Clover, 1966

The Night of the Generals, 1967

Battle of Britain, 1969

The Royal Hunt of the Sun, 1969

Waterloo, 1970

The Return of the Pink Panther, 1975

The Man Who Would Be King, 1975

Aces High, 1976

International Velvet, 1978

The Silent Partner, 1978

Murder by Decree, 1979

Hanover Street, 1979

Somewhere in Time, 1980

Wolf, 1994

Dolores Claiborne, 1995

The Insider, 1999

A Beautiful Mind, 2001

Ararat, 2002

Cold Creek Manor, 2003

Alexander, 2004

Syriana, 2005

The New World, 2005

LINKS TO OTHER FILMS

The Nun's Story (1959)

Six years before *The Sound of Music* this non-singing nun also has doubts about her vocation and is tempted by the love of a good man. She, too, chooses to relinquish her vows but not until a great deal more soul-searching than Maria.

West Side Story (1961)

Robert Wise finished the film version of the musical after Jerome Robbins had been fired, and it provided him with a grounding in the filming of musical numbers. This has more dynamism than his subsequent film, with the dance routines as integral to the story as its music.

The Great Escape (1963)

John Sturges' war film is typical of the trend in the 1960s to present war as a spectacular backdrop for some all-star heroics; it was war as blockbuster on a much larger scale than ever before. *The Sound of Music* shares this blockbuster mentality, where the spectre of war is not allowed to get in the way of a ripping yarn.

REPRESENTATION

Nuns

Nuns have been represented in a generally positive way for many years in films: in *The Song of Bernadette* (1943) Jennifer Jones suffers with grace; in *Les Anges du péché* (1943) Renée Faure is selfless; in *The Bells of St. Mary's* (1945) Ingrid Bergman is radiant; in *The Nun's Story* (1959) Audrey Hepburn is devoted; in *Thérèse* (1986) Catherine Mouchet is saintly and in *Dead Man Walking* (1995) Susan Sarandon is forgiving. But the picture is not always positive: psychotic Kathleen Byron in *Black Narcissus* (1947), the funny, but brutal Kathleen Freeman in *The Blues Brothers* and the sadistic Geraldine McEwan in *The Magdalene Sisters* (2002) all spring to mind.

Yet it is not the latter who tend to stay in the collective film-going memory as the epitome of religious life, but Maria, the singing would-be nun, whose humanity and generosity of spirit is seen as an extension of her spiritual life. She brings her goodness into the strict regimen of the captain's life and vaporises it with her innocence and integrity. It may seem clichéd to modern audiences but the enthusiasm of the representation is powerful and its ability to transcend fads and fashions has been proven by its subsequent history and popularity.

However, a more realistic representation can be found in the aforementioned *Les Anges du péché*, directed by Robert Bresson in Nazi-controlled France during World War Two. Here, the day-to-day work of an order of nuns is observed in detail as they attempt to care for women prisoners. The emphasis in the film is on the themes of guilt and salvation and the *mise-en-scène* is dominated by the results of a spiritual rather than a material existence; there is no opulence or finery, only the simplicity of a life of devotion.

Where, perhaps, there is some crossover with *The Sound of Music* is in the depiction of the world encroaching upon religious life and the tension between the two. Bresson also details the daily rituals and tribulations of a community which is both undermined and enriched by those who try to transcend their human, and fallible, frames. As such, the film delves much deeper than *The Sound of Music*. Its narrative, cinematography and acting are largely stripped of spectacle and clearly distanced from the traditional Hollywood representation of nuns as either wholly good or bad.

'One should never underestimate the effectiveness of the lead performances... There is also the unsentimental precision of Ernest Lehman's script... and the solid, unshowy expertise of Wise's direction, in which his editor's sensitivity to structure, rhythm, and rhyming juxtapositions is always evident.' Geoff Andrew, *1001 Movies You Must See Before You Die*, Cassell Illustrated, London, 2007

'[Robert Wise] also brought to the screen the appalling but grotesquely successful *The Sound of Music*.' David Thomson, *The New Biographical Dictionary of Film 4th Edition*, Little, Brown, London, 2002

KEY SCENE TEXTUAL ANALYSIS

Arriving at the von Trapp residence (8/9/10/11)

Maria has been sent from the abbey to start as governess for the von Trapp children; on her journey she sings *I Have Confidence* in order to allay her insecurities about starting this new life.

The final shot in the sequence shows her spinning and walking purposefully forward along the road, full of exuberance and freedom. The camera tracks backwards as she approaches, highlighting her dynamism, as if she is forcing the camera to move backwards.

The non-diegetic music and her singing stop abruptly as she arrives at the huge wrought-iron gates that front the imposing and immaculate chateau in the background. They look like prison gates, keeping *her* out and the house within. The shot is static, the frame poised, and no life can be seen within. It is a very formal shot compared with the movement earlier. Even Maria, previously centre-frame, is reduced to being a small part of this imposing structure with only her head and shoulders visible at the bottom of frame. She seems vulnerable and marginalised.

The reverse shot emphasises the prison motif. In Maria's walk up to the gates, she appears to be barred from this world. Her POV reveals a house that seems to be based on the principles of equilibrium and formality: two trees frame it, the formal garden lies centre frame and the windows are equal on either side of the front door.

The return to the previous shot, and Maria's juxtaposition with the large gates and handles, reiterates the imposing nature of the world that she is about to enter.

She tries to summon up courage. As she concludes the song and launches herself forward the camera again begins to move backwards as it has done before, seemingly in harmony with Maria's personality. But then it cuts to a long shot, which shows her stumble before cutting to a shot from the house. The camera is now more detached as she approaches this alien world outside the security of her cloister. This marks the beginning of Maria's struggle to wrestle influence from the captain, and in doing so, release the children from the chains of formality and order.

The *mise-en-scène* of the interior is a model of balance with two staircases, opposing columns and balconies, paired chairs and tables. The shot is held for some time, emphasising the structure, and Maria's furtive gestures are dwarfed by the surroundings. Her clothes and possessions also contrast with the immaculate room. She is dowdy and plain compared with the opulent entrance hall. Her simple carpetbag and old guitar case complete the picture of ordinariness.

In the previous scenes Maria's face has been brightly lit but now, as she enters another grand room, a shadow is cast across her face; she is in a very unfamiliar and unwelcoming environment. The long shot of this highly ornate room shows Maria walking from frame right to left covered in shadow. It is awe-inspiring but also sterile and devoid of

in static shots, suggesting their rigid upbringing. Their clothes, all precise and military-like, help to reinforce their straight-jacketed lives.

It is noteworthy that the first time all the children are seen out of their regimental formation is when their father leaves and they crowd around Maria, albeit to give her advice that is sure to get her sacked, and to plant a frog in her pocket. Nevertheless, it establishes the breaking up of their formation and a sense that individuality can survive in this environment.

Their first escape (18)

By this point in the film the bond between Maria and the children has been established and this sequence cements their friendship and the children's new identities.

humanity and only her gestures and movements imbue life into this hostile environment.

Her reverie is cut short by the captain's abrupt arrival; he is silhouetted and fills the door space as if signalling his ownership of the property. His face remains in shadow as she passes him and the next shot shows her recoiling away from the camera. She is not so sure of her place within the filmic space in this new context. His formal, smart, military-like clothes also contrast with hers to suggest austerity and authority. While they converse they are shown either in medium shot individually or together in long shot, but never close together. Rather, they prowl around each other, both wary.

The cinemascope frame is utilised to its fullest extent once the children have entered the film. The line formation emphasises their military uniformity and the camera pans as they parade down the stairs. That aside, the line is presented

This is the first escape from the confines of the chateau and the captain's rigid rules. The change of atmosphere is immediately signalled by the first shot, which disowns the formality of the house's front and the gate's prison connotations. There is a side-on view of the wall and gate, but it is the open tree-lined road, up which Maria earlier journeyed to the house, which is visible. It stretches into the distance and suggests endless possibilities and freedom.

The gate swings open and Maria twirls out; freedom of movement has returned. The children follow, but now they are not regimented and run out joyfully. Maria has made their clothes from the curtains in her room (something from the rigidity of their home has been subverted and liberated). They have a green pattern resembling something from nature and linking the children with the freedom of the natural world to which they are led in this scene. The harsh diegetic whistle and marching sounds of the previous section analysed are now replaced by the diegetic sounds of laughter and the non-diegetic music from the preceding scene, *My Favourite Things*, a song of defiance in the face of adversity.

In the next few shots the children bring life to the frame. They playfully run across the rigid bridge and are juxtaposed with the river, forced to run its course by the man-made banks; and they rush across the road and cars; cyclists and horse and carriage all divert from their path. The group is full of chaotic movement again as they pass a statue, contrasting with the straight line of those waiting for a bus and the three children walking in formation towards them. At the market the fruit and vegetables are in a neat row but Maria brings chaos by juggling and throwing the tomatoes.

As they leave the town and walk by the river the camera becomes more mobile, tracking with them. The lens is filtered to bring a softer, more dream-like and idyllic quality to the shot. Even the train appears to have lost any sense of rigidity as it curves through the frame and up to the summit, again hinting at possibilities beyond the horizon.

As the music comes to an end they now run through the long grass, free and euphoric without any hint of formality. No longer marching in and out of frame like actors making stage entrances and exits, they run at speed, almost crashing through to the audience, such is their new-found exuberance.

The shot of the immense mountains is juxtaposed with their childish freedom as the children draw just as much energy from nature as Maria. The picture-postcard shot is irreverently and joyfully matched by their free spirits, just like Maria in the opening scene of the film singing *The Sound of Music*, bursting through after a series of breath-taking aerial shots of the countryside with her own energy and inner beauty.

The remaining shots leading up to the next musical number, *Do-Re-Mi*, show the group in its element: green clothes blend in with the children's natural surroundings and they sit and play in a chaotic pattern as their journey from formality to a new organic state is now almost complete. In the song

that follows they learn to sing and the visuals reiterate their freewheeling sense of release, sailing over the meadow as Maria leads them towards true self-expression.

Jaws

KEY FACTS

Release Date: 1975

Country of Origin: USA

Running Time: 119 minutes

PRODUCTION NOTES

Production Companies

Zanuck/Brown Productions

Universal Pictures

Distributor

Universal Pictures

Budget

$12,000,000 (estimated)

Awards

Best Film Editing Verna Fields Academy Awards, USA

Best Music, Original Score John Williams Academy Awards, USA

Best Sound Robert L. Hoyt, Roger Heman Jr., Earl Madery, John R. Carter Academy Awards, USA

Anthony Asquith Award for Film Music John Williams BAFTA Awards, UK

Best Original Score - Motion Picture John Williams Golden Globes, USA

National Film Registry National Film Preservation Board, USA

SYNOPSIS

A young woman is dragged beneath the sea's surface after taking a late-night swim and the following day the chief of police, Martin Brody, finds her remains. The coroner suggests that she is the victim of a shark attack and Brody plans to shut down the beaches. Afraid that doing this will be detrimental to Amity Island's tourist trade, particularly with the 4th July celebrations approaching, Amity's mayor convinces Brody to reconsider. But a young boy is then killed by the shark and a massive search for the animal ensues, until a giant tiger shark is caught, which the majority of people believe is the culprit.

A marine biologist, Matt Hooper, summoned by Brody does not agree and they establish that it is not the killer shark when they examine the contents of its stomach. They then discover a fishing boat out at sea and the remains of a local fisherman, obviously another of the shark's victims. On the 4th July the mayor still refuses to have the beaches closed, but Brody insists on keeping a close watch of the area with numerous officers. A prank by two boys distracts the watching officers and the shark kills a man in another part of the resort and nearly attacks one of Brody's sons.

Brody, Hooper and a local shark hunter, the eccentric Quint, embark on a quest to find and kill the man-eater on board the *Orca*, Quint's boat. They sight the shark and fire harpoons, attached to flotation barrels by rope, into its flank in order to force the animal to the surface. But the shark, a massive great white, refuses to be beaten; Quint becomes increasingly unhinged and smashes their ship-to-shore radio, refusing any outside help and Hooper is lowered down in a cage in an attempt to kill the shark, but it destroys the cage and Hooper is presumed dead by the others.

Under constant attack by the shark, the boat begins to sink. As it slips beneath the surface the shark devours Quint, but Brody manages to throw an oxygen tank into its mouth, which he shoots as it swims towards him. It causes the tank - and shark - to explode. Hooper has, in fact, survived and he and Brody swim back to shore using two of the flotation barrels.

HISTORICAL CONTEXT

Amidst the political conspiracies and anti-war protests of the 1970s, Hollywood was producing films that reflected a decade when people questioned the structures of the Establishment and their relationship to the society in which they lived. It was a cinema of drifters and dreamers, characters displaced by modern society, where values and rules were breaking down. Don Siegel charted the clash between old world and new in his 1968 film, *Coogan's Bluff*, and followed it with *Dirty*

Harry in 1971, an essay on a modern society out of control.

Of course, Dennis Hopper's *Easy Rider* (1969) is the classic drifter, anti-Establishment text, but other films in the 1970s developed the concept of alienation; Bob Rafelson tackled the issue in *Five Easy Pieces* (1970), Martin Scorsese with *Mean Streets* (1973) and *Taxi Driver* (1976) and Francis Ford Coppola with *The Conversation* (1974). These maverick directors brought a fresh and direct approach to the world around them, just as Francois Truffaut and Jean-Luc Godard and the *Nouvelle Vague* of the 1950s and 1960s had done to a French cinema previously dominated by costume dramas.

Jaws, then, seems to be something of an anachronism in this context. It is the return of big and brash cinema, a hybrid of 1930's horror crossed with the exploitation films of the 1950s; in short, not the 'intellectual' cinema that proliferated at the time. Universal, the studio behind *Jaws*, had dabbled with the New Hollywood cinema, attempting to cash in on the lucrative youth market with films like Monte Hellman's *Two-Lane Blacktop* (1971), an *Easy Rider* on four wheels, and Douglas Trumball's *Silent Running* (1972), an *Easy Rider* in space. However, its heart seemed to be in spectacle cinema, producing the first blockbuster of the 1970s with *Airport* (1970), which it followed up with *Earthquake* (1974) and *Airport 1975* (1974).

Jaws achieved what studio chiefs had long dreamed of: it was a blockbuster but on a domestic scale, with enough time for some subtle character development and the occasional intellectual flourish. Lengthy filming delays due to bad weather and a malfunctioning shark meant that its budget rose to an estimated $12,000,000, exceeding both *Airport*'s estimated $10,000,000 and *Earthquake*'s $9,000,000. It was a massive investment for a film about a killer fish with a young director, but it was an enormous success, spawning sequels, imitators and the cycle of blockbusters that would jostle for position every summer thereafter. It *was* pulp, but it was a well-crafted archetypal audience-pleaser, winning plaudits on a number of critical levels.

Jaws proved to be Spielberg's launch pad for even

greater commercial success and heralded him, with George Lucas, as the most powerful of the 'Movie Brats'; he left Scorsese, Coppola and Cimino in his wake as he galloped through a number of box office smashes. Where the others floundered somewhat, he seemed to touch the popular nerve, going on to direct the Indiana Jones franchise and *ET* (1982) amongst others. Aggressive and imaginative marketing created a frenzy of interest in *Jaws* and every blockbuster from 1975 onwards would follow into the treacherous, but lucrative, waters of a summer launch.

SELECT FILMOGRAPHY OF MAIN PRODUCERS AND CAST

Steven Spielberg, 1946, Director, Producer

See *ET* in the SCIENCE FICTION section

David Brown, 1916, Producer

The Sugarland Express, 1974

Jaws, 1975

Jaws 2, 1978

The Island, 1980

The Verdict, 1982

Cocoon, 1985

Target, 1985

The Player, 1992

A Few Good Men, 1992

The Saint, 1997

Kiss the Girls, 1997

Deep Impact, 1998

Angela's Ashes, 1999

Chocolat, 2000

Along Came a Spider, 2001

Richard D. Zanuck, 1934, Producer

The Sugarland Express, 1974

Jaws, 1975

Jaws 2, 1978

The Island, 1980

The Verdict, 1982

Cocoon, 1985

Target, 1985

Driving Miss Daisy, 1989

Mulholland Falls, 1996

Deep Impact, 1998

Planet of the Apes, 2001

Road to Perdition, 2002

Big Fish, 2003

Charlie and the Chocolate Factory, 2005

Sweeney Todd: The Demon Barber of Fleet Street, 2007

Verna Fields, 1918-1982, Editor

Medium Cool, 1969

What's Up, Doc?, 1972

Paper Moon, 1973

American Graffiti, 1973

The Sugarland Express, 1974

Daisy Miller, 1974

Jaws, 1975

Robert Shaw, 1927-1978, Actor

From Russia with Love, 1963

Battle of the Bulge, 1965

A Man for All Seasons, 1966

Custer of the West, 1967

The Birthday Party, 1968

Battle of Britain, 1969

The Royal Hunt of the Sun, 1969

Figures in a Landscape, 1970

A Town Called Bastard, 1971

Young Winston, 1972

The Sting, 1973

The Taking of Pelham One Two Three, 1974

Jaws, 1975

Robin and Marian, 1976

Black Sunday, 1977

The Deep, 1977

Roy Scheider, 1932–2008, Actor

Klute, 1971

The French Connection, 1971

The Seven-Ups, 1973

Jaws, 1975

Marathon Man, 1976

Sorcerer, 1977

Jaws 2, 1978

Last Embrace, 1979

All That Jazz, 1979

Blue Thunder, 1983

2010, 1984

The Russia House, 1990

Naked Lunch, 1991

Romeo is Bleeding, 1994

The Rainmaker, 1997

Richard Dreyfus, 1947, Actor

American Graffiti, 1973

Dillinger, 1973

Inserts, 1974

The Apprenticeship of Duddy Kravitz, 1974

Jaws, 1975

Close Encounters of the Third Kind, 1977

The Goodbye Girl, 1977

Whose Life Is It Anyway?, 1981

The Buddy System, 1984

Down and Out in Beverly Hills, 1986

Stand By Me, 1986

Tin Men, 1987

Stakeout, 1987

Always, 1989

Rosencrantz & Guildenstern Are Dead, 1990

Postcards from the Edge, 1990

What About Bob?, 1991

The American President, 1995

Mr. Holland's Opus, 1995

Silver City, 2004

Poseidon, 2006

LINKS TO OTHER FILMS

Piranha (1978)

Joe Dante's film borrows heavily from *Jaws* with its narrative and darkly humorous approach to killer fish, but it is more of a parody compared to Spielberg's *homage* to earlier monster films.

Grizzly (subtitled *Claws*) (1976)/*Orca, The Killer Whale* (1977)/*Cujo* (1983)

Piranha, probably because of its talented director, Dante (who went on to direct films such as *Gremlins* [1984]), and its seasoned screenwriter, John Sayles, had a certain level of self-awareness, but *Jaws* did give rise to a number of inferior imitators, such as these three efforts which appeared in the wake of Spielberg's film.

Star Wars (1977)

George Lucas was the other wunderkind of 1970's American commercial cinema, making the other great pulp blockbuster of the decade. He borrowed from an earlier era of science-fiction film-making, making huge amounts of money at the same time and helping perpetuate the cycle of *Boy's Own*-style adventures.

The Deep (1977)

Peter Yates' film is another of the attempts in the 1970s to reap rewards from a connection with *Jaws*; it was a big-budget film ($9,000,000), it was based on another novel by *Jaws* author Peter Benchley and it even shared one of its stars in the form of Robert Shaw. But it fared less well commercially.

Raiders of the Lost Ark (1981)/*Jurassic Park* (1993)

Two later films directed by Steven Spielberg again displayed his talent at telling exciting stories and provided audiences with a rollercoaster ride of thrills and laughter. *Raiders of the Lost Ark* begins with great pace and knowing humour, just like *Jaws*, and both use action conventions to excite the audience, whilst revelling in the clichés. With *Jurassic Park*, computer-generated effects were used to fully imagine the creatures on a realistic scale, something that had been unavailable to him in the 1970s for his misbehaving mechanical killer shark. It might be argued that *Jaws* is the more artistically successful film for Spielberg had to concentrate more on creating tension with much more suggestion than in the 1993 film where the dinosaurs need not be hidden, and where the emphasis was too much on spectacle and not enough mystery.

REPRESENTATION

The sea

The sea plays a key role in *Jaws*; it is there from the very first shot as the camera prowls through the depths to the final long shot of Brody and Hooper swimming to safety, but looking tiny and vulnerable. In between, the shark causes terror and death, but it is the sea that broods, exhilarates, conceals and radiates; it is unpredictable and unfathomable. John Williams' brooding and menacing score, which builds to a frenzied climax as a shark attack occurs, also underpins that uneasy relationship of both fear and wonder that we have with the sea.

Where Jacques Tourneur's *Cat People* (1942) uses the dark to unnerve its audience, Spielberg uses the sea. Its beauty is first evidenced in the opening scene as the young woman glides majestically

through the water; the contrast between the still water and the brutal attack upon her is chilling. Her disappearance beneath the surface, leaving no trace, lies at the root of our horror of the deep; we can illuminate the dark but once upon the sea's surface we are especially vulnerable to the unseen.

Three years before *Jaws*, *The Poseiden Adventure* (1972) had brought the audience out to sea, but it was all too obviously studio-bound. Likewise, *The Perfect Storm* (2000) is strong in its representation of the fishermen's vulnerability amidst mountainous seas, but these are clearly CGI-generated in the latter stages of the film. Spielberg introduces us to the sea at the beginning of the film and by the end we are fully connected with all its foibles.

It harbours a multitude of terrors for the characters: Ben Gardner's decapitated head, the limb of the man in the rowing boat, and, worst of all, the beast itself. It is Brody's fear of the sea that is one of the dominant emotions in the film because the audience is placed within his world. It is his family that we eat with and we share his frustration at the mayor's refusal to close the beach because of loss of revenue (representative of the theme of political corruption which was a key focus for films in the 1970s, notably *The Parallax View* (1974) and *All the President's Men* (1976)). We connect with his pain when his son is attacked and he is wrongly admonished by the mother of a shark attack victim. Ultimately, it his journey of fear that we follow until he cannot avoid the water any longer as the boat sinks and he is forced to face his fear, clinging to a mast with the shark swimming towards him.

One of the most memorable moments in regards to the sea is Quint's true story about the ill-fated journey of the USS Indianapolis after it had delivered the A-bomb in World War Two. The torpedoed ship left, according to Quint, 'eleven hundred men… in the water. 316 men came out and the sharks took the rest.' Although not entirely accurate, this chilling rendition of the story encapsulates the fear of the sea and its uncharted depths.

The final long shot of Brody and Hooper as they gratefully paddle ashore is an iconic picture-

429

postcard shot of the sea breaking against a curved shoreline. It juxtaposes with everything that has gone before; the close-ups have been different and infinitely more terrifying. The sea can be both pleasurable or catastrophic. As the eponymous hero of Hemingway's *The Old Man and the Sea* suggests, the sea is 'kind and very beautiful' but also 'so cruel'.

'It is worth comparing Jaws with its most famous eco-precursor, **The Birds.** *Hitchcock's 1963 film has no civic authority plot or subplot, it is all about personal lives, emotions and relationships... Where nothing was innocent about the family in Hitchcock's film – it was riven with incestuous tensions – the only family we see in Jaws is so innocent that we'd all be happy to grow up in it.'* Nigel Andrews, *On Jaws*, Bloomsbury, 1999

'The blockbuster would eventually become synonymous with the effortless accomplishments of singular superheroes, but Jaws, from the outset, was an exercise in dramatic downsizing, attuned to the scruffy, low-slung heroism of ordinary men...' Tom Shone, *Blockbuster*, Scribner, 2004

KEY SCENE TEXTUAL ANALYSIS

Attack on the young boy (5)

Chief Brody knows that the body found on the beach was a victim of a shark attack, but his wish to close the beaches has been overruled by the mayor and town council. Instead, Brody, who has a fear of the sea, stations himself on the beach at the weekend where Spielberg's prowling camera offers the audience a number of likely candidates to be the shark's next victim.

First, there is the portly woman who we follow down to the water's edge, but then attention shifts as the camera tracks back up the beach with young Alex whose mother agrees that he can go back out for 10 more minutes. The tracking shot continues back up the beach with Alex as he goes to get his raft, finally coming to rest on a close-up profile shot of Brody. The tracking shot lasts about 40 seconds and is one continuous take, linking the two people to Brody in the same filmic breath; his pensive face betrays his anxiety.

His POV of the woman, lying squarely in the centre of frame on a calm sea, looks exactly like *she* might be the shark's next square meal. But, as before, another character diverts the camera away from our focus, playing with the audience's expectations as the camera tracks right with a teenager and his dog.

The dog runs into the sea to retrieve the thrown stick, in the process introducing another potential victim, along with the couple in the background. The camera is placed at a very low level here and throughout the scene (apart from the shark's POV), restricting the audience's view and connecting us with those on the beach and their lack of awareness and ability to see beyond the flat, seemingly benign surface of the water.

Our attention is drawn back to Alex who runs past his mother and then crashes onto the sea on his lilo. Both he and Pipit, the dog, are shown in medium shot with only the water around them, vulnerable and visually estranged from the land. Next, the woman is also seen with this watery framing, her visual connection with the land severed. Noticeably, however, the woman is still while the boy thrashes the water. The only diegetic sounds we hear are talking, shouting and a radio playing; typical beach noises portraying the normality that will soon be shattered. The camera then follows the dog as it splashes on the shoreline, waiting for the stick to be thrown again; perhaps he will be safe after all?

We now return to Brody. This time the camera is head-on and his face and posture look more relaxed. Perhaps nothing will happen, he appears to be thinking. However, the fact that he is not centre frame makes the shot unbalanced, indicating that maybe he is not so relaxed. The camera is then 'wiped' twice by passers-by, and each time the subsequent shot becomes tighter on Brody. It is a delicate and surreptitious way of signalling that he still feels tense, and that he is still firmly focused on the activities in the sea. Sure enough, his POV is the woman floating in the sea, who is again shown in just a watery context.

The screen is 'wiped' again by a passer-by, allowing a cut back to the woman. These blurred passers-by help connect the audience with Brody, whose gaze is fixedly on the sea; these visual interruptions are irritations in his lone vigil.

In fact, the shot of the woman reveals the first possible threat. An object moves towards her but before we can clearly make our judgement there is another 'wipe' and we are back with Brody as he takes a keener interest. We are denied an omniscient view, which furthers the audience's connection with him. The return to his POV shows that it is just another bather wearing a swimming cap and another 'wipe' brings us back to a relieved Brody, whose reactions indicate that he realises he is becoming paranoid. But the audience has also been fooled because the visual language has been so sparse and subjective; the subtle reframing of Brody, which looks as if it is happening without a cut (the cut is masked by the passers-by), has a disorientating effect on the audience, mirroring Brody's own sense of dislocation.

A side-on profile shot of Brody comes next with a friend coming into his filmic space. Until now he has been predominately seen in isolation. While everyone else seems to be enjoying their time on the beach, free of his preoccupations, he has taken a lone stand against the council's decision to keep the beach open.

The next shot looks rather comedic as we now see Brody peering over the friend's back in the foreground to maintain his vigil of the sea. Brody's POV is an optical effect which places the friend's face in extreme close-up, whilst the attention is focused on the figure in the sea. The face is a massive intrusion in the frame, oversized and obviously an annoyance to Brody; the highlighted

scream causes Brody to rise up above his friend, but again it is a false alarm.

From the dialogue we realise that Brody's sons are going towards the water and the next shot is again from a level close to the water as the children wade into the sea. The sound of their splashing is accentuated and the tension increases because we are already aware that noise and movement attract sharks.

Yet again, Brody's space is invaded, this time by an elderly swimmer. Everyone seems to be conspiring to block his view, frustrate him, and increase his anxiety. Because the shots have helped us connect with Brody, the audience now shares some of that anxiety. The frame is filled with the back of Brody's head and the old man, but again the focus is still clearly the sea beyond, full of horrendous possibilities for Brody's imagination.

Brody's sons are then identified running towards the sea's edge, adding to the potential victims who have already been introduced. Even the shot where Brody's wife massages his back is framed so that the couple are at the edge of frame, the emptiness signifying his mass of worries. The source of his worries is shown next in another long shot of the splashing children. The following sequence, a montage of childish excitement, has very sinister overtones with the implications of this noise and movement at the back of our minds; the noise of the splashing reaches a dangerous fever pitch.

The framing of the shot that follows connects the increasing danger with Brody's youngest son. On one side of the frame the boy with the dog looks anxiously out to sea, calling for Pipit, whilst the little boy plays in the sand singing an innocent song; the connection is made between extreme danger and vulnerability.

The cut to a medium shot of the teenager, as he continues to call his dog, has his figure surrounded by water, although he is still standing on the beach; his loss connects him with the unseen danger in the sea. The forlorn shot of the floating stick confirms Pipit as the first victim of the sequence. It is shocking for the audience because it has happened under Brody's nose without a ripple of water disturbed.

It is only after this lengthy build-up above the water's surface that the audience's, and Brody's, worst fears are realised. The underwater shot is immediately threatening, not just because it is obviously the shark's POV, but the brooding non-diegetic music begins, signalling an approaching climactic kill, the score echoing the shark's relentless and unstoppable attack.

The shark moves towards the large shape splashing above which is revealed as the young Alex, an unexpected victim. The camera crashes into the boy's legs. Yet the full horror of the moment is postponed as the camera cuts to a long shot; indeed, it almost looks innocuous, with splashing children carrying on in the foreground. It also reconnects us with Brody's, and the other sunbathers' viewpoint, and helps to highlight their impotence to intervene.

in Hitchcock's *Vertigo* when James Stewart climbs the bell tower). His sense of horror, disbelief and dislocation is captured as the camera tracks back from him as it simultaneously zooms in; together with a wide angle lens the effect makes the background heave and pulsate as the focal length is distorted by the combined movement and zoom. His whole world seems to shift as he watches this grotesque sight. Just as the shark contorts the boy, Brody seems to mimic this movement on land, connecting the two people and sealing Brody's destiny; he must take action. The straining strings pierce the soundtrack, mirroring this nightmarish moment (reminiscent of David Lean's *Oliver Twist* as Oliver's mother's pregnant pain is mirrored by a straining holly branch and a similar sound).

In the short-term there is nothing he can do, and as the swimmers realise what is happening and

The irony of the next shot is that, as the people on the beach begin to react to events in the surf, the boy's mother stays engrossed in her book. The non-diegetic music abruptly ceases, to be replaced with the diegetic sounds of joy and of pain.

The following long shot juxtaposes a horrific act, depicted by a fountain of blood and the boy's fleeting appearance above the surface (mimicking the carefree actions of the other children), with the children who continue to play: innocence and horror make for unnerving bedfellows.

The audience is then brought back into the full terror of the attack as the underwater camera captures the struggling boy and the diegetic sounds of his gurgled screams. Blood then fills the surrounding water and the climactic and violent brass score returns to maximise the impact.

Then, the 'reverse zoom' shot which really defines the complete upending of Brody's world (as used

lunge for the beach, Brody runs to the edge of the water. However, it is all the other people there who run out to save the swimmers, not him; he, of course, is scared of water and Spielberg shows him ineffectually running about with one shot even showing him looking down and ensuring that he is not going into the water. The music has gathered pace again as the panic ensues, juxtaposing the manic flailing of bodies in the water and on the beach. Alex's mother walks confusedly around and Brody's little son looks vulnerable amidst the panic. Ever since the attack has begun, the shots are short, the blur of images helping to convey the sense of horror and chaos.

The framing of the final shots show Alex's mother walking in the opposite direction to the rest of the people, towards the sea. The music and the panic have died down, allowing for her growing panic to be realised in a harrowing way. She becomes almost a lone figure in the long shot as she begins the emotional journey that the other people are just returning from. While their horror gives way to relief, she moves towards total incomprehension. Her clothes add poignancy to the moment with her floral swimsuit and floppy yellow sunhat, symbols of a carefree existence, juxtaposed with what the audience has just seen.

In visual terms the mother makes this journey as she moves from the back of the frame to the front, the close-up shot allowing the audience to clearly see her realisation and to highlight her complete isolation, in that she alone will suffer this moment of agony. Her plaintive call of 'Alex' accentuates the sense of loss, and the final images of the lilo's shredded remains and the blood in the surf are symbols of violent loss and helplessness. The shot is held longer than many of its predecessors to focus the audience's attention on the devastating

effect of the attack. The gentle lapping sound of the water contrasts with the guttural sounds of death that preceded it - a poignant and poetic vision of an elemental death.

The Last Emperor

KEY FACTS

Release Date: 1987

Country of Origin: China/ Italy/ UK/ France

Running Time: 160 minutes (Director's Cut: 227 minutes)

PRODUCTION NOTES

Production Companies

Yanco Films Limited

Recorded Picture Company (RPC)

Screenframe Ltd.

AAA Productions

Soprofilms

TAO Film

Distributor

Columbia Pictures

Budget

$25,000,000 (estimated)

Awards

Best Art Direction-Set Decoration Ferdinando Scarfiotti, Bruno Cesari, Osvaldo Desideri Academy Awards, USA

Best Cinematography Vittorio Storaro Academy Awards, USA

Best Costume Design James Acheson Academy Awards, USA

Best Director Bernardo Bertolucci Academy Awards, USA

Best Film Editing Gabriella Cristiani Academy Awards, USA

Best Music, Original Score Ryuichi Sakamoto, David Byrne, Cong Su Academy Awards, USA

Best Picture Jeremy Thomas Academy Awards, USA

Best Sound Bill Rowe, Ivan Sharrock Academy Awards, USA

Best Writing, Screenplay Based on Material from Another Medium Mark Peploe, Bernardo Bertolucci Academy Awards, USA

Best Costume Design James Acheson BAFTA Awards, UK

Best Film Bernardo Bertolucci, Jeremy Thomas BAFTA Awards, UK

Best Make Up Artist Fabrizio Sforza BAFTA Awards, UK

Best Foreign Film Bernardo Bertolucci César Awards, France

Outstanding Directorial Achievement in Motion Pictures Bernardo Bertolucci Directors Guild of America

Best Director Motion Picture Bernardo Bertolucci Golden Globes, USA

Best Motion Picture - Drama Golden Globes, USA

Best Original Score - Motion Picture Ryuichi Sakamoto, David Byrne, Cong Su Golden Globes, USA

Best Screenplay - Motion Picture Mark Peploe, Bernardo Bertolucci, Enzo Ungari Golden Globes, USA

Best Cinematography Vittorio Storaro Los Angeles Film Critics Association Awards, USA

Best Music David Byrne Ryuichi Sakamoto Cong Su Los Angeles Film Critics Association Awards, USA

Best Cinematographer Vittorio Storaro New York Film Critics Circle Awards, USA

SYNOPSIS

The story opens with Chinese Emperor Pu Yi's attempted suicide as the Soviet Red Army returns him to the People's Republic of China in 1950. This triggers a flashback to his youth when he became emperor at the age of three. The flashback charts his time in the Forbidden City, completely isolated from the outside world and surrounded by minions who cater to his every need. As he grows up, the emperor becomes increasingly frustrated and inquisitive of the world beyond the city's walls; his brother joins him but it is obvious that Pu Yi finds it difficult to accept that his mother has not stayed with him throughout his childhood.

When he becomes a teenager, a tutor called Reginald Johnston comes to the city and instructs the young emperor. Events beyond the city eventually start to have ramifications within its walls until he is eventually expelled and a divided China, torn apart by civil war, finally rids itself of a figure that sits incongruously with its modern anti-elite stance. Pu Yi goes into exile as a puppet of the Japanese until he is forced to return to communist China in 1950. There follows a number of scenes detailing his time in the communist re-education camp as he leads the drab and monotonous life of a prisoner.

By the time of the cultural revolution Pu Yi is a gardener, and he encounters his old prison warden who is now regarded as a traitor. The story ends with Pu Yi returning to the Forbidden City as a visitor and telling a young boy that he was once the emperor. It moves on to the city in modern day, full of tourists listening to the story of his life.

HISTORICAL CONTEXT

The Last Emperor appeared just two years before the fall of the Berlin Wall and the thawing of the Cold War. Its story of physical and mental imprisonment resonates with the struggles that were being played out around the world in the 1980s. In China, the 1980s had seen a great deal of economic reform and growth and, indeed, the film crew was given unprecedented access to the Forbidden City during production. The flipside to economic reform was seen in 1989 when students demanding greater freedom were silenced with force by the authorities.

Whilst the 1980s were a period of prosperity for many and a time of hope for others, China remained a place of uncertainty and uncertain change. Although the film is set in the decades prior to the 1980s, it still captures the Western outlook on China, with its vast land mass and population generating both wonder and a degree of fear amongst those observing its political and social machinations.

A decade later Martin Scorsese would also look at a venerated figure, the Dalai Lama of Tibet, and chart his progress from childhood to adult at the time of the cultural uprisings in China in the film *Kundun* (1997). It also illustrates how key historical figures can influence and be influenced by events around them in its detail of Chinese attempts to suppress his voice and that of Tibet's, a policy that remains as potent today as it was in the 1940s and 1950s when this film is set.

The Last Emperor is certainly a blockbuster in terms of its scope. It captures a huge swathe of important twentieth-century history, features an extremely large cast and uses many impressive backdrops. But for all that there is a discernible 'Art Cinema' sensibility to the film; its grandeur does not mask its depiction of intimacy and a careful observance of character, elements which are largely generated from the principal creators of the film. Its director, Bernardo Bertolucci, came to the production after many years of working on art-house films, notably *The Spider's Strategem* (1970), *The Conformist* (1970) and *Last Tango in Paris* (1973) with their often oblique and politically-motivated manner of story-telling.

Bertolucci had also shown himself to be adept at using an epic visual palette, as demonstrated in *1900* (1976) and *The Sheltering Sky*, made three years after *The Last Emperor*. Producer Jeremy Thomas also contributed to the film's crossover appeal - he has consistently worked with directors displaying a very distinctive and sometimes idiosyncratic narrative and visual style and has produced films for Nicolas Roeg (*Bad Timing*, 1980); David Cronenberg (*Crash*, 1996); Terry Gilliam (*Tideland*, 2005) as well as other Bertolucci films such as *The Dreamers* (2003). Director of photography Vittorio Storaro also brings a distinctive style to the film. He has collaborated with Bertolucci on a number of his projects, as well as working on Hollywood productions such as Francis Ford Coppola's *Apocalypse Now* (1979) and Warren Beatty's *Reds* (1981). His fastidious attention to lighting a scene results in frames that articulate ideas as clearly with light as do action and words.

SELECT FILMOGRAPHY OF MAIN PRODUCERS AND CAST

Bernardo Bertolucci, 1940, Director, Producer, Screenwriter

Before the Revolution, 1962

La via del petrolio, 1965

Il Canale, 1966

La strategia del ragno, 1970

Il conformista, 1970

Last Tango in Paris, 1973

1900, 1976

La Luna, 1979

La tragedia di un uomo ridicolo,1981

The Last Emperor, 1987

The Sheltering Sky, 1990

Little Buddha, 1993

Stealing Beauty, 1996

The Dreamers, 2003

Jeremy Thomas, 1949, Producer

The Shout, 1978

Bad Timing, 1980

Merry Christmas Mr Lawrence, 1983

Eureka, 1984

The Last Emperor, 1987

The Sheltering Sky, 1990

Let Him Have It, 1991

Naked Lunch, 1991

Stealing Beauty, 1996

Crash, 1996

Sexy Beast, 2000

The Dreamers, 2003

Tideland, 2005

Fast Food Nation, 2006

John Lone, 1952, Actor

Iceman, 1984

Year of the Dragon, 1985

The Last Emperor, 1987

The Moderns, 1988

Echoes of Paradise, 1989

Shadow of China, 1990

Shanghai 1920, 1991

M. Butterfly, 1993

The Shadow, 1994

The Hunted, 1995

Rush Hour 2, 2001

War, 2007

Joan Chen, 1961, Actress

Dim Sum: A Little Bit Of Heart, 1985

The Last Emperor, 1987

Wedlock, 1991

Heaven and Earth, 1993

Golden Gate, 1994

On Deadly Ground, 1994

The Hunted, 1995

Judge Dredd, 1995

What's Cooking?, 2000

Mo li hua kai, 2004

Saving Face, 2004

Xiang ri kui, 2005

The Home Song Stories, 2007

Se, jie, 2007

Tai yang zhao chang sheng qi, 2007

Tonight at Noon, 2007

Peter O'Toole, 1932, Actor

Lawrence of Arabia, 1962

Becket, 1964

Lord Jim, 1965

What's New Pussycat?, 1965

How to Steal a Million, 1966

The Bible: In The Beginning, 1967

The Night of the Generals, 1967

The Lion in Winter, 1968

Goodbye, Mr. Chips, 1969

Murphy's War, 1971

Man of La Mancha, 1972

Man Friday, 1975

Zulu Dawn, 1979

Caligula, 1979

The Stunt Man, 1980

My Favourite Year, 1982

The Last Emperor, 1987

High Spirits, 1988

Venus, 2006

Vittorio Storaro, 1940, Director of Photography

1900, 1976

Agatha, 1979

Apocalypse Now, 1979

Reds, 1981

One from the Heart, 1982

The Last Emperor, 1987

Tucker: The Man and His Dream, 1988

Dick Tracy, 1990

The Sheltering Sky, 1990

Little Buddha, 1993

Taxi, 1996

Bulworth, 1998

Exorcist: The Beginning, 2004

LINKS TO OTHER FILMS

Citizen Kane (1941)

Orson Welles' portrait of a great man who slowly loses his grasp on an empire has parallels with *The Last Emperor*'s portrayal of Pu Yi. However, their plights are somewhat reversed. The emperor becomes free of his imperial restraints and joins the masses, whereas Kane gradually becomes more removed and isolated from those around him.

55 Days at Peking (1963)/The Sand Pebbles (1966)

Hollywood has tended to depict the turmoil in Chinese history from an American point of view and these films are no exception. Nicholas Ray's 1963 film deals with the boxer rebellion of 1900, whilst Robert Wise's production is set just before the beginning of the Chinese Civil War, as various warlords and factions fought against each other and any Western influence.

Goodfellas (1990)

Like Pu Yi, Henry Hill is taken into a 'family', the Mafia, where he is protected from the banalities of ordinary life; and like the emperor, he ends his life, as Henry says at the close, like 'an average nobody... get[ting] to live the rest of my life like a schnook' (see pg. 122).

Farewell My Concubine (1993)

Chen Kaige's film details the story of an opera troupe against the background of political upheaval in China throughout a large part of the twentieth century, including many of the same events as *The Last Emperor*.

To Live (1994)

Zhang Yimou's Chinese film covers much of the same historical period as *The Last Emperor*, using the Chinese civil war (1927-1950), the great leap forward (1958--1960) and the cultural revolution (1966-1976) as historical backdrops to its story.

REPRESENTATION

The emperor

Chinese emperors enjoyed the same status as the kings and queens of medieval Europe, maintaining absolute control over their people with a divine right to rule. Of course, for the Catholic kings and queens the Pope was the ultimate authority, but many of them did not let that interfere with their particular whims and fancies. The emperor of China was related to the Western notion of royalty but he went beyond that narrow definition. He was divine, a representative of Heaven on Earth and his word was absolute. In China the power of the emperors lasted far beyond the kings and queens of Europe, who have been downgraded in authority during the last 400 years.

In *The Last Emperor*, the emperor is represented in a number of ways: he is the toddler with the biggest playground and toyshop in the world, but with no one to play with; the moody and inquisitive teenager; a flamboyant and irresponsible young man, and finally, aged and anonymous; in short, an ordinary man. These ages of man are placed within the context of the Forbidden City, with its codes and rituals stifling the human spirit, any pleasure and comfort achieved only in a diluted form or through acts of revolt against the system.

The film represents an impotent and vulnerable life, rather than one of power; the emperor is a puppet, manipulated by forces beyond his control. The image of him as a simple gardener, dressed in the uniform way of the republic rather than the extravagant clothes and possessions of his former life, symbolises something of a release for him. The suffocation of the opulence and the ceremony gone, perhaps he is content to be a 'him' rather than a 'Him'.

> 'The vast, gorgeous tapestry of visual delights is built around the question of one man's capacity for personal redemption...John Lone is superb as the sad mediocrity.' Geoff Andrew *Time Out Film Guide 14th Ed.*, Time Out Guides Ltd., London, 2006

'The Last Emperor
*was a masterpiece about a
reticent man pushed in so many
directions beyond his simple needs.
The use of color and space, of Peking and
history, of John Lone and Peter O'Toole were
all masterly.* The Last Emperor *is a true epic
but with an alertness to feelings as small
and humble as a grasshopper.'* David
Thomson, *The New Biographical
Dictionary of Film*, Little, Brown
and Co., London, 2002

KEY SCENE TEXTUAL ANALYSIS

Coronation (3; 14:03)

The film has many images of different types of barriers, symbolising the emperor's physical and emotional confinement in the Forbidden City. The first image of him as emperor is this medium shot of the three-year-old as he sits upon his throne. All the scenes in this part of his life are shot with rich and vibrant colours, a world away from what lies outside where drudgery endures; it is hyper-reality, intoxicating and otherworldly. The boy is encased in finery, as if he were a porcelain doll, and he is hemmed in on all sides by gold and gilt. As emperor, he has become a rigid part of a decorous and stifling environment. The long shot reveals the reverence with which he is held, but there is no physical contact and the three footmen are turned away from him; the shot foreshadows the life that lies ahead of him.

The frame is full of splendour, but it is sterile rather than magical. The monotonous tone of the chant adds to the dryness of the ritual. The cut back to the boy's face demonstrates his desire for childish japes and his discomfort with such restraint. The camera is either static or ponderously slow moving in its tracking shots, underpinning the rigidity of the proceedings. The medium shot of the boy as he flaps his arms emphasises his impatience. The shot, not quite fully face-on, allows the small figure to become divorced from the background

as he begins to assert his individuality in the face of so much conformity. He looks more like what he actually is: a mischievous toddler rather than a divine ruler.

The shot of the doors to the outside, billowing with a golden silk, is surreal and disorientating, something fluid and magical amongst the suffocating ceremony. This image of something light and free is juxtaposed with one of ritual heaviness. A weighty stamp is picked up and pressed on some delicate handwritten script, marking the paper with its disfiguring red seal, a portent for the weight of duty that will be brought to bear on the young child. For the moment, at least, his young mind is unimpressed by this burden and he gets to his feet and waves his arms in his desire to be free and to escape these unwanted and unintelligible rites.

As the courtiers around try to calm him, the camera comes to life, moving quickly towards the boy and then away from him in an excited POV. The previous two high angle shots of the men not only suggest their subservient place next to the emperor, but more importantly, the fact that he is placed upon an untouchable pedestal. A haunting and lyrical melody, beginning with a harp then wind instruments, begins as the child moves towards the fabric, suggestive of innocence and exploration. He runs almost up to the camera as if trying to break free of the frame's confinement and then we see him from behind, running towards the doorway, the incandescent colour of the fabric alive with magic and possibilities for the boy. The camera tracks behind him and for a moment it looks as if this is a gateway to freedom, his delicate child's laughter complementing the non-diegetic music's frivolity and contrasting with the earlier austerity of movement and sound.

As soon as he reaches the shimmering fabric it ascends away from him like a dream evaporating and reveals ranks of his followers in ordered and rigid lines. For a moment the touch of the material is soft and fun-filled, but his POV emphasises its elusiveness. The gentle non-diegetic music ends abruptly and is replaced with the harsh and formal shout of one of the guards; the camera becomes restrained once more, tracking along the massed inhabitants of the Forbidden City, all there to bow before the emperor.

From an impersonal long shot of the many, the cut is to a close-up of the one, alone, confused and frustrated. The camera tracks with him as he walks down the path, a tiny figure amongst many men who revere him without question. The camera cranes upwards as he reaches the end of the path, only to reveal another stairway leading to yet more subjects kneeling before him; from this viewpoint they are like multi-coloured ants, united in their devotion to the child emperor.

This impersonal regimentation is colourful, but affords the child no contact or comfort and the cut back to his face again shows his disappointment and frustration; everything is on a grand scale, there is nothing personal or on a child's scale. The next shot is a long shot with bowing men filling

world. Finally, there is something for his childlike fancy upon which to alight, a natural thing amongst man-made pomp.

Contact (8)

The teenage emperor's tutor comes to the Forbidden City, his white linen suit and straw boater instantly juxtaposing him with the dark-hued clothes of the city's inhabitants. This is further emphasised by the pushing of a bike, a thoroughly modern contraption amidst such age-old ritual and convention. The long shot of the large entrance gates and the tunnel leading into the city is a repeated visual motif in the film, highlighting the delineation and division between two worlds.

Building on this framing device, another tunnel is shown as the emperor runs through it; he may

the frame and the child just a small dot in the distance. It suggests a world filled with people, but only the spectacle of humanity rather than its companionship.

The single man's chant is perfunctory and cold, underpinning the atmosphere of loneliness. It seems that the boy will return to his throne (this has been an unscheduled departure from routine, much to the angst of those around him), but the sound of a cricket distracts him and the POV shot places the audience within his world as his ears strain for a deviation amidst the conformity. The camera tracks with him at his level, furthering the audience's identification with him as he tries to find the location of this welcome interruption to the ceremony. He wanders through a forest of finery until he finds the source of the sound, a container held by one of the kneeling ranks. The face of the man is full of character, a kindly face, a man who has brought life and fascination from the outside

be in flight but he is always enclosed. The camera tracks to reveal a group of men involved in contact sports but our focus is a large swathe of fabric that is unfurled to the length of the room. The camera cranes upwards to suggest its importance to the scene. Again, fabric is used as a symbol of something beyond the ordinary. Like the fabric in the coronation scene, its soft and billowing appearance sets it aside from the rigid decoration and symmetry surrounding the emperor. Young and older men stand on either side of the fabric, one line of men feeling the other side's faces in a moment of intimate contact, albeit filtered through a barrier.

Almost immediately the young emperor is left alone, tumbling along the fabric, a sea of hands grasping and caressing. Gentle music swells amidst the diegetic sound of laughter, contrasting with the surprised look of the English tutor into whose face the camera tracks forward, his look of surprise juxtaposing with the frivolity within. The emperor luxuriates as he wallows in the touch of those on the other side. Of course, mere mortals could not touch him in the normal course of events, so this is an opportunity to feel the warmth of human contact.

The lilting music conveys his sense of pleasure; he is delirious in this abandonment to the senses. It is both a sensual experience for him yet also an intimation of the love that has been denied him by not having a mother with him. It is all short-lived as the tutor's voice cuts through the scene of physical adoration (all the men are huddled in a mass of physicality), and crashes the bicycle hard on the ground - a new sensation and experience for the emperor to try, but one without physical comfort.

Titanic

KEY FACTS

Release Date: 1997

Country of Origin: USA

Running Time: 189 minutes

PRODUCTION NOTES

Production Companies

Twentieth Century-Fox Film Corporation

Paramount Pictures

Lightstorm Entertainment

Distributor

Paramount Pictures

Budget

$200,000,000 (estimated)

Awards

Best Art Direction-Set Decoration Peter Lamont (art director), Michael Ford (set decorator) Academy Awards, USA

Best Cinematography Russell Carpenter Academy Awards, USA

Best Costume Design Deborah Lynn Scott Academy Awards, USA

Best Director James Cameron Academy Awards, USA

Best Effects, Sound Effects Editing Tom Bellfort, Christopher Boyes Academy Awards, USA

Best Effects, Visual Effects Robert Legato, Mark A. Lasoff, Thomas L. Fisher, Michael Kanfer Academy Awards, USA

Best Film Editing Conrad Buff IV, James Cameron, Richard A. Harris Academy Awards, USA

Best Music, Original Dramatic Score James Horner Academy Awards, USA

Best Music, Original Song James Horner (music), Will Jennings (lyrics) For the song 'My Heart Will Go On' Academy Awards, USA

Best Picture James Cameron, Jon Landau Academy Awards, USA

Best Sound Gary Rydstrom, Tom Johnson, Gary

Summers, Mark Ulano Academy Awards, USA

Best Director Motion Picture James Cameron Golden Globes, USA

Best Motion Picture - Drama Golden Globes, USA

Best Original Score - Motion Picture James Horner Golden Globes, USA

Best Original Song - Motion Picture James Horner (music), Will Jennings (lyrics) For the song 'My Heart Will Go On' Golden Globes, USA

SYNOPSIS

In the 1990s, Rose Dawson Calvert returns to the site of the *RMS Titanic*'s final resting place, joining Brock Lovett on his treasure hunting ship, which has located the wreck of the sunken liner. Rose, a passenger aboard the *Titanic*, arrives with her granddaughter after a drawing of her is discovered on the ship and shown on television. The treasure hunters are searching for an immensely valuable necklace called the 'Heart of the Ocean', and the drawing of a nude Rose shows her wearing it.

The 101-year-old woman tells the story of the necklace, beginning with her arrival on board the ship. She is part of the upper classes, engaged to wealthy but ruthless Caledon Hockley, about which she becomes increasingly depressed. She is prevented from committing suicide by lower-class Jack Dawson, an artist and free spirit, who liberates her from a strait-jacketed existence. They drink and dance together, but when her fiancé finds out about her time in the lower decks he forbids Rose from seeing Jack again.

As the days pass, Rose and Jack fall in love and he sketches her in the nude wearing the precious necklace – a symbol of their love and an act of defiance against Hockley. He sends his manservant, Lovejoy, to find Rose but the two lovers evade him and make love hiding in a car stowed in the hold. Hockley decides to frame Jack by having Lovejoy plant the necklace on him; the plan is successful but by this time Jack and Rose have witnessed the *Titanic*'s collision with an iceberg and the ship is sinking.

Regardless, Jack is still handcuffed in a room deep below the deck for his 'crime', but on deck there is a growing sense of unease as the ship begins to list. Rose manages to free Jack, but by now the water is filling all the lower decks. To add to their problems some of the stewards are preventing those on the lower decks, the poorer passengers, from escaping to the top deck. They eventually fight their way through only to discover that the evacuation of the ship is descending into chaos as panic grows. Rose and Jack survive the sinking and Rose clings onto some flotsam, holding Jack who is in the water. He dies, apparently from hypothermia, but she is rescued and the old Rose finishes her story back in the present day. Later, Rose climbs onto the stern of Lovett's ship with the necklace, which she has had in her possession since the sinking, and she drops it back into the sea.

HISTORICAL CONTEXT

A common debate about film-making in Hollywood often centres on the conflict between 'dumb' big budget films and smaller, more human, films which tackle issues seriously and develop believable characters. It is estimated that *Titanic* cost somewhere in the region of $200,000,000 to make; a colossal amount, but it recouped a figure approaching two *billion* dollars. These are staggering sums and it is easy to see why smaller budgeted films were being squeezed out of Hollywood at the time. Its scale was epic and the box office return ensured its place as the most financially successful film of all time (unadjusted for inflation), as well as receiving numerous awards, including 11 Oscars.

It needed two major Hollywood studios to finance the film, perhaps having learned from previous expensive flops that had almost or totally destroyed studios. If the film had been a financial disaster the consequence might have been more, smaller budgeted films being produced, focusing on characterisation and stronger plots, but it is not necessarily true that its success killed off the smaller film. Indeed, its financial returns could well have helped the production of other, more independent-orientated, films by the production companies involved.

Seeing its success, other studios were inclined to continue to invest in big budget films, hoping to replicate its financial returns. Ever since *Jaws* (1975), Hollywood has tried to make its really big money through the summer blockbuster. Occasionally they get it very wrong: *Ishtar* (1987), *Hudson Hawk* (1991), *The Postman* (1997) and *Alexander* (2004) have all failed to recoup their production costs. For every success there are numerous failures and film-making is one of the riskiest businesses to be in as an investor or as part of the production process. There are so many variables involved with the film-making process that it is little short of a miracle when a film actually succeeds, both critically and financially.

The film also pushed CGI to a new level; ever since *Jurassic Park* it was obvious that this technology had progressed sufficiently so that it could replicate the extraordinary and make it look real. Initially, it seemed that its possibilities lay in the science-fiction and fantasy genres, recreating the impossible. James Cameron's earlier films used CGI to bring the 'non-human' to life, as in *The Abyss* (1989) and *Terminator 2: Judgement Day* (1991). However, it was the recreation of the *RMS Titanic* and its many passengers using CGI that demonstrated that these technologies could mimic the massive sets and crowds that had been used in earlier blockbusters like *Ben-Hur*. Digital Domain's CGI work on *Titanic* also helped to pave the way for succeeding films like *Gladiator*, which also used CGI to recreate an epic vision of history.

SELECT FILMOGRAPHY OF MAIN PRODUCERS AND CAST

James Cameron, 1954, Director, Producer, Screenwriter

Piranha Part Two: The Spawning, 1981

The Terminator, 1984

Aliens, 1986

The Abyss, 1989

Terminator 2: Judgment Day, 1991

True Lies, 1994

Titanic, 1997

Ghosts of the Abyss, 2003

Aliens of the Deep, 2005

Avatar, 2009

James Horner, 1953, Composer

Star Trek II: The Wrath of Khan, 1982

48 Hours, 1982

Gorky Park, 1983

The Dresser, 1983

Cocoon, 1985

The Name of the Rose, 1986

An American Tail, 1986

Aliens, 1986

Willow, 1988

Field of Dreams, 1989

Glory, 1989

Patriot Games, 1992

The Pelican Brief, 1993

Clear and Present Danger, 1994

Legends of the Fall, 1994

Apollo 13, 1995

Braveheart, 1995

Titanic, 1997

Deep Impact, 1998

The Mask of Zorro, 1998

The Perfect Storm, 2000

Enemy at the Gates, 2001

Iris, 2001

A Beautiful Mind, 2001

Troy, 2004

The New World, 2005

Apocalypto, 2006

Leonardo DiCaprio, 1974, Actor

This Boy's Life, 1993

What's Eating Gilbert Grape, 1993

The Quick and the Dead, 1995

The Basketball Diaries, 1995

Romeo + Juliet, 1996

Marvin's Room, 1996

Titanic, 1997

The Man in the Iron Mask, 1998

The Beach, 2000

Gangs of New York, 2002

Catch Me If You Can, 2002

The Aviator, 2004

The Departed, 2006

Blood Diamond, 2006

Body of Lies, 2008

Revolutionary Road, 2008

Kate Winslet, 1975, Actress

Heavenly Creatures, 1994

Sense and Sensibility, 1995

Jude, 1996

Hamlet, 1996

Titanic, 1997

Hideous Kinky, 1998

Quills, 2000

Enigma, 2001

Iris, 2001

The Life of David Gale, 2003

Eternal Sunshine of the Spotless Mind, 2004

Finding Neverland, 2004

Little Children, 2006

The Holiday, 2006

The Reader, 2008

Revolutionary Road, 2008

LINKS TO OTHER FILMS

Titanic (1953)

This version of events is similar to that of James Cameron in that it attempts to tell a domestic story of family conflict and love against the backdrop of the tragic sinking of the ship, thus giving a face to an event that is already familiar to audiences.

A Night to Remember (1955)

This is a British version of the ill-fated ship, which takes an approach akin to that of a docu-drama and focuses on the story of the voyage from a crew member's point of view.

The Terminator (1984)

This was James Cameron's breakthrough film, made on a fraction of the budget of that for *Titanic*, but already showing his penchant for use of special effects, which would be further honed in his subsequent films, particularly *The Abyss* and *Terminator 2: Judgment Day*.

REPRESENTATION

Class System II (for 'Class System I' see *Kind Hearts and Coronets* in COMEDY pg. 279)

The subject of class is a perennial favourite in British films, and Britain's long-lived love affair with class has invited much satirical parody. It has occupied writers for hundreds of years, beginning with Irish writer Jonathan Swift's satirical idea for dealing with the 'problem' of the poor in Ireland in his work, *A Modest Proposal* in 1729, by feeding poor children to the rich. In slightly more restrained terms, but with as much wit, Jane Austen dissected the English class system in the early 1800s, while Charles Dickens detailed the minutiae of the lower and upper classes in Victorian England. The latter two writers have formed a rich vein for film-makers in Hollywood and elsewhere where class systems are represented in historical terms.

Other costume dramas that have dealt with the subject include Jean Renoir's *La Regle du Jeu* (1939), Carol Reed's *Kipps* (1941), Robert Hamer's *Kind Hearts and Coronets* (1949), James Ivory's *The Remains of the Day* (1993), John Madden's *Mrs. Brown* (1997) and Robert Altman's *Gosford Park* (2001). However, the representation of class systems is not the preserve of solely costume dramas. Film-makers like Mike Leigh and Ken Loach have put their own contemporary spin on the issue in films such as *Secrets and Lies* (1996) and *Riff-Raff* (1990) respectively.

The representation in *Titanic* uses the ship as a metaphor for class division, with the British and American upper classes enjoying the luxury and splendour of the upper decks with the predominantly Irish lower classes relegated to the bowels of the vessel. The prejudice of those above for those beneath them is clearly represented in Jack's journey into the rarefied atmosphere of the magnificent dining rooms, and when those below are actually barred from reaching the deck as the ship sinks.

The upper classes are represented as being bound and stifled by their self-imposed rules of behaviour and etiquette whilst Rose encounters a world of free-wheeling excitement, generosity and unaffected joy with Jack and those partitioned below. Only Rose and Margaret Brown, played by Kathy Bates, are welcoming to Jack. Indeed, Margaret herself is barely tolerated by the other first-class passengers because she is 'new money', and she is the one person who is Rose's kindred spirit, accepting and helping Jack as he moves into the alien world of the upper decks.

'While not by any means an intellectual film (and far less an intellectual's film), *Titanic* nevertheless prompts viewers to pose to themselves questions about our society's divide between rich and poor, the nature of love, the meaning of sacrifice, and modernity's faith in, even obsession with, technological prowess and mastery over nature.' David M. Lubin, *Titanic*, BFI, 1999

Titanic is the Gone with the Wind of the contemporary Hollywood period. Directed by James Cameron and grossing a record-breaking $1.2 billion in its first year, the film is a blueprint for the term *'blockbuster'.'* Michael Hammond, '*Titanic*', in Williams, L. R. and Hammond, M. (eds) *Contemporary American Cinema*, McGraw Hill/Open University Press, 2006 pp.349–351

KEY SCENE TEXTUAL ANALYSIS

Hitting the iceberg (16)

The scene opens with Jack and Rose spilling out onto the deck after escaping from both her fiancé's henchmen and the master of arm's men. Their loving embrace brings a smile to both a ship officer's face and the two lookouts watching them. The soft Celtic music adds to the lightness of the moment, particularly in contrast with the frantic chase of the previous scene.

It is at this moment that Cameron stages the ship's collision with the iceberg. No shots of the iceberg are included before this point; in fact, everything is done to distract the audience from the inevitable course of this film. Because the outcome is so well-known he instead concentrates on the romance, the conflict of different social classes and the pursuit.

With such distractions the iceberg collision is as surprising as it can be, given our prior knowledge. The expression of disbelief, then fear, on the two lookouts' faces is the first indication of danger. The camera moves towards them to suggest the impact of the sight; then it is their POV: an iceberg barely discernible in the distance.

A threatening and brooding orchestral score, dramatic and suggestive of the approaching catastrophe, replaces the gentle music and the diegetic bell cuts through the non-diegetic music, signalling the onset of the panic. The score then shifts to a faster pace, a quick drum sound underpinning the approaching drama and chaos. As soon as the lookout utters the word 'iceberg' a much faster and dramatic score takes over.

The camera follows the officer in charge as he speeds back to the bridge. There is a whip pan as

The officer in charge of the engine room does a classic double take - on seeing the signal for a change of course the camera moves in on him and as he moves towards the camera his screamed command is given an even greater level of intensity. It is then back to a close-up of the wheel, and then wheel and man, both tighter shots than before, signalling his increasingly desperate efforts. It is low angle again and the resulting low ceiling hems him in, suggesting that he is locked into this struggle with the wheel. The perspective then returns to the iceberg and it seems as if these frantic efforts, despite this speed, have been in vain: the ship seems to be still heading for the iceberg.

Back into the engine room the camera loses any sort of equilibrium that it may have had as it jerkily follows men down the steps. The audience is drawn into the heart of the action as we become one of

he and another officer shout orders at the sailor on the wheel and the camera move matches the rush of adrenaline that courses through each man's veins. A low angle shot of this sailor, as he desperately spins the wheel, emphasises the enormous power that rests on his shoulders. How fast he can do this may determine the ship's fate and it is a shot that binds the man and wheel together in the frame; they are one and the same as he puts his all into the action. The first officer rushes past the other, knocking the tea out of the second officer's cup, for this, it seems, is enough of an emergency to ruffle even the stiff upper lips of the English.

The camera follows the officer's frantic efforts as he attempts to alter the ship's course. It then tracks towards the sailor and the wheel as the intensity of his battle continues and the music thrusts the action forward with its vicious stabbing chords.

the ship's crew. Men run through the frame and the camera sways dangerously from side to side, as if events are now almost out of control.

A red light flashes and we reach the bowels of the ship, having made a journey from top to bottom. The men on deck are treated to a clear night sky with stars above. They wear smart uniforms and have the freedom of the deck while, below, the harsh light glares on the engine room and the men are clad in working clothes. In the depths, meanwhile, the men feed the voracious appetites of the coal burners and grime, sweat and the incessant assault of the fires obscure their humanity. The light is dim and their clothes are without identity. We have made the journey down through the sailor ranks, just as we constantly see the divide between rich and poor amongst the passengers and, of course, between the lovers, Rose and Jack. Here, however, the ranks are momentarily united by the common threat. We see another frantic whip pan and a high angle tracking shot, firmly placing these men at the bottom of the hierarchy.

In the engine room another wheel is turned, the close-ups of gauges underlining the tension. The fruits of all these human endeavours are then shown as we see the propellers changing direction: all this collective action by so many is needed to tame this beast of a ship. Next, a very high angle shot of a massive piston, with a small figure beneath, shows the fragility of man in relation to these structures.

The *mise-en-scène* is cluttered with huge machines, pistons and gauges; steam and shouts disorientate the viewer as the tiny figures clamber around these mammoth structures. It is both incredible that the technology should work but also frightening how vulnerable the men are in

We come back to the human element and the reactions of the men with close-ups of those above deck and their expressions and utterances. The camera slowly tracks towards the first officer's face as his anxiety grows. There are cuts back to his POV, with a tiny figure at the very prow of the ship, to put the enormity of the ship and the iceberg into perspective, heightening our awareness of the massive impact to come, and intensifying our growing expectation of that impact; the repetition in the musical score heralds the coming disaster.

The contact comes with a screeching of metal. On the score strings take over, mimicking the adrenaline rush as the ship scrapes along the iceberg; even Jack and Rose's kiss is disturbed. Shots of those onboard and the effect on them physically is shown: hands shudder, bodies move, glasses shake. We are taken on a whirlwind

comparison. A CGI shot of two men reacting with fear as the giant pistons change direction reiterates this juxtaposition of power and frailty; these men may be able to operate these machines but once in motion their course is very difficult to check.

Cameron ensures that human figures are in the frame or come into frame with the pistons to reinforce the immense power of the ship. It is almost the equivalent of Frankenstein's monster, a force that its human creators can do little to control.

We lose the diegetic noise from below as we return to deck level. Just the brooding score remains as the pace of editing slackens and the shots become more static; everything has been done that can be done and now the nerve-shredding wait is documented as the vessel bears down on the iceberg.

tour of the ship's clientele as the iceberg has a democratising effect; all are united in feeling its power. While things above shake and rattle, the truly devastating effects below are revealed. Tracking shots follow the rupturing of the hull, the invasion heightened by the diegetic sounds of metal exploding and water surging in.

On deck, the iceberg looms menacingly above Jack and Rose. The music is urgent, but restrained; while back in the bowels the water crashes through and here the music is frantic.

The editing is fast-paced again and the camera shots are jarring and erratic. The camera itself is placed down at the level of the men, now being covered by water, enveloping the audience in the action. The shouts and screams of the men add to the impact; steam finally filling the frame and blocking our view of their plight; we are aware of the complete disorientation of their world.

With another CGI shot of this immense ship, as Jack and Rose look over the side at the iceberg, we return to a frantic pace. The camera moves more quickly and back down to the fleeing men to take us amongst them down in the water. We follow others through closing doors, feeling their panic and claustrophobia as some escape and others become trapped.

The cut back to the display panel in the ship's bridge, showing the lights coming on to indicate that the watertight doors are shut, is a chilling short-hand representation of what is actually happening below deck: sailors will become entombed in the bowels of the liner.

The remainder of the sequence consists largely of close-ups of the officers and sailors on deck as well as of the captain when he finally appears. It shows us the intensity of relief and of the dread that still remains; the music is now calmer, but the repeated horn refrain speaks of danger only lurking just below the surface.

The final shot of this sequence shows the captain looking down at the only visible signs on deck, some lumps of ice, which are frighteningly deceptive (as we know the true damage). The shot looks down from above the captain: he is in frame with the ice and is shown to be vulnerable through the use of such a high angle shot. This look back towards the iceberg, which seems to be now out of view, is poignant and suggestive of a man who knows that his fate has been sealed.

Spider-Man 2

KEY FACTS

Release Date: 2004

Country of Origin: USA

Running Time: 122 minutes

PRODUCTION NOTES

Production Companies

Marvel Enterprises

Laura Ziskin Productions

Columbia Pictures Corporation

Sony Pictures Entertainment

Distributors

Columbia Pictures Corporation

Sony Pictures Entertainment

Budget

$200,000,000 (estimated)

Awards

Best Achievement in Visual Effects John Dykstra, Scott Stokdyk, Anthony LaMolinara, John Frazier Academy Awards, USA

SYNOPSIS

Peter Parker is finding it increasingly difficult to juggle the demands of living an ordinary life as well as being a superhero. His friend, Harry Osborn, son of Norman Osborn (whose alter ego, Green Goblin, was defeated by Spider-Man in the first instalment), is financing a fusion experiment conducted by scientist Otto Octavius. The experiment goes wrong and metal tentacles become permanently fused to his spine. It makes him unhinged and he destroys a hospital surgery, determined to continue his experiments whatever the cost.

J. Jonah Jameson, editor of *The Daily Bugle*, to which Peter supplies photographs, dubs him 'Doctor Octopus' or 'Doc Ock', as he undertakes a crime wave in order to fund his experiments. Peter and his Aunt May happen to be at a bank he attacks and Spider-Man has to rescue his aunt after the scientist takes her captive. After this, Peter, who is increasingly frustrated by his superhero persona, decides to leave his crime-fighting days behind him. He tries to re-establish his relationship with Mary Jane Watson, the girl he has loved since he was a child, but she is unwilling as he has let her down on so many previous occasions and she is also engaged to John, J. Jonah Jameson's son.

Doc Ock threatens to kill Harry if he does not supply him with the final component for his experiment, and Harry strikes a deal with him: he will give him what he needs if the scientist delivers Spider-Man to him so that he can avenge his father's death. Doc Ock abducts Mary Jane in order to lure Spider-Man. Peter is forced to become the superhero again and goes off in search of Doc Ock; they clash and Spider-Man saves a train full of people that the scientist has tried to destroy. In doing so, Spider-Man's power is depleted and Doc Ock takes him to Harry Osborn as agreed. Harry unmasks Spider-Man and is shocked to discover his real identity; Peter convinces Harry to let him go and rescue Mary Jane.

Doc Ock has nearly completed his fusion experiment, which may cause massive damage if completed. Spider-Man manages to subdue the scientist, revealing his true identity and convincing him to destroy his experiment. Doc Ock does this, killing himself in the process. Mary Jane also sees the superhero's true identity, but Peter cannot commit to a relationship with her because of his superhero responsibilities. Harry discovers his father's secret lair where all his Green Goblin paraphernalia is hidden, and he realises his father's true identity. Finally, Mary Jane calls off her wedding and commits to Peter with the understanding that his role as a superhero must always come first.

HISTORICAL CONTEXT

Hollywood rediscovered the superhero film in the noughties: the three major superhero characters, Spider-Man, Superman and Batman have all been revived and generally well-received by audiences and critics alike. Previous decades had seen the production of superhero films, with the Saturday morning serials of the 1940s, the Superman and Spider-Man films of the 1970s and 1980s and the

Batman franchise of the late 1980s and 1990s. The initial films in the series (with the exception of the Spider-Man films) were successful, but as the sequels piled up, their credibility and success diminished, culminating in the disappointing *Superman IV* (1987) and *Batman and Robin* (1997).

There had also been a number of live action and animated versions of these stories through the decades and audience familiarity with these characters has remained high. But why the successful reinvention in the noughties? Like the Bond films of the 1970s and 1980s, the tone of many of the sequels became more parodic, but the noughties gave rise to films with a harder edge, often closer in tone to the original comic books or graphic novels. Films such as *Spider-Man* (2002), *Spider-Man 2*, *Spider-Man 3* (2007), *Batman Begins* (2005), *Superman Returns* (2006) and *The Dark Knight* (2008) present a more psychologically complex profile of the superhero persona than had been seen before, seemingly reflecting the increasingly complex issues that are facing the world in the early years of the new millennium.

It is also unsurprising that there is a resurgence in the superhero subgenre after the 9/11 terrorist attacks in the United States. These had a profound effect on the American psyche, their borders having been breached in such a catastrophic and momentous manner, and perhaps this new breed of superhero taps into a search for answers that are raised by such attacks. These American superheroes are the embodiment of an American spirit to fight the 'baddies'. Indeed, in *Superman Returns*, the hero (the ultimate symbol of an American superhero), prevents a plane crash.

These films also fit into a whole sub-genre, the 'apocalypse' film, where civilisation (usually represented by the United States) is under threat from a hostile 'outsider'. In superhero films the villain is usually a mutant, representative of man's folly, and even the hero is just on the flipside of this, sometimes barely suppressing his inner demons. The 'apocalypse' film tends to become even more prevalent at times of moral panic; the dawning of the new millennium gave rise to a series of films that tapped into the sense of unease (Peter Hyams' *End of Days*, 1999, for example), and the new century has been littered with visions of world destruction. Flu pandemics, global warming, worldwide economic collapse, famines, nuclear war and increasing natural disasters have all bred films, such as *28 Days Later* (2002) and *Doomsday* (2008), that continue to tap into humanity's deepest fears.

In this context, the superhero film takes on even more resonance as the main protagonists battle against forces which mirror our own very real demons. 2008 saw the release of *The Incredible Hulk*, *The Dark Knight* and *Hancock*, all superheroes trying to vanquish our enemies, but even our heroes are becoming less easily defined, darker and more ambiguous, casualties of an 'apocalyptic' epoch.

SELECT FILMOGRAPHY OF MAIN PRODUCERS AND CAST

Sam Raimi, 1959, Director, Producer, Screenwriter

The Evil Dead, 1981

Crimewave, 1985

Evil Dead II, 1987

Darkman, 1990

Army of Darkness, 1992

The Quick and the Dead, 1995

A Simple Plan, 1998

The Gift, 2000

Spider-Man, 2002

Spider-Man 2, 2004

Spider-Man 3, 2007

Tobey Maguire, 1975, Actor

This Boy's Life, 1993

Fear and Loathing in Las Vegas, 1998

Pleasantville, 1998

The Cider House Rules, 1999

Ride with the Devil, 1999

Wonder Boys, 2000

Spider-Man, 2002

Seabiscuit, 2003

Spider-Man 2, 2004

The Good German, 2006

Spider-Man 3, 2007

Kirsten Dunst, 1982, Actress

Small Soldiers, 1998

The Virgin Suicides, 1999

Bring It On, 2000

Get Over It, 2001

Crazy/Beautiful, 2001

The Cat's Meow, 2001

Spider-Man, 2002

Mona Lisa Smile, 2003

Eternal Sunshine of the Spotless Mind, 2004

Spider-Man 2, 2004

Wimbledon, 2004

Elizabethtown, 2005

Marie Antoinette, 2006

Spider-Man 3, 2007

LINKS TO OTHER FILMS

Batman Begins (2005)

Both Batman and Spider-Man were given a twenty-first century makeover with younger actors in the lead roles. Their non-superhero sides are given the most attention, making them more human and more prone to everyday angst, addressing questions of their role in society and their private relationships.

Superman III (1983)

Although this was not received favourably by audiences and critics alike, it still addresses the dichotomy of a superhero life, the split personality that is required to function successfully in both roles. In the course of this film and in *Spider-Man 2* the central characters face a struggle in overcoming their inner demons.

Pleasantville (1998)/ *Get Over It* (2001)

Both Tobey Maguire and Kirsten Dunst have come to this blockbuster by way of films aimed at the teenage market, and indeed, *Spider-Man 2* contains a number of conventions found in these two films. It is, in some ways, a teenage film of anxieties and love on a blockbuster scale.

REPRESENTATION

Adolescence

In 2006, American television network, NBC, launched its new teen-orientated series entitled *Heroes*, where a group of disparate and outwardly ordinary citizens discover that they have incredible powers. The emphasis is on their characters and how they react to their powers, plus the conflict between the power and domestic issues. *Heroes* positions the characters very much amidst the banalities of everyday existence and a number of them are adolescents who have as much trouble with growing up as they do with being a superhero.

In *Spider-Man*, Peter Parker is seen dealing with issues many in the audience can readily identify with: losing his job as a pizza delivery boy, his aunt's house being repossessed, keeping up with college assignments or guilt over his uncle's death. Never has there been such an ordinary superhero. In *Superman* (1978) we see the bumbling antics of a young and innocent Clark Kent as a foil to Superman's later persona of assured masculinity. Peter Parker's ordinariness and awkwardness are realistic. He is the geek in a world of adolescent angst; it makes him approachable, believable and helps the audience connect to a character that has a depth of personality. Just as Jesus was reinvented for teenagers in the 1960s with Jeffrey Hunter's portrayal in *King of Kings* (1961), dubbed *I Was A Teenage Jesus*, so *Spider-Man* is re-imagined for the very people who flock to these films.

'I can't remember any Hollywood film so preoccupied with anxieties of impotence, but Parker's puppy-like resilience in the face of trauma certainly makes for a more likeably vulnerable protagonist than you usually find in superhero films. Raimi successfully maintains the first film's sense of outright ordinariness, both of Spider-Man's off-duty life and of his existential predicament. ...All this makes his tragedy - so much power, and no emotional gain - the more poignant, giving Spider-Man 2 the edge over all those self-consciously moody and significant comics movies, such as Burton's morose Batman, Ang Lee's oedipally traumatised Hulk, and Bryan Singer's flashily unfocused X-Men.' Jonathan Romney, *The Independent*, 18th July 2004

'Molina makes a great bad guy, less of a caricature than Defoe's Green Goblin and more menacing. Overall, a superior blockbusting sequel with both heart and brain.' Dave Calhoun, *Time Out Film Guide 14th Ed.*, Time Out Guides Ltd., London, 2006

KEY SCENE TEXTUAL ANALYSIS

Doc Ock at the hospital (17)

A crane shot reveals the hospital location. It is dark and the façade is bathed in shadow. The American flag flies above the entrance; it seems to be the embodiment of American solidity and safety, but the shadows disfigure this public building, perhaps a taste of the monster that lies within. The non-diegetic orchestral music is sombre and forbidding, helping to set the tone for the scene.

The old-fashioned cross-wipe echoes older films, particularly the serials (*Flash Gordon*), from which this borrows in terms of its tongue-in-cheek approach. It also bears some resemblance to the classic Hollywood cycle of science-fiction/horror films (1930s-1950s) with the first images of the surgical theatre, a doctor pointing to hi-tech images of Doc Ock's injuries, and Doc Ock's accident itself. They are all reminiscent of films like *Doctor Jeykll and Mr Hyde* (1931) and *The Fly* (1986).

The crane shot in the theatre retreats from the computer images and pulls back to reveal a room full of surgical paraphernalia and a large and threatening-looking circular saw unexpectedly flashing into view (its appearance accompanied by a heightened diegetic sound effect of screeching metal) as it is picked up by one of the surgical team, pointing to the rather unorthodox nature of the procedure to follow and foreshadowing the violence

again sets up tension.

A cut to an extreme close-up of his eyes as we hear another sound is the first real indicator that something is about to happen. As well as the saw stopping to show its vicious edges, a supporting hook is shown to be moving, but nothing more. The only sound at this moment is that of the heart monitor beeping, something that is usually a positive sign but here it is used for sinister effect.

With a cut back to the previous shot the saw whirs into life and then the surgeon slowly moves it towards the metal limb. A moving tentacle is only glimpsed in the next shot, a reflection in an observing surgeon's goggle lens, to further raise the tension and the audience's expectation of violence.

The surgeon sawing must see it or sense the movement because he suddenly turns to face the

to come. As the camera pulls further away another surgeon tests another implement, the sound resembling the pump action of a shotgun.

The camera finally comes to rest with a long shot of the room, showing the uneasy spectacle of the four massive metal tentacles that they are about to remove; the fact that they are draped with surgical sheets adds a surreal inflection to the *mise-en-scène*. The cut to the low angle shot of the surgeon as he brandishes the saw above the metal arm, which looks like an animal's backbone, adds another frisson of tension.

As the main surgeon jokes with the others we see them dressed in their surgery garb like a group of surgical super-heroes. A range of masks, goggles and headgear hide their identities. The medium close-up of the main surgeon shows the now rotating saw in the foreground, covering part of his face; the juxtaposition of jagged saw and flesh

camera. It delivers the first jolt to the audience, intensified by the fast zoom to an extreme close-up of his eye as the tentacle speeds into his face and hurls him away. The shots last for a few frames only, adding to their shock value, but also mirroring the way that these arms respond to Doc Ock's thought patterns. The surgeon's somersault ends with a spectacular impact on a large sheet of glass at the end of the theatre; the noise brings the serenity and quiet of the room over the previous few shots to a shattering end.

The impact is synchronised with a cut as glass flies towards another member of the team. Her scream again pierces through the previous calm as a fast zoom towards her intensifies the moment. The next long shot shows all the tentacles now moving, enveloping the room and its occupants, resembling a mythical beast; tables and objects are scattered and small pyrotechnics contribute to the chaos.

A tentacle then pulls free of its leash, its three pincers moving, ready to pounce. This is a low angle shot, empowering this metallic beast (for that is what the tentacles have become, fuelled by Doc Ock's dark side), whilst the next person to be attacked is shown from a high angle, connoting her vulnerability.

The pincers come towards the camera and then we track after a nurse who attempts to flee. As the tentacle follows and grabs her, another one fastens onto a colleague nearby; the audience is placed squarely in the middle of the attacks, helping to plunge us into the visceral terror.

The second colleague is lifted and we see his plight in shadow as he is flung across the room. He then enters the frame, quickly followed by three large surgical lights. The shadow is eerie and the lights, which explode, literally blind the audience, again pushing our noses right up against the celluloid

transported out of frame.

Again, we see the fear in someone's eyes as the tentacles attack; he backs away from the foreground of the frame and there is a cut to an extreme low angle as he is lifted up, adding to the vertiginous and frightening nature of the shot, as he is electrocuted in a light fitting. To make an already busy frame even more chaotic, another body is tossed across it and the lights flash violently off and on.

We then see a body crash into the ground, a disorientating close-up tracking shot of legs being pulled through the air, and then the front of that person as she stares at the camera. Indeed, she is holding onto the camera as if we were her last chance, yet all she achieves is to drag us along with her. The camera then follows another body, horribly held by the head, as it is flung around like a puppet on a demonic string.

screen, as close to the action as Raimi can get us. The shot is static, but this only helps to accentuate the chaos; the structure of the frame is ripped apart by the marauding tentacles.

The same effect is created in the following shot as another sinister shadow looms over a human shadow, the stuff of children's nightmares, like a snake rearing above its prey before the fatal bite. As it descends on the defenceless shadow another of the tentacles cuts across the static frame, dissecting it, and looking more serpentine than ever.

The serpent opens its 'jaws' as it moves towards its next victim and the cut to a moving shot adds even more energy to the scene as we follow it, crashing through tables to latch onto its victim's face, just like the alien all those years ago in *Alien* (1979). The camera follows but cannot keep up as the body is

Until this point all the audience has seen are the tentacles that have been made to look like a beast, but now a shot shows us the source of their power - Doc Ock. He is lying face down and blindfolded on the bed, the conductor of this diabolical symphony. His calm and static position contrasts with the chaos he is creating. Although he is prone and facedown, the low angle shot slowly moving towards his face empowers him and makes the events all the more sinister, his metal arms gyrating in the background.

The next long shot again shows the general mayhem of the room as people are tossed around. We then return to the girl being pulled along the floor. She screams straight at the audience, but this time she is pulled from the sanctuary of the camera. Her nails scratching the floor add to the terror until her final immersion into the darkness at the back of the frame seals her fate.

Another surgeon is also in one tentacle's grip; as he is buffeted back and forth against the wall he sees another saw and the camera zooms into his eye as he senses possible salvation. The camera connects him with the saw by matching the zoom into the saw in the next shot. But we are denied a continuation of that vignette for the moment; instead we see another mechanical arm lashing out. Cutting to another man the camera zooms in and then he is blasted against a wall, causing it to disintegrate behind him. This hyperactive 'millisecond concentration span'-style editing helps to connect us with Doc Ock's 'thoughtful' attack; indeed, if James Joyce had written an action scene for a blockbuster then this would have been it - a celluloid stream of consciousness violence.

The audience is then returned to the surgeon and the saw; the close-up shows his eyes looking towards something as he is in the tentacle's vice-like grip. His hand comes into focus as it reaches towards the front of frame and us, again using this technique of almost crossing the divide into our world. We also are forced to focus on his desperate face and connect with his plight as his hand is pulled away and he is forced to the ground. The saw falls with him but the audience is left once again on tenterhooks as the camera's focus shifts once more.

This time the camera tracks in close-up with another metal serpent as its mouth opens. It cuts to a woman, her face almost in darkness, as its shadow passes across her face. The camera is at a dutch or tilted angle, highlighting the madness of the moment as she retreats into the corner of the frame, reminiscent of the clichéd way of framing a damsel in distress as she screams, circa 1950 (*The Blob*, 1958, for instance).

Returning to the man and his saw, we now only see the table as the man makes one last stand. The following sequence has intertextual links with Raimi's own *The Evil Dead II* (1987) where the hero uses a chainsaw to cut off his own possessed hand; just as we think we may see this particular battle to its conclusion Raimi cuts yet again.

Another victim is pulled backwards through the static frame, but the real focus of the shot is the jaws of a tentacle coming up into the frame and staring directly at the audience, so that we understand some of the terror the characters are feeling.

This prepares us for the next shot, which is the tentacle's POV. We swoop up and over objects, taking in the petrified face of a woman on the floor and connecting with the perpetrators of the violence (just as director Michael Powell does in *Peeping Tom*, 1960).

Two sets of jaws then face the camera in the next shot (the man with the saw's POV), and we see their double POV with a split screen shot. We are tossed between the two viewpoints just as the victims have been; the central white light and surrounding red lights of each 'jaw' help to underline their vitality and their nightmarish quality.

A third tentacle joins them from its POV and they all surge towards the camera, their inner white lights changing to red, a sign of their growing wrath; how dare he attack one of their own. The three rush towards the camera, the red light of one seen in extreme close-up, connecting the audience with the man's inevitable fate.

The four-shot split screen POV reveals his horror even more intensely. One shows his whole screaming face, whilst the others just show fragments of his face, suggesting a grisly fate. The camera zooms in on each POV and we almost jump into his screaming mouth. The final image is that of the eye, the top right screen ending with half an eye, a distinctly Buñuelian image.

The camera does not show the effect of their attack, leaving that to the imagination of the audience, only giving us a frame into which the saw drops with a lifeless hand attached. It is an image of defeat and vulnerability next to the power of these 'creatures' whose reflection we see in the saw and whose shadows cross victoriously over it. The four return to their master, as much a part of him as Medusa's serpentine hair.

The kinetic power of the sequence is ably aided by rapid cutting. From the moment the first metal arm is seen moving, it has more than 50 cuts in under 70 seconds, effectively jabbing the audience with images in a frenzied editing attack.

There has been no non-diegetic music throughout the sequence, just the heightened screeches of the humans, the thud of their hurled bodies, the crash of metal and the whirring of the saws. The horror and the excitement of the scene is derived aurally in these diegetic sounds rather than from a musical score.

Hectic movement of both attackers and victims has dominated the *mise-en-scène*, along with lighting sourced in huge surgical lights. Its destruction allows for more and more noirish swathes of shadow to underpin the horror of the sequence and the theatre. The room itself is full of the trappings of modern technology yet walled with coloured bricks and carvings and a high ceiling of curves and arches, suggesting some of the Gothic rather than a modern, sterile surgical space.

There is horror, action, tension and no small measure of black humour here. The film language echoes many another film, paying homage to and parodying a variety of film styles and films, particularly those of the 1950's science fiction genre and early horror. Most notable is the use of chiaroscuro lighting that characterised German Expressionism in film, as seen in *The Cabinet of Dr. Caligari* (1920) and *Nosferatu* (1922), and later transferred to Hollywood's early horror output in films such as *Frankenstein* (1931). *Spider-Man 2* emerges from this gamete of filmic influences as a blockbuster with the heart of a magpie.

Bibliography

Altman, R. *Film/Genre*, London: BFI, 1999

Andrews, N. *On Jaws*, London: Bloomsbury, 1999

Barber, N. 'Shaun of the Dead' in *The Independent*, 11 April, 2004

Bould, M. *Film Noir*, London: Wallflower, 2005

Bradshaw, P. 'Children of Men' in *The Guardian*, September 22, 2006

Bradshaw, P. 'Dark Water' in *The Guardian*, 6 June, 2003

Buscombe, E. *100 Westerns*, London: BFI, 2006

Buscombe, E. *The Searchers*, London: BFI 2000

Buscombe, E. *Unforgiven*, London: BFI, 2004

Callow, S. *The Night of the Hunter*, London: BFI, 2002

Christopher, J. 'Crash' in *The Sunday Times*, 11 August, 2005

Clover, J. *The Matrix*, London: BFI, 2004

Cook, P. & Bernink, M. (eds) *The Cinema Book 2nd edition*, London: BFI, 1999

Cornea, C. *Science Fiction Cinema*, Edinburgh: EUP, 2007

Cousins, M. *The Story of Film*, London: Pavillion Books, 2004

Darke, C. *501 Must-See Movies*, London: Bounty Books, 2004

Dawson, A. *Studying the Matrix*, Leighton Buzzard: Auteur, 2008

Ebert, R. http://rogerebert.suntimes.com

Fischer, L. *Sunrise: A Song of Two Humans*, London: BFI, 2002

Fox, K. & McDonagh, M. (eds) *The Tenth Virgin Film Guide*, London: Virgin Books, 2001

Frayling, C. *Mad, Bad and Dangerous?*, London: Reaktion, 2006

French, P. 'Brokeback Mountain' in *The Observer*, 8 January, 2006

French, P. 'Pan's Labyrinth' in *The Observer*, 26 November 2006

French, P. *Westerns*, Manchester: Carcanet, 2005

Hardy, P. *The Encyclopedia of Western Movies*, London: Octopus Books, 1984

Hirschhorn, C. *The Warner Bros. Story*, London: Octopus Books, 1981

Körte, P. & Seesslen, G. (eds) *Joel & Ethan Coen*, London: Titan Books, 1999

Lubin, D.M. *Titanic*, London: BFI, 1999

McBride, J. *Searching For John Ford – A Life*, London: Faber and Faber, 2003

Neale, S. *Genre*, London: BFI, 1980

Newman, K. *Cat People*, London: BFI, 2001

Nowell-Smith, G (ed.), *The Oxford History of World Cinema*, Oxford: OUP, 1997

Paglia, C. *The Birds*, London: BFI, 1998

Parkinson, M & Jeavons, C. *A Pictorial History of Westerns*, London: Hamlyn, 1984

Pym, J. (ed.) *Time Out Film Guide 14th edition*, London: Time Out/Penguin, 2006

Quinn, A. 'Dark Water' in *The Independent*, 6 June 2003

Roberts, I. *German Expressionist Cinema*, London: Wallflower Press, 2008

Romney, J. 'Spider-Man 2' in *The Independent*, 18 July 2004

Sargeant, A. *British Cinema*, London: BFI, 2005

Schneider, S. J. *1001 Films You Must See Before You Die*, London: Cassell Illustrated, 2007

Shone, T. *Blockbuster*, London: Scribner, 2004

Sragow, M. 'Extra-Terrestrial Perception' in *Rolling Stone*, 8 July 1982

Thomson, D. *The New Biographical Dictionary of Film 4th edition*, London: Little, Brown, 2002

Williams, L. R. and Hammond, M. (eds) *Contemporary American Cinema*, Maidenhead/New York: McGraw Hill/Open University Press, 2006

Stills information

The credits below pertain to the film still at the start of each case study and each section's title page. The framegrabs that illustrate each case study's textual analyses are in each instance taken from the current Region 2 DVD of the film.

The Western

Frontispiece – *The Searchers* (BFI); *The Iron Horse, Stagecoach, The Searchers, Pat Garrett and Billy the Kid* (Joel Finler Archive); *Red River, Young Guns, Brokeback Mountain* (Aquarius Collection); *Once Upon a Time in the West, Unforgiven* (BFI).

Drama

Frontispiece – *The 400 Blows* (BFI/image.net); *Sunrise, Angels with Dirty Faces, The 400 Blows, Saturday Night and Sunday Morning, Goodfellas* (Joel Finler Archive); *The Killers, Apocalypse Now, Crash* (Aquarius Collection); *Wings of Desire* (BFI).

Science Fiction

Frontispiece – *Alien* (Aquarius Collection); *Metropolis, Things to Come, A Connecticut Yankee in King Arthur's Court, 2001, ET* (Joel Finler Archive); *Invasion of the Body Snatchers, Alien, The Matrix* (Aquarius Collection); *Children of Men* (Universal/image. net).

Comedy

Frontispiece – *The General* (Joel Finler Archive); *The General, Duck Soup, Kind Hearts and Coronets, Mon Oncle, The Graduate, Raising Arizona, Delicatessen* (Joel Finler Archive); *Young Frankenstein, Shaun of the Dead* (Aquarius Collection).

Horror

Frontispiece – *The Birds* (Joel Finler Archive); *Nosferatu, The Birds, A Nightmare on Elm Street, The Silence of the Lambs* (Aquarius); *Frankenstein, The Night of the Hunter, Halloween* (Joel Finler Archive); *Cat People* (BFI); *Dark Water* (Kobal/Kadokawa Shoten).

Fantasy

Frontispiece – *King Kong* (Joel Finler Archive); *The Thief of Bagdad, Hidden Fortress, Brazil, Edward Scissorhands* (Joel Finler Archive); *King Kong, A Matter of Life and Death, Jason and the Argonauts, Soylent Green* (Aquarius Collection); *Pan's Labyrinth* (Warner Bros./Aquarius Collection)

Blockbuster

Frontispiece – *Titanic* (Aquarius Collection); *Intolerance, Gone with the Wind, Bambi, Ben-Hur, The Sound of Music, Jaws, The Last Emperor* (Joel Finler Archive); *Titanic, Spider-Man 2* (Aquarius Collection).

Index

This index includes all references to the key 63 case studies; all key personnel listed as integral to these case studies; and every film listed under each entry's 'Links to Other Films' subheading. Foreign language films are listed under their English language titles where it is commonly known as such (e.g. *Pan's Labyrinth*).